What makes consultancy work
- understanding the dynamics

International Consulting Conference 1994

Editors

Roger Casemore, Gail Dyos, Angela Eden,

Kamil Kellner, John McAuley, Stephen Moss

SOUTH BANK
UNIVERSITY
PRESS

ISBN 1 874418 07 1

South Bank University Press
103 Borough Road
London
SE1 0AA
United Kingdom

British Library Cataloguing-in-Publication Data. A catalogue record for
this book is available from the British Library.

Originated by Roger Burnett, Creative Services, South Bank University.
Printed and bound by Ashford Press, Southampton.

INTRODUCTION

Consulting to organisations is big business. Many organisations are using the help of consultants to cope with complex changes. Some are encouraging their professional staff to become independent consultants, others are developing internal consulting services. Consultancy is a developing profession, but is it thriving?

In this growing and increasingly complex market both clients and consultants are raising questions about effectiveness and value of consultancy. The question "what makes consultancy work ?" brought 50 contributors and 350 delegates from UK, Europe and USA to a weekend conference at South Bank University to explore the demands and complexity of consulting.

The event was designed as a learning conference, and used a structure which involved five plenary presentations, three parallel sessions at which 42 papers were presented, and four meetings of facilitated learning review groups.

The aims of the conference were:

* to examine the interventions that can be used in consulting with individuals, groups and organisations;
* to consider the effects of consultation on the dynamics of an organisation;
* to explore the complex relationships between the consultant, the client and the client system.

The conference design intended to address the following key questions:

* Do we understand what makes good consultancy for the client and the consultant?
* How does the nature of the relationship between the client and the consultant effect the process and outcome of the consultancy?
* What influences the choice of interventions by the consultant?
* What impact can these choices have on the development and capability of the client system?
* To what extent do the dynamics which lie beneath the surface - within and between individuals, groups and organisations - really determine the thinking and behaviour arising from the relationship?
* How does this impact on the ultimate outcome of the interventions for the client organisation, and its long term performance?

1

The conference started with a session on
NEW PERSPECTIVES ON ORGANISATIONS
and then mirrored the phases of the consulting task by use of series of inter-related sessions focusing on:
BUILDING THE CONTRACT
WORKING IN ORGANISATIONS
CLOSURE AND IMPACT OF CONSULTANCY
REVIEW AND APPLICATION
When we, members of the conference planning group, started planning the event we had in mind a small conference which we could manage easily and we had no idea how large our task would become. Very soon we realised to our delight that we were meeting a need. We received well over 100 responses to our call for papers and found ourselves negotiating with major national and international figures in the consultancy world who wanted to appear; we sent out some 14,000 invitations to potential delegates, filled the conference to (or perhaps beyond) capacity with 400 people, and in the end had to disappoint nearly an additional 100 people who also wanted to attend.

We would like to thank everybody who contributed to the success of the conference, contributors and delegates. We are grateful for support from Association for Management Education and Development and Institute of Management Consultants, sponsorship from Allied Irish Bank, BT and Parks Bookshop, and the generous efforts of countless South Bank University staff.

In the pages that follow are the papers presented by the keynote speakers at the plenary events, the papers or abstracts of papers presented by consultancy practitioners from a variety of fields in the parallel workshop sessions, a brief description and report of the Learning Review Groups process and a conclusion giving some suggestions of what might arise as a consequence of this conference.

Kamil Kellner
on behalf of the planning group, May 1994

2

CONFERENCE PLANNING GROUP

Roger Casemore, Principal of Kasmor Consultancy, experienced in community development, economic regeneration and in human relations training and consultancy

Gail Dyos, Training Manager with the London Borough of Lewisham and an OD and MD consultant

Angela Eden, Internal Consultant at BT specialising in organisational and cultural change

Kamil Kellner, Course Director of MSc in Human Resource Development at South Bank University and an OD and MD consultant

John McAuley, Director of Postgraduate Studies at Sheffield Business School and a practising OD consultant

Stephen Moss, Principal of Moss Consulting, working with organisations, teams and individuals facing significant change

Antoinette Dixon, conference organiser at South Bank University Enterprise Services

NEW PERSPECTIVES ON ORGANISATION DEVELOPMENT

The Conference was opened by two speakers who addressed the conference theme - What Makes Consultancy Work - from the perspectives of the client and the consultant.

Millie Banerjee, a senior manager from BT, drew on her experience of many major change projects and variety of client roles. She focused on the importance of the consultant's recognition of the complexity of the client system and subsystems, empathy with and sensitivity to the situation of the different members of the client system, and appreciating the needs and stresses of the busy manager in the middle who never asked for the consultant's intervention in the first place. What makes consultancy work for her is the consultant who speaks hers, rather than his own technical language, who is available and not intrusive and imposing, and who develops a collaborative relationship in which he shares her pain and does not add to it.

George Lapsley, President of the Institute of Management Consultants, stressed the need for professionalism of consulting through development of better standards and continuous development of practitioners. In his view "what makes consultancy work" is the quality of the client - consultant relationship. This relationship is founded on five elements: clarity of the specification, selection of the right person in terms of "technical competence", the right person in terms of character and personality, consultant's interest in clients' objective being from a place of detached involvement, and consideration of time span of recognisable impact in designing the contract.

Both of these views, and the assumptions of many of the delegates were challenged by the presenters of the opening keynote paper, **New Perspectives on Organisational Development (or Adrift in a Sea of Change)**, **Dr. Petruska Clarkson** (metanoia in Organisations) and **Prof. Ralph Stacey** (University of Hertfordshire), which are printed below. Their perspectives on organisations and their development as emergent turbulent systems offer an understanding and explanation of the conception, development and temporary existence of this conference as an organisational system. More importantly, these perspectives provide a paradigm which challenges the orthodoxy of organisational change as a plannable and planned process and explain the difficulties faced by majority of change agents.

NEW PERSPECTIVES ON ORGANISATIONAL DEVELOPMENT
(OR ADRIFT IN A SEA OF CHANGE)

Professor Ralph Stacey. *University of Hertfordshire*

The principal paradigm whereby most practitioners understand and practice the discipline of 'Organisational Development' is still that first proposed by Lewin. From this perspective, successful organisations are seen as systems that are normally in a state of stable equilibrium and adapted to their environment. When the environment changes, the organisation must move to a new position of adapted equilibrium if it is to survive. In order to do this it must pass through the 'unfreeze' stage, a state of some turbulence in which new behaviour patterns are propagated. Then, once the new patterns are sufficiently established, they constitute a new 'freeze' state which lasts until the next environmental change comes along. Consultants in the OD tradition believe that this process can be managed through the medium of comprehensive programmes of planned change. Firstly the appropriate new equilibrium pattern of behaviour is identified analytically, then education programmes are designed to convert members of the organisation to the new pattern, and finally these programmes are implemented.

This Lewinian paradigm is based upon a number of assumptions about the systemic nature of organisations which are rarely questioned. One assumption is that success is a state of equilibrium; that is, internal harmony and consensus, in which the system is adapted to its environment. Other assumptions are that this state of adaptation is achieved primarily through the prior intention of members of the system; and that there are clear-cut, identifiable links between the actions of members of the system and their long term outcomes. When they make these assumptions about the nature of the system, consultants understand their role as (a) intervening to assist in identifying the desirable new equilibrium, and (b) designing and facilitating the education programmes which will convert an organisation's members to the new pattern of behaviour required for successful adaptation.

Naturally, if we find reasons to question the fundamental assumptions upon which the discipline of OD is built we will develop new perspectives, and we will have to reappraise the nature of consultant interventions.

The reasons are to be found in the modern science of complexity, which is concerned with the behaviour of non-linear feedback systems. Such systems are now seen to characterise almost all of the systems of nature. It is furthermore, not at all difficult to see that when humans interact they always constitute non-linear feedback systems. As soon as I say or do anything in relation to another person, that other person has to discover the consequences, choose how to respond and then respond. That response immediately has consequences for me and I must discover what they are, choose how to react and then react. In this way, each I speak, act or refrain from speaking and acting, this has consequences which feed back and determine to some extent my next word, action or omission. These feedback loops constitute a non-linear as opposed to a linear system. In a linear system, any action I take can lead to one and only one response; but in fact any action I take can lead to more than one response - such multiplicity of 'solutions' is the hallmark of non-linearity. Another hallmark is that groups are more than the sum of the individuals constituting them. When we interact, the system we constitute cannot be understood simply in terms of each individual. We can understand linear systems by decomposing them into their components, examining those components and then putting them back together again. However, we cannot do this with non-linear systems because in them the system is more than the sum of its components.

Human groups and organisations are this networks of non-liner feedback loops. It has been discovered that these networks have certain fundamental properties, no matter where they are found - in nature or in human systems. The notion of an attractor is a pattern of behaviour which a system will settle down to and continue to follow, given certain control parameters. All non-linear feedback networks have at least three attractors - typical patterns of behaviour, or dynamic, which they will settle into given certain kinds of control. The first attractor is stable equilibrium such as a perfectly constant sequence of behaviours or various perfectly regular fluctuating patterns of behaviour, or cycles. A second attractor is some form of explosively unstable behaviour, or some form of highly random behaviour in which it is practically impossible to discern much pattern. Attractors of both the stable and unstable kinds have been known for along time to be properties of feedback systems.

However, it has recently been discovered that, as feedback networks are pushed from stability to instability they pass through a phase transition in which they are paradoxically both stable and unstable at the same time. There is a distinctive attractor in this phase transition at the edge of stability - here behaviour is fluid, not frozen into rigid regularity and yet it has recognisable pattern. At the edge of stability there is an intertwining of order and disorder. There are patterns to behaviour, but they are irregular. In this state the links between cause and effect, between action and long-term outcome are lost in the details of what happens. The sensitivity to initial conditions means that tiny changes can be escalated by the system into major qualitative changes in behaviour.

Thus at the edge of stability, feedback networks are capable of spontaneously generating endless variety but what form that variety will take is inherently unpredictable and unknowable. It follows that no central agency can forecast the future of a system operating at the edge. Instead the future emerges from the interactions of members of the system. It emerges from a process of spontaneous self organisation - each member of the system follows local rules of conduct and out of this, overall patterns of behaviour emerge. The important point is that only when a system operates at the edge is it creative and innovative. Only then is it changeable and evolvable. We are beginning to understand that the process of natural selection actually weeds out all systems that are attracted to either stability or instability - those that survive are the ones operating at the edge because only then are they changeable and evolvable. the universe itself may well be a non-linear feedback system poised at the edge of stability, at the edge of chaos. Because it is so poised in this fundamentally paradoxical state, it is continuously creative.

Taking this conclusion back to the field of organisational behaviour leads us to a fundamentally new paradigm, to the proposition that successful human organisations are those that are poised at the edge of chaos, for only then are they innovative, changeable and evolvable. However, at the edge, all the fundamental assumptions of OD are overturned: changeable systems are not those in equilibrium adaptation but those held far from equilibrium, at the edge where they are intentionally not adapted to their environments. Successful organisations are then not stable, harmonious, consensus-based systems but rather systems characterised by continuous turbulence, by difference rather that sameness. Such systems change and evolve not as a result of the shared intention of their members since the future is unknowable, but through a self-organising process in which members engage without knowing what the outcome will be - the links between designed actions and long-term outcomes disappear.

If successful human organisations are characterised by dynamics of this kind, what can we say about the nature of consultant interventions? Clearly, when consultants design and install a comprehensive programme of planned change it will succeed only by chance and then only for a short time. Science becomes a matter not of predicting but of explaining and understanding. The role of the consultant becomes one of trying to assist members of an organisation to make sense of their experience, rather than one of converting members to intentional forms of behaviour.

New Perspectives in Organisational Development *(or Adrift in a Sea of Change)**

Petruska Clarkson, *Metanoia in Organisations, London*

We live in an organisational, cultural and scientific world in which the old paradigms seem to have lost their usefulness, inspiration and sometimes their values. The nature of change itself, whether through evolutionary development or revolutionary, radical quantum leaps, has changed; and it appears that it will only continue changing. The quantity and quality of change (or **metanoia**) itself is changing, at the same time as the tempo of change is accelerating. Managers and developers need to enable themselves and empower others to survive these turbulent, unpredictable conditions and transform them into opportunities for survival, if not growth.

If organisational systems have to be revisioned, consultancy skills and organisational development concepts will also have to be revised. Reporting some experiences of organisational consultants in our current climate, Gerry Moult wrote bravely: 'We don't know what we are doing and we don't know what's going on'. What we <u>do</u> know is that, with the eruption of quantum physics, postmodernist cultural theory as well as chaos and complexity theory, organisations and organisational consultancy have changed in fundamental and shockingly unpredictable ways. Yesterday's solutions have become today's problems and tomorrow's nightmares. What used to be good professional practice in organisational development and consultancy may have to be reworked in ways which have previously been unthinkable, if not unimaginable.

In this late 20th-century climate of escalating quantities and qualities of change, of disruption and unpredictable turbulence barely cohering, managers, trainers and consultants to organisations are finding a particular set of themes are increasingly coming to the fore. I am not for a minute suggesting that these themes apply to everybody in all situations - 'if it works, don't fix it'. But, as certain of these new conditions become more manifest, the new demands on consultants are mandating new ways of being, thinking and behaving. In researching, defining and teaching these themes we can of course highlight them in different ways. However, for the purposes of this short exposition, I would like to flag up five directional markers. These are themes postmodern consultants are engaging with in chaotic organisational systems now.

From the analysis of parts to the appreciation of wholes

We are moving from a sensibility where problems were solved at the level of separate parts to be analysed and fixed, to a recognition that in complex systems like organisations, little can be achieved without an appreciation of the whole system.

From chaos theory we learn that the most minute part of any system is whole in itself, yet also a microcosm of the organisation. No matter how small the size to which it is reduced, the essential features of the field will remain present and available to inspection in roughly the same shape as on the larger maps.

That means that consultants are thinking less analytically and more systemically all the time. We are having to work in the knowledge that any segment of an organisation, however unrepresentative or unrelated it may appear, encodes all of the organisation in the same way that a single cell from your body can be used to clone the complete person whom you are.

Introduced to this way of thinking, many members of organisations find some relief from the years of assertiveness and responsibility training and resonate to the sense that they are engaged in patterns larger than themselves that shape them and are shaped by them; day in, day out.

Instead of respecting an organisation's formal boundaries or working with closed groups, consultants are working with open boundary systems - people coming in and out of events as they are affected or impacted by them, notwithstanding hierarchy or organisational roles. They also work with multiple sponsors and clients; client relationships are not as tidy as was once held desirable.

From causality to non-linear feedback tracking

Instead of linear cause-effect explanations of organisational events, management consultants are questioning every cause-effect assumption the client gives. Systems are now characterised by a very complex interdependence, which makes causal chains highly questionable. Consultants help their clients map these interdependences in order to be alive to them, rather than to explain them.

Non-linear feedback tracking means that small things lead to big changes, and big changes such as large-scale cultural change can have very small consequences. Unfortunately, we do not always know when these conditions apply, but we know that they sometimes do. This dependence upon initial conditions is known in science as the 'butterfly effect'; the idea that a butterfly stirring its wings in America can cause major storms in China. This notion must make the work of organisational consultants exceptionally difficult, particularly when they try to attribute changes to their intervention. However, it does mean that perhaps even small inputs into our world may have profound results.

As we know from physics, the observer always influences the field, and vice versa. So it seems to be more representative of the complexity of client-consultant transference and countertransference interactions to represent these different forces in a circular, dynamic relationship to one another. To seek first causes in such a complex, dynamically interactive situation can be futile and misleading.

From mission to meaning-making

Since the Enlightenment project, human beings have been engaged in a process of trying to find a 'grand narrative' or an overarching story to explain and give stability to human experience. In this way, we have had fashion after fashion in organisational development, replacing each other in some kind of perhaps childlike attempt to find the truth, the whole truth and nothing but the truth. Now, many or all of these stories are true or felt to be untrue. The metaphor of chaos reflects the psychological experience of people in many organisations as well as proving helpful in making sense of current conditions. There is no longer any one story.

Organisational consultants are now moving from providing missions and 'solutions' to helping clients make meaning from multiple narratives. They are helping people to create a variety of frequently-changing metaphors and models to orient people in turbulent times. Effectiveness lies in being able to configure the field in many different ways - herein lies the powerbase of effective people in chaotic systems. To be 'outcome-orientated' takes on new meaning as the focus shifts from planned objectives to a readiness to respond to the unpredicted and unpredictable outcomes of consulting work now. In this sense, long-range planning is disappearing in favour of emergent strategy. Consultants are increasingly not designing more than one step ahead - the horizon at which things become uncertain or change in unexpected ways seems to be very close.

From learning to unlearning

Any cycle of learning of significance or any genuine competency probably requires a similar cyclical process. We are always learning as well as unlearning, becoming stale in the same kind of process as well as becoming more masterful or more competent in any area of endeavour. In any kind of learning that has to do with growing and changing we can never rest on our laurels. Life itself and the forces which surround us will keep challenging us to the survival of the fittest. This, in the original Darwinian sense does not necessarily mean the strongest, the most ferocious or the best. It does mean those organisms (people, groups and organisations) who adapt themselves soonest and most effectively to changes in the environment are most likely to survive and thrive. Even more likely to survive or thrive are those who change the environment itself.

More and more consultants are going from knowing what to do, to knowing what to do when you don't know what to do. Humour, creativity, spontaneity, a real capacity for collaboration - all these are needed to help self and others avoid the paralysis of fear of the unknown. A university professor from Tokyo came to visit a famous Zen master to attain wisdom, and was invited to a tea ceremony. The Zen master poured the tea into the professor's cup until it overflowed onto the table, but he still continued to pour. When the professor remonstrated, the Zen master likened his visitor to a full cup. He pointed out that in order to have one's cup filled it needs first to be empty. Emptiness, letting go, unlearning.

From equilibrium adaptation to the boundary

Organisations often try to reach a state of equilibrium or balance but we know from chaos theory that creativity happens at far from equilibrium conditions. Consultants may now have to relinquish the human, but perhaps outdated desire for stability or equilibrium adaptation. There is a move from tinkering with formal structures to learning to work the informal structure overtly in terms of self-organising political power. The fluctuating ebbs and flows of canteen gossip and political allegiances are as important as minutes of meetings and managerial directives.

Consultants have to become more open to disorientation, turbulence, confusion, conflict and difference, in the light of an unknowable future. Teaching knowledge or skills or claiming to have privileged access to answers has a certain reassuring appeal to that part in each one of us who wishes some higher authority to solve these incredibly complex problems. But it takes a greater kind of courage to be willing to let go and experience the creativity, innovation and disturbance which comes about when we risk the outer boundaries of trying to maintain a balance (whether between conscious and unconscious, past and present, masculine and feminine) and the terror and excitement of living, training and consulting at the edge of chaos.

With gratitude to Patricia Shaw for her input.

Further Reading

P. Clarkson (1993) 'New Perspectives in Counselling and Psychotherapy (or Adrift in a Sea of Change)', pp. 209-232 in P. Clarkson, *On Psychotherapy*, London: Whurr.
P. Clarkson (1993) 'A Small Kitbag for the Future', in papers from 'Order, Chaos and Change in the Public Sector', the third Public Sector Conference organised by the Association for Management Education and Development 18-20 Jan 93, pp. 17-27. Also accepted for publication in *MEAD*, the Journal of the Association of Management Education and Development.
P. Clarkson (1993) 2,500 Years of Gestalt - From Heraclitus to the Big Bang. *British Gestalt Journal* 2 (1), pp. 4-9.
˙ The title of this paper is taken from the title of the chapter 'New Perspectives in Counselling and Psychotherapy (or Adrift in a Sea of Change)' in *On Psychotherapy* by Petruska Clarkson - published by Whurr (1993).

BUILDING THE CONTRACT

This session examines the process of beginning or renewing the client-consultant relationship.

The keynote speaker, **Dr Neumann** explored the issues that arise, especially when there are difficulties present in the contracting phase. She offers a model for examining this. The papers and abstracts which follow reflect the rich mix of contributors' backgrounds; mainstream management consultancy, psycho-therapeutic, group relations, academia. They raise questions about ethics, power and psychodynamic influences. The development and renewal of the contracting process is discussed from practice and theoretical perspectives, giving considerations to the impact of difference (especially gender), the emotional problems facing client and consultant, and cultural and historical influences on approaches to the relationship.

What seems to emerge from all of this is that contracting is an iterative process involving responses to individual, systemic and cultural/historical factors. The theme of this section coincided with the early stages of the conference itself, experienced by many participants as 'a difficult beginning'. A melange of expectations, diverse cultural influences and newness of the temporary institution gave us a real sense of what it is like to be "working at the edge", in which the boundaries are in the process of being established.

DIFFICULT BEGINNINGS: CONFRONTATION BETWEEN CLIENT AND CONSULTANT

Jean Neumann, *The Tavistock Institute, London*

ABSTRACT

The start of a new consultancy relationship can be a time of excitement and anxiety for both consultant and client. The same can be said for beginning a new phase of a long-term project which takes the consultancy process further down through hierarchical levels or further out into additional sections of the organisation. Such beginnings usually involve consultant and client in negotiating those details which constitute an organisational development and change project.

Embedded in these negotiations lie crucial questions regarding roles and responsibilities as well as philosophies about the nature of authority and leadership in organisational change. A successful beginning, one that results in something that the relevant parties consider to be progressive, requires a satisfactory working through of such questions and philosophies. Often, working assumptions between client and consultant are similar enough to move things forward with little difficulty. But sometimes, differences in values and opinions - along with unconscious dynamics - result in confrontation between client and consultant and/or failure to progress the change project.

Using material from two cases of action research, this paper illustrates difficulties with beginnings as they became apparent during confrontations between client and consultant. One case is a success story; the other is a failure story. Psychodynamic concepts are used in combination with organisational development theory to examine those dynamics in operation during the confrontations. Propositions for consultancy competence in dealing with difficult beginnings are offered.

INTRODUCTION

My purposes with this paper are to develop understanding about the functions served by confrontations between a client and consultant during the early stages of building a working relationship, and to contribute potentially useful ideas for dealing with such difficult beginnings in consultancy practice. I will start by describing the problem as I have experienced it during the course of my practice. Then I draw together four bodies of literature into a conceptual framework which helps identify working hypotheses to be examined in the paper.

After a brief word about method, I use the conceptual framework to analyse two cases: one in which difficult beginnings eventually led to a productive consultancy and another in which confrontations led both parties to terminate the relationship.

I return then to the working hypotheses to consider the question of what functions are served by difficulties in the early stages of a consultancy. Finally, I use these analyses and considerations to generate some propositions about how the consultants might assist both clients and themselves in working through confrontations when they arise.

1   THE PROBLEM I HAVE EXPERIENCED

During the course of the twenty years in which I have been practising as an organisational consultant and researcher, I have noticed an increase in the frequency with which confrontations between myself and my clients occur, especially during the initial stages of crossing the boundary and building relationships. I can understand this experience both in terms of my own career development, with resulting changes in my preferred domain of consultancy, and in terms of shifts in the types of client systems with which I work and their agendas for change.

For example, I started my career as a freelance consultant in the early 1970s in New England, specialising in small to medium-sized service organisations for which changes towards greater participative management and employee involvement was a significant part of their organisational ethos. I obtained work exclusively through referrals from former clients, friends and colleagues. The congruence between my values and those of my client systems, often thought of by themselves and others as "alternative organisations" and staffed predominately by women, was very high. I specialised in short-term organisational development interventions: data feedback, team building, conflict resolution, leadership development, and staff development programmes. Whilst difficulties and confrontation frequently formed the problems around which I had been invited to consult, I experienced little negativity between myself and my client systems, certainly during the early stages of consulting.

By the early 1980s, I began to be attracted to, and recruited for, work in larger, more established enterprises. Whilst completing doctoral study in organisational behaviour at Case Western Reserve University in Ohio, I became interested in the efforts being made by many corporations to introduce participative management and employee involvement. I also began to shift my consulting focus from short-term work addressing interpersonal, group and inter-group issues to longer-term work on organisational structure, job design, human resource management, and cultural change. With this shift in both sector and size of client system, I began to experience difficult beginnings with clients.

Normally, because I was consulting to companies within the very traditional commercial and manufacturing sectors of the industrial Mid-West I was attempting to cross the boundary and build relationships with men in senior hierarchical positions. Instead of participative decision-making being something they believed in and valued deeply, their motives were orientated towards overcoming resistance coming from their labour forces to significant change. These managers wanted to stop the pain which they were experiencing without actually changing their behaviour or the structures of their organisations too much. Confrontations during the early stages of negotiating a contract usually centred around such magical thinking.

With my move to England and The Tavistock Institute in 1987, the scope and complexity increased of the change projects to which I was invited to consult. In all of our 16 client companies during this period, the significant stakeholders have demonstrated ambivalence throughout their 2 to 5 year developmental projects. The "buzz words" have changed since the early 1970s: now managers are talking about changing their organisations towards greater employee empowerment, flatter hierarchies, more open and extensive communications systems, and less rigid adherence to departmental boundaries.

But the intentions of those commissioning consultancy have become even more instrumental since the early 1980s: now they are not just talking about motivation, they are talking about "cutting head counts", "flexibility", and competing internationally with Japan and the Continent on quality and innovation. In this political-economic environment, the relationship between such instrumentality and the values which I hold similar to many organisational consultants whom I know, tends to result in increased confrontations in the early stages of developing a consultancy relationship.

Yet, I do not think that my own career development and the societal changes which blur the distinctions between "alternative organisations" and established commercial and manufacturing organisations fully capture what is going on during the difficult beginnings which I seek here to understand. Sharing my war stories with colleagues and hearing their own convinces me that a more broadly shared phenomenon is taking place. The fact that employee involvement, in some form under some "buzz word", is now considered a matter of business survival by many companies means that it is crucial that a broader, social scientific eye be turned on this phenomena.

2   TOWARDS A PRACTICAL CONCEPTUAL FRAMEWORK

2.1   Opening thoughts

When I and my colleagues experience difficulties with new clients we usually feel upset and confused. We try to make sense of what is happening by using what we know about ourselves, the representatives of the client system, and the particular issues around which a confrontation arose. But I, for one, have felt the need to think more systematically across more than one case with a practical theory to assist such reflections. The types of relevant theory seem logical.

Something about the stages in organisational development consultancy points to the purposes and issues characteristic of the initial steps of crossing the organisational boundary and building relationships. Literature on clients' expectations of the consultancy relationship provides ways of thinking about the various roles that consultants and clients negotiate. Any contributions related to confrontations and difficulties, offered by consultant and researchers more experienced than I, helps avoid recreating the wheel. In my opinion, there is no theory better than psychoanalysis applied to groups and organisations to help illuminate messy, stuck relationships. And, finally, organisational theory and sociology which explains resistance to organisational change strike me as a necessary piece to this puzzle.

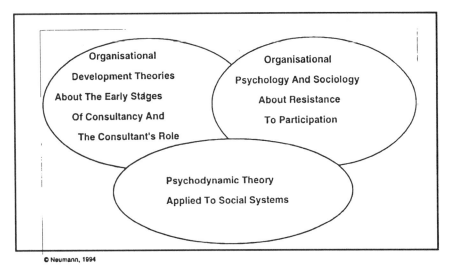

© Neumann, 1994

Accumulated Knowledge of Logical Relevance to Difficult Beginnings

Figure 1

2.2   Stages in organisational development consultancy

Fortunately, the practical literature on organisational development offers widely accepted definitions of the purposes and issues characteristic of the stages in this type of consultancy. For nearly 25 years, few authors have improved on Kolb and Frohman's (1970) formulation of seven basic stages. These are: scouting, entry and contracting, diagnosis, negotiating and planning intervention, taking action, evaluating action, and either starting another round or terminating the relationship.

The first two stages, and some elements of the third, constitute what we mean by the early or initial stages of crossing the boundary and building a working relationship: scouting, entry and contracting, and negotiating the initial diagnosis, including how and with whom the findings will be worked through. "Scouting" is a term that comes, I believe, from North American history when an individual or small group would be sent ahead to check out the territory into which the large party would be travelling, to assess "the lay of the land" and to check for potential dangers.

Indeed, scouting retains some of these connotations as the first contact(s) between potential consultant and client. Before investment of resources on either part, both sides of the interaction attempt to assess what is on offer and how closely it matches conscious and unconscious needs. Cherniss (1976) labels this "pre-entry" during which the consultant ought to ask "should one provide consultation in this situation?", "whose interests will the consultant serve?" and "what will be the primary focus of the consultation?". Call it scouting or pre-entry, this is the first point at which both parties take an initial decision to proceed or not.

Typically, the telephone or a brief meeting at a conference or other unexpected venue will be the vehicle for scouting. Issues for consultants include hearing the presenting problem, understanding the type of consultancy being requested, and judging the degree of fit between themselves and this client system. Should the yes/

no decision of this stage be positive on both sides, and agreement needs to be reached on the next step - almost always some sort of meeting - and the financial arrangement and logistics for this activity.

Two other issues on the consultants' minds provide an overlap into the entry and contracting stage. They begin to ascertain the status of the client representative(s) to determine whether or not the appropriate people, with the corresponding decision-making authority for the type of problem and consultancy being proposed, will be present at the next step. Also, certain intuitive feelings about psychological compatibility are experienced. Menzies Lyth (1988) describes the initial contacts as enabling "the client organisation and the consultant to explore each other as personalities, with their own particular orientations to the problems of social organizations" (p168).

If this exploration barely gets started during scouting, it rushes ahead at full speed during entry and contracting. We tend to think of this second stage of consulting as having the dual task of negotiating a formal agreement to work together - to let the consultant into the organisation or to keep him out - and of negotiating an informal psychological contract (Sherwood and Glidewell, 1971) of mutual needs and expectations. Schein (1969) adds to the tasks of formal and psychological contracting that of defining the relationship, by which he means the support and involvement of the consultant needs from the client and commitment of the senior managers to proceed. The workload of this stage is mind boggling.

In addition to re-visiting several issues discussed only briefly during scouting, a clearer definition of the problem needs to be discovered and the client needs to be identified. Schatzman and Strauss (1973) extend the scouting metaphor further by preferring the idea of "casing the joint", for the purposes of assessing suitability, feasibility and suitable entry tactics. They are writing as ethnographic researchers, thus thinking about entry as going deeper into the organisation almost immediately. Most practitioners writing on this subject, refer to entry with an individual or sub-group representing the larger client system.

We find that elements of beginning to understanding the client system get mixed in with establishing objectives for the consultancy and clarifying the overall scope of the organisational development(s). Many questions must be asked on both sides to discover, and then to decide, elements of both the formal contract - eg objectives, timing, fee and confidentiality - and of the informal contract. This latter tends to include negotiating the role of both consultant and client, about which I will say more in a moment, as well as to explore and experience the concepts being used by both parties to explain and make sense of the situation sufficiently to take a decision if and how to move forward together.

Agreeing a few overall issues about the initial phase of diagnosis tends to involve both sides in gathering data about how the other works. Block (1981) summarises these issues as "the boundaries of your analysis", "the kind of information you will seek", "the product you will deliver", and identification of the people to whom a feedback will be presented (p46). Another decision needing to be taken, often but not necessarily as a part of entry and contracting, includes access to significant stakeholders and records and documents of relevance to the problem for which the consultancy has been requested.

As this decision, in particular, raises questions about how broadly across and deeply into the organisation the consultant will be allowed, examination of assumptions about the definition of the problem, possible solutions, and identification of the client tend to re-emerge. The representatives of the client system authorised to engage in this examination tend to be those people who attend the contracting meeting, set the objectives for the project, approve any action to be taken, and receive the report on the results of the initial diagnosis (ibid, p56).

Frequently, these people are known as "the client"; however, several other aspects of the client system will need to be considered at this stage. Lippitt and Lippitt (1984) remind us that in addition to this body with which the initial contract is agreed, there are target clients (ie those who are supposed to change in some way), leverage clients (ie those who can make or break a change effort), and beneficiary clients (ie those who will benefit from the efforts of others).

I know that the beginning stages are over with my new clients when I have a formal and informal contract, and have agreed timing, sequence and duration of the initial consultancy activities. Frequently, issues of internal and external confidentiality and publicity need to be resolved in order to establish sufficient trust to begin. And finally, a first attempt at determining who will be included and who will be excluded from "steering" roles has been made.

From this literature on the initial stages in organisational development consultancy, we learn that the sheer volume and complexity of issues which must be explored, negotiated and/or addressed in some degree of satisfactory resolution are enormous. A great deal is at stake for both the consultant and the client. In this context, one might be forgiven for thinking that beginnings which are not difficult are suspect, not the other way around.

2.3 Client's expectation of consultancy relationship

Many practitioners and researchers have written about clients' expectations of the consultancy relationship and the various roles that consultants and clients negotiate. In my experience, both I and my new client operate different versions of our mutual contract, despite carefully worded formal and informal agreements, until one of us violates the expectations of the other. This violation signals the need for re-negotiation, what Sherwood and Glidewell refer to as a "pinch" (1971), often announced in the form of a confrontation from the party experiencing the violation in expectation. The volume of literature in the area of roles, and negotiating them, suggests that I am not alone.

Many clients operate on the basis of what Sherwood, in another paper, (1980), calls "traditional assumptions". According to these, the client considers that she has already effectively identified the problem or that it is the consultant's responsibility to decide the nature of the problem. Sufficient information is assumed already to be available to decide the direction that the consultant will take. Therefore, data collection and diagnosis are a waste of time and money. The consultant's report and recommendations should be given directly to the person in authority who will approve, modify and implement.

This view of the consultant's role differs dramatically from the assumptions favoured within the organisation development professions as they have been evolving themselves since 1947. A belief in collaboration, or cooperation as some people prefer to call it, lies at the heart of the discipline. In the "collaborative approach", the entire organisation is the client, not just the boss. The client, in some form, plays an active role in identifying the problems, conceiving solutions and actions, implementing, and evaluating or reviewing. As expressed by Steele (1975), "By the consulting process, I mean any form of providing help on the content, process, or structure of a task or series of tasks, where the consultant is not actually responsible for doing the task itself but is helping those who are" (p3).

Many authors echo some version of these thoughts. The theory of organisational development emphasises the importance of involving clients in the solutions to their own problems rather than assuming that the solutions lie with the consultant (Steele, 1975, p12). It is considered illegitimate to take authority from the organisational members for their right, derived from their organisational legitimacy, to plan and implement changes.

Further, consultants can be trapped by accepting responsibility for the success of consultations for several psychodynamic reasons which I will address shortly. Resisting potentially unacceptable outcomes of the project can then combine with resisting the consultant who has taken on responsibility for that project. Many a consultant has been kicked out of an organisation as a scapegoat, a way that organisational members get rid of the organisational change they find intolerable.

Block (1981) summed up this literature by identifying three ways consultants and managers can work together: the expert role, the pair-of-hands role and the collaborative role. In the expert role, the consultant has full control and the clients awaits the expert driven outcome. Ignoring or even stifling a client's creativity and initiative are dangers of this role. In the pair-of-hands role, the positions are reversed. The client retains complete control and the consultant completes the assignment as specified to him. The collaborative role, clearly the one that Block advocates, involves both parties in joining together to address the client's problem or opportunity. The consultant contributes expertise and the client contributes knowledge of the organisation. In his book, Block advises that a "good contract with the client" ensures that "responsibility for what is planned and takes place has to be balanced - 50/50" (p12).

As much as I value this typology, I would like to add two other roles which I have become aware of since moving to England. The first is that of a neutral observer. In this role, the consultant observes and interprets, taking no responsibility for process or outcome. The client carries on pretty much as usual with the option to use the interpretations or not. A danger of these roles is that the client flounders without sufficient assistance offered from the outside expert. I feel compelled to mention this one because The Tavistock Institute frequently gets blamed for this role, which some people mislabel, "the Tavistock approach".

Whilst we at The Tavistock Institute do, on occasion, play the role of the neutral observer - especially during process consultations - mutual engagement more accurately describes the current biases of myself and several of my colleagues. The consultant contributes expertise in content, process, and/or inquiry depending on her domain of speciality. She values a successful outcome for the client and can be prepared to play a variety of roles as appropriate. The client contributes knowledge of the organisation as well as taking initiatives in the content, process and inquiry of his own change project. He takes full responsibility for process and outcome also playing a variety of roles as appropriate at different points in the consultancy relationship.

From this literature, we see that roles and responsibilities of both parties provide fertile ground for difficulties and confrontations in the early stages of working together. The tension for the consultant seems to be to find a balance between too little responsibility and too much when negotiating her role. Clashes about exactly what collaboration does and does not mean can be expected; especially, when the client will have experienced, interviewed, or heard about other consultants who work along the lines of more "traditional assumptions".

2.4   Psychodynamics between client and consultant

Psychoanalytic theory contributes to this building conceptual framework for understanding "difficulties" and "confrontations" by suggesting unconscious reasons for why messy dynamics emerge between consultants and clients. This is a massive field to try to summarise in so short a paper; therefore, I have chosen to review this literature in an order of accessibility to the client and of possible intervention for helping the client to move forward. I propose that the following psychodynamics are of relevance to the topic of this paper: task anxiety, group and inter-group defences, transference and counter-transference, and individual defences.

In order to engage with the application of psychoanalytic theory to the study of groups and organisations, it helps to shift one's attention off of the individual and the pair and onto the group and organisation as a whole (Rioch, 1985). This can be challenging because most of us live our conscious lives aware of personalities and inter-personal relationships. The goal is to be able to identify patterns of behaviour within the group and the organisations that feel or look or sound "off" in some way.

The gist of this approach is that the individual is acting not just as an individual but as a member of a social group or groups (Marrow, 1969, p108). The group is so important in shaping the behaviour of individuals because it is an essential element in the overall working "life space" of that person. The individual seeks out, consciously or unconsciously, "relevant situations in the external work which he can identify...with psychic structures within himself. The two situations must resemble each other to some degree...Once it does happen, elements of the external situation come to symbolise elements of the internal situation" (Menzies Lyth, 1989). This leads to an organisation being made up of people with a strong proclivity for joining with others in creating and acting out a socially structured defence against shared feelings of threat.

Even taking some healthy scepticism into consideration, I think the argument that individuals search to find a match between their inner worlds and the external organisations to which they join strengthens for employees with a greater freedom of mobility and discretion in their career choices. We can disagree about specific individuals and about those lower down the hierarchy, but senior, middle, and technical personnel often overtly engage in such a search and can articulate those aspects of their search which they consciously understand. Certainly the mutual search is even stronger between a consultant and his client, almost providing a prototype of this matching between inner world and outer organisational reality.

When a group or organisation creates their social defence system, they are hoping to avoid the experiences of anxiety, doubt, guilt and uncertainty. They accomplish this by, as much as possible, "eliminating situations, events, tasks, activities and relationships which cause anxiety or, more correctly, evoke anxieties connected with primitive psychological remnants in the personality" (ibid, p63). We see here one of the most difficult aspects of organisational culture to diagnose and to influence toward change.

Task anxiety, then, can be understood as those policies, routines, structures, and rituals which allow members to avoid genuine fears, anxiety, doubt, guilt and uncertainty. In particular, task anxiety refers directly to undertaking activities necessary to the primary task of the organisation. Menzies Lyth provided, what is still one of the most well known examples of this psychodynamic, when she wrote of the socially structured defence system of nurses dealing with seriously ill patients. Several elements of the organisation of their work helped them, usually unconsciously, to avoid becoming attached to any one patient: eg a shift rota and work allocation system which meant they were never in any one place with any one patient for very long and a dispersed system of authority with prevented any one nurse from feeling responsible for the death, or lack of recovery, of patients.

Any occupation in any sector carries its own anxieties and other emotions which members experience as unbearable, requiring some blocks to awareness - even the consulting profession. By the very nature of the profession, role, position, job or identity group, members are "at considerable risk of being flooded by intense and unmanageable anxiety " (ibid, p50). Clients can often be helped to become aware of ways in which they are managing their anxieties which are not productive to their roles and the primary task of the organisation.

They are not always so amenable, however, to understanding how they do not perceive the ways they blend "with others in groups...to reduce anxiety and maintain a coalition in the face of anticipated trouble or disagreement" (Menninger, 1975, p272). It is this psychodynamic, known as the basic assumption group, which Bion (1961) discovered in the 1950s. He maintained that every group is simultaneously two groups: one devoted to working on the task, or the work group, and one devoted to avoiding anxieties, doubts, and uncertainty which Bion named the basic assumption group. The term "basic assumption" builds on the work of certain object relations theorists, notably Melanie Klein, by stating that socially created and enacted defences, for example between a group representing the client system and a consultant, have their roots and resulting dynamics in defences basic to all human beings rooted in infancy. One can predict that the basic assumption group is in action when "work-group activity is obstructed, diverted, and on occasion assisted, by certain other mental activities that have in common the attribute of powerful emotional drive" (Bion, 1961, p14).

The three types of basic assumption groups postulated by Bion are the basic assumption dependency group, the basic assumption fight/flight group, and the basic assumption pairing group. In each type, group or organisational members assume, as a basic motivation for their behaviour, a joint stance towards the authority figure or consultant acting "as if" such and such were the case. In other words, the basic assumption group shares a joint fantasy.

The basic assumption dependency group acts as if the group has met in order to be sustained by a leader on whom it depends for nourishment, material and spiritual, and protection. The essential aim is to attain security through and have its members protected by one individual. Members act as if they know nothing, as if they are inadequate and immature. Their behaviour, including sometimes expressed wishes, imply that the leader, by contrast, is all knowing and all powerful (ibid).

The basic assumption fight/flight group acts as if the group has met to fight something or to run away, to flee, from something. The assumption is that the group needs to preserve itself and that can only be done by some essential action: either fight or flight will do, it doesn't really matter. If an individual must be sacrificed that is of secondary importance to the preservation of the group (ibid, p93). Their behaviour implies that the leader, or consultant, is unbeatable or uncatchable.

The basic assumption pairing group acts as if the group has met for purposes of awaiting a better, brighter future which will come through two of its members joining together and saving them. Two people get together, on behalf of the group, to undertake some sort of creation while everyone else looks on. The genders of the pair are immaterial to the feeling of hopeful anticipation that a type of reproduction and birth of something that will save the group is taking place. The group's behaviour implies that ignoring the consultant and the immediate present is necessary because the leader who will take them out of their misery is still unborn (ibid, p95).

These basic assumptions operate on the psychological mechanisms of "massive splitting and projective identification, diminution of effective contact with reality, lack of belief in progress through work and suffering" (Menzies Lyth, 1989, p21). That means that individuals cooperate in labelling some aspects of their situation as all bad and some as all good and then identify with one or the other. They think their problems can be solved by the consultant, for example, with little effort on their part. Or, paradoxically, they act as if their problems can not be solved by themselves or by the consultant.

This already complicated picture of group and organisational defences is made even more complicated by the interpersonal processes of transference and counter-transference. Transference is a psychological process by which individuals transfer from the past into the present elements of unresolved experience. The healthy impulse is to resolve the experience in the present and be done with it. The unhealthy impulse it to be driven, usually without awareness, to repeat the experience because something about the present has evoked something similar from the past.

For our purposes, the client is perceiving and responding to the consultant as if that person were an important figure from the past (Kets de Vries and Miller, 1985). This is achieved by projecting oneself or part of one's impulses and feelings into another person and then experiencing them as coming from that other person. The essential expression of the transference is "an unconscious intrapsychic fantasy that distorts an individual's perceptions and interactions" (ibid, p184).

There is a tendency then for the person to act according to the projected images they have accepted, or introjected in the psychodynamic language. Counter-transference is the same process but from the consultant towards the client in reaction to that which the client is projecting. Transferences can be of three types: idealising transferences of both a relatively normal intensity and those character-ised by clinging behaviour; mirroring transferences whereby behaviour is almost obsessively matched; and persecutory transferences whereby feelings of hostility, moral suffering, and envy predominate (Kets de Vries and Miller, 1985).

All human relationships rely on the processes of projecting of certain mental contents from one person onto another and the resulting alteration in the behaviour of the targeted person (Klein, 1959). However, realistic transferences tend to be appropriate to the situation whereas distorting transferences do not. Such psychodynamics block and confuse productive working relationships between consultant and client. We experience them as especially difficult to unravel in a consultancy situation because of the degree of closeness between the personality of the consultant and her or his role.

Lastly, other individual defences will be present in the consultant and client interaction, but usually due to persistent patterns of psychological behaviour which are not necessarily caused by or evoked due to the presence of the consultant. In other words, the person behaves this way most of the time. The labels for these defences have entered the popular vocabulary. Repression involves memories, desires, emotions, thoughts and wishes which are made unconscious and divorced from awareness. Regression results in reverting to modes of adaptation and behaviour more appropriate to an earlier stage of development. In identification, the person thinks, feels, or acts as he conceives the other does, including the idea of identifying with an aggressor.

In my experience, these individual defences do appear in members of the organisational systems to which I consult. However, they do not play as important a role in difficulties and confrontations as denial and reaction formation. In reaction formation, one of a pair of contradictory attitudes or traits is kept unconscious and hidden by emphasising its dramatic opposite. For example, being a participative manager while hiding the authoritarian sides of oneself. In denial, one literally denies the existence of an external fact of reality. This defence, I find, appears most often in relation to task anxiety.

These psychodynamics add to the challenges already posed by negotiating the early stages of crossing the organisational boundary and building a working relationship with a client consistent with the role one would like for oneself and which the client would like enacted. Socially created and maintained defences like task anxiety and basic assumptions are "motivated by anxiety and the desire for protection and typically involve some conscious pretence, emotional suppression, or cognitive unawareness concerning the factors that induce fear" (Kets de Vries and Miller, 1985, p136). Together with transferences, countertransferences and individual defences, they create a terrain in which productive work requires a consultant capable of working with the resulting blocks and confrontations.

2.5   Organisational issues relevant to consultancy remit

If psychodynamic theory addresses the subjective terrain, organisational issues relevant to the consultancy task constitute the objective terrain. Difficulties and confrontations surrounding questions about how to proceed with the initial diagnosis, and working with the findings, rapidly uncover all sorts of information about the organisation. Therefore, a practical framework for understanding confrontations and difficulties requires organisational variables.

Since my work focuses on those organisational changes which result in increased individual autonomy, greater group responsibility, and more effective system-wide influence (Neumann, 1989), I have been particularly interested in difficulties related to that consultancy brief. Depending on the main focus of your consultancies, other types of organisational theory might be of more use to you. From research we have been pursuing over the last decade, three categories of explanations have emerged for why people might resist participation in organisational change (ibid). These categories are grouped into structural, relational, and societal explanations.

Structural explanations include organisational design, work design, and human resources management. The three factors refer to predetermined systems which shape human behaviour by requiring specific socio-technical boundaries, flows of information, connections between subsystems, sanctions for activities, and strategies for motivation. When it comes to organisational structure, people are less willing to participate when: a) the real decisions of the organisation are made outside of participative forums; b) their individual jobs do not require them to use participation: and, c) participation is not reinforced via the personnel mechanisms which communicate the organisation's pivotal norms, ie required behaviour.

Relational explanations for non-participation include the actual management of the participative effort, the dynamics of hierarchy, and the individual's stance towards the organisation. These three factors refer to relationships between individuals and groups which pose contradictions and dilemmas by introducing emotionally laden issues. When it comes to relationships in the organisation, people are less willing to participate when: a) the effort is managed in such a way as to discourage participative competence; b) rank and status continue to be more important than mastery and competence; and, c) participation conflicts with non-work roles and needs.

Cultural or societal explanations for non-participation include primary and secondary socialisation, ideology of work, and the social history of politics. These factors exist prior to and outside the boundaries of a specific enterprise. They impact on organisational life through a steady, sometimes imperceptible influence on the individuals who make up the workforce. This cluster of explanations captures how individuals make sense of the structures and relationships in an organisation. When it comes to culture, people are less willing to participate when: a) they have been socialised successfully to avoid behaviours which threaten hierarchical authority; b) participating challenges deeply held beliefs and values, especially those about what it means to be a "good" employee, boss and company; and, c) adversarial politics, both in the past and present, have resulted in and continue to support protection of self and others.

For consultancies in which involvement of employees matters, regardless of the level of hierarchy, these organisational issues are the raw materials from which organisational changes must be crafted. Since involvement is also a core value of the collaborative and mutual engagement approaches to organisation consultancy, confrontations with the consultant almost always mirrors some organisational issues requiring attention. Meetings with representatives of the client systems, therefore, become a microcosm of the larger organisation wherein problems of involvement are re-enacted in front of and with the consultant.

2.6 Working hypotheses

I have taken a great deal of space in this paper to review these four bodies of literature in order to build a practical framework about what is going on between client and consultant during difficult beginnings. From the literature on stages in organisational development consultancy, we can identify the three stages of scouting, entry and contracting and negotiating the initial diagnosis as defining what beginning with a client means. From the client's experience of the consultancy relationship, we begin to understand that in negotiating the details of the early stages we are also negotiating complementary roles between consultant and client.

These tasks are full of fears, anxieties, doubts and uncertainties that can explain difficult beginnings and confrontations. Both client and consultant mobilise various psychological forces and processes in order to defend themselves against these feelings. Further, significant data about organisational structures, relationships, and culture emerge during these early stages which complicate to address the psychodynamics and role conflicts.

In considering what contribution these bodies of literature can make to our understanding, we take these as variables for analysis. In other words, in studying a particular difficult beginning, we ask ourselves questions about the issues being negotiated during the three early stages of the consultancy, about the client's expectations of the consultant, about the psychodynamics being enacted in the interaction, and about the organisational issues relevant to the consultancy brief. The questions can be arranged in a matrix for analysing particular cases or across cases.

		Socio-Psychological Aspects of Early Stages		
Issues to be Negotiated		Mismatch Between Consultants' and Clients' Expectations of Consulting Relationship	Organisational Issues Relevant to Consultancy Brief	Psychodynamics
During the Early	Scouting	Expert	Structure: •Organisational Design •Work Design •Human Resources Management	Task Anxiety Group Defenses: Basic Assumptions
		Pair-of- Hands		
Stages Which Might	Entry and Contracting	Collaboration	Relations: •Management of Participation •Dynamics of Hierarchy	Transference and Counter- Transference
be Resolved	Initial Phase of Diagnosis and Working With Findings	Neutral Observer Mutual Engagement	Culture: •Primary and Secondary Socialisation •Idealogy of Work •Social History of Politics	Individual Defenses

© Neumann, 1994

Grid for Analysis of "Difficult Beginnings"
Figure 2

The working hypotheses embedded in this matrix are:

(a)   confrontation takes place between consultant and client around numerous overt and covert decisions inherent in building a new working relationship;

(b)   the particular psychodynamics which underlie difficult beginnings enact both the client's expectations of the consulting relationship and organisational issues relevant to the consultancy brief;

(c)   during confrontations, especially concerning the initial diagnosis and the roles of both parties, data emerge about the organisational issues which are relevant to the consultancy brief; and,

(d)   successful working through of difficult beginnings requires the consultant to address, in some fashion, all three aspects of the difficulties: ie, the client's expectations of the consultant's role, the organisational issues relevant to the consultancy brief, and the psychodynamics of the interactions.

3.   METHOD OF ENQUIRY

The data which we analyse in this paper were collected during the initial stages of consultancy with two different clients. We have gone back through the accumulated field notes from contacts with the client to analyse them according to the four variables suggested in the practical framework. One case is that of a success story and the other is that of a failure.

We shall call the organisation in the success story, Basepaper, because they make and fabricate paper for sale to wholesale and industrial customers. The production process is that of continuous processing being undertaken in eight plants on five sites across three countries. The company itself is over 150 years old with nearly 2000 employees. During scouting, entry and contracting, and negotiating diagnosis, we worked with a client representative group of four executive directors. Our brief was to help them develop a "people strategy" which would reinforce behaviours supportive of their business strategy. There were 59 contacts between consultant and client - by telephone, post, and in person - during these early stages. The client was funding the project themselves by paying consultancy fees and signed the formal contract during month 10. A productive working relationship has been ongoing for three and a half years.

We shall call the organisation in the failure story, Carsystems, because they design, make and assemble various mechanical systems for sale to vehicle manufacturers. They use a batch production process in two plants on one site. About 20 years old, the company broke off from a larger corporation and employs 350 employees. Our main client representatives were six people sitting on a managerial project group. Carsystems was one company of eight cooperating with us in a research and development project funded by the UK's Department of Trade and Industry. Therefore, the client was receiving money for participating in the project, not paying the consultants. The purpose of the consultancy was to assist Carsystems in developing and reinforcing group-based working or "teamwork" which they had started on the shopfloor. There were 26 contacts between the consultant and client during the initial stages. Although the client signed the formal contract during the first month of interaction, by mutual agreement the contract was terminated after month 8.

The methodology being used in both cases was that of action research (Marrow, 1969), meaning that we study the organisational issues through iterative cycles of diagnosis, intervention, review or evaluation undertaken with the client. Action research as a consultancy approach provides the double benefit of allowing us to gain intimate access to the client system for the purposes of offering service and generating knowledge which might be of use more broadly beyond the immediate consultancy project. By combining organisational development practices with qualitative data collection and analysis techniques, we usually can engage in longitudinal field research - between two and five years in any one organisation - tracking the developments over time.

The data used for this paper are field notes and semi-structured interview notes for the 59 contacts in Basepaper and the 26 contacts in Carsystems. The researchers use participant observation and related ethnographic methodologies developed by natural sociologists and social anthropologists. A notation system developed by Schatzman and Strauss (1973) is used for each client contact. Observational notes are separated from speculative, theoretical notes which are in turn separated from methodological notes. This encourages the researcher to record sensory observations - ie what she actually hears, sees, touches, smells - whilst also having a category for recording inner reactions, thoughts, guesses, and working hypotheses.

Once the above practical framework was developed, the accumulated field notes for each case were analysed. Analysis took the form of studying the data for a series of interactions and illustrations according to the following questions.

(a)   What issues being negotiated during the initial stages of consultancy were problematic?

(b)   What expectations of the consultancy relationships did the client express, especially during difficult interactions and confrontations?

(c)   Which organisational issues related to the consultancy remit might have influenced the difficulty and confrontations between consultant and client and how?

(d)   Which psychodynamics emerged during the initial stages of consultancy, especially during difficult interactions and confrontations?

4   THE SUCCESS STORY

My first contact with Basepaper came through a telephone call from the Chief Executive Officer and President of the Board. He had gotten our name from an association specialising in issues of industrial involvement and participation. He and his executive directors needed "expertise and a sensitivity to help us develop a strategy" for how they increased the involvement of their employees in the organisation. The President described a very progressive ownership structure, spoke explicitly about believing in worker control, and invited me to travel, at their expense, for an initial chat after receiving a copy of the brief they had developed for the project.

It had been nearly a decade since I had consulted to a senior manager who actually believed in participation. I was delighted. My delight was somewhat dampened by the brief which read like a textbook on the "traditional assumption" model of consultancy. I was amongst several other consultants being invited to tender for the task of "reviewing, formulating, making recommendations and then working with managers to ensure that they understood the recommendations, viewed them as practical, and initiated action". I intended to renegotiate the brief, and went ahead on my scouting mission because (and my counter-transference was already starting) it sounded like the perfect client.

My delight was reawakened during an initial face-to-face meeting where the President and I discovered several mutual interests and common values. I met, and briefly interviewed, all the executives and came away with a pretty good idea of the situation and felt confident that I could negotiate a role more suitable to the kind of work I do. I agreed with the President to send a two page letter summarising how I understood their situation and my ideas for how to proceed. I did so quickly, allowing myself to express the expert side of myself and being very explicit about one of my guiding principles, "using participation to get participation".

Months passed without a word. Several attempts to reach the President by telephone finally paid off. He explained that they had been delayed but were "urgently ready to take the next step", another round of interviews with short-listed consultants. I explained that I would be willing to attend one additional meeting without payment but after that, no more. Now a days, I wouldn't even have done that.

When I showed up for the second scouting meeting, the executives hadn't even read my proposal. They were waiting for me to make a presentation "like all the others". I gently refused and waited while they read my document. The conversation which followed unearthed the task anxiety most of the executives felt about the project. They had been pressured to invest more in people by the non-executive members of their Board. They had initially decided, with a non- executive member, that they would hire a Group Personnel Director (this is a Group of companies); after the non-executive member left their meeting and they had "slept on it", they decided to bring in a consultant instead. This was also the first conversation we had about whether it was my job to decide for them how to proceed.

However, half of the executives really didn't see a "people strategy" as a priority. They were in the midst of a very expensive acquisition downstream, during a period of growing international competition, and having to travel all over the world for business. They weren't sure if they needed help on "people strategy" or "capital strategy". The last consultants brought in by the President had recommended changes which resulted in a 15% cut in people. The President was the only person expressing "total commitment to people" and "pushing very hard" for the project to go ahead. I wrote in my notes at the time "I would love to work with this man. I think I am projecting too much goodness onto him"; I was suffering from an idealisation counter-transference.

The executives had also begun to transfer onto me their concern for treating employees well and for employee involvement. Frequently during that meeting, I had to counteract assumptions that I didn't care about managers and only cared about shopfloor employees. Occasionally, this argument was targeted at the President. In the group's mind, we seemed to be paired in favour of creating this better future of harmony and balance between business needs and people needs. I left that meeting still interested in working with the client but concerned about the degree of conflict amongst the executives.

Months passed. I did receive a telephone call from the Managing Director of one of the companies inviting me to tender for a short-term consultancy with his site. I declined explaining that I felt it would be too confusing for me to be working simultaneously with two parts of this particular system. Finally, I received a "holding letter" from the President, praising me and asking me, in a very personal tone, to please wait a bit longer. He assured me that they wanted "someone steeped in the philosophies you have been talking about".

The executives had decided to hire "an expert in group dynamics to help us sort out some of the differences between us" and then to come back to me later. I felt confused, but once again responded with my expert hat on and encouraged them to not spend too much time avoiding thinking through how to involve others more broadly in whatever they were going to do. That letter resulted in a very rapid telephone message to "begin work together urgently" and a rushed meeting between the President and I at his club in London, after which he asked me to arrange for the "minor details for finances and contracts".

Seven months after that first telephone call with the President, a meeting was scheduled for what I consider to be the start of entry and contracting. The confusion about objectives for the consultancy brief continued: some executives thought the focus should be on ownership and structure and others favoured activities to deal with low morale and resistance to several technical and organisational changes. Throughout these conversations, I was struck with the confessional tone as executives admitted to less savory aspects of how they treated their employees. These confessions were frequently followed by expressions of terror about the business climate: competitors were being bought by bigger international corporations and they had to find a way to avoid being taken over. The various companies, managed rigidly as profit centres, weren't doing as well as needed and couldn't afford any improvements for people anyway.

I considered that this first entry and contracting meeting had effectively started the tasks of coming to a common picture of the situation and identifying the complex client system with which work would need to be undertaken. Finding a date for a meeting to continue this work proved difficult. I was dealt with sharply by the President's secretary for not re-adjusting my schedule to suit these "very busy men". I prepared for the second meeting by thinking through various scenarios for undertaking an initial diagnosis and identifying a suitably representative group with which to work through the findings.

The meeting began with three of the four executive directors confronting me. I had "not cooperated" with the executive secretary in scheduling the meeting, an act which they didn't consider very "people-orientated". The previous meeting "was a mess, without any positive action resulting". It was "ambling" and "not focused". "If that's how you lead a meeting with us, it would be a disaster to have a bigger meeting with people present from all over the company, we wouldn't get anything done!". Once they had calmed down a bit, the President explained that he usually acted as chairman for their meetings, and "it is the job of the Chairman to move things along and make things happen". Another executive complained that I hadn't "created a spark, engendered excitement, inspiration, enthusiasm". In a softer tone, the other two spoke of needing to hear me "regularly refer to other work and situations"; "you don't employ testimonials like other consultants".

I interpreted this outburst as a combination of basic assumption fight mixed up with the client's expectations of an expert role for the consultant. Clearly, anxieties had been stirred up about moving outside their small group of four and into the next two layers of management, plus involving the trade union representatives. They felt they had to stay in tight control of any progress related to "people strategy", due to number of organisational factors relevant to the consultancy brief. At the same time, they wanted to feel reassured that they had an expert on whom they could depend or whom they could easily reject. They couldn't fully do either with me.

We worked through this difficulty explicitly by talking first about conflicting expectations in roles and responsibilities, and second about the issues of authority, leadership, and involvement in managing a change in their complex organisation. The executive directors were in disagreement about initiating change throughout the entire group of companies or within each individual company. They also couldn't agree about working through the existing chain of command or using existing employee involvement mechanisms. The rest of that meeting and all of the next meeting was spent in sorting out these details of the initial diagnosis and a representative structure for working through the findings. The contract was actually signed between these meetings.

The day after they appeared to have agreed to go forward together as an entire organisation, I received a letter from the President. After I had left, the executive directors had "searched their souls" and decided that they couldn't go forward in the largest company. They were going to have to announce redundancies there and didn't want The Tavistock Institute accused of these cuts. So, they had decided that I would go ahead with the four smaller companies, which constituted a separate division. For the first phase of work, then, I worked with the executive director in charge of this division and his four boards of directors, alternating with quarterly meetings with the executive director group.

5   THE FAILURE STORY

I first met the infamous Managing Director and Chairman of the Board of Directors of Carsystems at a consortium meeting for the eight firms which had applied for government funding to study "teamwork" in their companies. He had written an angry letter to the Department of Trade and Industry complaining that they weren't giving him enough money for participating: the DTI responded by giving him ten times the grant of any of the other consortium companies. The Chairman was well respected throughout certain manufacturing communities for his flamboyance, his technical achievements, and his economic performance.

During what constituted the scouting phase, he bragged about how far ahead his company was, about how he had had no trouble with the trade unions, and how he knew exactly what kind of help they needed from the consultants. Apparently, he read widely amongst popular management books about the role of the chief executive in leading organisational change. His own language was peppered with phrases like "breaking down the barriers" between departments and "empowering the supervisors to lead the cultural change" on the shopfloor. These two areas of concern - the role of supervisors in improving workers' motivation for group-based working and increased cross-functional cooperation - were recurring difficulties he had "not yet managed to crack" at his company.

The Chairman agreed at this consortium meeting, as did the representatives of the other seven companies, to convene a body of people within Carsystems representative of those stakeholders most likely to make a contribution to developing and reinforcing "teamwork". This group would then meet monthly with the consultants, steer actions within the enterprise, and review progress. When the consultant rang to arrange the logistics for the first entry and contracting meeting, the Chairman stated that it would be premature to convene a representative body until after he had "set the scene" for us as outsiders. Further, he wanted two groups instead of one - one for shopfloor supervisors and one for office-based managers - and he wanted to be sure that "we have invented the future before moving into it".

We understood that he might wish to engage in more formal and psychological contracting with us before involving others and accepted his idea. We agreed to meet with him and two others in the morning and, then, to meet with a slighter larger group in the afternoon. The agenda for that larger meeting would ritualise the start of the DTI project and could go ahead with a management-only group.

What actually happened was different. After being kept waiting for a period which started to feel insulting, we were led into the Chairman's office. There, for the next two hours, the Chairman - with occasional affirmations from the meek Personnel Manager - lectured at the consultant team on the stated topic of "our interesting background for you to see where our heads are". They emphasised that Carsystems was "a brownfield site", with the workers having "a docile, regionally-based mentality" different from what they preferred. They had both worked at a well known automobile manufacturer during a period of nationally published strikes; in fact, Carsystems had been a part of that company 20 years before. They didn't believe in "jaw jawing" with employees.

It is important to mention that, in addition to a consultant from The Tavistock Institute, the other consultant was a Senior Industrial Relations Officer from ACAS. The Chairman had known that involvement of the trade union was an explicit part of the contract he had signed. He then went on and described his negative impressions of The Tavistock Institute consultants whom he had met during the 1970s: "the men all had long hair and the women were bluestockings".

As the DTI project was contractually both a research and consultancy project, the consultants gathered this information as data. We asked a few questions, but didn't attempt to stop the flow. The lecture session ended with a factory tour, during which the Chairman - who had a powerful voice and a relatively quiet shopfloor - gave us electronic earphones to wear on the tour so he could continue to speak and we wouldn't miss anything. At one point, he turned to the woman on the team and asked if she knew who Frederick Taylor was, when she said "yes" - adding that organisational behaviour was her field of study, he interrupted her and proceeded to give a lecture on Taylorism and how he was trying to do something entirely different on the shopfloor.

Indeed, the shopfloor was impressive from a technological point of view. It was obvious that a great deal of money had been invested in equipment and machines. Also, the jobs appeared to be well structured into cells around particular products and processes. We knew they had managed to change the payment system from individual piece rate to one which rewarded group productivity.

Upon return from the tour, we were joined by the Acting Manufacturing Manager. In the past six months, the Chairman had removed the previous manufacturing manager from post, lost the previous managing director to another company, made 25% of all employees redundant, eliminated three layers of middle management, and put in place the new supervisors - called "team leaders". The Acting Manufacturing Manager, paid as a full-time consultant, had been the main implementor of these activities.

The Chairman introduced this man as his "exorcet missile", a title which seemed to please the Acting Manufacturing Manager. Not being familiar with this military metaphor, the consultants asked what it meant: the "missile" answered by describing himself as "putting a bomb under complacency, making rapid fire decisions, like SAS work, takes hills, leaves debris, makes two years of change in three months". The Personnel Manager, who had been practically silent through-out, suggested that the employees were a bit "shell shocked". The Chairman countered that "they are not shell-shocked, just unsettled".

Throughout the rest of the meeting, the Chairman frequently interrupted the consultants and the other two managers to correct their language: not "mission" but "creating the future"; not "problem" but "opportunity"; not "organisational structure" but "business process". The three Carsystems managers did eventually identify some next steps for themselves and agreed to extend the project group to include two supervisors and one office-based manager. The Chairman refused to involve anyone from the shop-floor, but agreed to communicate the results of this meeting to the trade union representatives and employees in face-to-face meetings.

When we arrived for the second entry and contracting meeting, we were greeted by the same triumvirate. They wanted us to "structure our day for us". When we attempted to plan with them, they began to complain that they didn't know what we were going to do for them, "what valued-added do you bring to the party?". Straightforward attempts to answer these questions only evoked more resistance. We then instigated a lengthy, difficult conversation about roles and responsibilities. The Chairman and Acting Manufacturing Manager tended to dominate the discussions, as before, with the Personnel Manager being silent. After about 45 minutes non-stop of confrontation, the consultants spoke for about 5 minutes about our understanding of the situation.

On the one hand, we interpreted the first meeting as communicating the client's expectations that we would be a "pair-of-hands", as if we were there to do the bidding of the Chairman. On the other hand, we were now being treated as outside experts. The explicit contract for the project - discussed at length on three separate occasions at consortium meetings - was one of mutual engagement. The client needed to carry on with tasks they had identified as important for developing and reinforcing "teamwork", sometimes with the consultants' assistance in various roles. For example, at the previous meeting, the triumvirate had identified two tasks they were going to do, how had those gone? It was apparent from the reaction that the client didn't remember having agreed to anything, even though the Chairman had written the notes from the previous meeting.

At this point, we were attacked. The Chairman said "you want to move faster than we want" and "there is no ownership on the team". There "was a smelly fish in the room": he resented our attempt to establish a forum at which their "right to manage might be challenged". When we reminded him of the contract he had signed as a requirement for joining the consortium, the Acting Manufacturing Manager said we were "just engaging in willy wagging". The Chairman stated that he had only joined to learn from the other companies and not to engage in the research and development activities. "We are moving ahead fast, we can't be held back by research, that's not value-added." The possibility of collaboration with a consultant seemed as foreign as the possibility of genuine collaboration with employees.

The consultants were sent off into the staff canteen to eat lunch alone while people were collected for the fuller meeting. About 10 minutes before that meeting was to start, the Acting Manufacturing Manager called the consultants into his office to meet an additional three consultants. These men were his "team of collaborators in crime", all retired or made redundant production engineers. They handed their business cards to The Tavistock Institute and ACAS consultants, and expressed deep concern about the human and organisational issues which continued to block full implementation of the technological changes. When we suggested that these sorts of issues were the raw materials of the DTI project, the Acting Manufacturing Manager insisted that this was not the case.

Eventually, a fuller meeting was convened and the entry and contracting agenda of the first site visit was repeated with this larger, more representative group. Throughout, the Chairman corrected people's language, set up an atmosphere of intimidation, and then asked people directly to reassure him that they were not inhibited from speaking their minds openly and honestly. Interventions from consultants focused on decreasing the time and space taken by the Chairman and inviting silent members to speak. Again, members identified actions they wanted to take for themselves before the next monthly meeting.

The Chairman and the Acting Manufacturing Manager complimented the consultants on the meeting afterwards. In chatting with the Chairman alone, the consultants suggested that some sort of diagnosis was now necessary for them to be of use to the client. He agreed and encouraged them to undertake as small number of interviews to look at the issue of cross-functional cooperation.

Two weeks later, the Acting Manufacturing Manager sent a fax to the consultant saying "Did not think much of last meeting - woolly, fluffy, and no context!". To this note, he attached a one page description of research being undertaken by another institute which was more technologically orientated. This was the second confirmation the consultants had received that even the "exorcet missile" didn't feel that he could be open in his communication.

A week after that, the Chairman sent a thick packet of data on "an internal consultancy" which he had been undertaking to "break down the barriers erected by the specialists and bureaucrats". He had been holding frequent off-site sessions, at which he both led and consulted, with both senior and middle managers separately. In the enclosed letter, he explained that his latest attempt to find a managing director had failed. He was in negotiation with the three senior managers to take over the role, so he could step down as Acting Managing Director.

As the next meeting approached, both the Chairman and the Acting Manufacturing Manager contacted the consultants to say they would not be present but to go ahead without them. The former would be on holiday and the latter was interviewing for a permanent position. The Acting Manufacturing Director sent a fax indicating that he had personally ensured that all tasks had been completed. Clearly, there was a feeling that the consultants were in some sort of police or school mistress role.

The day before the meeting, he rang to say that he "wanted to change the direction of how the company is organised". He thought the Chairman's approach at internal consultancy was a "waste of time". He lamented the continued difficulties he was experiencing in getting the "team leaders to take on the task of cultural change on the shopfloor". He was starting to understand that "forcing is not for all types of changes, I have problems in those areas of change where forcing does not work".

We arrived on site for our third meeting, hoping to negotiate initial diagnosis. We met with the group of supervisors and managers, led by the Personnel Manager. He was lively and talkative throughout. The group began by reviewing work they had undertaken since the previous session, although they insisted that the work the Acting Manufacturing Manager said was done had not been done. They, then, engaged in an analysis of shopfloor "teamwork" and identified one or two actions they felt would be useful next steps. The Personnel Manager was very excited that his own ideas were to be taken forward. For the rest of that site visit, the consultants collected data of relevance to the other topic of cross-functional cooperation, in preparation for a promised written report on the first six months of the project.

Three days later, the Acting Manufacturing Manager sent a fax saying that he liked what he had seen of the outcome of the last meeting. However, the Personnel Manager's idea was "scrapped because it wouldn't work" and other ideas were being implemented. With the Chairman, the consultants agreed to forego the next monthly meeting as a new managing director had been found and he was still in negotiation with the senior management team. Instead, we agreed to send a lengthy letter summarising the situation as we understood it and suggesting directions for development.

Our feedback letter addressed both topics of shopfloor "teamwork" and cross-functional cooperation. Because we felt that we still did not have a mutual picture of how to work together as client and consultant, we made a point of discussing both topics in the light of unresolved contracting issues and of organisational issues relevant to the consultancy brief. By this point, we had decided to raise the question of termination with the client. Therefore, the feedback letter was written as a formative evaluation of the current situation, in the hope that the document might prove of use to them after we were no longer around.

Both key actors wrote lengthy letters back in response. While the details were different, both men thanked us for our thoughtful comments and defended the status quo. They reiterated their opinion that they were "light years ahead of anybody else" they had seen. Further, any "improvements to the current picture are ones we are already aware of and have in hand".

The Chairman also sketched out the new management structure, reported that he was backing out of daily operations - including the DTI project, and indicated that he wasn't going to force the new management team to stay in the project. He wrote that he had participated in the project for a number of reasons, including: "listen to 'experts', eg Tavistock, take care with such input until I/others here am/ are comfortable with it, such input is optional, note that my previous experience was a Tavistock conference in 1973/74".

Further, he stated, "I agree we cannot order attitude changes etc, but leadership setting context can do more than a shipload of participation (tried that in previous company - what a waste of everyone's time)". He was "setting up a context" in which the next senior management team could decide "how this project contributes to our 1993/94 plan: does it add value? if no - withdraw, if yes - how can we get optimum value?". He also noted that the Personnel Manager was "no longer with us, he was made redundant".

In speaking on the telephone, the Chairman and I agreed that termination was a option for both of us. We agreed to meet with the senior management team, after interviewing them individually, in order to take a decision whether to proceed or not. He had set "stiff financial objectives which they have to achieve - if teamwork helps them, fine, if not then drop it, it is not a priority, it is my job to hold them to account". "I told them that if I was the managing director, I'd continue it...We've done all the mechanistic things but we are not getting the numbers. We are not getting people enrolled to meet the established aims and values." In written form, he had also told them "do not stay in this just because of the money from the DTI" and "only stay in it if it is going to help you meet your financial targets".

In this conversation, the Chairman was reflective about his reaction to me. "I have been wary of your input. That 1973-74 experience meant that I had a past view of Tavistock. It is something I've had to fight against. You have something of value to input, it is up to us to access it. I have an 'already listening' for you, an impression I already got, that's what I'm doing to you."

During the individual interviews, we learned that each of the senior managers felt under severe pressure to meet the objectives set by the Chairman. In fact, they would lose tremendous financial rewards if they failed, and possibly also lose their jobs. The Acting Manufacturing Manager was on his way out. The new Managing Director prided himself on his ability to work well with people and with the trade unions. The Finance Director informed us that the company was being prepared for sale in one to two years.

Armed with this information, we were no longer willing to continue working with the company. The senior managers came to the same conclusion. The Finance Director explained, in a telephone call, that they needed someone "to teach us how to do it" and to "give straight answers" which they "felt we would not do". Further, they "were very busy" and "needed time to get the new MD on board". His closing comment was "being a salesman myself, I know how you must feel. I've lost some deals in my time." Needless to say, this conception of Carsystems as "a deal" with which to work had not been our experience as consultants.

6   SOME PURPOSES SERVED BY DIFFICULTIES

These stories about Basepaper and Carsystems illustrate how the proposed conceptual framework can be applied to analyse difficult beginnings between client and consultant. The cases were described according to the dimensions of the grid. I will now use the grid further to make connections between the various dimensions and psychodynamics, which can prove to be so messy. From these connections, some ideas about the purposes served by of difficulties can be interpreted.

Consider, for example, the relationship between the client's expectation of the consultancy relationship and psychodynamics. At Basepaper, the executive directors preferred an "expert" role for the consultant with a corresponding basic assumption dependency. During that first telephone call with the President, he stated as much, "We need expertise and sensitivity to help us develop a strategy". The copy of the brief which he sent described the job of consultant as "to review, formulate, and then to work with managers to ensure that they understand recommendations, view them as practicable, and initiate implementation". During the surprise attack launched by the executive directors, they complained that I hadn't taken charge of their meeting, hadn't ensured a "constructive outcome", and hadn't provided them with "excitement, spark, and inspiration". Further, I didn't feel the need to sell myself to them by referring to other clients and past successes.

We were able to work out a more mutually engaging relationship. Even so, throughout these early stages, my most successful interventions were "expert advice" letters which I wrote to influence their decisions.

Carsystems, by contrast, preferred a "pair-of-hands" role. This was apparent from the sheer numbers of full-time consultants working as employees inside the company, eg the Acting Manufacturing Manager and his "collaborators in crime". The Chairman announced repeatedly in various types of meetings that he would decide whether or not to use the consultants' input. He lectured the consultants in areas for which they had national reputations: organisational change theory, job design principles, and industrial relations practices. He tried to give the consultants "homework" assignments to be carried out between monthly meetings. A variety of psychodynamic explanations for this can be considered; however, the one for which we have the strongest data is the transference the Chairman and Personnel Manager were experiencing on The Tavistock Institute female consultant. They both enjoyed telling the story about having met Institute consultants in the 1970s when they consulted to their previous employer, including the punch line: "the men had long hair and the women were bluestockings". The Chairman confided to the Managing Director of another consortium company that "that woman has a lot to give but I can't get at it". Finally, he told the Institute consultant directly that he had realised that he had "an 'already listening' for you, an impression I already got, that's what I'm doing to you": he had transferred unresolved feelings from a 1970s Tavistock Working Conference onto the present.

The individual psychodynamics of leaders play an important role in both of these cases, influencing both the early stages of the consultancy and also providing useful information relevant to the brief accepted by the consultant. For example, the Basepaper President engaged in reaction formation as an individual defense. For him, one of a pair of contradictory attitudes or traits were kept hidden while he emphasised its dramatic opposite. On the one hand, he was known throughout the group of companies for being philosophically committed to employee ownership, employee involvement, and participative management. He had made great strides in moving the ownership structure and formal consultation mechanisms in these directions. At the same time, he defined so narrowly the degree of genuine participative decision-making available in these meetings that employees found them boring and meaningless. The President would attack "taking care of people" as an old "paternalistic" notion, insisting that "involvement in the business" was the progressive way forward. He tolerated poor personnel practices and refused to address the issue of financial structure which kept those practices in place.

In Carsystems, the Chairman defended himself with projection and denial; this defense set up a dynamic of hierarchy within the company where employees enacted basic assumption dependency behaviour and basic assumption flight behaviour. In short, he dominated all meetings, told people which words to use, blocked any comments coming from the consultants, and then complained that they didn't contribute. Employees were intimated into silence and, simultaneously, worshipped the Chairman as the one who was going to make sure that everything was alright. The fact that he intended to sell the company suggests that this trust might have been misplaced. When his own managers stated that employees were "shell shocked" from the pace and style of organisational and technological change, he insisted that they were only "unsettled". He waxed elegant about his plans for cross-functional cooperation and then supported the behaviours of his "exorcet missle" which undermined that very cooperation. Finally, he bragged to the point of alienating others that he was further down the "teamwork road" than anyone else at the consortium meetings; and, then, he puzzled repeatedly about lack of motivation and responsibility for operating his technically perfect job designs.

These examples illustrate how the matrix can be used to analyse difficult beginnings. Many more examples from these cases could be drawn from the data presented in this paper alone.   The reader may have noticed the counter-transference from the consultant onto Basepaper as "good client" and onto Carsystems as "bad client". Ideological differences - values clashes - could be another fruitful avenue for analysis, as could the mismatch between participative approaches to managing change during periods of severe economic pressures.

I would like to consider the purposes served by difficult beginnings or confrontations between client and consultant in the early stages by linking the organisational development literature with the psychodynamic literature. These two disciplines rarely speak to each other through the scholarly and trade publications, although practitioners and researchers all over the world are becoming increasingly interested in their synthesis. I believe this synthesis promises greater understanding of difficult beginnings.

From the organisational development literature, we learn that feelings are an important source of data for the consultant, the "affective side" versus the "technical/business problem or project" in the words of Block (1981, p11). From the psychoanalytic literature, we learn that "conflict and anxiety are inevitable, existential givens which occur within each individual, group, and social system, though in differing ways and degrees" in the words of Miller and Rice (1967).

Feelings, anxieties, and conflict emerge in the face of the mutual task of establishing a "goodness of fit" between consultant and client. Congruence of values and complementarity of roles matter precisely because both parties are engaged in the "special case of the attachment of a new person to an existing social system" (Glidewell, 1969, p20). In developing a relationship with a person who is to be only temporarily involved with their organisations, clients are concerned, reasonably so, to establish a basic criterion for predicting that the consultant will contribute positively to the ultimate values and immediate goals which the client consciously and unconsciously holds (ibid, p21).

For the consultant, there are two concerns around which she intends to exercise her authority. The first concern, and the one more easily discussed openly with the client, has to do with influencing the content and methodology of the project. Lippitt and Lippitt (1984) consider this to be yet another aspect of consultancy role, that is the degree to which the consultant advocates the choice of particular goals, values and methods to be used by actors in defining and solving problems or undertaking tasks.

The second concern for the consultant, and the one less easily discussed by its very nature, has to do with examining possible discrepancies between the "presenting problem" and the "real", or deeper, more complex nature of the problem, to quote Menzies Lyth (1988, p158). The concept of "presenting problem" comes from the clinical professions in which "presenting symptom" can be understood as the client's understanding of his problem due to a lack of expertise or some unconscious reason why he might not be aware of the real problem. The client, in carrying out his own diagnosis, might identify as a problem "an area of organisational functioning where the 'pain' is most severely felt or can be most easily formulated. Or it may be used as a 'displacement area' because the real disorder "is too difficult to be disclosed or to be accepted as amenable to change" (ibid, p169).

The stages of scouting, entry and contracting, and negotiating the diagnosis and feedback place both parties in a situation in which the power to define the situation is shared. Managing such a lateral relationship, in which there is no clear boss/ subordinate relationship, creates a power imbalance open to ambiguity and continuous negotiation (Block, 1981). In the face of resistance - another way of looking at difficulties and confrontation- the consultant struggles with the decision to push harder for her opinion or to let go and accept the opinion of the client. This is especially true in collaborative consultancies.

But the early stages are the points of maximum leverage for the consultant. To quote Block, yet again, "client commitment is the key to consultant leverage and impact. We can not order the client to take action. Having leverage requires confronting the doubts at each stage of the consulting process." Kets de Vries and Miller (1984) define confrontation as the process of "making problems or events explicit so that persons involved will recognise what is happening" (p193). Their emphasis is on aspects of behaviour and issues which appear to the consultant to be being avoided.

I think it is part of a consultant's responsibilities to assist the client to face that which has been avoided, as it relates to successfully addressing the brief for which they have retained me. Frequently, the client agrees an objective and almost immediately begins putting up obstacles to making progress on that objective. I understand this to be due to inner conflict within the organisation which has prevented the members from progressing and has motivated them to seek consultancy help. Therefore, resistance which seems to be directed at me is "a reaction to the emotional process taking place within the client" (Block, 1981, p113). This process, one of emotional and/or political conflict results from the process of taking up the role of client. The client experiences "the opposition of approximately equally strong field forces", as Lewin's force-field analysis educates us (Marrow, 1969, p62): these forces might be pulling between two positives, two negatives, or one positive and one negative, as they relate to change the client consciously wishes to make.

Such forces will be unique to each client; however, we can predict - and the framework I am building here for analysis of difficult beginnings assumes - that the forces will be related both to psychodynamics and organisational issues of relevance to the consultant's brief. Hirshhorn (1985) postulates that at the moment of taking up a role, a person is pulled in the direction of reality and external threats and, simultaneously, pulled inwards towards the threats rooted in one's psychological past (p346).

This inner conflict between external organisational realities and internal psychological fantasies gets played out in relation to the consultant in a variety of ways which might look like difficulty, a confrontation, and/or resistance. I provide only a few examples as readers can, no doubt, think of their own. Needless to say, the literature abounds with consultant's frustrations. Miller and Rice (1967) speak of a client system seeming "at times rigid with their desire to avoid discussion of irrational motivation" (p248). Block (1981) finds himself or the client explaining something for the third time as a strong clue for difficulty. Hirschhorn (1985) describes experiencing himself as "stepping out of role" and responding in an unprofessional way with clients (p146). Other than being directly attacked by clients, I have also learned to consider ceaseless negotiation and lack of progress being made between meetings as dependable signals that something is wrong.

Why would a client go to the time and expense of bringing in an external consultant and then resist the very task for which they requested assistance? To quote one of my favourite poets, Robin Morgan, "excuses for not moving are - in number, age , diversity, and sheer prolific art - the baroque high genius of the slavebrain" (1972, p79). I will only mention a few. Block (1981) suggests that "preoccupation with the consultant selection process means the manager wants to start a project, but does not want anything to really happen" (p93) or, perhaps, such delay expresses underlying fears that they really can't be helped. I and my colleagues can echo these thoughts and add the observation that some clients seem to want the consultants to fail so that they are vindicated in their own inability to have solved the problem before hiring outside help. Carsystems illustrates this problem.

Kets de Vries and Miller (1985) echoes these thoughts from a psychoanalytic perspective: deriving benefits such as care and attention from symptoms; avoiding pain of discovering roots of one's difficulties; feeling unworthy of deserving relief; fearing criticism of one's past performance. They also mention wishing to retain current allocations of power and authority, competing between factions for power and engaging in destructive political behaviour. This indicates that the dynamics underlying difficulties and confrontations between consultant and client can have roots in political as well as psychological dynamics. There are reasons why managers can not be publicly seen to accept help and be open to suggestions which have very little to do with how they feel about the consultants. For two of the four Basepaper executives, this was certainly true.

Miller (1985) speaks of a "system of political relationships and relatedness, the micro-politics of the immediate situation, not only the task and roles of this occasion but roles in other political systems" outside, for our purposes, the contacts between consultant and client in the early stages. As newcomers, we are handicapped in our ability to be fully aware of this network of political systems which characterise organisations, especially in the scouting and entry and contracting stages, regardless of how effectively we attempt to collect such information. We can be on the receiving end of conscious or unconscious manipulation - i.e. covert political activity - without being aware of it. Or, when funding is coming from a source other than the client, the client might feel under coercion and inadequately in control of the situation.

Bexton (1975) defines covert politics as "the social field of alliances, pressure groups, and power influences operating within" a change process "in unexamined ways unrelated to overtly stated" objectives, concerns, and constraints (p346). The picture is further complicated by the consultant also being involved in the political activity of advocating particular goals and methodologies for the consultancy. And, so, the dual dynamics of psychology and politics interweave with the numerous tasks of decision-taking, role negotiating, and relationship building inherent in the early stages of scouting, entry and consulting, and diagnosis. The knots of difficulty and confrontation almost seem inevitable.

So, several functions might be served by difficult beginnings. Confrontations allow both parties to establish the congruence of values and complementarity of roles which constitute "good of fit". The experience of mutual influence, or lack thereof, educates both client and consultant about the degree to which they can predict one another's behaviours.

Achieving a match in problem definition, and in style of problem resolution, is another function of difficult beginnings. Presenting problems and desired consultant approaches need to be tested and explored for readiness to learn on behalf of both sides.

So several purposes might be served by difficult beginnings. Successfully working through confrontations allows both parties to establish the congruence of values and complementarity of roles which constitute a "goodness of fit". The experience of mutual influence, or lack thereof, educates both client and consultant about the degree to which they can predict one another's behaviours. Achieving a match in problem definition, and in style of problem resolution, is necessary for a productive working relationship.

"Presenting problems" offered by the client and approaches preferred by the consultant need to be tested and explored for readiness to learn on both sides. Discovering rigidities within the client system provides important data about the topic for which consultancy has been requested as well as about the degree to which individual and group members learn. Similarly, discovering rigidities with the consultant system provides important data about the degree to which a standardised approach (even an overtly "un-standard" one) is on offer and can or can not be adjusted in response to developing needs within the client system.

Establishing mutually acceptable roles for both client and consultant constitutes one of the most important purposes of confrontations. Usually, when difficulties turn into confrontations, the dimension of power is being addressed. How much power will the consultant be allowed to exercise in this client system? How much power will the client retain? Which people within the client system, or consultant system when more than one, will be or are most powerful in relation to the topic of the consultancy?

The ability and willingness to work through difficulties, confrontations, and resistance is a core competence for both consultants and clients. The approach taken to working through might differ early on, but needs to develop some commonality if a working relationship is to succeed. In psychodynamic terms, the entry of a stranger into an organisation mobilises the socially structured defence of the client system (and probably the consultant system, as well) to mould the stranger into someone safe, someone who will not upset the defences too much.. Such a mobilisation takes place precisely because the consultant has been asked, by virtue of being asked to address lack of progress on a particular brief, to work with resistance to change.

Activated defences enact the same blocks in the client system which organisational members have been struggling with alone. The combination of politics and the psychodynamics of splitting and projection allow some individuals and groups to represent forces in favour of the change and some to represent the forces against the change. The vary process of selecting and beginning to work with a consultant serves the purpose of attempting to co-opt a consultant into representing one side more than another.

7   PROPOSITIONS FOR PRACTICE

Just like the consultant, the client system will be aware of some purposes served by difficulties and confrontations more than others. As the consultant becomes more aware of the range of possible issues underlying difficult beginnings, she needs to take decisions about which issues to raise in what manner. Sometimes, awareness dawns in the heat of a battle with the client ; equally, the heat of the battle releases emotions on both sides and new insights emerge after the fact.

Having a practical framework in mind during the initial stages of crossing the boundary and building a relationship can help both to prevent difficulties and to work with them as they arise. My goal with this paper has been to propose such a practical framework, expressed as a grid for analysing difficult beginnings. From a theoretical viewpoint, the consultant can use the questions suggested for analysing Basepaper and Carsystems.

     (a)   Which issues related to scouting, entry and contracting, and initial diagnosis have not been negotiated to satisfaction?

     (b)   Which expectations of either the client's or consultant's role and responsibilities appear to be in dispute?

     (c)   What information is emerging about organisational issues relevant to the topic for which the consultancy has been requested?

     (d)   Which psychodynamics on the part of client and/or consultant are contributing to difficulties in addressing (a), (b), and/or (c)?

The working hypotheses direct the consultant towards these four questions of analysis. The suggestion is that these variables provide a useful picture of the causes of difficult beginnings. Once understanding is achieved, then the likelihood increases (provided the competence and willingness is present) that the consultant can act in a way to assist the client in working through the difficulty.

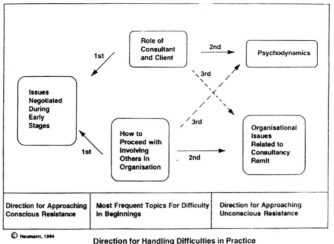

Direction for Handling Difficulties in Practice

Figure 3

In Figure 3, I propose a further development of the conceptual framework; this time, I am visualising directions for handling difficulties in practice. As Basepaper and Carsystems illustrate, my experience of most difficulties during the initial stages of consultancy focus on conflicts about roles and responsibilities or conflicts about the initial diagnosis. It is my proposition that both conflicts have an aspect to them that is conscious or that can be brought into consciousness relatively easily through intervention with the client. That aspect is the same - contractual issues to be negotiated. By taking difficulties back to contractual points - depicted on the left side of the figure - difficulties might be unstuck. I propose that a consultant's first approach to working through difficulties might be to ask herself and the client whether or not there are contractual issues that are causing the difficulty.

Practically, working explicitly with two of the variables will always direct attention on the relationship between the client and consultant. Issues of negotiating a formal contract and questions about roles and responsibilities implicate both parties. In my experience, the client willingly discusses these variables during messy situations. They can accept the ideas of negotiation and contracting as familiar to them from other tasks they undertake in their roles, eg selling products and agreeing industrial relations changes.

However, working explicitly on psychodynamics and on organisational issues relevant to the consultancy brief can be more difficult This is depicted on the right side of the figure. Sometimes, starting with the contractual issues that might need to be clarified resolves a difficulty. Other times, starting with the familiar makes it possible to move into the less familiar. I propose that a consultant's second approach to working through difficulties differs slightly for the topic around which the difficulty has arisen.

For example, the second approach for working through difficulties around roles would be to address the psychodynamics being enacted in the relationship. The client wishes to have an expert upon which he can be totally dependent and have all his problems solved without any effort on his part. The client wishes to retain all the control and to treat the consultant as a recalcitrant employee to be managed harshly and kept at a distance from the organisation. The client appears to be treating the consultant like a stern father who will punish them for not being a big enough success.

For example, the second approach for working through difficulties around the initial diagnosis (ie how to proceed with involving others in the organisation) would be to address the organisational issues emerging as they related to the objectives of the consultancy. The client wishes to have employees involved and committed in making changes but wants to behave contradictory to that goal. The client wishes to remove the terror from the company culture but plans to announce major redundancies the last working day before holidays. The client wishes to understand how people are feeling or thinking but wants to avoid having to be face-to-face employees when they express themselves.

For both sorts of conflicts, I am proposing that if the first and second approach fails to resolve the difficulty, there might be a third approach possible. If addressing the contractual issues and the psychodynamics hasn't resolved difficulties related to the role of consultant and client, then perhaps there are organisational issues that need to be addressed. If addressing contractual issues and organisational issues hasn't resolved difficulties related to the initial diagnosis, then perhaps there are psychodynamics within the organisation that need to be addressed.

These propositions from practice come from my review of the three areas of relevant literature, from my analysis of Basepaper and Carsystems, and from my own experience in working through difficult beginnings with a variety of clients. It is possible that my particular developmental needs dictate that issues of role and initial diagnosis are those most frequently appearing in my practice. Another consultant might evoke different difficulties. The conceptual framework and these propositions are not meant to be exclusive or complete. I would hope that additional research will be reported from other researcher/consultants on the topic of this paper.

8   SUMMARY

The purpose of this paper was to increase understanding about what is going on when clients and consultants experience difficulties and confrontations with each other during the initial stages of consultancy. Literature was reviewed from organisational development theories about the early stages of consultancy and the consultant's role, from organisational psychology and sociology about resistance to participation, and psychodynamic theory applied to groups and organisations. Working hypotheses and an analytical grid was then presented as an aid in understanding two cases of difficult beginnings. Contractual issues, roles of client and consultant, psychodynamics, and organisational issues relevant to the consultancy brief were identified as the four variables of importance in analysing difficulties. A discussion of the purposes served by these difficulties led to propositions for practice. First, second, and third approaches for working through two particularly frequent difficulties - the issues of roles and of how to proceed with initial diagnosis - were offered.

REFERENCES

Alderfer, C. P. and Brown L. D. (1975) *Learning from changing organizational diagnosis and development.* Beverly Hills: Sage Publications.

Argyris, C. (1970) *Intervention theory and method: a behavioural science view.* Reading, Massachusetts: Addison-Wesley Publishing Company.

Bayes, M. and Newton, P. M. (1985) Women in authority: a sociopsychological analysis. In Colman, A. D. and Geller, M. H. (eds), *Group relations reader 2.* Washington D C: A K Rice Institute, pp 309-322.

Bexton, W. Harold. (1975) The architect and planner: change agent or scapegoat? In Coleman, A. D. and Bexton, W. H. (eds). *Group Relations Reader 1.* Washington DC: A K Rice Institute, pp 343-358

Bion, W. R. (1961) *Experiences in groups and other papers.* London: Tavistock Publications. New York: Basic Books, Inc.

Block, P. (1981) *Flawless consulting: a guide to getting your expertise used.* Austin, Texas: Learning Concepts.

Cherniss, Cary. (1984) Pre-entry issues in consultation. In Lee, R. J. and Freedman, A. M. (eds), *Consultation skills reading.* Arlington, Virginia: NTL Institute, pp 47-52.

Colman, A. D. (1975) Group consciousness as a developmental phase. In Colman, A. D. and Bexton, W. H. (eds), *Group relations reader 1.* Washington D C: A K Rice Institute, pp 35-42.

Glidewell, J. C. (1984) The entry problem in consultation. In Lee, R. J. and Freedman, A. M. (eds), *Consultation skills reading.* Arlington, Virginia: NTL Institute, pp 47-52.

Gould, L. J. (1985) Men and women at work: a group relations conference on person and role. In Colman, A. D. and Geller, M. H. (eds) *Group relations reader 2.* Washington DC: A K Rice Institute, pp 163-172.

Hirschhorn, L. (1985) The psychodynamics of taking the role. In Colman, A. D. and Geller, M. H. (eds), *Group relations readers 2.* Washington D C: A K Rice Institute, pp 335-352.

Kernberg, O. F. (1985) The couch at sea: psychoanalytic studies of group and organizational leadership. In Colman, A. D. and Geller, M. H. (eds), *Group relations reader 2.* Washington D C: A K Rice Institute, pp 399-412.

Kets de Vries, M. F. R. and Miller, D. (1984) *The neurotic organization.* San Francisco: Jossey-Bass Publishers.

Klein, M. (1959) Our adult world and its roots in infancy. *Human Relations,* 12, pp 291-303.

Kolb, D. and Frohman, A. (1970) An organizational development approach to consulting. *Sloan Management Review,* 12, pp 51-65.

Lippitt, R. and Lippitt, G. (1984) Consulting roles. In Lee, R. J. and Freedman, A. M. (eds), *Consultation skills reading.* Arlington, Virginia: NTL Institute, pp 35-36.

Marrow, A. J. (1969) *The practical theorist: the life and work of Kurt Lewin.* Annapolis, Maryland: Basic Books Inc.

Morgan, Robin. (1972) *Monster.* New York: Vintage Books.

Menninger, R. W. (1975) The impact of group relations conferences on organisational growth. In Colman, A. D. and Bexton, W. H. (eds), *Group relations reader 1.* Washington D C: A K Rice Institute, pp 265-280.

Menzies Lyth, I. (1988) *Containing anxiety in institutions, selected essays, volume 1.* London: Free Association Books.

Menzies Lyth, I. (1989) *The dynamics of the social, selected essays, volume 2.* London: Free Association Books.

Miller, E. J. and Rice, A. K. (1967) *Systems of organisation.* London: Tavistock Publications.

Miller, E. J. (1985) The politics of involvement. In Colman, A. D and Geller, M. H. (eds), *Group relations readers 2.* Washington D C: A K Rice Institute, pp 383-398.

Neilsen, E. (1984) *Becoming an OD practitioner.* New Jersey: Prentice-Hall Inc.

Neumann, J. E. (1989) Why people don't participate in organizational change. In Woodman, R. W. and Pasmore, W. A (eds) *Research in organizational change and development, volume 3.* Greenwich, Connecticut: JAI Press Inc.

Ruma, S. (1984) A four-phase developmental model. In Lee, R. J. and Freedman, A. M. (eds), *Consultation skills reading.* Arlington, Virginia: NTL Institute, pp 45-47.

Schatzman, L. and Strauss, A. L. (1973) *Field research: strategies for a natural sociology*. New Jersey: Prentice-Hall Inc.

Sherwood, J. J. and Glidewell, J. C. (1971) Planned renegotiation: a norm-setting OD intervention. In Jones and Pfeiffer, *The 1973 annual handbook for group facilitators*. La Jolla, California: University Associates Publishers Inc.

Steele, F. (1975) *Consulting for organizational change*. Amherst: University of Massachusetts Press.

Weisbord, M. R. (1984) Client contact: entry and contract. In Lee, R. J. and Freedman, A. M. (eds), *Consultation skills reading*. Arlington, Virginia: NTL Institute, pp 63-66.

KNOWLEDGE-BASED OR SPECULATIVE CONSULTANCY

Professor Andrew Ehrenberg, Bruce Lloyd and John Scriven
South Bank Business School, London

Abstract
The paper contrasts consultancy which falls at opposite ends of a spectrum:

(a)   those dealing with recurring problems, where at least part of the answer should be based on firm knowledge

(b)   those dealing with unique changes, where the answers are new and speculative

It examines the requirements of the client organisation, the inputs of the consultant, and the skills needed to perform the task well.

1.   INTRODUCTION

Just as there are many different strategies for a business, which Porter classifies into three generic types[1], so there are many different types of consultancy which we propose to classify on a spectrum with two extremes, namely Knowledge-based and Speculative.

In Sections 2 and 3 we characterise the two extremes. The former is rooted in "formalised" experience obtained from previous similar situations and is associated particularly with providing incremental improvement in client company performance or understanding. Speculative consultancy, on the other hand, deals with situations which are apparently new and different from previous experience. These situations are often associated with more radical and discontinuous change, sometimes even chaos, in the client organisation.

We will argue, however, that much of what appears to fall into the Speculative category is not truly dealing with a new problem and an unknown future, but rather an incomplete grasp of the past. The situations have not been encountered often enough or studied enough to be assimilated as reliable knowledge. Therefore as experience becomes formalised, these categories could also move towards being more knowledge-based. Furthermore we join the growing band that questions the wisdom of radical discontinuous change except in desperate circumstance.

The inputs and outputs to each type of consultancy are quite similar. The client organisation needs to develop its understanding of a situation and needs guidance towards implementing the resulting knowledge. The consultant's role is to provide the basis of the understanding and to facilitate the client learning process. As such, the key skills necessary are elements of those of:

(a)   the researcher, to develop the knowledge or experience base

(b)   the teacher, to implant the knowledge in the organisation

(c)   the project manager, to ensure its adoption.

2.   KNOWLEDGE-BASED CONSULTANCY

The term knowledge-based is applied to consultancy that draws on firm under-standing of processes that are known. This understanding will have come as a result of systematic study of the processes concerned, either from a historical or scientific perspective. Scientific knowledge is associated with known "facts"; empirical results that are the same under widely varying conditions and possibly even grounded 'models', ie models with a theoretical basis that is consistent with the generally observed results. Understanding of the process is therefore rooted in well-grounded theory[2]. Historical knowledge is less due to observing the same results, but rather to drawing insights into the process from observing a range of one-off results where some of the elements are similar.

The aim of knowledge-based consultancy is to get individuals and companies to be aware of, and to use, things that are known and understood by others.There are many types of consultancy that fall into this category.

We start with an example from our own particular sphere of marketing, concerning the repeat buying loyalty of frequently purchased consumer products. It has been established for many years[3] that there are a number of regular patterns in repeat purchase of consumer products that occur irrespective of the product field (over 50 studied), the country (UK, USA, Germany, Japan), the brand or its positionig (hundreds studied). Three such patterns are:

(a)   Double Jeopardy, whereby a small brand is not only bought by less people, but those buyers also buy it less frequently (eg small brands Brim and Maxim average 2.3 purchase occasions v larger brands Maxwell House and Sanka average 3.5 in Table 1 below for the US coffee market)

(b)   your brand's customers (in a year, say) are mostly other brands' customers who occasionally buy you, ie buyers of a brand buy other brands in total more often (eg buyers of the average brand in Table 1 buy the brand 2.8 times, but buy any coffee 9.5 times and therefore buy other brands 6.7 times)

(c)   loyalty is in effect simply an ongoing propensity to buy.

Whilst points (a) and (b) can be easily seen in Table 1, point (c) is impicit in the specification of a stochastic model called the Dirichlet[4] which produces the theoreti-cal results which fit so closely in this and other cases.

Table 1 Patterns of Purchase and Repeat Purchase

INSTANT COFFEE (USA - 12 months)	Market Share	Pene-tration	Av. Purchase Per Buyer of Brand of Category			
	%	%	O	T	O	T
Any Instant	100	67	-	-	6.7	-
Maxwell House	19	24	3.6	3.3	9.3	8.6
Sanka	16	21	3.3	3.0	9.2	8.8
Tasters Choice	14	22	2.8	2.9	8.8	8.9
High Point	13	22	2.6	2.9	8.5	9.1
Folgers	11	18	2.7	2.9	9.4	9.2
Nescafe	8	13	2.9	2.8	10.3	9.4
Brim	4	9	2.0	2.6	9.4	9.4
Maxim	3	6	2.6	2.6	11.2	9.4
Other Brands	12	20	3.0	3.0	9.3	8.9
Average Brand	11	17	2.8	3.0	9.5	9.0

O - Observed values

T - Dirichlet model predictions

There then follow many implications for the likely success of different types of marketing activity, eg that small brands with a highly loyal user base (the so-called niche brand) simply do not exist, or would be far more exceptional than is generally thought.

The establishment of quality control standards is another good example of knowledge-based consultancy. This entails the study of variability in a manufacturing process and an understanding of the relevant statistical theory of probability. Job evaluation could be considered somewhat similar, with the application of well considered methods of assessing job content and skills to the abilities of the job holder. The extension of this to the currently in-vogue method of performance-related pay is perhaps an example of a knowledge-base that needs some perfecting!

Most Professional services fall into the category of knowledge-based consultancy. Lawyers are hired for their knowledge of the process of law, an accountant or banker for their understanding of financial practice and a market researchers for their ability to draw a sample from a population, frame a questionnaire and analyse the responses. It is perhaps best to stress in this context that just because the consultancy is knowledge-based, it does not guarantee a "correct" answer, or that the knowledge is correctly applied.

In terms of general application, the need in the client company is for an understanding of something that affects their operation, a learning process whereby they can absorb the knowledge and an application in which they can see the benefit of the knowledge acquired. It is an evolutionary process of change that is brought about, with steady absorption and improvement, not a radical discontinuous one. The objective is to become more literate about one's situation. Sometimes the client does not even perceive the need for this type of consultancy, and it may be necessary to sell it quite hard, because the benefits are less obvious than when a problem is perceived.

3. SPECULATIVE CONSULTANCY

Speculative consultancy arises from situations which are apparently new and unique. They seem to the client company to be very different from their previous experience, with elements which are peculiar to their own situation. It is felt that little if anything can be known about them. In many cases they result from difficult situations such as lack of profitability, market decline or new competitor entry and are associated with the perceived need for radical change, with its associated upheaval.

Examples where this sort of unknown position arises currently cover areas like the deregulation of Nationalised Industry and the growth of capitalism in the former Communist Eastern Europe. The early days of the healthy eating trend may not have foreshadowed quite the effect to come in many food markets such as yellow fats and yoghurt, nor the Green Issue on washing products. And if the full extent of the PC revolution was forecast, why did it catch IBM out so badly?

Many situations, however, although new and different to the client are not unique in the wider scheme of things.

Examples occur in consultancy associated with restructuring, either of whole companies or of functions within them. The problem may be new to the company that has it, but the issues have been faced by others before. New product development is another area where the results of the development process may be new, but the process itself is not. In both these cases, the solutions offered by consultants are mostly similar to those they have offered before (the "house style"). If the processes involved were studied more, or there were more cases available to study, they would be better understood and may even move towards being knowledge-based.

If there is uncertainty about the future it is not because the future is inherently unpredictable, but that the past is not yet fully understood. We cannot predict the dollar exchange rate because we do not know why it is what it is today.

So we see that much speculative consultancy can also be based on previous experience, if not quite as formalised as in the knowledge-based case. Only in the case of real one-off changes, many of which are ephemeral, not predicted or not recognised as important at the time, is there a need for consultancy with no base in experience. Consultancy rooted in experience makes transition more gradual and less traumatic.

This leads on to the question why do organisations find themselves needing to make radical changes? Is the incidence of unpredicted environmental change that prevalent, or is there a greater case to be made for continuous, slow evolution? Is it that too many organisations do not pay enough attention to the evolution process, opening up too big a gap between where they are and where they want to be? A gap which they try to close by taking radical steps driven by the vision of where they want to be, instead of being rooted in incremental steps from where they are now. Why cannot organisations plan to evolve more slowly? In fact many do, very successfully, eg Coca Cola, McDonalds, Hanson, Shell, Unilever.

Apart from the truly one-off situation, where the client needs a consultant with a better crystal ball, or just some-one to hold their hand, the needs for Speculative consultancy are not that different from the knowledge-based case. That is some reference to prior knowledge, insights or even just nostrums which will aid identification and clarification of the issues involved, give guidance towards the solutions and help in implementation.

4. THE CONSULTANT'S ROLE AND SKILLS

In the first type of consultancy, consultants bring the knowledge base and experience of using it to bear on the client's problem. They also bring an outsider's perspective, which may be invaluable. The result should be greater understanding within the client, and an ability to integrate that to the application, with the consultants' help. This is the process by which the client organisation learns, individually and collectively.

In good examples of the speculative case, consultants are performing a similar role. They bring experience, which may move towards knowledge as it becomes more formalised, leading to understanding. In many cases the consultant will define as well as help to implement the application.

A truly successful consultant's primary role is as a catalyst in the client learning process. The analogy is not quite exact since a catalyst does not itself change, which a good consultant must do also as part of the learning process. Consultants who see their role as merely doing the job will not ultimately be as successful. Helping people to learn is a central part of the consultant's function and implementation is critical. Effective learning is the oil that lubricates continuous improvement. Organisations can only change and progress by learning something new. If learning does not occur faster than the rate of change, then chaos will surely result.

In order to perform the task, a consultant or consultancy organisation needs to blend the skills of three different disciplines:

(a)   the researcher, to develop the experience or knowledge base

(b)   the teacher, to disseminate it

(c)   the project manager, to use the knowledge in ensuring implementation.

It is success in achieving this blend, and not pre-eminence in any one that will produce outstanding consultancy.

5.   SUMMARY

This paper has attempted to contrast the nature of consultancy at two ends of a spectrum: one based on knowledge, the other of the speculative variety, dealing with one-off situations.

The first type is associated with a simple need in the client organisation to understand some process better, and to implement that knowledge in an operational context. It is also associated with a more evolutionary development path.

Speculative consultancy stems from more complex client situations, where they feel they have encountered a situation which is new and different. They do not think that the situation has been encountered previously, but nevertheless feel the need for outside help in resolving it. It is often associated with more radical discontinuous change.

Some of the speculative situations are not as new as they might seem. They have been encountered before by other organisations, and consultants may well have provided similar solutions.

Whichever type of consultancy is being offered, the requirements of the consultant are similar. They need to provide a knowledge or experience base that addresses the issue, a means of assimilating the relevance of the knowledge to the situation (hence understanding), and help in implementing the solution.

The skills necessary to perform these tasks include elements of those of the researcher, teacher and project manager. Who said a consultant's life was easy?

REFERENCES

1.   PORTER Michael E, 1980, *Competitive Strategy: Techniques for Analysing Industries and Competitors*, New York: The Free Press

2.   EHRENBERG Andrew S C , 1994, "Theory or Well-based Results: Which Comes First?", *Research Traditions in Marketing* (eds. G Laurent, G Lilien and B Pras), Dordrecht: Kluwer (in press)

3.   EHRENBERG Andrew S C , 1959, "The Pattern of Consumer Purchases", *Applied Statistics*, **8**, 26-41

4.   EHRENBERG Andrew S C, Gerald J Goodhart and Chris Chatfield, 1984, "The Dirichlet: A Comprehensive Model of Buying Behaviour", *Journal of the Royal Statistical Society A*, **147**, 621-655

5.   MUMFORD Alan, 1993, "Improving the Experience of Learning", *efmd Forum*, **93/1**, 26

RESISTING THE RESISTANCE TO CHANGE

Teresa Howard, *Independent Consultant, London*

ABSTRACT

This paper describes my experience as an internal consultant to a large inner London local authority at a time of chaotic change. Ideas from the domains of knowledge relating to systemic family therapy, social constructionism and psychoanalysis are drawn on to inform a struggle that sought to make sense of an experience that felt incomprehensible. The main focus is a search for patterns in the chaos which both informed me about what was happening at a dynamic level in the organisation and enabled me to move out of my own resistance to change.

INTRODUCTION

This paper was written 'along the way' as a way of understanding my experience as an internal consultant, providing staff and management support, to a large inner city local authority at a time of huge legislative change. It tells the story of my struggle to make sense of the chaos that surrounded and, at times, invaded me and finally triggered me into thinking about the processes that were pushing me into feeling demoralised and exhausted.

This story is informed by my previous role in the organisation as an operational manager for nine years and by some external consultancy to a number of other public sector organisations which gave me some key bearings in the turbulent sea I was attempting to sail through.

I did not set out to reveal an objective truth or reality about the organisation or myself. But, I did expect to map out how the belief systems of the people who manage the organisation, work in it, and expect to receive a service from it, influence the way it functions. What I discovered was a pattern of contradiction that seemed to pervade every interaction and ensure demoralisation and confusion at every level.

"Anna's soul was at peace between them. She looked from one to the other, and she saw them established to her safety, and she was free. She played between the pillar of fire and the pillar of cloud in confidence, having the assurance on her right hand and the assurance on her left. She was no longer called upon to uphold with her childish might the broken end of the arch. Her father and her mother now met to the span of the heavens, and she, the child, was free to play in the space beneath, between" *D. H. Lawrence, The Rainbow*

"It is only when you pull back the curtain a bit that you can see what the light is like." *A comment from a client after a stress management session.*

1   THEORETICAL PERSPECTIVE

The emotional state that triggered this paper could be described as burnout. Burnout has been defined as detachment from one's own work and/or clients. It is a psychological answer to stress experienced by professionals in their job.

Laura Fruggeri and Sheila McNamee (1991) developed the hypothesis that the usual preventative explanations about job stress given by experts actually contribute to burnout. From their theoretical viewpoint of Social Constructionism, they would say that the beliefs we have about the world construct our realities. These are then maintained through social interaction and reflexively confirm our original beliefs.

Instead of job stress being explained in terms of a cause being located either inside or outside the person, or as a disequalibrium between the two, the social and interpersonal processes that maintain it are investigated. Moving from looking for a cause, to understanding the processes that maintain the experience of burnout, we begin to see a reflexivity between actions and meanings in social contexts. Belief systems create social realities as much as social processes create belief systems.

If the usual kinds of explanations for stress are taken seriously, we can find ourselves caught in an inner tussle between the negative connotation that we are somehow not up to the job or that we are too idealistic. The resolution of this tussle lies in either giving up on our own ideas in order to become realistic or by accepting the idea that we are not good enough to get it right. The resulting experience is a sense of alienation resulting from the idea of being completely determined by others. A prolonged experience of alienation results in burnout.

In order to survive, I had to find a way of changing my belief system about what was possible. Remembering that stress is not just a mechanical answer to some objective cause but an answer to an impossible situation, I had to give up on any messianic notions I had about leading this organisation out of the mess it was in. My solution was to redefine my daily role to one of learning and research. I decided that I would start charting the interaction of my own emotional state with that of the organisation and to track whether the feelings that I found myself having to deal with were in fact a microcosm of the organisation as a whole.

By seeking to observe the organisation from within, some people would say that I was asking too much of myself. But, no observer is entirely objective. The Chilean biologist Maturana and his colleague Varela (1987) have argued that all living systems are organisationally closed and strive to maintain an identity by subordinating all changes to the maintenance of their own organisation as a given set of relationships. There is no beginning or end because the system is a closed loop of interaction. In order to discover the nature of any system, it is therefore necessary to interact with it and trace the circular interaction through which it is defined. From this perspective, it is necessary to risk being immersed in the organisation and literally to feel it to understand how it functions.

In all systems, patterns repeat themselves. It is sometimes referred to as parallel process or resonance. Because the architect in me tends to understand most things in the form of visual images, I see these repeating patterns as a metaphorical version of what Mandelbrot, the French mathematician, described as a fractal (1987).

In contrast to mainstream mathematicians he liked to think about problems intuitively using his visual ability to recognise patterns and shapes. As a result, he noticed that in apparently random fluctuations in any naturally occurring phenomenon that he cared to look at, there was a symmetry across scale. Small scale fluctuations had the same pattern as large scale fluctuations in the so called chaos of nature. He found that the world seemed to display a kind of regular irregularity, or a pattern of similarity across scale. No matter how much the image or a part of the image was magnified, it always looked similar, like a pattern within a pattern, always with the same degree of roughness or irregularity. It is possible to zoom in on a fractal an infinite number of times and still find the same degree of roughness or irregularity.

What emerged in this system was a fractal like pattern *of contradiction* that connected apparently random events like a hall of mirrors reflecting itself in me and at every level and in every activity of the organisation. Its relentless quality replicating the Batesonian double bind (1972).

2   BACKGROUND

Since the abolition of the GLC and the ILEA in 1986, this organisation was forced to cope with one unwanted and externally enforced change after another. Initially a huge absorption of staff and responsibilities, was rapidly followed on by the introduction of the Community Charge and subsequently, the Council Tax. Increasing competition with the private sector had been legislated for together with an accompanying reduction in funding, forcing increased customer orientation and staffing cuts. Despite all this upheaval nothing fundamentally changed.

Three years ago, I was appointed from within the organisation to set up a Welfare Unit "to urgently address staff morale." On appointment, I was aware that there was a prevailing notion that welfare was a kind of soothing balm which would make things better and relieve managers from having to deal with difficult staff.

3   CULTURE AS PATTERN

There seem to be as many definitions of organisational culture as there are observers of organisations. Essentially culture relates to the ability of human beings to give meaning to their experience of life. It includes thought, speech, action, that are taught to or adopted by successive generations and embodied in the typical behaviour or, customary beliefs and social forms of a particular group. Baker (1980) described it as shared meaning that holds an organisation together like glue.

Have you ever pondered on how it is that the culture at places like Oxford University maintains itself through hundreds of generations of students whose average stay is only three years?

Maturana, developed the concept of the linguistic domain to describe the interactional system through which meaning is created. We create and live in a world that exists in language and social exchange. Problems exist in conversation with others and are resolved by changing what we say to each other and then by what we believe. In this way, culture is co-constructed by talking to each other about what we have on our mind. Every interaction embodies the pattern of culture.

Meanings are socially generated by the conversations we have with one another and are changed in the same way through what he called 'consensual social constructions'.

Kenneth Gergen (1991) reminds us that,

> *'words are not mirror like reflections of reality, but expressions of group convention. Various social groups possess preferred vocabularies, or ways of putting things, and these vocabularies reflect or defend their values, politics, and ways of life. For participants in such groups, these forms of talking (or writing) take on a local reality'.*

Adrian McLean and Judi Marshall (1988) described the way culture is relayed through both high profile and low profile symbols. It is the low profile or covert symbols that maintain persistence in the system. In this organisation, I became increasingly aware of the disjunction between the organisation's stated aims and objectives and the way it actually operated and delivered its services. *This was the first observable pattern of contradiction.*

The high profile symbols sought to demonstrate that this was a supportive organisation with sensitive employment procedures and service delivery objectives based on a clear commitment to equality of opportunity.

The low profile symbols completely contradicted this picture. Directors were consistently appointed without an understanding of, let alone a commitment to, equalities. The most recent Chief Executive was appointed after the suspension of standing orders to avoid having to make an appointment according to its own rules!

The developing workaholic ethic was also in direct opposition to the Equalities culture that the organisation overtly espoused making it very difficult for senior women, in particular, with child care responsibilities to meet the increasing obligations to attend never ending evening meetings and to meet unrealistic deadlines.

Overtly, there was a commitment to house the homeless but homeless people needing help were constantly being bundled out of the Town Hall using the police if necessary. Despite statements to the contrary, confusion about the organisation's financial situation continued. Some trading accounts were suspected of making enormous losses and continued confusion avoided accountability.

Not surprisingly, staff morale tumbled as the contradictions about the organisation's covert and overt objectives increased. Services were poor and the Internal Ombudsman was over run with complaints from the public. The main belief system that operated for senior managers was that the organisation was full of lazy staff who needed a good shake-up. The only solution was to tighten belts and to get tough. If they could hire and fire like the private sector all their problems would be solved. This belief system absolved them from having to do anything about developing their workforce, further contributing to staff feeling poorly motivated and undervalued.

Another contradiction began to unravel itself. Ostensibly I had been appointed to help improve morale. On a daily basis I was working with those people who were having most difficulty functioning. At the same time, I discovered that few inside the organisation wanted to acknowledge that anyone was having difficulty. I had been appointed to deal with a problem on behalf of the organisation in the hope that it could avoid having to address it. Clearly a ludicrous proposition but it often happens.

Many people think that change can be implemented by carefully preparing staff and managers for it. This is an idea that Maturana describes as, *instructive interaction*. He rejects the notion that it is possible to force a new idea on an individual or an organisational system against their will, and maintains that it is 'the structure of the system' that determines how it will respond to an interaction, not the force instigating it. Having some sympathy with this idea, I was clear about what I could not do! There was not much mileage in trying to tell anyone what they should do or how to improve things because of the implied negative connotation that they had got it all wrong. Nobody likes to be criticised least of all managers who had thought they had appointed someone to deal with the problem on their behalf.

The implication of my appointment was that by counselling staff, I would somehow or other solve the problems of the organisation. What I did not realise then was that although I was being told that there was problem of morale, I was also being told covertly not to draw attention to its origins.

Isabel Menzies Lyth(1970), in her classic text about the nursing profession, made the observation that counselling seemed to be the current remedy. Wait until the nurse is on her knees; then counsel her with all the implied messages that the fault or inadequacy was hers. The same remedy was being applied again in a different environment.

I was stuck with *a contradiction* that I could not resolve while I maintained the idea that I could make a difference to the organisation. Like the alcoholic, I had to give up the idea that I could control any reasonable outcome. The clue about how to proceed came from looking very closely at my own experience.

4   THE PATTERN OF MY EXPERIENCE

Almost from the time of my appointment, I began suffering a loss of energy which made no sense. I was pleased to be given the opportunity to use my skills and felt that I had something unique to offer. At the same time, I noticed a recurring feeling of being undervalued, over worked and almost panicky. These feelings were not usual for me and they continued for almost a year until I came across an article called Counter Transference can be the Therapist's Compass (1991) and realised that I had found myself caught in a circular, yet almost invisible, process that Melanie Klein had termed, mutual Projective and Introjective Identification.

Projective Identification is the unconscious process of projecting unwanted, often painful parts of oneself, on to others. Introjective Identification is the complementary process of taking in and identifying with the projections of the other, usually without quite knowing it. In this way, projective and introjective identification become the vehicles for unconscious communication and understanding in all human relationships. This process can also become the basis for shared unconscious misunderstanding and consciously destructive ways of behaving. I had taken in the confusion and powerlessness of many senior people. But why? What had led me to be so receptive to these feelings? I had to look within myself and to my history for the answer.

I was the eldest daughter of a refugee from the holocaust growing up in New Zealand, and as a result of this experience learnt very early on in life to take in incomprehensible and contradictory messages, to store them until I could begin to make sense of them later. Ann Beaglehole, in her book , A Refugee Childhood in NZ (1990) describes, "the way such children were brought up in a kind of limbo world where they received few clear messages from their families about how the old ways fitted into the new or about the merits of either cultural world. Many received neither a Jewish education nor a Christian one. A consequence of such an upbring-ing was that these children grew up feeling uncertain about which community they belonged in and about how to behave in the world outside the home.......In fact it was the children who very often interpreted the ways of the new society to their parents, and advised them on what was acceptable behaviour and what was not.... A reversal of the usual role of parents and children."

For as long as I can remember, my stance in life has been one of a search for understanding and meaning. I had developed what Silvia Brinton Perera, referred to as the Scapegoat Complex (1986). I had learnt that in order to survive in the world I had to support the system that was supposed to be supporting me. Almost without realising it, I unconsciously provided the missing links to maintain its stability. She would say that I had developed, "The capacity to endure discomfort as a result of an early experience of not feeling adequately physically held leading to an uncertainty about the body-ego's ability to resist fragmenting, merging with the environment or being overcome by unconscious forces. The sense of having fallen out of touch, of not having or never having had the protective-containing embrace, is central to scapegoat-identified individual's experience, for they are identified with exile and with only parts of the whole - primarily with what Jung would call, the 'shadow parts'."

These are the unwanted, unacknowledged, destructive thoughts, feelings and actions that exist despite conscious intentions to the contrary. To resist this sacrificial role requires a capacity to hold a conscious position or meta perspective outside that of the group, in this case, the organisation. I also discovered quite recently that my father had been expelled from school for, "putting himself outside the community by his own actions." by walking out of assembly when being asked to sing a song that referred to Jews as scum and traitors'.

I had emerged from my childhood with a very clear understanding of the way in which words could be used to sanitise massively destructive processes to avoid outrage and to manipulate the belief systems of a whole nation. This personal experience linked with my position as the unacknowledged but vitally necessary emotional support in my family, led me to suffer intense distress when this historical context revealed itself around me in my work environment.

With these reflections in mind, I realised that my life experience had provided me with a very useful tool for understanding what was happening in this organi-sation. I had grown up having to manage a powerful pattern of contradiction on a daily basis that I understood very well.

5   THE PATTERN AT DIRECTOR LEVEL

Soon after my appointment, I hypothesised that the degree of forced change and the resulting panic could not be acknowledged by any of the senior management team and I was having to hold the contradiction of their unwanted vulnerable and frightened feelings.

Having arrived at this hypothesis, I had it reinforced by the discovery that many of the directors, were in a state of crisis that they appeared unable to acknowledge either collectively or individually to one another. They were not coping with the problems they were facing but were unable to admit it. Because these high levels of anxiety could not be addressed within the existing culture, they waged a war of criticism against each other as a way of defending against the anxiety of not knowing what to do and as a result, further increased their stress by persecuting each other.

Although appointed to manage, directors were clearly not managing themselves let alone the organisation. Increasingly, I noticed that these extremely high stress levels amongst this group was denied almost like a badge of honour. Blind to their own state, stories of people dying in other local authorities of asthma attacks, alcohol misuse and suicide abounded. The experience of survival reinforced their strong men and women images of invincibility as their denial increased to cope in an ever upward spiral. Unrealistic expectations of themselves and their staff increased tension as a result of increased demands being placed on them by elected members and the government. Not surprisingly, blind to their own self abuse, many turned to addictions such as chain smoking, alcohol and overwork. Directors were often reported being seen in the pub long after lunch time despite contrary exhortations to their staff.

Barbara Killinger (1991) described workaholism as a kind of self abuse. Work becomes the drug of choice masking,

"an insecurity fed by unconscious inner struggles to overcome unresolved childhood fears of helplessness, dependency, and loss of approval and affection, and the workaholic's life becomes dominated by, perfectionism, obsession and narcissism. In periods of chaos, consolidation, or downturn, where many changes are required, workaholics do not do well. They are often in a confused state and no longer function well enough to be competitive and resourceful."

In a study of 45 Managing Directors and Chief Executives in the UK, Cox and Cooper (1988) found that a surprisingly high number had learnt self sufficiency and responsibility early on in childhood as a result of feelings of aloneness. A high proportion had suffered some kind of bereavement during childhood particularly loss of the father and or separation from parents through evacuation or by being sent to boarding school at an early age. A number reported feelings of strength through adversity. Early traumas seem to have resulted in a successful testing out of their 'survival skills', a 'psychic tempering', leading to a basic feeling of strength, self sufficiency and independence, which they felt served them well in their later careers. In common with the findings of this research, I discovered on an ad hoc basis, that this organisation had more than its fair share of directors and managers with traumatic childhood experiences.

John Bowlby (1980) drew attention to the long term effects of the lack of an opportunity to mourn the lost parent available to children because of the remaining parent's preoccupation with their own grief and wish to protect the children from sadness. He documented two outcomes resulting from these childhood experiences.

The first is similar to that described by Cox and Cooper where individuals grow up tough and hard. Bowlby claims that although many of these people may be competent and to all appearances self-reliant, and may go through life without overt sign of breakdown, they are likely to be difficult to live and work with. In later years they run the risk of depression, alcoholism and suicide. Even if they do not become psychiatric casualties themselves they can often be responsible for the breakdown of others, their spouse, colleagues or employees. The problem is that they learnt early in life that attachment is a sign of weakness, that crying is contemptible and that all expression of feeling should be frowned upon. A belief system is thus developed that defines ordinary human frailty as an indication of poor management ability.

The second outcome is a predisposition towards compulsive caring arising from having to look after an ailing parent. What usually happens is that these people select someone who has had a sad or difficult life so that the compulsive caregiver can attribute to the cared-for, all the sadness and neediness that they are unable or unwilling to recognise in themselves, the cared-for person can be regarded as standing vicariously for the one giving care. Sooner or later those, who avoid all conscious grieving in this way, break down usually with some form of depression.

Alice Miller (1983) documented the way unmet need in childhood can have catastrophic consequences in later life as displayed in the wider world beyond the family. In particular she draws attention to the way in which the forbidden expression of anger, rage or sadness in childhood leads to a betrayal of our own inner needs as adults as well as those of our friends, colleagues and children. For those who were alone or felt alone in childhood and had to keep a stiff upper lip and be brave, they are unable to find a haven within their own soul for the helpless child and grow up to persecute these same qualities whenever they appear.

My experience after over 20 years in local government is that many people enter this area of public service to meet the unmet needs from their childhood. This phenomena operates simultaneously at two levels. For some, the organisation is seen as if it were the parent, they never had, with a consistent sense of justice. These people usually become managers. They then construct a culture that maintains feelings at arm's length while maintaining a belief system that systematically avoids feelings of vulnerability. A management culture that is distinctly unsupportive is thereby evolved.

Most senior women managers found that in order to be taken seriously and to reach director level, they had to relinquish any qualities that could be faintly labelled feminine in order to survive. Anyone who did not behave in what might be thought of as stereotypically masculine, did not usually reach through the glass ceiling and if they did, did not survive.

The second level is more complicated and arises from an unconscious wish, to be the parent that they themselves did not have by working to make a difference to the lives of those less fortunate than themselves. These people usually end up in front line services. This way of meeting unmet personal need continues for as long as the worker can feel valued by the client and by the organisation and a safe distance is kept between the worker and the client. It falls apart the moment the worker no longer feels valued and the client's needs can no longer be met. This process of meeting one's own needs through giving help to others requires a clear definition between the helper and the receiver of help to maintain the emotional stability of the helper.

For as long as the conventional role of the Local Government Officer was clearly defined and resided safely at a distance in the Town Hall, staff could continue to be ministering angels. With recent demands to become more sensitive to consumer needs and to work 'out in the field', staff had to become much more involved. At the same time as the clear boundaries between council officer and community user became blurred, the necessary support stuctures and systems were steadily removed, leaving staff stuck with the contradiction of trying to provide a service they felt good about in an environment that did not facilitate them in this task. As individuals struggled to make sense of this situation, referrals for counselling steadily escalated

6   THE PATTERN AT MEMBER LEVEL

At elected Member level, a contradiction again existed between intent and action. Although the Council was predominantly left wing, it was in effect hung politically with the left being divided into several factions that found it difficult to agree about such fundamental issues as the level of community charge to be set. This inability to agree had the effect of leaving every difficult and therefore important decision until the last possible moment. Often council meetings would finish in the small hours of the morning long past the eleventh hour!

Many Members lived on Council estates and were elected with the expectation that they could improve the lot of their neighbours and constituents. Most were very accessible to their constituents and were therefore subject to constant queries and harassment. Personal requests for special treatment and stories of poor treatment by the Council were their daily experience. Once elected they discovered that need far outweighed resources and therefore found it difficult to reconcile budget limits with political ambitions. As if this was not uncomfortable enough they found themselves having to tow the Conservative government line by making cuts to avoid having their budget capped. They had to deal with an almost intolerable amount of ambivalence that could not be acknowledged. As a result, Council Officers became the butt of Councillors frustration of dealing with a contradiction they could not resolve.

Compared with many Councillors, Officers receive very high salaries. They were seen as 'fat cats' who were paid too much and deserved to be kicked around. Recently an ex assistant director told to me that one ex Chair of Housing had told him that he would do what she f.....ing well wanted or else, despite the fact that most of her demands were unreasonable!

7 THE PATTERN AT THE COMMUNITY LEVEL

Elisabeth Rohr (1993), drew my attention to a very important phenomenon which informs this situation very well. She describes the way an organisation can take in the culture of the surrounding environment that it is set up to serve. The daily multiple encounters with people from the community have a powerful effect on the functioning of all relationships and systems within.

This authority was serving one of the most deprived communities in Britain with a high level of unemployment, poverty and homelessness. The accompanying alternative culture of survival through begging and criminal activity sat quite literally on our doorstep. It was what many would describe as 'streetwise'. Increasingly the culture within the organisation mirrored that outside and further reinforced the pattern of contradiction. The written and the unwritten rules of operating were quite opposed. Unfortunately, it was the unwritten and 'streetwise' modes of operating that dictated what happened.

8 CONCLUSION

Being stuck in the middle of this sea of contradiction led me to thinking further.

Cronen and Pearce of the University of Massachusetts developed a theory called the Co-ordinated Management of Meaning in the late 70's. (1989) Their view is that communication is not fundamentally an individual problem of correctly describing some objective truth but a social process of co-ordinating action and managing meaning within particular structural contexts. We are all social actors and organise meaning both temporally and hierarchically and all social structures entail ways of managing consciousness of various elements of those structures. These emerge from conjoint action and are always continuing to emerge. Their view is that we always conceive meanings as hierarchically organised so that one level is the context for interpretation of others.

There can be any number of levels of hierarchy. In this situation I have already defined six, the community; the organisational culture, elected members, directors, staff and myself. One important level that I have not so far defined is that of the external influence of the government. Again a contradiction arises. Working for a council committed to left wing policies at a time of conservative government is confusing at the best of times but what was even more confusing was the contradiction between the overt expression of political slogans informing the community that their services would be protected at the same time as they were being covertly cut.

This pattern of contradictory messages at all levels created a culture that was at worst double binding, and at least, destructive and confusing. Accepting this belief system made life much easier to survive and to feel creative in. It gave me the opportunity to control of my own destiny and to develop an expertise in diagnosing and working with extremely complex and difficult large group organisational dynamics.

9   END NOTE

In the discussion, it was noted that a further twist to the contradictions that existed in this organisational system could be tracked. It was noted that the conservative government is currently facing continuing and apparently unresolvable difficulties with the economy that cannot be acknowledged. A recent TV documentary revealed the way the British economy has continued to decline since the second world war despite numerous attempts to 'do something'. The prevailing culture in Britain is one in which the vulnerability of not knowing what to do and the consequent material, emotional and intellectual poverty are not able to be acknowledged. As a result all formal communication is manipulated to deny what is happening. This cultural norm creates a high level context for maintaining the idea that those at the top of any hierarchy can only be seen as 'knowing what to do' despite all the information to the contrary. In this organisation, the not 'knowing what to do' was again very formally clothed in a 'knowing what to do' framework of structures and systems that existed to maintain a silence about the non achievement of the primary task.

Is there anything more confusing than being employed to contribute to the primary task of an organisation that cannot achieved?

10   REFERENCES

Bateson, Gregory (1972) *Steps To an Ecology of Mind* New York: Ballantine

Beaglehole, Ann (1990) *Facing the Past, Looking Back on a Refugee Childhood in NZ in 1940's to 1960's* Wellington :Allen and Unwin

Bowlby, John(1980) *Loss: Sadness and Depression* London: The Hogarth Press. Reprinted London Penguin Educational, 1981.

Cox, Charles J and Cooper, Cary L (1988) *High Flyers: An Anatomy of Managerial Success* Blackwell.

Frugerri, Laura and McNamee (1991) 'Burnout as a Social Process' *New Systemic Ideas from the Italian Mental Health Movement* London: Karnac Books

Gergen, Kenneth J (1991)*The Saturated Self* USA: Basic Books

Gleick, James (1987) *Chaos: Making a New Science* New York: Viking Penguin Group

Killinger, Barbara (1991)*Workaholics: The Respectable Addicts* Toronto: Key Porter Books Ltd

Maturana, Humberto (1987) *The Tree of Knowledge* Massachusetts: New Science Library Shambhala Publications

de Maré, Patrick (1991)*Koinonia: from Hate, through Dialogue to Culture in the Large Group* London: Karnac Books

McLean, Adrian and Marshall, Judi (1988) Cultures at Work Local Government Management Board

Menzies Lyth, Isabel (1959,1961,1961b, 1970) 'The functioning of social systems as a defence against anxiety' in *Containing Anxiety in Institutions* London: Free Associations Books, 1988.

Miller, Alice (1983)*For your own Good* London: Faber and Faber.

Palazzoli, Mara Selvini, Boscolo, Luigi, Cecchin Gianfranco, Prata, Guiliana (1980) 'The Problem of the Referring Person', *Journal of Marital and Family Therapy January*

Pearce, W Barnet (1989) *Communication and the Human Condition* USA: Southern Illinois University Press

Perera, Silvia Brinton (1986) *The Scapegoat Complex* Inner City Books,

Rohr, Elisabeth (1993) *Der verlorene traum. Zur supervision von gewaltverhältnissen. (The lost dream. On supervision of violent relationships)* Heidelberg: To be published in proceedings of the Ninth European Symposium in Group Analysis.

Schaef, Anne Wilson and Fassel, Diane (1988) *The Addictive Organisation* San Francisco: Harper and Row.

Scharf, David E and Savege, Jill, (1991)'Counter Transference can be the Therapist's Compass' *The Family Networker* Volume 15 No 5: 73-81

de Vries, Manfred FR Kets and Miller, Danny(1984)*The Neurotic Organisation: Diagnosing and Revitalising Unhealthy Companies* New York: Harper Collins. Republished New York: Harper Business Paperback Edition 1990

Watzlawick, Weakland and Fish (1974) *Change: Principles of Problem Formation and Problem Resolution* New York: W W Norton and Co. Inc.

ENCOURAGING UNPLANNING
How Organisations Can Cope With Uncertainty

Peter Jones & Gina Lawrie, *YKW Consultants, London*

ABSTRACT

We have been involved in change management for many years and have regularly applied programmed approaches to planning for change. These have been in line with common paradigms like "where are we now, where do we want to be, how do we get there". But we had doubts, and these were firmly and colourfully reinforced by research we have undertaken with senior managers of change programmes.

We now favour an 'emergent' approach for complex and badly defined problems such as change in organisations. This approach is characterised by: clarity of purpose; acknowledging that we cannot know for certain the consequences of our actions so being prepared to take action and respond to the consequences; the planner of change finding change strategies as much as creating them; and a focus on learning from our experiences on the way.

So, how are we as consultants to work in a new way with clients (not least when there is a strong pull to carry on in the old way)? We need to recognise that the sense of control that programmed change appears to give is illusory. When working with clients we now talk of 'building an agenda for change', rather than planning for change. This is a rigorous process that provides the context within which to take action and react to and learn from experiences on the way.

INTRODUCTION

In this paper we question whether programmed, structured approaches to "managing change" are effective. We include details of the findings from a research study we have carried out, talking to top managers to obtain a practising manager's view of what helps and hinders bringing about change in organisations. We then set out what we can do instead. We believe that an 'emergent' approach to planning is more helpful, and we describe what this is in practice. We finally consider the significant implications of this approach for the role of consultants.

1. A STORY OF CHANCE AND DISCOVERY

For several years we have been involved in helping clients to "manage change" or with "change management programmes", programmes often lasting several years. We have regularly applied structured project planning techniques to this work. We told ourselves, and our clients, that this had a number of benefits. It can if done well, we said, highlight the best progression of tasks, and the interdependence of tasks, which if missed will often lead to bottlenecks and hold-ups in achieving change. It also highlights the resource implications of a change programme, which are often horrendous - planning can highlight the enormity of taking on change whilst maintaining the current activity of the organisation.

While clients found this type of planning very reassuring we were beginning to question its usefulness. The plan often felt constraining, was usually beset by unforeseen circumstances, and we wondered if it left us blinkered to opportunities that were arising along the way. This sense of unease developed markedly when we undertook a research project to look at what Chief Executives thought made change work, and what made it fail. What they said to us was not what we expected.

Our own exploration of new theoretical perspectives on change was going on quite independently of the research, as part of our own development. This exploration also pushed us to question how we were helping clients with change programmes. We began, therefore, to look in earnest at the assumptions behind how we carried out the planning of change and to think about alternatives.

This paper is the story of our voyage of chance and discovery, a voyage which has led us to work with clients in a new way. We have had to recognise that the sense of control that structured planning seems to offer is often illusory. We have moved away from a programmed approach to change towards a more 'emergent' approach.

2. COMMON PLANNING PARADIGMS FOR CHANGE

Many of us have grown up with, or been exposed to, the most common paradigm for planning change: "where are we now, where do we want to be, how do we get there?" It is widely quoted, and widely used.

This simple framework has been developed and elaborated in a number of ways. There are also different, more detailed approaches to change (see for instance Greiner [1]). What all of these approaches have in common is the sense of a programmed achievement of change. There is a *right order* in which to do things, and a steady progression from stage to stage.

This structured approach also leads to many people hoping that successful change can be simplified into a number of 'laws' so that "...the constituent parts of the effective management of change can be frozen into a set of recipes, awaiting the microwave oven of application."[2]. Hence the runaway popularity of Total Quality Management; and in the near future Business Process Re-engineering will no doubt be equally prevalent.

This programmed approach was very much the background to the way we had operated as consultants. It was also what we thought that Chief Executives would say they believed.

3. OUR RESEARCH PROJECT

Change for an organisation is complex and destabilising. Trying to achieve change can frequently feel almost impossible. We have all heard the stories of customer care programmes derailed by a rise in complaints, TQM programmes abandoned for cutting productivity, a mission statement that creates cynicism among staff, last year's favoured acquisition suddenly shed in a "return to core business". Yet, the stories don't seem to deter others from trying to reform themselves radically - attempting to generate success that has either slipped away over time, or was never quite achieved.

Our research was prompted by talking to senior managers well into change programmes, and hearing them reinforce the stories of failure. We heard comments such as: "we seemed to have lost impetus and direction"; "we haven't actually achieved anything"; or "the text books don't tell me what to do now". We wondered how common these feelings were, and if they were common, what we should do about them.

Our objective in the research was:

To discover the views of top managers on the experience of leading major change programmes, particularly eighteen months in.

We conducted interviews with top managers of thirteen organisations, in utilities, banking, health, retail and engineering. We wanted a practising manager's view of the challenges posed by change. The interviews covered:

- planning
- leadership
- techniques for achieving change, and
- people.

4. OUR RESEARCH FINDINGS

Our sample of top managers gave us a very strong, and unanimous message in one of our area of interest: planning for change. It was a message we hadn't been expecting. Also, not only were the views expressed consistently held, they were given to us with passion.

We found top managers saying, that from their experience detailed, structured planning for change:

- does not deliver the goods
- is unresponsive
- is unrealistic, and
- can make you look stupid!

Table 1 gives some quotes of what these top managers actually said to us.

Table 1
<u>Quotes from top managers about planning for change</u>

- "It is important to take a voyage of discovery"
- "...we never had a grand scheme, we allowed it to evolve"
- "...change itself induces further change...it is not completely controlled"
- "Success is a matter of chance and insistence"
- "Grand plans do not look intelligent from the bottom, and are bad for morale"
- "...planning is for the birds..."
- "Decide what you want to do...go for it...and tidy up the knitting afterwards"
- "...[planning was given up because] we needed something more live and real"
- "Taking an evolutionary approach you are less likely to put your foot in it"

5. NEW THEORETICAL PERSPECTIVES

Our research findings gave us great food for thought, as did our parallel exploration of a range of new theories about change. These theories are posing questions about the way we work with organisations.

In particular we had been exploring chaos theory, quantum theory and post-modernism. The application of these theories to organisations is at a very early stage. Their real relevance is not yet proven, but if their insights are valid when applied to organisations the implications are profound. A danger with theories from a quite different discipline is that we misapply them, but some of the implications do seem to tie in with our practical experience of working with organisations.

5.1. Unpredictability

Both chaos theory and quantum theory present the issue of unpredictability. Chaos theory suggests that we often cannot predict the behaviour of complex systems; the information and computation requirement is simply too great. Quantum theory alternatively suggests that systems can be inherently unpredictable. Practically they result in the same outcome: how do we operate, plan, and make choices in an unpredictable system?

5.2. "Both / and" - the decade of paradox

We struggle to grasp how, as quantum theory tells us, light is both a wave and a particle at the same time. It feels unnerving to many of us that this can be true, and we battle to understand how to live with this change in perspective. Yet equally difficult paradoxes face us in our working lives. As organisations become more linked and intertwined we face the dilemma of needing to *both* compete *and* collaborate with other organisations. Within our own organisations we need to find a way of being *both* stable *and* unstable at the same time. Our organisation needs to be stable to exist, and not explode or disintegrate. Yet our organisation must be unstable to innovate, change and be creative, without which it will not continue to survive. The 1990s is likely to be the decade of such paradoxes.

6. QUESTIONING OUR BELIEFS

We became very excited when we found our research findings and our exploration of new ideas suddenly coming together, starting to connect, and to reinforce each other. The practical experience of top managers surprisingly aligned itself particularly to the issue of unpredictability.

This double nudge led us to really question how we went about planning and the assumptions behind what we did. We went back to think about our assumptions and those behind much organisational consulting, and how they apply to change. We summarised them as:

- *managers can / should:*
- decide in advance the outcomes of change
- decide the degree of change required
- specify sequences of tasks to achieve the required change
- *managers can / should therefore*:
- set up a process for smooth transition to a future desired state.

Yet clearly we must recognise the complexity of organisations. It is not possible to anticipate:

- all of the interactions between the many members of the workforce who will make choices based on their own needs and values
- the wide range of feedback loops throughout the organisation, that can reinforce or dissipate changes put in place.

As if this wasn't enough, every organisation sits within an increasingly complex environment, which constantly makes demands upon it, many of which are unpredictable in the short term, never mind the long term.

Given this complexity it is impossible to predict accurately how any attempt at change will take root. Given the complexity of organisations it is vital to realise that:

- **each action will always have unplanned consequences,** and
- **each successive step of change reveals new information.**

The new information, and the unforeseen consequences of previous actions *must* be taken into account when deciding subsequent steps, or for rethinking strategic direction.

7. EMERGENT PLANNING

So, if programmed approaches to change are unlikely to work, and organisations are unpredictable places in which to try to bring about change, what do we do? Do we give up all hope? Or do we decide its time to change career - setting up refuges for uncertain executives might well be lucrative!

We know that smart will never be smart enough to predict accurately how an organisation will respond to change, so our first step in getting to grips with the situation has been to move towards using 'emergent planning'. The term comes from Henry Mintzberg, who talks about "emergent strategy" in the field of business strategy. He talks about the need to "craft" strategy, to allow it to emerge, much as a potter at a wheel crafts her output:

"At work the potter sits before a lump of clay on the wheel. Her mind is on the clay, but she is also aware of sitting between her past experiences and her future prospects. She knows exactly what has and has not worked for her in the past. She has an intimate knowledge of her work, her capabilities, and her markets. As a craftsman she senses rather than analyses these things; her knowledge is 'tacit'. All these things are working in her mind as her hands are working the clay. The product that emerges on the clay is likely to be in the tradition of her past work, but she may break away and embark on a new direction."[3]

In formulating our approach to *change* we also, we believe, need to take a more emergent approach.

8. EMERGENT PLANNING IN PRACTICE

What does emergent planning mean in practice? We believe it has a number of elements.

8.1. Clear purpose

In trying to bring about change we must have a clear purpose. Without purpose there is no impetus behind change. The potter at her wheel will anticipate an approximate outcome of her work: is she making a jug or a plate? We should have a similar clarity of purpose - while knowing that the unexpected may happen along the way.

8.2. Take action and respond to the consequences

Given the unpredictability we face we must accept that whatever action we take is part of a voyage of discovery. We cannot know for certain what the consequences of our action will be, or what information or insight will be revealed as we go forward. Flexibility, responsiveness, and sensitivity to opportunities, are the hallmarks of an emergent approach.

8.3. Detect emerging patterns

The emergent approach is less about systematic analysis, although this has its place, and more about detecting emerging patterns, helping them to take shape, and choosing where to put our influence. The planner of change *finds* change strategies as much as creates them. People throughout the organisation are in touch with different aspects of the organisation, and how it needs to change. The reality, as Mintzberg points out, is that strategies for change "grow like weeds in a garden", wherever people have the capacity to learn. We can help these strategies to take shape, and from the patterns we detect, decide to put our influence behind those that look most productive.

8.4. Focus on action then learning

Unlike programmed approaches to change, an emergent approach fosters learning along the way. In the face of the complexity of the organisation, and the unpredictability this causes, we need a sense of humility about how much we don't know. Learning allows us to take sensible next steps in the light of new information. That information includes unexpectedly good and bad outcomes, reactions from within and outside the organisation, noticing 'resistance to change', and trying to understand what it tells us about the organisation and how we are acting.

9.   EMERGENT PLANNING OR MUDDLING THROUGH?

One of the potential dangers of the emergent planning approach is that it could drift into getting by, or muddling through, or as an excuse for not really applying ourselves. There are four words which contain for us the difference between an emergent approach and muddling through: **purpose, insistence, learning, rigour.**

Purpose and insistence allow us to hold onto change as an imperative for the organisation. Change can be hard. Without insistence it is all too easy to let things drift, to return to the comfort of stability, rather than the discomfort of instability.

Learning, and rigorously doing the best we can in our thinking, acting and feeling, will give us the best opportunity to take the most appropriate action, and then build productively on the consequences.

10. CONTRASTING APPROACHES

In Table 2 we have set out some comparisons of the programmed and the emergent approach to planning for change.

Table 2		
Contrasting Approaches		
PROGRAMMED		EMERGENT
• rigid		• flexible
• formulated		• forming
• programmed		• crafted
• directed		• mobilising
• omnipotent		• humility
• analytic	*and*	• intuitive
• single loop learning	*and*	• double loop learning

Programmed change is formulated at the outset, and has a rigidity to it. Emergent change is more flexible and continues to form as more is learnt. Programmed change is also directive, and decided almost with an assumption of 'we know everything that needs to be known'. It is in essence controlling. The emergent approach recognises the limits of what individuals at the top, or consultants, can achieve alone. The emergent approach also *builds* on the analytic, by detecting emerging patterns, and adding the use of intuition; and it aims to build double loop learning into the process.

It is important to stress at this point that we are not saying that programmed planning is wrong, and emergent planning is right - each is appropriate to different situations. The emergent approach is relevant to complex, open, badly defined problems, such as change within organisations. Programmed planning is relevant to running the day-to-day operations of an organisation, or building a bridge. A humble, intuitive plan which is still forming, is not what you want for making sure your products are manufactured to the right quality, and delivered by nine o'clock tomorrow morning.

The difficulty for many of us is that we have grown up dealing with more controlled or contained situations to which a programmed approach is more relevant. We then have to deal with a different order of complexity when we are trying to bring about and handle change, but continue to use the old tools.

11. TOP MANAGERS BELIEVE IN EMERGENT PLANNING

Our research suggests to us that top managers know from their experience that an emergent approach is needed. They were clearly saying to us:

- You don't know what you don't know
- Take a step and see what happens
- Be responsive
- Make the most of opportunities.

Our question now is: how do we make the most of this approach?

12. THE IMPLICATIONS FOR CONSULTANTS

Even though we know we need to work in a different way, we find ourselves drawn to continuing with what we had begun to call 'traditional' planning for change. This pull seemed to come from a number of sources:

- clients expect clear project planning, and want to know outcomes
- traditional planning provides a familiar framework
- with an illusion of predictability, an illusion of 'we know what's going on'
- it is a linear, 'hard-edged', approach which is highly valued in most situations
- traditional planning methods replicate the prevalent top-down, controlling management style of most organisations.

And, let's face it we need to earn money.

But it's not just about going along with clients' expectations. Breaking away from a sense of knowing cause and effect is one of the hardest steps we can take.

13. RESISTING THE PULL

We are still working on how we resist the pull of the old way of planning! Clearly, however, we need to stop believing we have the power to predict accurately what will happen in organisations as they try to change. Sharing the basis for the emergent approach with clients will help to sell a different way of working, and help to set the ground for appropriate expectations. The early contracting with clients, and client organisations, becomes even more crucial if we are not to have difficulties from the outset. What we hold on to at the moment is a belief that what looks safest is actually most dangerous - it won't deliver.

14. PRACTICAL FIRST STEPS

We called our paper "Encouraging Unplanning", because we believe that giving up the old programmed way of formulating change is the vital first step. What we can put in its place is shown in Figure 1. (This builds on the work of Stacey[4].)

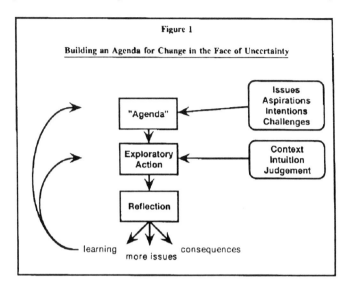

Figure 1

Building an Agenda for Change in the Face of Uncertainty

We now talk to clients about 'building an agenda for change' rather than planning for change. We work with the current, live issues and challenges of the organisation, and with today's real aspirations and intentions both of the organisation as a whole, and of those we work alongside. This set of issues, challenges, intentions and aspirations builds an agenda for change that provides the context within which to decide what action to take.

This action will, of course, be what we believe will be most likely to lead to the consequences we want, but we recognise nonetheless that it is exploratory - it will give us new information, greater insight, and cause unanticipated results, both good and bad. We therefore need to reflect on what we have learned, and move on to further action, or to resetting our agenda.

This process grounds action in the real needs and desires of the organisation, and is a practical route forward in the face of uncertainty. The consultant can play an important role in this:

- in promoting an emergent approach
- helping members of an organisation to build their agenda for change
- helping to find the right tasks, the right exploratory action, which will move the organisation forward most effectively
- providing personal support in dealing with uncertainty.

15. SUMMARY

We believe that structured and programmed approaches to "managing change" are not helpful. The research we have conducted gives a very strong view from top managers that in practice a structured approach to change is too unresponsive, and does not deliver the goods. This was a surprise to us, given the strength of prevailing practice in the consulting world is towards "programmes of change" which are often highly structured, and that programmes such as TQM, and Business Process Re-engineering are massively popular. Indeed our own practice was to use project planning techniques in formulating change strategies.

The views of top managers align themselves to some current theoretical thinking which suggests that trying to bring about change in complex systems (which organisations clearly are, given the large number of individuals and groups pursuing their own goals, and the wide range of feedback loops in the organisation), is an unpredictable business. New information is revealed as each step is taken, and actions have unplanned consequences.

This combination of new ideas with the strong views of top managers has led us to adopt a new approach to change, based on emergent planning. This new approach demands a clarity of purpose and an insistence to bring change about, but combines it with flexibility, responsiveness and learning. Emergent planning also focuses on detecting developing patterns from within the organisation, helping these to take shape, and then putting influence behind those that look most productive.

One practical outcome of this shift is that we now talk to client organisations about 'building an agenda for change' rather than planning for change. Plans are out of date almost as they are written. Their rigidity becomes a positive hindrance. Instead we work with the current, live issues and challenges of the organisation, and with today's real intentions and aspirations. These provide the energy to bring about change. They direct action; but we act knowing that the unexpected may happen along the way, and that we will constantly need to reset our agenda for change.

The difficulty for many of us that change presents a difficult, complex, open-ended, badly defined problem, and we are used to dealing with more controlled situations. We need different tools for dealing with change to those we have typically used. Emergent planning is, we believe, one such tool.

Treating change within organisations as if it is controllable may make us feel more comfortable, but we can end up adding little value to organisations. The more certainty we assume at the outset, the lower our chances of success in bringing about useful and sustained change.

REFERENCES

[1] Greiner, Larry, (1967) "Patterns of Organisational Change", Harvard Business Review, May-June

[2] Wilson, David, (1992) "A Strategy of Change", Routledge

[3] Mintzberg, H, (1987) "Crafting Strategy", Harvard Business Review, July-August

[4] Stacey, Ralph D (1991) "The Chaos Frontier", Butterworth-Heinemann

THE SALE OF CONSULTANCY, CLIENTS' AND CONSULTANTS' VIEW

Michael Kearsley, *Wordcom Associates, Walton on Thames*

ABSTRACT

There has been much written concerning the consultancy relationship. This would include the role of the consultant within an organisation and the various method-ologies and processes open to consultants in their work. Other writers have looked at the impact of consultancy and some of the ethical and moral considerations involved. This paper is concerned with what is, for many professional advisers and consultants, the most difficult aspect of consultancy - the process of actually getting a client. This paper shows that the consultancy sales process is a difficult and emotional problem for both clients and consultants. It presents data taken from the author's own doctoral research into sales reluctance in professional advisers. The dialogue following is based on a series of foils which formed the basis of the presentation.

1.   INTRODUCTION

Management consultants are one form of a group which may be loosely defined as professional advisers. Others in this group would include accountants, engineers, tax advisers, financial services advisers and lawyers. For many of these profes-sional advisers, finding and developing clients can become the most important part of their work. Many professional advisers may work for firms which already have a large existing client base. Professionals within these firms may have felt for some time that it was not necessary to put too much effort into business development and the most important part of their work was their technical expertise.

Greater competition, combined with the recent recession, has shown this to be an increasingly erroneous view. Maintaining "utilisation" - that is paid time - becomes paramount in difficult times, and it is perhaps this concern that has brought many people to this Conference. Many professional advisory firms have now realised the importance of sustained business development. This has high-lighted a need for skills above and beyond technical expertise and this has presented a number of difficulties for many firms.

There are only three ways to gain consultancy work.

> ITT (invitation to tender) is a variation on the traditional way that professional advisers gained clients; that is, the clients came to the adviser.

The difference with an invitation to tender today is that very often the consultants are being asked to bid for a job rather than being offered a job. In a recent tender for a project management assignment in East Europe for example, 69 consultancies were asked to bid. Bidding for work involves much time, effort and money - and the result may still be rejection.

- **Selling on** is when a consultant seeks to extend involvement with a client perhaps even into areas outside of the immediate consultant's expertise. Many firms now offer a wide range of services. The process of selling other services available through the firm is often referred to as cross-selling.

- **Selling in** is when firms are actively contacting prospects in order to develop new clients.

These three processes need three different types of skills. The invitation to tender requires the traditional skills of analysis and writing ability. Selling on involves the consultant much more in relationship building and thus highlights the need for trust and empathy between consultant and client. Selling in is the most difficult area and requires tenacity and practical selling skills. It needs to be remembered that in this third area, the consultant may well be approaching the clients of other consultancies and professional advisory firms. Selling in involves the firm in much time, effort and money. It is the area which most consultants will admit they do not enjoy. It is also the most expensive way of developing business. An invitation to tender may frequently involve aspects of selling in. Even selling on to a subsidiary or separate division will involve aspects of selling in.

2. THE CLIENTS' VIEW

There are many different kinds of clients which form a spectrum from a relationship based on a fleeting activity of a few hours to perhaps a decades long relationship. There are many levels of demand from perhaps the services of a lone consultant to multi-level, multi- disciplinary teams.

Whatever the mechanics of a consultancy assignment, clients are likely to seek a consultant for many different reasons. Sometimes the consultant's immediate contact did not initially request help. Sometimes consultants are being asked to save the day. Sometimes the consultants are being lined up as the scapegoat - someone to blame when the inevitable occurs. Sometimes the consultants are there simply to rubber stamp what someone has already decided. Sometimes the consultants may be there to give credibility to what may even be a fraud. In short, when someone sells themselves as a problem solver, they are likely to find that the problems are deeper and more complex than they may have at first envisaged. This will come as no surprise to professional management consultants.

Service versus Product

Accepting however that the consultancy purpose is useful and honourable, the client is quite likely to be a buyer of many other goods and services. There is a significant difference between buying products and buying services. Clearly there is a much greater element of trust involved in service selling. The consultants cannot divorce themselves from the sales process because they are, in fact, the product being sold. There is often a substantial difference in the view of consultancy and client with regard to fees and performances. Consultancy firms will often wish to bill the time of their consultants on a daily basis at a fixed rate with no guarantees of results. The client, on the other hand, is buying only the results.

Often the need for consultancy is not planned. It is very difficult, therefore, for consultancies to have the correct number of consultants with the correct skills for every available client problem. From the clients point of view, the need for consultancy is often complex and uncertain, in comparison with buying products. The choice of consultants is difficult to make because of the difficulty of comparison and the fact that value criteria are often vague.

It is often difficult for clients to understand the value of a consultancy project as opposed to the daily price for the consultants and, of course, the client is often actively involved in the production of the consultancy assignment. The client can thus more readily see how things are done and when things are going wrong.

All consultants would love to be able to provide real tangible benefits. These may include reduced costs, improved productivity, increased sales and faster implementations. Very often, however, the benefits of consultancy are intangible - improved communications, more cohesive management time, improved morale and clearer direction.

Some clients may be guilty of expecting that the consultant will guarantee their success in business - perhaps with minimum effort on their part, minimum cost and no risk. This may sound a little extreme but sales people and consultants quickly learn that clients, as human beings, are primarily emotional creatures, pretending to be logical.

Emotional Factors

In every consultancy assignment, there are always underlying emotions - fear, envy, pride and vanity may often take precedence over profit, efficiency and utility. The difficulty often experienced is in finding out what the underlying emotions actually are. As a justification of this, one might consider how many excellent consultancy reports are never actually implemented. This can be very difficult for specialist enthusiasts such as management consultants to accept.

Another factor which influences clients behaviour is the perception of the risks involved in implementing consultancy advice. Most solutions involve some kind of risk. When risks are small and benefits are small, a decision to proceed is perhaps easily made. Sometimes however, the risks are much greater especially in the mind of the client. This highlights the great need for consultants to extract from their clients, *all* the concerns they have. For many clients the act of introducing a consultant is, in itself, a major risk. The importance of benefits versus risks as perceived by the clients is one of the most fundamental reasons for client inactivity.

Clients in fact, may not buy consultancy services for a number of reasons.

Perhaps the client has a problem without knowing precisely what they want. Perhaps also, clients do not know what a consultancy might offer or have a wrong impression of the technical strengths of a consultancy. Some people see consultants as a means of educating themselves without actually buying anything. In many cases, however, rejection has a very simple cause - the clients simply don't like the consultants. In a world where many consultancies can offer virtually the same advice to the same level, it is only the style and behaviour of the individual consultant which may make the difference. Dunn & Bradstreet, in a 1988 survey, questioned why customers stopped buying from their suppliers. 82% reported that they had terminated their supplier because they were unhappy with the supplier. This unhappiness was often revealed to be a relationship problem rather than the quality of the goods or services.

Survey Results

As a result, many firms have realised the importance of asking clients what they want. A number of surveys have been conducted and one in particular, which involved the clients of 14 major UK consultancies, revealed some interesting information. When asked how the organisation had first come to know of the consultancy which now handled their account, the 5 leading reasons given were by recommendation (16%), through a long standing relationship (12%), through the reputation of the firm (8%), because the firm were also auditors (8%) and personal contact (7%).

Only 4% could recall that the consultancy had first contacted them and only 1% said they had been influenced by advertising. The percentage figures may be suspect but it seems clear that clients had responded to people they knew or who were recommended to them.

When asked what dangers and risks could be associated with using a management consultant, the responses indicated many emotional concerns. The danger of paying a lot of money for little benefit, not unexpectedly, was the leading concern. Fears were also expressed, however, regarding confidentiality, incorrect solutions, adverse affects on staff morale, loss of control, failure to understand needs, disrupting the company, fielding inexperienced staff and providing cosmetic solutions. The consultancies involved in the survey often excused these comments by indicating that such comments reflected what *could* go wrong rather than what *had* gone wrong.

When asked what was the most important factor in selecting or assessing a management consultant, value for money was again, not surprisingly, the leading response. Interestingly, however, clients commented on the chemistry and rapport with staff, professionalism, presentation, adaptability, flexibility, and integrity.

When asked what was the most effective sales and marketing method which a consultancy could use in order to gain entry into an organisation, the three major responses, accounting for over 40% of responses, centered on personal contact, reputation and recommendation. It seemed clear that clients were indicating the overwhelming importance of the personal relationship and reputation of consultancy firms. This was far in excess of advertising, seminars and cold contacts. In short, clients seemed to be saying that they wanted to deal with people that they know and like, and who perhaps were recommended by those they trust.

What is presented here is the difficulty of selling in, and the tremendous influence that the behaviour, manner and approach of consultants has for the success of its consultancy. This is in addition to good technical knowledge and may appear to even transcend technical knowledge.

With so much importance placed on the behaviour and skill of the consultant, it is perhaps pertinent to now consider what the consultancy sales interaction means from the consultants viewpoint.

3.   THE CONSULTANTS' VIEW

There is a lot of advice now available from supposedly successful consultants on how and why they achieved success. [Cohen 1985, Gray 1985, Tuller 1992, Markham 1993, Lambert 1993].

Many of the books written by successful consultants will highlight the skills which the author considers are the most important skills for success. The ability to diagnose problems and find solutions were shown to be, often of secondary importance. In describing success skills, the authors used such terms as bedside manner, communication skills, ability to work under pressure, ability to handle people, sensitivity to others, tolerance for the consulting life and strong personal drive.

The message was very clear. All authors emphasised the overriding importance of interpersonal skills as well as a tolerance for the consulting lifestyle and an inner drive and persistence. These may conflict a little with the job specification first presented to prospective management consultants. My own view is that success in consultancy (as in anything) is a combination of three things: *organisation, skills and attitude*. The consultants that I have known and have trained over many years, have been successful (or not) through the effects usually of all three of these factors.

Organisation

Increasingly, management consultancy is a continual hunt for new business and a farming of existing business. One difficulty that consultancies may face is that they do not have the support systems to influence total market and national communities. They may not employ marketing people or outside agencies. Because of this, a lot of the activities which would have been undertaken by marketing people is not done. This would include such things as prospect database development and sustained marketing programmes.

It is difficult to sell to people when they do not know you exist, when they do not receive your invitations and when they do not receive your brochures or proposals. Even the biggest consultancies are often remiss in their record systems and particularly in monitoring sales performance. They thus continue to repeat many of their mistakes despite internal attempts to the contrary. Internal training departments may lack the necessary authority to change this. Many firms do not have a co-ordinated and authoritative training structure. Many other firms do not have training at all. My experience has been that whilst many firms are willing to accept that they cannot possibly be doing everything right, they are nevertheless often unwilling to accurately detail and quantify what they are doing wrong. It is difficult to gain acceptance of this particularly if firms have experienced great success as occurred throughout the 1980's. Chris Argyris [1991] at Harvard has also shown through his research how difficult it can be, particularly for management consultants, to acknowledge that in fact they may be failing at something. He found that management consultants were the most difficult group to accept that they were in any way personally inadequate.

If firms wish to increase their sales success rate, there are really only two ways of doing it. The first is to increase the number of prospects and thus play the numbers game. The second is to improve their effectiveness in the process of selling. Both of these require skills beyond technical skills so it is appropriate to perhaps now look at the second issue of skills.

Skills

Consultants have usually spent a great deal of time, effort and money in developing technical skills. They will often spend little or no time, effort or money in developing their sales and interpersonal skills. My own doctoral research with four of the big six accountancy/consultancy firms revealed that these firms often provided a wide range of personal skills courses. A typical selection would include selling skills, presentation skills, writing skills, negotiation skills, time management, stress management, interviewing skills, process consulting, various business development programs and client relationship initiatives. In one part of my research which was predominantly with accountants, tax advisers and some management consultants, the participants were spending on average 10 to 20 days a year in various technical training initiatives - yet no one in that particular part of the study had more than 2 days per year of total personal development training of the kind described.

Management consultancy divisions within these firms may argue that they provide more personal development training than this but one could consider that the biggest of these firms may have more than 1000 consultants. If a firm was to run, for example, a three day selling skills course every week, it would be over two years before all had attended. Most major consultancies would probably only run a sales course monthly, perhaps even quarterly. The calculations are easy to make and the situation is further compounded by a situation which many management consultants in larger firms will be familiar with - that of being withdrawn from a sales training course perhaps a week before it is due to run owing to client demands.

Management consultants, as with other professional advisers, have often invested very heavily in their own technical training. This may have included university courses, evening courses and the purchase of significant numbers of books, articles and papers. In my study, which involved predominantly managers, senior managers and partners with many years of professional activity, I asked when each participant had last purchased a book which was concerned with sales or personal development along the lines of the courses which have been described.

62% had never bought a book on sales or personal development. A further 22% could not remember purchasing a book within the last year. Those who had purchased a book, could often not recall actually having read it. These books are available, of course, on every railway station and in every bookstore for often less than six or seven pounds. Consultants may argue that they are lacking in sales related skills or that they are not provided sufficiently with the kind of training described but in my study, at least, they did not appear to be rushing to do anything about it themselves. In fairness, many of the participants were not unduly concerned about this and it perhaps says more about their attitude to sales activity than to anything else. It might thus be pertinent to now look at the third area of success, that of attitude.

Attitude

My research has revealed some attitudinal problems which are experienced by many consultants and professional advisers. To put it simply, most are not very enthusiastic about selling. My experience has been that most professional advisers are also very willing to admit that they are not very good at selling. Their first line of defence in this is that the organisation they belong to does not support the sales activity by, for example, giving them too much other work to do. Some will argue that they have extensive management responsibilities and that always the clients' requirements come first. I have conducted programmes when, to assist participants, these inhibitions have been significantly reduced and at this point, many professional advisers will move to a second argument.

The second argument to justify sales inhibition is a lack of sales skills, i.e. that they have not received selling skills, negotiation skills or similar training. As with the first argument, there is always an element of truth but when the necessary training has been provided and sales activity has not flourished, a third argument is often provided.

The third inhibition they will argue is a lack of the correct personality for selling - they will argue that they are not the "sales type". As part of my research, I used a profiling technique that has its origins in the work of Chomsky [1957] and transformational grammar. Called the LAB Profile (language and behaviour), the profile is acquired through a 15 to 20 minute conversation during which the participants' language patterns are used to indicate some 14 motivational and attitudinal traits.

Whenever I have used the profile, I have fed back to participants what the profile appears to be revealing and overwhelmingly, participants have agreed that it is a fair reflection of their attitudes, motivational and working traits.

Lab Profile Results

The profile is presented as a trend towards two extremes of behaviour and my own training experiences have revealed that while we may all argue that our personality is "in the middle" somewhere, we often, in fact, reveal a tendency to more marked behaviour. The profile revealed some interesting trends amongst the hundreds of professional advisers and management consultants who were tested. It should be stressed that there is great individuality within groups and these trends are grossly simplified. However, there was a tendency amongst accountancy and tax people towards reactive behaviour whereas management consultants were slightly more proactive. It should be stressed that their is no value judgement in this. Proactivity is not better than reactivity. The nature of many professional occupations is, in fact, reactive and individuals who are more reactive by nature will be comfortable operating within them. Sales development, however, requires greater proactivity and at a level higher perhaps even than many of the consultants profiled.

All groups showed a tendency towards independent behaviour and this questioned just how much professional advisers actually do like to work together rather than doing their own thing. Accountants were often much more procedural whereas management consultants were often attracted to change and to options. The consultants often had less interest in detail and specific information, preferring a much more general overview of things whereas the accountants and tax advisers often needed a great deal of information before making a decision. Management consultants seemed more content with much less information before they came to a judgement.

Many professional advisers showed a strong internal tendency - that is, a security in that what they thought was right must be right. This also reveals itself in an unwillingness to consider other points of view. Many were very task centered, preferring the work and the achievement of technical problems to pleasing the people involved.

Further to this, many of the advisers were motivated by the interest of the work itself rather than the amount of money that they might make as a result of doing the work. For many, money was considered to be rather unimportant. Many of my participants were not really interested in helping other people, preferring to pursue their own interests, tasks and ambitions. There was, however, an interesting difference between management consultants and other professional advisers in that whereas the accountants and tax advisers were often influenced by avoiding unpleasant situations, the consultants were often much more motivated by what they could acquire or gain from a situation, often in the form of learning or new experience.

Many of the accountants and tax advisers revealed a dislike of major change. This was different to many management consultants for whom travel, new situations and new challenges were often attractive. These consultants were in danger of becoming bored more readily if the task remained too stable.

It should be stated, in fairness, the participants in my research were often well suited to the technical aspects of the jobs that they had been hired to do. Unfortunately the nature of the job had now changed and included a much stronger sales and business development element. For many participants, the real job still continued to be the technical analysis and problem solving aspects and sales activity clearly did not coincide with this.

Sales Reluctance

Sales activity, by its very nature, is different in many respects to the technical aspects of consultancy. Sales can often be physically, socially and psychologically separating. It requires great flexibility and innovation. It may involve the playing of multiple roles some of which reduce the importance and status of the individual. It requires great persistence and self motivation and is full of uncertainty and conflict. The results of sales activity can often take a long time to become apparent.

Sales activity can therefore be disturbing to many people and when asked what they felt of sales activity during my research, participants, even the consultants who sought major change, revealed some deep concerns.

There were often feelings of manipulating and forcing things on to people. Participants felt that to be involved in sales activity was to equate with a common salesman, lacking in status and importance. Many others reported the feelings of apprehension and even danger associated with a sales situation. This expressed itself in quite dramatic bodily reactions - heart racing, sweaty palms, worried state etc. Participants reported that they frequently became muddled and jumbled in a sales situation. One participant summed it up by reporting that selling was like being stopped by the police.

What all of this clearly reflected was the deep sales reluctance or "call reluctance" as it is sometimes more narrowly called. There are many kinds of sales reluctance each with its own cause. For example, a fear of failure is a very strong inhibitor for management consultants who often have a history of success. The idea that selling is dishonest and immoral may be based on actual experience but often seems to be a stereotypal approach in which a low status activity must be associated with low status people. Many regarded selling as a politically dangerous activity, fearing criticism not just from the clients but their own colleagues and superiors. The fear of rejection from clients was a widespread concern. Included also was the lack of belief in the service or the firm itself which became obvious with a number of participants. Sometimes this was reflected in a lack of belief in the individual and an underlying assumption that the client has more power and is more important.

Of course, despite all of the inhibitions described, some individuals within every firm show themselves to be very good at getting business. I asked my research participants (who incidentally did not largely number themselves in this band of superior performers) to describe someone whom they knew to be good at selling within their firm. A most interesting phenomenon occurred. The first positive comment (such as talks well, confident, gregarious, knowledgeable etc) was often followed by a secondary negative, critical comment - e.g. "she's very knowledgeable - but of course it's bluff" or "he always has ready answers - but of course it's not always true". It was almost as if participants were saying that because a certain colleague was good at selling that there had to be something wrong with them. It was as if they were saying (and this was more strongly reinforced elsewhere) that to be good at selling was a negative rather than a positive attribute.

4. CONCLUSION

This paper has presented some of the difficulties which both clients and consultants experience in the consultancy interaction. These difficulties have been seen to center on the interpersonal difficulties rather than technical difficulties. Clients and prospects have described the range of risks which are present when management consultants are used. They have described their great need to know and trust the consultants that they use. The behaviour and attitudes of the consultants thus becomes of great importance in the development of this trust and confidence.

Consultants, for their part, are faced with a greater task than the identification and solution of technical problems. Consultants are dealing with human beings and thus must bring to the consultancy interaction a whole range of interpersonal skills. Consultants are always selling themselves whether they like to or not. They cannot divorce themselves from the product of consultancy because they are the product in consultancy. One way or another, every organisation that wants to compete in the increasingly competitive consultancy marketplace, will have to face some of the issues that have been raised by this research.

The attitudes and beliefs which many consultants and professional advisers have with regard to the consultancy sales process and to selling can be a serious inhibitor for business development. Many internal training courses do not address this problem and some may even reinforce the problem. Those employed in major consultancies may have the luxury of an existing body of clients and an existing volume of work but their future success may depend increasingly on their ability to come to terms with their sales reluctance. For those wishing to create and develop their consultancy, overcoming these inhibitions will become even more important.

Some firms already have a reputation as more aggressive business developers and this was reflected in my own research in the amount of sales training undertaken and the attitudes of their professional staff to the sales activity. This has a cost in both time, effort and money - a cost, however, that those who wish to compete will have to bear.

REFERENCES

ARGYRIS C, 1991. *Teaching Smart People How To Learn*, Harvard Business Review, May/June,

BENNETT R, 1990. *Choosing & Using Management Consultants*, Kogan Page

CHOMSKY N, 1957. *Transformational Grammar*, Department of Linguistics, MIT, PhD Dissertation

COHEN W A, 1985. *How To Make It Big As A Consultant*, American Management Association (Amacom)

GRAY D A, 1985. *Start & Run A Profitable Consultancy*, Kogan Page

KARISON D, 1991. *Consulting For Success*, Kogan Page

LAMBERT T, 1993. *High Income Consulting,* Nicholas Brealey Publishing

MARKHAM C, 1987. *Practical Consulting,* ICA - IMC

MARKHAM C, 1993. *The Top Consultant,* Kogan Page

MCDONALD M & LEPPARD J, 1986. *How To Sell A Service,* William Heinemann Ltd

PARRY R, 1991. *People Businesses - Making Professional,* Business Books Ltd, Firms Profitable

RASSAM C & OATES D, 1991. *Management Consultancy, The Inside Story,* Mercury Business Books

SCHEIN E H, 1987. *Process Consultation - Volume 2,* Addison Wesley

TULLER L W, 1992. *The Independent Consultants - Q & A Book,* Bob Adams Inc

VAUX A, STOCKDALE M &SCHWERIN M, 1992. *Independent Consulting for Evaluators ,* Sage Publications

VINEY N, 1992. *Bluff Your Way In Consultancy ,* Ravette Books

THE POLITICS OF SALVATION AND REVELATION IN THE PRACTICE OF CONSULTANCY.

W. Gordon Lawrence, *Director IMAGO East-West London*

The working hypothesis to be explored is:

> *within the practice of consultancy there is occurring the beginnings of a paradigm shift from the politics of salvation to the politics of revelation.*

If you will, there is the beginnings of change in the 'mind set' that consultants bring to their work. In particular, I am concerned to explore the covert 'scientific' thinking and related, latent values which structure how consultants see the work relationships between their client-partners and themselves.

What are the processes of thinking that are leading to this change in perspective?

THE TWENTIETH CENTURY HERITAGE OF THINKING.

Business, and consultancy, would be impossible without thinking and thought.

> *'...thought has a creative function... to create what is there. In fact, almost everything we see around us in the world was created from thought, including all the cities, all the buildings all the science, all the technology and almost everything we call nature.' (Bohm and Edwards, 1991, p. 8)*

To give a striking example: It was the capacity to think that caused Neolithic people at the end of the Stone Age in about 2,500 BC to start growing cereals, to begin to domesticate pigs, sheep, oxen and goats. This remarkable leap in thinking transformed human beings of the time from being exclusively nomadic hunters, fishers and gatherers of food to becoming settlers. From these beginnings agriculture as we know it developed All of it has been achieved by thought.

The thinking and thought of our present century is characterised by a reliance on science and technology. This has been the century of staggering scientific and technological advances. The twentieth century began with one version of the natural sciences and is ending with another. Similarly, the thinking which has formed the social sciences has also been transformed, but to a lesser degree. This is because, for example, the methodology of psycho-analysis as it has developed since Freud, but particularly through the leadership of Jung, has always been striving for a celebration of the subjective and a recognition of the prime importance of the conscious and unconscious mind for the act of thinking.

The paradigm shift in the natural sciences in this century began with what can be labelled Newtonian-Cartesian ideas. They were founded, first, on an ontological assumption of separateness. The study of being and essences was conducted through the :

> *'separability of observer from observed; of man from nature; of mind from matter; of science from religion; separateness of "fundamental particles" from one another; separability of the parts of a system or organism to understand how it "really" works; separateness of scientific disciplines'*
> *(Harman, 1992, p. 48)*

The second assumption was epistemological (the theory of knowledge) which saw any scientific picture of reality as being based on empirical evidence derived from physical sense data. As Harman points out from these two metaphysical assumptions have followed beliefs as to how knowledge of phenomena are gained

The most important of these are: objectivism, i.e. the assumption that there is an objective world 'out there' which can be studied by observation. Positivism assumes that the real world is what is measurable; and reductionism which assumes that we come to understand phenomena by studying its elemental parts, such as 'fundamental particles':

The ontological and epistemological assumption with which we began this century have their roots in the experiences of the greatest catastrophe to befall human beings in the known world. This was the Black Death which began in Cathay in the 1330s and ended in London in the 1660s. It was an overpowering experience in that it carried off two thirds of the known population. Lasting as it did in time for over three centuries it brought about a substantial shift in the way that people regarded their environment.

Both poor and rich were subject to the plague. The catastrophe caused people to become paranoid. They could no longer trust their environment or, for that matter, the version of God which had informed their daily lives. They did not know the cause of the Black Death, and it took them a long time to discover ways of mitigating its consequences. Such a a powerful, destructive force ever-present in people's lives had an effect on their thinking. Their thinking changed in two domains: that of spirituality and that of science. In actuality the two were interdependent.

In the domain of the spiritual;

(a)   The Divine was identified as being transcendent to the natural world. While this undoubtedly facilitates a deep and intimate Divine-human relationship it can also be seen as separating any idea of, what I shall call, god-ness from the natural world. If you will, the natural world becomes more profane and looses any quality that we might call 'sacred'.

(b)   Within the Judaeo-Christian tradition the focus in our western spiritual tradition started to be on salvation dynamics to the almost exclusion of creation dynamics.

(c)   There begins to be a constant presentation of Man as being transcendent to the Natural world.

(d)   There grew a gradual belief in a transcendent future to which everyone should aspire and which is expected to usher in the millennial bliss. (McDonagh, 1982)

Each of these assumptions of transcendencies has had far reaching effects, if only unconsciously, in the minds of the peoples of the western world or, to update this, of the northern hemisphere. The first and second transcendencies separates man from the Earth-Cosmos creative dynamic. The third and fourth separates man from the natural world and the fourth, in addition, shifts Man's perspective from the 'here and now' of existence to some future bliss be it communism, fascism, democracy, or any form of millenarian belief.

All these transcendencies together constitute a spiritual position. The word 'spiritual' I use in the sense of 'linking together'. In particular I am thinking of the linking 'in the mind' of human beings to the Cosmos. In actuality, any previous linking together was ruptured. The Church of the times had the final say in what the nature of this linking was. But in a real sense the Church had failed and disappointed the people who had survived the Black Death.

The important consequence was that 'in his mind', Man became 'dissociated' from his environment which had now become persecuting. T.S. Eliot called this the 'dissociation of sensibility' (Eliot, 1953, p. 117). More particularly, this transcendent~scientific perspective that was forged as a result of the experience of the Black Death produced resultant concepts, metaphors and perceptions which give expression to 'three pernicious dichotomies, as identified by Lawrence Cahoone (1988). These are: the split between subject and object, i.e. mind and body, the inner and the outer world; the split between the individual and his or her relationships (the solipsisitic view point); the split between human culture and the biophysical processes in which it is contained.

In the domain of science, and the associated technology which it spawned, the ability to be an outsider to, or split-off from, the environment meant, particularly through the invention of the telescope, that the world's phenomena were no longer seen as being part of a cosmic wholeness but rather parts of a complicated machine. This was the 'new science' of the times.

From Galileo through Bacon, Descartes and Newton there developed the version of scientific thinking which has just been described. The important point was that they were freed from the teachings of the Church and were able to explore reality as it seemed to be. This dissociation lasts till well into our present century. The result has been that human beings have come to see themselves as being in charge of their environment and that every problem of it can be solved by them.

This particular 'mind set' of transcendent perspectives, which led to this version of science and of technology, is what lies behind the 'Politics of Salvation'.

Here, my working hypothesis is: the imago of the cosmos in the mind directly influences the nature of human beings's behaviour in and to their environment in which they make their experiences and co-create reality, This reality becomes a representation of the cosmos. Similarly the cosmos in the mind is a mirror of the environment. They are mutually constructed through the psychic processes of projection and introjection.

The corollary is that: if there is a change in the understanding of the nature of the cosmos it will affect human beings' behaviour in the environment. This will include business behaviour.

For example, whereas at the beginning of the century people had a picture of Heaven and Hell as part of the cosmos, we end the century with no substantial belief in these. Piero Camporesi (1990) argues that the fear of hell has now virtually disappeared. For Mediaeval people, living through the Black Death this was not the case. For most of us as we near the end of the century we have come to realise painfully that people make their heavens and hells on earth through their behaviour

THE POLITICS OF SALVATION.

What do I mean by 'politics'? I use the word in the sense of 'influence' of one person or party, over another. By 'salvation' I refer back to the salvation dynamics that were launched by the Black Death - in particular to the idea of a transcendent future.

The politics of salvation can be clearly seen in the missionary effort of the churches. The idea was to convert the heathen, i.e., save them for Christ.

And countries who developed empires were also caught in the same dynamic. To be sure there were other reasons but I am arguing that the principal rationale was to bring enlightenment to the savage.

The politics of salvation have been demonstrated through the '-isms' that have been a hallmark of our century: communism, fascism, capitalism and, of course, democracy.

I took the idea of salvation, originally, from the 'rescue phantasy' which can operate in therapeutic situations when the therapist loses sight of the task and becomes involved in trying to save the patient from whatever psychic ill they may be experiencing. In the dynamics of consultancy this is translated into 'seeing the client system as being a system to be "cured' and so offering solutions as a way of analysing unconscious material (Dubbane and Lee, 1980).' (Lawrence, 1986, p. 62) There is in such situations an avoidance of the existential reasons for the consultants and client-partners to understand their present political, psychic and spiritual condition.

In the practice of consultancy I think the politics of salvation can be seen in all the 'packages' of interventions that are offered. One example, in particular, is the Quality of Working Life Movement. While this movement has laudable and the best of aims in a social justice sense it is, nevertheless, based on the idea that the workers have to be saved from their conditions.

This century has seen the development of ideas on 'social engineering'. Essentially, I see the politics of salvation as giving solutions to people and not allowing them to define their life-situation for themselves and taking their own authority to alter it.

THE EMERGENT THINKING OF THE LATE TWENTIETH CENTURY.

What helped to cause the paradigm shift in the sciences in the twentieth century?

The discovery of quantum mechanics, to be sure. It was physicists exploring quantum mechanics who realised that could not be like the classical scientists standing behind a glass screen and observing, so to speak.

Scientists had to participate. Participation is the key word: It has two meanings now: 'One is to "partake of". We partake of the whole within ourselves. The other is "to take part in it actively". Both are necessary.' (Wijers and Pijnappel, 1990, p. 31)

Wheeler states this new understanding of 'participation' thus:

'May the universe in some sense be "brought into being" by the participation of those who participate? The vital act is the act of participation. "Participation is the incontrovertible new concept given by quantum mechanics. It strikes down the term "observer" of classical theory, the men who sharply stand behind the tick g;lass wall and watches what is going on without taking part.' (Reference lost)

The point here is that the scientist was no longer 'dissociated' from the phenomena being studied. This method of experiencing through participation has been leading to new discoveries by scientists of all kinds resulting in a new version of creation dynamics which turns on its head all previous notions of how the cosmos is organised and, therefore, the nature of the relatedness of human beings to their environment, i.e. the ecosystem.

This change in orientation to methodology has far reaching consequences. In particular it has contributed to a new version of science. Now we have two new assumptions, They are:

' (a) an ontological assumption of oneness, wholeness, interconnectedness of everything and (b) an epistemological choice to include all the evidence.' (Harman 1992, p. 49)

By 'all the evidence' Harman includes:

1. Those data admissible in the strict logical empiricism - namely measurements of physical parameters.
2. Data depending on the connoisseurship of expert judges, such as those on which systematic (taxonomic) biology is based.
3. Data which are essentially self-reports of subjective experience obtained in an environment that promotes high levels of trust and candour, subjected to sophisticated skepticism because of our known capability for self-deception, and checked in other ways wherever possible.
4. The subjective self-reports obtained by "inner explorers" of various cultures. This includes the so-called "perennial wisdom" distilled from esoteric core experiences of the world's spiritual traditions.' (Harman, 1992, p. 50)

The ontological assumption of wholeness has been given substance by James Lovelock. He found when studying the atmospheric chemistry of the earth that it could only be explained in terms of regulatory processes. Life on earth began, according to fossil records, 3500 million years ago. Conventional theory is that species evolved in ecological niches. This, argues Lovelock, is far too simplistic as life would have died out because of the natural processes of physics, chemistry and biology which would have destroyed the conditions that sustain life. Lovelock argues that life goes on because the the the atmosphere, the seas and the Earth's crust together with all living things all form part of a single, living organism. He calls this living organism "Gaia" after the Greek goddess of the Earth.

> *'The science of Gaia is new, exploring the planet wide homeostatic processes in which we share. But the concept is old, a rediscovery of what all earlier peoples have known. We are in Lovelock's words, "part and partners in a very democratic entity." Formed of the fabric of Gaia, living amidst the web of interdependent species and the traces of past lives, we cannot conquer nature without defeating ourselves. Recognition of this truth is fundamental to peace.' (Barnaby, 1988, p. 10)*

The idea of Gaia expresses the interconnectedness of everything that exists on Earth. Here we can talk of 'symbiosis' This is the mutual dependency between two organisms such as a cow and the bacteria which enable it to digest grass which the cow could not do on its own.

There is another kind of symbiosis, however. This is the interdependence between the universe as whole, which is inanimate and not an organism, and the second partner which 'is alive, but is not any particular organism. It is not even an entire species. Rather the second organism is all organisms - life itself.' (Greenstein, 1988, p. 189). Here, what is being pointed to is a gigantic symbiosis at work in the universe.

To understand this kind of symbiosis we have to take account of the Anthropic Principle which Greenstein has propounded. This is: 'The only things that can be known are those compatible with the existence of knowers.' His hypothesis is that the cosmos brought forth life in order to exists. His argument is that for a single particle to exists, it must be observed. Subsequent steps in his argument are:

> *'The first is to argue that what is true of a single particle is also true of a collection of particles: stones, planets - even the universe as whole. The implication is that the very cosmos does not exist unless observed. And the second step will be that only a conscious mind is capable of performing such an observation.' (Greenstein, 1988, p. 223)*

It is this kind of thinking that has made us realise at the end of the twentieth century that we live in an ecosystemic environment in which everything is linked to everything else. This holistic-ecological perspective is now fundamental. Systems theory, biology and psycho-analysis are all holistic and, so, ecological.

> *'Now this deep ecological world view is ultimately spiritual. When you look at the essence of spiritual experience or religious experience, it is the sense of being connected to the cosmos as a whole, of belonging to the cosmos as a whole. In fact the very word 'religion' means binding...The connection between science and spirituality is through the ecological world view of science.' (Wijers and Pijnappel, 1990, p.67)*

My working hypothesis is that:

> *this paradigm shift causes a shift in the way that we conceptualise consultancy.*

To state this as succinctly as I can: the preoccupation of the politics of salvation is with change, i.e., it is imposed from the outside on individuals or systems by others holding power. The politics of revelation is preoccupied with the conditions and resources for the exercise of transformation which comes from inside the person or system and is brought about through the people revealing what may be the truth of their situation to themselves and taking authority to act on their interpretation.

THE POLITICS OF REVELATION.

What follows I have to put in personal terms because the thinking that goes into the politics of salvation can never be completed because by their nature they are always in an unfinished state.

My concern in consultancy and action-research is to create the conditions and resources for the politics of revelation to be realised on the part of the client-partner. This rests on the view that everyone who takes up a role in an organisation has the capacity to manage him- or herself in that role. The idea of management of self in role was formulated by Miller and myself in the 1970s (Lawrence and Miller, 1976) but has never fully been realised generally. Ideas on Quality Circles intervened, for instance, which, if only unconsciously, were designed to give workers the impression that they were responsible for the management of their work. Essentially Quality Circles never shifted the basic worker-management dynamic. It is an excellent example of the politics of salvation.

Now the idea of 'empowerment' is to the fore. Miller describes his own work as directed at offering individuals methods for understanding the unconscious social processes they can be caught up in in order that they can gain greater influence over the environment in which they live and work. I am in complete agreement with his observations on the notion of empowerment. He writes:

> '*It is a term I avoid because of its ambiguity: between becoming more powerful and making more powerful. The notion of giving power is inherently patronising - it implies dependency - and hence is of itself disempowering. Power cannot be given, only taken. That having been said, power and dependency are central issues for a consultant working with organisations.*' (Miller, 1993, p. xvi)

In the terms of this paper giving power implies salvation, i.e. rescuing the other from their situation.

Consultancy and action-research I see as being conducted within a frame. This idea came in the late 1970s when with some Tavistock Institute colleagues I conducted an acion-research study to launch democracy in a company which I shall refer to as The Firm. The project hinged around the concept of System Future. Its primary task was: to provide opportunities for the people in the Firm to explore what it was like to work there and consider what it could be in the future. As was written subsequently,

> '*Perhaps the most controversial aspect of System Future has been its initial organisation. System Future was separate from the Firm. It started in our minds as being a symbolic space to which people could come on their authority to talk with us (the consultants) about their feelings, beliefs and wishes. We wanted to have the idea of people "seconding" themselves from the Firm to System Future for an interview or a discussion..."Space" in this context also implies a time space, e.g., the duration of a discussion; a time out from life which would allow for reflection; a time in space to stand outside the skin of the Firm, so to speak.*' (Lawrence, 1980, pp. 72-73)

The encounters with the client-partner take place in what I now call, borrowing from Winnicott, the 'third space' between the consultant and the client-partner. The key thought of Winnicott is:

> *'From the beginning the baby has maximally intense experiences in the*
> *potential space between the subjective object and the object objectively*
> *perceived, between me-extensions and non-me. The potential space is at*
> *the interplay between there being nothing but me and there being objects*
> *and phenomena outside of omnipotent control.' (Winnicott, 1980 edn., p.*
> *118)*

This potential space between mother and baby is a metaphor for the third space between the client-partner and the consultant. It is a cultural space in which meanings can be discovered. In the third space the 'meanings' of the situation can be explored. Just what is meant by 'planning' for example. What conceptualisations are there?

Winnicott writing in his context describes the 'play' that takes place between mother and baby which is the grounding for cultural experience. In the context of consultancy and action-research with adults in work roles I refer to the idea of 'generativity' because the term 'play' carries infantile associations.

What are the areas of generativity? The short answer is thinking and thought. Given that all business is reliant on thinking, not only for its day to day operations and the management of activities of conversion but also for anticipating the future by bringing new markets into being, the capacity to thinks is the major asset of the people in any enterprise.

Here it is useful to take the ideas of David Armstrong (1991) on thinking. He distinguishes between two kinds of thinking: Thinking 1 and Thinking 2. The former is characterised by thought or thoughts which come out of the process of thinking and owe their existence to a thinker. Such thoughts are capable of exegesis, justification and falsification. Epistemologically, thinking is prior to thought. In Thinking 2 thought and thoughts are epistemologically prior to thinking. Bion (1984) expresses the idea thus: 'Thoughts exist without a thinker...The thoughts which have no thinker acquire or are acquired by a thinker.' (p. 165) Such thoughts are able to be voiced through the practice of attention and awareness.

All my consultancy work in the last decade or so has been pointing me to trying to find ways of providing a third space between the client-partner and myself in role to be available for Thinking 2 because it is through this kind of thinking that innovation is more likely to happen.

Here, Bollas's idea of the 'unthought known' is also useful. In consultancy we are preoccupied with the unconscious condensed material that is present in every encounter. We are vigilant to identify 'systems of defence against anxiety' following Menzies (1988), for example. It also is apparent to me that every encounter is pregnant with the thoughts about experiences in the client enterprise which are known, at some level (the unconscious) but have not yet been thought and voiced. Bollas refers to geneticaly-based knowledge which has not yet been thought of and constitutes 'an inherited set of dispositions that constitute the true self' (Bollas, 1989, p. 10). In the context of an action-research project there are thoughts which are there in the enterprise, held by people about their experiences of work in the enterprise which are unthought. The thoughts are in search of a thinker. The consultant becomes a temporary container for these thoughts to become available. It is this kind of thinking work that leads to insight. In my terms these are thoughts which come to be revealed, i.e. they are a products of the politics of revelation. The essential point for me is about working with the partner-client in order to enable them to find their authority to interpret the psychic, political and, possibly, spiritual realities in which they are working.

Even if there ha been no paradigm shift in the natural and social sciences the changes that are occurring in enterprises because of the use of Information Technology would cause consultancy to shift towards the politics of revelation.

Information Technology is transforming organisations. Everyone who has access to a personal computer can equally know about the information that is needed to manage. The old style organisation where only senior managers had access to such information is on the wane. There is an inevitable democratisation process let loose in organisations because of IT.

Information Technology has been necessary because of the quantity of data that any enterprise needs to process into information for decision-making. Peter Senge makes a general point about organisations in the contemporary world:

> 'In an increasingly dynamic, interdependent word it is simply no longer possible for anyone to "figure it all out at the top" The old model, "the top thinks and the local acts." must now give way to integrating thinking and acting at all levels.' (Senge, 1990)

The requirement increasingly is that people manage themselves in their roles at all points in the organisation. The thinking that is required for people to do so is more likely to happen through the politics of revelation than those of salvation. Salvation is linked to the idea that there is someone who knows all and the others have only part of the information.

In terms of leadership we may have to rethink our conceptions of how leaders and followers are to be related in the future. Gilmore highlights one aspect of this in the context of changing forms of institutions.

> 'We may be approaching what Toffler calls "adhocracy". Our organisations are no longer the enduring institutions of old but assemblages of parts. The assemblage of a French designer, an American marketing organisation, and a Korean manager who join to produce a line of shirts may, within a year, shift some or all of its parts. Like movie-producers who assemble and disassemble the elements of a film, leaders and followers have to develop their skills at recruiting, joining, direction setting, organising, and managing change among short-lived teams of people.
>
> 'We need to match hopes of finding leaders who can articulate a genuine vision, infuse the organisation with a sense of purpose, moderate conflicts, and defend the integrity of the enterprise with the realities of the instabilities of key relationships.' (Gilmore, 1988, p. 247)

One consequence, in Senge's terms, is that the leadership task of tomorrow will be that of designers and not, in his terms, 'crusaders', i.e. saviours. He sees the the leaders task as being that of designing the learning process 'whereby people throughout the organisation can deal productively with the critical issues they face, and develop their learning mastery in the learning disciplines' (Senge, 1990, p.345)

Following on these ideas I want to introduce the concept of 'symbiont management' which is a concept of organisation that I am developing in a number of enterprises, and take the opportunity to signpost in this paper.

I take this concept from the ideas of Greenstein. If we have an imago in the mind that we are in a symbiotic universe such an imago can can structure the way we see actual relationships between ourselves and others and the environment in general and, what is our concern, relationships in the world of work. Symbiont means an organism being in a state of mutuality with another. (Reid, 1962, p.99)

One of the persistent myths of the late twentieth century is that individuals are autonomous - and this has spilled into the work enterprise. The idea of autonomy has been part of the aggressive posture that is often held in work enterprises. Aggression in work, particularly as associated with ruthless ambition, ultimately can destroy a work enterprise, as, in time, it destroys the aggressor. In Britain aggression marked the seventies and eighties. For example British Airways set out to destroy their major competitor Virgin Airways. Indeed, one could go as far as to say that some managers involved in this plot became, in effect, temporarily psychopathic, i.e., acting without taking account of values, or ethics, or conscience.

We have tended to see business as being in competition with each other. However, I note the changes that are occurring. Managers of businesses are beginning to realise that they need to have, what I am calling a symbiont relationship with their suppliers, and, of course, their customers. The motor industry, for example, which has always been characterised by aggressiveness to their employees and suppliers has moved to 'lean production'. What this means is that the authority for organising work is in the hands of the people in the shop floor. What is also happening is that suppliers have long term contracts which contributes to high quality components.

CONCLUSION.

I have tried to outline ideas on the possible changes in consultancy practice from the politics of salvation to those of revelation. This is coming about through the changes in the methodologies used, and resultant conceptualisations of, the natural sciences. At the same time, however, there are changes in enterprises themselves with the arrival of Information Technology which changes authority relationships in the organisation. What is also emerging is a greater emphasis on mutuality and support between role-holders rather than a reliance on competition, conflict and aggression to execute particular primary tasks. This mutuality between role-holders questions ideas of individual autonomy, which has been a convenient myth of the twentieth century; for it has allowed people to justify their being dissociated from their environment of other people and whatever the cosmos may be.

REFERENCES

Armstrong, D. (1991) THINKING ALOUD; CONTRIBUTIONS TO THREE DIALOGUES. Grubb Institute, London.

Barnaby, F. (1988) THE GAIA PEACE ATLAS. Pan Books, London.

Bion, W.R. (1984) SECOND THOUGHTS. Karnac Books, London.

Bohm, D. and Edwards, M. (1991) CHANGING CONSCIOUSNESS. Harper, San Francisco.   Bollas, C. (1989) FORCES OF DESTINY. Jason Aronson Inc., New Jersey.

Cahoone, L. E. (1988) THE DILEMMAS OF MODERNITY. State University of New York Press.

Camporesi, P. (1990) THE FEAR OF HELL Polity Press, London.

Dubanne, E. and Lee, A.P.N. (1980) Countertransference and the Rescue Phantasy. Paper: Canadain Psycho-Analytic Society.

Eliot, T.S. (1953) SELECTED PROSE. Penguin Books, Harmondsworth.

Gilmore T. North (1988) MAKING A LEADERSHIP CHANGE. Josey-Bass, San Francisco.

Greenstein, G. (1988) THE SYMBIOTIC UNIVERSE. William Morrow and Company, New Yorl.

Harman, W. (1992) Shifting Assumptions and Extended Science. ICIS FORUM, Vol. 22, No. 3.

Lawrence, W.G. and Miller, E.J. (1976) Epilogue. In E.J. Miller, ed., TASK AND ORGANISATION. John Wiley and Sons, Chichester.

Lawrence, W.G. (1980) Citizenship and the Work Place. In B. Sievers, ed. ORGANISATIONSENWICKLUNG IN DER DISKUSSION. Wuppertal.

Lawrence, W.G. (986) A Psycho-Analytic Perspective for Understanding Organisational Life. In G. Chattopadhay et alia, WHEN THE TWAIN MEET. A.H. Wheeler and Co., Allahabad.

McDonagh, S. (1982) THE EDEN BLUEPRINT. Columban Fathers.

Menzies Lyth, I.E.P. (!988) CONTAINING ANXIETY IN INSTITUTIONS. Free Association Books, London.

Reid, L. (1962) THE SOCIOLOGY OF NATURE. Penguin Books, Harmondsworth.

Senge, P. (1990) THE FIFTH DIMENSION; THE ART AND PRACTICE OF THE LEARNING ORGANBISATION. Doubleday, New York.

Wijers, L. and Pijnappel, J. (1990) ART MEETS SCIENCE AND SPIRITUALITY. Academy Editions, London.

CONSULTANCY DYNAMICS IN A POST MODERN WORLD

- some implications of the Death of God, Science and the Subject for assessing the quality of Management Consultancy

Del Loewenthal, *University of Surrey, Guildford*

In the post modern era both client and consultant do not speak their language, instead they are spoken by it. This paper examines such questions as: In the dynamics of the consulting relationship how do we see the other? Does the other become at best part of a supporting cast established to enhance either the managerial or consultancy order? Can consultants and clients be ethical? Such models as 'client centred' and 'consumer' are examined from various post modern psycho dynamic perspectives in order to explore how we see the other in consulting relationships. In assessing the quality of Management Consultancy this paper gives primacy to the consulting relationship. In so doing it examines the notion from Levinas (1969) of one being responsible for the others responsibility. By taking therefore what can be seen as a more Hebraic than Greek logocentric argument, appropriation is examined particularly in respect to knowledge.

The article starts by questioning egocentric, client-centred and consumer approaches to being with the other: Do your clients wish for you to become only part of a supporting cast in a drama set up to preserve their privileges and protect their approach? To what extent do you go along with this conspiring to be a bit player on your client's stage because really you think unknown to them that they are really just a bit player on your consultancy stage? Is management consultancy about enabling people to think for themselves which does not necessarily mean by themselves. However, is what managers and their consultants call thinking and speaking very often only a succession of egocentric monologues. To what extent is the consultant's responsibility for the manager's responsibility such as to facilitate the manager responding so that he or she need justify their egocentric attitudes and do justice to the other in their thought and in their action? Not apparently with macho general managers. So are we really any nearer to having action and justice? It can be argued that in some ways management theories have changed from manipulating the other like a machine to manipulating the social aspect of the other to manipulating the other as part of a system. Nowadays we have what George Bush called 'this vision thing'.

According to Levinas (1969) totalitarian thinking accepts vision rather than language as its model, it aims to give an all inclusive panoramic view of all things including the other in an impersonal neutral life. To what extent is the aim of Management Consultants and their clients to develop further totalisation thinking such that what is produced through the consulting relation or what might be termed 'totalizers' rather than 'infinitizers'.

The 'totalizers' are satisfied with themselves and with the systems they can organise around themselves. The 'infinitizers' are dissatisfield and strive for what is other than themselves. The former seek for power and control the latter for a quality of life which perhaps comes through a responsibility for the other's responsibility for the other's quality of life. It is being suggested that it is a contradiction in terms to have a systemised approach to the quality of life. However, systematic thinking establishes the power structure which produces the goods in the so called good life but when this is extended it can constitute violence. Furthermore, the individual can be seen to become free and responsible not by fitting into a system but rather by fighting against it and by acting on his own (ibid p.18) So is it possible for consultants to help others not do violence to others? Is it possible for managers not to interpret their own and others 'continuity' making them play roles in which they no longer recognize themselves, making them betray not only commitments but their own substance. Postmodernism and its method deconstruction is useful here as it is concerned with what are the standards. First Christianity formed the standards, then the scientific method, until it became clearer that there are different scientific methods and (as with e.g. sexuality) at any one time there are certain standards that are done and not done. One way of trying to impose standards is by force and domination, another way is in terms of administration - yet another way is by perversion whereas yet another way is to ask what is natural. Foucault (1971) has explored the relationship of power and knowledge. Thus one way of imposing standards is to say that you know. Consultants can create pseudoknowledge. Jargon and technical knowledge can be an management trick whereby words are used in special ways and then played back as if it is normal. This is done on a wide scale and often this is difficult to work through the jargon to see if something new is really being said.

One question concerns where do our values lie. When are perversions intolerable? When in imposing standards are we treating others as puppets?

To what extent have we moved to an era of individualism where the standards are centered on the person so that what is good are the goods we pursue in the good life and this becomes the basis for standards e.g. self-managed learning and the customer become the standards. So we move from God to Science to the person - so is the person the new God, and which person is it: the consultant or the manager? In fact consultancies with a behavioural, humanistic existential and in most cases psychoanalytic orientation create delusional systems in that they would have a client believe that they are the core, the centre, the subject. The reason for this is that they attempt to understand as if the subject is independent of the structures imposed by language (Lacan, 1988).

REFERENCES

FOUCAULT, M (1971) Madness and Civilization, Penguin
LACAN, J (1988) The Seminars of Jaques Lacan, Cambridge Univ.Press
LEVINAS, E (1969) Totality and Infinity, Duquense University, Penn.

THE CONTRACTING PROCESS

Brian McEvoy, *McEvoy Consulting, London*

Contracting is about more than just agreeing in detail the task to be achieved, and the fee, in order that the client has an assurance that something will happen and the consultant has some assurance of being paid. Though those who are used to public sector competitive tendering might be forgiven for believing that is often the limit of the procurement department's interest.

No, my definition of the contracting process is that it is the method by which the consultant and the client attempt to establish:

* where all the key players to an intervention are coming from
* what they all expect to get out of the consultation
* what they all expect to put into it
* how they will know when they have done it.

It is about ensuring the success of a consulting intervention by being clear about assumptions and expectations and by establishing a framework which allows regular checking in to see whether those expectations are being met in a dynamic situation.

We should start by being clear what kind of consulting we are proposing to engage in, as that can be the source of much misunderstanding. Most of my work is to do with helping top management groups become more effective and I find that their effectiveness in achieving their goals is related to three broad questions:

* Do they know enough about the technical or operational problems they need to address?
* Is the approach they are taking to the task likely to deliver the results?
* Is there enough holding the team together to encourage them to want to complete the task successfully and grow in the process?

These questions, though they are connected, are different in nature. The first is about content issues, the second is about process issues related to the task, and the third is about process issues related to the maintenance of the group. So that we are clear we are using the same language, let me detour slightly to summarise what I mean by this.

We are all fairly familiar with the split between content and process issues. Content is about **what** we are trying to do. Process is about **how** we do it.

Content includes the subject matter of the problem, the data surrounding it, the objectives, the concepts and the tangible technical and operational issues. Process includes the methodology and approach, the inter-personal relationships and group dynamics.

Professor Brendan Reddy from the University of Cincinnati first introduced me to the value of distinguishing between the different sorts of process issues and to him I owe the diagrams 1 and 2 which follow.

Process can be divided into those activities which help to take the task forward - procedural and taskdriven - and those which relate to individuals' own reactions to those events. They are different, but interact closely as Diagram 1 illustrates.

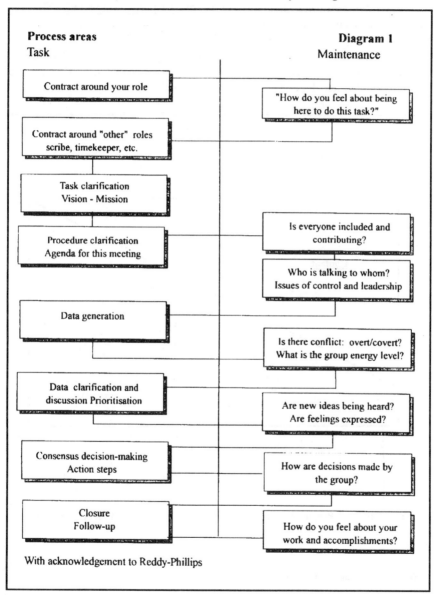

Process areas   **Diagram 1**

Task   Maintenance

Contract around your role

"How do you feel about being here to do this task?"

Contract around "other" roles scribe, timekeeper, etc.

Task clarification Vision - Mission

Procedure clarification Agenda for this meeting

Is everyone included and contributing?

Who is talking to whom? Issues of control and leadership

Data generation

Is there conflict: overt/covert? What is the group energy level?

Data clarification and discussion Prioritisation

Are new ideas being heard? Are feelings expressed?

Consensus decision-making Action steps

How are decisions made by the group?

Closure Follow-up

How do you feel about your work and accomplishments?

With acknowledgement to Reddy-Phillips

Task process issues are generally overt, can often be learned and appear regularly on the agenda of consulting skills courses. They include: defining roles, clarifying the mission, agreeing agendas, brainstorming, prioritisation, getting consensus, getting closure, action planning.

Maintenance process issues are more often covert, are sometimes not recognised and have a bigger impact on our ability and willingness to do things and be committed to the outcomes than most of us are ever prepared to admit. They are mainly about feelings and include inter-personal issues of inclusion, influence, affection; group behavioural patterns related to unwillingness to address issues, to politeness, ambiguity, frustration, to emotional responses to the task willingness to enter into negotiation and collaboration; and all the leadership issues around dependence, counter-dependence and inter-dependence.

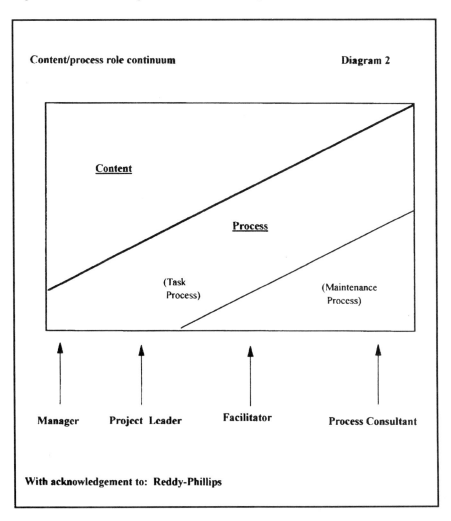

Table 2 is a simple model designed to show that the balance between content and the different sorts of process can vary in different kinds of intervention. At one end it represents the traditional concept of a bottom-line driven manager who focuses most of the effort into ensuring the content issues are addressed whilst placing just enough effort on task process to keep the ball rolling. At the other end of the continuum is a process consultant who focuses primarily on team maintenance process issues and task process issues, expecting the team members to make the necessary content contribution.

The significance of all this for the contracting process is that you need to be clear:

* where on this continuum you intend to consult
* that your client agrees that is where you should be
* you have the opportunity and the freedom to operate there.

When you are establishing and when you are updating the contract is the best opportunity you have to create and maintain that understanding about your relationship, or to recognise and adjust to the changing circumstances.

If we go back to the three questions about effectiveness (What are we trying to do? How are we going to do it? and How will we hang together?), we see it gives a broad agenda for the contracting discussion. The relative emphasis that you give to each of these three questions will accord with where you are expecting to operate on the content-process continuum. In summary, the issues break down as follows:

Question	Nature	Issues
1 What is the group trying to do?	Content	Technical, operational or functional issues
2 How is the group going to do it?	Task Process	Task, procedural and managerial issues
3 How is the group going to keep together productively and grow?	Maintenance Process	Relationships and feelings

This sounds as though it could be complicated. It does not have to be. If you are clear in your own mind and have established a rapport with your client, you can summarise a contract on one page of A4, as the example by Marvin Weisbord in Appendix I illustrates.

Establishing that rapport is not always easy and most consultants eventually (if not sooner!) have to face the question of whether they should consult at all in a particular situation.

Failure to address this issue invariably leads to problems later. When considering whether to consult a particular situation, you should think about whose interest the consultant will be serving - not forgetting the consultant's own interests. Think also about what will be the primary focus of the intervention.

Cary Cherniss of the University of Michigan offered some possible criteria:

* is there a congruence between the values of the consultant and the consultee?
* are there sufficient resources available to do justice to the task - including sufficient time by the consultant?
* can you work with the client? (Chris Argyris says he will only consult to those who are "open to and capable of learning" and "provide access to the power points in the client system")

Some other issues you might want to think about include:

* is it the kind of work you particularly want to do?
* do you have to do it because your boss insists?
* is there a greater than 50% chance of success?
* is the client willing to work with you in a way that makes you feel comfortable?

There are rarely "Yes . . No" answers to these questions. But exploring them in the contracting phase helps you cope better with the consequences of contracting or declining to contract.

There may be a case, particularly if you are operating at the process end of the spectrum, to have an entry contracting phase before you contract to do the job. It might look like diagram 4.

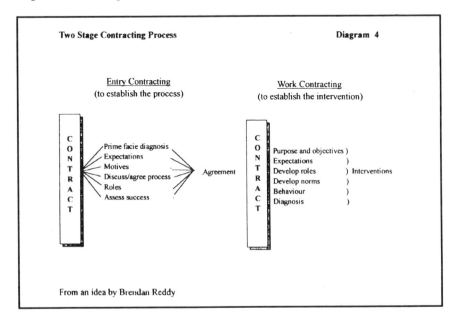

Two Stage Contracting Process   **Diagram 4**

Entry Contracting
(to establish the process)

Work Contracting
(to establish the intervention)

CONTRACT

Prime facie diagnosis
Expectations
Motives
Discuss/agree process
Roles
Assess success

Agreement

CONTRACT

Purpose and objectives)
Expectations   )
Develop roles   ) Interventions
Develop norms   )
Behaviour   )
Diagnosis   )

From an idea by Brendan Reddy

The entry contracting phase acknowledges the need to establish clarity and agreement with your client in advance about the process you intend to use during the project. It is then much easier to negotiate the contract about the content, which can often be done later.

Are there any guidelines we can use on how to contract, based on practical experience? The following ground rules were developed by Claire and Mike Reiker. I find them very powerful and they have helped me understand better what my relationship can be with clients. Some sound a bit obvious, but many of them are ignored in the anxiety which surrounds most contracting sessions.

Contracting Guidelines

1. Responsibility for any relationship must be joint, otherwise it will collapse. So too with the contract.
2. The contract should be freely entered into.
3. You cannot get something for nothing. There must be mutual consideration.
4. All wants are legitimate. You cannot say "You should not want that".
5. You can say no to what others want from you. Even clients.
6. You do not always get what you want, but you will still survive and have clients in the future.
7. You can contract for behaviour, but you cannot contract for others to change their feelings.
8. You cannot ask for something the other person does not have.
9. You cannot promise something you are not in a position to deliver.
10. You cannot contract with someone who is not in the room (e.g. clients' bosses). You need to talk to people and look them in the eye to know if you have agreement with them.
11. Write down contracts when you can. Most contracts are broken out of neglect, not intent .
12. Social contracts are always renegotiable. If someone wants to renegotiate, be grateful they are talking to you about it and not just doing it.
13. Contracts require timescales and duration.
14. Good contracts require good faith and often accidental good fortune.

What has become clear to me in my consulting career of some fifteen years is that knowledge and expertise are not enough to be a good consultant; nor are good consulting techniques and procedures. If you are operating at the process end of the continuum, in particular, clients seem to be looking for something in addition.

Talk to clients about why they decided to bring in consultants and how they made their selection and you get some interesting responses. You find that although the decision to call in consultants was generally logical and left-brain driven, the choice of who to use was invariably very right-brain and intuitive, even emotional. This can be a difficult predicament to resolve for clients who work to a very formal procurement procedure.

Part of the "something in addition" is what the individual consultants bring to the process, and the relationship they establish with clients. Clients can be very ambivalent towards consultants. They admire and respect them for the same sort of rational reasons they decided to go down the consultation road. But at the same time they dislike, fear or are resentful at the idea that they have to depend on these outsiders. This ambivalent attitude makes for an uneasy relationship. Clients will say they are looking for a consultant they feel comfortable with. What they often mean is someone who will not make them feel threatened or inadequate, whilst at the same time delivering results they and their team may not be in a position to deliver.

The danger is that even with the best will in the world consultants may go wrong at this stage. By simply trying to help they can end up putting the client into a deeper dependency relationship. And that will lead to an unsatisfactory consultant-client relationship, a poor consulting process and lack of ownership by the client organisation of the results of the consultation.

You need to establish a trusting relationship in which you can discuss these things. And you start that relationship in the contracting process. In my experience the best way to do this is to be as open and transparently honest as you can. Consultants are often advised to be authentic. What does that mean? I think it means being honest with yourself and not being manipulative. It means telling the truth as you see it and not trying to mislead. This authenticity needs to influence everything you do, not just in the contracting process but throughout the project. It makes your consulting unique to you. It also provides a base line you and your client can come back to later in the project when things start getting difficult and misunderstandings arise. I acknowledge that this may seem less significant if you operate exclusively at the content end - installing technical or professional systems, for example. But, at some stage there will be problems around implementation, when the apparent definitiveness of the technical solution is being questioned. That is also when the credibility of the consultant will be challenged.

To conclude, I would offer you the following step-by-step process for negotiating a consulting contract. Peter Block does this in great detail in his book, "Flawless Consulting". (That is an excellent work which I recommend to you. I learned a lot from it.) This is my simplified and very practical version of a one-stage contracting process based on my own experience.

1. **Set the tone for the relationship early**
   You start establishing the psychological relationship right from the first meeting. Time is short, so say plainly what this project means for you. Let your clients know where you are coming from. Tell them you are pleased to be working on this project, if that is true. Make them feel comfortable and show them they can trust you, but be honest with yourself.

2. **Outline the problem**
   Do not do a diagnosis on the spot, before you have started the project. But in your own words, show your understanding of the issues and acknowledge why your client considers them so important. This

demonstrates knowledge and understanding but it also helps to make sure you are both talking about the same thing.

3. **Find out what your client wants and is prepared to give**

    Making this a two-part question emphasises the two-way nature of the relationship and the joint responsibility for its maintenance. Being up-front with your requirements helps make the relationship one of equals rather than master-servant.

    Clients usually want answers, solutions, recommendations or reports. And they are frequently operating under some difficult constraints over what they can give in relation to time, cost and resources. Get them to be open about this, and discuss the implication for the project - frankly.

    You need to indicate candidly what you think is feasible and what is not, and assess how much flexibility your client is operating under. You need to start establishing where on the content-process continuum you are to operate and get clarity not only about the content objectives but also about the process issues.

4. **Make clear what you intend to deliver and want in return**

    Part of this is your convincing the client that their unique and almost impossible problem is soluble by the proposed approach. But it is also about being frank about your needs for support, information, access to people, facilities etc. It is about establishing an effective relationship and being kept informed. It is better to avoid jargon and use simple straightforward language.

    Be practical and maintain a realistic balance in the relationship. Your client will probably take the way you handle this part of the contracting process as illustrative of how you will handle the sensitive parts of the project itself.

5. **Negotiate Agreement**

    You will not get all you ask for - and this will not necessarily be the end of the world because there are lots of different ways of doing a project. Look for and test different approaches. But do not roll over and capitulate. That is no way to establish a partnership of equals. (If that kind of relationship is your objective, by the way, say so up front so everyone can see what you are getting at.)

    You are trying to establish an agreement which satisfies the needs of both of you; and to establish joint commitment to joint success, so there needs to be give and take, and understanding of each others' position. Do not forget the commercial aspects either - including how much time it will take, how much in fees and expenses and, not least, how long they take to pay their bills.

6. **Check the Process**

    I put this step here for convenience but in fact you can check how the process is working at any stage - indeed at any time you feel uneasy at the way things are going. Describe simply what you observe. Say what you are thinking. Ask for feedback. Listen to what they say and see if you can modify your approach in response.

Trust your instincts. If the process does not feel as though it is going right, it probably is not. There may be a problem somewhere. Get it out into the open where you can see it and influence it.

7.   **Test for Commitment**

You need to know how secure your agreement is and only your client knows this. Ask them. Say something like "Are you happy with the way we have set this up? Are you convinced it is going to deliver what you want?" If they are not convinced then you have a potential problem. Find out why and modify your contract accordingly.

8.   **Summarise the Next Steps**

Close the discussion by moving from the big picture down to the detail with something like: "So, you will brief your colleagues tomorrow on the purpose, objectives and approach, and Jill and I will start here on Monday".

But do not forget that your clients may feel they are taking some momentous steps too. Be encouraging, be supportive, be optimistic, enthusiastic and, above all, be confident in your joint future success.

This is how you establish the contract and the relationship initially. It is also a good framework for checking progress as the project continues, except that you should start by reminding everyone what the last agreement on the contract was so that any emerging differences can be identified.

There is nothing startling or new in all this. I have just taken the best ideas I have come across over the years and modified them in the light of my practical experience as a consultant. It is largely common-sense combined with good listening skills. But most of all it is about establishing a dependable, trusting relationship in which it is acceptable to be open about what you and your client honestly think is feasible, and being able to come to terms with the consequences of that at the beginning and throughout the relationship.

Appendix 1

Contract in the form of a letter

Dear . . . . . .

This will confirm our discussion of last Monday. As I understand it, you want to begin a more intensive development activity with your managers. We agreed that a short off-site workshop for the top team should be the first step. The objectives would be to:

*   clarify your expectations and goals for people reporting to you
*   do the same for their expectations of you
*   more clearly define relationships between line and staff managers, including ways they can help each other
*   develop a work plan for the top team i.e.. frequency of meetings, agenda, action plans between meetings)
*   examine ways to improve communication, decision-making and problem-solving skills of top team
*   provide support and ideas to your vice-presidents for developing their own staff and management teams.

I propose the entire team be involved in setting the agenda for the workshop. I will conduct a one hour interview with each person in advance. Questions might include those on the attached list, plus others to be worked out between us. All responses will be combined anonymously into a diagnostic report. Only items approved by each participant will be included. The report will be given out at the start of the workshop.

My role will be to help you identify high-priority agenda items and consult with you and your team as you work on them. I will also be ready to introduce specific procedures should the interview data suggest that would be helpful. The final format would be based on a discussion of the data between you and me on the day the workshop is to begin.

I propose we start on Wednesday afternoon and run through Friday afternoon, with work sessions on both evenings. This will give us a solid 2.5 days. Interviews, preparation of report, and the design and implementation of the workshop will require six days of my time at a cost of £ . . . . . plus expenses.

I look forward to working with you.

Yours sincerely,

Acknowledgement to Marvin Weisbord/NTL Institute, Alexandria Va

WOMEN & MEN WORKING TOGETHER: GAINING REAL COMMITMENT TO EQUALITY AT WORK

Carol Pickering with contributions from Jean Woollard
Jean Woollard Associates, Brighton

SUMMARY

This paper, which is based on our practice as consultants, examines some of the obstacles towards equality of opportunity in the field of gender. It describes the principles and practices which underpin our approach to working with organizations on this issue and which we have found helpful in dealing with such blocks to bring about effective cultural change.

It argues that many initiatives which have focused on gender have (unintentionally) alienated many men by blaming them for the status quo and that we need to win the hearts as well as the minds of such men. It suggests that this will be achieved partly by exploring the destructive effects of men's conditioning. It recognises that women too have been alienated and argues that the culture to which men's conditioning gives rise explains some of women's reluctance to break through the glass ceiling. It advocates the importance of "both-and" thinking which allows us to acknowledge that both group's conditioning has negative effects and paves the way for better understanding between women and men.

It shows how, by working in mixed gender groups, with single gender subgroups, it is possible to create sufficient safety and structure to explore and celebrate difference and to allow the expression of feelings all of which is essential to winning people's real commitment to change. It describes some questions which we have found powerful agents in this process and which we have used successfully across other "boundaries" such as race, class and role differences,eg customer and supplier. It shows how the application of a cultural change model can effectively move people towards achievable action on the issue of gender.

Finally it argues that there is a strong business case for gender initiatives which needs to be advanced **at the same time as** enabling individual women and men to see that they have more to gain than to lose in organizations which combine the best of male and female cultures.

INTRODUCTION

"progress (towards greater equality) continues to be blocked either by what appears to be a somewhat seige mentality amongst the male junior and middle managers or by the lack of awareness that turns many of them unwittingly into benign saboteurs." (Lady Howe, Chair of Opportunity 2000) [1].

As consultants, we are constantly asked to assist organizations, teams and individuals to come to terms with, and more effectively handle, the major changes that face them. From this and our own life experience, we know that such changes can only be effectively assimilated by us if we are allowed the time and space to explore them at a "heart" as well as a "mind" level. That is, when we are encouraged both to give expression to our **feelings** about the proposed change, however irrational, and to examine our **thinking** about the new situation facing us. When this dual process has been engaged in fully, we can begin to commit ourselves to take the action necessary to move ourselves and the situation forward. Conversely, if we are denied the "heart" stage and moved too quickly from thinking to action, we may regress and become "stuck" in a rose-coloured, pre-change past, from which vantage point we either passively resist the change, by denying its existence, or more actively work to sabotage its progress and success.

As the quote by Lady Howe suggests, many Equal Opportunities initiatives have been less than wholly successful because they have failed to win the hearts as well as the minds of the men concerned. Even apparently small steps forward for women have been perceived by many men as a threat and have resulted in a backlash of resistance, either passive or aggressive, to further attempts to equalise the workplace. Indeed, in some cases, women themselves have reacted negatively and have shown a marked reluctance to take their place with men.

Given that men still hold most of the formal power in organizations, we cannot, as change agents, afford to ignore this resistance, hope to work around it, or succeed despite it. We have to learn to work more effectively with it. However, to work only with the resistance shown by some men is not sufficient either: we must also address why women hold back.

How can our experience as consultants to other change projects inform us in our approach to promoting greater equality at work? How can we hope to gain men's commitment to Equal Opportunities initiatives when they have, apparently, so much to lose by them?

How can we help create organizational cultures which are not only "woman-friendly", but in which both sexes can flourish?

In this paper, we describe some processes which we have found helpful in gaining both men and women's commitment to these issues and which will assist us in translating awareness into positive and productive action.

1. WHY PROGRESS IS SLOW

1.1. Crime & punishment as levers for change

Since the introduction of the Sex Discrimination Act in 1975, there have been many developments aimed at promoting equal opportunities in the workplace. Positive changes have resulted, but progress has been slow and the evidence is that we are still a long way from eliminating discrimination:

"research and statistics show that women are generally still not in posts where they can make their full contribution to economic life and prosperity" [2].

It is a commonplace from our work in organisations that attempts at cultural change lead to resistance; work on gender is no exception. The reasons are complex; legislation in itself is never enough. It has provided a big incentive to make changes, yet inevitably this can lead to mere compliance; better than nothing, but not the goal.

Punishment has come not only from the law, but, more often and more damagingly, it has been sometimes unintentionally yet inextricably woven into the fabric of many of the change initiatives themselves. When we have aimed to raise awareness by making discrimination and conditioning visible, or got caught up in exploring causes, we will undoubtedly have met with strong negative feelings. The dynamic which often emerges is between men as guilty oppressors and women as innocent victims with a thirst for retribution. It would be dishonest if women did not admit that seeing men's unease has brought some comfort, though it has been short-lived. Feeling blamed and with apparently everything to lose and nothing to gain, men have, with some exceptions, been slow to commit themselves. Yet, with crime and punishment as the twin and blunt instruments used to advance equal opportunities, is it surprising that progress has been slow ?

Blamed for women's lot, men have retaliated by blaming women, both for conforming to the stereotype associated with their conditioning and for deviating from it. In response, some women have also blamed each other: "Don't know what all the fuss is about; I've never experienced discrimination myself." Both groups are left feeling negatively about themselves and the other group.

1.2. Women's reluctance

There are many women who will own up to having experienced the effects of unequal treatment. Where they have held back it has been for different reasons. Two contributory factors which play a part are self-reinforcing. The first is their lack of self-belief and self-esteem borne of years of conditioning as a woman. Women-only training programmes have been vital in enabling women to recognise the limiting effects of their conditioning, validate their experience and learn from each other how best to move beyond these limitations.

As a result, they are better prepared to break through the glass ceiling, yet still little sound of breaking glass. Why? It is not only that the winds of demographic change which were forecast to speed women's passage were no match for the effects of recession. Another important factor, is their clarity about the costs of breaking through it into (more of) men's current culture. Infuriatingly disabling as women's self doubts are, they have also acted as a friend. Although they have led women to question their abilities, they have also asked them to question the desirability of the requirement to leave themselves behind as women, to act in accord with men's conditioning and to endure what men endure.

The process of men's conditioning is a harsh one: its ultimate goal is to toughen men up so that they are ready, even eager, to kill or be killed, should their country need them. Thankfully, many will never be asked to make this sacrifice, but the process operates anyway, with disastrous consequences for men and women. There is time only for a glimpse at the results of men's conditioning, (which barely does it justice), but it is enough to make the point.

If it works, the process of men's conditioning produces "real men" who overwork to provide for a wife and family, see little of them as a result and are more distant from their children than they would like. It leads them to expect to be uprooted from their homes in search of promotion. It asks them to be uncomplaining in the face of the disruption which this causes to the lives of their families. If they decide to leave them behind to become weekend partners and fathers, it asks them not to mind the separation and loneliness which this may bring. It trains them to compete with other men at work and keep their relationships with them at a relatively superficial level. In order to help men forget some of this mistreatment, it encourages them to mistreat themselves, by eating or drinking more than is good for them. It leads them to die, on average, earlier than women. Faced with this prospect, is it surprising that women have held back?

1.3. Why consider men's conditioning?

If they are to be successful, initiatives for the future will need to address the lack of appeal which "a man's world" has for most women. This will come in part from a better understanding of men's conditioning. "Not men again!" you might be saying and here we meet another obstacle to progress.

Let us briefly explore the effects of the growing awareness that men have not remained unscathed from their part in the male-female dynamic. This understanding has begun to emerge from the depths of the whose-fault-is-it-anyway discussion and has led some organizations to create programmes, exclusively for men, to address the impact of their conditioning on them. This has met with derision from some women who, finding themselves in the minority in meetings, teams and training programmes, consider men have enough arenas where they are the primary focus of attention.

The idea that time should be devoted to considering that men's lot is also not a happy one has incensed many women and led them to compete to be the more oppressed group. A view I have often heard expressed has been that, power and the benefits which accrue from it, should be compensation enough for any kind of suffering men may experience and that, if women had as much to grin about as men appear to, they would certainly be better able to bear the difficulties of which men complain.

This is a response from inside the mental cage of dualistic thinking which dominates much of our perspective on the world and trains us to see things in terms of "either-or". Women see men's expressions of difficulty and hurt as a denial of their own. They think that to acknowledge what men experience will again put men one-up, which in the "either-or" syndrome, leaves women only one place to go: one-down. It is a desperate response. Anne Wilson Schaef has this to say about the "either-or" syndrome:

> "Once ... the dualistic thinking process is engaged, conflict and
> misunderstanding usually ensue. One cannot value women and men

too. One must choose-and one had better make the "right" choice, leaving the other to be labelled "wrong," since two differing rights are conceptually impossible." [3].

Another factor which has kept women from hearing the truth which lies beneath men's expressions of difficulty and dissatisfaction with their position, has been the confusion between men and male conditioning. As Nancy Kline puts it:

"The two things are very different. Men, like women, are creative, generous, courageous. Male conditioning, on the other hand, is rigid, predatory, controlling and disconnected. Male conditioning is that set of messages that men must endure, believe, live out, in order to be seen as "real men". Male conditioning is destroying the world, and its first victims are men themselves." [4].

She argues powerfully that women need to know about this conditioning so that they can recognise it and stop being a victim of it. She describes where I believe we currently are in the process of bringing about change between women and men:

" When we think that men and male conditioning are the same thing, we lose our power, and we abandon men in the process." [5].

1.4. The gender dynamic at work: an example

Understanding each other's conditioning is an important part of altering the negative dynamic that can, too often, operate between women and men. An incident on a recent gender workshop for women and men probation officers illustrates this point.

The women and men concerned worked in partnership on joint case-loads. Many of them worked with serious sex offenders and other clients that were categorised as potentially dangerous. As the workshop progressed, it became clear that the male officers were habitually over-protective of their female counterparts. The women officers felt frustrated and patronised by their behaviour but, at the same time, allowed themselves to fall victim to it. The men made assumptions about the women's ability to handle what they judged to be high-risk situations and often jumped in to offer assistance or take control of the situation before the woman officer had even asked for help. Having experienced this kind of behaviour from their male colleagues in the past, some of the women officers responded by no longer asking their partners for help, even when they genuinely needed it. They feared that to do so would make them appear too vulnerable in the eyes of the men and that this would inevitably reinforce the view commonly held but seldom publicly expressed, that the work they were engaged in was best done by men. These women had developed the veneer of toughness that protects many women who operate in a predominantly male environment.

Both sexes felt trapped in this dynamic. The men genuinely wanted to help the women but had no model for doing so other than playing "rescuer" to the women's "victim". A key part of men's conditioning is to take control of difficult situations, particularly those in which women are at risk. The women, on the other hand, wanted the support of their male colleagues but not at the expense of their visibility and status. Neither sex could see a way out.

The workshop was being jointly facilitated by a woman and man tutor team. On this, as on all our gender workshops, the woman consultant was in the leadership role, supported by her male colleague. This arrangement deliberately contradicts the traditional male/female roles of man as leader and woman as supporter.

At that moment on the workshop, the woman consultant was unable to decide what to do next. Instead of handing over the responsibility to her male colleague, she and he decided to use this as a "live" issue to illustrate how men can support women in ways which do not undermine their leadership.

The consultants set up a "fish-bowl" with themselves in the centre and the participants on the outside observing. The woman talked freely about her feelings of self-doubt, incompetence and confusion. She expressed her fears about the consequences of making a mistake. Her male colleague listened attentively and encouraged her to speak. However, instead of "buying in" to her "distress", that is, to the limiting effects of her conditioning as a woman, he held a mirror up to her of her true potential. He reminded her of her skills and abilities; of her successes in similar situations in the past and, most importantly, he encouraged her to **think the situation through for herself** rather than offer her suggestions or advice about how he would have handled it. The result was that after 5-10 minutes she was again confident enough to proceed.

The impact of this short but significant episode on the participants was gratifying. The men could begin to see alternative ways of supporting their women colleagues, rather than rescuing them, and the women recognised the empowering effects of having the men help them in a way which neither diminished them nor robbed them of their credibility.

2.   A WAY FORWARD: THE IMPORTANCE OF THE "BOTH-AND" APPROACH

Part of the way forward is to remain clear about the importance of the distinction between men or women and their conditioning, even when our feelings rise to confuse us. Another element is to side-step "either-or" thinking and move to a "both-and" position. With the understanding that **both** groups suffer from the effects of their conditioning, we are in a better position to create a climate and opportunities which enable women and men to talk and listen well to each other and avoid the conflict and misunderstanding which have dogged our earlier attempts.

It makes sense to do this in mixed gender settings, as these also provide scope to work in single gender sub-groups. In this way, opportunities which are only available in mixed settings are combined with benefits of women- or men-only training. Mixed groups offer the chance to explore the male-female dynamic directly; they give women and men the chance to get useful information from each other about what helps and hinders good relationships between them; and they provide a supportive environment, reflecting the composition of the world at large, to begin the process of transferring what they have learned.

3. OUR APPROACH

3.1. Overview

In our approach to working with women and men, we pay particular attention to creating a positive climate which is relaxed and robust enough to allow women and men to explore and celebrate difference and to decide on specific next steps for change. There are productive outcomes and in the process there is also upheaval. We have found it important to create sufficient structure and safety to enable this to take place and to allow the confusion, feelings and difficulties which this usually entails to surface. In this way women and men can gain a better understanding of each other and of the part they themselves play in the male-female dynamic. If this is done well, without blame or criticism on either side; applying "both-and" thinking (which recognises that **both** women and men are hurt **and both** need to change) and from a position which distinguishes between the human being and their conditioning or stereotype, we have found a readiness to take action which leads to change.

In addition to those elements referred to above, there are several others we have found to be central:

(a) the effect of feelings on thinking and listening and the need to handle feelings well;

(b) self-esteem;

(c) narrowing the gap between women and men, by providing an opportunity for people to see the rich differences of individual women and men;

(d) the application of a model which is widely used in implementing other change initiatives: the change cycle

(e) pre-requisites and "safe" structures for exploring and celebrating difference

(f) vision and action

We will examine each one and describe their practical application to a three-day workshop for women and men on the issue of working more effectively together.

3.2. Feelings

The Disincentives to Expression

Feelings, seldom handled productively in gender work (and other areas of difference), have kept the needle stuck on the same old tune and prevented women and men dancing outside the dynamic which binds us. Whether women or men, we are brought up to treat feelings with suspicion and to give them short shrift. We learn that there are some occasions where it is considered appropriate to express them, but only with the volume turned down and not for too long.

If we go beyond this we may incur a range of reactions including: silent embarrassment, accompanied, if we're lucky by a fumble for the Kleenex; distraction and anaesthetic, with a cup of tea, a G & T or a cigarette; containment, with the suggestion that we have said enough/too much; first aid, with the suggestion that it will look very different in the morning or that worse things happen at sea and many more. Expressing feelings is seen by many as the first sign that we, like Humpty Dumpty, will have a great fall and that those around us will be unable to put us together again.

Our particular conditioning as a woman or man will make it more or less appropriate for us to express certain feelings. If we are unguarded enough to do so, we lay ourselves open to a scheme of interpretation which not only devalues us, but threatens to scupper our chances of equality forever. The tunes are many and varied, depending on the gender and emotion expressed, but two old favourites are:

- if you cry and you are a woman, you are irrational, incapable of sound thought and will find it difficult to stand up to the pressures of a "man's world";

- if you cry and you are a man, you are like a woman and all the above applies, and, therefore, not a "real" man.

So Why Bother?

Given such powerful disincentives, why bother? There are good reasons. In addition to the argument that storing up feelings can lead to ill-health and, in extreme instances, suicide, feelings **do** affect our capacity to think clearly. Not in the "either-or" sense that if we express them we cannot be rational, but in the sense that, **whilst** we are full of feelings and fighting not to express them, we have little free space to think well. They also affect our ability to listen well to others. If we are to free the stuck needle, change the record and play a different tune, we all need to think and listen better than we currently do.

Working Productively with Feelings

What helps? It helps to take the view that expressing feelings is a natural process which, if uninhibited, speeds recovery. Rather than "getting over" feelings, it helps to think that the best way round is through them. If we are relaxed and allow their expression, people usually do regain their equilibrium, though some may take longer than we have the nerve for. It helps to ask what the person wants from us, if anything. It could be a Kleenex, it could be a cuppa, but as well as, not as a signal to stop, expressing feelings. It helps if we can stay believing in their competence and sanity, alongside seeing that they feel strongly.

As part of the process getting the workshop started, we spend time forming agreements about how we want to work together. We ask women and men to be explicit about how they do and do not want to be treated during the workshop and we raise the issues of feelings and encourage the standpoint outlined above in as light a way as possible. We have found this is often met with relief mixed, naturally enough, with a little anxiety. Making the distinction between feelings being welcome and being obligatory can help with the anxiety. With this out in the open, we are a step further in the cumulative process of building the safety which we consider an essential basis for some of the more difficult later work.

3.3. Self-esteem

How we feel about ourselves is an integral part of the dynamic between men and women. Popular myth has it that this is a women's problem. Though the manifestations may be different, it has currency for both genders.

For Women

The negative messages which their conditioning installs affect all women. The undermining effect that these can have on their self-esteem will vary with the individual. In their darker moments many will wonder whether some of these messages are really true. The effects of this are insidious and cumulative. Whenever a woman hesitates to voice an idea at a meeting for fear it might not be relevant; or has a concern about something which she does not make public because it is "just a feeling" which is difficult to substantiate with logic (but which later turns out to have been well-founded); or undervalues what she knows because she thinks that everyone must know it, that it is obvious and not worth mentioning; or hands over to the men when in doubt about a decision to be taken or where to go next, we can see this conditioning at work. In general, this conditioning leads women to question the validity of their thinking and decision-making in the world at large and tells them that men, not women, are leaders. Whenever **women** doubt their ability to think, make decisions and lead, they hold themselves back just as effectively as any other barrier which faces them.

For Men

Growing up under the regime of male conditioning is a brutalizing process. We hear few men describe it as such because, neatly, male conditioning requires men to brave brutality in silence. Those who do not conform, even in apparently minor ways, run the risk of being likened to women, with all the resultant implications of inferiority. This impacts on men's self-esteem and debilitates them, though in different ways to women. They become workaholics, miss out on the lives of their children, alienate those they love through anger, addiction and, at the extremes, violence. It makes them ineffective and prevents them learning: they feel unable to make mistakes or admit that they do not always know what to do. Gloria Steinem comments on the research which forms the basis of her book on the subject :

> "The more I talked to men as well as women, the more it seemed that inner feelings of incompleteness, emptiness, self-doubt, and self-hatred were the same, no matter who expressed them, and even if they were expressed in culturally opposite ways."[6] .

She quotes Vaclav Havel's 1990 address to the Czechoslavakian people:

> "Only a person...self-confident in the best sense of the word is capable of listening to the voice of others and accepting them as equal to oneself." [7].

The implications for successful work on gender (and all other difference) are clear. In practice, this means that we regularly encourage women and men to say what they value about themselves, as well as what they appreciate about their colleagues. We do this at appropriate intervals throughout the workshop, giving it particular attention when exploring and celebrating difference (see below).

3.4. Narrowing the gap

Another early step in the process of laying a strong foundation from which to explore and celebrate difference is to get closer to at least one other person, preferably of the other gender, by self-disclosure, using a given question: "What has made me the woman/man I am today?" and some ground rules:

- a period of time individually to write and/or draw their thoughts before speaking them aloud to their partner;

- each person takes a turn to talk for an equal amount of time;

- the listener is asked to interrupt only to encourage the other to express their thoughts more; to ask interested, non-judgemental questions and, at the end, to say, briefly, what they were struck or moved by from the other's account.

The partnership which results from this process is built upon and used a means of reviewing learning, getting support and planning action as the workshop progresses.

3.5. The Change Cycle

This simple planning cycle provides a flexible and progressive structure for this workshop (and for much of the change work in which we are involved). It can be applied to any issue or problem where we want to see improvements. In this case, our focus would be the issue of women and men in organizations:

Figure 1

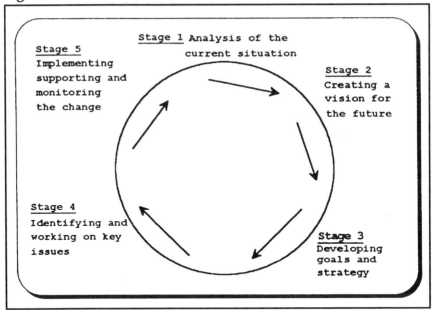

The process of moving through each of the stages will have limited value if we approach it in a single-track, linear and purely logical way. The stages provide us with the necessary structure, but, at any point in the cycle, (and we may journey round it more than once), we may make the intuitive leap in our understanding which allows us to see the whole situation and our part in it from an entirely new perspective. For this reason, we need to engage our intuition, our creativity and our feelings in this process, as well as our logical, deductive thinking and our rationality.

At each stage and throughout the process as a whole, we encourage a balance between left and right brain activities, or what may be referred to as "male" and "female" energies. We use drawing, visualization, guided imagery and other creative means to help us get in touch with and engage our subconscious in this process and we combine this with more logical, deductive work such as analysis, planning and goal-setting. This "marriage" of opposites within ourselves, models in microcosm some of the positive outcomes that can be gained from the effective working together of women and men.

This paper does not offer a detailed account of every stage to the issue of gender. However, it does highlight our approach to three of its elements:

(a)   analysis of the current situation

(b)   creating a vision for the future

(c)   action, which occurs in stage 5.

3.6. Analysis of the Current Situation: exploring & celebrating difference
Creating safety

With clear agreements made, the issue of feelings discussed and some in-depth (as well as some more general) introductions complete, the climate is usually sufficiently relaxed and robust enough to begin looking into areas of difference and potential difficulty. These agreements and introductions are important, if apparently simple and obvious, pre-requisites for this aspect of gender work. They build a foundation of trust and connection between individuals without which real progress is difficult.

In addition to these pre-requisites, we have found that clear structures and processes create sufficient safety for this to happen. For, as Simon Caulkin noted in his recent article:

> "...diversity is volatile and difficult to handle- which is why most companies have attempted to "manage, that is limit, cultural difference rather than celebrate it", according to Rob Goffee, associate professor of organizational behaviour at the London Business School."

These structures and processes provide an embracing framework which has the effect of "holding" women and men whilst they deal with the risky and difficult issues which arise from difference. Within such a framework, and with opportunities to handle feelings productively, it is possible to work with the upheaval which inevitably surfaces and still move towards productive outcomes and understanding. At one level, the change cycle itself is such a structure: it encourages us to be forward looking, optimistic and to commit ourselves to realistic actions. However, in itself this is not enough, particularly at this first stage. In analyzing the current situation, it is important to share our different perspectives as women and men in some detail but without falling into the abyss of history, the nature-nurture debate or blame and criticism. In short, it asks us to forgo the pleasures of intellectual argument in favour of listening with an open heart or being a "witness" to what others have to say.

Being a "witness"

Being able to listen without comment and with an open heart is not easy but, done from the perspective of "both-and" thinking and from a foundation of knowing what we value about ourselves as well as what others value about us, it moves within reach. Knowing that we will have our turn to speak also makes it easier. The questions which follow provide another helpful structure within which to explore and celebrate difference whilst we are listened to well. We have found it effective to work on this topic first in single gender groups. We use a series of questions (see below), which enable individuals to think aloud in a pair before voicing their thoughts within their group. Then they meet as a mixed group to present their collective thoughts to the other group.

We give the first opportunity to speak to women, as the oppressed group. This usually creates have enough free thinking and listening space, unclouded by feelings, for them to be ready to hear men's stories and acknowledge them as also true.

Questions which explore & celebrate difference

What we value
1. What do you value about yourself as a woman/man?

This question works on the principle that if you are going to love your neighbour as yourself, you first need to love yourself. From this basis, we are more genuinely able to value the other group:

> "Man finds woman by first finding himself and woman finds man by first finding herself. Begin with the self to find the other. Togetherness arises out of separateness." [9].

It also challenges what Pat Dixon calls the "Hermaphrodite Solution" :

> "Many men (and some women) deny making distinctions between the people they work with. "It makes no difference to me what sex people are- I treat them all the same." It's something they believe and are proud of, because it seems to demonstrate liberal attitudes to half the population, and the rejection of the old imbalance. But it leads them down the garden path: if people are all the same, any acknowledgment of difference has to be sexist (doesn't it?)- and therefore beneath contempt. The motive for taking this tack is admirable, but the tack itself is misguided and premature. It is the result of interpreting "equality" as "sameness"- doublethink which results from far too narrow an interpretation of the aims of equal opportunities in the workplace." [10].

It is important to acknowledge our gender, our difference, however risky this may feel. Otherwise, women have no option but to wear the strait-jacket of male-conditioned behaviour in order to move forward, rather than bring in what is valuable from their culture; this road limits men too.

2. What do you value about the other group?

The rationale at 1. also applies here.

3. What they do that helps us.

This step may be seen as unnecessary if you take the view that: "they ought to be doing this anyway, so why waste time on it?" This view feeds the practice of many managers and leads those they manage to feel undervalued as a result. In the same way that it is important for managers to notice and comment on competent performance, it is vitally important to reinforce what the other group does in relating to us that is already productive. The more specific and concrete this feedback is the better.

These three questions are first by design. We believe our potential to learn and to change is dependent on a positive view of ourselves and our contribution. Our ability to listen to constructive criticism seems to increase if we have first been genuinely appreciated. It seems even more effective if the positive outweighs the negative.

What we find difficult
4. What we find difficult about working with the other group.
Rather than a long list of criticisms, it helps to apply what is known about the practice of giving constructive criticism:

    (a)   be specific

    (b)   be selective (focus on the things which are the most significant)

    (c)   avoid labelling the person (e.g. as insensitive). Instead,

    (d)   describe the effect they have on us

    (e)   if a change in behaviour is called for, say what
             would be more helpful.

The effect of the positive climate already established together with the first set of questions, lays the foundation for the responses to be as well received as possible.

5. How we think they see us.
This question exposes the stereotypes and messages from our conditioning which we have all internalized. This is important because, like it or not, these messages still affect us and hold us back from our true selves. To name them is to begin to have power over them. The expression of these thoughts and beliefs has gone underground as a result of work on gender and the climate of political correctness. If they remain unmentionables we are liable to get lip-service to equality and little real change.

6. How do we most undermine our relationship with them?
This question challenges us all to own up to our part in the dynamic and to take joint responsibility for moving forward. Both groups are usually quick to spot and ready to admit the ways in which they still collude to hold the dynamic in place. The thinking which this question asks women and men do about relationships they have with the opposite gender paves the way for them to take the first move in changing the old dance they get stuck in. There is no need to wait until your dance partner is ready. As the old saying goes: "It takes two to tango!" and if one of you begins to waltz something has to change. You may fall over in the process, it may feel awkward, but, if **we** have decided to change, the dynamic will too.

After each presentation, we ask the presenters to invite two or three of the listeners to say what they value about the other group and what they have heard. This done, we encourage everyone to deal with whatever feelings or implications may have emerged for them whilst listening, using the debriefing questions below. This is done in single-gender pairings or groups.

Debriefing
7. What did you like/were you moved by?

8. What did you find difficult to hear?

9. What are the implications for you?

Often this is the point where real insights and shifts in position occur. I remember our work with a group from a mixture of private and public sector organizations, which had as a member a woman who, on hearing the men report back, saw very clearly that men do have feelings and have difficulty in expressing them. She learned from them that a more helpful response than anger or irritation might be to summon the patience to ask them how they felt, particularly if they looked as if they were feeling nothing. This was a significant insight which has positively affected her work with men.

We find all these questions can be adapted to work in a variety of settings:

    (a)   within a group of women (or men), to explore where we support and undermine each other;

    (b)   for work across other groups, to explore issues like race class, sexual orientation; even customer and supplier; shop-floor and management.

3.7. Vision & action
Now we would like to focus on two important aspects of this cycle which exemplify the "marriage" of apparent opposites referred to earlier: vision and action.

Combining the masculine and feminine
Vision is more concerned with "being" than "doing". It requires us to take an inner journey to the future whilst action is generally directed outward. To get in touch with our vision we need to invite, through creative and expressive means, our subconscious mind to help us. Action, on the other hand, requires us to engage with our logical thinking in its planning stage and our will in its implementation. We could say that vision is more readily described in terms of the traditional "female" attributes, whilst action is more "masculine" in its origins.

> "Vision without action is merely a dream. Action without vision just passes the time. Vision with action can change the world." [11].

As the quotation above suggests, the combination of vision and action is a powerful one. Together they are key contributors to the change process. Taken separately they are of limited value. Without a commitment to accompany it with purposeful action, vision-building can be dismissed as mere day-dreaming; the powerless yearning for a "never-never land" which is rarely if ever arrived at. We may wish for change in our lives, yet fear taking the necessary but often difficult steps to achieve it. A clear vision can inspire and motivate us when the going gets tough and help keep us on track amidst the confusion and chaos that can threaten to engulf us when we are in the process of transition.

Resistance

Understandably, many people greet the prospect of vision-building with a high degree of scepticism, fearing to engage in an activity that may, temporarily, raise their expectations and hopes for the future but which could ultimately lead to further disappointment. "We have allowed ourselves to dream before," comes the cry. "Can we risk our dreams not coming true again?"

It is perhaps not surprising that when asked a question like: "How would you really like it to be in this situation?" some people respond initially with a mumbled, "I don't know." Such expressions of hopelessness are common in the early stages of vision-building. As consultants and facilitators, we need to remain optimistic on behalf of our clients. If we can encourage and support them whilst gently persisting with this process, we may be rewarded by a glimpse of the idealist that can inhabit the frame of even the most hardened cynic.

Most of us carry our visions close to us, like secrets. Fearful of ridicule, we resist revealing them in public. In expressing our visions we are expressing our innermost hopes and desires and this makes us very vulnerable. Creating a safe environment in which people's visions can be received in a spirit of appreciation rather than derision is vital, therefore, to the success of this process.

A thorough exploration of the current situation is a necessary and fruitful way into visioning. Before we can consider the possibility of an ideal future, it seems we need to explore

at the level of both heart and mind, how things are for us now. Similarly, the process of "witnessing" referred to earlier in this paper, helps create readiness for an exploration of how things might be different in the future.

The temptation, however, is to side-step vision and move directly from the current situation to action. We do what can be done right now, irrespective of its value. Many of us are addicted to action. It keeps us busy and we feel productive even if we are not. The syndrome of the "headless chicken" is all too familiar to anyone who has experienced an organization in crisis. To stop and reflect before we act may mean having to feel something, perhaps fear, anger, regret or sadness about the situation in which we find ourselves. While we exhaust ourselves with action, however unfocussed or directionless, we can convince ourselves that we are still in control. Paradoxically, in order to be truly "in charge" of change we must first learn to give up this kind of control. We must learn to "let go" enough to allow our intuition, spontaneity and creativity to come to the fore and guide us. This will not happen as long as we are involved in frantic activity. We will need to create a quiet space for ourselves, a point of calm and stillness at the centre of the storms of change, where we can allow our "inner voice" to speak to us.

Men's conditioning is strong on control: control of themselves, of other people, of their situation and, most importantly, their feelings. Action is often the means to hold troublesome feelings at bay. Women's conditioning on the other hand, equips them better to express feelings but does little to prepare them for taking decisive action in the world outside. Of course, there are many exceptions to this general rule. There are many women and men who stand outside of this conditioning: women who confidently take decisions and act upon them and men who are reflective and able to express their feelings easily. What is interesting to note is how gender conditioning seeks to deprive each sex of the ability to operate successfully in both spheres. When working with women and men on the issue of change we need, therefore, to be aware of these potential limitations and the relative degrees of discomfort each sex may feel at certain stages of this process. Our aim should be to empower both sexes to work effectively in both spheres.

The commitment to action

Purposeful action is vital to bringing about change of any kind and this is especially true of change associated with gender issues. Awareness-raising alone will not, in itself, change things for the better. Increased understanding of our own and the other gender must be coupled with a commitment, from each of the women and men concerned, to do something or to do something differently as a result. Each of our workshops ends with such a commitment.

Whilst having high expectations about people's ability to change their behaviour and attitudes, experience shows us that old habits die hard. Trying to change ourselves is often a slow and difficult process. Without support and encouragement the best planned actions may fail. It is important, therefore, to build in to any action plan the right degree of support for ourselves. When our will to change is weakened by the uphill nature of the task, we will need the right combination of encouragement and challenge to keep us en route to our vision.

The action stage is a time for being practical and down-to-earth, even for discouraging the grand scale which rightly characterises vision-building. One group of teachers we worked with in 1992 on the issue of leadership and gender began to falter at this point. The demands of the national curriculum and the pressures they were under from all quarters made them doubt their ability to achieve their individual visions. We asked them the question, "What do you already do that is consistent with your vision?" They each produced a long list which they shared with the whole group. The effect was two-fold. Firstly, it reminded them of their resourcefulness in the face of everyday demands. The things that they identified which aligned with their vision were significant, yet they were also "ordinary" and achievable. Two examples were:

(a) asking students to bring in tapes of music they liked (outside of formal lessons) to encourage them, through chatting about the contents and asking staff about their own tastes to relate more equally, person-to person, rather than to the role of teacher

(b) finding opportunities to laugh with students before and during lessons, based on their belief that lightness and laughter make learning easier.

Secondly, it inspired others who could see that there were so many more specific actions within their grasp, which they had not considered, that would make their own visions live. As consultants, we must not underestimate the impact of apparently small actions; they can lead to bigger things. Two months later a junior school teacher from the same group told us of some changes she had made to her classroom practice. Over a period of time she invited every child (rather than selecting a small sample) to read a piece of their writing to the whole class. Applying some of the principles outlined in the description of exploring and celebrating difference above, she asked the rest of the class to listen attentively telling them that, at the end, she would invite two or three of the listeners to say what they enjoyed about what they had heard. Without exception, the effects on each reader's self-esteem were positive and their enthusiasm for and interest in writing grew steadily. When, through pressure of other work, she halted the practice for a while, the children were quick to ask when they were going to resume!

"Effective visions are lived in details not broad strokes." [12].

4. CONCLUSION

At the time of writing, some British organizations, concerned to stay ahead in an increasingly competitive market, are announcing big reductions in their workforce as well as record profits. Work on gender which fails to address the business benefits is unlikely to get very far. The case is a strong one:

> "The link between equal opportunities and corporate performance has formed the cornerstone of equal opportunities initiatives taken by companies such as Xerox and Digital. Their work has pointed persuasively to the direct relationship between improved communications, effective team work and productivity increases, brought about in part through equal opportunity, and higher profits." [13].

However, this focus on the bottom line may make some of us involved in work on gender uneasy, especially if we have argued the case from the moral and legal high ground. We need to be wary of rejecting the good which may come from economic necessity on the grounds that change is happening for the "wrong" reasons. In the other work we do as consultants, we do not expect organizations to implement change initiatives unless they can see some business advantages, nor do we dismiss them as ill-founded because of this: why should it be any different for those which focus on gender? It will help to work with the grain of economic necessity, that way everyone can benefit.

This is not, however, an argument for compromising the integrity of this work. For its effects to be long-lasting, we need to work with organizations and individual women and men in a way that wins their hearts as well as their minds. This will mean enabling men (and women and organizations) to see the destructive effects of men's conditioning on themselves and others and to explore their feelings of resentment, fear and loss about what they are "giving up", so that they are readier to consider what they might gain. It will mean enabling women to see the limiting effects of their conditioning so that they can trust their own abilities to think, make decisions and lead. It will mean valuing and making good use of the diversity which women bring and of the positive skills and attributes which women's conditioning engenders:

> "The Swedish car-maker Volvo recognized that women were an under-utilised talent in the company. When women were more fully

involved in the workforce, efficiency improved and a better working atmosphere was created. In product design women brought a new perspective to an area once solely a male preserve." [14].

Inevitably we will all make some mistakes, so it will also mean finding what Charles Handy calls "the missing forgiveness"[15], which he sees as central to developing organizations whose womenand men are ready to learn and change.

REFERENCES:

1. Hammond, V. & Holton, V. Ashridge Management Research Group. (1991) "A Balanced Workforce? Achieving cultural change for women: a comparative study"

2. Hammond, V, op. cit.

3. Wilson Schaef, A. (1985) Women's Reality: An Emerging Female System in a White Male Society. Harper & Row, San Fransisco.

4. Kline, N.(1993) Women and Power. How Far Can We Go? BBC Books.

5. Kline, op. cit.

6. Steinem, G. (1992) A Book of Self-Esteem: Revolution From Within. Corgi Books.

7. Steinem, op. cit.

8. Caulkin, S. (14/11/93) Minorities Get the Vote. The Observer.

9. Grigg, R. (1989) The Tao of Relationships. Gower Publishing Group.

10. Dixon, P. (1993) Making the Difference: Women & Men in the Workplace. Heinemann.

11. Barker, Joel.

12. Peters, T. (1987) Thriving on Chaos. Macmillan.

13. Hammond, V. op. cit.

14. Hammond, V. op. cit.

15. Handy, C. (1989) The Age of Unreason. Arrow Books Limited.

CONTAINING THE CONTAINER

How to Create An Environment That Will Allow Staff Members to Take Risks, Push Out The Boundaries and Reach Their Creative Potential In Their Work Setting.

Gabrielle Rifkind, *consultant in the NHS, Social Services and the Voluntary Sector. London*

SYNOPSIS

We live in an emotionally illiterate climate. We have little shared language to describe our experience. We reward ourselves for managing and achieving things, but we are part of a culture that is contemptuous of vulnerability and of needs. These are perceived as weakness. The price we pay for this is a split in our culture that often leads to burn-out, paralysis and an unhealthy environment at work.

If we apply this to a work team of professional, we often have a group all pretending to be coping. Inside, they are often feeling incompetent and fearful of taking risks, they fear humiliation and therefore their response is often defensive. This environment creates anxiety about change and new ideas.

In a staff consultancy group, one is striving to create a climate in which one is free to express one's emotional neediness without feeling scorned or bankrupt. Such recognition allows the person to feel strengthened and not overwhelmed by their experience. This allows for the potential of the worker to both feel and think. The bringing together of these two parts of the self via the language of emotional illiteracy, allows the potential for more creative and effective work.

It is my experience of running these groups for the past 10 years that the quality of work is thereby substantially improved. It can encourage and facilitate the longer life of it's workers and the potential for more adventurous work. It creates a more stable environment with a greater sense of trust in which difficult work can take place.

INTRODUCTION

It is a well acknowledged theme that in the world of social workers, probation work, community work and counselling, there is a high risk of burn-out. Those people having the courage to work with those on the boundary of society find themselves in an isolated and critical world. They frequently find themselves blamed by the client, the media and government of the day. They often become the scapegoats of society, on whom we dump our inability to tolerate those vulnerable members. To acknowledge them and recognise their needs would only touch on our own vulnerabilities. We therefore split off this sector of our community so that we can remain isolated from it, and ask a professional group of caregivers to get on with the task. There is little attempt to acknowledge the stress involved in working with HIV positive clients, drink and drug addicts, homelessness, despair and general disillusionment. It is little wonder that there is a high level of burn out, job changes and people leaving the caring professions.

If we are to take this work seriously, we must acknowledge that, if we expect caring profession to provide a containing safe environment for the high risk groups with which they work, it is necessary to provide a containing safe environment for them.

In my experience of ten years of running weekly or fortnightly staff consultation groups for social workers, probation officers, mental heath workers, women's refuge workers, etc I have come to the view that the provision of this kind of safety net substantially improves the quality of work. The group encourages the longer life of its workers. It also facilitates more adventurous and creative work. It creates a more stable environment for difficult work to take place.

In this paper, I would like to explore the need for the provision of staff consultation groups to "contain the containers" or workers in the caring professions. I will then outline some of the factors to take into account when setting up these groups. Then I will comment on some important aspects of the group process particularly the role of the group conductor focusing on the differences between staff group consultancy and group analysis. I will give examples from my own work throughout.

I.   THE NEED FOR "CONTAINING THE CONTAINERS"

Susie Orbach's concepts seem particularly relevant here. She is concerned with creating an environment in which the individual can find a language of emotional literacy to describe their experience. In the article "Feeling our Way Through" she writes "Our emotional experiences get exploited rather than addressed. We reward ourselves for achievement, for managing everything, for not collapsing and most fundamentally for not needing." This communication permeates every aspect of our culture Orbach says: "To recognise a feeling, is not as some fear to succumb to it, be driven by it, to be in its sway. Recognition allows us to experience it directly, digest it as it were - be done with it". She writes that we have no shared language to describe the experience. "This leaves us emotionally illiterate. We therefore split off our emotional needs for fear that we will be experiences as too needy or too demanding."

If we apply this to a work team, we have a group of professionals all pretending to be coping but feeling incompetent inside and fearful of taking risks. Therefore Orbach says: "This emotional connectedness we crave for should inform our cultural practice". Such concepts are central to the climate that we strive to create in a staff consultancy group - an environment in which one will be free to express one's emotional neediness, without feeling scorned or bankrupt. Such recognition works towards the person feeling strengthened. (Group members often fear they will be swamped and overwhelmed by being in such a group. In practice they usually feel strengthened by the experience, and if they can find a language to express themselves it allows the potential space to both).

As a staff group consultant I am aiming to help facilitate the communication in the group. If there are underlying tensions and strains within the team, one's intention is to help bring to the surface these and help the group make sense of them. One's aim ultimately is always in the hope that it will further the quality and depth of work that is possible. My own belief is that staff tensions, rivalries and conflicts often inhibit the potential for developing good practice. It is only when these are addressed in a collaborative supportive environment, that team members have the potential to develop the quality of their work.

For example, when a member of the team declares in exasperation that she does not need any help from her colleagues, we might then be able to get behind this facade. it might be that she fears that a request for help betrays a weakness. She perhaps feels her request will not be heard or responded to. In order to understand the process of what is going on, we may think of the group as creating a noise, and the group members filling the silence but without necessarily communicating. We have over the years developed very sophisticated defence mechanisms that some-times serve us well, but also act as a screen covering the very things underneath, which we want to communicate but feel prohibited from doing. In a staff group, it may be very difficult to acknowledge feeling hurt, trampled on, or undermined. We feel the pressure to claim that we are coping with change and doing a good job. We feel that acknowledgement of our own vulnerable points will lead to being attacked or criticised. It is therefore one of the essential tasks of the staff group to be able to create an environment, where the vulnerable parts of ourselves which have been shielded by our defences, can be responded to and understood.

II.   SETTING UP STAFF CONSULTANCY GROUPS

1.   What is a staff consultancy group?

(a)   Staff consultancy groups can provide an opportunity to examine staff working relationships and the way this affects the work. This would involve creating a climate in which primitive emotions such as rivalry, envy, competitive and destructive impulses can be ex-plored openly without the fear of harming one another. When these emotions go underground they can be potentially far more destruc-tive.

(b)   A consultancy group can also allow the exploration of work with the client group. Individuals can examine what is being stirred up as a result of their work. This can in practice mean looking at the transference, counter-transference and projective identification, both within the existing group and with their client group. In practice, one is helping the group to put feelings into works. This can have the effect of reducing the power of the stirred up feeling and can give people more control over their experiences, allowing them to locate feelings where they belong.

(c)   Another function of consultancy is to look at the relationship between the small group and the large group. That is, the relationship
between the team and the wider institution. The dynamics of the
team may be microcosm of the dynamics of the wider institution.
The relationship between the individual, group and organisation is
constantly changing and we therefore need to examine this as part of
the group process.

2.   The Contract

It is important to differentiate with whom one is negotiating the contract for a
group. If one is working in the voluntary sector it might be necessary to ensure that
team or one's self has informed and has the approval of the trustees. If one is
working in Social Services, the Health or the Probation Service it might be of critical
importance to have ensured that such a group has been negotiated with sanction
from the managers. If one omits to anticipate this in the negotiations, it is possible
that the group may be undermined, not supported or ended prematurely by the
management group.

Group analysis and consultancy work stress the critical importance of establishing the setting of the boundaries in which the consultancy is to take place. Unless
these foundations are established fairly early in the early stages of the group they
will reverberate through the group later.

I have learnt over the years, that before entering an agreement with the group,
we need to satisfy ourselves that we can each work with the other. I therefore need
to give the group the opportunity to explore what they are hoping to get from the
group, and whether there is sufficient common ground. In practice, members of the
group may have a hazy picture of what the potential for such a group is. Some of
them may have had previous experiences, that have left a residue of confusion and
frustration. It is necessary to recognise all these responses at an early stage. Of
course groups are often confusing and frustrating - the process of change usually
is. However, in a staff consultancy group one is attempting to establish clarity at
this stage. It is not like an analytic group where the tension of uncertainty may
create the environment for change. The methods of this should be translatable to
other settings, eg: industry, civil services, government groups. Hence the need for
maximum clarity and the definition of its aims.

3.   Setting the Stage - Dynamic Administration

In group analysis, the behind the scenes organisation is known as the dynamic
administration and is critical to the establishment of a potentially healthy functioning group. Behind the scenes tasks such as establishing the setting time and length
of sessions and arrangements for fees will be some of the foundations of one's task
as group consultant. It can be compared to the behind the scenes task of parenting,
the "holding in mind" tasks, the preparatory thinking which enables the child to get
on with the task. As the staff consultant I am attempting to establish a firm
boundaried environment in which the group will be able to translate feeling into
words and thoughts.

In the preliminary stages, it is important to establish, as in group analysis, the physical environment where the number of people involved in the group can get around in a circle. This will involve a commitment to not being interrupted by the telephone or going out to see clients. There is a choice whether one establishes these limits as part of the foundations of the group, or uses it as part of the early learning in the group. My own practice is to establish these boundaries in the early stages of the group as it works to quickly strengthen the culture and increase its safety.

It will also be necessary to negotiate the frequency and length of the group. This will be dependent on the nature of the organisation in which one is working. In the voluntary sector, groups tend to be less anchored into other networks or hierarchical structures. Voluntary organisations can easily feel isolated and more vulnerable, and may need to meet more often than those anchored in the statutory section. The role of consultant may be one of "containment, holding in mind", increasing the anchoring of a project. Holding this role is a delicate one, because one is never the manage or decision-maker, but is enabling group members to perform these tasks by the act of containment of the group. Some consultants work with the institution on a less frequent basis. Critical to the decision is a clear understanding of one's task. The more of the consultancy will permeate the working culture of the institution.

It might also be necessary to determine the fee. It is important to do this at the beginning and to be clear about the amount and the form in which it is to be paid. This might be something to be negotiated with the group independently or for them to negotiate with their management. Clear boundaries in this area are an important part of establishing the foundations.

III   CONDUCTING THE GROUP

Having set the scene as a staff group consultant, I see my task as facilitating communication that may be unintelligible, 'autistic' and 'illiterate' into an understandable shared language. I am consciously trying to enable the group members to have a clearer understanding of themselves as individuals in the organisation and as members of a team. Primarily I am concerned with the members of the group as "workers". My task is to help facilitate and deepen their understanding of the work. This in practice will usually enhance the quality of the work. Various aspects of the group process seem particularly important in those groups.

1.   Boundaries

As a group consultant and group analyst, one is constantly working on the boundary of the group. Hence the importance of establishing where the boundaries or structures lie in the early stages of the group. This enables group members to feel the safety of the boundary which in turn will allow them to challenge it. It becomes a safety net in which work group members can take risks, explore similarities and differences. Without these limits the group world might be threatening. It may be likened to the limits set by parents which allow children to take risks.

Helen Durkin in Von Bertalanfy's "Model of Living Structures" makes a very useful contribution to the understanding of the group boundaries. She examines the relationship between General Systems Theory, G.S.T. and psychoanalysis. Psychoanalysis provides information about every familiar experience while general systems theory about boundary structures and the effect of opening or closing boundaries. Analytical groups and consultation groups fluctuate between thinking and feeling. Closing the boundary within the group will encourage thinking, opening a boundary with exploration will encourage feeling. this is very relevant when thinking about the facilitation of groups. A group consultant may choose to close down a group if they feel it is turning into a therapy group, conversely they might open up the system if they feel it would be useful to explore the emotional content in relationship to the group process. The following example will illustrate my opening of the group boundary.

Example

A member of the group was unusually withdrawn - he had recently commented that the consultant was too distant and did not reveal sufficient of herself, and there was too much of a split between the professional and personal boundary of the conductor. On this occasion it seemed important to help the group member to open his personal boundary and explore in more depth what was being stirred up. At first he was reluctant, but he was able to share his won feelings of being overwhelmed by the work. There has recently been a number of deaths of young people with whom he had been working. The pain of this had left the worker feeling impotent and very critical of himself. He later acknowledged that this had led to his splitting off his professional self and his real self which had left him feeling withdrawn and depressed. This had been the very thing he had been challenging me for doing, so this led to some very useful exploration.

An example of closing the boundary and not encouraging exploration but helping the group to think and not feel was the following.

Example

A young woman who as a mental health worker was having great difficulty holding any boundaries at work. She was often late, disorganised, fearful of work and not pulling her weight. It became apparent that her own history of deprivation and inadequate parenting and personal problems was surfacing in the current setting. The boundary I was to set was to recognise the pain and distress she was experiencing but that she needed more in-depth help outside the group. I thereby reinforced the boundary that it was a work and not a therapy group and helped her to think about other possibilities. I was prepared to offer her a session outside the group to help her think about a referral for personal therapy.

2.   Working Collaboratively

As a consultant, one is essentially working with colleagues. One's contribution is as a specialist in this particular area, in understanding the group process and how organisations function. There will be many areas of their work at a grass root level in which the group will be more experienced and knowledgeable. This does not need to be inhibiting as it may facilitate the exploitative process. By working collaboratively one is able to confirm, validate and empathise with their experience.

I have found that it is important to use interpretations carefully and sparingly with these groups. As Robin Skynner in "Institutions and how to survive them", "Interpretation place the professional in a childlike dependent role and turn them into patients - one shares issues from a different but complimentary position". I see myself as a resource to the group. I will sometimes take on the role of teacher, explaining these ideas to them. This might involve explaining the development of behaviour in one of the clients, or helping the group to explore the appropriate developmental tasks of the person being discussed. It might involve enlightening the group when some powerful transference might be operating between a group member and the consultant. Whilst it might be useful to explore this process, it is experience as less patronising if the process is explained and how it comes about. This allows the adult part of the group member to be reached and does not induce a dependency culture.

It is very easy for group analysts, group therapists and group consultants to indulge in "therapy speak". By this, I mean the sue of therapy jargon, for which I have to acknowledge my own participation in the past and present. It would however seem important to be vigilant of this because it is usually not understood by group members and can be experienced as creating distance and lack of communication between group members and the consultant. The language one chooses would seem most appropriate if it reflects the culture and environment of the group in which one is working. If one is working "responsively" to the group then this will reinforce one's empathetic listening if one carefully reflects their language, such as their term for their clients, for example, "residents" in the case of a unit for clients with alcohol problems or "people with learning disabilities" in the community day unit.

If one pays attention to such factors, it can contribute to a feeling of collaborative work. Such collaborative work is likely to lead to the strengthening of the group culture and the recognition of itself as a 'thinking and insightful resource'. It is probably true to speculate that most men and women working in the helping professions tend to devalue their contribution and any apparent 'overvaluing' is seldom based on an authentic sense of their own worth. In such groups they are able to discover and develop their sense of having an 'impact' on one another and facilitate the understanding of the group process. The following example illustrates this.

Example

I was consulting to a group of workers who were feeling very unsettled, devalued and marginalised. Most of them described themselves as having very few qualification for the job; they were working in the field of mental health. At the time of calling me in, their hidden agenda was that I would help them get rid of the senior worker and that I would help them provide sufficient evidence for him to be dismissed. The following session I described here is where the senior worker is absent.

The group began by telling me they had had a meeting with their management committee that evening. The aim of the evening was to provide confirmation about their senior's incompetence. I quickly set the limits that I did not see that to be my function. I could help them to look at what had been going on in the team and what had led to such a deep polarisation. The group were as first reluctant to think about this, described how the communications were unresponded to, and words seemed to fall into the empty air, I wondered what was not being said. Slowly, the group began to discuss how their past tow senior workers had had affairs with members of the team. I asked them if this made them feel devalued, not the chosen special one. Members of the group then talked about "climate of isolation" and feeling disconnected. This had been mirrored by the patterns of communication in the group. There were complaints that the quality of supervision was very poor, boundaries were unsafe and they did not know whether they could trust him. (We had previously done some work on the organisation's need to set boundaries that were consistent and clear and how this was further feeding into the high anxiety level.) Certain members of the group were then able to develop the theme of isolation and creatively respond to it, by describing their own experiences of isolation. They moved from blaming to recognising the isolation they all felt and how the senior worker's role was even more intensely isolated. There was recognition for the need for support, understanding and being responded to and how these needs had been expressed in the form of 'affairs' and exclusion.

This example illustrates the collaborative creative potential of the group and how it is able to extend the matrix of the group. This was made possible by the workers feeling heard, understood and taken seriously by the group consultant. This enabled the group culture to be extended and group members were able to begin to value each other's contributions. their feeling of worthlessness and powerlessness had been projected onto their colleagues as a way of protecting themselves from their own pain. These feelings had been reinforced by the setting in which they were working and the uncontained boundariless atmosphere. They had built up a climate of criticising each other and had forgotten how to value one another. Such a climate is very common in the helping professions, increasing the potential for staff burn.

3. The Style of the Conductor

I have already talked about the importance of working collaboratively with a group and of the need to be vigilant in the use of interpretations. I want to deal here, in more detail, with the general style of the group consultant. It is the practice of certain consultants in the field to develop detachment which would demand an emotional distance or barrier between the consultant and group. I consider the aim as consultant is to try to reduce transference and unconscious fantasies. This is not an analytic group and we are not actively trying to induce the transference. The central point here is in the consultant's ability to be real.

Ernest Wolf's theoretical model of the disruptive - restorative process in relation to individual therapy is most helpful here. Wolf says that the analyst can never provide "total and perfect empathic intuneness with the patient/ At some point the patient will feel outraged, often thinking the therapist seems more interested in his or her own agenda".

For Wolf, what is essential to the healing process is (1) a sense of being understood by the other and (2) a sense of one's own efficacy (impact) as regards the other. These ideas are critical to both group analysis and consultation work. if one retains all the power in the relationship then one does not recognise the genuineness of the other group members experience. It is as if one holds a theoretical position which does not take into account how group members are actually experiencing the group. This could be further developed as the idea of the group conductor being able to acknowledge when an intervention may not have been appropriate or helpful.

My own experience is that, the more real: and less defended I am able to be, the more effective I am when the group touches any raw nerve. If I defend against them by becoming distant, I am less effective as a group conductor.

4.   The Group as a Microcosm of the Wider Institution

When working with a group it is useful to be attentive to the group as a communication of the wider institution in which it is located. The communication taking place in the group may be a template of the group's relationship with management or it may in some way echo the experience they may have with the client group with whom they are working. It is critical to be vigilant to these issues otherwise one might miss another layer of communication that is unknown to the staff group.

Example

I was invited to an introductory meeting with a group of workers who were working on a Needle Exchange Project. The client group were HIV positive and drug addicts. On the telephone the workers had communicated to me that they had been looking for a staff group consultant for over a year, and they had not been able to go ahead because management had not agreed to the funding. They had been recommended my name and I was led to believe in the telephone communication that they were very eager to work with me. Within 30 minutes of our assessment meeting, two members of the group communicated very clearly that their level of trust and support in the group was very high and that my presence might destabilise this. They also suggested that the structure that I had imposed, of asking them to sit around in a circle, and inviting to share with me, why they had invited me, was too formal. I was putting too much pressure on them and they had thought they would be able to smoke, eat and sit around casually, rather than in a circle, talking with me. I was aware that inside I was feeling pretty useless. They didn't seem to want the skills that I thought I was bringing. They were also communicating their mistrust of me. My first reaction at the time was that perhaps I did not want to work with this group of people, I already had too much work, I told myself. Stepping back from these feelings, I suggested to the group that I felt it was important that we met again before we made any decision. I also wondered with the group whether the mistrust, suspicion and pressure they were feeling from me was perhaps a microcosm of what they experienced from their client group who would often have those feelings towards them, I also picked up the theme that perhaps their suspicion towards me also reflected their relationship with management. In their experience management was not to be trusted. It let you down and did not come up with the goods. I wondered if they though this way how I would treat them. Certain members relaxing a little more at this point in the group, other members retained their position of suspicion. I needed to pay attention to how uncomfortable and difficult that work setting was. this response to me was a very clear communication of this.

In the internal dialogue with myself I was obliged to address my own narcissistic response. I had gone into the group feeling needed and had very quickly felt rejected. It was necessary for me to look at the underlying communication. I was also told that they had seen three other consultants in the previous year and nothing had come of it. The first option of them deciding that they did not wish to work with me, would have increased their destructive fantasies, mirroring the e experience of their client group. The mood of the group very powerfully reflected the client group with which they were working, and the rejection they experienced by management.

5. Outside and Inside

Essential to the work of the staff group consultant, is the relationship between the group process and the context, in which the group takes place. The task of the facilitator, is to help the group to be "Janus faced", ie learning to look inward in forms of the group process, and outwards in terms of the wider structure and what is happening on the outside. This is particularly relevant at present, in the context of so much political change within the NHS. It is not sufficient for the group to be examining its staff group dynamics, without understanding its wider environment. So for example, there might be a great deal of tensions and rivalry in the team at a given time. this might be a reflection of an internal dynamic within the team, or it might be a response to peoples insecurity about losing their job, because of cuts being made. The function of the consultant is to help the team identify where the tension point might be, and what they might be able to do about it. A common response to anxiety about management's power, is to feel powerless and ineffective, to feel there is no possibility of influencing decisions.

Example

A team of mental health workers I recently worked with, were being threatened by cuts in their staff group, the possibility of being dismembered as a group and absorbed into other teams. Their response was one of feeling powerless, ineffective and a passive acceptance of their lot. They complained amongst themselves. They felt persecuted by management for this radical cuts. What however became clear, was that although they would tell each other why they were doing important work and why they needed to survive. This was not communicated to management. Management was experienced as distant, not interested in them and holding all the power. We had a two pronged task. Firstly, we needed to acknowledge their own feelings of powerlessness, and examine where this came from. Was this because they genuinely had no access to influence the system or were they handicapped from some internal feelings of powerlessness, a sense of not being entitled to influence. Once we were able to address this, it allowed us to look carefully at the structure, to examine where power lay and how change came about. The knowledge lay within the group, but it had been previously unknown to them. They moved from a position of "wondering" amongst themselves, to asking for a meeting with management, sending clear memos to management about their function and communicating clear messages to management about why their work was important in the community. They moved from a position of passive withdrawal to speak with a coherent voice as a group. It was a clear example of communicating at the right level with the right people they were able to be heard. At the time of completing my consultancy with them, they were a strong and integrated team, with little risk of being dismantled.

This example may read to some like a fairytale story, many readers will say the world outside is much more irrational and random. The key to our work, however, is to balance both the inside and the outside. We need to help groups to understand the structures that exist, how decisions are made, where power lies and what potential they have to influence things. Simultaneously, we must facilitate group members to understand what may handicap them in finding a route through this labyrinth. Is it their won internal sense of powerlessness, or a structure that is closed and unavailable to influence?

CONCLUSION

It is in this climate that "Caring for the Carer" may not on the surface be a fashionable concept. Our political environment is such that stress levels, disillusionment, burn out and staff turnover would seem to be particularly high in the statutory sector. If one is committed to a high quality of work, new initiative and pushing out the boundaries, it is necessary to provide a containing and supportive environment for workers. Paradoxically, those members of society who we ask to work with high risk group (eg drink and drug addiction, HIV positive and those people living on the edge of society) are often unsupported themselves. It is my experience that if one is able to provide staff consultation groups for these professionals, they are able to practice more in depth work, take more initiative stay longer in the job and be less likely to experience burn out.

Acknowledgements
I would like to thank the following organisations for enabling me to write this paper. * I feel over the past years we have learnt an enormous amount together. The key to the learning has essentially been collaborative and exploitative. I have had the task of holding the group boundary and facilitating a safe enough environment in which the group has been able to take risk and deal with often painful and uncomfortable areas within the group.

   *   Basement Project, private Tenants Rights Project, Earls Court Housing Association & Advice Line, Women's Refuge, MIND, Focus (all these projects are in the voluntary sector). Harvey Centre School's Project, Clare Nursery (Social Services), Community Mental Health Project (NHS), 431 Project, Needle Exchange Project, Inner London Day Training Centre (Probation Service).

REFERENCES

BACAL H A & KENNETH M NEWMAN - Theories of Object Relations Bridge to Self Psychology

BAKER H S & BAKER M N - Heinz Kohurt's Self Psychology: An Overview

KOHUT H - How does analysis cure? University of Chicago Press.

MARRONE M - Aspects of Transference in Group Analysis. Group Analysis XVII/3 (179-90).

ORBACH S - The Emptiness Within - The Search for Intimacy - paper delivered Auckland NZ 1989.

PINES M & MORRONE M - "Group Analysis". The Group Psychotherapists Handbook. Kulash & Wolf Ed. Columbia University Press.

SKINNER R - Institutes and How to Survive them. Mental Health Training and Consultation. Edited by John Schlapobersky.

VON BERTALANFLYS - Models of Living Structures (Chapter by Helen Durkin).

WINNICOT D - The Naturational Process and the Facilitating Environment. Hogarth Press 85.

WOLF E - Treating the Self - Elements of Clinical Self Psychology. The Guildford Press

WOLF E - Hollowness and Ruinous Disorders. A process approach to psychoanalysis and psychoanalytic therapy.

CATASTROPHE, CONTAINMENT AND THE USE OF PLAY IN ORGANISATIONAL CONSULTANCY

Vega Zagier Roberts, *Independent Consultant, London*

ABSTRACT

This paper examines examples of consultancy work with organisations where there is a sense of imminent catastrophe. The interventions used have in common the introduction of an element of play designed to contain organisational anxiety, so as to enable participants to recognise previously unacknowledged aspects of their difficulties. The presenting problem can then be reframed and more creative responses become possible. Three case studies are discussed with reference to the work of Bion on thinking, and of Winnicott on playing.

1. INTRODUCTION

As consultants, we are brought into organisations for a variety of reasons. Our brief may be for teambuilding, organisational review and development, conflict resolution, or the management of change, to name but a few. In this paper I will start by considering two situations where the presenting problem was extreme anxiety in the client system, associated with a sense of imminent catastrophe. In both, the use of a consultative invervention involving an element of play proved useful in clarifying the sources of the disabling anxiety and in shifting how people construed their difficulties, so that they could begin to think about new ways of addressing these.

The design served as a 'container' for anxiety, in situations where containment within the organisation were inadequate or had broken down.

The case studies previously described are then re-examined in relation to Winnicott's ideas about playing, with particular attention to the importance of being able to surprise oneself. Designing a consultative intervention which makes playing and surprise possible can contribute greatly to organisational development. However, when anxiety is too great, play becomes impossible. The last case-study describes work with a team which had lost the capacity for play, and how the ensuing block to development was overcome.

The idea of playing is then extended to 'playing with ideas'. This requires sufficient containment of anxiety so that purposiveness can be suspended temporarily, thus allowing for discovery and creativity.

2.   CASE STUDY 1

As part of massive financial cuts across the whole education authority, the South Trenton Resource Development and Training Department, an advisory service for South Trenton schools, was about to be disbanded and its staff redeployed.

A colleague and I were asked to design a training day on managing transitions which might help the staff to cope with their anxiety about the impending changes. We were sent a mountain of documents to help us prepare for the day - policies, proposals, job descriptions, and so on - written in an in-house jargon that we had great difficulty making sense of. Eventually, buried in the pile, we discovered two critical bits of information. The first was that the cuts to this particular service were vastly disproportionate: fifty per cent of the total savings of the education authority were to come from a service representing only one-sixth of the overall budget. No mention had been made of this when we were briefed, and our link-person professed surprise when we asked her about it. The second was that the proposed changes were going to affect some of the thirty staff far more than others. It seemed likely that a small group would continue offering a training and advisory service, which would have to be self-financing (bought in by schools), while the remaining staff would return to classroom teaching.

By the time we actually met the group, their trade unions had been mobilised and there was an excited smell of battle in the air. Yet within minutes of starting the day one person admitted that she, for one, had no energy for the fight; they had been through a similar process less than a year before and this time she wanted just to sit back and see what happened. The union representative immediately said that they <u>must</u> all stand united "or they will pick us off one by one."

The first exercise consisted of a role-play. Participants were divided randomly into three groups, one to speak as the managers of the education authority, the second as the staff of the training department, and the third as the users of the service (heads of schools and members of school boards of governors). Each group was to prepare a statement to present to each of the other two groups. The 'managers' group found it very difficult to say anything, and at the debriefing afterwards explained they had found it unbearable to stand in those hated shoes even for a few minutes. The 'staff' group defended their position in a predictable way, insisting on the importance of providing support and advice to teachers and school heads. The 'users' group, however, were very energetic in criticising the service, saying they had never really been clear what it was for, and that they foresaw no great loss to the schools if it were to be closed down.

Up to this point, the value of the service had been treated as a given, the identified problem being that 'they' - the managers who were proposing the cuts - cared only about numbers and not about the welfare of the teachers. That the 'users' could voice their scepticism so readily suggested that there were depressive anxieties within the team about the value of what they were offering, very near the surface but not possible to talk about and hence not addressed. The selectiveness of the cuts, which we had inquired about, might well have felt like 'just deserts' - their privileged life away from the classroom was to be taken away. 'Talion dread', or fear of retaliation in kind, had led to projection of their self-blame onto the management.

Here we see the interplay of internal and external threat. The depressive anxieties about the usefulness of their work pre-dated the crisis for which the consultation was requested, but had been suppressed. The proposed cuts served to shift the team from feeling guilty to feeling persecuted, that is, from depressive to paranoid anxieties. As a result, instead of being able to consider ways of improving their service, or to negotiate effectively with their managers, they resorted to splitting and projection, banding together to blame their problems on outside enemies. Hence the excited but incoherent and ineffective fight group we found at the start of the day, which felt so threatened as soon as there was a breach in their unanimity. The shock of recognition resulting from the role-play made available and public thoughts which had previously been too dangerous to voice, and thus constituted a first step towards planning how to face the future.[1]

3.   CASE STUDY 2

Champion Hill was one of several residential units in an organisation set up for the resettlement of people leaving long-stay mental hospitals to live in the community. It consisted of a block of twenty flats in a pleasant suburb, each flat providing independent accommodation for one or two tenants. A team of twelve were available to help the tenants develop independent living skills, for advice and counselling, and for a range of other services designed to help the tenants make the transition from the institutions where most had spent many years to 'normal' life in an ordinary community. When I first heard about Champion Hill I thought it sounded like a dream come true. I had been consulting to a number of other organisations working with similar clients, and was aware of a gap in available services, in that there seemed to be nothing intermediate between shared houses where tenants had their own bedrooms but limited independence, and essentially independent housing where people with chronic severe mental health problems had to manage with little or no support at all. At Champion Hill, there was twenty-four hour staff cover and support, yet tenants had the same privacy and freedom of choice as any other member of the community.

I was asked to consult to the Champion Hill team some two years after the project opened. The brief was for five days' work, comprising teambuilding, a review of service aims, and establishing objectives for the coming year. In my preliminary meeting with the managers, I was told that the team seemed to be in disarray: morale was low, and there was considerable disagreement and uncertainty within the team about what they were trying to achieve and how they should work with tenants. The managers were dissatisfied with the quality of the service, though they could not specify what was wrong, and were perplexed by the high levels of staff stress and sickness. Sleeping in was experienced as extremely onerous. Although all the staff were experienced residential workers, well accustomed to being on duty alone at night, they apparently found sleeping in at Champion Hill frightening. They were aware of tenants' distress and isolation at night, but had no way of checking on their state of mind or even their safety, since respect for tenants' privacy was the foundation-stone of the team philosophy. Staff entered the other flats only when invited, or when there was actual evidence of danger to tenants' safety. It was as if distress and even madness hung in the night air or oozed through the walls into the staff flat, disturbing their sleep but too intangible to deal with. By day, there was often uncomfortably little to do, since tenants did not approach staff directly for help very often and the team considered it inappropriate to interfere with how tenants chose to manage their day or use the staff on duty. The dream seemed to have become a nightmare.

Having been led to expect considerable resistance to the consultation, I was pleasantly surprised by my first meetings with the team. They seemed to be very pleased to have the opportunity to review their service, and engaged with me warmly. Bit by bit we began to build up a picture of what they hoped they could offer their clients, and of some of the strengths, shortcomings and dilemmas of the work at Champion Hill. But something was missing: the staff distress which had been described to me so vividly was not coming into the consultation. Indeed, in some fundamental way, the tenants were not coming into the consultation either. So I began our third meeting by inviting the team to participate in a role-play. I handed out short briefings to four team members. The scenario was that a prospective tenant, accompanied by a social worker, was visiting Champion Hill for an informal meeting with two current tenants. The visitors were asked to prepare questions which would help them decide whether they wanted to pursue arranging for the prospective tenant to be referred to Champion Hill. The current tenants were asked to answer questions truthfully, one emphasising all that was positive and the other all that was negative in their own experience of life in the flats.

I had designed this exercise in the hope that it would provide a relatively safe way for the team to express their concerns about weaknesses in the service and to criticise it openly without worrying too much about shaking the new sense of team cohesiveness we had achieved. But the outcome took us all by surprise. It was not the negatives but the positives that proved disturbing. The tenant who extolled the virtues of life at Champion Hill described how he was allowed to watch television all night and to sleep all day, that he was not forced to eat proper meals at set times but could live on chips and crisps if he wished, that there were no obligatory group activities or therapy, and that he hardly ever needed to leave his flat. There was no mention of staff being available for advice and support, nor of the communal activities on offer at Champion Hill, let alone of taking advantage of opportunities in the community outside. It was appalling and compelling. This man had described a life as narrow as the one he had had in hospital; the only change was the absence of rules to govern his days and nights. His praise seemed to make a mockery of the team's mission statement, which was to provide tenants with opportunities to develop their potential and to become integrated into the community.

In the debriefing following the role-play, and in our subsequent work on re-examining the purpose of the service, this aspect of the tenants' experience came to be referred to as 'the empty core'. For the first time, the real implications of long-term mental illness were discussed in the team and taken into account in service-planning. In particular, the hands-off approach which had always been taken for granted was reviewed. As part of a new, more pro-active approach to their work, the team developed a structured day with regular appointments three times a week to meet with each tenant. This served both to contain their own anxieties and to facilitate the tenants' making more use of the considerable staff resources which had previously been so grossly under-utilised.

4. CONTAINING ANXIETY IN ORGANISATIONS

In both of the cases described above, the sense of imminent catastrophe was stirring up disabling anxiety. At South Trenton, this was ascribed to the proposed cuts and re-structuring of the department which would break up a group invested in working together. Their repressed doubts about the value of their work made for further threat, both to their self-esteem and to their survival in a competitive marketplace where schools might well elect <u>not</u> to purchase their services. At Champion Hill the source of anxiety was harder to locate. There was no external threat, but rather there was an undefined dread and sense of helplessness arising from the nature of the work itself.

According to Bion (1967), the capacity to think, or even to distinguish reality from fantasy, is severely compromised by primitive anxieties such as those aroused by the kinds of situations these organisations were in. Thinking depends on 'alpha-function' which transforms sense impressions into usable thoughts or alpha-elements. When anxiety is not contained, other mental contents, which Bion called beta-elements, cannot be thus transformed, but can only be evacuated as violent projective identifications. In the earliest months of life, babies communicate anxiety using projective identification. Maternal containment, or reverie, 'permits the infant to project a feeling, say, that it is dying, into the mother and to reintroject it after its sojourn in the breast has made it tolerable to the infant psyche. If the projection is not accepted by the mother, the infant...... reintrojects, not a fear of dying made tolerable, but a nameless dread.' (Bion 1967, p.116) The mother can fail to contain the infant's anxieties in a number of ways: she can be too preoccupied to hear the infant's distress, or she may pick him up dutifully while conveying 'I don't know what is the matter with this child,' or the intensity of her own anxieties may render her incapable of 'metabolising' the projection, so that it is returned unchanged or made yet more dreadful, into fear of utter annihilation.

In organisations, this containing function normally comes from the management of the system, from firm boundaries and from the support and supervision managers provide. These days, however, such sources of containment are often inadequate. Boundaries are increasingly unreliable, as organisations undergo constant change (see Stokes 1994), and managers themselves are less able to provide containment since they are caught up in similar anxieties themselves. Obliviousness to need, or the 'I don't know what is the matter with you' response is all too common. When there is breakdown of containment within the organisation, consultants may well be brought in to provide the lost function. However, what is officially presented to the consultant is not usually a request for containment but is more likely to be a 'problem' requiring a 'solution'. In order to contain organisational anxiety, it is crucial that the consultant first contain his or her own anxiety to be seen to be doing a good job by responding too promptly to the presenting request. The consultant's state of mind and the framework of the consultative intervention can then serve to transform immobilising dread into a worrying but tolerable and nameable difficulty which can be thought about. Once the capacity to think has been restored, the presenting problem can often be 'handed back' to the organisation, and the risk of the consultants' allowing themselves to be used as alternative managers - a risk which pervades consultancy work - can be avoided.

The formal briefing for the consultancy work at South Trenton was to design a training day on managing transitions. Our preparatory study of the written information sent to us suggested that significant aspects of the situation were being denied. Our hypothesis was that there was something going on which it was not possible to talk or think about. It seemed to us that, instead of seeking information, the agency was lost in a fog of supposition and speculation. This is typical of Bion's 'basic assumption' group mentality, characterised by the 'absence of even rudimentary scientific curiosity', loss of the ability to think and to learn from experience, and the search for an omnipotent leader who will protect the group from anxiety (Bion 1961).

By the time we actually met them, the prevailing basic assumption seemed to be fight-flight. There was a flurry of excited activity focused on fighting the cuts, and considerable pressure on individuals to maintain a united front. When the manager of the department introduced us at the beginning of the day, it felt as though the expectation was that we would somehow fill the group with the magical strength they needed to win their battle, or at least prevent the defections that threatened to sap the force required to fight the enemy.

At Champion Hill my brief was to help the team review their aims and objectives, in order to remedy the apparent lack of effectiveness of the service in enabling clients to live more fulfilling lives in the community. Staff complaints about sleepless nights and anxious days were treated almost dismissively as an unfortunate hindrance to service development. However, my early encounters with the team gave me the impression that their dogged adherence to established routines, however unsatisfactory these were, and their repetitive arguments over details and rules, were obsessional defences against being flooded by the tenants' distress. Like the South Trenton group, they were locked into defensive positions, unable to think. In both cases, it was imperative to find a way to help participants stand back from the pressure to act, and to look at their situation from a fresh perspective.

5. PLAY AND THE CAPACITY TO BE SURPRISED

When clients are locked into a particular defensive position as described above, it is often very useful to introduce an element of play into the consultative intervention. At South Trenton, the group was stuck in an entrenched us-and-them polarisation. The exercise was designed to help them shift out of this by introducing a third position: instead of addressing the conflict between the department and the managers of the education authority directly, we widened the field of study to include the users of the service. In addition, inviting two-thirds of the participants to step out of their everyday work-roles and to stand for a while in other shoes, so to speak, was intended to provide them with a playful opportunity to think about their situation from an unaccustomed vantage-point. The essential element of the intervention was the setting of a task which was close enough to the real situation not to be dismissed as 'just a game', but not <u>so</u> close as to arouse the same degree of anxiety.

The exercise as a whole, based on a design by Eric Miller, offers a kind of transitional space where issues get highlighted very quickly because the element of play temporarily removes participants from the immediacy of their anxieties and the pressure to find solutions. When the three groups come together to exchange the statements they have prepared, everyone has a chance to hear something new. Specifically, in this instance, the design made it safe enough for the 'users' to articulate what, at some level, everyone knew but had been unble to acknowledge, that the department had failed to provide a service that felt relevant to the schools they intended to serve. Had this observation been put to them from outside - by a manager, or a school head, or by the consultants - there is little doubt that it would have been rejected. Since, however, it came from within, the statement evoked a shock of recognition, and made available a crucial insight. The second crucial insight came from the 'managers' group. Although they had been very reluctant to take the management position, even briefly and in play, one or two members of this group diffidently and apologetically pointed out that cuts <u>did</u> have to be made. Together, the two statements paved the way for the group as a whole to begin to re-own what had previously been disowned and projected, namely the need for cuts and the doubts about the relevance of the service. With this it became possible for them to begin to think about alternative ways of providing a more efficient and effective service.

Winnicott makes two statements about playing which seem relevant here. One is that 'playing has a place and a time.' The place is neither inside oneself, nor outside in the repudiated world, but rather in what he calls the 'potential space' between child and mother, self and other. The other statement is that 'the significant moment [of play] is that at which the child surprises himself or herself.' (Winnicott 1971)

So, too, the design of an intervention involving play is about providing a place - one which is neither 'real' nor 'not real' but rather intermediate between the two - <u>and</u> a time for playing. Place and time together provide a container for anxiety, and can create a space where it is possible for the players to surprise themselves. This is quite different from being surprised by someone else, for example by a clever interpretation by the consultant. The crucial function of the consultant is to manage the boundary conditions needed for a dependable setting where play and discovery can happen. The 'as-if' ness of the situation also means that insights occur when the players are ready for them, and not before.

At Champion Hill, the design of the role-play allowed team members to put aside their pre-occupation with what to do (for example, whether or not to knock on doors at night). Instead, they stood in the tenants' shoes and discovered the power of the 'institution within'. The largely unconscious anger and anxiety they had felt at not being approached oftener for help, which had made them feel useless and rejected, gave way to recognition that being given a key to their own front door was not enough to liberate the tenants, nor were respect and opportunities for self-development enough to fill the 'empty core'. Their decision to be more pro-active meant they would have to struggle constantly with the tension between, on the one hand, drawing their clients out of their locked worlds, and on the other, respecting their right to choose what use they made of the opportunities offered. This fundamental and inevitable tension in the work was one the team had been evading. Once they faced this dilemma, they became more able to use expertise within the team, to go out and learn from others, and also to use their own managers as a resource, less anxious that displaying a need for help would lead to their being 'put away' again and losing their cherished autonomy.

However, as Winnicott also points out, playing is inherently precarious. The necessary space between me and not-me, between fantasy and external reality, can be eroded when the contents of the fantasy too closely approximate what is feared and repudiated in the outside world. In this case, playing becomes impossible or is spoiled. Indeed, the capacity for playing is itself a sign of health. I would now like to consider an example of a group who were unable to play.

6.   CASE STUDY 3

Queen's Lane was a large bungalow on the outskirts of London, staffed by a team of residential social workers, and providing accommodation for eight elderly men and women, most of whom had spent several decades in psychiatric hospitals. The team's philosophy was very similar to that of the team at Champion Hill, and I had a similar brief, to assist them in reviewing their service and drawing up new aims and objectives. There was considerable conflict in this team, often quite bitter, which centred on opposing views about how staff should work with the residents. Most team members felt strongly that they should do as much as possible to care for the residents, given how profoundly disabled they were by age, ill health, and having spent most of their lives in institutions. The managers and a few of the staff felt equally strongly that showing respect to clients and providing opportunities to develop each individual's potential, as their mission statement said, meant that every effort should be made to encourage residents to do what they could for themselves: the staff-role was to help and support, but not necessarily to do things for the clients. Their colleagues accused them of being unrealistic, of forcing their expectations on the residents, and thereby undermining and persecuting them.

Since the ethos of this team was so similar to that of Champion Hill, and since I thought some of the difficulties might be similar too, I decided to use the same role-play here, in the hope that the service users' views would introduce the missing 'third position'. Initially, several team members refused to participate, saying that the role-play was disrespectful of the residents. However, eventually they went through the motions of cooperating, though without any enthusiasm. Each player responded quite briefly and blandly, and as far as I could see the exercise was a total failure. I felt baffled by the antagonism the team had shown towards the exercise, and quite stuck as to how to proceed. At this point we had used half the total available time for consultancy and seemed to be no nearer to understanding or shifting the conflicts in the team than at the outset. It felt as if every idea or intervention I introduced was killed off so that nothing new could emerge. Presumably, the team were unconsciously communicating to me what it was like for them to work at Queen's Lane, by ensuring that I too had the experience of feeling that nothing I did was of any use in bringing about change. But this thought was of no help to me in planning how to proceed, and I was quite relieved when our next meeting was cancelled because over half the team were unable to attend.

For various reasons there was then a long hiatus before another meeting could be scheduled, and in the interim I met with the project managers and the manager of the service of which Queen's Lane was a part. They too felt rejected and useless, and expressed some irritation at the constant barrage of complaints from the team about their management style, disrespect for others' rights and views, and so on. At one point, the service manager said perhaps the rest of the consultation should be cancelled, since the team was refusing to make use of this expensive resource, and my services could then be offered to another team which was asking for consultancy.

Up to this point, our conversation had felt rather desultory, with a similar absence of effective engagement as had characterised my earlier work at Queen's Lane. This last remark, however, was said in a way that felt aggressive and punitive towards the team. I fell silent, musing as to where this dissonant note was coming from. Until now, we had been bending over backwards to be understanding and patient, and now, suddenly, there was an opening to 'get back' at this group of ungrateful people. The idea was rather appealing, not least because it offered an acceptable way for me to get out of an unusually onerous piece of work.

I found myself thinking of the residents I had seen in the lounge, their bleak faces and grudging greetings. Surely the staff must sometimes long to get back at <u>them</u> for making the work so cheerless. Yet they were unfailingly kind and friendly to the residents, reserving their aggression for the managers. When I shared my thoughts with the others, a stream of associations followed, of gifts offered and rejected, and of other cruel attacks by the clients on staff members' self-esteem. The service manager recalled an incident from many years before, when she had been working in another residential unit with a similar client group, of being presented with an elaborately wrapped and be-ribboned gift on Christmas Day, only to find the contents were human excrement. I felt flooded with horror, and the pain of that long-ago event was palpable in the room.

Suddenly I felt able to think again. I was able to remember Menzies's classic paper (Menzies 1960) on social systems as defenses against anxiety, and much else that I knew from my own experience about socially sanctioned ways for staff to express aggression towards patients in traditional institutions; for example, how nurses can be 'too busy' to respond to a patient who needs help to get to the toilet, or can punish unco-operativeness by refusing to give out cigarettes. I recalled Winnicott's paper 'Hate in the Counter-transference' (1947) and how he referred to the end of the psycho-analytic hour as a permitted way for the analyst to express hate towards the patient. At Queen's Lane, none of these were possible. Indeed, it had been set up to prevent just such abuses of power by carers. Always there must be respect, treating all with dignity, so that cruel withholding of cigarettes or help with toiletting could not happen. Nor was there an end of the hour: a shift was many hours long. Suddenly it seemed obvious that the team's determination to respond unstintingly to clients' demands was a defense against unbearable hate and rage. With nowhere else for these unacknowledged feelings to go, was it any wonder they found their way into endless carping at management, formal grievances, and high absenteeism ?

My own inability up to this point to use any of what I knew was, I believe, an indication of how powerful the defenses were in this unit against recognising these unacceptable feelings. The role-play in this case had probably been too close to the psychic reality of life at Queen's Lane, so that the team's defenses became more rigid than ever, making playing impossible. It was too dangerous to run the risk of being surprised. Perhaps I too had unconsciously avoided surprise by using a role-play which had worked well elsewhere, rather than devising a new one based on my experience of this particular team, as I normally would. My meeting with the managers away from the rest of the team had given us a space where we could recover our own capacity for play, this time with ideas. One outcome of our discussion was that the managers decided to set up a series of team meetings to review each client in detail, with particular attention to the feelings the work with each stirred up in the workers. They hoped that if they as managers could openly acknowledge their own negative feelings towards the clients, this would free their staff to face feelings they had previously denied. Furthermore, since time was running short, we agreed that the managers would draft an aims statement, based on the work done in our first three meetings and on further discussions in team meetings.

When I next met with the team some two months later, the atmosphere was different. The aims drafted by the managers were accepted by the team as accurate enough representations of their contributions, and only minor amendments were suggested. We were then able to proceed with the task of setting objctives for the coming year, and the entire team participated in this task with energy.

7.   PLAYING WITH IDEAS

In this last example, it was the period of more random free associating that made it possible for us to be surprised and to discover something new and useful. Winnicott regards all cultural and creative activity, and also free association as used in psychoanalytic work, as adult forms of playing. Like playing, he locates them in the intermediate area between me and not-me. And like playing, they require trust in a dependable setting. Excessive anxiety, and also excessive purposiveness, make all of these activities impossible, since they erode the space within which to be surprised.

However, both anxiety and purposiveness are characteristic of most consultancy. The client is often in a crisis, and is almost certainly intent on 'getting somewhere' as a result of the consultation. The consultant is likely to be more or less anxious from the outset to be helpful, and is also prey to taking in and experiencing clients' work-related anxieties. Yet it is often only at the point where both client and consultant can temporarily abandon their purposive attempts to find solutions that they can be surprised and thereby discover something new.

Achieving this relaxed non-purposive state is difficult. In my work with individual managers, I find that with some we never get past the struggle to find better ways of addressing their presenting problems. While this is certainly valuable, and many such clients tell me they find our time together very useful, it is quite different from my experience with those where we find a way to play with ideas. For example, in a session with the director of an organisation working with people with severe learning difficulties, a chance remark of his about a staff member's apparent stupidity led to an hour of random associations to the meaning for him, his management team, and the different residential projects across his organisation, of intelligence and stupidity. For a time, we both wondered if we were not straying rather far from the point, for he had brought an urgent difficulty in one of the units to the session. It was within the last quarter hour of the session that all the apparently random bits fell into place. He left in a very different state of mind than that in which he had arrived, feeling able to handle the crisis, without my having made any specific suggestion about it.

I find that in my work with groups, it is often even harder than with individuals to preserve a space for self-discovery, particularly when the available time is very limited, as in the case-studies described in this paper. It is in these situations that I am likely to design into my intervention an element of play, usually in the form of an exercise which involves participants taking on roles related to, but different from, their usual ones. While these 'role-plays' fall far short of true playing in Winnicott's sense, they are often very useful in reducing anxiety and the pressure towards purposive problem-solving. They provide a containing structure within which it becomes safe enough to be surprised, to discover something new, and to re-discover what the participants had previously not dared to know. As a result, presenting problems can be reframed in ways that make new and more creative responses possible.

8. SUMMARY

Consultants are often brought into an organisation because there is a sense of imminent catastrophe which cannot be managed without outside help. In some cases this is due to external threats to survival such as cuts in services and redeployment of staff. In other cases the danger is more vague and cannot even be named or thought about. Instead, there is a retreat to primitive defences, including denial of reality, splitting and projection, which undermine the capacity for effective action. This indicates that there has been a breakdown in the ability of the organisation to contain the anxieties stirred up by the external or internal threats.

This paper describes a number of consultative interventions which have in common the introduction of an element of play into a fraught situation. This is intended to enable participants to stand back from the everyday pressures towards action and quick solutions. By serving as a temporary 'container' for anxiety, the design provides opportunities for participants to recognise in the here-and-now previously unconscious aspects of their experiences at work. One outcome can be the reframing of the presenting problem in such a way that new and creative responses become possible.

Some clients, however, seem unable to play: they can neither engage with the intervention as offered, nor 'play with ideas'. Just as the loss of the capacity to play is a serious symptom in children, often indicating a fragile ego and rigid defences, so too the inability to play during consultancy needs to be taken very seriously. The temptation may be to abandon the experiential approach in favour of more task-focused interventions in order to decrease both the consultant's and the client's anxieties. While time constraints, among others, may dictate proceeding in this way, it is important for the consultant to work at understanding what is inhibiting the consultancy process, and to try to create a space within which it is safe enough for clients to let themselves be surprised, to discover something new and to re-discover what they had previously not dared to face.

REFERENCES

BION W.R. (1961) *Experiences in Groups*, New York: Basic Books

BION W.R. (1967) 'A Theory of Thinking' in *Second Thoughts: Selected Papers on Psychoanalysis* London: Heinemann Medical (reprinted London: Maresfield Reprints, 1984)

MENZIES I.E.P.(1960) 'Social Systems as a defence against anxiety: an empirical study of the nursing service of a general hospital', in E.Trist & H. Murrary (eds.) *The Social Engagement of Social Science*, Vol.1, London: Free Association Books, 1990.

MOSSE J. AND ROBERTS, V.Z. (1994) 'Finding a Voice: Differentiation, Representation & Empowerment in Organisations Under Threat' in Obholzer, A. and Roberts, V.Z. (eds.) *The Unconscious at Work*, London: Routledge.

STOKES J. (1994) 'Institutional chaos and personal stress' in Obholzer, A. and Roberts, V.Z. (eds.) *The Unconscious at Work*, London: Routledge.

WINNICOTT, D.W. (1947) 'Hate in the Counter-transference' in *Collected Papers: Through Paediatrics to Psycho-Analysis*, Hogarth Press and the Institute of Psycho-Analysis 1958.

WINNICOTT, D.W. (1971) *Playing and Reality*, Harmondsworth: Penguin Books

APPROACHING ORGANISATIONS - AN EVOCATIVE ROUTE TO COMPETENCE IDENTIFICATION

Graham Stickland with Roger Stuart, *University of Ulster*

ABSTRACT

Set in Northern Ireland in the context of a research project looking at managerial competence, the paper invites readers to engage their own powers of evocation as they are taken to meet one of the companies concerned.

It then explores the value and power of evocation as a means of investigating and understanding organisations. It compares and contrasts the results from such an approach with those from other methodologies, particularly repertory grid analysis.

The paper illustrates the extent to which the responses and reactions of the consultant are inextricably linked to the organisational context and, indeed, the wider environment and how these can be a valuable source of insight.

1. INTRODUCTION

The stimulus for this paper came from the synthesis of two seemingly disconnected elements. First was a growing awareness of the power of evocation as an important source of information in consulting assignments. Second was an opportunity to join a research team investigating the question of competence in small to medium sized enterprises in Northern Ireland.

Evocation as an approach features strongly in Gestalt with its emphasis on phenomenology and awareness and Nevis has written specifically about the concept of an "evocative mode of influence" in organisational change work. Put simply, it is the ability to allow free rein to our responses and reactions to a particular context and to trust those reactions as a potential source of relevant data and useful energy.

As part of the initial stage of the research project, each participating company was visited. The purpose of the visit was to enable the managers involved to be fully introduced to the project and to alert them to the steps in the data collection process which was to follow. This would use repertory grid methodology to identify their own constructs of managerial competence. The visit also enabled us as researchers to develop an understanding of the background of the organisations which were to be studied in the sample.

It quickly became obvious that this entry point provided us with an excellent opportunity, as an off-shoot of the project, to consider the value of evocation as a process of enquiry compared to more mainstream methodologies such as repertory grid.

To this end, the first part of the paper, (APPROACHING THE ORGANISA-TION), is written as a narrative taking the reader along to meet one of the companies and inviting him/her to share in that experience. There are a number of pauses at key points in the text to encourage the reader to reflect on what is being evoked by the story.

2. APPROACHING THE ORGANISATION (NARRATIVE)

"To know what is happening, push less, open out and be aware. See without staring. Listen quietly rather than listen hard. Use intuition and reflection rather than trying to figure things out. The more you can let go of trying, and the more open and receptive you become, the more easily you will know what is happening." (The Tao Te Ching)

The plane landed on time at 1640. It was my first time in Northern Ireland and I was glad I wasn't alone. We made our way off the plane and followed the signs to the baggage hall. My colleague lit up a cigarette. He had been coming over to Belfast for a while now and seemed quite relaxed about it all. People always say about Northern Ireland that the more you go the less you worry. Now I know that's true. I even catch myself saying the same to others but it offers little comfort when you've just arrived and are about to start travelling around the place on your own. I had received a letter a few days earlier with an itinerary of sorts. It gave company names, addresses and times. I picked my suit-carrier off the carousel and as confidently as I could made my way to the taxi-rank.

Sitting in the back of the taxi, I felt safe again. It was as if having the car around me somehow provided a sort of barrier against the outside world. I was taken care of and could relax a bit. This was a sensation I was to have a number of times during the next few days. We headed for Belfast, through the permanent checkpoint on the road out of the airport and on through Templepatrick towards the motorway. I looked eagerly around, taking in as much as I could and all the time being struck by how normal everything seemed. It was early Sunday evening and an elderly couple were walking their overweight dog, stopping every now and again to urge the creature to catch up. A man was filling his car on a garage forecourt talking to his small son whose head was half out the back window. His wife was on her way to pay the cashier. The road signs were the same shape and colour as in England. Somehow these "normal" things had a significance for me and settled me down a bit. We came to a set of traffic lights near some roadworks and, as we slowed right down, I suddenly found myself gazing at a slightly scruffy semi-detached house. What drew me to it was the huge red and blue flagpole coming out of the front wall at an angle of forty five degrees. On its end was a Union Jack fluttering provocatively in the breeze. On the upper front wall was a crest and underneath it was painted in new, shiny black paint the words, "No Surrender". The windows were closed. There was no sign of life. In a few seconds my sense of calm had disappeared. I was anxious again and, although I don't think I realised it at the time, I was just beginning to learn one of my first lessons about Northern Ireland.

Somehow the place demands of you a greater level of alertness to your surroundings. You need to quickly weigh up the significance and possible impact of what is going on around you. Your safety depends on it.

To get to our hotel we skirted round the northern outskirts of Belfast. The city sprawled out below us with its teeming houses, cranes and blocks of flats. I couldn't help wondering how people lived there, what they did and how they coped with life from day to day. Which part is west Belfast? Where's Harland and Wolff? Which area is that? Is that a safe pub? I began to realise how full of questions I was.

I felt like a small boy out for the day somewhere with a grown-up, excited and scared, brimming over with reactions and responses to all around him and desperately trying to put everything into a frame that made some sense and could explain the world. But I wasn't a small boy out for a weekend trip. I was a consultant working in a project team about to research the question of senior management competence in small business. For the next eighteen months or so we would be working closely with a number of volunteer companies to arrive at a relevant framework of competence for Northern Irish businesses. We were to have our first team meeting later that evening. I checked into my room and immediately phoned home. I had only left a few hours earlier and already I had lots to talk about.

The purpose of the meeting was to introduce us to the companies in the first phase of the research as well as signal the formal start of the project. We had a room set aside.

It was one of those conference rooms that you find in virtually every hotel. The tables were covered with green baize tablecloths and arranged in a horseshoe. On top were little bowls of mint imperials placed at regular intervals and bottles of water and fruit cordial. At each place was a pencil and a few sheets of paper inside a folder that carried the hotel name. At the open end of the tables stood a flipchart easel and a large white screen next to a table with a projector on it. There was a faint smell of felt-tipped pens. I felt in very familiar surroundings.

We filed in, half a dozen of us, a mixture of men and women, half of us English and half Northern Irish. Two of us were in Northern Ireland for the first time. Apart from my colleague who had travelled with me, I had not met any one of them before. We spent a little while introducing ourselves and, probably because it was Sunday evening, quite quickly got down to work. The idea was that we would confirm together the purpose of this first phase of the project and then spend some time swapping any information that was available on the companies and people we were about to visit over the next couple of days.

It was a fascinating couple of hours. Again I was aware of my urge to get more information about where I would be going, who I would be seeing, what I might expect, whether or not I'd be going anywhere near trouble spots and so on. I eagerly questioned the others and remember feeling a bit uneasy as we began to talk about the journeys we would be making. I recognised just how many of the place names in Northern Ireland evoked in me images and memories of destruction and hostility. They are certainly ingrained in our English subconscious and have a significance that is not easily explained. Probably like most first time visitors and especially those from the "mainland", I needed to do something about my fear and vulnerability and one way was to fire off questions in an attempt to fill in the picture as fully and as quickly as possible; the hope is that I wouldn't then feel so exposed and ignorant about what to expect and would feel more in control. It didn't work, though.

One Northern Irish member of the group seemed to take pleasure in dropping in the odd bit about a bomb having gone off there recently or cars being hijacked in that area or a particular pub being used by some organisation or other. He would then, in the next breath and with a broad smile, say there was nothing to worry about, though, and so and so was a terrific guy or such and such was a beautiful place and you'll be alright.

I have experienced this kind of exchange any number of times between Northern Irish people and visitors. Taxi drivers from the airport are past masters at it. I guess it's both a way of acknowledging the extremes that exist in Northern Ireland, the everyday normality and the periodic atrocity, as well as an attempt to suss out new arrivals. The first few times though I found it very unnerving and unsettling.

Still you get used to it!

I hope all this is helping you arrive in Northern Ireland too. I want to continue in a moment and take you with me to one of the companies I visited but, as in any process of evocation , I wanted to pause for a while first and allow some time for you, the reader, to check your reaction to what I am describing. . . . . .

2.1 Pause

Back in our conference room, we agreed that the purpose of the initial interviews was to begin to build a story about not only the history and development of the business but also the background and personality of the key person or people running it. We needed both in order to provide a context for, and to add richness to, the subsequent data we would be gathering about competence.

There wasn't much information to be had about the first couple of firms on our list. One of them, a manufacturing company in Belfast, had only a few days before agreed to join this first phase and the other, an electronics firm, had not been in business all that long. One of my companies, a metal company, came next.

"You're going there, aren't you?", said Pete, emphasising the "you're" and smiling slightly. "It's the arse-end of Northern Ireland, you know". I didn't know at all and suddenly felt my anxiety rise again and a string of questions start to stream through my head. What did he mean? Did he mean dump or trouble-spot or was this some kind of local joke that you can only understand when you have been let into the secret? I composed myself enough to ask him what he meant.

"Oh, you'll see when you get there", he replied with another broad grin and added, "only the English would settle in a place like that". I withdrew and felt a bit awkward and unsure. Perhaps noticing that, he then, true to script, began to say how it wasn't actually all that bad and how I'd be perfectly alright really and so on.

I'd already taken a look at the map. The place was some way from Belfast and looked a bit off the beaten track. Pete went on to talk about Dave Stephens, the M.D. and described him as a "good Prod" and how he had moulded the company into what it was. I began to realise that the term "arse-end of Northern Ireland" was less likely to be indicative of Pete's view of the countryside and more likely to be a comment on the people that lived in the place, or perhaps a bit of both. Why else would Dave's Protestantism be important? He mentioned Angela, too. She was Dave's secretary and was obviously the person to speak to in order to make any contact with him.

That night, back in my room, I reflected on what I had found out and tried to picture the next couple of days travelling around on my own and talking to these people. I realised that I didn't have much factual data at all about the metal company or any of the others for that matter. I'd got a bit about company size and main products. I knew, though, that Dave Stephens was a Protestant and that his company was probably in a predominantly Nationalist part of Northern Ireland. I knew that "he had knocked the company into shape". I had sensed too that there was some amusement that I was going to go to the place. Quite why, I just didn't know. I decided that there was nothing more I could do other than just go and see what happens. I still felt a bit scared and unsure and decided that I would call the company first thing in the morning to confirm that they were expecting me and to check the best way to get to them. I pulled up the duvet and switched off the light. I'd been in Belfast about six hours and I felt exhausted. It was certainly going to be a demanding couple of days...............

2.2 Pause

"Good morning, The Metal Company, how may I help you?"
"I'd like to speak to Mr. Stephens' secretary, please.
"Certainly, may I ask who's calling? Thank you. Just one moment Mr. Stickland."

The efficient female voice was suddenly replaced by some music. The tune was "Thine is the glory, ever conquering Son..." Halfway through the third bar it was interrupted by another female voice, this one much softer.

"Hello Mr. Stickland, I'm Angela, Mr. Stephens' secretary."
"Hi, I'd like to confirm my appointment for ten thirty today with Mr.Stephens.
"Yes, that's in Mr. Stephens' diary. Mr. Stephens has asked me to ask you how long you will need?"
I hesitated a bit as I felt sure the letter they'd been sent had said two hours.
"I'd have thought a couple of hours would be fine."
"O.K. that's no problem, Mr. Stickland."

I then asked her for directions and picked up my pen to make notes. Next to me on the bed was sprawled out my map of Northern Ireland.

"Where will you be coming from, Mr. Stickland?"
"From Belfast, probably along the Motorway."
"O.K. Then..."
    For the next five minutes or so she proceeded with meticulous instructions on where I should head for, what I should look out for and what I should do if I missed any of her landmarks. She finished with a "once you've got there you can't miss us" and paused to let me catch up. I scribbled it all down, half looking at the map and at the same time trying to trace the route she was suggesting. Some of the place names she mentioned I had heard of before, almost certainly on the TV news or in the paper and I felt a bit like an outrider being briefed before being despatched on some mission into dangerous terrain. I concentrated very hard. Her voice sounded kind and re-assuring.
    "If you get lost at all just give me a ring and we'll try and put you right. O.K., Mr. Stickland, we'll see you at ten thirty then."

I looked at my watch. It was twenty to nine and I decided to get going. It was a crisp, bright morning with the threat of the occasional heavy shower. I folded my raincoat on the back seat of the hired Ford Fiesta, which had been delivered to the hotel early that morning, and arranged my briefcase and roadmap next to me in the front. I had my scribbled directions from Angela as well, tucked into the fold of the seat behind the map. Not that I particularly needed them; I had already got the route off by heart, the number of times I had looked at it!

I felt confident about the first bit out of Belfast as I'd noticed a sign to the motorway outside the hotel. I set off, though, a bit like someone who has just passed his driving test and is out for the first time on his own, eagerly looking ahead for every sign. The prospect of getting lost somehow had an edge to it!

The first part of the journey on the main roads went very smoothly and I began to relax as I chugged along the motorway at 65mph or so. Somehow that sense of familiarity, that I'd been aware of in the taxi the day before, had returned and I began to think about the meeting with Dave and what I was going to ask him.

When I turned off, though, things became less straightforward. I began to go through some very beautiful, lush, green countryside along roads which were not only deserted, apart from the odd tractor or farm vehicle, but also, like most rural roads everywhere, were practically bereft of any direction signs. I began to get a bit uneasy. I seemed to be the only car on the road and felt very conspicuous, though the chances of anyone seeing me were fairly remote as there was no-one else around.

That realisation only seemed to make matters worse as I lost all sense of direction thanks to a couple of T junctions with no signs at all. At one there was a white flagpole with an Irish tricolour flying in the breeze and "victory to the IRA" daubed in white on the small stone wall next to the road. I pressed on beginning to get worried about the time and nervous about getting lost in an area not that well-disposed to a "British presence". I felt a wry smile at the thought that probably not many English Management Development consultants had beaten this particular track as part of their work, or as part of anything else for that matter!

Suddenly, almost out of nowhere, I came across a sign for the place I wanted and eagerly turned left along another deserted country road. It began to rain heavily. About five minutes later, as the shower died down, I noticed one or two houses ahead. Soon I was passing the fortified RUC station on the right and some more houses on the left and I realised that this must be the place. I arrived at what was obviously the top of the main street which stretched wide and empty in front of me. A few vehicles were parked on the left and I saw some small shops on the right. A tractor pulling a trailer was crossing the road directly ahead so I slowed right down and looked around.

It was the sort of place that you suddenly found yourself in without any obvious signs that you were approaching it. Similarly, out the other side would be the same. Suddenly you'd be in the country again. With the hills behind, the mud on the road and the farm vehicles, it reminded me of a wild west, frontier town. It certainly felt rural and isolated and I felt very conspicuous. I drove slowly down into the main street, half checking Angela's directions and half looking out for the turning.

It was as she had said, just along on the left. I turned in and a short way up the rising road, on the right was a high, blue, metal fence. Was this the place? There was nothing to

tell me. I drove past to make sure and turned round just before some greyish, white houses.
I pulled up outside the locked main gates and pressed the intercom. A woman answered.
I said who I was and she asked me to wait and someone would come and let me in.

I'd no sooner got back into my car when an oldish man, in dark blue overalls shuffled
towards the gates, unlocked them and with a grunted good morning and a nod of the head,
let me in pointing to a row of parked cars where presumably I was to put mine. I pulled up
next to a Jaguar. That must be Dave's, I thought. I somehow couldn't imagine him in any
of the other, smaller vehicles that were there.

2.3. Pause

I felt nervous as I headed towards the entrance to the building. What was this man Stephens
going to be like? He certainly had a reputation for toughness and was also obviously well-
respected as a businessman. One of the people the day before had described him as a "tough
man". I couldn't help thinking that this was a tough environment too, miles from anywhere,
rural, agricultural, unsophisticated and insular.

I walked through the door and into the reception area. On my left was a desk and a young
woman greeted me with a smile and asked me to take a seat. She said she would tell Angela
that I was here. I sat down and looked around. The decor was a soft, pastel pink and the area
had a plushness and a sort of Laura Ashley elegance that seemed so out of keeping with the
town I had just driven through. Some glossy brochures about the company and its products
were thoughtfully arranged on an angular glass coffee table. Every now and then the young
woman would politely answer the 'phone, her voice exuding the gentle friendliness that had
re-assured me the day before. Every caller seemed to want Mr. Stephens. After a few
minutes I became aware that in the background, beyond the soft pink walls, I could hear
the muffled sound of metal being bashed and finished. It reminded me that this was a
metalworking factory and a successful one too!

Soon a tall, elegant woman in her mid thirties, dressed smartly in a dark blue suit came
over and said with a smile and a soft intonation that I immediately recognised;

"Hello, Mr. Stickland? I'm Angela, Mr. Stephens' secretary, would you like to come
through".

I I stood up, offered her my hand and began to tell her about my journey as she led me
along a short corridor into a space where she had her desk. Adjacent to it was a mahogany
door, half open and leading to what was obviously Dave's office. The carpet, pink walls and
dark brown door reminded me of the corridors and rooms you get in the "Executive Suite"
areas of modern, business hotels. We paused for a few seconds while Angela glanced at some
papers on her desk and then she showed me in

2.4. Pause

Before we meet Dave though, I'd like to break again from the narrative for a while
and give you some time to see what kind of picture you are beginning to paint of
this company. I did the same with two friends who had read this far.

One, a woman, said she was struck by some of the contrasts; tough, hostile
environment and warm, caring welcome; hard, shiny, noisy metal and soft, pastel

pink; male and female. She said that she had a picture of a company shaping something out of raw materials, working against the odds, a bit out on a limb geographically and psychologically in terms of what it stood for. She said she imagined that perseverance and getting results would be particularly valued.

The other, a man, said the narrative strongly reminded him of a mythological tale with a traveller embarking on a dangerous quest to some distant castle. The traveller, as all such travellers do, is setting off with the barest essentials and yet, amidst the dangers, there is also the hint that some value and worth will be gained from this trip. Access to the castle through the kingdom can only be arranged with the help of the wise woman, a custodian figure who allows the king to get on with the job of ruling. He said the castle contrasts with its surroundings giving rise to all sorts of intriguing questions about its purpose and role. It's been built through sheer, hard work against the odds and, above all, that is what it stands for and upholds.

2.5. Pause

Dave Stephens was sat behind a largish, mahogany desk in a crisp, white shirt with his sleeves down to his wrists. He stood up and we shook hands. He had a strong, firm grip. He was shorter than I imagined, thick set without being fat. He spoke very quickly and in bursts, in a voice that was clipped and sharp. He asked Angela to bring in some coffee and almost in the same breath began to ask me about the research and what the benefits from it would be. I'd only been in there for a couple of minutes and already we were focussing on the outcomes.

I was aware of suddenly feeling nervous and under pressure and thinking rapidly about the best way to respond. Somehow I felt that my answers needed to be as tight and clear as his questions. Fortunately Angela returned almost immediately with the coffee and biscuits and the inevitable interruption enabled me to settle down a bit and prepare my response. Dave then asked about the purpose of our meeting and I went through my prepared patter about the aims and method of the research and how I came to be part of it. I again noticed that I was feeling the need to hurry up and get to the point. He agreed to the interview being taped which meant that I did not have to spend all the time scribbling furiously; something I was particularly pleased about given how quickly he spoke. It also meant that I could observe him more fully.

I set up the tape recorder as quickly as I could feeling like the Saturday boy in Dixons or Currys, tentatively going through a demonstration of a product to a customer and hoping that I'd got the right leads in the right sockets!

In the first part of the interview, he talked very knowledgeably and passionately about the company; how it had started as a community project in an area of high unemployment; that he had become MD ten years after and the business had been in profit ever since; how from its early agricultural links it had expanded and diversified; that it had won two Queens Awards to Industry and that the target was to double turnover five years out. Sitting opposite him across his desk I couldn't help noticing his piercing blue eyes that every now and then would lock in a fixed stare for a few seconds, breaking the contact between us. I found it hard to interrupt him when I wanted some explanation or clarification. He knew what he wanted to say and got on with saying it. Fortunately, there was one interruption which not only let me frame some further questions but also provided more insight into the man. It took the form of a phone call.

2.6. Pause

The call was from someone who obviously wanted to talk through with Dave the planned appointment of a new teacher at a local school. He gave his view on the individual and crisply went through what should happen and who should be spoken to. His standing and authority clearly stretched into other arenas as well.

Later on though, when I asked him to talk more about himself and his people, I was struck by how his demeanour changed. The sense of control and assuredness disappeared and he spoke more slowly.

He needed little encouragement to share some of his ongoing frustrations; that colleagues wouldn't challenge him enough; that they wouldn't take responsibility; that there was no-one who he could trust to run the place when he was away; I that he too often ended up having to sort others' mistakes and that, if anything, he was getting busier and more stressed and certainly no younger. At one point he stopped, and looking hard at me said that he wasn't used to having conversations like this with anyone. I asked him why not and he said it was because I was prepared to ask him to say more rather than accept immediately his reason or response. "I wish the people here would do more of that", he added. I imagined that it was also to do with the fact that he was not accustomed to speaking to people without having the answers.

Before I left he showed me round the factory. He brightened up and again talked eagerly about what was going on and what plans there were for improvements to the systems and processes. I was struck by the order and tidyness of the place and there was an industriousness that was very evident. Every now and then Dave would pick up a piece of finished metal and admiringly show me a feature. He loved the stuff.

We went outside to the Stores area where Dave again beamed with delight as he showed me how little stock they had on hand. I was introduced to the Stores Manager, one of his top team. Dave tried unsuccessfully to include him in his account of how the stock ordering process had been improved.

The individual hovered nervously and only spoke when Dave asked him a direct question and then it was largely to add his endorsement to what had already been explained. My thoughts went back to Dave's gripe that no-one challenged him and I could almost feel the unease that this individual would experience at such a prospect.

We walked back to Dave's office to collect my briefcase and Dave asked me what was planned next. I explained that the next stage would involve him and his managers being asked to do some analytical work aimed at identifying areas of top team competency for the company and that he would be hearing from some of my colleagues soon. I thanked him for his time and shook hands. It was about twenty to one. We had been together for just over two hours.

Back in my car I began to reflect on my visit. The project team had fixed a project team meeting for Wednesday to enable each of us to talk through how our interviews had gone and to share with each other our data and hypotheses about what would constitute *competence in the companies we had been to. I began to reflect on my time with Dave and the thoughts I had about the company he was leading.*

But first a few moments for you, the reader, to gather your thoughts and reactions and perhaps have a go at forming your ideas of what you imagine this company would regard as competence.

2.7. Pause

3. OUTCOMES OF EVOCATION

That concludes the narrative part of this paper. In the remaining part, I intend to compare and contrast the conclusions I came to about competence from my visit to The Metal Company, with the results of the systematic, objective, analytical work undertaken by other research colleagues who made subsequent visits. In this way we may reach some conclusions on the comparative power of evocation as a methodology for approaching/understanding organisations.

So what was my initial stab at the sort of things that would constitute competence at The Metal Company?

What I shared with my colleagues was my image of a John Wayne character, forging a business in a hostile, wild environment where for him toughness, resolution, conviction and a preparedness to give it all are what matters.

I talked about how the man and the environment seemed made for each other and that Dave seemed to revel in the power and status he had as a successful and respected businessman in this part of Northern Ireland. I was struck by how much pressure I felt in his presence to hurry up, get to the point and demonstrate my competence and professionalism. I felt there was no room for hesitation or uncertainty. The way he spoke reminded me of gunfire, sharp, staccato and clipped. Metal too seemed entirely appropriate for such a man. It is hard, definite, resilient yet with a smooth finish that Dave delighted in when we were on the shopfloor. Like the metal the company had developed a smoothness which was evident in the reception area and the way Angela dealt with me. This care and attention, however, did not remove the strong sense of isolation and lack of support which I was aware of when listening to Dave and which he described as mutually reinforcing. I was also struck by the deference and attention that was afforded him by people in the company, some even repeating what he had just said.

For sure you would need to know what you were doing and to get on with it in a way that made it certain that targets were hit, plans were fulfilled and schedules were met. During most of my talk with Dave I was conscious of time and the need to get through what I was there for. Decisions would need to be quick, sharp, snappy and demonstrate that you were in control of your bit. Being seen to be in charge would be important as would be your readiness to stand up for what you believed in and carry that through despite opposition or indifference. Leading from the front you would be able to suss out the terrain and beat the competition by keeping one step ahead all the time.

Supporting this, however, would be your ability to plan, organise and schedule. Good plans not only enable you to keep your eye on the target but also ensure there is no energy or time wasted in unnecessary diversions or luxuries. I was fairly sure that relationships too would be subject to the same focussed, economical approach. Despite Angela and her care and the stuff Dave had shared with me about his isolation and loneliness, I did not get a sense that people talked that much to each other. There was something significant in the fact that the Stores manager, the only employee I really met apart from Dave and Angela, only spoke to reinforce what Dave was already saying. I imagined that he and other top team members were unlikely to be party to Dave's private thoughts and emerging agendas and it would be interesting to see if, and how, this would influence the subsequent data from the company.

Overall, my expectation was that the competence data that would emerge from the company would emphasise the aspects of toughness, control, quickness and self-sufficiency that had been so strongly evoked in me during my time with Dave.

4. EVOCATION AND ELICITATION COMPARED

Let us now look at what actually did emerge from the subsequent analytical work which was begun in the following way.

The first step involved Dave Stephens taking part in an elicitation process which used repertory grid analysis to arrive at a series of competence domains for top team members in his organisation. This raw data on competence domains, along with similar data from other participating companies in Northern Ireland, was then pulled together in the form of a competence domain supergrid which was then subsequently completed individually by top team members from The Metal Company. These were the Quality Manager, the Production Manager and the Finance Manager. (For an in-depth description of this approach and methodology, see Lindsay, Stuart and Thompson; "The Competence of Top Team Members: A Framework for Successful Performance" (In Press)

If we start by taking a look at Dave's data and the sort of competence domains that he viewed as important in his top team, we can classify it broadly into two distinct bands. There is a clear primary focus on "managing and increasing sales", which he sees as an overriding priority, and which came out as his core competence domain, supported by "ensuring and maintaining customer satisfaction" and the need to "install and make good use of computers" and "harmonise standards". His secondary concern is the development of the people in the management team, which is reflected in constructs like "obtaining and growing quality people for growth", "developing the management team" and "lack of engineering ability".

His (Dave's) full list is:

- Managing and increasing sales (Core Competence Domain)

- Developing the management team

- Obtaining and growing quality people for growth

- Ensuring and maintaining customer satisfaction

- Harmonisation of standards
- Installing and making good use of computers

- Lack of engineering ability (Not a domain, but a competency concern)

Sales management is his major priority, but beyond that, there is a distinct developmental flavour to his domain constructs.

The data from the three top team members took the following form:

Analysis of Individual Responses to Supergrid of Competence Domains

Competence Domain	Production Manager	Quality Manager	Finance Manager
Leadership	/	/	/
Developing Competitive Advantage		/	/
Setting and Meeting Sales Targets	/	/	
Operational Planning	/	/	
Benchmarking			/
Control of Company Finances	/		
Managing Profitability			/
Making Sound Commercial Judgments		/	/
Marketing	/		
Understanding Markets		/	/
Identifying and Addressing Markets			/
Developing Sales & Marketing Teams	/		
Quality Awareness	/		
Satisfying Market Needs	/		/

The data is interesting from a number of perspectives. The top team members clearly indicate a strong emphasis on selling. This echoes Dave's own priority. What is different, though, is that there is very little individual or collective prioritising of development for the management team, or for the human resource in general. Their data is much more about doing it, making it happen, making the figures. It has a short term, operational and control feel to it. Dave's personal concerns, reflected in his data, about building a team and becoming less indispensable simply do not feature in what the top team members see as important. Given the extent to which his influence and stamp can be seen in their data, we can safely assume that he has kept this so private that it hasn't influenced anything out in the company yet.

What is surprising is the number of constructs relating to marketing that emerged. On the whole, this represents an area not strongly evoked in the visit to The Metal Company and therefore gives rise to an interesting question. Is marketing at the heart of the company or is it a bolt-on, like the reception area? Is it what is apparent away from the company rather than on-site? Clearly further follow-up would be necessary to arrive at the answer.

The relative consistency across the top team data is worthy of note. It seems to demonstrate the extent to which the individuals do it Dave's way, in the manner prescribed; clear, focussed, sharp, controlled and planned. It is economical, operational and to a degree functional in that some of the differences between individuals seem to reflect their different responsibilities rather than different styles or personalities. It should be stressed that between them the top team members identified a total of only 14 competence domains required of an excellent top team member of The Metal Company. The supergrid they responded to consisted of 36 possible domains and included things like:

- Developing the management team
- Promoting a sense of teamworking
- Management of Human Resources
- Training and development
- General staff development
- Matching skills and motivations to jobs and tasks
- Legal aspects and requirements
- External awareness
- Strategic planning
- Public relations
- Innovation
- Research & development of existing products and services
- Company flexibility

None of these feature. Again, many of these represent a longer term and developmental viewpoint.

5. SUMMARY

The marketing issue apart, there is nothing in the data that emerged from the analytical work that could remotely constitute a surprise. The conclusions formed as a result of my being open to my experience and my environment have been in large part underpinned by the subsequent data generated by more systematic, conclusion making approaches.

Indeed, I would go further, however, and claim that what emerged from the systematic, analytical work is not only fairly typical of the sort of data that comes out of such an approach but also, in comparison to the evocative approach, is lacking in richness and depth. It does not give us the flavour of metal, the battle against the environment and the sense of toughness that permeate the company. More importantly, it does not allow us to form a picture of the climate and context within which managers are performing and needing to develop. It is as if we get the skeleton without the flesh; the bare bones without the life.

This paper has set out to illustrate that when we, as consultants, can in the course of our work remain truly open to ourselves and our environment, we have available to us a good deal of information that can throw light on our clients and what is happening for them.

In choosing to test this hypothesis in the arena of work on competence identification, where traditionally more analytic approaches have dominated, I have hopefully demonstrated that such an approach can also have a high degree of accuracy when compared to the more frequently used systematic approaches. Beyond this, the nature of the data that can be gathered through a process of evocation can often have a richness and depth that simply cannot be gained using more structured and analytical methods.

REFERENCES

Nevis, E. "Organisational Consulting: A Gestalt Approach". Gardner Press Inc. New York. 1987.

SITUATIONAL ANALYSIS AS AN INTEGRAL APPROACH IN CONSULTING TO ORGANISATIONS

Dr Emanuela Todeva, *South Bank University, London*

1. INTRODUCTION

In this **introductory section** are stated some of the key principles of our argument in relation to organisational consultancy and the foundations of situation approach.

Organisational consultancy has three dimensions: expert evaluation of the organisational parameters (including contextual and environmental); assessment of the management problems by the consultant; and projected managerial activities.

All three elements require extended experience and knowledge of the basic theoretical perspectives of organisational analysis in order to apply the most appropriate ones. The diversity in theoretical approaches corresponds (although in an indirect way) with a variety of practical schemes for consultancy work. The emphasis of the theoretical overview in the **second section** of this paper is on the strengths and contributions that each conceptualisation of work and business organisations may provide.

Our main concern is not only the explanatory strength of the organisational theories (in relation to past and present events), but the potentials for an application of particular theoretical approach to evaluate present and foresee future events. This in terms of organisational analysis means to construct a phenomenon that will become a reality in the future with some probability.

However, our believe is that the experience is a better judge than the mathematical calculations. Consequently, one objective of this paper is to integrate to certain extend the accumulated knowledge in organisational and management research. This is particularly focus of the **third section** of this paper in which a new integrated theoretical model is proposed.

The application of this theoretical model is discussed along with some new studies in consultancy work in the **forth section** of this paper.

The social reality is a complex and dynamic system, built up by social subjects and their activities, by material objects and cultural values. The actual reality is built out through the specific **actions** and **practices** of individual and socially organised **subjects** and the **meanings** that the later attribute to different objects as well as to their own activities. (1*)

The social subjects constantly enter in immediate (direct) and intermediate (indirect) interactions and interrelationships - between each other, as well as with the overall environment. These interactions are carried out always in concrete piece of time and this defines different situations in historical time.

The situations as subject of analysis have been in focus of different social sciences - sociology, psychology, social psychology, anthropology, economics, politics, management and others. Most of these scientific disciplines look over the situations from a particular point of view, but almost all of the authors use the concept 'situation' in its natural language meaning without formulating precise definitions related to the framework of its interpretation and understanding.

Our definition for this key concept is the following: **Situation is a particular relation between the individual** (his/her role, position, location, status) **and the external to him/her circumstances** (conditions, surrounding, relationships with the environment and specific duties) **in a particular moment** (critical point, coincidence) **in reality.** (Based upon the definitions from 'Chambers English Dictionary' and 'The Oxford English Dictionary'.) (Fig. 1)

From this perspective we made an attempt to conceptualise a new approach for organisational analysis and consultancy, that will both satisfy the definition and will allowed evaluation of all well known and well explored elements of a work situation.

2. APPROACHES FOR ORGANISATIONAL RESEARCH AND CONSULTANCY

If we follow the debate, starting from Weber, one of his methodological contributions in **action theory** was the situational approach in social analysis. Later on, in **social and cultural anthropology** it was laid as a basic method **casus analysis** and **situational analysis** without pointing out the difference between the two. In **management theory** situational approach was formulated - as 'theoretical and practical means' for studying an organisation. Different types of situations are described, characterised, analyzed, by diverse criteria that are based on various theories.

The natural centre for most of the research approaches is the relation 'individual - environment', characterised by the description of behavioral effect from the influence of concrete objective 'stimulus' presented as 'situational factors'.

What was not considered was the reverse effect that the behaviour has upon the objective 'stimulus' and how this effect changes the interaction process as a whole. Therefore, our effort was to look at the process itself, with its independent variables (starting up the interaction) and dependent variables (both as effect and cause for further changes).

2.1. System Thinking

The organisational and management theory from its very beginning has been based upon conceptual models attempting to present the existing organisational realities in a meaningful and scientific way. A whole range of approaches and models have been developed to facilitate research and consultancy.

The majority of them portray the organisations as systems of organisational and individual elements. The categories that are being used are at different levels of abstraction and usually describe diverse and indirect relationships. The research in management as a whole has been developed mainly on the basis of including new categories as more significant and replacing others -as non-relevant.

There is a very close relationship between system theory, system approach and system thinking. We see System Theory as this extensive body of academic thought which has been developed as a result of system thinking and application of system approach while analysing complex entities.

The most distinguished feature of **System Approach**, according to Brown, is that it characterises organisations as systems in a way that their behaviour is held regardless of the nature of groups and individuals who compose them. (Brown, 1992)

It seems that the term 'system' conceptualises any social structure which by definition is composed by individuals and their structured activities.(2*) System thinking appears to be the most powerful mean to conceptualise organisations. Everything is a system. Even the individual is a system of features and characteristics.

Under the auspice of system thinking a number of approaches and perspectives have evolved. The **Universalistic Approach** in management theory has developed on the premise that by analysing all particular instances it is possible to derive a series of general principles and practices that operate within organisation. (Ritchie, 1993) The hope is that the application of the best of these principles will lead to improvement of effectiveness and efficiency of organisations in all possible management situations.

The background assumption here is that of a complete system of organisational principles and practices which is impossible itself because of the endless variety of real life situations and characteristics.

If we take as a focus the concept of 'management', rather then 'organisation', we face system thinking in the majority of theoretical approaches. According to the **Technical Perspective**, management is conceptualised as a rationally designed and operationalised tool for realisation of predominantly instrumental values with the systematic coordination of social action. (Reed, 1989) The assumption is that of a formal organisational structure to secure the systematic coordination of activities. This is the view of organisation as a system of managerial positions, roles and control mechanisms in which managers can exercise some limited control over the pace & direction of structural redesign.

The system itself is determined by the economic and political interests of the ruling class, as it is conceptualised in the **Critical Perspective** (Reed, 1989), or by the production technology, as conceptualised in the **Technological Perspective**.

The assumptions are, that organisations are functionally indispensable mechanisms that institutionalise individual values and objectives into human collectivities and those institutionalised patterns of social relations (in the form of management systems) impose themselves on the individuals in organisations. (Reed, 1989)

The most sophisticated of all approaches developed under the dominance of system thinking is the **Contingency Approach**. To certain extend it is a restatement of **The Open System Theory**.

By identifying key variables in the external and internal environment of the organisation, Contingency Approach aims to determine whether there are relations between them. The uncertainty of their appearance is a key element of the analysis. Those relationships are used to classify the nature of organisation's environment and are transformed further into some guidelines and prescriptions for decision-makers. (Ritchie, 1993)

All Contingency Approaches differ by the way that the environments are structured. Lawrence and Lorsh (1967) have appraised the relationship between organisation structure and management style.

The **Aston Programme** for research identifies six key dimensions of organisational structure and eight key contextual variables that effect the organisational performance and efficiency of decision making. These are the following: **structural dimensions** -specialisation of activities, standardisation of procedures, formalisation of documentation, centralisation of authority, configuration of positions, flexibility; and **contextual dimensions** -origin, size, ownership and control, technology, location, resources, interdependence. (Pugh et all., 1963; Pugh and Hickson, 1976)

Child (1970) has discovered positive relationship between decentralisation of authority and specialisation, standardisation and formalisation. (3*)

In relation to the guidelines and prescriptions, initially it was suggested that the decision makers should react in response to the environment (both external and internal). Later on it was discovered that a complete match between the two environments can not be achieved in reality and Child (1977) suggested that a certain compromise may be necessary and what may matter for the performance of the organisation is the internal consistency of structural arrangements.

This analysis reveals that the underlying assumption in Contingency Theory is that the organisation is an open system, exposed to the uncertainty of its external and internal environments and it is a managerial task to mediate the process of adjustment and to direct the organisational behaviour and performance.

As it was stated above the focus of our analysis is not to enter the theoretical debate on organisations by criticising, but by incorporating different approaches. In this context, system thinking is seen as a very fruitful theoretical form of analysing the social phenomenon called 'organisation'.

2.2. Action Thinking

The argument has evolved in developing a number of other theoretical models trying to overcome the constraints of system and contingency theories. According to the **Population - Ecology Model** the main concern is not the single organisational unit but it is the classification of forms and populations of organisations that fill niches in the environment. (Hall, 1991) The appropriate fit of the organisations with the environment is only a matter for their existence, but not for their structure.

Similar to this approach is the so called **Institutional Model**. According to it, organisations exist in 'fields' of other organisations and organisations are increasingly homogeneous within those fields. (4*) The organisation according to this model are seen as an institutionalisation of structures, practices and power.

According to the **Resource Dependence Model,** no organisation is able to generate all the resources it needs and therefore, it is dependent on the environment. (Marple, 1982) As organisations consist of 'actors', the decisions and actions of the latter are oriented towards perceiving, interpreting and evaluating the environment in order to provide the necessary supply of resources (including finance, personnel, services, production operations). (Hall, 1991) The focus in this model is on the 'strategic choices' that the actors make.

Both the Institutional and the Resource-Dependence Model develop a new perspective, which focus upon the actors' practices, decisions, and acts. With similar focus is also **The Political Perspective.** It conceptualises management as consisting of a "plurality of competing groups or coalitions that often come into conflict over decisions concerning the choice of organisational design". (Reed, 1989)

Political perspective focuses upon the continually shifting balance of interests and power within management and treats the individual managers as "knowledgable human agents, functioning within a dynamic situation where both organisational means and outcomes can be substantially shaped by them". (Reed, 1989, p. 6)

Even though the Political Perspective has not attracted much research efforts, it is important to consider its argument as a powerful interpretation tool in organisational dynamics. The focus on managerial power, political skills and manipulative control over decision making places this model in the filed of action thinking approaches.

The 'system elements' such as: formal control systems, hierarchy, rules, procedures, regulatory codes, monitoring techniques (Reed, 1989), are seen as a background context, subject to continuous renegotiation. This reveal the relativistic logic that supports the action thinking approaches.

Further evolution in that direction of application of relativistic logic is the so called **Practice Perspective** exploring the concepts of management and organisation as points of intersection for a wide range of 'social practices'. Those practices are subjected to various 'institutional strategies'. Main objectives of this theoretical perspective are to link together the behavioral, organisational and institutional level of analysis and to theorise in a systematic way the "interrelationship between managerial work, control strategies and macrostructural constraints". (Reed, 1989)

However, this perspective has been applied primarily to studying managerial work, rather than individual practices in general. It excludes also the temporary dimension, which is a primary concern in any real business situation.

An attempt for an integration of system thinking and action thinking is offered by the **Situationalist Approach.** As it was stated, it is based on the premises that all organisations are unique, which stem from the differences in each organisation's external environment, internal structure and culture, processes, goals and objectives. (Ritchie, 1993)

The first problem here is that the notion of action and practice is build in the concept of organisation's culture and processes and in a sense it is diluted in the meaning along with other notions like values, believes, symbols.

The second problem is that the concepts 'structure' and 'processes' are used in such a broad sense that in fact it means everything. If we look at the individual practices in work situation, they are structured actions (as they are organised in a particular way) and also they are part of a process (production, communication, management process, etc.).

This was challenging enough to attract our attention on an attempt for an integral view over the main theoretical domains in organisational theory, incorporating both system and action thinking and altering the analysis by applying both deterministic and relativistic logic.

The presented theoretical model for a situational analysis is a result of the efforts to clarify the existing levels of organisational analysis and to develop an integral approach for their complementary use in practical research.

It is also an attempt to overcome the theoretical opposition and contradictions between the technocratic and the humanistic approaches in organisational and management research.

Another major task of this work is to operationalise some of the abstract theoretical concepts in order to be used in practical research at a field.

3.   THEORETICAL MODEL

The model itself has been elaborated primarily for analysis of a work (business) organisations as it has been established on the basis of a study conducted in a manufacturing enterprise in Bulgaria in 1988. With relevant modifications it could be adopted for organisational research in all types of social organisations by changing mainly the elements related to specificity of the main organisational activity, the necessary conditions for it and the final results (or products).

The major criterion in the elaboration of the model has been to identify the main factors, as **necessary and sufficient conditions**, determining the actual dynamics of the situation (including labour and management), and characterising it in depth.

From the adoption of system thinking for the development of our situational model we have accepted the view of organisations as systems with a particular structure, which elements are interconnected and ruled by managerial decisions for to achieve maximum efficiency. Following this deterministic logic we accept a framework of major principles defined in theory:

A.   Organisations are interactive, highly complex, open systems with a great deal of internal and external uncertainty (Dawson, 1993);

B.   Changes in one of the sub-systems (or elements) generate changes in the other sub-systems. As being limited, the sub-systems make the results of changes predictable (Klein, 1984);

C.   In each formally described system there are both 'expected' and 'unexpected' (or casual) consequences, and the casual ones proceed from the social processes themselves (Klein, 1984);

D.   The 'behaviour' of the organisation is manifested as a series of processes ('responses') within a given framework (Klein, 1984); (5*)

E.   Organisation's resources are always scarce and all strategic choices have financial and social costs (Dawson, 1993);

F.   The individuals in organisations operate together in a number of interest groups which perform in patterns of consensus and conflicts (Dawson, 1993);

G.   Individuals in organisations face a variety of constraints and opportunities within which they have an element of choice. (6*)

H.   There is no one best way to act in organisations. The aim is to find an appropriate fit between the variety of elements of the system (Dawson, 1993);

J.   The activities of the individuals, their reasons and outcome constitute four levels of analysis - individual, management, organisational and environmental levels.

System thinking, however, can not answer questions related to the 'social processes' in organisation, how consensus between groups is achieved, how

Incorporating action thinking three more principles are suggested as relevant to any organisation:

K.   Organisations tend to institutionalise individual practices by selecting 'the best' in order to increase efficiency and to provide standards and quality. The choice

L.   Strategic choices (decisions) are on one hand determined by the elements of the organisational system, and on the other - they are determining the system through resource supply.

M.   Each organisation needs a form of consensus between different interest groups in order to exist. Therefore, adaptation and adjustment are primary objective and process.

As Richard Brown points out, "the whole sociological endeavour implies a view of social life in which the whole is greater than the sum of its parts and social entities, like social institutions, organisations, have 'an existence' in some sense independently of the individuals who constitute them". (Brown, 1992) The elements of the work organisation and the institutionalised practices that exist in particular time in it provide those additional situational characteristics of organisations.

In the model for situational analysis I intend to incorporate elements and variables from the existing models in the organisational theory that are explored in a wide range of conducted studies. These features will be treated as objective factors which characterise the social processes in an organisation. Each of these features (factors) will be viewed simultaneously as an independent variable (cause), and a dependent variable (effect). This multi-variance and reversibility of the action appears as a major feature of the interaction between the acting subjects and the industrial organisation as a working environment, in result of which any particular situation is generated.

All the factors, defined in the model and logically organised in blocks, are operationalised in a certain way for an expert assessment and evaluation. The main elements defining the situations at work are presented in Fig. 2 and Fig. 3.

The 'elements' in these figures are provisional definitions of the main situational groups of factors and form 18 major blocks. Each 'element', in terms of the model structure, is represented by certain 'characteristics', defined in a range of scales. These characteristics are the factors directly involved in the situational dynamics, as opposed to the 'elements', which represent indirect relationship. The location and the time (not presented in the figure) are determinative in regard to the physical and historical borders of the situation but are not treated as its elements or characteristics.

The **first circle** in the diagram consists of the most general characteristics of the organisational system. They normally are used in structuralist and system analysis based upon the notion of ideal type of organisation. As dependent variables, in their distinctive form, the general characteristics are result both of the influences of external to the system factors ('environmental factors' - blocks 13.A, 13.B and 13.C), and of the particular individual activities. (7*)

The **second circle** includes seven major blocks constituting independent sub-systems of management characteristics within the frames of the main organisational system. They also are treated both as dependent and independent variables. This level represents the main part of the usual organisational analysis, focused on particular managerial or organisational problem. (8*)

The purpose of defining the blocks has been to systematise and to take into account all the major characteristics that determine the development of each possible work situation - either routine or a conflict one. The allocation of the characteristics in blocks has been made after a logical analysis of their direct influence upon each other.

The **third circle** consists of the subjective elements of labour situation or the elements characterising the so called 'psychological situation'. These are characteristics usually involved at a psychological and social psychology level of analysis, centred on the individual interpretations of the situation at work and individual performance and behaviour. They also are viewed both as dependent and independent variables.

At this personal level - the level of 'psychological situation' -the distribution of grades for the characteristics varies in a wide range for different individuals. This requires the subjects to be grouped according to particular characteristics in order to make a description of the common features of their psychological situations and their 'group' activities.

In Fig. 2 an additional block is placed - 'environmental factors' - determining the most general parameters of the social situation and the most general preconditions for its realisation. The analysis of the contextual factors is of significance at a macro-level of analysis, where the organisational system is studied in relation to its business performance and as a whole entity, without considering its separate elements.

The factors of the environment are particularly important in a comparative analysis of different types of organisations functioning under the same or under comparable cultural, economic and political conditions. This is the level of studying the economic system, the basic social relations, property relations and economic performance, social and political order in general.

4.   APPLICATION FOR RESEARCH AND CONSULTANCY

If we look at the practical aspects of organisational consultancy there are three dominant paradigms: (1) There is no best way to organise; (2) It has not been proved possible to develop a universal set of strategic choices that can be applied routinely in all major decisions; (3) The primary objective of managers is to match the strategy to the environment. (Ritchie, 1993)

The main question is: if there is no one best decision and choice in managing organisations, how can we justify consultancy advice? The practice has shown that a good consultancy in its essence is sharing experience and knowledge. The art of consultancy is to identify the real problems and to relate the experience and knowledge to them.

This detailed model for situational analysis provides an integral and deep perspective for identifying contradictions in management; strengths and opportunities for development; threats from both external and internal environment; weaknesses in structures and resources. It is a good instrument for SWOT analysis and strategic decision making, based upon evaluation of activities and systems.

The model reflects the uniqueness of the business organisation, its temporary situational element, and the individual perspective of the consultant. It is particularly appropriate for analysis of the most contemporary forms of business organisation - networks, matrix and nebulous organisations, as described by Philip Powel. (Powel, 1992) What is specific about these new forms is that their structure could only be described as relationships between the unified parts. Its flexibility and dynamics require application of relativistic logic rather than the standard deterministic analysis.

The change in paradigm from 'organisational efficiency' towards 'the sovereign consumer' (Paul Du Gay, 1992) require more and more swift in analytical approaches - from 'organisational performance' towards 'individual's activities'. In terms of system thinking and action thinking it is perceived that both will be required to grasp business systems and to understand their problems.

5.   NOTES

1[*]   The term agency will not be used in this paper as though it is believed that it has more technocratic value, and more complex meaning in comparison with the term "subject". The last is understood as closer to the term "agent" or "actor", but broader in a sense that the "subject" is not only acting, but also reflecting, evaluating, judgments and decisions making, generalising, coding, decoding, expressing and being impressed, and a numberless line of hidden mental activities that stand behind the actual action. The subjects would be called some times individual subjects, some times - social ones, but this aims only to put an accent on a part of the subject features, relevant to the concrete analysis, and it is not related to differences in the meaning of the concept.

2*   Structural approaches will not be discussed separately in this paper as they are seen within the framework of system thinking. The conceptualisation of organisations as structures of elements, functioning in a particular way, is still based upon the assumption of a system that has a structure and functions.

3*   These are only some of the leading examples of organisational research in this area. Throughout the conducted research three levels of analysis could be distinguished - first, the level of organisational structure and functioning, second, the level of group composition and interaction, and third, the level of individual personality and behaviour. (Brown, 1992)

4*   The main reasons for that are the following: 1.coercive forces from the environment (such as government regulations and cultural expectations); 2. using the experience of the others in the field and 3. the normative pressure from the management and the working force (such as professional training and networks). (Hall, 1991)

5*   Some of the dimensions of this framework are determined by the organisation itself, like 'formal organisational structure', 'pattern of feedback and control', 'remuneration system'. Others are determined by the system of informal relations, based on the social and deep psychological nature of the individuals - expressed in features like 'seeking remuneration', 'attempting to achieve relevant status and fulfilment' and others. (Klein, 1984)

6*   The relative balance between constraints, opportunities and choice varies between groups and individuals and over time (Dawson, 1993)

7*   The general organisational characteristics on their part appear as independent variables, or causes, influencing both the interaction between the elements of management (from the second circle of the model) and the activities of the people (or the subjective personal elements of the situation within the third circle of the model).

8*   The distribution of the characteristics at this level of analysis in blocks is to some extent relative, due to the transfusion and mutual influence of the factors. This determines the existence of a number of marginal characteristics of the system. The planning and selection of the personnel, for example, can be viewed first as a characteristic of the 'management', second, as a characteristic of the staff/'personnel' (the actual selection and allocation of the people), and third, as a determining factor of the 'social relations'. As all characteristics in the model only map out an interlink with other element, it was decided that their meaning and interpretation is more important than their actual placement within the model structure.

6. REFERENCES

1. Arnold, H. & Feldman, D. (1988) Organizational Behaviour. N.Y., Mcgraw-Hill Book Company.

2. Brown, R. (1992) Understanding Industrial Organisations: Theoretical Perspectives in Industrial Sociology. Routledge.

3. Chambers English Dictionary. (1988) Chambers, Cambridge.

4. Dawes, P., Dowling, G. & Patterson, P. Criteria Used to Select Management Consultants. In: *Industrial Marketing Management*, Aug. 1992, Vol. 21, 3, 187-193.

5. Dawson, S. (1993) Analysing Organisations. Macmillan Press.

6. Etzioni, A. & Lehman, E. (1980) A Sociological Reader on Complex Organizations", 3rd. ed., Holt, Rinehart and Winston, London.

7. Farr, J. (1985) Situational Analysis: Explanation in Poli-tical Science. In: *Journal of Politics*, Vol.47, 1985.

8. Flippo, E. & Munsinger, G. (1978) Management. Allyn & Bacon, Inc., Boston.

9. Hofer, C. (1975) Towards a Contingency Theory of Business Strategy. In: *Academy of Management Journal*, Vol. 18, 4, Dec 1975, 784-810.

10. Paul Du Gay & Gream Salaman (1992) The Culture of The Customer. In: *Journal of Management Studies*, Sept. 1992, Vol.29, 5, 615-634.

11. Hall, R. (1991) Organisations: Structure, Processes and Outcomes. 5th ed., Prentice Hall.

12. Jay, A. (1974) Organization and Management: A system approach. 2nd ed. New York: McGraw-Hill.

13. Kakabadse, A., Ludlow, R. & Vinnicombe, S. (1988) Working in Organisations. Penguin Books.

14. Klein, S. & Ritti, R. (1984) Understanding Organizational Behaviour, Kent Publishing Company, Boston.

15. Lester, T. (1992) The Rise of the Network. In: *International Management*, June 1992, Vol. 47, 6, 72-74.

16. Marple, D. (1982) Technological Innovation and Organisational Survival: A Population Ecology Study of Nineteenth Century American Railroads. In: The Sociological Quarterly, 23, 107-123.

17. Powel, P. (1992) Beyond Networking: The Rise of the Nebulous Organisation. In: *European Management Journal*, Sep. 1992, Vol. 10, 3, 352-356.

18. Pugh, D., Hickson, D. & Hinings, C. (1988) Writers on Orga-nisations, 3rd ed., Penguin Books.

19. Reed, M. (1989) The Sociology of Management. Harvester Wheatsheaf.

20. Ritchie, B. & Marshall, D. (1993) Business Risk Management, Chapman and Hall.

21. Silverman, D. (1972) The Theory of Organisations: A Socio- logical framework. Heinemann, London.
22. The Oxford English Dictionary. (1989) 2nd ed., Vol. XV, Clarendon Press, Oxford.
23. Thompson, J. (1993) Strategic Management: Awareness and Change. 2nd ed., Chapman and Hall.
24. Thorne, P. (1992) Patent Remedies: Remedies for Organisational and Managerial Problems. In: *International Management*, July-August 1992, Vol. 47, 7, 72.
25. Todeva, E. (1991) Methodology for Situational Analysis of Work Organisations. Dissertation, awarded from Sofia University, Bulgaria.
26. Whyte, W. (1959) Interaction approach to the theory of organization. Wiley, N.Y.

NOTE:

In the original paper, the main blocks from the theoretical model are presented in details as an example of application of the proposed methodology. For a copy of the original paper, please, contact the author at the following address: Dr. Emanuela Todeva, South Bank Business School, IBL, South Bank University, 103 Borough Road, London SE1 0AA, tel: 071-815-8296, fax: 081-887-0188.

PENETRATING LARGE-SCALE ORGANISATIONS; A STUDENT/ PRACTITIONER PERSPECTIVE

Peter Elsmore, *South Bank Business School, London*

The paper addresses both empirically and theoretically the author's study of two large-scale organisations during a period of full-time research in 1992-1993. The concept of organisation culture is used as an opportunity to demonstrate the utility of postmodern methodologies. Discussion is made concerning why four other large scale groupings were not able to make themselves as available as those with members who did participate.

The sociological notion of counter-culture is borrowed as a helpful way of examining (understanding/explaining) some of the processes surrounding social-psychological and psycho-dynamic organisational activity.

The work concludes with a brief thought about research outcomes.

Full copies of the paper are available from:
Peter Elsmore, South Bank Business School, 103 Borough Road, London, SE1 0AA

DEALING WITH DISTANCE: CULTURAL BARRIERS IN INTERNATIONAL CONSULTANCY - A CASE STUDY

Dr.Richard A.Rooke. *South Bank Business School, London*

This paper addresses the problem of how the consultant, unlike the normal employee, needs to adapt to working for an organisation where access to normal channels of inter-relation are more difficult. Emphasis is placed on communication as a key to efficiency within group dynamics especially across the field of cultural barriers.

Full copies of the paper are available from:
Dr.Richard A.Rooke, South Bank Business School, 103 Borough Road, London, SE1 0AA

Session 2

WORKING IN ORGANISATIONS

The papers in this session were chosen to reflect the middle phase of working in consulting assignment. The range of papers and workshops reflected the different CONCEPTS, THEORIES, ETHICS, VALUES AND LANGUAGES used in consulting work. The dialogues presented were about the concepts of the unconscious, conscious systems, economics and business. An extension of these issues is the need for training, support, consultation or even therapy to help consultants withstand boundary stresses. The continuing debate is a concern about skills and competencies for meeting the demands of a professional working relationship.

None of these themes were answered fully, but the issues were encapsulated in the keynote lecture from **Larry Hirschhorn.** His paper, shows the personal, political, and professional elements that makes this work in organisations a vulnerable and exciting experience.

TRANSFERENCE, THE PRIMARY TASK AND THE PRIMARY RISK

Larry Hirschhorn, *Centre for Applied Research, Philadephia, USA*

INTRODUCTION

THE TRANSFERENCE

What do we mean by transference in organizational psychoanalysis and psychotherapy, we mean that the patient brings into the psychotherapeutic relationship, the quality and feel of his or her primary experiences of relating to other people. The patient then acts out these relationship as if the therapist were his or her parent, sibling and intimate friend.

In consultation, we say that the client brings to the consulting engagement, to the relationship with the consultant, the most salient experiences of his or her work, how difficult it is, how risky it is, how one collaborates with others to accomplish it. It is this focus on the nature of work that distinguishes consulting from psychotherapy.

In this paper I want to highlight certain propositions.

The client's transference and our response to it remain the bedrock of the consulting process.

Up until now we have relied on the concept of the primary task to help us link unconscious experience to the world of work. We ask in what ways does the work people concretely do, such as make loans, control a computer directed lathe or heal patients affect the content and quality of their unconscious life at work.

The concept of the primary task I will argue however, is not sufficient. As the social and economic environment itself becomes more turbulent, and people at all levels of the organization must help to shape and implement its strategy we must look at the organization developmentally and discover what I will call its primary risk, as opposed to its primary task shapes its members' experience. The primary risk is the core risk that animates the organization's strategy.

THE PRIMARY TASK AND THE TRANSFERENCE

Let me first explore the impact of the primary task with two examples from my consulting practice, foster care services, and a law firm.

Foster care workers, in my experience find group life and organizational functioning to be very difficult. For example, I have found that they are very reluctant to participate in large group discussions. To be sure, it is hard for people take up roles in large groups, but I found that foster care workers are the most inhibited group of human service workers I have worked with.

Moreover, when I work with foster care workers I often experience myself to be at the edge of some significant mistake. I worry that I will be left out, alone or rejected if I try to join them.

Using the transference enables us to construct three hypotheses about the client's experience. First, I am experiencing the case workers' feelings of being isolated and alone. Second as you will undoubtedly recognize the case worker has internalized and then projected onto me the feelings of the children they serve.

Third, looking at my experience as transference reveals a more subtle process and defense. Being alone is painful, but in light of one's despair being with other's can be even more painful. It is better to fragment your awareness and reject the group. I felt alone, because foster care workers feel to much pain when being together.

As this example suggests, the transference when effective as a tool of consulting renders experience whole but muted. This helps us understand our client's experience without having to cope with its full import. This is also the central character of empathy.

Let me give another example. Jim is the managing partner of a law firm that represents workers who are injured on the job, helping them get a good financial settlement from their employers.

Jim's problem appeared to be delegating. Another partner in the firm and Jim's assistant Joan, was eager to assume more responsibilities and felt that Jim was not allowing this. He supervised her too closely. I met with Jim and Joan together and with Jim separately. I experienced the meetings with the two of them as lively, and the meetings with Jim alone as lacking spontaneity. He appeared inhibited and I felt constricted. There was however no anger. '

Reporting on his progress at one session, as the result of the consultation, Jim said he felt ambivalent. While he had given Joan more authority there were still some responsibilities that he did not want to delegate to her or his other partners. He felt he had strong business and professional values to protect.

If we look at his communication as part of a psychotherapist encounter, we might interpret his as "resistance" to the consulting and as some reflection on his character.

But this is to confuse consulting with psychotherapy. Talking with Jim, I mentioned that clients sometimes reported their dreams to me. Jim then asserted that in his dreams about work he sees maimed bodies. In fact he must frequently decide which gruesome pictures of this clients he should present to a jury.

His unconscious work life is thus tied to visions of injured bodies. This suggests that his resistance is not just about his character but reflects as well the "silence of the dead" the experience of dismemberment that can render us mute.

I thereby gained a better understanding of his delegation difficulties. The close relationship Jim had with Joan in fact revitalized him in the face of an organization, which he noted, thrives on the basis of others suffering. Jim wanted Joan for himself not to control her but to stay alive emotionally. He did not delegate to her because he could not bear to be alone.

As these examples suggest, the transference gives us insight into how people experience their work at the unconscious level. Following in the Tavistock tradition we see how the organization's primary task, such as protecting neglected children or defending maimed clients, shapes people's experience, their transference, and our subsequent experience of their experience

THE PRIMARY RISK

I suggest however, that focusing on the primary task as a source of meaning of people's anxieties is limiting. An organization has two interdependent relationships to its environment: a relationships of exchange and a relationship of development. The relationshiop of exchange refers to how value is created by converting raw material or information into goods and services for customers. This indeed is the organization's primary task.

The relationshiop of development highlights the conscious or unconscious strategy leaders pursue to gain profit in an uncertain environment. Leader enact such a strategy by assuming a core risk, a risk that animates the vision of the organization. I call this risk, the organization's primary risk.

EXAMPLE OF WAL-MART

Wal-Mart, the huge US retailer provides an example here. It's primary task, its relationship of exchange, is to sell to as many people as possible, non customized, good quality and low-cost merchandise. Its primary risk however while related to the task, goes beyond it and can be discerned by examining Wal-Mart's founder Sam Walton and his animating strategy.

Walton took the risk of building big stores in small towns, a risk based on a vision of a growing rural America in the aftermath of World War Two; a rural America with an increasingly prosperous middle class and a developing interstate highway system. People would be increasingly willing to drive long distances for quality goods at a fair price. Walton conceptualized the environment in developmental terms and created a strategy that took advantage of emerging geographies, markets and opportunities.

In retrospect, this was a brilliant move; but at the time it entailed huge risks. Could small towns support big stores? What logistics would be involved? And so fourth. What is important here is to grasp that this primary risk is what animates the organization's vision and forward motion. The consulting challenge becomes to understand how this risk expresses the hopes and plans for the organization's future. and to use the transference to experience the emotional meaning of this risk.

RISK: DEFINITION AND AN EXAMPLE

Any risk has three dimensions, stakes, novelty and depth. Stakes refers to the financial exposure incurred by a particular risk. Novelty implies how unusual the risk is and depth suggests the moral dimension, the degree to which the risk evokes feelings of good and bad, truth and falsehood, what is valued or devalued. The greater the stakes, novelty and or depth, the more likely we consultants are to experience the character of the risk in the transference.

Let me give you an example of a risk's depth. Our team is currently working with the planning committee of a hospital trying to reduce its costs by 30 million a year by using a "quality process" meaning essentially, calculating the costs of every step and procedure, workload or system that can be imagined. The group is using a tight-fisted methodology to uncover and analyze inefficiencies. Members cannot improvise, nor rely on their intuition to jump ahead of the facts.

We could surmise that this quality process functioned as a useful social defense, helping people organize their thinking and interaction in an ongoing and controlled way. But if we are alert to the primary risk and its dimensions we can begin to discern the committee's anxiety and my reactions. At stake was a considerable sum of money and the redesign was novel; committee members had little to go on. But most importantly the risk's depth, its moral dimension was great.

The committee is composed of nurses and support professionals 80% of whom are women. While the climate of committee meetings is serious I also experienced the discussions as obsessive, as if imagination and creativity were not allowed. In one meeting I angrily defended the role of nurses as leaders in the restructuring of the hospital's delivery system. Yet my stance was greeted with silence and discomfort.

As I reviewed these dynamics I realized that gender was the issue. Nurses and support personnel, traditionally women, do not overtly presume leadership, but coax physicians and administrators, traditionally male, into changing their ways. So women assume postures of good soldiers rather than generals. What I responded to - the transference— was based on the limits women face in taking up the mantle of authority. My anger reflected the moral dimension, - the depth of the primary risk, female nurses and other staff "usurping" the leadership role of a traditionally male dominated institution.

WHAT DOES MANAGEMENT REALLY MEAN?[1]

HOW PSYCHO-ANALYTIC AND SYSTEMIC THINKING INTERACT TO ILLUMINATE THE MANAGEMENT OF INSTITUTIONS

Jean Hutton, John Bazalgette & David Armstrong
Grubb Institute, London

1 INTRODUCTION: Our underlying thesis

The thesis we will explore in this paper is that:

> *the effective management of any institution is built upon the principles that are generated from an understanding of the 'core technology' which that institution frames and the ways in which this technology interlinks with the experience of all those working with the institution, both from within and without.*

We define this 'core technology' as the primary process through which inputs are transformed into outputs, that together realise the purposes of the institution in its context.

During the two decades after the Second World War, Eric Trist and his colleagues at the Tavistock Institute of Human Relations demonstrated, in a series of pioneering studies of industrial organisations, that technological considerations alone were inadequate to determine organisational structure. Besides considering the machinery, attention always had to be given simultaneously to the human dimension, not simply as an independent variable, but as an integral part of what they termed a 'socio-technical system'. It was an understanding of this system which provided the only sure basis for 'organisational choice'.[2]

The interpenetration of human and technological dimensions becomes even more salient in service enterprises, where technology itself cannot be specified without reference to the complex interactions between the providers of services and the client or customer. In schools, hospitals, social agencies; but also in service industries generally and probably in most of the newer businesses working with soft technologies, the primary process driving the enterprise will always involve attention to and interpretation of human exchange.

It is this process which underpins and defines the core technology of the enterprise. Our hypothesis is that this process is not self evident' it requires discernment. We suggest that the act of discernment takes place as managers bring into view and reflect of what we call the **organisation-in-the-mind.** By this we mean the mental picture of the institution in its context which is informing the managers' experience, shaping their behaviour and influencing their working relations, both overtly and covertly.

The task of management evolves from this act of discernment. That task can be stated as being to create the conditions which support, maintain, adapt and if necessary transform the primary process so as to deliver desired outcomes. Management is effective to the extent that it defines the process, recruits the resources (human, physical and financial), develops structures and practice and provides leadership, in ways which define and optimise these conditions for carrying out the purpose of the institution.

It follows that ideas about management derived from other contexts (eg financial management from business applied to running a university or a hospital) must always be scrutinised and assessed in terms of their goodness of fit with the institution's core technology. In recognising this particular quality, we have called it **'X-generated management'**, where X equals the combination of ideas, ethos, skills and values of a particular profession, be it medicine, education, business, the church, probation and so on.

Without awareness of the embedded principles of the core technology, consultancy aims at bringing about organisation change, strategic development, new role definitions, appraisal methods or installing new performance indicators may tear the heart out of the original raison d'être of an institution, leaving it lifeless rather than capable of making its hoped for new contribution to its context (customer, market, users, owners or even society as a whole).

2 TWO BASIC PERSPECTIVES

We present here a line of work and thought which is still in progress but which we have been developing with our colleagues at The Grubb Institute for some ten years or so. The origins of this work stem from applying the approach to understanding organisations and their management which was first opened up by the Tavistock Institute referred to above.

This approach brings together and seeks to integrate two perspectives on human behaviour in organisations:

> **psychoanalysis** and in particular a psychoanalytic approach to understanding experiences in groups.

> **open systems theory** as developed in the United States, and first applied to organisational thinking in Eric Trist's studies of coal mining.

One of the contributions that we have valued from those Tavistock pioneers is Ken Rice's way of describing an institution diagrammatically, drawing a boundary around its activities which separate them from the context, and then systematically investigating its inputs, conversion processes and outputs[3]. This enables the institution to be visualised in a dynamic relation with its environment.

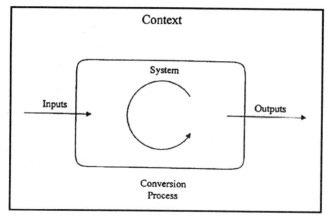

Diagram 1: System in context, illustrating interactions with its context

By applying this model rigorously a variety of key issues come into view which are responsive to both psychoanalytic and systemic understanding of institutions and the ways in which they interact with their contexts. This will be more fully explored later in this paper, but the significant point to note is Rice's formulation of management as a function on the boundary, monitoring and influencing the transactions inwards and outwards. The significance of this conception of management will emerge later in this paper.

Whilst psychoanalysis and open systems thinking have had an uneasy relation to each other, we believe that both continue to be fundamental to an adequate understanding of organisational life, its dilemmas and challenges. Indeed the tension between them creates a dynamic which is fertile for developing new understanding.

The psychoanalytic approach is fundamental to a recognition of the **centrality and significance of emotional experience** in all human endeavour, both at a conscious and unconscious level. What the systemic approach contributes is a recognition of the essential **inter-relatedness of emotional experience.** On this view, emotional experience is not bounded by one's own individual skin, is not the property of the individual alone. Rather, it is bounded by the system or systems in which individuals interact - in collaboration or in conflict - with each other and with their context.

3   THE ORGANISATION-IN-THE-MIND

The Grubb Institute's characteristic way of working is to engage in a collaborative relationship with client organisations. From this collaboration, thoughts emerge about the issues being addressed. Both client and consultant have these thoughts, which are stimulated by working together within the framework of the client's system(s) and which get applied in practice in the way the client works, develops structures or manages the organisation.

The consultant's method - known as **Organisational Role Analysis (ORA)** - is an analytic one which seeks to bring into view to both parties in the working relationship, the organisation-in-the-mind of the client. In this phrase we refer to the way the client patterns in their mind the realities of the organisation, patterning them in ways which give expression to the emotional realities present in the experience of the client and in the organisation, indicating where the client is drawing the organisation's boundaries and what the nature of its interactions with its context are about. Some of those realities may be overt but others - often the most influential ones - are not obvious to consultant or to client. Clues to some of these are often embedded in the way the client describes a critical incident, where feelings indicate assumptions about role, system and purpose which may not be immediately apparent to either participant in the consultant/client relationship.

The consultant works to share the experience of the client's emotional reality. From this, access is given to the primary process of the institution in its context through participation in the consultant/client relationship. This cannot be discovered from 'outside' but emerges from the experience within the institution, which is communicated to the consultant through a process comparable to transference in psychoanalysis.

In parenthesis here we need to note a distinction from much other psychoanalytically oriented work with organisations which has been largely concerned to emphasise and uncover defensive structures: mechanisms through which the organisation and its members defend against anxieties generated by the nature of the work and/or its social setting. By contrast the focus of ORA is rather on emotional experience as disclosing the heart of the matter: what is essentially involved in carrying out the organisation's task, whether acknowledged or not.

To borrow a telling phrase from the British psychoanalyst, Christopher Bollas, what the patterning of emotional experience gives access to is something known but unthought[4]. In turn the formulation of the 'unthought known' discloses what we are terming the 'primary process' - the core technology of this organisation now. Once this is formulated, options for managing come into view which were previously inconceivable or at least 'unconceived'. The formulation itself, once articulated, may seem obvious: its importance is that the change of perspective it opens up contains new possibilities, often transforming threats into opportunities, causing existing resources to be re-evaluated, and leading to the reassessment of relationships. Perhaps most importantly of all it means that authority and power are construed in new ways.

Most of the findings we will outline in this paper have emerged from ORA sessions held with a Chief Executive on a one-to-one basis over a period of time lasting four months or more. However, we have also developed ways of discerning the client's organisation-in-the-mind and in its emotional realities through working with groups of managers.

It is these studies of experience within bounded social and organisational space, and how they interact with their environment that constitutes the raw material we want to explore and illustrate in this paper.

Managing an open system is the activity of regulating transactions across the boundaries between the internal world of the system and its contexts; carrying out the regulation of these transactions in such a way as to create the optimum conditions both for the system's survival and for its development in a changing and often turbulent environment. Effective management is about the survival and development of the system in relation to the purposes and values it embodies and strives to realise in its context

Given that institutions exist not for their own good but because they serve purposes in society, which will differ depending upon the differing needs of society - creating wealth, governing justly, preparing future generations, curing the sick or despatching the deceased - the activities by which each system relates to its context will correspondingly vary. Hence it follows that, while there may be some very general principles of boundary management which can be observed in all systems, the significant differences between the purposes of systems mean that those principles cannot in themselves lead us to a usable general theory of management which applies across the board.

4   INTRODUCING 'GENERATED MANAGEMENT'

In our view, management and the experience of managing need always to be seen and understood in relation to the particular process which an institution frames through its corporate interactions with the context. This arises not simply from the mechanical factors (nor financial or statutory ones) but from the key human interactions within the institution which enable its members to realise the purposes (overt or covert) given to it from the context within which it exists. For example, in a school, the myriad day by day interactions between teachers and pupils in classrooms, assembly halls, laboratories, gymnasia, playgrounds and corridors, together express a process which relates to and depends on that school and its context. This will embody intentions, knowledge, values and skills which are distinct to schooling, or more exactly to **this** school in **this** context here and now. But at the same time intentions, knowledge, values and skills do not by themselves **define** the process, which develops rather from the dynamic human exchanges which are in practice determining the quality of the school's outputs: the difference it is making to the education and development of children as pupils. It is the identification of this process which establishes the 'core technology', and it is establishing that technology (for the time being, since circumstances and contexts do not remain constant) which sets the management agenda.

We have come to describe this approach to managing a core technology as **'generated management'** - business generated management, school generated management, church generated management and so on.

The principle behind 'generated management' is that management in any professional field grows from an understanding of what it is that underlies **existing best practice at the point of service delivery**, the point at which the contradictory demands of the stakeholders/employers/customers/society/parents/children/ taxpayers/doctors/patients and so on - are in practice reconciled and prioritised. The act which delivers the service between provider and recipient is what Jan Carlzon, when President of Scandinavian Airlines System, called the **moment of truth**[5].

While one can, as a result of study, begin to develop some general guide-lines, in truth the requirements of management can only be fully understood when applied to a single example: **this** company, **this** school, **this** hospital and so on. One can draw abstractions from examples of similar institutions, but these will indicate what to look for rather than something to be imposed. This has important implications for the practice both of management and consultancy, which we now turn to and illustrate.

5   THREE CASE STUDIES

The examples we propose to explore here are drawn from work done by one or other of the Institute's staff during the last two years. In the first two examples the method used was mainly individual ORAs with key executives and managers. In the third the principles of ORA have been used within events for groups of managers in a conference method called 'Working with Experience'. In all three we are still in client relations with them and new understandings continue to unfold as work develops.   In ORA work the consultant attends carefully to the feelings experienced in the working relations with the client. The reason for this is that the method is designed to enable the client to surface in these sessions the emotional experience of being in his or her place of work. The way those experiences are transferred to the consultant provides data for interpreting what the primary process might be that the client is managing.

In the first case study, one of us had worked with the chief executive and the unit managers of a body responsible for managing psychiatric provision for convicted offenders, whose dangerous behaviour is related to mental conditions which require treatment under high security conditions.

The second is a college responsible for the education of those over 16 and who have left the school system, in an inner city area which has always scored highly in any ratings of deprivation including violence (especially related to racist attacks) and urban decay. For many years the college has been a focus of attention in the world of further education and has recently been grappling with the transfer from local authority control to incorporation under the control of its own Board of Governors and the Further Education Funding Council (FEFC).

Our third example is drawn from work we are doing with the aviation industry, based at Heathrow Airport. Although this is still in the early stages and therefore more speculative, we include it here to show how the theme of generated management has application in a rather different, more commercially oriented organisational context.

5.1   CASE STUDY 1: FORENSIC PSYCHIATRIC INSTITUTIONS

The social and political context

The work of these institutions involves the provision of psychiatric care for patients convicted of serious, often violent offences, where there exists an inescapable tension between the claims of security and those of treatment. For a number of years they have been the responsibility of a statutory authority set up to manage them and with a remit to introduce a broad programme of change designed to enhance the primacy of therapeutic goals. In reality, the hospitals concerned are subject to pervasive and deeply ambivalent public attitudes, which make the task of managing them perilously difficult.

On one hand they are seen as places of confinement for mentally disturbed but dangerous offenders, who represent a potential threat to the public at large, both in reality and symbolically. From this perspective the boundary between special hospitals and context is conceived of as if it were physically impermeable, containing the threat felt by the public. On the other hand they are expected to treat and care for such offenders with humanity and dignity, offering hope of bringing about change which will enable offenders eventually to be discharged into the community. Viewed in terms of the boundary conditions, the institution's boundary is here seen as permeable after rehabilitation has taken place.

These public attitudes are not necessarily inconsistent. Nonetheless it is striking how, over time and in a kind of cyclical pattern, such hospitals will be blamed, sometimes simultaneously - not always by the same people but often enough by the same media - both for releasing patients into the community who then commit violence or cause hurt to themselves and to others, and for inhumane treatment in retaining patients who should be released.

In the course of this work, we were, as one would expect, made aware of a number of differences between our clients in the ways in which the issues of management and leadership were being tackled. These differences had to do mainly with differences in style, rather than with the organisational constructs involved, and also with the respective weight given by different people to the management and leadership components of the job.

However, these differences were less significant than the similarities.

About half way through the work with the chief executive he wrote a 'Working Summary on Key Issues Identified' as an aide memoire for himself. It was striking how many of the themes he had listed reappeared in the issues and experiences recounted by the unit managers themselves in their ORAs: the experience of 'isolation and vulnerability' (a theme we will return to later); the communication of mission; the relation of management to clinical goals; devolution and the tension between centre and periphery; corporate accountability at unit level; the relations of operational and functional management; how to measure progress; and how to counter resistances to change.

The implication to be drawn from this was that anyone who had management and leadership responsibility for a whole unit - either in the Authority overall or one of the constituent hospitals - was encountering similar dilemmas, challenges or opportunities. The difference was simply in the boundary within the system for which they were responsible.[6]

Perhaps this was not surprising. But what it seemed to indicate was something about the commonality of the internal and external forces with which all general managers in the hospitals were having to deal. Could one identify more clearly the nature of this commonality? If so, were there pointers for the ways in which the

Authority and its units were addressing policy, strategy, structures, development and change?

The dynamics of change

At one level one could argue that what was common to general management in the Authority was a reflection of the dynamics of change on which the Authority had embarked since its inception. This fundamentally involved a two-fold transformation of an existing culture.

One intended change was from a culture of confinement and control to a culture of care and treatment. The other was from a culture of dependence to a culture of autonomy, where the accent was on devolution of responsibility, integration of tasks and aims and accountability for results.

Much of the work we did with the managers had been concerned with their understanding of these dynamics of change and how to effect it in the face of a variety of resistances: historic, structural and cultural. The analysis of those resistances, both overt and covert; and how to address the need for change in a way that enabled staff to take ownership of this for themselves, preoccupied the early sessions, without always appearing to take things further.

The fundamental challenge

There was, however, quite a different thread from the challenge of change which ran throughout the work, though it related to it. This concerned the very nature of the job that these hospitals do and are charged by society with doing. In the Chief Executive's aide memoire, referred to earlier, one theme identified had been, as he put it, "isolation/vulnerability of the Chief Executive, particularly in an organisation which has no counterparts and in an organisation which is new with high profile and ambitious aims".

In responding to this aide memoire at the time, the consultant had speculated "how far are you focusing on feelings which are more widespread throughout this organisation? Seen in that way, could your own experiences of isolation and vulnerability be understood as part and parcel of being in touch with the life of the organisation?".

In fact, all of the managers we worked with, from time to time, communicated similar feelings from their position. Events which happened over this period, including a widely reported public enquiry, contributed to this undertow of vulnerability. There were sessions with managers in which, in different ways, work on this aspect of their experience wholly preoccupied us.

We were also aware of the number of occasions when sessions had to be cancelled or postponed because of illness. It could be said that vulnerability is an occupational hazard in the management of institutions which are both highly sensitive and, when things go wrong, susceptible to public criticism and anger. The experiences reported by the managers could simply be seen as a personal response to this reality, and be understood as an example of occupational stress.

But such an explanation missed something which came more clearly into view as the consultant became aware of the feelings of vulnerability aroused in **himself** in the presence of his clients. It was as if one were caught up in a pervasive emotional undertow, which was more than a matter of the particular exigencies of one's own role.

At some stage during the consultations the consultant looked up 'vulnerable' in Webster's Dictionary. It is defined as 'capable of being wounded; liable to injury or criticism; subject to being affected injuriously or attacked'. To be in a special hospital at all, it then occurred to him, whether as patient or staff, is to put oneself in a position that **exposes oneself to being vulnerable, in just this sense**.

Moreover, the reason patients are committed to such hospitals in the first place is precisely because their behaviour has in turn exposed or exploited the vulnerability of others. (We recognise of course that in many instances this may have involved the patients' **own** feelings of vulnerability, projected into their 'victims'.)

Seen from this perspective, the managers' experiences of feeling isolated and vulnerable could be understood as registering in themselves an emotional experience that was part and parcel of the life of the organisation as a whole; that arose out of and in turn illuminated the very nature of the task upon which **all** members of the organisation were engaged, staff and patients alike. As such these experiences were not so much an 'occupational hazard' as the raw material for work: work on the process given to the organisation by society.

We could express this more paradoxically by saying that if the chief executive and his managers were **not** in touch with such experiences in themselves, they would, and by the same token the organisation would, **really be** both isolated and vulnerable. Indeed, it gradually became clearer to us that it was precisely when our clients were not alert to these feelings in themselves that their judgements were most questionable and most questioned, by themselves as much as by others.

Correspondingly, the monitoring of these experiences and their fluctuations within oneself, could be seen as a central aspect of the practice of management and leadership, of keeping in touch and of being in touch.

On a broader view, this perspective opened up a new interpretation of the emotional reality which underlies what these hospitals do and are charged with doing. **This could be aptly described as the process of 'managing vulnerability', (more exactly of managing the experiences of being vulnerable oneself and of making others vulnerable): in the relations of patients to themselves and to others; in the relations of staff to patients, and of staff to staff.**

Recognition of this reality in turn enabled the issues of change, ownership and accountability which had set the management agenda of these institutions to be seen in a new light. The challenge for management and leadership could now be restated as 'how do I in my role act in a way which enables and supports staff in containing and working creatively with experiences of vulnerability in their day to day practice in the wards?' And 'how do I work across the boundary of the institution to enable the public at large, through its stakeholders, to acknowledge, give value to, and shoulder the responsibilities and risks of such a task?' The problem that is raised is that the more changes that were brought about, the greater the risks that staff had to carry.

There are several implications of this recognition. What we identified was not a great flash of new insight: it was the recognition of something that had always been present within the relations between the hospitals and their environment but which became reframed in a different way. This showed that resistances to change may not be due to a failure to adapt, but were more likely to be based on a deep-seated understanding of what was really at stake. As government initiated changes were introduced - for example purchaser-provider models of resourcing or performance indicators - they were most likely to be effective in supporting staff if they were related to managing vulnerability.

If evidence of vulnerability is seen as something to be got rid of or denied, the emotional experience will go underground, become exacerbated and erupt in less manageable forms. If change is introduced from outside, say by government, without a proper appreciation of how the experience of vulnerability is being worked with at all levels of the organisation, the place where the reactions to it will be most likely to surface will be amongst the patients - and their characteristic response is to react dangerously to the experience.

Those in authority in special hospitals have to find ways of handling relations with external authorities which enable them to take back responsibility for working with these elements in society.

5.2   CASE STUDY 2: AN INNER CITY COLLEGE OF FURTHER EDUCATION

The Context since the 1960s

The college with which we worked has evolved from the steady combination of various technical colleges in an East London borough over the last twenty years or so. The population of the borough is largely immigrant, having arrived as if they had floated up the Thames. It is an area which has traditionally hosted such people: economic and political migrants, refugees, sailors who jumped ship and so on. The old style cockneys are now in the minority and feel it. Since successful people have generally climbed out of the area, those remaining convey a feeling of being stuck and depressed in their stuckness.

The docks which gave the area a historic sense of significance, have closed down, leaving behind a pervasive air of dereliction and decay. The towers of the City of London, especially the Natwest Tower, tell of the existence of international business. Though the Big Bang meant that some of the sharpness of cockney traders could be used on the dealing floors, those without that bounce or with the 'wrong coloured skin' or gender did not see the City as a place of opportunity.

Not surprisingly the local authority was one of left wing persuasion, with a sense of responsibility for those of its citizens whom it saw as depressed or deprived. In its various institutions and services - schools, colleges, youth service, social services and housing - the local politicians sought to compensate for the difficulties that were manifest wherever they looked. Faced with the policies of central government over recent years, the authority had been squeezed and driven into a corner.

The consequence of these different factors was that an atmosphere existed within the borough of low self esteem both at the personal and the corporate level.

Response

In the 1970s the College recognised the pain and depression amongst the local people, including the 16-year olds leaving the borough's schools and the adult population. Seeing the waning employment opportunities, staff set out to create conditions that would compensate for that loss and respond to the apparent needs of the marginalised people who lived in the borough. Within its structure, the College set up groups of unemployed people, support groups for refugees from war-torn countries, crèches, single parents groups, lesbian and gay groups, and so on. There were a range of courses being run, but these did not necessarily lead to qualifications, nor to progress on to higher education, nor to employment. This did not imply that nothing was happening in respect of such progress, but the raison d'être of the college became one of care and nurture rather than one of gaining qualification and advancement through teaching and learning.

The College and its then-Principal won a reputation for imaginative and dedicated work in such a setting. Given the circumstances, the demands and the assumptions of the time, this was probably well deserved.

Change

The massive development of Docklands resulted in the Canary Wharf Tower and all the associated buildings pushing their way onto the horizon. The Docklands Light Railway changed the transport situation. The City Airport brought a totally new form of transport into the heart of the area. The debate about the Channel Tunnel rail route suggested that the borough might be chosen for a major transport development. The 'East Thames Industrial Corridor' began to be talked about. However the depression of the late 80s meant that the expected boom in employment which could have justified the disruption to this environment (housing, transport and the sense of community) remained unrealised. To some extent the slow pace fed a feeling amongst members of the community of intrusion and cynicism about whether there was anything for them in this brave new world.

At the same time, a new Principal was appointed to take over from his retiring predecessor. He was alert to the growing demands of the changing context and also aware that the existing culture of care and nurture meant that the College had been massively overspending during previous years. He set out to discover the facts and found that there was much looseness in the financial controls of the college, as well as a substantial number of things happening that could not be justified as 'educational activities'. The sums of money that had been spent, with little accountability either for the College's budgeted income or for identifiable outcomes, were very large indeed. The College had become a kind of spreading chestnut tree, under which anyone could come to rest for as long as they liked, a tree that went on growing without regard to its financial cost.

As the Principal began to seek out ways of tackling the financial and professional problems he was faced with, legislation was passed taking colleges out of the control of local education authorities and placing them under the centrally funded Further Education Funding Council, which would allocate resources in direct relation to students served. Its governors now became more clearly accountable for what happened in the College. In terms of management the governors had a real responsibility to take up their role in the boundary of the institution.

The Grubb Institute began a programme of work with an individual Organisational Role Analysis for the Principal a few months after he had taken over the post. He had heard about ORA but he was sceptical about how he might be helped. However he was concerned enough to begin the consultation process, analysing his experience in his role in the College. After several sessions for himself, he persuaded the Chair of Governors to begin an ORA on her own account and, in due course, also involved the new Executive Team through a 'Working with Experience' Conference. This work supported the Principal as he went through a period of attacking the problems of the overspend, identifying its extent, how it had come about and how to deal with the consequences. He also thought out and established a new organisational structure which reduced the overall staffing, changed the profile of top management through careful, professional selection from inside and outside the College, and set about creating a new culture and image for the College.

Managing Poor Self Image

Through this work, consultant and client developed an analysis, collaboratively worked at, of the primary process that was being carried out day by day through the College. This emerged as a result of investigating the college as a system in its context and also reflecting upon the Principal's experience of working within it.

In reflecting upon the history of the College over recent years, the Principal and the consultant came to the conclusion that a common thread lay at the heart of the management of this College, both in its former time and in its present state. The borough and its people over time had acquired what could be described as a poor self-image. The area's loss of the economic and commercial base of the past; hosting people who have come into the country short of money, driven out of countries by oppression, poverty, famine or civil war; with the local public authorities under criticism and pressure from a central government radically at odds with local politics; all these meant that the College existed in a context where self image was low individually and corporately.

As the ORA sessions progressed and the Principal began to tackle the issue that confronted him, he described the way he was being perceived by segments of the college staff: in particular he was described as heartless, calculating, a hatchet-man acting for others with little understanding of the immense needs of the students. Whereas he was doing the best he could to address the dire situation that confronted the college and, while he did not accept these descriptions as being real, he could not help wondering whether there might be some truth in what was being said of him. At the same time the consultant himself experienced a sense of not being up to the job in hand, not having the intellectual capacities and the grasp of government policy and its administration that seemed to be required.

Thus the client and the consultant, in ways relevant to their own responsibilities, both experienced a poor self-image. They both found themselves challenged to resist being controlled by that self-image, to manage it rather than be managed by it. As this was identified, the consultant realised that it gave a clue to the nature of the College's primary purpose.

In the earlier phase, the College had failed to manage the boundary with the community and had allowed itself to be captured by that culture and to become saturated with it. It was remarked that staff became like the students in dress and attitude. Progressively they became as dependent as those they were there to serve. As evidence about the overspend of previous years accumulated, there were those who argued that the dire deprivation of the population justified, even sanctioned, such profligacy. As a result poor self-image was as unmanaged as were the finances and educational performance.

In the latter phase, poor self image amongst potential students has been faced up to. It has been seen as a motivator to raise people's performance. "Men and women - if you feel unqualified, unable to progress, want a better job than you have, could raise your income if you could gain skills which you can put to use in the economy - then this College has something to offer you".

As the College responds to the new opportunities of commerce, travel, industries that have seedlings in the borough, the borough's image of itself can begin to be enhanced. "Employers, if you want to hire modern, skilled workers, the College can supply them. If you want advice about engineering, management, personnel training and business, you don't need to go outside the borough; what you need is already on your own doorstep."

In this way, **managing in this College can be seen as managing poor self-image.** This means tackling the self-image of those who come as students carrying with them real social burdens. It requires that the staff, under criticism from central government and elsewhere, face that criticism frankly and courageously. It means that the local community itself, with its national reputation, begins to address rather than to exploit poor self-image. Since a college of further education in an inner city area exists to contribute to its local community in exactly this way, this work lies at the heart of its core technology.

5.3   EXAMPLE 3: THE AVIATION INDUSTRY[7]

Our final example is deliberately more speculative. In the last year we have been working with companies in the aviation industry that use Heathrow Airport[8]. We have been developing approaches to raising the quality of management exercised by first line supervisors across the airport. This is to enable the work done by the teams that serve the customers through their direct activity, to be transformed to world class standards. We have used a model we call a 'Working with Experience' Conference to apply ORA principles. The work is still at an early stage and we have much to learn.

As we have engaged with the aviation companies (including carriers and the airport itself), working with men and women who run baggage handling teams, teams of engineers servicing planes, load control staff, members of the fire service, telephone sales staff, cargo handlers and accountants, there appears to be a thread which runs through all their work.

It is evident that the aviation industry works within a culture which of its nature, is characterised by unpredictability. Changes in weather, mechanical faults, human error, overload, anxious passengers, sickness, security alerts, industrial relations issues and volatile economic conditions - combine to make the setting within which people work one which is subject to constant changes of plan, sometimes of a radical nature and with very short notice. These changes cannot individually be planned for and hence cannot be 'managed' in a conventional sense, but sudden changes permeate the whole working environment. In our experience we have not previously encountered such high levels of unpredictability as a basic fact of life in an industry and this has been corroborated by other consultants.

In carrying out this project, we have been faced with constant changes often at very short notice, especially last minute changes of availability. Within the events, those of us staffing the courses have experienced powerful pressures to change our plans (which we have resisted). One of us has said that he was reminded of his experience of being a front row forward at rugby who has three yards to make to the try-line and most of the opposing pack in his way: conviction about what must be achieved has produced the determination and impetus to cover the ground and achieve results against the opposing forces.

Managing the interaction between stability and turbulence

Our current hypothesis is that the thread running through the aviation industry is about managing the interaction between stability and turbulence so that the result is creative. In all cases that we have studied so far, it is evident that employees in the industry are seeking to create a setting for customers which is tranquil and secure, in which they are shielded from the impact of the unpredictable factors which surround them. On arrival at check-in, those being attended to are handled by a staff member who works calmly and methodically, while other passengers stand back behind a mark on the floor; the transition from 'land-side' to 'air-side' is a tightly controlled boundary crossing; there are departure lounges; passengers are separated from flying staff and so on.

As we have thought about this we have realised that the forces which keep an aircraft in the air are forces which come into play as stability (a wing) comes into a dynamic relation with turbulence (the effect of passing through the air at speed). The aircraft flies because of this dynamic engagement between stability and turbulence, and it flies effectively because the interaction is 'managed' by the pilot's skill.

This has led us to the formulation that **management in this industry is that which creates the conditions where managing the dynamic interaction between stability and turbulence is constantly kept in view.** It is this 'management' which enables passengers to feel safe and to trust themselves and their possessions to the carrier. It may be far fetched: after all this is a physical conception, but for the present it provides a way of thinking which takes us beyond some of the simplistic notions about 'customer care' which flood the industry at the moment, ignoring this reality. Evidence from our most recent work on this programme indicates that effective customer care in this industry entails being able to know what a company can **guarantee** to deliver under these prevailing conditions and to be frank with customers about that. To quote the distinguished Chief Executive of Scandinavian

Airlines System, this is the type of management which sustains and relies on "the moment of truth" between customer and service deliverer[9].

What this means for managers is that each of them must take into themselves the experience of the turbulence and its interactions with the stability and manage that relation inside themselves. If they split the two apart - which is the natural psychological defence against the stress of their relatedness - the latent anxiety of the passengers will immediately be triggered into consciousness. This will result in apparently excessive, indeed apparently irrationally high reactions. Cases have been reported to us where there have been almost violent scenes over what are in themselves simple things; the availability of trolleys, the slowness of information to appear on information boards, the discovery of un-emptied ash trays in an executive jet, and so on. For the traveller, who is naturally apprehensive at this mode of travel with its inevitable risks, these may be signals of other underlying problems, anxiety about which can be triggered to the surface.

6   SOME IMPLICATIONS FOR THINKING ABOUT MANAGEMENT

Thinking about the 'organisation-in-the-mind' is work still in progress. The three case studies we have explored have been of specific institutions or groups of interacting institutions within one business. As our future work develops in these and other areas, we would hope to extend our understanding across a broader range of organisations and contexts. It is implicit, however, in the stance we have taken, that such understanding is always linked to what is specific.

In this sense there can be no generic basis for organisational consultancy, no reservoir of organisational 'say how' that is universally applicable. One always consults to the particular case: indeed to the particular **human** case. Consultancy in this sense is a 'positional' discipline.

Thinking about 'generated management' is also work in progress. There are other fields of professional specialism in which The Grubb Institute has worked in the past which have been subjected to substantial change in recent years: the probation and prison services are two examples; business, voluntary organisations, schools and churches are others. In all of these we are seeking ways to conceptualise how the **characteristic** processes in each field are managed so as to ensure that the human realities underlying those processes have priority. This is especially true for human service organisations, where the temptation under the present political climate in schools, hospitals, and even churches, appears to be to seek out prevailing principles (especially financial ones) that will supersede the complex, qualitative, work of attention and interpretation. Professional businesses such as partnerships of accountants and solicitors are also having to address what 'management' means in their institutions[10], in particular examining what is involved in managing the boundaries across which the inputs and outputs pass.

Though we still have much to learn there are, nonetheless, some implications arising from these ideas which we can tentatively advance now. We recognise that in a political climate based on the assumption that 'privatisation' provides the ingredient that will raise the effectiveness of many public services, what we say will have political implications. We also recognise that the current calls in the UK to go 'back to basics' and to return to 'family values', which seem to us to be the political response to a human dynamic perceived to be at work in society, have thrown up problems for the British government. To us this is evidence that to take human realities seriously is not to be done without disciplined understanding of what one is getting oneself into.

We have written this paper to open up a new perspective on professional thinking about managing. If we are on the right lines, we may be able to offer a way to achieve some of the best of what is sought by the various advocates of change. What is central to our thinking is that if the propositions we advance are taken seriously, when shifts and changes take place in economic and social conditions, the details of managers' behaviour will need to be construed in a different light. This is especially true when those factors such as finance, the law and conventional 'wisdom' are commonly treated as determinants of what happens and how managers think, without any critical reflection. Yet, just as Trist and his colleagues showed that the physical and technical environment were not wholly determinant of what happens in the work place, we believe that we have demonstrated that neither are finance, law, or 'business' sense.

The propositions we would like to advance for testing are these.

- *Management which is effective in releasing the resources of men and women (and children in such places as schools) engaged within a system is management which is homologous[11] with the system's primary process.*

- *The challenge posed by our first proposition is how to create the structures which enable that primary process to come into view at all levels of the institution. By 'structures' we mean not simply those things reflected in an organisational diagram but anything through which the organisational processes are channelled and realised: for example, remuneration and benefit systems, communication methods, record keeping practices, induction procedures.*

- *The main obstacle to keeping the primary process in view is the assumption that finance and administration in themselves provide the best indicators of effectiveness, rather than their providing only some of the evidence about the process itself and the fulfilment of the professional purposes of the institution in its environment.*

- *Understanding the emotional experience of living and working within an institution is key to understanding what its primary process is and what has be done to manage it.*

- *The fact that in every kind of institution work on aims, purposes, missions and core values are virtually all-pervading, suggests that there is a general search going on for the primary processes of institutions. We are suggesting that the line of thinking we have outlined here opens up the possibility of taking such work much deeper by analysing **all** the realities with which the institution works, including especially the emotional realities.*

> *To the extent that the primary process can be identified and articulated, managers at all levels can use the fine-grain of their experience - in our examples their feelings of vulnerability, low self-image or managing stability within turbulence - as being central to their work, not peripheral or self-indulgent. By treating their experience in context seriously, they will find themselves connected to others within the organisation in surprising ways, ways which will otherwise be hard to tackle. This will release the currently untapped resources of its staff.*

We began by outlining a thesis that emotional experience in the institutions we have been working with was the clue to identifying their primary processes, to identifying the organisation-in-the-mind of the client and what the management is that is generated from the key interactions within it and across its boundaries. In our three case studies we have indicated that the relation across the institution's boundaries to its context was vital to understanding a system's primary purpose. To work with one's experience in such a way as to understand a relation to context and to understand what the institution is being used for, requires skill, a skill that is not yet necessarily present in many human series organisations that have been subject to radical change. To the extent that the managers of a system do not have the skill to work at understanding the institution's relation to the context, they become prisoners of that context: they will not then be able to work with statements of aim that define the organising principle upon which their institution is functioning because, just like the teachers in the college, they cannot understand what they and their clients are embroiled in.

This leads us to continue to recognise more clearly that the principle behind 'generated management' is that managing in any professional field grows from understanding and relating two things to each other:

> *The **management of the core technology** of the institutions; in a school it is the education of children; in a hospital, the treatment of the sick; in a prison the secure containment and rehabilitation of prisoners; in a residential institution, the care of the handicapped or the aged.*

> ***Managing the factors which influence and impact upon the core technology;*** *in particular managers need to understand the emotional and value based factors as they manage the state of the system.*

The former is about the internal world of the system and the activities which transform its inputs into its outputs. The latter is about the interface between the system and its context, the elements of which are embedded in the experience of the men and women (and children) who move in and out of the system day by day. The effective management of the institution handles the interface at the outer boundary, identifying what these are, what they mean for the running of the institution and how they might be handled. Leadership within the institution involves demonstrating to colleagues in practice and behaviour how the interface is handled by individual human beings within themselves and in their own experiences.

We have explored these ideas from different angles. We currently take the view that in a world which has gone 'management mad', where 'management' has been assumed to be the practices used by business and industry to manage its affairs.

What has happened has been the covert introduction of practices that are at odds with what is really required to manage most organisations, practices incapable of handling the human realities which are both part of the primary process and of the context within which the process takes place. This is even true of some businesses! Our prediction is that, unless the primary process and core technology are central to the thought processes of managers and enable them to work with their experience, the work for which the institution was originally set up will suffer. We have a sense that unless some of the political initiatives which bear on the cases discussed above are 'managed' in the light of the realities set out in this paper, the longer term effects of present policies will be to reduce the quality of work done corporately.

The ideas of 'generated management' and 'the organisation-in-the-mind' offer a way forward. Consultants have a part to play in enabling quality to be enhanced in institutions, but it is managers and executives in post who make the real difference.

REFERENCES

Bollas C, 1987, The Shadow of the Object: Psychoanalysis of the Unthought Known, Free Association Books London.

Carlzon J, 1989, The Moment of Truth, Harper & Row.

Emery F E, 1974, Freedom and Justice Within Walls, Tavistock Publications.

Emery F E & Trist E L, 1960, 'Socio-technical systems' in Churcham C W & Verhulst M (eds), Management Sciences, Pergamon.

Hirschhorn L, 1990, The Workplace Within, MIT Press.

Miller E J & Gwynne G V, 1974, A Life Apart, Tavistock Publications.

Rice A K, 1963, The Enterprise and its Environment: A system theory of management organisation, Tavistock Publications.

Scholes K, 1994, Strategic Management in Professional Service Organisations, Sheffield Business School.

Trist E L & Bamforth W, 1951, 'Some social and psychological consequences of the long-wall method of cost-getting', Human Relations 4.

NOTES

[1]   Earlier forms of this paper have been delivered to seminars in Australia, one to the Faculty of Business at Swinburne University of Technology, Melbourne and another to an audience of senior executives invited to the occasion by KPMG Peat Marwick, Sydney

[2]   See for example, Trist E L & Bamforth W, 'Some social and psychological

consequences of the long-wall method of coal-getting' **Human Relations 4,** 1951; Emery F E & Trist E L 'Socio-technical systems' in Churcham C W & Verhulst M (eds), **Management Sciences,** Pergamon 1960; Rice A K **The Enterprise and its Environment: A system theory of managment organisation,** Tavistock 1963. The approach was further developed in human service organisations for example Emery F E, **Freedom and Justice Within Walls,** Tavistock 1970 and Miller E J & Gwynne G V, **A Life Apart,** Tavistock 1974.

3   A K Rice **The Enterprise and its Environment: A system theory of management organisation,** Tavistock Publicaitons 1963.

4   Christopher Bollas, **The Shadow of the Object: Psychoanalysis of the Unthought Known,** Free Association Books London 1987

5   Carlzon J, **The Moment of Truth,** Harper & Row 1989

6   The definition of 'boundary' offered by Hirschhorn is valuable here. In **The Workplace Within,** (MIT Press 1990), he defines boundary as the point at which uncertainty is translated into information and decisions.

7   It has been interesting to draw on the original work of Miller and Rice, which included a study of issues concerned with this industry (op cit 1967).

8   This project has been carried out in conjunction with Brunel University and sponsored by the West London Training and Enterprise Council.

9   Jan Carlzon, op cit

10   See for instance Scholes K, **Strategic Management in Professional Service Organisations,** Sheffield Business School 1994

11   **Homologous** - Related or similar in structure, origin, nature or value (**New Webster's Dictionary**)

UNCOVERING AND THINKING ABOUT ORGANIZATIONAL SECRETS

Francesca Cardona, *Independent Consultant, London*

ABSTRACT

This paper describes three different situations of consultancy work.

It illustrates different ways in which I worked at creating a space where it was possible to identify and discover the core issue, or the hidden organizational secret, which was impairing the teams' capacity to think and to function in an effective way.

The Lambert team of social workers was experiencing a lot of difficult changes in their department and painful conflicts among themselves. They could not think about their organisation until their 'secret' was disclosed: I saw my function to create the space for this to happen. The first step was to help them to own their central problem and to translate what was perceived as one individual's personal problem in an organizational one.

Green Lodge is a residential establishment for difficult adolescents which was experiencing an uncertain future. Management and staff were not openly acknowledging the threat of closure. Only when I became aware of the situation, when the 'family secret' was disclosed, the staff became able to articulate the problem, to voice their anxieties, concerns and, finally, to take a more active role in the death or survival of their organization

The St Mark Trust is a a small residential establishment for delinquent boys. After a few years of great instability and recurrent crises, it was enjoying a period of development and growth. Important issues on the nature of their work were starting to emerge. The central theme of bullying and being bullied, abusing and being abused is discussed in relation to the role played by different staff members.

INTRODUCTION

This paper illustrates that it is only when people are willing to *own* their organizational problems, to talk directly about the previously hidden organizational secrets, only then can change occur. Without this very little can be done.

I explore here three case studies from a psychodynamic perspective, which illustrate how organizational secrets can impair the capacity to think and function effectively.

1.   THE LAMBERT TEAM

The Lambert Team of psychiatric social workers is currently going through many difficult changes in its department and experiencing painful conflicts. The team is located in a run down, disadvantaged area with many residents from ethnic minorities. Although formally one group, the team is still perceived, by the staff, as being divided into two subteams: one based in the psychiatric hospital, the other in the community. I was asked to provide a few consultancy sessions to help the staff to look at their internal conflicts and the issues related to the restructuring of the service.

After a couple of sessions, in which we seemed to get nowhere, I met them again and realised that my proposed structure of looking at priorities and aims of the service was 'de facto' rejected. It did not work. Participants were very tense, frustrated and somehow quite resentful towards me. I had to find another strategy.

It seemed to be up to two of the most sophisticated members of the team to try to keep the conversation going. I felt an enormous pressure to do something, but knew that my previous attempts had only created disappointment and had not helped to advance the team's thinking.

I felt increasingly annoyed with Paula and Roger, two of the most senior members of the team, who filled up a valuable space with general and unemotional issues. Then, gradually realised that the team members have probably experienced my professional approach in a similar way: an external and quite distant framework was brought in and imposed on them in order to examine their organizational problems, unable to address their central difficulties and pain. Because there was much pain.

I invited Paula and Roger to abandon their "code" language and to start to relate their feelings to what they were saying, to explain their 'code'.

This intervention seemed to release the tension. After a brief exchange, a black member of the team, Jim, made a remark about British hypocrisy and said that he had not spoken because if he started he would still be talking tomorrow morning!

It was a highly emotionally charged moment.

Paula invited him to share his feelings.

Jim says that people in the district have been labelling him, expecially in relation to what happened to one of his patients.

I asked for more details. He explained that a few months ago the patient in question killed his own child. Colleagues commented that the tragic event could have been avoided if Jim had not closed the case.

He didn't want to close the case. He said it was Alan, the team leader, who insisted on closure because the client was not keeping appointments.

Alan, is always regarded as the 'good' guy. Jim, is the one who often takes all the blame.

This major problem, I discovered, was never discussed by the team before. Another staff member linked what happened with lack of a support system within the team. After having listened, stunned, to this account, I entered the discussion quite forcefully. I pointed out how the first step was to make the team own the problem. What has happened is not Jim's problem but the problem of the team as a whole: he acted on behalf of the team, while the team behaved as if this tragic event belonged exclusively to him. Support can only take place if the staff recognise the problem and are prepared to own it. Jim was upset, bitter. His distress was genuine.

My initial proposal, in thinking about the aims of the organization, had to change. I perceived a developing anxiety and some resentment diverted towards me, without understanding the reason for it: people wanted to talk and to be open, but they did not know how. Through the analysis of my countertransference feelings I was able to show them how to do it, in a way that which challenged the 'sterile' exchange between the two senior members of the team, in order to provoke a break through.

The situation was ripe for development, but it was essential for me to acknowledge, within myself, that I had to bear, with them, the slowness and the arduousness of the process and my initial failure in trying to help them. They could not think productively about their organization until this 'secret' was disclosed: I had to allow the space for it to happen.

Staying with the situation, bearing some of the pain and anxiety of getting nowhere, without forgetting the need for creating organizational frameworks and structures, was essential to this approach.

In the next meeting everyone was relieved to see Jim back. He apologised to Alan for some rude remarks he had made.in the previous session. Jokes were made about his role; who was going to be the ogre now ? There was a feeling of reparation and a shift in focus.

The people acknowledged that the conflicts took a lot of energy away from investing in the team and creating an organizational framework. It was time for planning, for looking at the priorities and aims of the service.

I had the impression that this brief consultancy was the first time that the Lambert team experienced themselves as one team, despite their differences. Some 'emotional bonding' and sense of reparation took place in that context.

Another important function of the consultancy was to translate what had been perceived mainly as personality problem and lack of professionalism to an organizational problem.

The first step was to help them to own what was, at that time, their central problem. The reflective work on what happened became a developmental experience for the whole team and created a transitional structure which has continued.

People working in the mental health field are particularly subject to projections from their clients, and also from society which often does not want to know about such marginal and difficult client groups.

It is almost impossible not to be caught up in some kind of projection, both from the clients and from society. I wondered if what I have described was also a 'repetition', within the team, of what happens in society when people try to ignore and marginalise individuals who represent complex and painful realities.

2.   GREEN LODGE*

Green Lodge is a residential establishment for adolescents situated on the edge of a big city. The request for consultancy followed the re-opening of one of the two units and the consequent reorganization of children and staff. The management felt that there was a need for reflection on the impact of these changes on the unit which seemed to be experiencing considerable stress.

When I arrived, I was struck by the sheer size of the campus, the wide spread of the buildings and the absence of a physical centre. What was immediately noticeable was how much the environment was lacking in character, and the absence of children around the place.

The community seemed empty and isolated.

The coldness of the place was in sharp contrast to the warmth of the first meeting with the management. They seemed eager to discuss their concerns, which centred on the stress experienced by the staff of the newly re-opened unit. I felt it was important to try to understand this within the context of the organization as a whole.

The format I proposed was, therefore, to have a number of meetings with each of the different sectors. I would then have a final meeting with representatives from each level and discipline.

In the first meeting with the management group, a few months later, I discovered there had been quite a high level of sick leave in staff in recent months. The union had been called in by the staff, who found it impossible to cope with the level of aggression and misbehaviour of some of the children, and were blaming the management for their difficult work situation. The management felt there was a contradiction in the complaint of being 'abused' by the children, when the task of Green Lodge was precisely to work with and care for very abusive and difficult children. It seemed that over the months since my initial visit, the distress previously located mainly in one sector - the newly re-opened unit- was now pervading the whole organization.

Clare, the Head, mentioned that the number of children was very low, but that there was no immediate threat of closure.The optimistic re-opening of the unit had not happened. Clare explained that she was involved in developing a plan for reorganising residential resources in the district that might bring some positive changes by proposing alternative uses of the community.

I came out of the meeting overwhelmed by a sense of hopelessness and resignation in the face of a situation that management did not seem able to control. On the one hand, they were part of a complicated bureaucratic system which apparently governed and controlled even their smallest decisions; on the other hand, they had an angry and unsatisfied staff group who did not want to accept the very essence of their work. I could not see any clear sense of purpose to guide and support them in tackling all these issues and conflicts.

The emptiness I had been so struck by on my first visit, the absence of a physical centre, seemed to mirror the lack of a centred and coherent approach, and also the

* **This work has been described in greater details in a chapter of 'The Unconscious at Work ' by A. Obholzer and V. Roberts , Routledge (Forthcoming)**

distance between a well meaning but ineffectual management and an angry staff group. These feelings were confirmed in the following meetings.

Gradually I began to realise that the community was facing a very uncertain future. Although mentioned to me only in passing, the number of children was very low and there was not much hope of an increase in the number of referrals in the short term. Green Lodge had become a very expensive under-utilized structure, which could not survive in an increasingly competitive market place. I also learned that the lease of the premises was due to expire in two years. What was surprising was that these serious threats to the survival of Green Lodge were not identified earlier, nor indeed discussed as problems at all, merely as a background element to the conflicts and difficulties between management and staff, and between staff and children. As one of the managers put it, the potential closure was more a rumour than a stated fact. It was natural to be protective about this issue with the external world, of which I was a representative.

My slowness in putting the evidence together was a strong indication of what was going on in the staff group. People were complaining about a number of things, but were not talking about what really bothered them: the possibly imminent closure

I began to see that my main area of work had to be to try to help the organization to focus on its future. I knew that to accept the invitation to concentrate only on the working practices and the internal changes would mean colluding in denying the main problem of the organization, yet I felt painfully anxious about saying what needed to be said.

My function came to be one of disclosing this 'family secret', stating openly, on every possible occasion, facts that were known to all the community. As I did so, I became more and more in touch with the feelings of death and impotence which pervaded the whole community.

As I continued talking with the different groups, I started to build up a picture of a very fragmented organization in which layers of different cultures and contrasting models coexisted with no real interchange between each other. Most staff derived their professional identity from their previous positions rather than from their present ones. For instance, the teachers still related very strongly to their past experience of Green Lodge as an approved school, where they had felt more contained, with clearer boundaries, more discipline, and less uncertainty about their task.

My impression, listening to their views, was that their difficulties in dealing with the children had much to do with the absence of a clear and shared understanding of the task of Green Lodge Was the community a custodial institution with a caring component? Or was it aiming to create small family units where children could be looked after in a closer and more containing environment? Outside the community, both options had been considered by the local authority, and either could have been implemented, but not both.

As I came to understand it, the basis of this muddled sense of purpose was due to the combination of its origins as an approved school, with a bureaucratic model derived from the local authority. This had in some way impaired Green Lodge capacity to create a more independent, innovative, and coherent approach; an underlying dependency culture affected the functioning of the whole organization.The community provided for most of the basic needs of both children and staff. In this situation staff seemed to have lost some of their own ability to take initiatives, projecting upwards in the hierarchy , and outside the organization itself. This attitude could also be seen as a projective identification with the adolescents, who did not feel in control of their own lives, and who both wanted and resisted containment of their impulses. As a result, both staff and residents found it difficult to move towards a more active role, using their experience, resources and ideas to make an impact on their reality. Authority was experienced as distant and indistinct, but at the same time very powerful, and sometime even abusive.

I was struck by how anxious and lost people felt with regard to their future; how difficult it was for them to plan and take responsibility in a working environment which they felt they could not control or influence. The staff showed quite a lopsided vision of their situation; they were mainly preoccupied with themselves. The managers, on the other hand, were more in touch with the idea of positive potential scenarios for the community in the outside world, but they were somehow unable to communicate these hopes effectively within the system.

In thinking about my intervention I frequently wondered what I had been trying to achieve. Looking back, I think I had tried to inject some energy and ideas into the system through my own presence, fostering the hope of productivity which had been generated at the first meeting. My aim was to shake up the dependency system and to help staff and management to exercise more authority over their situation and their future.

It was up to the management and staff to decide how and if they wanted to make an impact on their future- just as, in the end, it was up to the children to decide what they would make of their lives.

The hypothesis that I developed during my work with the community was that only through an open and public acknowledgement of the real problem of the organization- the possible imminent death of the community- could people accept some ownership and shared responsibility for their future.

3.   ST MARK TRUST

The St Mark trust is a small residential establishment for delinquent boys. After a few years of great instability and recurrent crises, it was enjoying a period of development and growth. Important issues on the nature of its work were starting to emerge.

The central theme of bullying and being bullied, abusing and being abused, is discussed here in relation to the role played by different staff members. Bullying and being bullied are linked. They are part of a vicious circle

In the case of severely mentally and physically abused children we can find examples of both. In the St Mark Trust the bully and the bullied were often split between two different staff groups.

It was very difficult to acknowledge the existence, within the team, of anything to do with aggression, bullying or abuse because of the everyday experience of working with abused boys. How could the staff identify with the people who had so severely damaged the lives of the boys in their care?

Many staff were not fully aware of the background of the boys they looked after, in a way that suggested that they were trying to protect themselves from the extremely painful realities of their clients, of the aggressive and violent world from which they came.

It was left to a few members of staff to carry out the function of the aggressor and the bully within the team.

Mary was often the person who initiated the meetings, many times with complaints about how things are run in the unit. This time she started the meeting complaining about another staff member who had forgotten to pick up a child from school. "This is a terrible thing to do, people can't forget such things. If this is allowed to happen we accept a very low standard of practice".

Explanations were given: Tracy, who was a new staff member, still found it difficult to remember the routine of the unit, all the things that needed to be done. She was very apologetic and genuinely sorry about what happened. Mary seemed untouched by her response and justifications: what had happened was unforgivable, it should never have happened. She went on and on about Tracy's negligence.

The rest of the team, including senior members of staff, were sheepishly silent and seemed unable to stop a clear aggressive and bullying behaviour from one member of staff to another. Only a few people intervened, but without any clear assumption of authority or firmness and without a real will to confront Mary's behaviour. I too felt impotent and very angry: my attempts to bring people into the discussion and to try to broaden the issue that Mary has raised had little affect. Nobody seemed to want to stop Mary and assume the difficult role of taking a clear stand against her behaviour.

Tracy was absent from the next session , because she was on sick leave, while Mary was somewhere in the building, due to join the meeting later. Suddenly, the silent group of last week became very vocal about what happened in the previous session, pointing out how unacceptable Mary's behaviour was towards Tracy, who was probably absent today as a consequence of last week's attack.

It became clear to me that they were only able to express their feelings openly and forcefully because Mary was not there. Mary was very convenient in her role as bully: she could take on that role while other members of staff could distance themselves from aggressive feelings towards each other and towards the children. They can be the sophisticated professionals who will never raise their voices or risk being accused of authoritarian and undemocratic behaviour.

When Mary joined the meeting I made the link between the two sessions: the inability of very articulated senior staff members to stand up for Tracy or to confront Mary's attitude when she was present; and later, in the following session, the sudden freedom of expression and sense of outrage when Mary was absent.

It seemed to me that this organizational dynamic was reproducing something characteristic of families where physical and mental abuse take place: a passive attitude and an inability to confront the aggressor which colludes with the aggressor's behaviour.

Looking at what happened in the two sessions, linking it with their everyday experience made it possible for the team to start to own some of the aggressive feelings implicit in their work, without necessarily having to split them in some of their colleagues.

An over identification with their clients, a strong wish to rescue them from their terrible past formed the basis of their difficulty to be in touch with their own aggressive feelings towards the boys.

Acknowledging some of the complexity of the work which could not completely separate good and bad and the implications of taking the role of the colluding parent or sibling who does not want to see or know what is going on.has opened some further possibilities of looking at the dynamic between the victim, the perpetrator and the passive parent and the function of the unit in this triangle.

4.   CONCLUDING COMMENTS

Fundamental to this consultancy approach is being open to the experience and to the projections of the people to whom you are consulting. This often implies experiencing very uncomfortable feelings.

It is important to realise how the client uses you, what the organisation and the individuals in it project on to you, make you feel.

Only through a constant review of your own feelings and emotions and holding on to the uncertainty of the experience, resisting the pressure of giving immediate and precise advice to the client organisation is it possible to reach some understanding of the underlying dynamics which affect the whole organizational process and to uncover the core issues or the organizational secrets they are struggling with.

It is often extremely difficult for organizations and staff to consider the possibility of change, even if it means moving on from a situation of great uncertainty, paralysis and unhappiness, to something possibly better, or at least more clearly defined. Changes inevitably threaten established individual and organizational defences, and however unsatisfactory these defences may be, they are hard to give up.

5.   SUMMARY

This paper presents three examples of organizations which have used the consultancy work to uncover their 'family secrets' and to become aware of the organizational dynamics which were impairing their capacity to think and to function effectively.

This paper shows that until people could name the danger which is threatening them the anxieties it stirred up would continue to get displaced, or into the children or into individual members of staff. Denial as organizational defence disables people from thinking and therefore for bringing about any change.

Facing reality can restore some confidence in their ability to use their authority, to influence their destiny, even if some external realities cannot be overcome.

REFERENCES

Adams, A. and Crawford, N. (1992) Bullying at work, London: Virago

Menzies Lyth I.E.P.(1988) Containing anxieties in Institutions: Selected essays, London: Free Association Books.

Miller E.(1993) From dependency to autonomy - Studies in organization and change London, Free Association Books

Trist, E and H. Murray (eds) (1990) The Social Engagement of Social Science, vol 1: The socio - psychological perspective, London: Free Association Books

CONSULTANCY IN THE COMMUNITY - INVADING FOREIGN LANDS. IT'S TIME TO DO THE UNTHINKABLE

Roger Casemore, *Kasmor Consultancy, Rugby*

ABSTRACT

This paper sets out to describe an innovative approach to consultancy on community development in a highly disadvantaged inner city estate in North London. The paper outlines a conceptual approach combining some of the methodology used in the management of change in organisations along with a radical approach to harnessing resources within the community, in order to effect change at both a macro and a micro level in the community. The paper also examines the pressures on the external consultant and their impact on him.

INTRODUCTION

Much is known and has been written about inner city estates with extreme levels of poverty, crime and drug abuse. Considerable government effort has been put into diverting resources to meet these concerns, through aid programmes such as Urban Aid and City Challenge. So far there appears to have been only limited success as a number of these estates have become literally "No Go areas". They are largely but not wholly populated by black and minority ethnic communities which are difficult to penetrate or to communicate with, for traditional central and local government agencies. Traditional policing methods to combat drug abuse and other criminal activities often exacerbate the problems rather than alleviating them. If these problems are to be resolved and these communities enabled to access some of the government and other resources which could be available to them, has to be found to enable these communities to take responsibility for dealing with their own problems. The traditional approach of encouraging a dependency model by parachuting Outsiders in to deal with the problems is plainly ineffective. There is clear evidence of the difficulties which occur when community developers are parachuted in, set up solutions to problems and then leave again, at which point the solutions they have set up usually collapse again.

Community and Economic Development in multi-ethnic inner city communities is a highly problematic field of consultancy. Consultants who are usually white, specialists with expert knowledge, are employed by outside funding agencies to enable change to take place in the community. Such Consultants are usually viewed as invaders with vested interests and with no real knowledge or understanding of the community. and in the past their success has been very limited. This paper describes a different approach to community consultancy on the Stonebridge Estate in Brent, which has been developed in recent years linking the external consultant with an internal change agent to harness resources within the community and enabling the community to identify and set up its own responses to community problems.

1   The Background

1.1   Stonebridge Estate sits within the Harlesden City Challenge Area and is renowned for its social and economic problems. It is typical of inner city estates in London and other big conurbations with high levels of drug abuse and drug related crimes. Harlesden City Challenge has used my services to devise a strategy which will have some impact on young people on the estate and lead to diverting them away from drug related activities.

1.2   Most of the tried and tested approaches used by local authority youth services and other agencies have proved to be of little use. Several agencies have tried to develop Outreach projects which have had a measure of success but largely they are ineffective and the young people they target are very suspicious of them. Particularly as they usually employ qualified, trained workers recruited and brought in to work from elsewhere.

2   History of the Approach

2.1   I was working in Coventry as Senior Education Officer for Community Education at the time of the Toxteth riots. As it was known that I had substantial experience of community development work with minority ethnic communities in different parts of the country, I was asked to undertake some community development work in the Hillfields Estate in Coventry to try to prevent riots occurring there. Purely by coincidence, at that time I came into contact with the Director of the Histadrut, the Jewish trade union movement, equivalent to our TUC.

2.2   The Director told me about a programme of work being developed by the Histadrut in inner city areas in Third World countries. They had identified the fact that in those communities, individuals with leadership skills and motivation managed to get themselves out of the slums and on to courses to train as community workers, social workers, teachers etc. However, having trained and qualified they then usually moved somewhere else and did not return to their home community. The Histadrut was developing a programme to identify and train young leaders in the community with the express purpose of putting them back to work in their home communities.

2.3   With my tongue in my cheek I asked him if he would be prepared to accept Hillfields Estate in Coventry as a third world estate so that we could join his programme. To my surprise, he readily agreed to do this and to provide a substantial element of the funding. I managed to get support from the Leader of the Council to develop this project and some funding to match that being offered by the Histadrut. Over the next six months, we identified a group of twelve young men and women, from different ethnic backgrounds living on the estate. They were seen as having leadership potential and as key figures. This group then went with two council officers, to Tel Aviv, for one month to undertake the Histadrut Community Training Programme and develop skills that they could use in their community.

2.4   On their return, the group played a central role in developing a new Community Centre funded by the Urban Programme, on the estate. Some five years later many of those individuals are still living and working in Hillfields and have been involved in successfully developing a number of important community projects.

2.5   I suggested to the Chief Executive of Harlesden City Challenge that this seemed to indicate a possible strategy for Stonebridge Estate. What we needed to do was to identify and harness human resources from within the community, to work within that community, identifying strategies for dealing with the problems that were facing them. Part of the approach would be dependent on identifying more clearly what the needs of the community were in order to find ways of helping them to meet their needs.

2.6   The Chief Executive of Harlesden City Challenge then set up a meeting with representatives from Brent Council, the City Challenge Board and the local community, to discuss his concerns about enabling the residents of communities like the Stonebridge Estate in the City Challenge area, to get information and access to City Challenge funded schemes and projects. The meeting identified a range of social and economic problems experienced by residents of the estate and the difficulties that the usual agencies have in being accepted in order to work with the residents.

2.7   One of the major problems for City Challenge as for many other agencies is to carry out a real needs analysis in the community, largely because communities are suspicious of the motives behind the exercise and of the people who carry it out.

3   The   Initial   Proposal

3.1   On the basis of my previous experience I suggested recruiting a team of young, black adults living on the estate, whom we would then train and develop so that they could first of all carry out a systematic needs analysis, action research programme. Having completed that, they would then move on to use that information to work as a community outreach team, developing programmes to help their community to meet the needs that were identified.

3.2   I pointed out that in order for this work to be credible in the community we would need to appoint individuals who may well have criminal records or who might be or have been, actively involved in drug dealing or other criminal activities. This really was the "unthinkable " part for an agency like City Challenge but I re-iterated my view that we should avoid appointing people with the "right" qualifications and appoint people who could actually do the job by being able to have effective contact with ordinary people in the community.

3.3   City Challenge were very much aware of the fact that the community on this estate was generally very suspicious of the Local Council, the Police, City Challenge and any other central or local government agencies. In order to work, this project would need to be delivered at "arms length" from any agencies.

4   Change Agents

4.1   In my work in managing change in organisations I had often used Schon's theoretical framework of "Dynamic Conservatism" [1] I also identified the principal often used in managing change in organisa-tions of teaming up an "External Change Agent" with an "Internal Change Agent", who work together to support each other in over-coming the resistances to change. On the estate there is a considerable investment by individuals in maintaining their economic status, income and individual power bases through drugs and other crimi-nal activities. These individuals would actively resist any changes in the community and might well take fairly forceful action to do so.

4.2   I discussed this with the Chief Executive and also identified that there would be a significant problem for me in actually running the project. That I was first of all an "Outsider" and secondly, "White". It would be essential to identify an appropriate individual with local credibil-ity who could work with me to develop the project, as the "Internal Change Agent", allowing me to operate as the external agent of change. We identified Leonard Johnson, a well known local black personality who runs the Bridge Community Project, as a possible partner for me. We agreed also to try to involve the Brent Youth Service Manager for the area, Elizabeth Sinclair, (Ghanaian by origin) who might then take on the longer term running of the project, in the future.

4.3   The Chief Executive of City Challenge (Black Afro-Caribbean by origin) then brought the three of us together to talk through my proposal and we reached agreement on a process of collaboration. I then met with Leonard Johnson and we produced a proposal for the pilot project which was approved by the Chief Executive and his board. (A copy of that proposal is attached as Appendix 1).

4.4   During this first individual meeting, Leonard admitted that he had done some research on my background to check on my credibility. He said he received very favourable references on me and would be very happy to work with me. He also said that he had very little experience of consultancy work and hoped that he would be able to learn a lot from me about that. Over the next few months I actually had to spend quite a lot of time helping Leonard to understand some of the dynamics of the consultancy/client relationship and the behaviours and language of public sector organisations. Throughout the project this was a continuing area of difficulty for him and at times the relationship between him and the City Challenge officers became quite strained. For me this meant continual attention to my role as liaison between him, the Outreach Team and the City Challenge and was to give rise to serious difficulties at the end of the Pilot phase of the project..

5   Developing the Pilot Project

5.1   Harlesden City Challenge then employed me for three months, to oversee the development of the project, giving strategic direction, planning the action research and liaising with the City Challenge Office. My role was also to give guidance to Leonard Johnson who was employed to manage the team on a day to day basis.

5.2   We began by producing:
  i   a person specification and Job Description for the Outreach Workers,
  ii   an advertisement for the posts and
  iii   a revised budget to fit within the amount that had been allocated by the City Challenge Board.

6 Recruiting the Team

6.1 Rather than go through the usual official selection processes using the Brent Council machinery, it was agreed only to advertise on the estate via the local Employment Centre and various community networks. We also agreed to advertise on the local Pirate Radio Station and this was our most succesful source of candidates It was also agreed that City Challenge, Leonard and Elizabeth would target individuals known to them, to receive the information. A process for short listing and a selection process to enable us to appoint the team, were planned and organised by me, which would test for the aptitudes that we thought were necessary.

6.2 Both Leonard and Elizabeth began straight away agreed to use their networks to publicise the project and to gain community support for it and adverts were placed to appoint the team of four project workers.

6.3 Twelve people were short listed and some two weeks later a mixed group of individuals from the estate, with a variety of backgrounds were interviewed. All of them were unemployed, none of them had relevant, formal qualifications and one candidate was actually just about to come out of prison.

6.4 At the end of the selection process there were five individuals who it was felt could do the job and it was decided to appoint all five but to reduce the length of the Pilot Project in order to remain within budget. The four young men and one young woman who were appointed would have been unlikely to have applied for a local authority outreach project job and if they had none of them would have been likely to have been appointed. Several of the candidates interviewed are well known in the area and are very much part of the street scene in Stonebridge.

7 Training and Building the Team

7.1 Because of the nature of the individuals we sought to recruit and their likely backgrounds we knew that we would have to put them through some appropriate training at an early stage, to enable them to survive and to do the job. We identified a local black training agency -Stonebridge Community Learning Action Resources (SCoLAR) with a good reputation and local credibility. Leonard and I met with them and discussed our project and the training needs that we expected to have to met. SCoLAR collaborated with us in designing a training programme which would consist of a residential week-end followed by 10 half day sessions over the following months.

7.2   The initial course programme was planned to cover:
Time Management
Listening and Communication Skills
Assertiveness
Goal Setting
Problem Solving and Decision making Skills
Action Planning
Presentation and Public Speaking
Leadership Skills
Creative Thinking
Guidance and Counselling
Team Building

7.3   Immediately after the Outreach Team were appointed, they were taken away on a four day residential training course, staying at a hotel on the sea front at Brighton. SCoLAR ran the course with some specialised input from myself, Leonard Johnson and Elizabeth Sinclair and by the end had done a good job of bringing the team together and getting them committed to doing the job they had been appointed for. The course was a considerable experience for the five members of the team and to some extent quite a culture shock for them. None of them had stayed in such a hotel before and all of them were very anxious about returning to learning as a result of their unhappy experiences of school.

7.4   We started out by establishing a contract of openness and honesty and spent a substantial proportion of the time looking at the processes that were going on, as well as dealing with the content of the learning. Between us we helped them to settle in and to get involved with the training materials and learning experiences. We found that they rapidly became engaged and hungry to learn and I was particularly moved by the way in which the group accepted and related to me, the Outsider.

7.5   At the start of the course, I felt very anxious and aware of the suspicions of the new Team members. SCoLAR, Leonard and Elizabeth helped the Team to accept and understand my role and I worked hard to get myself accepted as an individual, with a commitment to supporting them and making the project work.

8   The Pilot Project

8.1   Two members of the Team started on the Monday following the course, to get the office set up in Stonebridge Park Community project premises and the other three started the following week. Once they were all in place, Leonard and I met with them and helped them to produce a questionnaire (Appendix 2) and to identify a target of completing 1,000 individual interviews of young people aged between 12 and 25, on the estate by the end of September.

8.2   I produced Diary Sheets and Recording Forms (see Appendix 4) to ensure a process of accountability for the Workers and then I worked with Leonard and the Team to produced the Questionnaire to do the needs analysis. I then spent several days with Leonard and the Team, helping them to work through the issues, such as confidentiality, and the approaches they would have to use to do the needs analysis. Leonard also regularly met on his own with the team to help them plan and organise their daily work routines. Throughout this time I was in almost daily contact by telephone with Leonard providing him with ongoing support.

8.3   In addition SCoLAR were meeting the Team on a weekly basis for the ten, half day session course. In addition to the originally planned course content, we added in sessions on data analysis, and helped all the team to be able to use a Word Processor and Spread Sheet.

8.4   Leonard supervised the team in a daily basis in carrying out the research and as one would expect, there were a number of hiccups arising from using a team of inexperienced, untrained people. There were also difficulties in getting enough copies of the Questionnaires produced and in the sheer logistics of getting the interviews done in the planned time scale. However, the team demonstrated full commitment to their work and seemed to be coping with the pressure. Difficulties also occurred because none of them were used to the routine of working and had to be taught how to answer the phone and deal with visitors to the office. Establishing accepted ways of behaving and encouraging conformity with   office management practises was dealt with effectively by Leonard, with some support from me.

9   The Research Approach

9.1   We expected the team to meet some suspicion and resentment about what they were doing and had explored with them the way they were going to be seen as "Targets" by taking on this work. In order to counteract this, we opted for two kinds of research to be carried out to obtain the information we wanted. First of all the team would carry

out some research by an **INFORMAL NETWORKING APPROACH.**
Visiting individuals and groups on the estate and talking to them
informally about the research and about City Challenge. Through
this process they met and talked to approximately 1,200 people. In
fact, they very quickly met some considerable suspicion and anger
and it is to their credit that they were largely able to dispel this.

9.2   They then went on to carry out the **FORMAL INTERVIEW AP-
PROACH** and managed to get 550 questionnaires completed and
returned from a circulation of 1,000. They were a little disappointed
not to achieve their target figure but we worked hard to reassure
them that to have in excess of a 50% response rate is very creditable
indeed in comparison to other formal surveys.

9.3   Again, in addition to the days I spent with Leonard and the Team, I
was in almost daily contact with Leonard dealing with queries about
the process and supporting him in managing the team.

10   Presentation of the Findings

10.1   The difficulties described above did cause some slippage and the
presentation of the results had to be delayed from 1 October 1993 to
18 October 1993, some two weeks later than had originally been
planned.

10.2   On 15 October Leonard Johnson and I spent a full day with the team
going through the information they had collected and helping them
to prepare their presentation. The Team then continued working on
analysing the data they had collected and preparing their presentation over that week end. They then made their presentation to Gerry
Davis the Chief Executive and members of his City Challenge Team
at their offices, on the 18th of October 1993.

10.3   The Team, with some help from Leonard and myself, produced a full
report analysing the results of their investigations. A copy of that
report is attached as Appendix 3. Bearing in mind the backgrounds
of the individuals concerned and their lack of confidence and nerv-
ousness at the start of the project, for them to have produced a report
at all after only ten weeks together would have been a major
achievement. To have produced a report of this quality is quite
outstanding.

10.4   The Team then made a verbal presentation of their report in the City
Challenge Company Board Room, using over head projector slides
and then responded to questions by the Chief Executive and his
officers from the City Challenge. This presentation was excellent and

greatly impressed the Chief Executive, particularly when they backed up their findings with their own local knowledge.

10.5   The Team raised with the Chief Executive, their concerns about the temporary nature of their appointments. He immediately confirmed that their contracts were to run until the end of November and stated that he expected that his Board would confirm the continued funding of the project for a further year.

10.6   Again it is important to note the performance of the team members, none of whom had ever made a formal presentation or been in a Board Room before. They had all made substantial learnings and skills development through the course by SCoLAR and support from Leonard and myself and had effectively translated these learnings into action.

10.7   After the presentation, Leonard and I agreed to produce a report on the Pilot Project for presentation to the City Challenge full Board. We then met with the Team to de-brief them on their presentation and to plan their work after the board meeting.

10.8   At the next meeting of the Board, the final report was presented by the Chief Executive along with several recommendations.

10.8.1 First of all we recommended that to take account of the ethnicity of the Stonebridge Estate and to improve the gender balance in the Team, there should be two additional appointments to the Team. Ideally we should seek to recruit two more female Outreach workers, one white and one black.

10.8.2 Secondly we recommended that the size of the managerial task of running this team needed to be appreciated, particularly as they would now begin to move on to developing a number of the projects identified in their report. This really indicated the need to appoint a Team Manager, again, preferably from within the community and possibly from within the existing Team.

10.8.3 Thirdly we recommended that a Project Steering group should be formed comprising mainly residents of the Estate, to take over the ownership of the project. This Steering group should be established as a voluntary organisation with charitable status to enable it to seek additional funding from other sources. This Steering Group would take over the running of the project and act as employers of the Outreach Team, although Brent Borough Council would continue to act as the "Paymaster".

10.8.4 Fourthly we recommended that alternative accommodation should be found for the Team preferably centrally located within the Stonebridge Estate.

10.9 The City Challenge Board warmly received the Report and confirmed their approval for the project to be funded for the remaining 4.5 years of the City Challenge funding. They also accepted all the recommendations and approved increasing the funding to cover the costs of appointing two more Outreach workers and a Team Manager.

11 The Saga Continues

11.1 At this point I had expected to begin to fade from the picture and only to provide some occasional support or consultancy. However the difficulties I referred to in paragraph 4.4 became quite serious at this point with relationships between Leonard and the City Challenge Officers breaking down quite badly. This was primarily to do with Leonard's lack of experience of the Consultancy role and its responsibilities. As a result of some of his actions the Chief Executive decided he did not wish to employ Leonard any further.

11.2 I was then approached and asked if I would continue to provide consultancy support and discussed with the Chief Executive how the Team could be managed on a daily basis. We approached the Brent Youth Service who agreed that one of their experienced black Detached Youth Workers already doing some work with young people on the Stonebridge Estate, would take over the day to day management of the Team, under my supervision, until a Team Manager could be appointed and the Steering Group set up. I agreed to provide three days a month consultancy to give ongoing support and direction to the Team and their new temporary manager.

11.3 At the time of writing, I am now working with the Team helping them to develop their ideas for projects arising from their research work. I have taken them through the processes of project management and helped them to prepare project proposals for the four projects they are planning to run.

11.4 This has brought me back into a different, much closer working relationship with the Team and their new manager, with rather different impacts on me and on them. For example, I have had to undertake some managerial direction of the team, insisting that they maintain expected standards of working behaviour, such as time keeping. So far this seems to be working well.

12   The Project Proposals

12.1   One of the exciting consequences of the Pilot project is the fact that the Team have identified four projects which they believe are a response to the needs they have identified in their community. For each project one member of the Team will act as the Lead Person with a second member of the Team as Support Person. For each of the projects they are starting out by setting up a small Project Steering Group of interested people in the community who they identified through their survey work.

12.2   Project One is based on the belief they have that there is considerable talent within the community which is being wasted. This Project will establish a Talent Data Base of individuals within the community who have talents and skills that could be marketable. These will include a broad range of employment and enterprise skills as well as those in the fields of Performing Arts, Crafts and Sport. The Project will then go on to find ways of marketing these talents regionally and nationally.

12.3   Project Two is based on their view that young people on the estate need alternative supportive opportunities for education. They may well be alienated from schools, but they are not ineducable. This Project will set out to establish a Supplementary Education Centre on the Estate targeting young people aged 12 to 15. It will offer attractive leisure activities as a "carrot" alongside of supplementary tuition in National Curriculum subject areas and facilities for supported home-work and individual study.

12.4   Project Three is based on their view that Black people are badly under represented in some sports and need positive action to enable them to reach national levels. This project will begin by targeting snooker and has an aim of trying to promote young black people into the professional snooker industry so that within two years there are several nationally known black snooker players.

12.5   Project Four is based on their view that young people do not get enough opportunity to participate in sports activities or to move outside of their estate very often. This Project will set out to organise a regular series of multi-sports tournaments twinned with other difficult inner city areas as a means of encouraging young people to visit these and develop contact which will enable them to see what other similar communities are like and how they are responding to their problems.

12.6 The effect of the Team's investigations and the news of the proposed projects has caused quite a stir on the estate and there is a sensation that a new change process has really begun, under community ownership and direction.

12.7 **Recent Progress Report**

At an early stage of planning, we informed the local police of our plans for this project. Early in January I met with the local Police to dicuss their continued support and liaison. They informed me that in their perception the level of drug dealing on the estate has markedly reduced since the Outreach Team began their work and that they are extrremely impressed with the results. They do however, continue to be anxious about the nature of the individuals we have employed and their particular past involvement in the drug scene.

13 Pressures and Impacts on the External Consultant

13.1 Being The Outsider

13.1.1 Just being the outsider going into an ordinary organisation to carry out consultancy work is in itself stress provoking. Learning the boundaries, hierarchy, language, culture, ethos, norms and systems of an organised public or private sector company is, finding ways to become accepted and acceptable in order to question challenge and enable change to take place is a highly sensitive and stressful task. To do this in the much more loosely organised and bounded macro systems of a community is even more difficult. The first impact on me has always been my own expectations of being seen as an outsider and planning out my strategies for presenting myself in a way that is acceptable and at the same time congruent with my own ethics and beliefs.

13.2 Looking and Sounding Different

13.2.1 At the start of any consultancy approach I always find myself considering what I should wear, what I should carry and reminding myself to pay attention to what I say, how I speak and my non-verbal communications. In consultancy work with a community like the Stonebridge Estate, those considerations are even greater. Not only do I find myself giving considerable time to thinking through the preparation, I also find myself replaying many of the conversations and interactions which occur, to check out my understandings of what happened and to monitor my effectiveness. This usually evidences itself when I come home from a day in Stonebridge in an almost manic "high", quite unable to sleep or relax!

13.3   Using a Different Language

13.3.1 The words we use, sentence construction, tones of voice and styles of speech are all important tools of the trade in consultancy work. In community consultancy particularly within minority ethnic communities language is an important component of acceptance. I believe that the ability to use some phrases like those for thanks, greeting and farewell, in the language of origin of members of the community is the least they should be able to expect from consultants working with them. With formal languages like Arabic, Urdu, Hindi or Tagalog, Russian or Polish, this may be difficult enough to manage and remember and may call for regular refresher courses. This does of course add to the feelings of being an outsider and makes the work even more tiring, trying to maintain an understanding of what is being said in conversations and ensuring that one is understood by others and do not cause offence can be quite tiring.

13.3.2 However, a non-formal language like Afro-Caribbean Patois is another dimension again. The speed of delivery and at times the use of deliberate convolutions to ensure that it is not understood by the outsider, make listening very hard work indeed. I have learned to be very "up-front" about this difficulty. I do not attempt to use the patois myself but make it clear that I am trying to improve my understanding of it and to openly ask for translations when I do not understand. I also raise the matter early in my negotiations with community groups asking them to make me translate to them if I say things they do not understand in the language I am used to using. At Stonebridge, I have come away totally exhausted from sessions with the Outreach Team, partly as a result of trying to keep up with their language but also partly through their boisterous extrovert style of behaviour and communication.

13.4   Crime and Fear

13.4.1 The very nature of the Estate and others like it in which I have worked means that serious crime, drugs and violence are often near the surface. To be warned by the Taxi Driver who deposits you at the Precinct that you shouldn't get out here because it is not safe for "people like you" can be either amusing or alarming depending on your frame of mind at the time. There have been several occasions when I have been seriously frightened and anxious for my personal safety. I have learned to walk with confidence and to be aware when real threats are present and how best to respond to them but there have been several times when I have questioned why I was doing this work. The awareness of the proximity of danger does have an impact, not only on me, but also on my family, that brings an unwelcome measure of tension to this kind of consultancy work, that is unavoidable.

13.5   The Pressure to Succeed

13.5.1 Coming into close contact with these communities raises ones awareness of the dreadful conditions in which people live and of the desperate need for change. It is essential to avoid the role of patronage or prescription but in this work I find myself being almost driven by the need to change the situation. My role has to be that of enabling people in the community to identify the need for change, to create the opportunity for change to take place and to empower them to make the changes they feel they need. This process, by its very nature, must be slow and evolutionary one. The impact on me of the effect of poverty, unemployment, drugs and serious crime is at times to leave me extremely depressed and frustrated. When the process begins to work as it seems to be doing in Stonebridge, it can be exhilarating and addictive. Both consequences can lead me to work too hard and to give considerably more than I have contracted to.

13.6   The Hit and Run Merchant

13.6.1 Unavoidably this kind of consultancy work like many other forms is what I call a "Hit and Run Job". I do not live in that community and it is perhaps important that I can come in as an aware Outsider with specialist skills and experience, do my job of empowering and enabling the community and then leave. Avoiding creating a dependency role and sensitively managing the withdrawal process is very difficult but essential. At the end of a project like this it is quite usual for me to experience a strange mixture of relief and release quickly followed by a sense of bereavement. It is important to look after my own internal psychological needs at all stages of this kind of process. Conception, Birth, Childhood and Adolescence are the stages of a project with which I am usually involved and they seem to follow each other very quickly in real time and tend to be charged with feelings of excitement and hope. At the end I have to walk away and ensure that I deal with my feelings of loss and review my learnings from that project in readiness for the next one. This returns me once again to the strong feelings of being "The outsider".

14 Summary

14.1 This paper has set out to describe a different approach to consultancy on community development in a disadvantaged inner city area, the activities that have resulted from that approach and some of the effects on the external consultant. The paper began by describing the history of the concept and the drawing together of community development and organisational management concepts into a new approach. The planning and setting up of the project is described including the approach of recruiting individuals from within the community who would not usually have been considered suitable, as Outreach Workers. The Action Research Community Needs Assessment excercise that this Outreach Team carried out is described, along with the ideas for four new projects which emerged from their research. Finally the paper identifies some of the pressures and the psycho-dynamic impact that the consultant experienced through his involvement.

15 References

[1] Schon Donald A **Beyond The Stable State,** Harmondsworth Press 1971

THE INTERNAL CONSULTANT; RESISTING THE UNDERTOW

ANGELA EDEN, *BT, London*

ABSTRACT

This paper is an exploration of boundary issues for the Internal Consultant . The hypothesis is that a consultant can be drawn inappropriately into organisational dynamics by pressures, politics and projections, and then diverted from their primary task.This diversion may be more easily managed by the external consultant. Two case studies will illustrate the discussion; one from the perspective of an external role, and the second as an internal consultant . Some strategies for resisting this unconscious pull are listed for consultants to consider in their own practice.

INTRODUCTION

Building professional standards for working as a consultant is a long and complicated journey. People embarking on personal therapeutic journey are often told that once the path is found the journey never ends. The same 'health warning ' could be given to people who wish to train as organisation consultants. In reality the two paths are closely linked , and an awareness of ones own 'pathology' and motivation is an essential framework for consultancy work.

One of the corner-stones of any consultancy is resisting the attractive unspoken offer to become integrated into the clients' system. There is too much written about transference, projection and seduction , from every discipline of the people industry, to consider here. However this paper will offer some personal thoughts and experiences drawn from the author's work as both an external and internal consultant and strategies for resisting the 'undertow' . It seems essential that as consultants we recognise, and deal with the pull towards intimacy and build a set of professional standards to maintain the appropriate boundaries.

1 AN IMAGE OF UNDERTOW

I have decided to go swimming at the seashore. I am familiar with that stretch of coast, and know that it is sometimes buffeted by heavy seas and strong winds. But today I am confident, as the weather report is good and the tide will be up near the shore; I feel healthy and ready for the experience. At the seashore I leave my clothes against a large familiar rock below a headland, and swim out into the bay and back. As I swim towards the sun I congratulate myself on my excellent judgment and gain confidence as my co-ordination becomes automatic and I swim steadily out from the beach.

After some time I begin to feel weary and turn back; as I look towards the beach

I have a moment of complete panic. The headland - my rock - the shore have all disappeared. Maybe I have swum further than I thought - maybe I am facing the wrong way or maybe I am dreaming. I swim back towards the coastline, which suddenly seems different. My co-ordination has gone - my breathing is shallow, my eyes smart, and I am getting cramp. This swim has turned into a nightmare as I realise I am swimming against a strong current. The outgoing tide has swept me along , and I am having to re-double my efforts to make any headway.

If there was to be a happy ending to this I would finally struggle to shore, find my clothes and go home with a reinforced learned to read the tide better and become better informed about the local dangers.

There is probably no need to labour the point and make the transition to working within a consultancy contract. How often have we moved confidently into a contract only to find ourselves out of our depth and off-course ? The argument for the paper is that an external consultant has more chance of resisting the undertow, but an internal consultant can be carried away from the contracted goal. This phenomenon will be linked to a theoretical base , two case studies , and some professional strategies to limit the dangers.

2 THEORY

The context for my professional development came through education - Community Development - Project Development - Adult and Management training and finally Management Development. I researched a variety of intervention styles from humanistic psychology, psychotherapy and co-counselling. I looked for a language that enabled people to use their own power, and attended the Advanced Consultancy course at the Tavistock Clinic . It was there that the range of theoretical concepts were woven elegantly into a set of professional standards. I came away from the course with this model:

A process consultant should:
- Remain objective
- Work beside the client
- The client owns their own problem and solution
- Be curious and questioning
- Have the courage to confront ambiguities
- Trust intuition and internal responses to address the transference
- Share my thinking and hypotheses with the client.

This list of professional standards was hard won through reading, experience, supervision and exploration. It is this framework that is challenged by the changing currents of organisational life.

3.0 CASE STUDIES

3.1 An External Contract

In my private practice I had a contract with a residential Homeless project. It was called "staff supervision" and the objective was to work towards respectful and honest communication within the team to enhance a sense of trust with each other.The project contained the range of staff difference in gender, sexuality, politics, race, culture, work experience and training .

I set myself the task of containing any issues that were raised.I wanted to model the ability to withstand discomfort , while working towards resolution. The contract allowed for a meeting in the main building of the project every three weeks for one and a half hours. I came early to attend to the dynamic administration of the group. I arranged the room for ten staff members and was ready to work at the appointed time. People came late ,carrying hot drinks and layers of outside clothing. Each week the group was a different size, with different membership and shifting alliances. There was a core group of three consistent people who came despite shift rota and their days' leave, but I never knew in advance who or what I had to work with. This seemed a direct reflection of the shifting population of their client group, and I had a strong sense of being punished for not having to suffer as they did.

Each session had a "ripe" issue to work on, and each session came to some resolution. But I never had a sense that the hard won gains were transferred to any other setting inside the project. It was as if we were encased in a "problem dome" that did not have a permeable membrane. This hypothesis was discussed with them, as an organisational intervention and still there was no change. I had to decide if being regular, loyal and containing was a good enough intervention, or if by closing the contract I would model that it was possible to make a change. Because I was external, I was able to explain and arrange the end of the contract. There was of course a group "payback" for my disloyalty, but I felt that I had escaped an ongoing and abusive collusion.

3.2 An Internal Contract

Before I describe a contract I want to describe critical difficulty about sharing my experience of organisational life - it is language. The systems, culture and procedures sounded like Martian when I joined the company. It was not just acronyms, but a different juxtaposition of words. No doubt my colleagues inside the company thought the same about my use of language and the way I described some concepts . However, I became moderately fluent, and the need to translate became less frequent. However this may be an indicator for become incorporated into the system. The issue of language and identity is another paper but it needed to be raised here as this case study had to be translated from organisation speak into a consultancy patois.

I was asked to consult to a project leader, to help clarify his aims, objectives and ongoing structure of the work. The project was set up to review a set of procedures and improve the work flow.It was a complicated set of procedures as it covered different disciplines, divisions, reporting lines, geographical sites and expertise. An additional difficulty was the technical nature of the procedure .However I set up the contract, attended meetings, made process interventions , designed and facilitated workshops.

The team was large - about 20 people - and meetings became overwhelmed with detail. I too felt overwhelmed by the enormity of the task and began to feel reluctant about contributing to the work. However in this case I could not negotiate a withdrawal, though I was feeling less and less potent in facilitating the project leader. There was a credibility issue for my unit, and this was high-profile work. As I became or felt less effective in my consulting role I tried to find alternative ways of becoming effective. It was at this point I made a shift from being a Consultant and lost my objective status. I offered to take charge of an area of work inside the project. My line manager agreed it was a good strategic move and the project needed that role to be filled.

I was clear at meetings about my double role, and was explicit about which role I was speaking from at any time. However I lost some of my wider vision, and gave up my right to address any deviation from the Primary task.

In some ways it was more comfortable as I could define a set of tasks and complete them. I was in there - "one of the lads" - getting my hands dirty, and I was getting credibility for my unit. I was thanked for being an active, participative consultant, though I knew I had moved away from my professional ideal.

4. STRATEGIES

The author has used a range of support systems to maintain her role as a contained and containing consultant. Over the years each contract has been supported , and the following list outlines the most successful.

4.1 Individual Supervision

A supervision contract is established with an experienced supervisor with expertise in the clients' arena. Sessions were booked between three meetings with the client , sometimes immediately after a meeting , sometimes prior to the next session. The importance of an 'expert' supervisor is the value they contribute about their specialist field. e.g HIV/ Aids support; Alcohol/drugs projects/;Housing; Employment; Training;Equalities issues.

4.2. Group Supervision

This entails working with a closed long term peer- group with a supervisor, who has expertise in group and individual work. The peer consultants all have ongoing 'live' contracts to contribute though they do not need to present at each session. Each presenter is offered impressions and interpretations from their co-supervisees, which give different perspectives to the work. The supervisors' role is to contain the input to allow progress rather than overwhelming input. The value of a long term group is the developing trust and depth of the work.

4.3 Problem Solving Groups

The concept is a development from Action learning sets, but includes the principles of group problem solving. Each group is managed by a rotating set advisor. The same process is used at each meeting; presentation-questions for clarity-new ideas - reflections and a new action plan. The main concept is the non-judgmental nature of the contributions and the interventions are controlled by the presenter. The value of the set is the collection of experience in the same field,e.g training, personnel,health, education, industry .

4.4 Expert Advice and Support

Working in complex contracts it is sometimes important to be fully informed of the clients world. Short expert knowledge should be sought to save time and avoid naive assumptions.e.g legislation; policies; similar projects; financial constraints;regulations; history and company procedures.

4.5 Networking

Being lost inside an organisation is a lonely business, and a number of colleagues can link together as an informal network. The regularity and structure of meetings is decided at each session. The agenda is built from the current needs of the group. The value of this internal network is sharing the same language and culture,and the problems can be solved and shared.

This list is hardly exhaustive and the author welcomes discussion and contributions from colleagues in the consultancy community.

5. SUMMARY

Resisting the undertow is the key task of a consultant. Being fully conversant with theoretical thinking, is only one strategy for surviving and behaving professionally. The consultant has to learn to live in and work with the undertow. This is part of the data the organisation is offering. Outside objectivity and support is an effective way of maintaining the consultants position ,on the boundary but involved with the Organisation.

6. REFERENCES

BATESON G Steps to an Ecology of Mind, Ballentine 1972

DEBOARD R The Psychoanalysis of Organisations, Tavistock 1978

MORGAN G. Images of the Organisation, Sage 1988

SCHEIN E.H Process Consultation, Addison -Wesley 1987

A PROGRAM OF STUDIES IN ORGANIZATIONAL DEVELOPMENT AND CONSULTATION

Kathleen Pogue White, Kenneth Eisold, Marvin Geller,
William Alanson White Institute, New York

I.INTRODUCTION

Good afternoon, I am Kathy White, Director of the Organization Development and Consultation Program at the William Alanson White Institute of Psychoanalysis in New York. I am here with colleagues from the Program — Ken Eisold, Director of Curriculum and Marvin Geller, a member of Faculty. Larry Gould, who is listed on the Program schedule for today, was unable to join us due to a family emergency.

For this conference on "What Makes Consultancy Work," we thought it would be useful to include some thoughts on the issues of training for consultancy that works. Our Program at the White Institute is just beyond its start-up phase. We thought it would be interesting to describe its philosophy, design and some of its problem areas and then join with you in a collaborative discussion on the developmental training issues that we are encountering.

II. HISTORY

The Organizational Development and Consultation Program is a course of studies at the William Alanson White Institute in New York. The Institute is a psychoanalytic training organization in the interpersonal tradition; it's primary task is the training and certification of psychoanalysts. In addition, it conducts continuing education programs for the professional public. There are many such training organizations in New York itself, as well as, along the east-coast corridor of the United States. Among these, the White Institute is competitively viable and enjoys a rather good reputation for the quality of its training program.

The Organization Program came into being when the Institute began to consider a strategic shift to re-enliven its historic mission, which had been to link psychoanalytic knowledge to social and cultural processes, and to apply this knowledge to social problems and dilemmas in the tradition of Sullivan and Fromm. The Institute began this enlivening process because the growing numbers of Institute graduates were having fewer opportunities to activate affiliation given the Institute's narrow task of training psychoanalysts. Members were taking their talents and energies to other organizations or to private enterprises; this began an organizationally depleting process of disaffiliation. (Clara Thompson, one of the Institute's Founders, is famous to us for the dictum "An Institute is not a home." This institutional attitude had severely affected the vitality of the Organization as a whole.)

At the beginning of the strategic shift, three graduates from the Institute's analytic training — Ken Eisold, Larry Gould and myself — were developing and teaching the application of psychoanalysis to processes in the workplace in the Institute's Continuing Education Division. Our combined courses were offered under the title "Irrationality in the Workplace." The courses were well attended, highly evaluated, and stimulated a great deal of interest in a diversified group of participants. As a result of the success, the Institute managers asked us to develop a full training program in application; in essence, the Institute asked us to become the pilot program for the development of their mission shift. (Subsequent to the development of our Program, two others have been inaugurated — the HIV Program and the Incest and Sexual Abuse Program, both of which are research and treatment programs. A third program is in the planning stage: The Research Center for The Study of Women's Life Crises.)

Background and Rationale

With Larry Gould in the lead, together with Ken and myself, we invited colleagues from the Center for Applied Research in Philadelphia to join us in research required to develop a rationale and potential design of a program of studies in the application of psychoanalysis to organizational life. We observed that conceptualizations on the application began with Freud's considerations of the Church and Army (1921), where he linked certain dynamic aspects of these organizations to his earlier hypotheses regarding the origins of social life - namely, the primal horde (1913). While Freud never directly followed this line of thought further, except generally in his later sociological works (1927, 1930, 1939), there has developed a rapidly growing and impressive body of literature on psychoanalytic conceptions of organizational behavior (eg. Bion, 1981; Kets de Vries, 1984; Jacques, 1951,1955; Kernberg, 1979; Levinson, 1972; Menzies, 1980; Miller and Gwynne, 1972; Miller and Rice, 1967; Rice, 1958; Zubeznick, 1967; Gould, 1985; and many others, some of whom are present at this conference).

Further, we noted that while the theory of practice had been slower to develop or to be systematized, there was a growing body of practice in the field of organizational development and consultation based on these conceptions. Despite such abundant interest and activity, we became aware there were scant advanced educational or professional training opportunities in this area for either psychoanalytically inclined clinicians or for organizational practitioners in the States. Nor were there many opportunities to stimulate interest in organizational practitioners by exposing them to psychoanalytic perspectives and insights on individual, group and social processes in the organizational environment. For example, to the best of our knowledge there were only two organizations in the States that offered some form of psychoanalytic education and training in this context.

The oldest was the A.K. Rice Institute which offered experiential opportunities to learn "first hand" about the dilemmas of group and organizational life through its group relations training conferences. Locally and nationally, it also offered a variety of symposia, lectures, workshops and scientific meetings. The A.K. Rice

Institute's particular focus derives originally from the object-relations tradition of M. Klein and W.R. Bion, and the open-systems theories and concepts of E.J. Miller, A. K. Rice and their colleagues at the Tavistock Institute of Human Relations in London.

The more recently developed organization — The International Society for the Psychoanalytic Study of Organizations (I.S.P.S.O.) - formed to provide a forum for theory and research. Its president-elect, Larry Hirschhorn, who spoke this morning, is a member of our Faculty. ISPSO is a pluralistic organization composed of academics, psychoanalysts and organizational practitioners who share a broad interest in the application of psychoanalytic theory to organizational behavior, development and consultation.

Although successfully satisfying affiliative needs of like-minded members, neither organization provided in-depth, systematic or advanced training for those who had a serious interest in applying the insights of psychoanalysis to their organizational work. As members of both organizations, the original core group of us had the repeated experience of being asked by participants in the activities offered by these organizations, how and where can they get further training. The unequivocal answer at that point was simple — there wasn't anyplace that offered such training either for psychoanalytically oriented clinicians who have an interest in making organizational work part of their professional practices, or for those trained in a variety of management and organizational disciplines who wanted to learn how to apply psychoanalytic principles to their work as executives, managers and consultants.

Hence, we found an intellectual tradition on which to base a rationale, and we anticipated a demand for a program offering. We reasoned that such a Program would be unique in the States, and we believed it would fill a major unmet need for advanced training in psychoanalysis and organizational psychology, as well as create the possibility that the William Alanson White Institute would take substantial intellectual and professional leadership in this rapidly expanding field of psychoanalytic theory and practice.

Program Aims

The theories, principles and methods we used and elaborated for the Program derived from two distinct intellectual traditions. One theoretical base rests on psychoanalytic formulations concerning the nature of individual, group and social processes - particularly the underlying, covert or unconscious aspects of such processes. The other theoretical base evolves from several sociological, social psychological and organizational perspectives such as open-systems theory, sociotechnical systems theory, and theories of organizational structure and the organization of work activities.

Taking the two intellectual traditions together, we developed the broad conceptual thrust of the Program: a socio-psychoanalytic perspective for understanding organizational enterprises by reconciling psychological and social aspects of human behavior, work tasks and activities, and the nature of the organizational environment within one general framework. The goal is to extend an understanding of the interdependence between psychological, structural and technical aspects of the organizational enterprise by providing a framework within which the independent contributions of these factors can be studied, evaluated and hopefully modified in the interest of both greater human satisfaction and organizational productivity. In practice, the Program is designed

- to develop a skill base in the practice of organizational assessment, design, development and consultation at all levels from the individual, to interventions with work groups and teams, to the organization as a total entity

- by providing its participants with a working knowledge of the conscious and unconscious psychological forces that profoundly influence the nature and quality of individual, group and social processes, and their relation to the success or failure of individuals, groups and organizations to accomplish their intended tasks.

Primary Task

In summary, we can say that the primary task of the Program, as it has developed over the past seven years, is to:

- join with the White Institute's historic mission to link psychoanalytic knowledge to social and cultural processes, and to apply this knowledge to social problems and dilemmas in the tradition of Sullivan, Fromm, Thompson, and Fromm-Reichmann;

- develop a teaching and consultancy training model designed to understand those "difficulties in living" that include the problems that individuals, groups and organizations have in working together productively to accomplish their goals;

- meld and integrate the psychoanalytic and the socio-technical/open systems traditions to inform the Program philosophy and design;

- bring from latency a *systematized theory of the practice* of applied psychoanalysis.

III. PARTICIPANTS

Given this primary task, we thought participants would represent four professional groupings:

- Psychoanalysts and psychoanalytically-oriented clinicians who had an interest in making group and organizational consultation work part of their professional practice.

- Professional organizational consultants (internal and external) and management development experts who wanted advanced training opportunities.

- Human Resource managers and executives who were responsible for either developing programs themselves, or for hiring outside consultants to conduct management training programs, executive education seminars, career development workshops and specialized training events.

- Executives and managers who wanted to increase their understanding of individual, group and organizational issues in order to enhance their own functioning and effectiveness.

The Program enrolled its first group of 15 participants in September 1990. We are now fully operational, having graduated the inaugural class in May 1992, and enrolling the fourth class for the Fall of 1993. Our participants, have a mean age of 47, and come from a broad range of backgrounds and interests — human resource executives, business managers, organizational consultants, law partners, university professors, psychoanalysts, psychotherapists, social scientists and small business owners. We are now a community of approximately 75 people.

IV. PROGRAM CURRICULUM & DESIGN, AND STAFF ROLES

Program Faculty

Let me say something first about the Program Faculty. The core group that originally proposed the Program and now continues to administer it consists of Larry Gould, Kathy White and myself. The three of us, as psychoanalysts who had graduated from the White Institute, were entrusted by the Institute with the task of setting it up. We knew each other and also felt able to address the job because of our extensive experience in group relations work, largely through the A.K. Rice Institute, as well as consulting work. In proposing the Program, we joined with three "outsiders" — i.e. non-Institute graduates — whose work consisted entirely of dynamically oriented organizational consultation: Larry Hirschhorn and Tom Gilmore, from the Center for Applied Research, (formerly connected to the Wharton School) and Jim Krantz who was at the time on the Faculty of Yale's School of Management. The six of us, then, combined in various degrees knowledge of psychoanalysis, experience with consultation, group relations training, and an interest in education.

Over the past several years, we have added colleagues both to share the burden of work and to bring greater diversity to the tasks of teaching. Marvin Geller, Director of Student Psychological Services at Princeton, an analyst and group relations trainer with a consulting practice, joined us the second year, as did Mal O'Connor, an anthropologist with the Center for Applied Research. Last year, Ellen Schall joined us, a Professor in the School of Public Affairs at NYU and former New York City Commissioner of Juvenile Justice. This year we added Rose Miller, an experienced group relations consultant.

Curriculum

From the start it was clear to us that the Program would be centered on practical experience. Thus the curriculum was designed to prepare our participants for their actual consulting experience and to support them during it.

Our idea is to spend the first semester — note our traditional academic terminology and thinking — focusing on the conceptual and personal contexts for their work. On the conceptual level, we offer a course on "Open Systems," a course that introduces them to the basic ideas and texts of group dynamic and organizational systems thinking that we are familiar with from our own group relations tradition: Bion, Menzies, Miller and Rice, etc. We also offer a course on Role Analysis, on a more personal level, a course in which our participants each present a role dilemma they currently face together with information about the organization in which that dilemma occurs and also their families of origin, particularly focusing on the roles they occupied in their families. The point of the course is to help each participant understand the dilemma both from the perspective of the organization and its problems and also from the personal perspective of the assumptions and unconscious patterns of relationship they bring with them to it. Our thinking is that in doing this work for themselves and each other they are also learning to understand how to approach such problems with potential clients.

At the end of the first semester, consulting teams are formed and, God willing, clients assigned. The second semester courses, accompanying the phase of beginning client work are (1) "Open Systems II," a continuation of basic systems theory, including socio-technical systems, and (2) "Organizational Diagnosis." As our approach to consulting assumes that each client system is a unique configuration of task and social defensive elements, it is essential to build into the consulting process a diagnostic phase in order to discern at a deeper level the nature of the client problem, of which the presenting complaint is likely to be symptomatic. This course, then, runs concurrently with the first phase of the consulting teams' work with their clients, proving them with the opportunity not only to think about diagnosis but also present their initial experiences of interacting with client systems.

The second year opens with two courses directly focused on client work. "Organizational Consultation" provides readings on the consultative process but also and, more importantly, opportunities for the consulting teams to present their work. The second course, "Organizational Design" focuses on how to think about designing organizational structures and presents a series of case studies.

The final semester offers a course we call "Advanced Consultation" in which we invite experienced consultants to come to present their work and respond to questions from the Program participants about their conceptions or underlying assumptions in consulting. The second course of this final semester is in the process of being revamped: up until this point we have offered a course on "Management Training" focused essentially on providing the tools of executive education. We are now in the process of replacing that with a course that gives our participants the opportunity to revisit the issues of role analysis and team development and also to reflect on particular cases.

In mentioning that this course is being revamped I don't mean to leave you with the impression that this is the only revamping we have needed to do in our now almost four years of existence. On the contrary. But we are essentially satisfied at this point that we have a sound and functioning educational curriculum. But two points need to be added.

The first is that we add to this basic curriculum workshops and additional educational modules. Workshops (generally on Saturdays) provide us with the opportunity to have visiting consultants engage our participants in particular issues: Clay Alderfer, for example, usually provides a workshop on "Imbedded Intergroups." Modules (which are Saturdays plus the preceding and following Wednesday class periods) provide opportunities for us to profit from our Faculty at the Center for Applied Research, Larry Hirschhorn, Tom Gilmore and Mal O'Connor. They may focus intensively on a topic such as "Post Industrialism" or present extended case material. There are other additional events scheduled throughout the year, such as "Social Dreaming" — but these are more in the nature of organizational interventions and I will discuss them somewhat later in this presentation.

We have increasingly built into the Program self-reflective and self-analytic aspects. Each course has a Convenor, whose role is to pay attention to the dynamics of the class. In some courses, particularly in the first year, a period of time is set aside at the end of each class meeting for the Convenor to work with the class on clarifying its own process. In other courses, the Convenor will interject comments or attempt to raise issues when they seem appropriate or when they seem to be interfering with the class's ability to work at its task of the moment. Frequently this analytic work can be related to the theories we are studying about group and organizational process. But it also tends to ensure that no significant problem concerning the relatedness of the participants to each other, with the Faculty or with the Program as a whole will go unnoticed for long.

V. PRACTICUM EXPERIENCE - THE OCS

In order to provide clients for consulting teams to have as part of their practicum experience, we set up the Organizational Consultation Service, the OCS. The mandate of the OCS is to provide low fee consultations to organizations — primarily but not exclusively not-for-profit or community-based organizations — which might otherwise not be able to afford them. Significantly, in so doing, we were able to carry out the mandate of our home institution, The White Institute, which has been since its founding by Erich Fromm, Clara Thompson, Harry Stack Sullivan and others in 1943 committed to addressing social issues through psychoanalysis. Indeed, our intention to set up such a service was a major selling point for our psychoanalytic colleagues in supporting the Organizational Program in the first place.

Administratively, the OCS is a separate entity in the Program. It sponsors the event in which teams are organized. (The dynamics of that event, by the way, are among the things which the teams are encouraged to study.) It assigns supervisors, contracts with clients, and collects fees. In effect, the consulting teams work for the OCS, and thus have to figure out for themselves how to make best use of the courses and supervision that are available to them to help with their learning throughout the practicum.

As you might imagine, it was not entirely easy at the start to find a sufficient number of suitable clients for our teams. But the situation has much improved as the word about the availability of this service has spread. Currently we have teams working with a department of the United Nations, the substance abuse division of a major hospital in New York, and a large nursing home. This past fall, we had the first opportunity to contract out to a team of Program graduates a client we could not assign to a team in the Program; our hope is that these opportunities will occur increasingly and give our graduates more chances to learn from experience beyond the formal Program boundaries. Several firms have formed out of the ranks of Program participants and graduates, and they would be eager to have the additional work the OCS could potentially generate.

VI. PROGRAM ISSUES

My part of the presentation centers on issues and concerns about the Program. Initially, I felt it was hard to find a role for myself, but ultimately relied on my experience as a Faculty member and conference presenter to illuminate some issues in the Program.

Upon my arrival at Southbank, I discovered that I had not been registered at the conference and at the last moment a makeshift name tag was given to me — a tag I chose not to wear. This experience provided me with further data about the lack of clarity of my role as part of the White Institute group presenting at the conference. This, in part, may have stemmed from the fact that I was not invited to attend the conference, but, rather, I had asked to come along.

As a result of my feelings and experiences, I was able to formulate three issues that I feel to be embedded in our Program:

Unclear Affiliation with the White Institute

The first comes from my personal experience. I have become aware that my ability to take on roles other than Faculty roles at our Program is limited by the fact that I am not a graduate of the White Institute. This simply points to one of the issues involved in being sponsored by and actually being a part of the Institute. While the Program managers were able to support my attendance at this conference, it was partial support and this required intense negotiations with the White on their part. This situation raises the question whether the Program is held as "otherly" in the Institute, and whether it is integrated as yet into its overall mission. The effects on membership morale need to be considered in this regard.

Effects of a Part-time Institution

The second issue which I had in mind before the actual presentation was the issue of the Faculty and administration of the Program being part-time. I used the fact that I had not been registered at the conference as an example of things falling between the cracks in a part-time institution. Students have feelings about our limited availability, and our part-time-ness also effects our work relationships, our communications with one another, and our boundary and role management efforts. The complexity of our lives mirrors the complexity of our students lives.

The question whether individuals taking up multiple work roles both within and outside of their organizations has limiting effects on Program cohesion and effectiveness needs to be addressed.

Problems with Collaborative Learning

The third issue is an example of the way we try to think about group and organizational life, especially our search for relevant covert issues. The issue I formulated, with the help of my colleagues, is the illumination of a covert agenda held primarily by the psychoanalytic wing of the Faculty. Those of us involved in A.K. Rice work have for years worked on the edges of organizational consultation relying primarily on the knowledge and experience gained through our group relations work. Most of us have not been as well informed on the socio-technical side of the work. Our Program, in bringing together the psychoanalytic an socio-technical perspectives, not only provides an integration of the two streams for our students, but also provides the psychoanalytic Faculty with opportunities to learn through teaching and working with colleagues. I think the desire to learn about the socio-technical in greater depth is conscious in the minds of a number of Faculty. The Program has provided a way for some of us to be students without acknowledging our deficiencies and without formally taking up the student role. I think as a group and as individuals, we always prefer to be "staff rather than members." I think that the unacknowledged ambition in the psychoanalytic Faculty sets us up as pseudo-experts and works against the collaborative learning that we say is the goal for our organizational culture.

VII. ORGANIZATIONAL SELF-REFLECTION

From the start we built into our management planning some of the conventional means of organizational self-reflection such as Faculty retreats and Program-wide meetings. These have proved indispensable in providing the opportunities to work at shoring up our relatedness and crafting solutions to particular problems. As you can imagine, with an "insider" and "outsider" set of Faculty roles there have been on-going tensions to be managed; and with a new educational design to refine, curricular problems and role confusion abounded.

But we quickly realized that such conventional approaches were insufficient. Not only did we feel the need for greater organizational exploration but also we felt driven to provide ourselves and our participants with exposure to new technologies of exploration. One has been developed by our colleagues at the Center for Applied Research: Histories of the Future. The other has been developed by Gordon Lawrence here in Great Britain: Social Dreaming. Let me say a few brief words about each.

Histories of the Future is an exercise in which different scenarios are explored for the organization's future. We set up two panel discussions, for example, both of which were imagined to take place five years in the future. One panel was convened to conduct a postmortem review of factors that led to the decision just announced to shut down the Program. In response to questions from the audience, the panel reviewed the history of the previous five years, attempting to identify the key factors and major turning points that led to this outcome. The other panel celebrated, five years hence, the decision of the Program to move into new quarters in order to provide space for more Faculty and expanded services. Similarly, the panel sought to identify the significant factors and events that led to this highly successful future outcome.

In going through this exercise — actually we have done it more than once — we were able to focus on a confusion we experience in the Program around primary task: are we really aspiring to train fully prepared organizational consultants or are we sidetracked by other objectives?

The second major interventionist technology, "Social Dreaming," involves the sharing of dreams in a matrix consisting of all Program members, including staff, with the assistance of several consultants. The task of the matrix is to explore dreams through association rather than interpretation. Thus dreams and their associations are woven together to produce images of the organization's collective unconscious life. Then, in other group settings, this material is related to Program issues. I refer you to Gordon Lawrence's writings on this for a fuller account.

The point I wish to make here is that this has given us a powerful look into our unconscious life and particularly into feelings about persecution and deprivation among participants and Faculty alike that have been present throughout our beginning years. Thus "Social Dreaming" has been enormously useful to use not only in identifying particular dynamics between participants and Faculty but also in fostering a spirit of openness and collaboration. And, of course, and by no means incidentally, it has given all of us greater access to tools and ideas for thinking about organizational life.

VIII. AFTERWORD

In our three planning years and four years in full operation we have gained in experience in melding and integrating the two intellectual and theoretical traditions that inform the Program design — psychoanalytic and socio-technical. We find that both our participants, as well as well as the expanding group of Program clients, public and private sector organizations are responsive to this development. In addition, the Program has provided some leadership for other psychoanalytically oriented consultancy training organizations that have sprung up subsequent to ours.

While we are enjoying some programmatic success, remain uniquely positioned in our country, provide leadership for some of our counterparts in their start-up phase, the Program is very much in its infancy, and if it is to thrive it must concern itself with its growth and development. We have discovered through the Social Dreaming Conference and the Histories of the Future Events that Ken mentioned that there are four potential mission streams for the Program:

> **Education** — a two-year, professional program with a regular academic mission;

> **Role Analysis** — a service to participants that can be applied in their work roles;
> **Consultancy Training** —a training program that develops a particu-

lar skill base;

Education, Role Analysis, Constancy Training — an integration of the three models.

While somewhat overlapping, these are different constructs that would require very different staffing, structure, marketing and budgetary strategies and ways of thinking and teaching. We are hoping that a collaborative discussion among us today will be mutually enlightening about these and other developmental issues in training for consultancy that works.

PRESSURES ON THE CONSULTANT'S INDEPENDENCE

VICTOR HOOD AND ELLEN NOONAN
The Advisors Group, London

ABSTRACT

This paper reports on three pieces of consultancy work which were positioned at different distances from the centre of the clients' businesses. The work is described in some detail, and is analysed in terms of the different pressures on the consultants' independence. The first, a series of individual manager assessments, can be thought of as taking place outside the boundary of the client company. The second, a graduate recruitment programme, took place on the boundary of the organisation. The third, a review of senior managers' experiences of joining the business in mid-career, took place deep inside the boundary.

The conclusion is that there is no simple progression along a scale of "pressures on consultants' independence" as distance from the centre varies. It is at the boundary that the greatest turbulence occurs, whereas work positioned clearly outside or clearly inside the organisation bears some quite evident similarities.

INTRODUCTION

We are members of the Advisors Group. This small consultancy group has been in existence in some form for nearly 50 years. It originated in the Tavistock Institute of Human Relations and the Tavistock Clinic with a group of psychoanalysts and psychologists who created a graduate recruitment scheme with Unilever designed to select young men who had the potential to become the company's senior managers. It remained within the Tavistock as a loose network of professionals with Harold Bridger at the centre until 10 years ago, when it became an independent organization. Aside from the particular relationship with Unilever, the group was active in other selection activity and in helping organizations manage the effects of change on its personnel and working processes. It also offered a career counselling service.

The distinguishing feature of the Group throughout is that the members have a thorough training and are actively practicing in clinical psychology or psycho-therapy in the psychoanalytic tradition. A significant part of the strength of the group lies in the fact that we are all part-time consultants with a substantial commitment to another professional activity. We hold senior professional and managerial positions in education, the health service, charitable and community mental health organizations, and research. Most members have a private psycho-therapy or counselling practice.

The impetus for this paper which aims to consider the pressures on consultants' independence came when an existing client for whom we have carried out selection work for many years offered us a retainer. This was complicated by the request that we also enter into a payment by results arrangement with them. Crudely this meant that the fewer candidates they had to process to achieve their recruitment target the better off we would be financially. Needless to say this offer had its appeal, but it also raised questions about how we could ensure that standards would be maintained and our professional integrity preserved. It also raised questions about our separateness from the company if we were to enter into this arrangement on the grounds that, as they pointed out, all the managers in their company (including the recruitment personnel) were subject to the payment by results agreement. There seemed to be a fundamental confusion about what kind of employees of the company we were.

Working from the anxieties generated by the offer, we thought that the answer to the question posed in our title today was that the further into the centre of the client organization we went, the more our independence would be threatened. In fact, that seems not to be true in our experience.

In this session we wish to present three different consultancy projects which vary principally in their boundary relationships, looking at a few selected issues relating to independence. By independence we mean the capacity to think and act without being unduly influenced by internal and external pressures, keeping faith with the basic principles and philosophy which underpin our practice. We are trying to focus on the psychodynamics of being a consultant, but we also demonstrate how we use our psychodynamic insight as consultants.

The first piece of work was carried out almost entirely outside the company, and the third piece was done at the heart of the organization. The middle piece occurred on the boundary of the company. We will summarise each section in terms of four headings:

    a.   The relationship with the client was characterised by:

    b.   The consultant felt identified with:

    c.   The pressures on the consultant's professional standards were:

    d.   The internal dynamic which the consultant tried to keep relatively free from was:

1. PROJECT 1 - WORKING OUTSIDE THE BOUNDARY

The beginning was a call from an ex-Unilever manager who remembered the role played by the Advisors group on his own selection board for the graduate management development scheme. He was currently Personnel Director of a fast-growing company which had recently decided to become involved in the take-over business, acquiring small to medium size manufacturing concerns and sorting them out. They were not asset-strippers, I should emphasise, but they certainly prided themselves on their ability to make a business more profitable through cost-cutting and through bringing in modern management techniques.

For my part, I was a self-employed consultant at that time, although with membership of a network which got together on various projects.

What he wanted was help in making some decisions about the management of their most recent acquisition. There had been a sorting-out process, during which some managers had left or been pushed out, and some of the company's own managers installed on a temporary basis: in the absence of any proper personnel systems, he felt quite in the dark about the abilities and potential for development of a number of key people. The task would be to carry out individual assessments of their talents, their immediate training needs, and their potential for further development.

My response was to establish my credentials, to convey my interest, to tell him what it would cost, and to suggest a meeting with himself and his Chief Executive. Privately I had reservations about the morality of these hostile takeovers, since people always seemed to lose their jobs, but the project sounded interesting and I was looking for work at that point. I had also read about the Chief Executive in the business press, and so I was intrigued, and a bit flattered, too.

The company's head office was attached to its oldest factory, well outside London, and I spent half a day there, meeting the Personnel Director and the Chief Executive, and looking around the factory. I found that the Personnel Director and I got on very well indeed, no doubt in part because of the Unilever contact. He had been interviewed on his selection board by Eric Trist, and I am sure that I benefitted from association with the great. With the Chief Executive, on the other hand, I had a great deal of trouble. He wanted to impress upon me the need for his managers to be incredibly tough, and so he proceeded to regale me with stories about his own toughness, using four-letter words all the time. In the end I said something rather debunking and probably flippant, and he spluttered and then laughed, but it was a tense moment. I suppose I was asserting my independence at that point, and that seemed to be important.

At the end of the morning the Personnel Director and I sat down to negotiate. I stressed the point that I was not able to provide a global assessment of a manager, which could then be applied in some universal way to any work environment. I could certainly use psychometric tests, and I could try to understand not only what the person had to offer to their work, but also what needs they tried to satisfy through their work, but I didn't make claims further than that. I would need to be asked specific questions about any manager which related to a particular work-place and work-group. It would be very important to stay in constant touch with him to understand the working culture and environment of the taken-over company as it developed, through the interaction between the old way of doing things and the new.

I went on to explain my procedure of spending one whole day with the manager, and how I discuss all my thoughts with the manager, including drafting the report, which the Personnel Director and I could then discuss.

He seemed surprised that I made so many provisos, and emphasised his need for straight answers, but he eventually accepted my view that the more I knew about his company the more likely he was to get straight answers, and he suggested that we have a trial run, as it were, with one man who had stirred up quite different reactions among the board. We agreed that apart from the usual information he would also send me his personal notes on his meeting with the manager, and a list of points he was interested in exploring further. Again this had not occurred to him as something which would be of value to me.

The most important feature about all this is probably what follows: for the next two and a half years, during which I carried out about thirty of these one-day assessments of their newly-acquired managers, I never set eyes on either the Personnel Director or the Chief executive again. The Personnel Director and I did spend time on the phone, including a series of six-monthly reviews of how the work had gone, but we never met face-to-face.

The psychodynamic feature I would like to draw attention to is the interplay of dependence and idealisation and omnipotence. At the outset, my experience was of the client apparently wishing to engage in a totally dependent relationship with me. I, in return, was to fall in with his idealised perception of what I could do, and behave in an omnipotent way. Thus his own ideas and his perceptions of people were to be of no relevance or interest to me, whereas I was supposed to be some kind of magician who could not only see all there was to see about a manager, but could also see into the future, and predict successfully how someone would work in an environment I was not familiar with, and alongside people I had never met.

From my side, I do find myself at times tempted towards omnipotence as a way of coping with life's anxieties, although of course that brings its own panics, since if you are meant to be omnipotent you are only as good as your last performance. On this occasion I had to struggle to work out what was professionally acceptable in a context of feeling tempted. For instance, I prefer the client to come to me for the day, rather than work on site. Again, I don't use any one battery of tests, but pick and choose depending on what the issues are. Further, I spend a lot of time in exploring the stages of childhood and adolescence with the person, using my clinical training, which yields very subjective data. Taken together, lots of potential pitfalls for me: lots of opportunities to be arbitrary, or idiosyncratic, or a bit mystical.

Firstly, what questions could I legitimately set out to answer?

Here are some examples:

> Has he the mental toughness to be a Plant Manager?
> Has he the innate intelligence to cope with a broader range of responsibilities?
> Is he an innovative person?
> Is he better suited to Marketing or Production?
> Is he better at presenting than achieving?
> What is his motivation - has he the drive to succeed?
> Are his decisions affected by his feelings?
> And the question about the first person I saw, the "trial run" -
> Is he the world's greatest bull-shitter?

These are not questions which can, or should, be answered by a straight yes or no, but they are certainly questions which can be addressed from different perspectives. I found that having that sort of question did provide a degree of structure, within which the manager and I could work. Inevitably other issues would also arise in the course of the day, since I use some exercises deriving from clinical work, and these often bring up less obvious matters for consideration. By the end of the day I would have worked through the material, discussed the questions and the findings with the manager, and outlined the headings of the report. It is my policy to discuss everything fully with the person there and then, and not to dodge any less welcome or palatable outcomes; this can make for a long day, on occasion, but it seems important to me, not least because it allows the person to make sense of the day and to integrate this particular experience into the rest of their life. It also sets a style of collaborative working which helps me to keep my feet on the ground.

It needs to be said, and not for self-advertisement, that the people who attended the one-day session with me almost invariably got a lot out of it; they remarked on the contrast with their experience of the predator company, but in any case they enjoyed the chance to reflect on their lives so far, and the sense that there were patterns and shapes to be identified and taken into account in their future planning. My function seemed to be completely different from everything else which the company organised for its employees.

In summary, then, one great source of tension and uncertainty for the consultant was the temptation to become a sort of mystical expert, with people beating a path to my door to receive my wisdom. The fact that I lived in a small village, which meant giving fairly complicated travelling instructions, perhaps added to the fantasy.

The second feature of note was the inaccessibility of the Personnel Director, who in truth spent much of his time visiting each of a dozen sites dotted around the UK. We communicated by telephone. For my part I was sure it mattered to discuss each report with him once he had received it, whereas his first response was usually that it was fine, just what he wanted etc; only after a few minutes did he realise that there were matters to be clarified, or discussed further, or very occasionally, to disagree about. Looking back, there was some reality in his attitude, in the sense that the company was very active, the businesses were going very well, and the share price kept going up and up.

I had mixed feelings about their success. I enjoyed the feeling of contributing to it, but I was becoming increasingly concerned about the lack of direct contact with the realities of the business operation. As time went on I was seeing managers who were working in factories I had never visited, and engaged in a different business entirely from the parent company. In addition, it was pretty obvious that there were several people, including the Chief Executive, who could have gained something through a regular review with me of the kinds of issues cropping up in the different functions and divisions, which I was gradually hearing more and more about, and in which they themselves were playing a part. In other circumstances I might have suggested such an overview, but partly through my uneasiness with the Chief Executive, I never really pushed that idea.

More importantly, I suspect, is the difficulty which a self-employed person can encounter in confusing one's professional worth with personal worth. What I didn't fully realise was how excluded I was beginning to feel, and the theme of being excluded from the centre of things is one which has a private significance for me. Looking back, there seems something quite hostile in my not asking more strongly for these meetings - first of all so that I could improve the quality of what I was doing, and secondly so that they could have feedback, without breaching confidentiality, on their personal styles as reported to me, on the worries or hopes people had, on the perception of Head Office, and on the central issues in the different cultures they were having to work within, and communicate effectively with.

From the Personnel Director's point of view, I suppose his perception of me was of someone essentially unchanging, someone concerned only with individuals, useful in making short-term decisions, but only reluctantly to be involved in the broader or longer-term development of the business through its people, and someone who tended to fuss too much, or was always wanting to check that everything was all right.

From my side, you could say that I was living in a kind of fantasy world. My image of the company was almost entirely formed at second-hand, through talking with people, one at a time, about their perceptions and their experiences of what went on. As the number of assessments mounted up I began to hear about managers I had seen earlier, from people who were new colleagues, and who occasionally carried a message for me. Sometimes there would be a piece in the business section which caught my eye, and I found myself reading it quite intently. There was an element of watching my favourite soap, episode by episode, as events unfolded. But I certainly felt more of a member of the audience than a member of the cast.

Turning to the four headings which we set out at the beginning:

a. The relationship with the client was characterised by:
Arms' length contact with the client but intensive work with the managers sent to the consultant
Pressure for the consultant to take up an omnipotent and aloof position
The consultant feeling excluded from the business operation and finding it difficult to insist on more involvement

b. The consultant felt identified with:
One person, and one function - the Personnel function. It was never clear quite what happened to the reports written by the consultant, but certainly the Personnel Director owned them
An aspect of the company which offered individual consideration to managers, in what was potentially a nurturing way. This seemed quite split off from the day to day running of the business, with its emphasis on the bottom line

c. The pressure on professional standards were:
Resistance to any real integration of the work into the ongoing life of

the company. It felt as if the consultant wanted to engage in a long-term view, and the client needed short-term answers and never mind the strategy.

d. The internal dynamic which the consultant tried to keep relatively free from was:

The take-over dynamic seems in retrospect to be very important. If the company's primary task is taking over businesses, then their primary anxiety is that <u>they</u> should not be taken over, and their response to the consultant can be understood as establishing a very firm boundary which he was not allowed to penetrate. Carrying on the idea of penetration, the exaggeratedly macho style from the top would further suggest a sexual symbolism attaching to the takeover activity, with the "feminine", nurturing function being split off into the consultant's work, thus freeing the top management from possible conflicts over their sense of purpose.

2. PROJECT 2 - WORKING ON THE BOUNDARY

This section is about establishing a relationship with a service organization, which wanted help with selecting a few graduates for a new elite programme designed to train practitioners through an internship and then sponsorship through an MBA. I was already working in the company as a 'selection expert' on another unique and experimental training programme and was known to the Personnel Director through this, but otherwise the groups of internal staff working on the two schemes were completely separate.

The original contact with the organization came through a Personnel Manager who had recently joined the company and whose career change had followed some individual consultations with me. So it was a personal invitation initially, although he knew of the Advisors Group and was happy with its policy that any work is shared within the group. The precipitating problem then was that in the first year of the scheme they had selected some trainees who had presented adolescent behaviour problems; they didn't know how to handle them and didn't want to make any more mistakes of that sort. We set up a selection process which, although rudimentary, the internal staff found exciting, effective, and fun - and which was initially foolproof since there were no more troublemakers.

I saw this as an Advisors Group project, with myself as the key contact person, so when the request came to discuss a second consultancy, I assumed it would be similar.

It was impressed on me that this was a very very special scheme, the company was investing a lot of money and trust in it, and it would recruit only the creme de la creme. Consequently they wanted only the best advice about it.

It was a complex selection problem. They wanted to find the brightest, most ambitious, most presentable graduates who had the potential to become directors, who would, without fail, be accepted for top flight MBA programmes in two years' time, but who would do fairly low level routine work in the early stages. As I had already experienced with this company, everything was being done at the 11th hour with terrible urgency. I was glad not to be on my own in the face of this kind of pressure and expectations and repaired to my Advisors Group colleagues for support and ideas regularly. One colleague actually attended a couple of meetings in the middle stages to talk about psychometric testing.

I was bringing to this my own manic ambitions: I had in my mind the ideal selection process, which would explore the conscious and unconscious elements of the match between personality and career opportunities. I was eager to try this out somewhere, and I imagined I had found a home for it in this company which seemed governed by the idea that nothing but the best and most elegant would do. I had a few twinges of anxiety about a conflict of interests, since this programme might compete with another I was a consultant to, but I justified this at the time by arguing that the other company had their own tailor-made procedure, so I was free to take these ideas elsewhere.

We had two weeks to get the thing up and running. It was part of their culture to drop everything if a customer required them, and they expected this kind of availability from me. I did my best to oblige. In all the fervour of the planning, I took insufficient notice of the undercurrents and underlying dynamics. If I had thought about it at all I could have anticipated that they would ultimately reject my ideal model because their mode of operation was one of very close control, and the notion of a rampant unconscious - although intellectually fascinating - would be anathema to them.

Day by day I would arrive for meetings to learn that another bit of my elegant programme had been nibbled away, leaving us finally with a shoestring format that was, incidentally, almost identical to the one devised for the first programme in the company. The significant difference for me was that I was not permitted to share the work with my colleagues: I was expected to work on all the selection days, and if necessary the schedule would be rearranged to ensure that. This was logical at a practical level, but I understood the meaning of it only later.

I certainly felt dependent and compromised in this process. The remains of the procedure were only just good enough for the task - but any guilt about my other client was relieved. I certainly felt that whatever they said about my expert status, it was paltry compared to their sense of knowing what's best for them. (In principle, I do agree with that, but somehow I felt diminished.) I felt positively isolated from my professional colleagues, culled out from the group like the calf to be branded. If I think about it in inter-group terms, I felt that I had been captured, my ideas and my expertise appropriated and modified by them without consultation: my professional identity and independence subsumed. And in a way I *was* branded, since I wore a company badge on the selection days, rather than having one with my own company name. This was in addition to a visitor's pass, which I also had.

Aside from the way the nibbling was done, a further indication I had of the extent of their control was the discovery that they had engaged three 'top-experts-in-their-field' consultancies in the planning stage and were keeping us firmly apart and unaware of what the others were contributing until their plan was complete. One disappeared unaccountably, but the other - an expert in psychometrics whose tests were to be used instead of ours - became my invisible partner. In the way the procedure was set up, apart from the briefing meeting described below, we were never to meet, and initially he never saw the candidates. I observed the candidates working on a task as a group and held brief individual interviews, and he sent in written reports of the computer analyzed results of tests that were administered by the internal staff.

However, he and I did meet occasionally by accident in the first year, and we took a certain delinquent pleasure in our clandestine relationship. He felt pretty much as I did about the way we had each been idealized and split, and about the wastage in a procedure which did not allow us to build an integrated picture of the individual candidates using our different and complementary data. We began to nibble back, and eventually we both attended the mid-day meetings. I think the client could see the advantage of this, but I think they also felt the loss of the control of a checks and balance system where he and I 'marked' the candidates in a double blind fashion, and they always curtailed any dialogue we might have.

Before the first selection day there was a briefing meeting to which all participants in the process were invited. I was frankly apprehensive about it. Among the items on the agenda was feed back of the results of an exercise carried out by my until then unseen partner. It perhaps goes without saying that this unit in wanting to attract the brightest, most ambitious, and most presentable young graduates was recruiting in its own image. Every manager and director of the unit had taken the tests the other consultant proposed to use with the candidates in order to provide a profile and baseline data. I was conscious of feeling envious that he'd been given that work and that I needed to watch my reaction to his presentation. I was soon diverted from such personal preoccupations, however. The results were presented anonymously, but it felt like being at a birthday party for five year olds when the prizes are given out, with everyone speculating about who had got the best and worst scores on any factor, accompanied by lots of raucous laughter and surprisingly provocative personal comments about each other.

Their mutual envy and rivalry was hardly disguised, and the infectious intensity of it alerted me to the absolute necessity of creating a positive working relationship with the other consultant lest we replicate it. Even so, during the mid-day discussions, when I would offer my observations of the group and his reports would be read out, sometimes I could manage to feel merely curious about how far we agreed about the candidates from our different perspectives, but more often I would feel competitive and hence vulnerable, especially since my bit depended on how on form I was on the day and how undefended the group was.

On the afternoon of the selection day, each candidate was interviewed by a director, a manager, a personnel officer, and myself. The others saw two or three candidates each, while I saw all candidates. In the decision- making discussion at the end of the day, the atmosphere was similar to the briefing meeting: the directors and managers were possessive about the people they saw and excited by their own interviews. It was evident that despite the extensive exercise of drawing up criteria for an acceptable candidate and the provision of a pro forma for the interviews, very idiosyncratic conclusions were being drawn from highly inventive conversations. They found it very difficult to allow anyone else to have an opinion about their candidates based on the shared group observation. Indeed, usually they left the room when their candidates were not being discussed, and had to be fetched back when it was their turn. It took me a while to realize that I was the only person in the room who had access to all the application forms. It was seldom possible to arrive at a firm decision about the candidates on the day.

The recruitment director (a calm, soft-spoken, self-contained man, clearly very bright, and clearly committed to excellence, but by understatement not by proclamation) was surprisingly inactive in this meeting, exerting very little control over and placing very little structure in the discussions. This was left to the administrator who was a young woman with little authority over the professionals. The pressure was definitely on me to manage this rowdy group - to keep them in the room together and to inject some rationality and order into the highly subjective material they provided. It felt like trying to sort out family squabbles, but it helped me to understand why it was inconceivable to them that I could share the work with a colleague: in no way did these people consider themselves to be interchangeable, in the way that I felt that I shared procedures and values with my colleagues.

As I gained the confidence of the recruitment director, he began to indicate to me that the real selection problem he faced - and why he had wanted external assistance - was located not in the candidates, but in the members of his unit. We had set up a system which placed the candidates in the paradoxical position of having to cooperate in a task while competing for limited favours, but the system as designed could not deal with exactly the same difficulty for the selectors, and it was exacerbating a problem of rivalry which was only latent in the everyday work. Furthermore, he was quite clear about who his favourites were, but he could not really afford to let those preferences show. Hence the silent pressure on me. It felt eerily like the reason I had been invited into the company in the first place: to eliminate misbehaviour which couldn't be handled. Once this was clear between us, I could suggest ways of adapting the programme and the format of the discussions. Even so, an idea I had put forward a year ago, and which had been received with some skepticism, has just been modified and put into effect. Although I was pleased to hear this, I once again felt the impact of their desire for control.

Just for a moment, too, I felt very identified with the candidates. When I am working inside, wearing the company badge, they can't quite figure out whether I am a member of the firm or not. Nor can I! Certainly I identify with - and am identified with - the selectiveness and the matching process, and I have been prepared to allow them to shape my contribution to fit their needs, but I have to work hard at maintaining my independence through how I think and act because if I am to be of any use to them at all I have to function as a member of the Advisors Group. This is very similar to the candidate's problem at the boundary: they have to 'be themselves' but they also need to try to figure out what is wanted; they have to show that they have something special to offer the company, but they also have to show that they are willing to let it be formed by the company training.

In reflecting on why this has been such a difficult, but engaging, piece of work to establish, I have concentrated on the activity at the boundary of my role as consultant. I have here perhaps portrayed both myself and the people I worked with in a questionable light through attempting to explore the dynamics of our interactions, and internal dynamics are seldom as pretty as what appears on the surface. I tolerated the original compromises partly out of respect for the quality of the service they provided. I wanted to work with them, but I was confronted with a deeply ingrained and tested culture, compared to which I felt quite insignificant at times. Another important reason was that, despite eroding the actual procedure, at no time did they denigrate the ideas behind it. In the hectic early stages of negotiation I felt neither safe nor strong enough to be ruthless and aggressive in my arguments. My aim became to preserve enough of the necessary structures to persuade them, eventually, that they could make good use of a more rigorous and coordinated process that called on the less obvious elements of selection and decision-making. At a deeper level, I felt that it would simply be counterproductive to become controlling, idiosyncratic and rivalrous in return. Not only would I almost certainly lose if it came to a confrontation, but I would have been contributing to the problem which they needed to resolve among themselves.

The real test of my independence arises in the work during the day itself, where it is my job to resist the delight in their individual eccentricities and to find ways to turn their sometimes pernicious rivalry into an asset. And of course to continue to think as an advisor to the process and not as a decision-maker or an opinion holder. This does require a ruthlessness with myself, because the danger is of being seen as a spoil-sport or a loony and as uncooperative, withholding and useless - and I do want to be liked by them and I want them to use my impartiality. It is encouraging that everyone now almost always turns up for all the selection events on time and stays to the end, that they comment on each other's candidates and try to reconcile their different perceptions, even help each other think about how to conduct a difficult interview. In fact, they often come early to have a chat - and a joke and a competitive joust or two. Although I no longer have to wait among the candidates in reception at the beginning of the day and the reception and security staff greet me by name, I am still escorted to and from the working rooms. This may be sheer manners, but I understand it to mean that I am actually just a visitor. I may not still be undergoing selection myself every day, but it is entirely proper for the effectiveness of the consultancy that I remain poised on the boundary.

I have not addressed the four elements in the format used for the other two projects, but they are outlined in the summary at the conclusion of the paper.

3. PROJECT 3 - WORKING INSIDE THE BOUNDARY

In this project Ellen and I were asked by one person, a senior manager just below Board Level, to take an interest in what went on when new managers joined the business in mid-career. The background is that traditionally U grew its own managers, through the graduate management development scheme mentioned earlier, and it is only in quite recent times that middle or senior managers have been recruited in any kind of significant numbers. This has come about from three different developmental pressures - firstly there was the very rapid growth of Information Technology, which meant bringing in talent from outside to give impetus and growth to its development within the business, secondly there was the great increase in take-over and merger activity, which brought in whole groups of new faces into the management structure, and thirdly there was a changing culture in which U lost people in mid-career in a way which hadn't happened in the past -the Big Bang in the City for instance attracted many people who could see a much more rapid career progression there, or simply a lot more money.

Our client was picking up concerns that these newcomers were not all settling in well, and had various anecdotes which could imply that there were forces of rejection coming into play. Some new managers were unhappy, some were apparently not performing up to the level expected, and some were actually leaving again, despite all the care that had gone into their selection. It was clear that U, despite its wealth of tradition and its strongly established style of managing, had no accustomed ways of helping newcomers to enter the concern at these higher levels, and what Ellen and I were asked to do was to establish whether there was a problem, and if so, to try to identify the issues at stake.

So we had an individual client, who had the go-ahead from the Board, and we were being trusted to look quite deeply inside the organisation. Our interim reviews of the project were conducted only with him, and his secretary handled all the administration of our visits, made the travel arrangements, and so on. The only other person we worked with was a younger manager in that department who went through the lists of European managers with us, sorting out a representative sample of what came to be called MCJ's, the mid-career joiners, drawn from the different functions, product groups and European countries.

What we did was to conduct quite lengthy individual interviews with the managers identified for the sample, meeting them on their own ground. In our interviews we wanted first of all to understand what the person's experience of joining had been, for better or worse, and then to make a judgment about that person's own attitudes to change, since it was clear that there was a wide range of attitudes which coloured what the person had to tell us about how they had been treated. For example, one person might say that they did not want any molly-coddling, and seemed proud of their ability to walk in unprepared and not especially welcomed, and get a grip on the job, while another might say that the lack of a proper induction and hand-over process was inefficient and costly, while yet another would say that for his new boss to say "Well, I expect you want to be left alone to form your own impressions - see you in a month", left him feeling lonely and unsupported - not worth bothering about.

It did seem that one person's challenge was another person's threat, so in order to evaluate what they were saying we would go through each manager's personal development with them, trying to see what formative experiences of change there might be. We might come across a trauma, or a series of events that formed a pattern and which helped or hindered in coping with a new situation; we needed to know what contribution, positive or negative, the individual had made to their transition from the old to the new.

The interviews were fascinating for us and helpful for the managers, or so they said. Some were pleased to sit down and reflect on their early years and see what themes and influences there had been, while others were pleased to be able to go over the joining experience and make more sense of what had gone on. Some were still upset by it, even after a year or more had passed, since they had not had the opportunity, or perhaps hadn't dared, to give vent to their feelings.

We also studied our own reception at the different factories and head offices and laboratories we visited, and learned something about how boundaries are crossed. We were interested in the mementoes and souvenirs and photographs and ashtrays and even cups and saucers which were to be found in some managers' offices, bearing the name of some other organisation.

It is worth giving an account of what we found, since it seemed to us to cast light on our own experiences as consultants relating to clients. Resisting the temptation to tell you some fascinating stories, the broad themes were:

There was an analogy, in the mid-career joiner's experience, with a transplant operation, in the sense that rejection processes are always potentially active in a healthy organism. Foreign tissue runs the risk of rejection - "we don't do it like that here", and a devaluing of previous experience with another business.

There was an analogy with someone joining a new school in the 4th or 5th Form, and having to find a place in a long-established group, having to learn the slang, the customs, the informal structures - and of course the acronyms. "I heard that at the PDRC they were discussing UCMDS and UEMTS, and whether there need to be separate IMCs organised by NPD." The acronyms are a most powerful way of keeping newcomers in their place.

There were cultural issues - "I have been a loyal servant of this company for X years" - equating continuity of service with moral worth, and leading to distrust of these flighty newcomers. This is a deep-rooted attitude; at one time Ellen and I were working on a project to understand why people did leave, since it was at that time still unusual.

There was envy, from those who felt trapped where they were, or who lacked the self-belief what could take them elsewhere. And from other work we know that people who do leave U tend to suffer a slow attrition of their worth, to the point where it may eventually be said: "Well, they were no great loss."

These were broadly the findings, which, as I say, offered us more understanding about our own experience of being kept away from the centre of things for so many years. We had done training and development work in some of the operating companies, and we had traced and interviewed people who had left, but gaining what we had thought of as trust took years. Now we were realising that we had been encountering some of the same resistances as had the mid-career joiners, or MCJs as inevitably they became known.

Turning now to the pressures which we experienced in this rather different setting, there were some similarities and some differences from the two situations which we have already described.

First of all, the inner temptation and the outside pressure to omnipotence. We were in that position again of dealing in highly subjective material and coming to our own conclusions. The main help here was the presence of a colleague. Ellen has one older brother, and a history of rivalry. I am an older brother, with a history of rivalry. So there was never much danger of anyone getting too complacent, never mind omnipotent. There was also, we felt, a reflection within our working relationship of the man-woman issue within Unilever, in that the vast majority of senior managers are men, and she became concerned that I seemed to be taking over the project.

Who we identified with was important. We found that in the interview setting we were starting to identify with the individual at the expense of the company, and losing some perspective in favour of gathering up horror stories. We realised that we could easily get into the position of the tabloid press, hungry for good headlines, which justify our price, as it were. We tried to counteract this by drawing out all the details but then asking ourselves a question: "What contribution does this person make to their own problems?"

There was none of the remoteness from the reality of the business which I complained about earlier in the first section. Though with the proviso that we were treated in the same way as senior managers, ie opulently, with the chauffeurs and the hotels and the first-class travel, which does get pretty remote from the business realities. In fact, it set up an uncomfortable pressure in us to be incredibly hardworking, in order to justify all this luxury, and we really overdid it sometimes, cramming too many interviews into a space so as to save on overnight accommodation. Sometimes we got tired and overloaded, without the space needed to just let each interview settle into place, along with all the others.

The only pressure on our professional standards concerned confidentiality. Sitting with our client, or mentor, it was all too easy to offer illustrations of a broad finding by talking about individual instances, and of course he might try to guess who were describing. It seemed a paradox that because we felt so trusted by him we were in danger of behaving in an untrustworthy way.

Otherwise, things went well. The interviewees perceived us as sympathetic and helpful, and the Centre saw us as good at this sort of thing. But the line was drawn at the stage of implementation. Once we had fully discussed our report with our client, that was the end of our direct involvement. The structures and policies which arose from the discussion of our report were handled internally, even although some of them, especially the group meetings of the MCJ's which were brought into being in order to smooth their transition, would have benefitted from our input.

The four headings can be responded to as:

a. The relationship with the client was characterised by:
    A high degree of trust in being allowed to conduct confidential interviews with senior managers
    On-site visiting for interviews, with all the opportunities that offers to see behind the scenes
    Some pressure to be omnipotent, but not to be aloof

b. The consultant felt identified with:
    One person, and one function - the Personnel function. The client owned our report, and negotiated its entry, discussion, and implementation without help from us

An aspect of the company which offered individual consideration to managers, in what was potentially a nurturing way. Although this was much less foreign to the company culture than that observed in Section 1, again the work was well-received by participants as representing the caring side of the concern

c.   The pressures on the consultant's professional standards were:
Forming a cosy, confidential special relationship with the client, in which we could relax the usual rules of confidentiality - it seemed as if he became identified with us, rather than the reverse

d.   The internal dynamic which the consultant tried to keep relatively free from was:
The centre of a multi-national spends much of its time and effort in balancing issues of freedom and control in relation to the various operating groups which go to make up the total enterprise. They mustn't be running Liberty Hall, and they mustn't become the Civil Service - as they say, the business needs operational managers who resemble "eagles that can fly in formation". The consultants felt that they themselves were seen in the same light - competent and enter-prising but needing to be kept under the centre's control.

4.   SUMMARY
Please see overleaf for the summary chart.

SUMMARY OF THE THREE PROJECTS

	Relationship with the client characterised by:	Consultant felt identified with:	Pressures on professional standards were:	Consultant caught up in internal dynamic:
1	Arms' length contact Idealised competence - omnipotence Exclusion - retaliation	One person Personnel function Head Office Individual regard, nurturing	Resistance to integration of the work into the business	The take-over dynamic, consultant not allowed to penetrate Need for control
2	Idealised competence Splitting the competence Conditional welcome	Selectiveness Recruitment Director Candidates	Cut off from colleague review Minimal information on which to work psychodynamically To be a decision maker	Envy and rivalry Being chosen Idiosyncrasy Need for control Wish to be the ultimate expert
3	Regular contact and site visits High degree of trust Some idealisation of competence	One person Personnel function Head Office Individual regard, nurturing	Temptation to break confidentiality at times, because of the close relationship	The Centre's need to control the operating groups, while allowing them freedom within limits

Noonan/Hood Advisors Group

STRATEGIC & INTIMATE MODES OF INTERACTION

John Leary-Joyce, *Gestalt Centre, London*

ABSTRACT
This paper will focus on the difference between strategic and intimate processes in human systems. All organisations have peer groupings within a hierarchical structure. For effective functioning the peer group needs to relate in a more Intimate mode i.e. trust, openness, mutual dependency, etc. However, in a hierarchy where power and control are an external reality, a more Strategic mode is necessary i.e. diplomacy, discretion and mutual respect.

I will address how to recognise and facilitate both dynamics from a Gestalt perspective.

1. INTRODUCTION

I would like to outline the journey that has taken me to this paper.

My background has been in Gestalt psychotherapy, working in personal development and training groups that primarily promote intimate relationships and spontaneous behaviour. These were therapist led peer groups focussing on honesty, self disclosure, closeness and affection, any hierarchy or power struggles were self-generated and covert. Later having been involved in family therapy and my own children's upbringing, I became much more aware of the power imbalance and strategic manoeuvering that is inherent in a family system while also recognising the importance of love and intimacy.

It was later when I came to be involved in team development and organisational consultancy that this balance between Intimacy and Strategy became more crucial.

I could see that in an explicitly hierarchical system, unlike the peer group, people would need to interact/behave more strategically and relationships would be more formal and distant.

When I use the word STRATEGIC in this context I am not talking about the whole raft of theory and method call Strategic Management or Strategic Development which is more about Direction, Purpose, Goals and Aims of Organisations, but rather behaviour to attain personal power, control and influence.

I think a trap that many consultants fall into when they become involved in the personal growth field is to assume that openness, honesty and directness are the best policy per se.

In fact, skilful manipulation of the environment is quite compatible with Gestalt theory. Our emphasis is on creating a balance between personal needs and environmental needs or the team's needs in relation to the organisational needs.

To achieve this depends on an ability to negotiate, compromise, maintain mutual respect and honour each others principles. An ability to Creatively Adapt to the demands of the situation, a flexible response to new challenges.

To maintain this flexibility and adaptability we must be able to behave strategically when necessary and also to form intimate relations which are appropriate to the situation.

2. GRAPHIC REPRESENTATION OF STRATEGIC AND INTIMATE ENGAGEMENT

We can express this graphically by having a Horizontal Strategic Behavioural axis and a Vertical Intimate Relationship axis (Figure 1).

The poles of the vertical axis are High Intimacy: openness, warmth, self disclosure and Low Intimacy: distance, reserve, closed.

The poles of the horizontal axis are High Strategy: power, control, influence and Low Strategy: spontaneity, equality, mutuality.

```
                    HIGH INTIMACY
                         |
    SELF DISCLOSURE      |    OPENNESS
                         |
                         |    WARMTH
                         |
HIGH STRATEGY            |                LOW STRATEGY
_____|_____
                         |
POWER INFLUENCE          |    SPONTANEITY MUTUALITY
CONTROL                  |    EQUALITY
                         |
         DISTANT         |    CLOSED
                         |
         RESERVED        |    UNAVAILABLE
                         |
                    LOW INTIMACY
```

FIGURE 1

This provides us with a map with four sectors in which we can describe the type of interactions that would occur.

2.1. High Strategy High Intimacy (top left sector)

If we look at the extreme type of interaction that occurs when we seek or engage in an High Intimate relationship and use Highly Strategic behaviour, we get pseudo friendship, seduction and emotional manipulation.

This is the stance of some facilitators and consultants who want to foster an atmosphere of trust without disclosing too much of themselves. It is often characterised by language which is inclusive and talks about "We..." or is apparently about emotions e.g. "I feel that....." but which are really disguised opinions and thoughts.

I find establishment religion can have this quality. The priest/minister draws us into a close relationship with God, assuming an intimacy in a very formal setting..

2.2. High Strategy Low Intimacy (bottom left sector)

If we look at the very High Strategic behaviour and Low Intimate relationships, we get a highly political, scheming, cold and calculating type of interaction.

Language is full of "It is......." highly impersonal, careful and indirect with non-disclosing questioning "Why.....?"

Characterised in party politics where everyone is guarding their back and every move/word is carefully thought out in advance. But also reflects the ability to function well in crisis, whether as a fire officer in an emergency or an executive making tough business decisions.

2.3. Low Strategy Low Intimacy (bottom right sector)

The extreme of this sector produces a lively, debating interaction. Discussing and analysing ideas and theories, whether highly intellectual or casual pub chat. I often find T.V. like this - interesting, but "so what......".

In consultancy, Brain Storming is an excellent example - it evokes an immediacy with low risk factor, stimulating ideas and working them over creates solutions to many material, factual and mechanical problems. Many expert consultants function successfully in this sector analysing the organisation and producing an efficient cost/benefit programme. Language is an impersonal "one....." or "you....", a talking about or talking over but generally direct.

2.4. Low Strategy High Intimacy (top right sector)

In the fourth sector High intimacy, Low Strategy has the combination of warmth, openness along with the desire of mutually and immediacy and therefore is typified in the extreme as: close friendship, affection and falling in love.

Varying depths of feeling, personal exchanges, physical closeness, desire for a genuine, honest meeting/communication is the interactive style of this sector. Martin Buber described this as an "I - thou" meeting. The language is personal "I" "Me - You" and is a dialogue, a Talking 'to' .... rather than 'about'.

This is the goal of most therapeutic and spiritual systems. But not, however, always appropriate or desirable in a business context.

The negative aspect would be someone over involved, can't see the "wood for the trees". Allowing personal feelings to run away with them, which can lead to all sorts of complications, poor judgement, preferential treatment, etc.

3.   KEY TO EFFECTIVE FUNCTIONING

For healthy and effective functioning, an individual within an organisation must have:

Self Awareness : full range of responses within each sector and the ability to move between sectors.

Environmental Awareness: sensitivity to the positioning of others, ability to assess the appropriate sector for a given situation and to proceed through the cycle of contact

3.1.   Self Awareness : This requires the individual to be able to access the full range of emotional and cognitive responses of each sector. This means being warm and open i.e. Low Strategy High Intimacy with colleagues and clients you know and trust while also being guarded and calculating i.e. High Strategy Low Intimacy when negotiating a competitive contract.

Boundary maintenance is also crucial so that one is able to contain feelings that might lead to inappropriate intimacy i.e. sexual relations between boss and subordinate or inappropriate distance, i.e. hanging on to old grudges and resentments: an inability to forgive.

Obviously, because of our basic personality, gender, culture, race, we each have a preferred style of interaction. However, it is important that through self development we keep breaking old habits and defenses to broaden that range of possibilities while also being aware of our limitations so that compromise does not become loss of integrity.

3.2.   Environmental Awareness :   Building an effective rapport means being sensitive to the operational mode of the other individual or team so you are able to respond at a level they can accommodate. It would be unproductive to be enthusiastic and friendly at a meeting with floor managers to discuss redundancies.   Similarly, a manager maintaining a reserved and formal position at an office social function would alienate her staff.

Within a Gestalt framework, every engagement has a cycle of Fore contact, Contact, Full Contact, Post Contact (see Appendix 2). The level of intensity and quality of the Contact varies vastly between the people involved and the situation.   However, using the Strategic/Intimacy graph, we can chart the optimal sequence of interactions as being:

3.2.1.   Fore Contact: The arrival and initial meeting is full of newness and the curiosity of the unknown.   Characterised by low intimacy and higher strategy i.e. shyness, awkwardness and reserve with those we do not know to enthusiastic questioning of "How are you?" with close friends.

Managerial behaviour includes Data generation, seeking and sharing information, reviewing performance history, environmental scanning.

3.2.2. **Contact:** Building an understanding of each others' needs or intentions and seeking ways of acting on them. This results in a mobilisation of energy and increased intimacy although the level of strategy would relate to the hierarchical nature of the relationship.

Managerial behaviour includes generating interest in the ideas and proposals presented, identifying differences, conflicts or competing interests, seeking maximum participation.

3.2.3. **Full Contact:** Moving into a sustained engagement, fulfilling the needs and intent and relating in a more personal and open mode. Having established the common ground there would be a lower strategic, higher intimate interaction.

Managerial behaviour includes: joining in a common objective, joint recognition of problem definition, indications of understanding but not necessarily agreement, choosing a course of action which is possible.

4.2.4 **Post Contact:** This is the resolution, closure and withdrawal phase of the exchange. There is a waning of intimacy in the process of leaving as one returns to a more internal perspective and considers "what's next?" Provided the previous stages have occurred satisfactorily then while intimacy diminishes, the level of Strategic behaviour also diminishes and a feeling of satisfaction, equality and immediacy is sustained in the saying "goodbye". Managerial behaviour also includes: checking for common understanding, reviewing and acknowledging what was accomplished and what remains to be done, generalising from what has been learned, pausing to let things "sink in" reducing energy and interest in the issue, turning to other tasks or problems e.g.developing, implementation and action plans and ending the meeting/project.

If the cycle is interrupted at any point or left unfinished, dissatisfaction, frustration and a drop in morale and therefore productivity results.

The challenge is to be able to understand and facilitate the interaction through these stages using the appropriate balance of Strategy and and Intimacy.

SUMMARY

The swing from the traditional autocratic management style to the concept of the "flatter" system with its emphasis on empowerment places much more responsibility on the individual whatever their position.

Teams are now being organised around tasks and skills rather than position and authority so the potential for confusion and chaos is high when there is ambiguity about role, power and control.

The perspective of Intimate and Strategic interacting can help clarify the ambiguity. Development the skill to adapt creatively both within the Self and towards the environment is necessary for effective functioning.

When there is no explicit authority structure then Strategy and Intimacy is negotiable. The optimal goals include personal openness and honesty, spontaneity, emotionality and friendship. Any hierarchy that develops is self-generated with strategic competition and power struggles tending to the covert. The evolution of constructive power and influence has to be dynamic, explicit and consensual.

In systems with a designed authority figure, the dynamic are quite different. As the overt power lies within the organisational structure, any openness and directness must be tempered with diplomacy and caution. A higher Strategic mode of interaction is necessary when there is an awareness of the politics and the "consequences of one's actions". The emphasis is on assertiveness and mutual respect rather than intimacy.

The key factor is the ability to negotiate, compromise, maintain mutual respect and honour each other's principles An ability to creatively Adapt to the demands of the situation. A flexible response to new challenges.

To maintain this flexibility and adaptivity we must be able to behave strategically when necessary and also to form Intimate relations which are appropriate to the situation.

ACKNOWLEDGEMENTS
In developing these concepts I would like to acknowledge Sonia Nevis for the initial insight, my colleague Graham Stickland and Jean Boulton, Peter Greatwood, Martin Hadland, Peter Jones, Richard Knight, Dolores O'Malley and Angela Terry who attended an experimental theme workshop and helped me put flesh on the bones of these ideas.

APPENDIX 1   STRATEGIC & INTIMATE MODES OF INTERACTION

HIGH **Openness,** **Self-** **Disclosure**	**INTIMACY** **Warmth**
INTERACTIVE STYLE: pseudo Friendship seduction emotional manipulation	INTERACTIVE STYLE: Love Friendship Affection Emotional Physical Closeness "I - Thou"
EMOTIONALITY: Guarded Heart	
LANGUAGE STYLE: "We ____." "I feel that ___." Talking *to* the other	EMOTIONALITY: Open Hearted
	LANGUAGE STYLE: "I ___ Me ___." "You (personal) ___." Talking *to*
HIGH STRATEGY	**LOW STRATEGY**
Power, Control **Influence**	**Spontaneity, Equality** **Mutuality, Immediacy**
LANGUAGE STYLE: Questioning "It ____." Talking about	LANGUAGE STYLE: Talking over "One ____." "You (impersonal) ___." Ideas Thoughts
EMOTIONALITY: Cold hearted	
INTERACTIVE STYLE: Political Scheming Planning Calculating	EMOTIONALITY: Hale and Hearty
LOW **Distant,** **Closed,**	**INTIMACY** **Reserved** **Unavailable**	INTERACTIVE STYLE: Directness Lively debating Discussing Analysing Brain Storming I - It

APPENDIX 2.

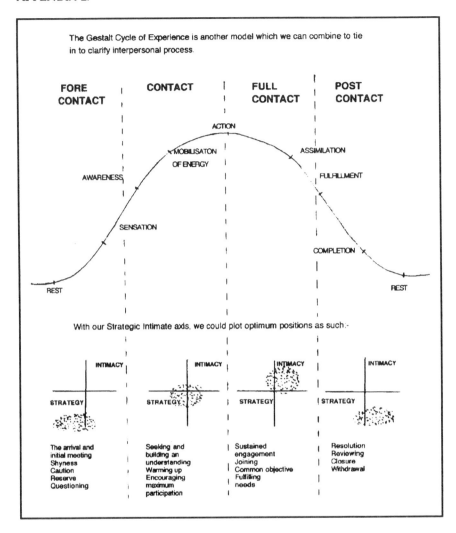

IN SEARCH OF SYNERGY: THE RELATIONSHIPS BETWEEN INTERNAL AND EXTERNAL CONSULTANTS

Lance Lindon & Steve Rathborn, *Sundridge Park, Bromley, Kent*

ABSTRACT

This paper explores the relationship between internal and external consultants and enunciates some critical differences in their roles as perceived by the client organisation. Using a model of the consultancy process, and the skills required to operate an intervention successfully, conclusions are drawn as to how best Internals and Externals can work together. This conclusion reflects both the realities of the commercial environment and the often differing approaches of internal and external consultants.

1. INTRODUCTION

As members of an operating practice within the PA Consulting Group, we act as consultants dealing directly with clients on organisation development. In addition we train internal consultants. From this blend of experience, it has become clear to us that the interrelationship between the external and internal consultant on change projects can be improved. At present, these relationships are at best tense, and at worst competitive and destructive - either to the goals of the change or the well-being of the consultants involved.

The purpose of this paper is to outline what we see to be some of the issues involved, and to place this within the context of the skills and processes that we have found to be effective in process consulting.

2. DIFFERENTIATION AND ROLE DEFINITION

At one level, differentiation between the external and internal consultant is easy: The external consultant is hired by the client organisation for a limited period and paid in fees to conduct a programme of agreed work, whereas the internal consultant is a full-time employee of the client organisation. At another level, this may become more fuzzy - for example when a Chief Executive hires a personal consultant on a full-time basis (ie not salaried, but paid per diem in fees) for a protracted period of time (ie years). In this case, there may be an absence of specific goals for the work, and the consultant's job is to help the CEO to manage better.

However, even this distinction is easier to make than that between an internal consultant and other staff roles within a client organisation.

Our public management development programme designed to train in basic consultancy skills - **Developing Professionals & Specialists** - typically attracts two groups of participants. One group has roles which demand that they influence without direct authority (such as Human Resources, Research & Development, Information Systems). The second group are those with the formal title of "internal consultant" (for example within the Metropolitan Police). What defines the difference between these roles? Is it merely that an individual is given formal organisational permission, through a role title, to be called an internal consultant, or is this more complex? Perhaps there is a parallel to differences between teamwork (ie using the skills required for collaboration and consensus) and teams (being part of an interdependent group with common goals), with specialists allowed to have the skills, but not the label?

Our observation is that "internal consultants" are deemed to have good process skills (facilitation, problem-diagnosis, communications etc) whereas this need not be expected necessarily of people working to improve operational practice from the perspective of their own function, such as HR specialists. This argument, however, does not advance our quest for clarity greatly, as it leads towards a position that everyone within the client organisation is, at least partially, an internal consultant if they are attempting to make improvements to organisational practice. After all, a key role for managers is to improve organisational performance through focus on task improvement. If this group is to be included, then our net widens to include all competent managers into our definition of "internal consultant"! This point fails to help us to make some meaningful distinctions of the internal role.

The OED defines "consult" in terms of 'to take counsel together, to deliberate, confer; to take counsel to bring about; to ask advice of; to have recourse to for instruction or professional advice'. This could help - if we are prepared to make distinctions between the expert consultant/manager (instruction and professional advice) and the process consultant (counsel together, confer). Many professionals and specialists seek to influence others to support the aims of their own discipline or function (for example, IT or Research). As such they may be seen as "experts" and consulted on the basis of their knowledge and expertise. Internal consultants, on the other hand, seem to be so labelled for their process expertise. Their knowledge is of social psychological processes without a specific task/function driven expertise. Hence, our working definition of internal consultants are "people who use their expertise in process facilitation to support their primary job responsibility - helping others to solve organisational problems they face".

External consultants may have either an expert or process focus. Experts may be hired for their subject, discipline or industry expertise (eg Marketing, Boston Consulting Group; TQM, Philip Crosby; Structure change, McKinsey; Travel, Speedwing). Typically, the client has already determined what the problem is (ie Marketing, Quality etc.) and hence wants expertise, not available internally, to help solve it. However, as the example of TQM shows, the external consultant's expertise may well be in process - ie facilitating change. The distinction is therefore somewhat theoretical, in the sense that all expert consultants must have a minimal degree of process skill, and all process consultants must have a minimal degree of perceived expertise - at least in people management. What is perhaps more helpful is to recognise that both 'expert' and 'process' consultants are experts, one primarily in functional/task skills, the other in processes. As such we define all 'experts' in terms of their functional competence. The following diagram may be helpful in defining the arena:

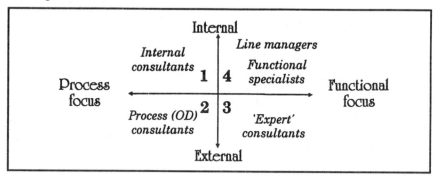

In broad terms, internal consultants are expected to fall into quadrant 1 - they focus on process. Those who are more aligned to quadrant 4 (such as IT specialists) are often expected to learn the process skills of quadrant 1 to become more acceptable to other functions. Their need to market themselves internally often requires such Internals taking on board both a broader business focus and making improvements to their interpersonal skills (ie understanding organisational processes and context better).

Externals can be engaged as specialists in either quadrant 2 or 3, but our experience is that it is unwise to expect quadrant 3 Externals to manage the human processes of implementation well. Their focus is as the expert bringing technical solutions. Our observation is that functional consulting has historically been bought by clients, yet the recent success of such relative newcomers to the UK as Proudfoot and Gemini (from whom powerful process consulting is bought to help manage complex change) is an interesting development. This suggests that process consulting per se is becoming more marketable - perhaps as best equipped to deal holistically with the complexities of cross-functional, organisation-wide change.

As internal and external process consultants' roles overlap, some considerable conflict between them is both expected - and seen. There are, however, some identifiable differences in practice betweenthe role of the External and the Internal:

(a)   the external consultant has 'detachment' and an 'objective' view through not being a full-time employee. It may be possible to tell an external person something too dangerous to share internally. This is a two-sided coin which may help, or hinder, the External's acceptability to the client organisation

(b)   typically the External's experience is of greater breadth than that of the internal (more experience of similar problems or needs elsewhere in equivalent businesses or operations)

(c)   the external consultant may have greater political access (for example, having the ear, daily, of the Chief Executive;

(d)   this access often brings with it control of sensitive and confidential information - information often denied to the internal consultant. The capacity of the external consultant to keep such data confidential (typically embodied in their contract of engagement) may also greatly affect the extent to which they can engender group support from members of the organisation. Similarly this can be markedly enhanced by the external consultant sharing results of research candidly with affected (or involved) employees and pulling no punches (for example, as to perceived shortcomings of the Board as seen through an organisational culture survey)

(e)   external consultants, simply by virtue of some of the above points, and through higher academic or technical qualifications, are often given a higher derived stature than their internal counterparts. Certainly the external consultant may well be attended to better than the internal consultant by senior people in order to get value for the high fees paid. Someone who is charging £1,500 per day typically will get more air space than an employee who is costing £200!

(f)   in contrast, the internal consultant is far more familiar with the workings of the client organisation, history, culture, norms, myths and legends. They will already have a network of people - both formal and informal, more or less productive - within the organisation

(g)   Internals are less likely to be perceived as a threat - after all as the 'bacon and eggs' analogy goes, the chicken is involved (like the external consultant) but the pig (the Internal) is committed. Internal consultants are far more likely to suffer the consequences of failure than the external consultants who are usually gone before these become apparent.

3. AREAS OF CONFLICT

Our argument is that internal and external consultants observe the needs for change from different perspectives and for a different paymaster. The Internal's great strength is intimate knowledge of what has worked, and is likely to work, within his or her organisational reality. The External brings an objectivity of view and a broader experience of other organisations to bear on the situation. Unfortunately however, the reality is that both parties are often motivated to compete rather than to co-operate. For example:

(a)   the Internal typically has a large network of contacts within the organisation at the inception of the programme, and may guard this jealously from the External;

(b)   the External may zealously guard knowledge of change techniques and processes in case these are pinched by the Internal and hence revenue to the consultancy firm is lost;

(c)   the External may over- or under - apply confidentiality so that at one extreme the Internal is denied all relevant information from top managers held by the External, whilst at the other, information is shared so freely that the Internal can feel compromised;

(d)   the Internal feels under threat when an External is brought in by senior management: This is seen as an implicit criticism of their competence. The External sees the Internals similarly, and for the same reasons, and hence fails to involve them on the basis that they may jeopardise the success of the project.   An allied factor is that Internals, who have already begun the process feel that Externals who are then called in will take all the credit for final success.

In addition, whilst often well-intentioned (in order to save the Client expensive external consultant fees) the External may well end up using Internals (or clients in general) as gophers - 'you can fix that, arrange this, brief them - it's cheaper'. This may devalue the Internal's self-esteem or conception of his or her role. Ironically, this may be exacerbated if it was the Internal who brought in the External (as typically he or she has greater budgetary constraints than is the case for senior colleagues).

4. OUR MODEL OF CONSULTANCY

To propose a more specific way forward, we need to apply these considerations to the model of process consultancy we use. This model, initially based on the work of Gerard Egan (Egan & Cowans, 1979), has been applied by the authors in a wide variety of organisations. Within PA, adaptations and enhancements have been made since it was introduced in the mid 1980s. The present operational model, with indicative goals and skills is given overleaf, whilst Appendix 1 lists our taxonomy of the basic skills and attributes required for effective process consulting.

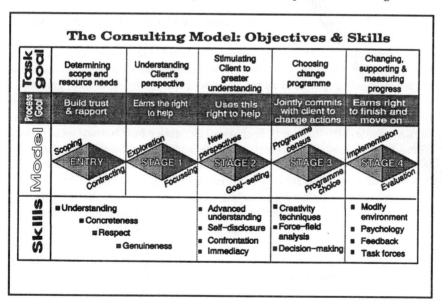

The Consulting Model: Objectives & Skills

	Determining scope and resource needs	Understanding Client's perspective	Stimulating Client to greater understanding	Choosing change programme	Changing, supporting & measuring progress
Task goal	Determining scope and resource needs	Understanding Client's perspective	Stimulating Client to greater understanding	Choosing change programme	Changing, supporting & measuring progress
Process Goal	Build trust & rapport	Earns the right to help	Uses this right to help	Jointly commits with client to change actions	Earns right to finish and move on
Model	Scoping / ENTRY / Contracting	Exploration / STAGE 1 / Focussing	New perspectives / STAGE 2 / Goal-setting	Programme census / STAGE 3 / Programme choice	Implementation / STAGE 4 / Evaluation
Skills	▪ Understanding ▪ Concreteness ▪ Respect ▪ Genuineness		▪ Advanced understanding ▪ Self-disclosure ▪ Confrontation ▪ Immediacy	▪ Creativity techniques ▪ Force–field analysis ▪ Decision–making	▪ Modify environment ▪ Psychology ▪ Feedback ▪ Task forces

Both internal and external consultants require, in our view, basic personal-emotional skills in such areas as:

(a)   analysis and understanding of their own behaviour

(b)   capacity to confront and act upon their own strengths and weaknesses

(c)   toleration of the ambiguity of their role.

Beyond this, there are relationship-managing skills which may be:

(a)   interpersonal (establishing and maintaining relationships of mutual problem solving and trust)

(b)   intragroup (within the consultant team, within authority groups of which the person is a member)

(c)   intergroup (problem-solving around group interfaces within the organisation)

(d)   organisational change management (management of projects and stages of organisational change explicit in the above model)

and finally,

(e)   diagnostic skills (in being able to determine appropriate skills and techniques for information capture and analysis, the creation of valid data, and to resist premature evaluation).

These skills are - or should be - common to both external and internal process consultants. Both parties should be working to a common, shared, overall consultancy process such as the model we use. However, our experience argues that internal and external consultants have different strengths at different points in our model: Strengths determined by the realities of their differing roles in practice.

Each stage of the model (below) involves an opening-out, data-gathering phase (the left hand of each diamond) and a decision-making or closing down phase (the right hand side of the diamond). Each stage is separated from the next by an explicit contract - or agreement - as to decisions taken and a commitment either to stop, or to move forward (jointly or separately). Hence, the client organisation may decide that external consultants are only required for Stage 2, or that internal consultants can complete Stage 4 after the preceding stages have been completed jointly.

It is our observation that functional consultants are most likely to be called in for Stage 2 (typically on strategy-related work) or for Stage 4 (for example, an information technology 'turnkey' assignment). For both of these stages it is most easy to justify using external experts rather than internal resources. In the former case the client specifically seeks breadth of experience and objectivity of direction: this is what Stage 2 offers. In the latter case it is likely to be more cost effective to the client to employ functional experts on a short-term basis (with skills that are not present in house) than to use internal resources (save for evaluation). This logic may be generalised to employing external process consultants as well.

274

For us, almost by definition, the Entry stage (requiring entry into the organisation) is the more obvious province of the external consultant. Internal consultants have already entered the organisation, even though their work may require them to enter new areas of it. Internals do, however, have a much greater understanding of the organisation in this event than the External at Entry. The behavioural skills required are identical to those of Stage 1. Similarly, the process objective of Entry (building trust and mutual regard) is a necessary part of Stage 1 (earning the right to help). Typically internal consultants are not expected to have the breadth of business knowledge required by the external process consultant as a prerequisite for Entry.

Stage 1 is often done well by internal consultants who may lack not only the level of access to top people, but also the detachment and knowledge of similar businesses often crucial to the selection of the external consultant. As such, Internals are less likely to move into sharing new perspectives (ie Stage 2) prematurely. In addition, their presence within the internal power structure urges greater sensitivity to client needs - clients who may be able to influence the career progression of the Internal. Externals may handle this process well, but our experience is that this is often skipped completely or given insufficient attention. Many clients complain that Externals 'never really understood the unique realities of our organisation or business'. Similarly the adage '(external) consultants borrow your watch to tell you the time' indicates a folk wisdom that this crucial stage is often not done adequately.

Stage 2 plays into the hands of the assessed skills of the External. New perspectives are often what Externals are hired to provide, by asking them such questions as 'How do other organisations do it?' or 'What are we not doing that we should?'. The External's knowledge of the operation of other organisations is critical in this stage, and hence, perhaps, the internal consultant should take a back seat. Similarly the detached, objectivity of the External typically enhances the quality of the specific goals set for the change process at the end of Stage 2.

In our experience, **Stage 3** is most often ignored by both sets of consultants. Perhaps both feel driven by mutual needs to 'get on with it' and begin change implementation as soon as goals have been agreed. This stage determines the best means to reach the ends defined at the close of Stage 2. In choosing the processes of change, both parties have a role, and a complementary role at that: the External to offer a range of means perhaps broader than that known to the Internal, the Internal, with greater depth of organisational knowledge, to determine which one(s) are most likely to work in his or her specific situation.

Stage 4 has typically been carried out by the Internal, although more and more frequently Externals are being involved as well. In this area the greater detailed knowledge of people, processes and culture possessed by the internal consultant is crucial to getting the details of implementation right first time. Besides, the Internal is more likely to be present continually in the organisation than the External, and hence is in a better position both to ensure the timely completion of action steps and to make needed adjustments.

We would argue that the final evaluation phase should not be done by either internal or external consultants involved in the process: Neither is likely to be objective as both parties have a vested interest in showing success. In principle we would support the notion of evaluation being conducted by a senior member of the client organisation with the objectivity required to determine if the change has a) been completed and b) worked.

5. DEVELOPING SYNERGY

At the conference in which the concepts in this paper were discussed, delegates were divided into two syndicates - one of internal consultants, and one of external consultants. From their practical experience, each group was asked to collate their thoughts on the strengths and weaknesses of working with the other group. The output from this work is given in Appendix 2, and offers additional insight and richness of example to the debate. We thank them for their contribution, and were pleased to note substantial agreement with our own observations. Several delegates were pleased to report little difficulty in working alongside their internal or external counterparts.

External and internal consultants operate under different sets of expectations from the client organisation. Externals are sought for objectivity, a breadth of view and often technical expertise in the project being considered. They are in general more costly - and perceived to be - than their Internal counterparts. Internals are sought to help managers operate more effectively and to offer a range of problem-solving skills or techniques. At the extreme, it is rare for Externals (and almost unknown for Internals) to be asked to operate as a vehicle for top management to 'take the heat' for unpalatable decisions (eg redundancies as a result of downsizing). As such we see External process consultants still being approached as if they were Functional consultants, with Internals seen typically far more consistently in process terms. Without doubt, Externals are seen as being more expert (they must be, otherwise there is no justification for high fees?) than the Internal. Typically, Externals are seen as more powerful.

In working together, internal and external consultants need to confront early the concept of mutual threat - to surface and deal with it.

The major distinction in approach may be between **detachment** and **compassion**. Detachment can be offered to a greater extent by the external than internal consultant. As a negative this may mean uncaring rationality; as a positive in helping clients to a more objective view of reality than that subjectively held within the organisation. Internal consultants typically have greater compassion for the human realities of existing in the organisation, and hence empathy, than the External. Yet this very ability to care may inhibit radical, or painful, solutions - however effective. Both the Internal and the External can overdo their strengths: The Internal's compassion can become avoidance of disharmony or conflict at all costs, whilst the External's detachment turns to avoidance of subjectivity and humanity. Both are necessary, and achieving a blend between them is crucial to achieving successful and enduring progress as a result of consultant interventions.

For us, achieving this blend would seem to result from two complementary approaches. The first is of mutual learning: Externals may need to learn empathy from the Internal - whilst Internals learn detachment from the Externals. The second route is together to recognise the distinctive or complementary approaches that each party brings to the process in order to balance the impact of people and task needs - compassion and detachment.

Synergy is possible if both parties are committed to the goals of the change, recognise and confront early the potential for conflict, and work continually to achieve collaboration.

6. SUMMARY

This paper has outlined the major issues involved in achieving productive collaboration between internal and external consultants from a practical perspective based on the authors' consultancy and training experience. Difficulties in definition - particularly of the internal consultant are explored, and a model of differences between the focus of Internals and Externals presented. In particular the authors argue that the term 'expert' consultant be replaced by a reference to functional focus to avoid confusion that process consultants are in some sense not expert.

Differences between internal and external consultants are explored, and their different areas of strength highlighted - based both on their perceived role by the client organisation and their own knowledge and skills base. From this analysis, the paper identifies key areas of conflict between Internals and Externals working together to achieve change, and briefly presents an overall model of consultancy to help clarify stages in which Internals or Externals may have greater expertise.

The paper concludes by highlighting key differences between internal and external consultants - the Internal's greater compassion as compared to the greater detachment of the External. The authors argue that mutual learning and/or an explicit recogition of different roles by both parties can offer the potential of synergy between internal and external consultants.

References:

Briggs Myers, I & McCaulley, M H (1985) "A Guide to the Development and Use of the Myers-Briggs Type Indicator" Consulting Psychologists Press, Palo Alto.

Egan, G (1976) 'The Skilled Helper; A Model for systematic helping" Brooks/Cole, Monterey.

Egan, G and Cowans (1979) M A "People in Systems: A Model for Development in the Human-Service professions and Education, Brooks/Cole, Monterey.

Appendix 1
The Skills of Process Consultancy

EARLY - INDIVIDUAL AND TEAM
Attention The skills of using effective non-verbal behaviour and body language.

Standard-setting Defining and agreeing ways of working with consultants and clients - procedures, timings and confidentiality (Contracting)

Basic Understanding Reflecting client statements to ensure understanding and clarity - the precis.

Respect Allowing the client to make his or her own decisions - to choose

Genuineness Consistency between verbal and non-verbal behaviours

Concreteness To get the client to give specific and detailed information - "Give me an example"

Probing To get more detailed information on areas of interest - "Tell me more..."

Sharing information Giving and receiving factual information accurately

Encouraging Giving praise to individuals for their contributions both to encourage further comments and to reward their present inputs

Compromising Having the self-confidence to admit mistakes and errors in a timely way

Summarising Precis of entire subjects/ meetings to ensure a) progress steps b) shared understanding.

LATER - INDIVIDUAL AND TEAM
Self-disclosure Relating personal experience of relevance to client issues

Advanced Understanding Valid summaries of client position going beyond what is known or believed by the client

Challenging Highlighting inconsistencies within client perceptions - including value clarification

Immediacy Confronting issues in the client-consultant relationship directly

Goal-setting Being able to set specific, observable, achievable, performance linked and time bound objectives that the client is committed to.

TEAM-ORGANISATION - THROUGHOUT
Process analysis Accurately sensing processes - interpersonal dynamics at work - in the client organisation, in meetings, within teams

Initiating and Structuring Proposing methods, processes or solutions to enhance client/team effectiveness

Gate-keeping Asking quieter people to contribute, seeking and achieving contributions from the unwilling

Harmonising Reconciling disagreements or conflicts between people - clients/or team members

Consensus-testing Testing for - and achieving - agreement to a course of action from all concerned.

PERSONAL SKILLS
Intervening Accurately determining when and how to intervene in client/ consultant and team relationships

Openness to change To be able to accept and take on board both negative and positive information and make personal changes to behaviour as necessary

Visioning To be able to develop a vision of the future and enable clients to accurately assess consequences of any actions taken

Environmental Modification Skills in changing the environment in which work occurs.

Process techniques Knowledge and skills and applying problem solving and decision making techniques e.g. force field analysis, brainstorming, rich pictures, cause and effect diagrams etc.
Presentation skills The ability to present conclusions in an informative and motivating way focusing on client needs.

Appendix 2
The External Consultants' view of Internal Consultants

THEIR STRENGTHS
Seek new ideas/open to and seeking new/external ideas

Intimate knowledge of organisation provides a) insights into management
b) a realistic sounding board/testing ideas

Opens doors/ gates

Have contacts

Know how things get done

Good advice on timing

Very good at accessing those with power/influence/insight and so provide constructive feedback

[If committed to work/intervention] will support it in the long term, after consultant has gone

Has big picture/access and insight into culture/ history
[Sub agenda for some - seeking external network prior to leaving]

Relationship and success of intervention can be the platform: a) for their personal growth, b) for their career development [Can become our next colleague/ally]

THEIR WEAKNESSES
They are destabilised by our [externals] very presence

They have a history/persona

More subject to internal pressures/politics

Being part of the culture can be a weakness.

Not necessarily the first choice/most effective point of contact

Can feel vulnerable/threatened/avoid disclosure

Afraid of telling tales

Concerned about externals on their 'territory'

Project may not be priority for them or perceived as having less impact

Can have very weak power base

Lack of clarity/role ambiguity

Professional jealousies   - withholding information or dis-information

"Dropping you in it"

[Can become our next competitor]

The Internal Consultants' view of External Consultants

THEIR STRENGTHS
Add value

Easier to get resources

Wider remit/vision

Don't carry baggage

Can focus on being a consultant/don't have functional speciality

Independent

New ideas/perspectives

Fashionable

Catalyst

Specialists

Respect/status

Can help internal person to grow

Perceived power

License to say what others cannot

Challenge

Access

Can leave

Flexible timing/singularly focused

May have wider pool of individuals

Trend setting

Done it before many times

Flexible, can get rid of them

Can help organisation to grow

More research time available

THEIR WEAKNESSES

Time to understand organisation

Time = Money

Language may not match culture

Lack of trust

Lack of earlier teamwork

Lack of loyalty

Fee-driven

Commitment?

Prejudice from previous experience

May be set up to take up hidden agendas
May be looking to build up CVs

Don't reap what they sow

Cowboys

May experiment with (or use favourite) tools and techniques

Confidentiality issues

Overuse could be a problem

Trying to sell something unnecessary

May not challenge enough

No social commitment

Costly

WORKING ONE-ON-ONE WITH SENIOR MANAGERS

Jenny Rogers, *Management Futures Ltd, London*

INTRODUCTION

In doing one-on-one work with senior managers I am often reminded of that bleak statement by F.D.Roosevelt:

> 'It is a terrible thing to look over your shoulder when you are trying to lead - and find no-one there.'

This seems to sum up so well why there is a need and a demand for one to one help in a role which has become so much more demanding and complex over the last few years.

My consulting practice spans three interwoven types of work: strategic work with teams, management development training which arises out of this work, and one-on-one work with senior managers. The one-on-one work is about a third of my practice and is growing. In doing this work, I frequently encounter conundrums and ambiguities. One significant problem is that there is no one word which really describes this kind of work accurately. *Development? Coaching? Mentoring? Personal training?* None is quite right. I don't know the answers to most of the questions this work raises and all too infrequently meet other consultants working in this particular area of organisational consulting. In this paper I therefore intend to explore some of these grey areas rather than to offer a one-size-fits all approach.

THE CLIENTS

My clients tend to fall into three groups.

- *Recently-promoted managers*, probably in their first significant managerial role. The typical pattern is a clever specialist who may have managed a project team before, but is now in a generalist role and has a big budget and a large number of people (or projects) to manage. There is usually an appreciable leap in responsibility between the new job and the old. This client is often young. One feature they have in common is that they have often eluded any form of management training. Now they are feeling a mixture of confusion, excitement, challenge, hope, and fear. They are usually acutely conscious that they need help.

- *The alleged 'problem performer'*. This client is usually in an exposed role in the organisation. He or she may have been in a newish job - perhaps for a year or so. The general perception is that they have been promoted to their level of incompetence. Often, some character feature which has been a positive advantage in the past, for instance, a task-driven approach to work, is now the very thing which is perceived to be de-railing them. Often, too, there is an inability to work collaboratively with colleagues. The old approach, that all colleagues are potential rivals who must be vanquished, becomes completely dysfunctional and is suddenly very public. However, someone - sometimes their boss, sometimes the HR specialist working with them - thinks that there is still hope, hence they are referred to me. Often, this client has a cheerfully thuggish attitude to leading people: subordinates must fall into line - or else. Such clients usually have little real idea of where and how they are getting into difficulty.

A different kind of 'problem performer' is the one who is perceived to be 'too gentle': lacking in the necessary protective toughness which will get him or her through organisational life successfully. Possibilities which must be considered with all 'problem performers' are that it is their manager, not they, who is the 'problem' or that it is the relationship which needs attention, not the individual.

- *The lonely boss.* This is a seasoned manager often working at or near the top of an organisation going through an unprecedented period of turbulent change. They feel, rightly or wrongly, that there are many issues on which they cannot consult peers, boss or direct reports. Typically, this kind of work grows out of conventional consulting assignments when a relationship of trust has already been built.

I am aware that describing clients like this makes them seem far more cut and dried than they ever are in reality. In practice, many clients do not fall so neatly into categories.

MY APPROACH
The approach depends on the client and the circumstances.

SETTING OBJECTIVES
If there is a 'sponsor' i.e. someone more senior who is paying the bill, one possibility is that after the initial phone call, I will spend about an hour and a half with the sponsor and the client clarifying what it is they want to get out of the process. Essentially I am facilitating a meeting which will uncover how we will all know if the work has been successful. I will challenge proposed outcomes which are unrealistic, unfair or vague. I look for behaviourally anchored statements which I can encapsulate in a letter I write to both parties later as a record of the meeting. At this meeting, I will also help both parties explore what responsibility each has for the current situation.

These are interesting meetings, and often the occasion for mutual amazement: 'So that's what you want me to do - why didn't you tell me before!' My presence has given both parties permission to achieve a level of candour that has previously been missing. Occasionally, this initial meeting is all that is needed.

At this meeting I set out my own conditions for doing the work:

> that the content of the session is totally confidential between me and the client: i.e. the sponsor has to take it as an act of faith that the work may achieve what we have agreed to aim for;
>
> that I am not a miracle worker and can only work with the grain of the person and the organisation;
>
> that the client and I have a private meeting at the end of this initial session where he or she can explore their reservations (of course they always have some) and decide whether or not they really want to go ahead with the work;
>
> that we can both withdraw from the arrangement at any time if it does not seem to be helpful.

Sponsor, client and I also agree that at the final phase of the work, there will be another meeting where we will assess how far these objectives have been met.

A DAY TO EXPLORE

The next phase could be a whole day to explore a number of issues. Usually I draw out a full biography; ask the client to undertake some simple career and life-mapping exercises; complete a battery of psychometric tests such as the 16PF, Myers-Briggs Type Indicator (MBTI) and FIRO-B; begin to sketch out the issues that they would like to address. I may also ask them whether they are willing for me to ask colleagues for feedback on them. If so, I will either use a '360° feedback' leadership instrument I have developed, or will ask them for names of people who can be interviewed by phone. The questions I will ask their colleagues are the simple but profound ones such as:

In what ways is X an effective leader/manager?

In what ways would you think he/she could be more effective?

How could the relationship between you be improved?

I do not ask to interview partners, though some consultants doing this work get good results from doing so.

FEEDBACK

The next session may last about 4 hours and will be devoted to feedback. I still find it staggering that so few managers have ever received any meaningful feedback from colleagues: often this occasion is a first. The impact of this session can be considerable. Finding out that all your colleagues think you rarely listen to them properly, or that all of them are afraid of you can come as a devastating surprise. Equally, there can be many positive and reassuring messages.

Wonderfully rich and complex instruments like the MBTI, FIRO and 16PF can be full of enlightenment, challenge and reassurance for clients, not just about how they behave themselves, but can also give insights about the puzzling behaviour of colleagues. This phase therefore cannot be rushed.

SUBSEQUENT SESSIONS

These usually last about two hours and are separated by periods of about three weeks. This is long enough to test insights or to try out new behaviour or put initial plans into action.

This is one way the work can develop. However, there are many others. For instance, the 'lonely boss' type of client will often have strategic issues on his or her mind and will wish to devote time to those issues first. The other work grows gently out of that. In these cases we will go straight to the two or three hour sessions and I will introduce instruments or feedback techniques only as and when they seem appropriate.

PACKAGES OR ONE OFFS?

With some clients I negotiate a complete package which is usually that I will give them about 25 hours of my time. This will include the time taken to interview colleagues, set and review objectives and write reports. With others, the whole process is loose and open ended.

VENUE

The sessions virtually always take place on my premises. There are several reasons for this. I find it is entirely beneficial for clients to be detached from their usual status symbols, their retinue of minders, interrupters and other distractions. Coming to me and sitting in a quiet room overlooking a garden helps them concentrate on the real issues. Another reason is that it helps me keep the cash costs to the client at a reasonable level.

WHAT DO CLIENTS DISCUSS?

The range is issues is enormous. The presenting problems may be purely at the level of creating what one client called 'the far horizon of the job': where he wanted his organisation to be in ten years time. Others may want a private tutorial in how to get closer to customers or to know how other organisations have coped with major change. Or there may be a perceived need to re-structure, introduce new systems, hire and fire staff. Sometime the issues are intensely personal: where am I in my career and life? What possibilities are there for me? Sometimes the issues are more immediate: how do I get on better with my boss or with others on the Board?

The approach I take is holistic. I am happy to devote as much time to the organisational issues as they need. However, I do not believe you can divide the work person from the private person. Issues in a manager's private life are often very similar to the issues in his or her professional life. Many of my clients face personal crises at the same time as the professional ones: that may be why they are willing to accept help.

The very first such client I worked with in this way was a young, apparently rough-and-tough 'problem performer' who told me within the first ten minutes that his marriage was at breaking point and that he had never experienced such all round misery in his entire life. He wept throughout most of our first session. I don't think we could have worked together as harmoniously as we subsequently did if this had not been possible. The assurance of being able to talk to someone who can be trusted not to judge, not to blab and not to get sucked into the emotion is an absolute prerequisite of this work, and that means being willing to look at the whole person, not just the work role.

WHAT ACTUALLY GETS DONE IN THE SESSIONS?

Most sessions follow the pattern of reviewing what has happened since last time; asking whether there have been any further issues arising which the client wants to discuss again after pondering; identifying issues that we should look at in the current session; reviewing the session at the end to see if we have dealt with them satisfactorily.

Within that framework, we might use a number of techniques. I have called on the techniques, for instance of Neuro-Linguistic Programming with its useful range of elegant ways to short-circuit feelings of failure or worry or of improving relationships. I don't hesitate to use simple, informal role-plays; sometimes I will use a straightforward coaching technique, explaining for instance what is known from research about how to motivate staff or run an effective team. However, a fly on the wall would mostly just see two people engaging in a concentrated discussion.

Very occasionally a client will suggest that I join him or her at work and 'shadow' them for a day or half day. This can be valuable data and can work well if the client is able to handle the curiosity of colleagues about my presence and as long as I bear in mind that it is impossible to be an observer at such events without also altering them.

ISSUES ARISING

There are a number of tricky issues that present in this type of work. In identifying some of them I am well aware that I cannot do justice to their subtlety or range, so these are headlines only.

WHO IS THE REAL CLIENT?

The person paying the bill is often not the person who gets the 25 hours of my time. So is my loyalty to the sponsor or to the person I have been describing here as the 'client'? Sometimes there is also an intermediary: an HR specialist who will know of my work and who is also a client of a different kind.

My own view of this is that the true client is the organisation. An effective organisation needs effective people, so while I am with the individual, my effort should be concentrated on seeing how that person might become more effective for that organisation. This will always involve the individual in feeling more comfortable with themselves. In some cases, the work we do may result in the individual deciding to leave the organisation - a possibility I always draw attention to in the first session with the sponsor. In many cases, the work diverges from the original brief for reasons that I feel are usually compelling, but this is a risk when the funds are coming from someone not present at the meetings.

WHO SHOULD BE DOING THE MANAGING HERE?

This issue arises especially with alleged 'problem performers'. Consultants doing this kind of work have to beware that they are not being asked to take on the task of actually managing the person concerned. For instance, I was once asked by a manager to take on a client whose problem was perceived to be inappropriate dress and a strong body odour. Instead of accepting this client, I suggested a session with the manager on how he might manage the issue himself.

MOTIVATION

Where the client refers and funds him or herself there is usually no problem about motivation: they are keen for help (and may, of course, also resist it, but that is a different story). However, when the client is referred, there may be problems. The client may want to please his or her boss, and may want to please the consultant, but deep down be uncommitted to the process. I try to deal with this issue by constantly checking with the client at the beginning and end of each session on what progress they think has been made and what they feel they are getting out of it. On the few occasions when I have terminated the arrangement, it has always been because I felt the client was politely role playing and did not have any real heart for the process. With one such client, his swift acceptance of this diagnosis made me feel that ending our sessions, with the promise of coming back for more when he was ready, was the right thing to do. So far he has yet to take me up on this offer.

WHERE ARE THE BOUNDARIES?

A particular question is where the boundaries are with therapy and counselling. I think the answer must be that the boundaries are fluid. I am not a therapist and do not pretend to be. Where clients clearly need other forms of help, I will always refer them to suitable and trusted sources. Some examples would be clients who declared a need for marital counselling, help with eating disorders, and treatment for depression, anxiety or obsessive-compulsive behaviour.

I find that clients are often initially confused about this issue themselves, and this may be something we usefully explore in early sessions. Some clients. for instance, say that if they have revealed to colleagues that they are starting working with me, they are on the receiving end of jokes about 'meeting the organisational shrink'.

One client said something that I thought was revealing and insightful about the difficulty of drawing the line between this sort of work and therapy when she said 'I know it's not therapy, but the effect is definitely therapeutic!'

Although it is not therapy, and the client is most certainly not a 'patient' or 'sick', the work does depend on using a number of the skills associated with a counselling/therapeutic approach. Among many others these would be: being 'fully present' for the client, listening attentively; being able to create rapport and empathy; being able to challenge appropriately; being able to give unconditional positive regard to the client. And of course, I need to be aware of phenomena such as transference, counter-transference and of my own 'hot buttons' as a consultant.

At the other end of the spectrum, clients may ask for help with aspects of organisational life where I have no expertise: setting up a new IT system would be a case in point. Here, again, I will refer them to an appropriate source of specialist help.

I am aware, too, that in this work I use a normative rather than a contingent approach to organisational values. For instance, I do assume that effective organisations will be ones with features such as: a participative management style; a determined equal opportunities policy; genuinely two way communication; a collaborative rather than competitive culture and so on.

CONFIDENTIALITY

The confidentiality rule is clear enough when it comes to the content of the sessions. I have sometimes been on the receiving end of subtle pressure from bosses to tell them about what so-and-so has said. None has pursued it when I have reminded them that we agreed there would be no feedback, other than anything the person themselves wished to say. In fact I find many clients are all too happy to tell others that they are meeting me. Some talk freely about the content of our sessions. 'Everyone should have this!' as one such client said. However, for others, it may well be something they do not want to share, especially if it is perceived as remedial treatment.

This may be a problem when it comes to obtaining feedback from colleagues. If there is any reluctance about this, I never pursue it.

ENDING THE WORK

My experience is that clients enjoy our meetings and feel regretful when it draws to a close either because we have exhausted the issues or because the funding has run out. However, I always invite clients to ring me at any time for an off-the-cuff consultation. I have never had anyone abuse this arrangement, and I am still in touch one way or another with many clients. Some contact me in due course for other kinds of work - for instance with their teams or for a fresh round of sessions because there is a fresh round of challenges. As one such client said in a letter to me after we finished the formal part of our work 'This kind of process is never really ended is it?'

SUPERVISION

I wish that the healthy tradition of 'supervision' as in social work, or 'Co-counselling' in other professions could become a reality for those of us doing this kind of work. I believe it is essential to find colleagues with whom one can discuss these and the myriad other issues which present in one-to-one work. The work itself is absorbing and, to me, deeply satisfying, but can also be emotionally draining. It would also be easy to become either complacent or discouraged. By definition, the process cannot be observed. Its real outcomes are hard to assess, since the underlying effects may only be apparent in the long term. There are ethical tripwires everywhere and it is essential to keep discussing these with others in the field. Given how relatively specialised and young this kind of organisational consulting is, this is often harder to arrange in practice than is really desirable and necessary.

SUMMARY

This paper discusses some of the practical and ethical issues involved in working one-on-one with senior managers in organisations. Three types of manager may present as clients: newly-appointed people in their first major managerial role, 'problem performers' or senior people who want a sounding board because there is no-one else they can consult. An approach to the work is described which typically involves meeting over a period of some months on the consultant's premises after an objective-setting meeting with the manager's sponsor. If no sponsor is involved, the work may be arranged more flexibly. The work itself may involve using psychometric instruments, training, discussion and NLP techniques. The approach is holistic. It may cover subjects ranging from personal issues to organisational ones. The paper discusses issues such as: unrealistic expectation; who is the 'real' client? confidentiality; motivation, consultant supervision and the boundaries between this kind of work and therapy. Whilst the work draws on a counselling approach and uses similar skills, it does not consider the client to be 'sick' and clients needing more specialised help are typically referred elsewhere. Also the approach to organisations is normative rather than contingent.

CHARACTERS IN SEARCH OF A THEATRE

Organization as Theatre for the Drama of Childhood and the Drama at Work

Dr.Burkard Sievers, *Professor of Organization Development Bergische Universität, Wuppertal, Germany*

ABSTRACT

Organizations are seen as theatres in which potentially two dramas are enacted simultaneously: the drama of one's childhood and the drama at work. Performance in either of these dramas is related to an experience of suffering. If this suffering becomes pathogenic, both people's health and performance at work deteriorates. Organizations have, however, the possibility of creating a setting in which this suffering can be creatively transcended.

Luigi Pirandello's play 'Six Characters in Search of an Author' serves as a metaphor to expand on both the interrelatedness of these two dramas and the possibility for creative transformation of the suffering involved.

Two case vignettes from organizations will be presented in which pathogenic suffering might be creatively transcended by exploring and reframing the conflictious situations they describe. They also demonstrate that unless people in organizations claim authorship and authority for the organizational roles in which they find themselves, they remain but 'characters' who tend to repeat their own drama of childhood, rather than of attempting to transcend it in a creative way.

"WE CARRY IN US A STORY OF TERRIBLE ANGUISH."
Luigi Pirandello

INTRODUCTION

The play 'Six Characters in Search of an Author' has not only made Luigi Pirandello famous as a playwright, but has also become one of the most significant innovations in modern theatre. When Pirandello began writing the play, he was just coming out of more than a decade of pure hell: His wife had mentally collapsed under the strain caused by the bankruptcy of the family-owned sulphur mines in Sicily (cf. Sciascia (1988), 66 ff.), and she was committed to a mental asylum in 1918. Pirandello had been forced into the marriage by his family in order to merge the two parental businesses and did not love his wife (cf. Rauhut (1964), 50 f.). What already had been part of the drama of his childhood, i.e. his father's greed to build an empire, had thus become part of his own family drama (cf. Bosetti (1971); Zappi (1928)).

Although Pirandello did not write in an autobiographic style, he occasionally assumes the role of author in his own plays. The destruction of theatrical illusion weakens the dividing line between the theatrical world and that of everyday-life. In Pirandello's later plays both the characters and the author himself carry in them "a story of terrible anguish" (Pirandello (1991), 8), in which the reality of his inner world and that of the theatre merge. Traumatic deprivation seems, as Bentley ((1972), 134) writes, "to be at the heart of things for Pirandello, and that is one reason why his work is dramatic. Theatre is shock because life is shock".

In 'Six Characters', a family of six mysterious figures enters the stage during a rehearsal of Pirandello's 'The Rules of the Game'. "Imagined but uncompleted characters burst into reality from an author's creative mind with an explosive, dynamic power" (Linstrum (1979), V). They bring their own story of anguish and, in search of an author, they force the producer together with his actors to put their family life on stage "with its disruption, adultery, prostitution, illegitimacy, nudity and potential incest" (ibid., V f.). In the beginning of the play Pirandello shows "us a group of easily recognized conventional Actors from the world of life faced with a group of Characters from the World of Art. The Actors are challenged to represent The Characters in a play on the stage, but by the end of Pirandello's examination the images have become reversed" (ibid., VI). "It seems that in this ongoing deliberate confusion between phantasy world and stage reality, life and illusion totally change roles the very moment the boy who is supposed to play his suicide actually shoots himself dead. This goes too far for the producer; he angrily sends the six characters away because they have robbed him of the whole morning's rehearsal. The characters leave; their attempt at gaining life on the stage failed. The performance of their failed attempt is the drama" (Huffnagel (1988), 528).

That family dramas are the stuff theatre drama is made of is not Pirandello's invention. It has been a constituent part of drama since its very beginning. "The classic preoccupation of the playwright has been with the family" (Bentley (1972), 158; cf. Simon (1988)). Oedipus Rex or Antigone are expressions of family anguish just as most of Shakespeare's, Ibsen's, Shaw's, Dürrenmatt's or Pinter's dramas are unimaginable without it. Often enough theatrical drama is the artistic narrative of a family drama. Although the story is often set centuries or even millenia ago, identification with the drama on stage is possible because family patterns of anguish apparently have not greatly changed since the beginning of civilization. The family still makes up, as Bentley ((1972), 36) writes, "the original cast of characters in the drama of life, a drama that we keep on reviving later with more and more people cast for the same few parts." Death and murder of a parent, a spouse or a child, marriage decisions, adultery, mésalliances and the dynamics of inheritance and succession are only some of the experience people have gone through either themselves or in others since the beginning of mankind.

Similar to the saga, myth and the fairy-tale, the written and performed drama offers every family member (and the child in particular (cf. Bettelheim (1976)) a relativization of the dramatic experience as a family member. His anguish in the family is shown not to be primarily an accident, a damnation or a unique catastrophe but, despite its pain and suffering, a 'normal' experience. Drama in its poetic and theatrical form is, from this point of view, both an artistic transcendence of the tragic (and comic) experience of the family drama and an encouragement and confirmation that one is not alone in the experience of pain and anguish of the family. It is an important function of the theatre to mediate and reconfirm for the audience that life is not exclusively a love story and that family life does not only take place in paradise.

Enterprises and other institutions in which people work are characterized by a less rigid and less clear discrimination of roles than in the theatre. In their everyday reality, organizations usually allow quite a degree of role-rotation in the sense that those who were part of the audience in one scene may well be actors, the playwright himself or the producers in the next one. To the extent that our adult world is rooted in our infancy (Klein (1959)), our dramatic competence and expression in the theatre of everyday life is influenced by the dramas we have been through in our families of origin.

THE DRAMA OF CHILDHOOD AND THE DRAMA AT WORK

Despite the fact that psychoanalysis has developed and offers a 'methodology' for studying and understanding the rootedness of our adult world in our childhood and infancy (cf. e.g. Lyman and Scott (1975), 101 ff.), the exploration of the relationship and interrelatedness between our adult world in organizations and our primary socialization in the family of origin is still quite rare and what has been undertaken is often very limited in scope. Although some attempts have been made to elaborate the relationship between the child's experience and the (unconscious) structure of work in organizations (cf. e.g. Kets de Vries and Miller (1986), Lawrence (1982), Pedersen-Krag (1951), Ulrich, David N. and Harry P. Dunne (1986), Volmerg ((1988) (1990)), the meaning and influence of the family as a system with its own history and drama is still widely ignored.

The notion of family-of-origin influence has in the context of family therapy gained wide acceptance; but - as Weinberg and Mauksch ((1991), 233) state - "considerably less attention (has been) given to extending this theory" to what is "occuring in the work environment". Unfortunately, the result of these two authors' examination of family-of-origin influences on life at work remains for me strangely sterile and almost mechanical: "Patterns of interaction to which people become accustomed in their families of origin often play largely unacknowledged roles in their lives at work and can contribute to unwanted pressures and stress on the job" (ibid.). What strikes me is the very limitedness of the metaphor these authors use; they refer to patterns of interaction which the child has become accustomed to and which, as an adult, it carries over into work situations. Reducing the drama of childhood and that of the family, in particular, into patterns of interaction is for me like comparing the Apocalyptic Horses to brewery horses: the fascination, the threat, the excitement and the scare are gone; patterns of interaction, like brewery horses, exclude tragedy, failure, anger and despair.

In my own consulting work, especially in 'Organizational Role Analysis and Consultation' (cf. Auer-Hunzinger and Sievers (1991); Berry and Tate (1988); Reed (1976); Weigand and Sievers (1985)) I am becoming more and more pointedly aware of the fact that the complicated way in which people are entangled in work episodes or in the organizational system itself and the way in which they get involved in conflict with colleagues (and/or clients) is not only dramatic, but cannot really be understood (and disentangled or dissolved) without relying on the working hypothesis that the main actors are actually working on at least two different dramatic levels, i.e. that the drama in the work situation - unconsciously and in a critical amount of the actors taking part - often invites and encourages regression into an earlier dramatic experience that is deeply embedded in the family of origin.

Often enough the combination of the family drama and the drama at work of each individual involved in the situation evolves into a competitive struggle as to which of the (hidden) plots will be accepted as the dominant one, who will be the producer and who will be allowed to assume the role of leading actress or actor. The competition and collusion between the various actors and characters is particularly intense (and threatening) if the majority of people working in an institution (unconciously) experienced a certain degree of similarity in their family dramas with respect to the dramaturgy, the role distribution and the tragedy enacted therein.

This is comparatively often the case in social, non-profit making institutions in which staff and clients often have comparable biographical backgrounds. Such a similarity may exist regardless of whether the institution is, for example, a self-help group for HIV-infected, a prison, or a convent of nuns caring for 'lost girls' (cf. Sievers (1992)).

Case: Child-abuse

The impact the re-production of the family drama has on the drama at work recently became evident to me again during my work with a group of social workers, each of whom had a managerial role for a particular area in the general social service of a city. A man in his early thirties began to present a case episode in which he had a conflict with an older woman within the group of social workers he led. The drama at work was based on the serious accusation made by the group leader that his older colleague had irresponsibly misbehaved in a case of severe parental child abuse towards an infant by his parents.

When we began to explore the episode it appeared quite obvious that the older colleague (who did not take part in the group I was working with) was 'guilty'; her incorrect conduct was supposedly 'explained' by the 'fact' that she was a well-known hardship case among the social workers in the city. It was considered more or less impossible to dismiss her, but nobody wanted to work with her. Without any prompting, however, another member of the working group, a woman of about the same age as the 'accused', began relating in extensive detail the biography and professional career of the accused. To me, it sounded as if she was reading from a public prosecutor's file, both in order to confirm the charge made against her colleague and to convince me that the original presenter of the case must be exonerated. I myself was not yet satisfied by the quick and one-sided acquittal and went on to ask the presenter of the case about his own biographic background. (This was within the frame of consultancy we had negotiated before starting work together.) We all, including the presenter, were struck by the similarity and reciprocity between what he told about himself and what had been reported about his colleague.

It became evident that the group leader had been caught in a kind of overidentification with the infant in the case of child maltreatment because at the time the conflict had escalated his own first child was only a few weeks old. Moreover, the main 'data' of the two protagonists' family dramas enabled us to perceive the conflict from an entirely different perspective. Despite the obvious differences in age and sex between the two people, it seemed as if both of them had almost exactly the same role in one and the same family plot, only that it had been performed at different times on different stages by different producers. Both of them were first-borns in their family of origin and had had to replace both their parents in the care of their younger brothers and sisters after father and mother in both cases had left the scene due to divorce, (natural) death or suicide. The enormous responsibility they had assumed for their younger siblings meant great sacrifice and gave rise to the feeling that too much was demanded of them and to a sense of inadequacy and despair. All this doubtlessly had an enormous influence on their decision to become professional helpers.

It also emerged that the older woman was forced by her colleagues into the role of an 'eternal spinster', a role which was collaborated and reinforced by a physical disablement she had since birth, the fact that she was still unmarried and that, not without considerable self-sacrifice, she was still caring for a younger severely anorectic sister and for her father (to whom she drove every weekend although he lived several hundred kilometers away).

This made it easier for the group leader to force his own family drama on her, leaving her no other role than that of the sacrifice. Only after this psycho-social collusion, which was not just limited to the two main protagonists, had been uncovered could the male social worker admit to his emotional overidentification and overreaction and to renounce it, thus opening the possibility for him and his colleague of finding a way of coping with and possibly solving the conflict in a more mature way.

As a consultant during this process I again and again felt much more challenged, moved and encouraged than I assume one would be by simply elaborating patterns of interaction. Occasionally I felt like the producer of a new, third drama, in which the main protagonist we were working with was sent on a journey through his life from the immediate past into its darker parts and back again into the present (cf. Bruner (1956), 464 f.).

Pathogenic and creative suffering

My experience with organizational role analysis and consultation has been guided and enriched by two very different ideas which have helped me to reframe organizations as a theatre where the drama of one's childhood and family is acted out in an interplay with the production process and the overall structure of the drama acted out at work. I first became really acquainted with the idea that what is happening at work (in the context of organizations) is a drama by reading Dejours

(1990). At the same time I myself had begun to look on organizational reality as a mutual quarrel about meaning, maturity and immortality among managers and workers (Sievers (1985), (1986), (1989), (1993)). To perceive one's family of origin as a family drama (which often extends far beyond the two generations represented by parents and children) was a lession I learnt by working with people in family owned businesses which in some cases went back more than four generations (cf. e.g. Calogeras (1987)). This is a perspective I was later able to expand using genograms in the same way these are increasingly used in family assessment and therapy (cf. Heinel (1988); McGoldrick and Gerson (1985); Roedel (1990)). When I first read 'The Drama of the Gifted Child' (Miller (1981)) I began to compare the vicious circle of contempt between parents and children with the drama of the gifted worker who, like his counterpart, the manager or the entrepreneur, is equally caught up in the organization drama, thus repeatedly performing the hopeless attempt to overcome the mutuality of contempt both sides are damned to perpetuate endlessly.

In his attempt to develop a new discipline of work-psycho- pathology Dejours (1990) not only bridges the theatre of childhood and the theatre at work, he also traces the development of the actors in the organizational drama into a pathological or, alternatively, into a creative environment. Working on the assumption that pleasure derived from work is a product of suffering (ibid., 696), he interrelates the suffering experienced during childhood with the experience of suffering at work (cf. Gabriel (1984)). Despite its attempts to struggle against the suffering of its parents, the child eventually shares its parents' suffering and anxieties, carrying these as an enigma into its own later adult life. In his attempt to transpose the former scenario of suffering into the theatre at work, where his partners are no longer his parents but fellow workers in a production-oriented environment, the young adult experiences ambiguity. On the one hand he feels tempted to reenact a scenario of suffering similar to his original one, on the other hand the new social reality makes new demands on his imagination and creativity.

Dejours ((1990), 693) calls this productive ambiguity 'symbolic resonance'; it subsists in the tension between the theatre of work and the theatre of psychic suffering. This area between the socio-historic context of the former and the psycho-historic context of the latter lends at least three aspects to the symbolic resonance that ensues: the choice of profession, the fact and the extent to which one actively can take part in the conception of a task (instead of merely executing it) and the ability to exchange the partners of sublimation in the sense that criticism and recognition of achievement is no longer derived from the members of a private world but from those in a social context.

Hidden in every worker is a suffering based on the desire to perform his or her work well. If this suffering is not resolved in a creative way, the individual will be caught in the vicious circle of pathogenic suffering, thus causing damage to his own health and diminishing the overall productivity of the enterprise. The psychic repression caused by permanent pathogenic suffering at work influences the economy of emotion in the family. The parent's transfer of his own paralysis of psychic disfunctionality to his children thus affects the theatre of childhood of the next generation, too; his children in their turn establish their own equilibrium by identifying with their working parents and the psychic economy they experience in the family (ibid., 699). The dynamics of this process show that "family life in advanced capitalistic society is psychotic" (Kovel (1984), 115).

Dejours mainly emphasizes the discrimination and interrelatedness of the drama of one's childhood and the drama at work, and almost completely neglects the surrounding context of the larger organization or enterprise. However, true to the metaphor used here, the organization can be perceived as a theatre (an institution with its building and ensemble), which has an identity and a history all of its own. These, together with many other factors, have an important impact on the way in which the drama at work is performed in any particular organization. In a more general way, it also influences the way in which the drama at work interferes (or even colludes) with the drama of childhood. The culture of an organization shapes the performance of the drama at work and has a decisive influence on whether this drama constitutes a primarily creative attempt to overcome and sublimate the suffering or whether it itself is no more than an ongoing performance of pathogenic suffering. Thus, the impact an organization and its culture have on the drama at work is comparable to the impact a theatre and its respective tradition have on its performance of a plot.

PIRANDELLO'S 'SIX CHARACTERS' AS A METAPHOR

Pirandello's play 'Six Characters' seems to me to offer a valuable metaphoric frame (a second-level metaphor; the theatre itself is its first-level counterpart; cf. Alvesson (1991)) in which the interrelatedness and potential quarrel between the psychic drama of one's childhood and the social drama at work can be represented.

As they rehearse another one of Pirandello's plays, the actors and producer on stage stand for the drama at work, whereas the six characters pressing onto the stage stand for their own family drama, which they want performed instead. Although the producer first tries to prevent the six characters from disturbing his own rehearsal of 'The Rules of the Game'(!), he and his troupe eventually get involved in the rehearsal of the family drama forced upon them. As it suddenly gets too serious for him through the death of two of the children, the producer breaks things off.

The attempt of the family to have their drama performed has failed and the hopelessness of their pathogenic suffering has reached its climax in the death of the two children. By adjourning the rehearsal at the end of the play, the producer draws on the frame in which he and his colleagues can maintain their roles and the characters left are sent back to their roles as mere trouble-makers. In the drama at work, represented by the former, death "has no symbolic value" (Baudrillard (1982), 261), it is exclusively a matter for the family drama. The former has won a victory over the latter. The four surviving characters are left alone in their grievance and despair and will have no future in the next rehearsal of 'The Rules of the Game'. The family drama on the stage is the performance of the futile attempt to find an author who will transform their story of terrible anguish into an art form which would relieve them of their pathogenic suffering. "The drama of their failed attempt is performed with all its tragic instead because these six characters have been rejected" (Pirandello (1930), 12).

The characters demonstrate very different ways of coping with this tragic. Whereas the two children die by accident and suicide, the son negates the drama intended to turn him into a character (ibid., 21). The stepdaughter runs out of the auditorium in a manic fit of laughter just before the last curtain falls. The drama of the mother is "the fact, not to know that she is a character (which) does not release her to be one" (ibid., 17). "But the father ... suffers the drama, he is not creative, he suffers it like an inexplicable undoing of himself and like a situation against which he rebels with all his force and which he wants to get in order" (ibid., 14).

Whereas reality on the stage is dominated by the hopelessness of the characters' suffering, the **play** itself symbolizes a creative suffering which overcomes the hopeless collusion between the family drama and the drama at work as seen from the reality level of the play. The discrimination between characters and actors is no longer valid and all roles are characters played by actors. In the end, after the last curtain, they all stand in front of the audience as actors, irrespective of the role they played during the performance. The play is a creative act giving the hopeless suffering on stage meaning and making sublimation possible. The pain and the fate of the characters are used by Pirandello to turn suffering into art. His "theatre represents not just life, but life mirrored through the reflection upon life" (Melchinger (1991), 104).

Pirandello as author appears in three different roles of his play: Like Alfred Hitchcock who liked to appear in short unimportant scenes of his films, Pirandello appears as author of 'The Rules of the Game' which is being rehearsed on the stage. As artist he thus uses his own previous art to create art (cf. Spitz (1991), 241 f.; Rank (1968), 7). He is also the author of the family drama, a character who himself does not appear, but is being searched for. "By making himself into such a character ... the author himself is carried away from his own reality. He no longer is Luigi Pirandello. He transcends reality" (Melchinger (1991), 101). Finally, he is the author of the play which forms a third level of reality, "a level at which a new 'reality' is created, i.e. that of art" (ibid., 103).

The drama of the failed search for an author is also an expression of the fact that the characters did not succeed in authorizing themselves individually or collectively. The father, who is **the** 'character in search of an author', is totally unable creatively to transcend the suffering from the drama (cf. Pirandello (1930), 14). The story of the characters' terrible anguish is all he is able to imagine. He is deeply caught in this anguish with his stepdaughter.

Since the characters are unable themselves to become actors on the stage because they cannot find an author, they also deny the authority of the producer and his troupe and deprive these of the ability to play their lives realistically. They resemble the neurotic in Rank's ((1925), 51) sense, who is so deeply caught in his own drama of childhood that he has to repeat it endlessly without the ability to take part in any other social reality (and drama) in which the rules of the game differ from the ones he himself has learned. Their own drama is the only one they can imagine, their pathogenic suffering is filled with despair and thus totally excludes any possibility for creative transcendence. Instead of liberating themselves from their history, they only repeat it (cf. Matthaei (1965), 346).

The actors and the theatre staff make an attempt to provide some kind of authorship for the drama of the family, but they ultimately fail because they do not realize that the drama is, in fact, a life-and-death struggle. The very moment death really does occur on the stage they lose all sense of compassion and interest and withdraw to the safer role of actors whose whole day's rehearsal has simply been spoiled. They live their drama exclusively at work, totally cut off from their characters' drama and from their own personal dramas of childhood, only committed to the task the producer sets them, i.e. to qualify for the production of Pirandello's 'The Rules of the Game'. Consequently, the characters the actors play as well as their drama have an author. They may have started the morning's rehearsal with an attempt at creative suffering, but they did not succeed.

The characters and the actors in their respective ways represent failed attempts at creatively transcending their own pathogenic suffering. They would ultimately have been lost in it, if the performance on the stage was the only reality. The fact that their performance of the dramas does actually attain the quality of creativity and art is only due to Pirandello, as the author of the play, and the 'real' producer of the performance. As the producer of 'Six Characters' - in comparison to the man on the stage attempting to produce 'The Rules of the Game' - he symbolizes and deputizes the authorship for the performance. It is this authorship which, on the stage, guarantees both characters and actors the possibility of acting either the search of an author or the failure of its attempt. The author is thus the guarantor that his play becomes the symbolic representation of creative transcendence.

As the integrator of both the family drama and the drama at work the author, on a metaphoric level, shows that the performance of a drama which in itself is a failed attempt can nevertheless be a creative act. A story of terrible anguish which people bring from their drama of childhood into the drama at work can be transcended by suffering, if that suffering is not self-destructive. The suffering individual can himself assume authorship or acknowledge such authorship in someone else, i.e. in a 'producer' or an 'author' of a 'play' in which he is actively taking part. Both the acceptance of one's own and the acknowledgement of another's authorship presupposes a sufficiently high degree of authority on the part of the 'actor'. To mobilize one's own authority in order to authorize oneself or another to be the author of a 'drama' expresses the hope and the confidence that suffering can be contained and transcended creatively; it will, however, also involve the risk that the attempt may fail.

'Six Characters' as a metaphor is not only a good example of how authorship and authority necessarily must be perceived as interrelated; it is also 'proof' that a productive attempt to overcome creatively the drama of suffering is more often than not a collective one: the authorship of 'Six Characters' (delegated to its producer) is a precondition for the members of the ensemble to have the necessary authority to act either as actors or characters. They know full well that the dramatic performance on the stage cannot be solved by calling for the police, but only by the strong belief that they will be individually and collectively capable of performing the paradox: the performance of the successful drama about the performance of the failed search for an author.

The risk entailed in this kind of play of paradoxes was impressively demonstrated on the opening night of 'Six Characters' on the 10th of May, 1921 in the Teatro Valle in Rome, which ended in a disaster - "Pirandello was jeered at and even assaulted by an angry crowd outside the stage-door as he tried to leave the theatre with his daughter" (Linstrum (1979), VI).

The interrelatedness of authority and authorship which 'Six Characters' elaborates both for the actor and/or the author also serves, on a metaphorical level, to explore the often complex and at the same time improbable context in which the management of one's own role takes place. In order to manage oneself creatively in a certain role it is necessary to become the author (or, at least the producer) of that role, otherwise one will get lost either in the nightmare of childhood or in the pain and humiliation of the drama at work. The ability to manage oneself creatively in one's role (Lawrence (1979)) presupposes a certain knowledge and awareness about the painful character of the two different dramas as well as a sense of challenge not to be destroyed by either of them. Whereas this is a necessary skill both of every actor and of every manager, the author in his capacity as playwright or producer has to have this creative capacity in a double sense. He must 'contain' (in Bion's (1984) sense) the hope and confidence that, at least 'in principle', the members of his troupe will not 'fail' to get their act together and put it on the road and that they will confirm the confidence the producer invests in them. The capacity to hold this kind of hope and confidence includes the conviction that both he himself as 'author' and the majority of 'the managers' in his 'ensemble' are prepared to suffer (and in a certain, non-masochistic sense are even challenged by) the pain and privation which the accomplishment of their work task to which their roles are related often requires of them.

As sketched so far, Pirandello's 'Six Characters' may well be taken as a metaphor to elaborate the interrelatedness of both authorship and authority as well as the links between the drama of childhood and the drama at work. Of course like any other metaphor it has its limits and its one-sidedness; every way of seeing is a way of not-seeing (cf. Morgan (1986)).

This became particularly obvious to me as I tried to think through the implications of the assumption that not only a **part** of an organization's members are characters (like in the play 'Six Characters' or in the case of the social workers described above), but that all members are, at least potentially, characters. With organizations in which there is either no 'author' or no 'plot' the members more or less deliberately tend to switch from 'characters' to 'actors' and vice versa. These organizations often resemble a mad-house in which a discrimination between inmates and wardens is not always congruent with that of madness and sanity (cf. Luske (1990)). Especially in non-profit making organizations I have often had the impression that, in a metaphoric sense, all members had at some stage handed up their role as actors and become characters instead. They are often so deeply caught in their own dramas of childhood that they actually go a step behind the search for an author to the search for parental figures.

Case: Foster-families

This was apparently the case with a public institution caring for families with foster-children in a city. Working in organizational role analysis with the psychologist in charge, it very soon became obvious that he and his colleagues (a larger group of social workers led by a female and a male director) had almost forgotten their original primary task.

The formal primary task of the institution was to help both 'normal' and 'professional' foster-families to get along. Meanwhile, however, a hidden primary task had gained the upper hand. This second focus regarded the foster-children as its object rather than the foster-families. What at the beginning of our analysis first appeared to be only a slight deviation on the organization's original course later turned out to have an enormous impact on the psycho-social dynamics of the institution and its main interface with its client systems.

It soon emerged that the prevailing identification of the staff with the foster-children could, with a certain degree of probability, be traced back to the assumption that several members of the staff themselves came from foster (or foster-like) families-of-origin (e.g. step-parents or situations in which for various reasons at least one parent was absent). Although in the limited frame of the organizational role analysis with the psychologist this hypothesis could not be definitely proven, the evidence we gathered clearly spoke in favour of this. After he had helped 'collect the data' on the biographical backgrounds of his colleagues, the psychologist was very astonished at the result. He became aware, for the first time, of how his own individual drama of childhood and his broader biography were interrelated with his professional choice of career as well as with the critical episode he wanted to work on in this consultation.

The personal part of the picture I had asked him to paint at the very beginning of our work mirrored a cobweb of foster-like family relations of which he himself had been a part. A grave indicated the tragic loss of his mother who had died when he, the firstborn, was twelve years old. The woman he had painted next to his father was crossed off; she represented the step-mother whom the father had married a year later, but with whom neither the psychologist nor his younger brother got along very well. From what he had painted, it also became evident that in his first marriage he had been a step-father himself to a girl whom he still loved.

I was not too surprised when some time later, after we had finished working on his case, he approached me to tell me that he had since then discovered further evidence that his choice to work in the field of foster-care was not coincidental. He remembered that his own father had lost his mother at the age of two, after which he had been brought up by his grand-parents. The realization that the fate of an incomplete family went beyond his own generation finally helped him to sympathize with his father and to begin to re-interpret crucial parts of the drama of his childhood.

More significant in the context of the thought developed here is, however, the perspective we approached with respect to the institution. Going on the assumption that a significant number of the staff members came from a foster-family-like background themselves, and that this was the reason for their preference for the hidden primary task of caring for the foster-children, it seems clear that they were in danger of being overcome by the temptation to act as 'characters', i.e. to become 'foster-children' themselves. This meant that the members of the institution were likely to repeat their own private early histories in order to free themselves of the memory of traumatic pain.

Once we were able to think along these lines and to look at the case from this perspective we realized that the psychologist and the social workers in their predominant identification with the foster-children maintained an unconscious alliance among themselves (as foster-children) with the 'real' foster-children they were dealing with in the drama at work. As members of a public institution, these people were very much isolated; they had more or less set their own individual tasks independently of those of the institution, and they avoided either challenging or criticizing one another. It seemed as if in their suffering they were reconfirming what Kundera ((1990), 249), the poet, called the 'haute école d'égocentrisme': "In the suffering the world disappears and each one of us is left to himself." Their own daily experience as consultants and supervisors of the foster-parents was often filled with feelings of inadequacy, inferiority and failure, an experience which, as long as it came from the regressive position of themselves being foster-children, could only be avoided by projection.

The result was that foster-parents were often regarded by the social workers as not being good enough parents, a projective identification which was very much in line with their own previous experience of their 'foster-parents'. Interestingly, the male and female directors were turned into an idealized pair of parents. They were highly respected by the social workers, one can only assume because they allowed them to persue the hidden primary task instead of the formal one, thus seeming to save the social workers from suffering the drama at work which the care of foster-families necessarily would have involved for them.

Although on a first view it seemed as if the identification with the foster-children and the change of the primary task made the work much easier and more enjoyable for most of the members of staff, it became evident on a more detailed analysis of the psychologist's role that the staff members were involved in a vicious collusion with the foster-children and that the joy of work and the lives of the people involved as well as the quality of the institution's work were severely diminished.

Taking Pirandello's 'Six Characters' as a metaphor for this case, we can say that the characters' search for their parents is simultaneously acted out on two different stages. On the stage of a normal foster-family, i.e. parents who in addition to their own children have one or two foster-children, there is always a high danger that the foster-child temporarily or continuously ends up as a 'character' vis-a-vis the 'real', 'natural' children, who are the 'actors'. Disappointed or angered by the specific dynamics of his foster-family, a foster-child almost always seems to have the narrow choice between either he himself not really being the object of his foster-parents' anger or idealizing his real parents, whom he looks forward longingly to be with instead. Just as the troupe of actors and the producer in Pirandello's play are not really good enough for the characters to transform their story of terrible anguish into a piece of art, foster-parents often seem to be convicted by their foster-children of not being good enough parents, because their parenthood is always questioned at critical moments. Whereas with 'normal' growing-ups it is more and more a constant experience of parents that their authority is questioned and that their children cast doubt on them, it seems that the same phenomena are much more difficult to bear in foster-relationships.

What happens on the stage of the foster-family seems to be repeated and elaborated on the institutional stage. In keeping with the predominant identification with their role in their dramas of childhood, the majority of staff work somehow below the level at which they should be professionally operating, while the directors are almost forced to show above-human competence in order to prove that they really are reliable foster-parents. There is good reason to assume that the decision to install a heterosexual directorship was itself only superficially guided by a principe of equality of gender. The fact that it unconsciously provokes all kinds of phantasies of parental and childlike identification was presumably neglected, as was the question of whether a triadic directorate including the psychologist might not have been a better 'solution'. The identification of the directors as an idealized pair of parents maintained and perpetuated a culture of dependency (cf. Lawrence (1982)) and in the case of a critical majority of the members of staff encouraged revitalization of their previous foster(-like) child-experiences.

Regressing into the respective emotional state helps to reactivate the past in the present, to become overwhelmed by feelings of loss, discrimination and privation, finally, to get caught up in the drama of childhood. This experience reinforces the staff members in their roles as civil servants, who regard themselves underprivileged in comparison to their colleagues in other public institutions of the city. Although the belief that they are underprivileged in comparison to other employees may be a general part of a social worker's self-identification, in this particular case it strengthens a feeling of self-sorrow and self-pity.

Instead of feeling pity and compassion with the foster-parents in their client systems and using this as a basis for mobilizing more mature skills to support the foster-families in their daily struggles, the social workers thus, both personally and professionally, tend to set themselves up as 'characters'. They do not take responsibility for their own ineffectivity, but instead accuse the foster-parents and find them guilty (cf. Gruen (1992), 286). By getting entangled in their own stories of anguish from the drama of childhood, they reduce or even lose their professional capacity to help the foster-families to cope with their own stories. Unconsciously, and pathogenically caught in the suffering of the drama of their childhood, the members of staff decrease their capacity and authority to help the foster-families to transcend the pathogenic suffering in the foster-family-dramas which, as a matter of fact, are the foster-parents' dramas at work.

The more this kind of psycho-social dynamic becomes predominant, the less likely it becomes that staff members or foster-parents can creatively transcend the suffering of their drama at work. The vicious circle makes it even more difficult for the foster-parents to keep their own self-esteem and to assume the authorship and authority which such a role requires if it is to provide children during the most important phases of their lives with security, a home and a 'family'. It would seem likely that if foster-parents cannot live their roles actively, they themselves will end up as 'characters'. Although such a dynamic must not necessarily end in the same tragic way as in 'Six Characters', Pirandello indicated that, of all the characters, 'foster-children' are the ones likely to suffer and to lose most: the girl and the boy in the play are dead at the end of the drama and the stepdaughter leaves in mania.

Because of the limited frame and time of this particular organizational role analysis we were not able to explore the case too much further. As this was also true for any reframing of the case and in particular of the primary task, it can only be hypothesized here what an attempt might have triggered off. It was obvious from a very early stage that the original formal primary task according to which the public institution and its members care for the foster-**families** in the city had to be reinstituted. Such a re-institutionalization could well be accompanied by a remythologization of the institution, which would consist of recapitulating and exploring which metaphors and myths originally inspired the institution and guided its initial founding process. The aim here would be to examine which of its basic values and energies might be revitalized (cf. McWhinney and Batista (1988)).

Reframing of this kind is the precondition for organizational processes of open discourse and exploration (cf. Dejours (1990), 704 ff.) that might enable all members of the institution to become more aware of their mainly pathogenic suffering, its relatedness to their dramas of childhood and of the damaging impact it has on the quality of both their work and that of the foster-parents. Such a process can be the beginning of a sublimation, of a creative transcendence of the suffering. It can only be initiated by the psychologist or the two directors, but cannot be prescribed or administered. Only if a critical mass of the members are prepared and able to manage this conversion in their professional roles will they be able to overcome their self-chosen 'characterness' and become 'actors', 'producers', and 'authors' both of their own work and the work they support in their client systems.

The more they accomplish this the more they will discover that the suffering from their own dramas of childhood can be an additional source, instead of a trap, from which they can draw competence and authority in their professional role of protecting the foster-families from getting hopelessly lost in the stories of anguish they are subjected to both from the foster-parents dramas of childhood and from the family drama of which they, their real and their foster-children, are part of. As former foster-children, these social workers may 'use' the affects and emotions provoked in them in their work in a mature sense. Their daily work experience may thus even enable them to experience foster care as a 'scandal' even if their role requires them to look on it as it is 'normal' or 'professional' (cf. Parin (1983), 66). The revitalization of the experience of their own conflicts from childhood and adolescence thus becomes a precondition for social and political involvement if the original suffering can be transcended.

CONCLUSION

The idea described here is that the search of characters for an author is not limited to Pirandello's play. Through overemphasizing the scars, wounds, and pains from the suffering of our dramas of childhood we all run the risk of not being able to perform any differently to characters carrying a story of terrible anguish full of resentment, rage and self-sorrow, and desparately in search of the parent, author or producer we cannot find in ourselves; characters who end in a hell of pathogenic suffering that even surmounts death.

The only hope often seems to be to find a stage on which the performance of one's drama may convince others to act it out and to take over authorship for it instead. And as the chances for most of us are pretty low that these stages will be in a real theatre, we often have no other choice than to revert to the organizations we work in instead. As 'characters' we walk into the rehearsal or the performance of the play performed at work, in which there is only space for the 'actors' provided in the official script. We thus get caught between two dramas, the one of childhood dominated by its 'games' and the one at work dominated by rules and rational economics.

There is no reason to assume that this kind of pathogenic interrelatedness and collusion of the dramas is limited to social, non-profit making organizations. The fact that the two case vignettes were taken from there is simply explained by the fact that these institutions, in comparison to enterprises, hardly allow any other conclusion and are often so conspicious that the point is easier to grasp. The collusion in social organizations would seem to be so plaintively obvious because they do not have 'products' around which people in other work contexts interrelate. Although, as Herbst ((1974), 212 ff.) convincingly argues, it is generally true of organizations, in social organizations, it becomes more evident that "the product of work is people". It also can be assumed that people working in industrial enterprises are less sensitive to remember previous suffering (Wedekind (1988), 69, 126) and are more used to cut off their childhood needs for warmth and love (Gruen (1992), 282).

Whether these people, however, will mainly be caught in an endless damnation of pathogenic suffering or whether they will be able creatively to transcend the unavoidable suffering at work ultimately depends on whether they are prepared and able to become authors of their own work, i.e. managers of themselves in their roles.

My description of the interrelatedness between the two dramas in the theatre of organizations necessarily has to remain a sketch in view of the wider dramaturgic range of constellations and dynamics this interrelatedness can have. What has been particularly neglected due to the limited available space is the fact that the organization as the theatre in which most of the dramas at work occur is neither a closed system nor an ahistorical entity. Just as the drama of childhood cannot be imagined without the surrounding family, its fate and its genogram, the drama at work is influenced by the organizational culture and the organizational genogram. The latter of these includes two different but equally important aspects for the suffering at work and the possibility of its creative transcendence: the history of the particular enterprise (which may, for example, have been moulded by several generations) **and** the history of labour which has given rise to different forms of institutionalization depending, for example, on the branches of industry and regional and political influences. It can thus be of enormous significance to determine whether labour, true to its original etymological meaning, still includes the experience of pain and suffering or whether it has been so drastically degraded into mere routine and monotony that makes almost any experience at all at work unlikely.

Family-owned businesses of small or medium size are often especially good examples for the very extended complexity and tragic overlapping of dramatic realities and performances. It is sometimes impossible in these theatres to discriminate who or what belongs to which drama or to decide whether the characters or the actors are the intruders of the rehearsal taking place on the stage. If the family drama dominates in an enterprise, the 'actors', i.e. the managers who don't belong to the owning family, might even get the impression that they are interrupting a family reunion (cf. Eliot (1964)) in which they as non-relatives have no authority, but are mere 'characters'.

Even in less extreme cases it often seems as if in addition to the family drama and the drama at work a third drama is put on scene dealing with inheritance and succession (cf. Sievers (1989a); Kappler and Laske (1990)). Although from the outside it may appear as a play in which only the nobility, kings and crown-princes are involved, it often dominates the whole royal 'court' and preoccupies everyone in the organizational theatre over an extensive time-span.

We can easily guess how difficult it will be in such an enterprise to successfully attempt any form of creative transcendence over the suffering of work, since the enterprise itself is crowded with characters who "are acting out the life stories behind them" (Bentley (1972), 59). Torn between characters of the owning family, the director of the enterprise and the crown-prince as the potential successor, it must seem almost impossible to take over the role of manager, i.e. to use one's own authorship and authority as a source for the role one is acting in the common attempt to achieve a creative form of transcendence.

There are many less complicated and less difficult constellations in organizations which still do not allow the kind of reflexivity over the meaning of work in organizations that Melchinger ((1991), 104) formulates for the meaning of life in Pirandello's theatre: it "represents not just life but life mirrored through the reflection upon life". For an enterprise or an organization to represent work creatively this would mean that work in it will be mirrored through the reflection upon work. It has to be acknowledged that the creativity of work, like that of art, is "deeply rooted in suffering" (Rank (1925), 48; cf. Kainer (1984)). This presupposes that a critical mass of the people working in an enterprise are, because of the work they are doing, not caught in the repetition of either their own private traumatic dramas of childhood or in those of the drama at work with its respective history.

In comparison to the theatre which is, as Wilshire ((1982), 238, 243) states, primarily "a metaphor for life" suffering and death in the metaphoric frame of the theatre applied to organizations and enterprises do not remain an illusion or a fiction. Organizations "promise us life and death" (Mangham and Overington (1987), 26). Unlike the theatre, suffering and ultimately death are facts of life in organizations and an unrenounceable prerequisite to creativity. Suffering and death can only be endured and transcended if a critical mass of people working in an enterprise become 'actors' who are capable of relating the meaning of the work they are doing to the pain they are suffering and its potential transcendence. If this can be realized in an organization we can well speak of it having a spirit. The spirit of an enterprise obviously cannot be grasped without this deeper insight.

REFERENCES

Alvesson, Mats (1991), The Play of Metaphors in Organizational Analysis. Studies in Action and Enterprise. Working Paper PP 1991: 3. University of Stockholm, Department of Business Administration

Auer-Hunzinger, Verena, Burkard Sievers (1991), Organisatorische Rollenanalyse und -beratung: Ein Beitrag zur Aktionsforschung. Gruppendynamik 22, 33 - 46

Baudrillard, Jean (1982), Der symbolische Tausch und der Tod. München (Matthes und Seitz)

Bentley, Eric (1972), The Life of the Drama. New York (Atheneum)

Berry, Tony, Diane Tate (1988), Success in a New Task. A Role Consultation. Management Education and Development 19, 215 - 226

Bettelheim, Bruno (1976), The Uses of Enchantment. The Meaning and Importance of Fairy Tales. London (Thames & Hudson)

Bion, Wilfried R. (1984), Container and Contained. In: W. R. Bion, Attention and Interpretation. London (Maresfield Reprints), 72 - 82

Bosetti, Gilbert (1971), Pirandello. Paris (Bordas)

Bruner, Jerome S. (1956), Freud and the Image of Man. American Psychologist 11, 463 - 466

Calogeras, Roy C. (1987), A Psychoanalytic and Cultural Study of the Krupp Family. An Inquiry into some of the Roots of German Character Formation. New York (Vantage)

Dejours, Christophe (1990), Nouveau regard sur la souffrance humaine dans les organisations. In: Jean-Francois Chanlat (ed.), L'individu dans l'organisation. Les dimensions oubliées. Les Presses de l'Université Laval, 687 - 708

Eliot, Thomas S. (1964), The Family Reunion. London (Faber and Faber)

Gabriel, Yiannis (1984), A Psychoanalytic Contribution to the Sociology of Suffering. International Review of Psycho-Analysis 11, 467 - 480

Gruen, Arno (1992), Schwache Sieger. Conversation with Gabriele Fischer. Manager-Magazin 22, 4, 280 - 286

Heinel, Peter (1988), Kontext und Kommunikation: Koordination des Genogramms (Familienstammbaums). Integrative Therapie 14, 365 - 375

Herbst, Philip G. (1974), Socio-Technical-Design: Strategies in Multidisciplinary Research. London (Tavistock)

Huffnagel, Gertraud (1988), Luigi Pirandello. In: Knaurs Großer Schauspielführer. München (Knaur), 526 - 531

Kainer, Rochelle G. K. (1984), Art and the Canvas of the Self: Otto Rank and Creative Transcendence. American Imago 41, 359 - 372

Kappler, Ekkehard, Stephan Laske (eds.) (1990), Blickwechsel - Zur Dramatik und Dramaturgie von Nachfolgeprozessen im Familienbetrieb. Freiburg (Rombach)

Kets de Vries, Manfred F. R., Danny Miller (1986), Personality, Culture, and Organization. Academy of Management Review 11, 266 - 279

Klein, Melanie (1959), Our Adult World and its Roots in Infancy. Human Relations 12, 291 - 303

Kovel, Joel (1984), Rationalisation and the Family. In: Barry Richards (ed.), Capitalism and Infancy. Essays on Psychoanalysis and Politics. London (Free Association), 102 - 121

Kundera, Milan (1990), Die Unsterblichkeit. München (Carl Hauser)

Lawrence, W. Gordon (1979), A Concept for Today: The Management of Oneself in Role. In: W. G. Lawrence (ed.), Exploring Individual and Organizational Boundaries. A Tavistock Open Systems Approach. Chichester (Wiley), 235 - 249

Lawrence, W. Gordon (1982), Some Psychic and Political Dimensions of Work Experiences. London (The Tavistock Institute of Human Relations), Occasional Paper No. 2

Linstrum, John (1979), Introduction. In: Luigi Pirandello, Six Characters in Search of an Author. London (1991), (Methuen Drama), V - VI

Luske, Bruce (1990), Mirrors of Madness. Patrolling the Psychic Border. New York (Aldine de Gruyter)

Lyman, Stanford M., Marvin B. Scott (1975), The Drama of Social Reality. New York (Oxford University Press)

Mangham, Iain L., Michael A. Overington (1987), Organizations as Theatre: A Social Psychology of Dramatic Appearances. Chichester (John Wiley & Sons)

Matthaei, Renate (1965), Die Dramaturgie des Unsichtbaren. In: Franz Norbert Mennemeier (ed.), Der Dramatiker Pirandello. Köln (Kiepenheuer & Witsch), 338 - 349

McGoldrick, Monica, Randy Gerson (1985), Genograms in Family Assessment. (New York (Norton)

McWhinney, Will, José Batista (1988), How Remythologizing Can Revitalize Organizations. Organizational Dynamics 17, 2, 46 - 58

Melchinger, Siegfried (1991), Nachwort. In: Luigi Pirandello, Sechs Personen suchen einen Autor. Stuttgart (Philipp Reclam Jr.), 99 - 112

Miller, Alice (1981), The Drama of the Gifted Child. New York (Basic Books)

Morgan, Gareth (1986), Images of Organization. Beverly Hills (Sage)

Parin, Paul (1983), Die Angst der Mächtigen vor öffentlicher Trauer. Psyche 37, 55 - 72

Pederson-Krag, Geraldine (1951), A Psychoanalytic Approach to Mass-Production. Psychoanalytic Quarterly 20, 434 - 451

Pirandello, Luigi (1930), Vorwort. In: L. Pirandello (1991), 5 - 22

Pirandello, Luigi (1991), Six Characters in Search of an Author. London (Methuem Drama)

Rank, Otto (1925), Der Künstler (The Artist). In: Twenty-eighth Journal of the Otto Rank Association, 15, 1 (1980), 5 - 63

Rank, Otto (1968), Art and Artist. New York (Agathon)

Rauhut, Franz (1964), Der junge Pirandello oder Das Werden eines existentiellen Geistes. München (C. H. Beck)

Reed, Bruce (1976), Organizational Role Analysis. In: Cary L. Cooper (ed.), Developing Social Skills in Managers. London (MacMillan), 89 - 102

Roedel, Bernd (1990), Praxis der Genogrammarbeit. Die Kunst des banalen Fragens. Broadstairs (Borgmann)

Sciascia, Leonardo (1988), Pirandello de A à Z. (Maurice Nadeau)
Sievers, Burkard (1985), Participation as a Collusive Quarrel over Immortality. Dragon 1, 1, 72 - 82

Sievers, Burkard (1986), Beyond the Surrogate of Motivation. Organization Studies 7, 335 - 351

Sievers, Burkard (1989), Führung als Perpetuierung von Unreife. Gruppendynamik 20, 43 - 50

Sievers, Burkard (1989a), "I will not let thee go, except thou bless me!" Some Considerations about the Constitution of Authority, Inheritance and Succession. In: Faith Gabelnick, A. Wesley Carr (eds.), Contributions to Social and Political Science. Proceedings of the First International Symposium on Group Relations. Washington, D. C. (A. K. Rice Institute), 155 - 173

Sievers, Burkard (1992), Das Unbehagen in der Organisationskultur. Wege zum Menschen, 22, 449 - 462

Sievers, Burkard (1994), Work, Death, and Life Itself. Essays on Management and Organization. Berlin (de Gruyter),

Simon, Bennett (1988), Tragic Drama and the Family. Psycho-analytic Studies from Aeschylus to Beckett. New Haven (Yale University Press)

Spitz, Ellen Handler (1991), Image and Insight. Essays in Psychoanalysis and the Arts. New York (Columbia University Press)

Ulrich, David N., Harry P. Dunne Jr. (1986), To Love and Work. A Systemic Interlocking of Family, Workplace, and Career. New York (Brunner/Mazel)

Volmerg, Birgit (1988), Der Arbeitsbegriff in der psychoanalytischen Sozialpsychologie. In: Helmut König (ed.), Politische Psychologie heute. Opladen (Westdeutscher Verlag), 73 - 93
Volmerg, Birgit (1990), Arbeit als erlebte Wirklichkeit. Überlegungen zum Verhältnis von Arbeit und Subjektivität. Psychosozial 13, 43, 80 - 91

Wedekind, Erhard (1988), Beziehungsarbeit. Zur Sozialpsychologie pädagogischer und therapeutischer Institutionen. Frankfurt am Main (Brandes & Apsel)

Weigand, Wolfgang, Burkard Sievers (1985), Rolle und Beratung in Organisationen. Supervision 7, 41 - 61

Weinberg, Richard B., Larry B. Mauksch (1991), Examining Family-of-Origin Influences in Life at Work. Journal of Marital and Family Therapy 17, 233 - 242

Wilshire, Bruce (1982), Role Playing and Identity. The Limits of Theatre as a Metaphor. Bloomington (Indiana University Press)

WHAT IS UNCONSCIOUS IN ORGANISATIONS?

Jon Stokes, *Tavistock Clinic, London*

ABSTRACT

This paper considers some of the ways that the concept of 'unconscious' can be used in understanding organisations.

The working hypotheses in the text were intended to illustrate the theme and also to provide a basis for discussion. They are based on real cases but disguised to preserve confidentiality.

INTRODUCTION

The term 'unconscious' is used in a variety of ways. Sigmund Freud uses it in a variety of senses, for example:

(a)   as an *adjective*, to describe the *state* of an idea or feeling

(b)   as a hypothetical *system*, that is a *place* in the mind of the individual with certain repressed contents. He also distinguishes between the *descriptive* sense of the unconscious (that which is presently not in consciousness but potentially available) and the *dynamic* sense (referring to feelings or ideas that are actively repressed or denied but which are constantly pressuring to becoming conscious, hence dynamic). He further distinguished consciousness from the pre-conscious (that which is potentially available but currently not accessed by consciousness, ie those memories, facts and ideas which are not repressed, merely out of current awareness).

These distinctions were later subsumed within a more complex topographical model of id, ego and super-ego with both ego and super-ego having unconscious areas. The contents of the id are the mental derivatives of the drives, an idea which is later elaborated by Melanie Klein and others in the concept of *unconscious phantasy*. These provide the deeper and thus generally unconscious emotional meanings to events both at the infantile and oedipal levels of psychological development. Psychoanalysis provides a means of understanding and mastering these unconscious infantile and oedipal elements in our personalities so that we are aware of their ever-present effects through out lives, rather than being unconsciously determined by them. For example, in our personal relationships, but also of course in our relationships at work and indeed our relationships with work. A psychoanalytic view is one that sees organisations and work as being influenced by what Wilfred Bion calls innate pre-conceptions - of a feeding breast, of a mother, of a father, a parental couple and their modification by early experiences of relationships in the family. Hence our most basic attitudes to the organisations and groups of which we are members are heavily influenced by our relations, both real and phantasised, with our parents, our siblings and the dynamics of the oedipus complex. For example, the organisation can be felt to represent a certain sort of providing mother with the chief executive as a certain kind of managing father with concomitant reactions to each being influenced by our internal mother and father figures. Certain parts of an organisation such as the canteen may come to be felt unconsciously to represent something to which it is closely akin such as mother and her breast and will be treated somewhat differently by each member of the organisation accordingly. Frustrations and a sense of deprivation with the organisation may be expressed towards canteen staff because of their unconscious associations with a mother figure.

WHAT IS WORK?

Before discussing what is unconscious in organisations further I want to consider briefly what is means by *work* from a psychoanalytic perspective, since this is the main purpose for which organisations are intended.

For Freud, to be able to work realistically was one of the two greatest human achievements, the other being to be able to love. He called these achievements because they each require facing rather than denying a reality beyond the self, they require the achievement of a capacity for relationship with separate others (*object relationships*) as opposed to forms of relationship where the other is there primarily to provide for the needs of the self (*narcissistic relationships*). Work involves both pain and pleasure. It requires a renunciation of wishful thinking and unrealistic fantasies and an acknowledgement of time, space and gender differences. In other words facing a reality which necessarily also involves at times a degree of frustration, limitation and non-satisfaction, as opposed to the use of delusion and hallucination in order to evade reality. The compensation is a sense of real achievement, of real satisfaction which bring more substantial though less immediate gratifications. This is important because an organisation's attitude to work, the collective 'work-culture', and especially the unconscious elements in this are clearly important. They inevitably involve a similar struggle at an organisational level between narcissistic and object relationships within and without the organisation, between manic or omnipotent states of mind and ambitions and more realistic and sober views of reality and what is possible. Indeed, the very act of taking up group membership poses this conflict for each member - between a joining with others in relationships with some shared purpose or a retreat to omnipotent phantasy. Group processes can reinforce either attitude, an evasion of conflict on the one hand or a potential space for psychological growth in the working through of conflicts on the other.

THE UNCONSCIOUS IN ORGANISATIONS

There are a variety of psychoanalytic approaches to organisations each deriving from different strands of psychoanalytic thinking (see Obholzer & Roberts 1994). My approach is one that could be called a psychoanalytic-systems approach drawing both on psychoanalysis and systems thinking.

I work as a consultant to organisations and when I receive a request I try to understand both the conscious and the unconscious requests, trying to keep in mind at all times what this part of the organisation might be representing and carrying for others. For example we were asked to provide some training for nurses on bereavement, but in the telephone call it emerged that there had been a recent series of deaths on the ward which had obviously distressed all the staff, not just the nurses. At a subsequent meeting with the nursing officer making the request for the staff it transpired that she had decided to leave for another post in another part of the hospital but was fearful of the response of her colleagues including of course the nurses. One could respond to this request at a number of levels and in a number of ways but I chose to work with the nursing officer in a role consultancy process on how she managed the announcement and manner of her departure and her feelings through this transition phase in the organisation's and her life. This incidentally also provided everyone with a real-live case of 'bereavement' which could be openly acknowledged and learned from. It would also have been perfectly reasonable to have provided a training course. 'Working with the unconscious' in an organisational sense always involves making decisions about at what level, with whom and how to intervene.

Unconscious processes in organisations can be distinguished at a number of levels:

(a)   The individual level

> Work provides not only a means of interacting with external reality with its concomitant pleasures and frustrations but also a potential for reparation (Klein 1959). By this I mean that it provides a medium through which the individual can build and repair which helps modify unconscious anxieties about destructive elements in the personality in internal reality.

The psycho-analyst Harry Guntrip (1964) describes how Anthony Trollope's early employment in the post office had an unconscious reparative function.

> "A friend of his mother was daughter-in-law to the head of the G.P.O. and begged a clerkship for Anthony. Though the first seven years were misery, his application for the post in Ireland opened out a new life for him, a life of constant travel usually on horseback which he loved. He developed a passionate attachment to the work of improving communications for isolated districts and lonely people, and there is no doubt that the driving force of his devotion to his work was a symbolic compensation for his own early loneliness *which still survived in his deepest feelings."*

Losing one's job is therefore a considerable blow not only at the external world level but also in the internal world since it deprives the person of a channel for reparative acts which provide a reassurance and a way of binding the forces of envy, hatred, and other destructive elements in the personality. The redundant employee suffers a double sense of impotence and depression at the obvious level of losing one's job but also at the unconscious level of losing a medium for reparative opportunities which help sustain a sense of internal worth and goodness. This loss of the means of psychological reparation may be even more catastrophic than the original external loss of job and colleagues.

Turning to the effect of certain individuals on others, it is a common experience that the personality of the head of an organisation has a great impact on the organisation as a whole. For example, in education a head teacher's personality and attitudes, and thus unconscious attitudes, can have a pronounced influence on the atmosphere and running of the school. In a business setting the 'nice' manager often needs to have a second-in-command who is forced into the role of being the 'nasty' one. He has become through unconscious projection the embodiment of the denied aspects of the leader.

Working Hypothesis 1

A chief executive's "unconscious" fear of women leads to repeated failures to recruit female members of the board despite a conscious desire to do so. The personnel director is blamed.

(b)   The group level

I have written elsewhere (Stokes, 1994) how the basic assumptions identified by Wilfred Bion (1959) underpin the main emotional dilemmas in the helping professions - medicine (dependency), therapy (pairing)) and social work (fight-flight). In this way unconscious group dynamics can become the foundation for the patient-professional relationship. Tim Dartington (personal communication) has used the same basic assumptions in distinguishing types of voluntary organisations:

(i)   mutual support (pairing dynamics)
(ii)   campaigning (fight-flight dynamics)
(iii) expert service provision (dependency dynamics)

In this way group dynamics come to influence the state of mind of the whole organisation and thus its relation to the environment.

> *Working Hypothesis 2*
> A geriatric team's "unconscious" anger with their patients leads to endless debate about whether or not to provide them with an electric kettle. The "unconscious" wish to attack their patients is expressed in the fear that they will scald themselves accidentally. The patients are prevented from having access to a kettle.

(c) At the level of task

Gordon Lawrence (1977) has distinguished between the various levels of awareness of tasks at work as follows:

(i) what we say we do
(ii) what we believe we do but don't always say
(iii) what we do unconsciously

For example as Anton Obholzer (1987) argues the NHS says its task is to provide for the health of the nation but implicitly those who work in it do so also because of their belief that it will provide a more equal society whilst unconsciously it is viewed by us all as the 'save us from death' service. This unconscious task leads to some of the more extreme reactions to efforts to change the NHS - in whatever way, since they are felt to threaten the loss of access to a service with deeply unconscious meanings.

> *Working Hypothesis 3*
> A mental health unit "unconsciously" pushes one of the fragile members of the staff team to the edge of a breakdown and beyond in order to establish the boundary between madness and sanity and to project all the madness of everyone into one person. Having driven one member out the group continues to hunt for the next victim.

(d) At the level of the whole organisation

I have already referred to this above with regard to voluntary organisations. Within an organisation there can be an unconscious structuring along the lines of the body with its clean parts (eg administration) and its dirty parts (eg the factory) and with individuals consequently becoming identified with and behaving according to these unconscious divisions. Alternatively "immaturity" can be located only in the junior members with "maturity" in the seniors but leading to an inevitable breakdown in communication between these two groups within the organisation and an artificial stultifying split inside each individual leading to a false-self atmosphere in the staff in the organisation. As Isobel Menzies-Lyth (1959) has shown such splitting processes can lead to the resignation of good junior members of the organisation when they feel they are being constrained not to fully utilise their abilities. Current exercises in `delayering' frequently suffer from a failure to understand these dynamics and how much is unconsciously invested in retaining the various layers of an organisation. Whilst there may be conscious wishes to change there may be unconscious investments in keeping things as they are.

Working Hypothesis 4

The collective organisational defence against the fear of inevitable redundancies in a public industry leads to an "unconscious" resistance to change expressed as a mobilisation of those with obsessional characters to become even more bureaucratic then normal.

Unconscious processes can also operate at the boundary of an organisation with the outside world and the management of this boundary.

Working Hypothesis 5

A department store "unconsciously" chooses a `scattered brained' individual to deal with complaints from customers who eventually give up in confusion and frustration. This saves the store money in the short-term but ultimately loses customers.

(e)   At the level of the social

Finally whole sections of society can come to represent areas of unconscious feelings for society as a whole. So that all madness is felt to reside only in those who are currently psychiatric patients, all criminality only in those in prisons and so forth. These large group processes are extremely powerful and play a central role in determining many individual lives and careers. Essentially, however, the processes are similar to those in smaller groups - a splitting off of unwanted aspects and a projection of these into others who are felt to be identified with these split-off parts.

In organisational terms these social processes may be expressed in the relations between different groups who are viewed stereotypically such as men and women or between the young and the old or between different social classes. Whilst these are social phenomena they also involve unconscious psychological dynamics such as those concerning envy, rivalry or idealisation.

> *Working Hypothesis 6*
> British fear of losing their island defence leads to "unconsciously" motivated delays and mistakes in the construction of the Channel Tunnel.

IMPLICATIONS FOR CONSULTANTS AND TRAINING

Knowing about the unconscious is very different from knowledge obtained from a book or a teacher. It is a knowing through acquaintance, through being in a particular state of mind. It also requires a willingness to be affected and not to move into action immediately, by painful as well as pleasurable emotions, to stay with the experience of not knowing, without a restless seeking after certainty (cf Keats' negative capability). As a consultant one is often used as a repository for emotions and states of mind that the client organisation is denying or simply cannot cope with, much as the parent of a child has to tolerate and contain fears and concerns that the child cannot. Thus working in this way with organisations and managers requires some degree of personal awareness and the capacity for self-reflection that can best be obtained from the experience of personal psychoanalytic therapy. But, as important too is the understanding of group process that can be obtained from group relations training workshops and conferences. Intellectual insight about psychological processes is easily and often used as a defence against *experiencing* the emotional dilemmas of an organisation. The experience of a personal psychoanalysis and group relations conference work provide essential means of staying in contact with the deeper levels of the emotional life of organisations. However, a concentration on the emotional life of an organisation at the expense of attention to its structures and environmental context is also misguided. An understanding and attention to unconscious processes in organisations is a powerful contribution to diagnosis and understanding but should never be to the exclusion of an analysis of both systems and structure.

REFERENCES

Bion, W.R. (1959) 'Experience in Groups'. Tavistock, London.

Guntrip, H.J.S. (1964) 'Healing the Sick Mind', Allen & Unwin, London.

Klein, M. (1959) 'Our Adult World and its Roots in Infancy' in Klein, M. Envy and Gratitude, Hogart, London 1987.

Lawrence, W.G., (1977) 'Management Development... Some Ideals, Images and Realities', in Colman, A.D. and Geller, M.H., Group Relations Readers 2 (1985), A.K. Rice Institute, Washington DC.

Menzies-Lyth, I. (1959) ' The Functioning of Social Systems as a Defence against Anxiety' in Menzies-Lyth, I., Containing Anxiety in Institutions, Free Associations, London 1988.

Obholzer, A. (1987) 'Institutional Dynamics and Resistance to Change'. Psychoanalytic Psychotherapy, Vol 2 pp 201-5.

Obholzer, A. and Roberts, V.Z., 1994, 'The Unconscious at Work', Routledge, London.

Stokes, J.H. (1994) 'The Unconscious at Work in Groups and Teams' in Obholzer, A and Roberts, V.Z.

Abstract

CREATING HEALTHY TEAMS

Dr Marlene Spero, *Institute of Group Analysis, London*

We all need healthy environments to develop our full potential and to respond creatively to the outside world, environments where we feel valued, recognised and listened to, where we feel safe and nurtured and have a sense of belonging. To have healthy environments we need healthy people but it seems that "health" is rarely taken into consideration when thinking about how to enable organisations and teams to be more effective, creative, productive and satisfying.

The paper considers some psychoanalytical, group analytical and systemic ideas that facilitate healthy development. These include the notion of the holding environment and the transitional object (Winnicott); mother as container (Bion); mirroring and the intertwining of self and other (self psychologists). All are seen as crucial to the healthy development of the individual. Group analysis sees the group as a holding environment, providing a skin to contain all the communication and interaction processes which "pierce the individual mind". The individual is a nodal point in this dynamic system who by putting words to feelings and seeing himself reflected by others begins to develop a stronger ego and sense of self. Communication and exchange, the mechanisms of change occur at different levels of consciousness. Finally reference is made to the the Timberlawn studies that point to qualitative differences between the attitudes, communication and interaction patterns of healthy vis a vis dysfunctional families.

These ideas are applied to the organisational setting. The group analytic consultation (working with a team, department or small organisation) is seen as a transitional space where individual members can share concerns and anxieties; where they can learn about group and psychodynamic processes, their own behaviour and that of others and where they can learn to work with differences and deal with such feelings as rivalry and envy as well as working with the task. The aim is to facilitate a shift in interaction and communication processes and the culture of the group to enable change. The role of the consultant is explored.

The case study illustrates how a team of highly dependent managers in a large financial institution who felt persecuted, vulnerable and under attack,who were too frightened to talk to each other, competed with each other and underperformed transformed themselves into a team that was able to share, to trust, to cooperate and deal with many of their anxieties. As they became stronger, more proactive and vociferous they become more professional, healthier and creative and to their amazement, the highest producers in the region. Working separately with the "client" system (the boss) also resulted in significant changes.

CLOSURE AND IMPACT OF CONSULTANCY

One theme of the papers presented in this part of the conference is concerned with the relationship between the consultant and the client, and an exploration of some of the features that make for successful/unsuccessful working together in the management of change. **Bill Critchley** talks of the disappointment that managers often experience with the more conventional, linear "management of change" models and draws a useful distinction between "improvement" which is essentially ameliorative and the more radical "fundamental shift" needs that are present in many organisations. Using Gestalt theory he looks at some of the different ways in which we can approach fundamental shift, and at some of the responsibilities of the consultant in engaging in this process. There is a good linkage between this paper and that of Bill Cooke who looks at the different sorts of issue concerned with "Big" and "small" consultancy practices and the impact of these on the client organisation.

His assertion that "fundamental change" relates closely to understanding the culture of the organisation in deep and significant ways links in with the preoccupations discussed by Lionel Stapley in his innovative work on culture. He sees organisational culture as the fundamental property of the organisation, rather than being a dependent variable. In his view, culture is what the organisation "is", not something that the organisation "has". As with Critchley, the implications of this view for consultants is about treating culture with the greatest of seriousness. In her exploration of some of the psychodynamics of organisations, Hilary O'Donnel looks at some of the issues of co-dependence in the organisation. She suggests that this is a "process addiction in which one person tries to control another and to be responsible for the consequences of the behaviour of that person." She discusses the implications of this both for the client group and for the consultant.

This links neatly with the paper by Michael Walton who "considers how insights from psychotherapy can be used to complement conventional logical-rational approaches to reviewing behaviour in organisations." He is also concerned to explore the effects, in the consultancy situation of "the embedded organisational dynamics and the pre-occupations and concerns of the author." This paper links well with the work of Russ Vince who looks at the ways in which a psychodynamic, group relations approach "makes it possible for managers to understand and work effectively with the management of change, both at a personal and an organisational level."

At a somewhat different level, the paper by Paul Tosey discusses the need to work "with the energy" of organizational members in undertaking the processes of change. Linked, perhaps, to the notion of Gestalt in Bill Critchley's paper, Tosey suggests the development of theory in which are embedded "notions of energy and healing in relation to approaches to organizational change", and the development of a perspective which envisions organisations as "flows of energy". It may be that there is some contrast here with the paper by David Casey who discusses his work with top management teams, in which he "warns against an over-emphasis on working with feelings when working with top teams."

There are then a number of papers which deal more specifically with issues confronted by the consultant in the developing relationship with the client. Philip Boxer and Barry Palmer explore some of the ethical and epistemological issues surrounding the consultancy act which help us to explore the "consultant-client conversation." The view expressed by Tony Berry and Kate Oakley is that consultancy can usefully be looked at as having three primary tasks - Knowledge Creation, Praxis (a fusion of theory and action) and Application. They discuss the ways in which consultants operate, within these three features and the consequences of the mix, and the ways in which consultancies see themselves. The paper by Maureen Scholefield takes a different line; she looks at the concept of the umbrella consultancy - one in which there shelter many different sorts of consulting expertise in a collaborative venture - and the benefits of this structure for consultants and clients.

Change - Evolution or Revolution?

Bill Critchley, *Ashridge Consulting Group, Berkhamsted*

INTRODUCTION

Many change programmes fail to live up to their expectations, and it is hard to find either managers or consultants who claim to have experience of a 'managed programme of change' which has gone according to plan. The experience is more often of frustration and bewilderment, while the goal of **real** change remains elusive. This is against the context of a massive number of such programmes, when more managers seem to be putting change at the top of their need to know agenda than any other subject, and the world of management education and consultancy is responding enthusiastically with theories, models, frameworks, methodologies, and the accompanying lexicon of obligatory slogans and phrases.

This paper explores some possible reasons why despite the tide of interest and the surfeit of books and papers, the phenomenon of organisational change remain stubbornly resistant to attempts to manage it. My starting point is to draw a fairly broad distinction between two types of change which I have called 'improvement' and 'fundamental shift'. While improvement is doing things better and is something which all managers are paid to do, fundamental shift, as the phrase implies is a shift in some of the deepest held assumptions about the particular organisation, and indeed about the nature of organisation itself. Unfortunately these assumptions have by definition sunk out of awareness, so that when I challenge one of your assumptions your first response will be to dismiss me as a crank, as someone who clearly does not understand organisations, or even life. It follows that our attempts at change will derive from our current assumptions; we cannot after all set out to shift something which we do not know exists. Herein lies the paradoxical problem in 'managing change'.

I will then look in more detail at some problems with current approaches to 'managing change' in particular the use of visioning, and what we have come to call 'resistance'. My hypothesis is that most of these approaches are derived from an 'improvement' paradigm, and that they can by definition, only produce more of, or less of, the same. Finally I will offer an approach to working with change which is in itself paradoxical; it advocates a **deep** exploration of 'what is', out of which will emerge the energy and the possibilities for something different. This 'theory' of change derives from Gestalt Philosophy.

The views and hypotheses in this paper arise from my fairly lengthy experience both as a practitioner in the field of organisational change and as an individual psychotherapist, and from observing and experiencing the interconnectedness between the two fields.

CHANGE - METAPHORS AND DEFINITIONS

Gareth Morgan in his book 'Images of organisations'(1986) pointed out the way we use different metaphors to inform the way we think about organisations. The metaphor in use, he suggested, acts like a filter which enables us to see certain colours and not others; thus we pay attention to some aspects of the phenomenon we call organisation and not others. For example, people who see them as machine-like in the way they work, are likely to pay attention to achieving role definition and relational clarity, establishing standards and monitoring procedures and building control mechanisms etc. They would be unlikely to pay the same attention to culture, and in his excellent book, Morgan elaborates very fully the possible implications of using different metaphors.

These metaphors, (the imago of an organisation we carry), contain our assumptions about their nature, and it seems to me they will also contain an implied model of organisational change. In my experience, despite some shift in language and conscious thinking, the predominant model of change is still one of 'managed improvement', and the underlying metaphor from which this springs is essentially a mechanistic one, with its associated assumptions of hierarchy and control. It appears to me there is some loosening of this collective organisational mind-set; 'new paradigm' thinking has of course been in the ether for some time, and many managers now talk of chaos as a phenomenon which has entered the realm of things 'to be managed'. And there we have it. Merely understanding something barely makes a dent on a powerful unconscious set of assumptions.

I think as consultants we also get wedded to our change metaphors and come to believe in their comprehensive explanatory power, rather than their partiality, their contingency and their temporality. It is interesting to briefly survey a number of different definitions of change currently in vogue, and notice the metaphor in use which may underlie the definition. For example we can reasonably infer a machine metaphor from the term 're-engineering'. Transformation on the other hand can either suggest a biological metaphor, implying a physical transformation of the caterpillar into butterfly variety, or a spiritual one implying a shift in personal awareness towards enlightenment. The quality movement seems to have its roots in a 'service' metaphor, with its well know focus on continuous improvement. Each of these metaphors contains different assumptions about the nature of change, and offers some kind of change model. The problem is that in most cases the assumptions are not surfaced and articulated, so the model tends to be left suspended as an article of faith, and articles of faith acquire ardent believers rather than collaborative enquirers.

An organisation is a unique phenomenon, and I think that theories from the natural sciences, from cybernetics, from engineering, from psychoanalysis, from biology, from quantum mechanics can all inform and broaden our perspective, but should not be allowed to dominate our thinking and practice. So I believe part of our job is to help managers broaden their perspectives, to find new ways of thinking about and seeing their organisations.

MY ASSUMPTIONS ABOUT CHANGE

In the spirit of enquiring into different assumptions and models of change, let me put my own cards on the table. I am unhappy about the idea that we can manage change; my own assumption is that change is a natural phenomenon over which we have no control. Natural cycles and forces are constantly at work, such as the process of cellular renewal in a human being, or the yearly drift of continents, and we do not manage them, indeed we are barely aware of them. Man's attempts to dominate and control his environment seems nowadays to be widely disputed as a viable, let alone sensible, enterprise, although our **interactions with** our environment may produce unintended modifications to some patterns, such as climate, which may in turn produce some modifications to patterns of human life, and so on. It seems that change is both cause and consequence of our interactions with our environment, although as the magnitude and the complexity of the whole system in which we live is, by and large, beyond our comprehension and even imagining, we could say that God holds all the cards; all that we can seek to manage are our own **responses** to our environment.

If we assume for all practical purposes that our 'environment' is beyond our control, and that it is in a constant process of change, what becomes focal for human beings and organisations is our capacity to adjust, to stay in harmony with it. In the field of Gestalt, the capacity to stay in healthy relation to one's changing environment is referred to as **'self-regulation'**, and it is this process of self regulation which constitutes my field of enquiry.

One of the assumptions in Gestalt thinking is that self-regulation is **natural**, and only becomes interrupted by environmental interferences, such as parents, events, experiences which are neither bad nor good but inevitable, hence the extent of alignment or misalignment between the subject and its environment and any impairment of the capacity for self-regulation broadly defines the problem area in any therapeutic initiative. Although some of the assumptions may be different we can see how the approach is similar in many psychotherapeutic models which are concerned with how the natural development of the child is interrupted and how **fixed patterns of interaction** are sustained.

EMBRACING DISEQUILIBRIUM

An organisation is not the same as an individual and the psychotherapeutic metaphor can be applied with the same disregard for what it excludes as other metaphors; nevertheless there is an important similarity. As with individuals, organisations are maintained by a system of beliefs, about how to survive, how to relate to their environment etc. Indeed we might argue that the essence of an organisation is the system of beliefs and perceptions that constitute it. The balance sheet may be what defines it for an accountant, but for those who work in it, it is a phenomenon, part shared and part personal. The shared beliefs are what is often described as 'the glue'. Edgar Shein, in his book "Leadership and Organisation Development", talks about 'basic assumptions' as the roots of organisation culture. These basic assumptions inform all transactions both internally and externally and give rise to **stable patterns and routines**. Here the direct parallel between individuals and organisations ends, because for most organisations the basic assumptions began as conscious choices which led to success, as opposed to unwillful and mainly unconscious adaptations in order to survive. The stable patterns and routines are therefore embedded in powerful, historically validated assumptions, which lead to valiant efforts to maintain and improve them.

Most of our experience with organisations is of periods of relative stability, which seem to be getting shorter, punctuated by short periods of turbulence or disequilibrium, which we are given to believe are becoming more frequent. During the period of stability organisations concentrate on improvement, and during periods of turbulence they seek to 'get back' to equilibrium; the process of continuous improvement (evolution) is viewed as the norm, and periods of disequilibrium as an unwelcome aberration. It is understandably difficult to embrace the disequilibrium, the period of inevitable seismic adjustment when the old pattern of beliefs can no longer accommodate the new order, and yet this is the problem that many organisations, at this point in their history appear to be facing.

REASONS FOR THE FAILURE OF CHANGE INITIATIVES

In these organisations there is a heightened sense of the need for change. We should remember that a manager's job has always been to improve things, to promote the long term gradual evolution of the organisation. Clearly managers are experiencing a new phenomenon which is not susceptible to conventional management techniques. My contention is that many organisations have reached that point where a fundamental shift in their assumption base is needed, and they are not yet seeing this distinction between improvement and fundamental shift. My hypothesis is that organisations tend to tackle what are essentially revolutionary changes by applying improvement techniques, so what results is more of the same. At a recent workshop with Richard Pascale, who is a proponent of the need for a fundamental shift in what he calls the organisation's 'context - the underlying assumptions and invisible premises on which its decisions and actions are based', one manager eventually burst out: "I don't believe in breakthroughs - fast incremental change is what gets results".

This problem is perhaps best described by Watzlewick, Wheatland and Fish in their seminal book entitled 'Change', as "Second Order Change". First order change is synonymous with improvement, when one is working within the current box or frame. The frame is described by a set of assumptions about 'how things work'. Within this frame things can go on being improved until the limits of the frame are reached, at which point a paradigm shift needs to take place. Thomas Kuhn wrote extensively about the creation and destruction of paradigms in his book "The Structure of Scientific Revolutions"; the technologies for managing improvement, such as planning processes, project management techniques, performance management etc. are well known; however they only work within the current paradigm because they derive from it. The most frustrating experience for managers engaged in change initiatives is that despite their best endeavours, they do not experience the real shift they had planned for; plus ca change, plus que c'est la meme chose. According to Watzlewick et al. this is inevitable; to move to a second order of change something quite new is required, but exactly what, of course, cannot really be known. Hence, while improvement is incremental, fairly predictable, usually imposed from top to bottom and therefore mainly plannable, second order change is discontinuous, unpredictable and unplannable. It is usually a response to some significant external event or major turbulence.

It is of course very hard for managers who have struggled to the top of their organisations, to accept that the rules they played by need to be fundamentally changed. They are usually willing to make substantive changes to the way work is done, often involving what appears to be quite major restructuring, but they are understandably unwilling to question the fundamentals, such as the distribution of power, the inherent hierarchy and related principles of reward; the role and purpose of management, the purpose of the organisation, in effect the deep cultural patterns, routines and assumptions of the organisation which lie at the heart of the current paradigm. Paradoxically, one of the assumptions in the whole field of organisation and management is that change is the order of the day, one of the major priorities for managers; if you were to challenge this assumption you would be thought as mad as if you had challenged one of the older assumptions such as the need for growth or profit; but it may be that many organisations do **not** need to change; at a recent seminar run by Ashridge Consulting Group, a major theme running through the day was organisational exhaustion. For many organisations 'change' is becoming a tyrannous obsession, preventing, like all obsessions, the organisation from being what it really is, from fully realising its current capability. However, those who really do need to undertake fundamental change are more likely to achieve it by abandoning the tried and tested techniques of improvement. It will probably prove more challenging, but much less exhausting.

PREVALENT APPROACHES

1 THE ROLE OF VISION

Visions can of course be a source of inspiration, although as such they are usually associated with a particular individual's capacity to inspire, and it is unfortunate that many of the expectations of modern leadership stem from the association of good leadership with this rather rare personal attribute. Henry Mintzberg in an article in the Jan. 1994 edition of the Harvard Business Review described vision as "an integrated perspective of the enterprise, a not too precisely articulated vision of direction". In a later passage in this article which was actually a critique of strategic planning he says: "The problem is that planning represents a *calculating* style of management not a *committing* style. Managers with a committing style engage people in a journey...........everyone on the journey helps shape its course". The important qualities of a really helpful vision suggested here are its 'not too preciseness', the sense of it as an **integrating perspective** rather than a desired state, and most importantly the notion of it as a process which builds commitment.

Many text books take the creation of a vision as the <u>beginning</u> of a change process, and would argue that it is a necessary precondition of an effective change strategy to create a vision that articulates the desired future state, and forms the basis for alignment between 'the organisation' and its members. In my experience this is the approach which many change initiatives actually adopt and is one of the most common causes of failure. There are three major problems with applying vision in this way; firstly in treating a vision as a desired future <u>state</u> which has to be reached, it assumes a fixed quality; secondly it encourages a linear, top-down way of thinking about change, and thirdly it tends to exclude the majority of the organisation's members from participating in shaping the vision. Let us now look at some of the potential negative consequences of describing an idealised future condition as a future imperative - what tends to become the **only** alternative to what is, by definition, the undesirable present state. This creates a number of effects;

- Idealised states are unattainable; we know that perfection is impossible; therefore while the vision may be inspiring to some, there are many who know at the outset that it is unattainable; if they voice their scepticism they become labelled cynics. Those who were initially inspired ultimately become disillusioned; the overall psychological effect is that the organisation becomes depressed.

- The 'vision', by this time immortalised in company statements, enshrined in company folklore through countless presentations, ark-like, proves elusive. When it becomes apparent that it is not being reached, rather than modifying it, or abandoning it, efforts are redoubled to reach it; it is of course part of the current paradigm that to modify or abandon the vision would be perceived as 'failing' or giving up, or would appear seriously indecisive. Hence senior management become heavily invested in maintaining it and proclaiming its necessity for organisational survival into the future. This rather fervent proselytising can have two further ill effects:

- it implicitly denigrates the present and past; staff who have built their career with the organisation will derive part of their sense of self-worth from their achievements and their identity with it, and this is now being undermined, so they may feel a mixture of guilt, (because they are now 'not OK'), and anger as well as a sense of loss;

- also the gap between the desirable future condition and the present state is so great that people get scared, not least because they assume from previous experience that in the end, despite all the talk of participation, empowerment and the rest, the vision will be imposed from the top.

These understandable reactions are then labelled **resistance**. The logical next step of course is to overcome it, and treatises on this subject abound in the change literature. I discuss the notion of resistance later in this article; meanwhile I would like to conclude on the role of vision in the change process.

I will argue later that future possibilities emerge out of immersing oneself in the nature of the present; that the main well-spring of energy for moving forward is created through fully experiencing that which is unsatisfactory in the current way of being and doing, and that hence vision is mainly emergent rather than a priori. However, there seem to me to be two reasons why some degree of *a priori* visioning is useful, provided it is not experienced as an ideal future state, rather as a starting **point.** One reason is that people in most organisations are used to being led; they expect leaders to provide a sense of direction, and to cross that expectation too early in the change process, even though ultimately the intention may be to build a much wider leadership franchise, would be to create a void of unbearable confusion. Secondly the human spirit needs and responds to a sense of purpose; we need our lives to make some sense, have some meaning, and if this has just been lost in a welter of downsizing, or re-engineering, or whatever terminology has been used, then this void needs to be filled if chronic and disabling anxiety are not to take its place.

So in addition to the qualities suggested earlier, a useful vision needs to have two further qualities; it needs to be **aspirational** to appeal to our need for purpose, rather than inspirational, and it needs to be **practical,** to provide us with a sense of meaning and context, so that we can see how we fit and how we relate. In a financial services organisation I was working with recently they had produced a vision that they were going to use as their starting point; this provided the aspiration, but it was not enough; the leaders ended up providing a 'blueprint' which described their initial thoughts on how tasks would get done in future, the likely form or structures, the new role of managers, and some new processes for developing and rewarding people. This provided a starting point for holding workshops to begin the dialogue with staff. The process for vision building was described as **shaping and co-creating** which captured the inherent and inevitable tension between the need to **provide** vision as a starting point for the process, and the ultimate aim of spreading ownership and enabling 'leadership from within'.

2 'RESISTANCE TO CHANGE'

Fundamental change is a phenomenon which cannot be understood in a linear cause-effect paradigm, and resistance is a **consequence** of applying 'change management' thinking which is embedded in that paradigm. Kurt Lewin's force-field theory suggested a long time ago that opposing forces maintain a state of equilibrium, and that increasing one force, or pushing, merely increases the resisting forces. As a result of trying to 'manage change', we have come to assume that resistance is natural, that everyone is reluctant to change. This is not surprising if we are pushed, sometimes implicitly threatened, if the process requires that we feel bad about ourselves. However, my experience with individuals is that they want to change; sometimes they find it hard, usually they are a bit afraid of letting go of familiar and comfortable routines, but mostly they are excited by the possibilities.

A new assumption is emerging, that by and large people have a natural desire and capacity to learn, grow and change. This seems to be reflected in the increasing importance many organisations are attaching to the development of people as a core process; indeed development is gradually coming to be seen as a primary source of motivation and reward.

So if we were to start with the assumption that change is natural, and a potential source of energy, our model of how to work with it would be different. The question which arises for those seeking to influence the change process, is how to release this natural potential within the organisation.

THE PARADOXICAL THEORY OF CHANGE.

As a psychotherapist it is taken as axiomatic that you would not offer a client any prescriptions, moral injunctions or exhortations. You start with your client, helping them explore and uncover their current reality, deepening their awareness of themselves in their current context, their beliefs about themselves and the world, and their feelings, the patterns they create in their relationships, how they come to be in their present situation, how they keep themselves in that situation, **how they would like to be different and what they need to do to change.** Note the order; it is out of their deepening awareness that the need to change takes shape and the possibilities become apparent. The need to change is theirs, no-one else's. The question of ownership never comes into question. Thus the 'Paradoxical Theory of Change' runs:

"One must first fully experience what is before all the alternatives of what may be, are revealed".

In organisations with their multiplicity of stakeholders it is not quite so simple; nevertheless the same principles apply. With a colleague, I worked with one of the large management consultancies who wanted to build a public and shared set of values; the job they hired us for was to help them craft their values statement, which they were then going to launch amidst a fanfare of publicity. We managed to dissuade them from this course of action and instead conducted a number of group workshops designed to surface the currently 'enacted' values. The groups sliced across the organisation mixing status and function and occasionally selecting special interest groups like 'long-servers'. They were asked to select typical or critical incidents and describe behaviours surrounding those incidents, re-contacting their own feelings and finding recurring patterns of behaviour and emotion. This process went deeper than traditional diagnoses, cutting through presenting symptoms, going beneath the standard problem formulations to the deep cultural layer. It generated a great deal of energy, revealing profound dissatisfaction with certain aspects of the organisation and making the need for change starkly apparent. This example is referred to in more detail in an article by Critchley and Casey entitled "Organisations Get Stuck Too" (The Leadership and Organization Development Journal, no.4 1989).

CONCLUSION

Fundamental change, or second order change, or 'revolution' involves making changes at a deep cultural level. The culture of an organisation is underpinned by some deep, taken for granted beliefs about the nature of organisations, the nature of people, and hence the nature of management. Some of these seem generic to our socio-economic culture and some are organisation specific. These basic assumptions constitute the boundaries of the prevailing box or frame of reference, the constraints to our thinking, the limits to our ability to solve a new order of problem. Confrontation at this level usually evokes powerful feelings and hence is often done badly or not at all.

My main proposition has been that we cannot apply methods and techniques designed to effect improvement, to the problem of encouraging fundamental shift in organisations. Ways of proactively working with this phenomenon are not really understood, despite the plethora of books and articles which would suggest the contrary. There are some pointers; I have suggested that we need to pay more attention to uncovering the present, in particular some of the assumptions and dynamics which lie embedded in current practice; we need to be more circumspect in our deployment of vision and values statements and their like. There is a lot of evidence that we try to take on too much, try to change everything in a big bang and scare everyone to death. It also seems likely that we pay too much attention to 'the top' thereby perpetuating the paradigm that we say we are trying to shift. In my view we need to work with the authority system and with the 'energy for change' simultaneously, sometimes treating them separately and sometimes together. We need to create new forums for dialogue, which involves breaking down existing structures, to enable conversations between people, functions, departments, levels, to take place which would not normally take place. I also think that sequential modes of working, starting with diagnosis, moving on to planning, action and so on, support the linear, improvement model, particularly in the separation of diagnosis from action. Here I think some of the thinking from Chaos theory is really helpful; it suggests that at times the necessary thing to do is for managers and consultants to "create the chaos that flows from challenging existing perceptions and promote the conditions in which spontaneous self organisation can occur; (thus) they make it possible for innovation and new strategic direction to emerge" (Stacey; "Strategy as Order Emerging from Chaos"; Long Range Planning, Vol. 26 1993).

A final word on the consultant's role. There are many treatises on consulting methodology, and on consultancy skills, but not enough discussion on the elusive X factor; what is it that an individual consultant actually brings to a situation which differentiates him/her from anyone else? Can anyone with reasonable intelligence be a consultant, or is there a particular personal quality required? All I want to say here is that the consultant's way of **being** seems to me to be as important, if not more important than what she does. Ed Nevis in his book "Organization Consulting", defines this quality as **presence**, which is a Gestalt concept describing the capacity to be fully aware and present in an encounter; a colleague of mine is exploring the idea of consultant as witch doctor, and I notice that there is a current surge of interest in shamanism. It seems a fine way to end this paper with some different metaphors for seeing the role of consultant, and the suggestion that we might fruitfully open ourselves to a wider and more rigorous exploration of **the act** of consultancy.

MANAGEMENT CONSULTANCIES: KNOWLEDGE, PRAXIS AND APPLICATION

Anthony Berry and Kate Oakley, *Manchester Business School*

ABSTRACT

Management Consultancies are significant actors in diffusion of knowledge and hence in organisational change and development. More significantly, they are significant actors in the creation of both discourse knowledge and of practical knowledge. This paper stems from a research project in knowledge firms.

Management Consultancy is viewed as a process involving three primary tasks which we call (a) Knowledge Creation, (b) Praxis, which here is viewed as the fusion of theory and action, and (c) Application. In this paper these three tasks are shown to encompass other typologies of management consultancies and through the results of a survey, undertaken in 1993, of 25 of the largest consultancy firms in the UK we show that the typology provides a reasonable fit to reported work. Further, this typology provides a basis for examining the differences between the work, revenues and organisation of these consultancies. Significant differences were found in the mix of work undertaken by firms and hence in the patterns of revenues and organisation. There were further differences between firms that were primarily domestic as opposed to having significant international business.

In addition to these observations we found that consultancy practices viewed themselves as developers of both discourse knowledge (in a minor role) and of practical knowledge (in a major role).

Hence a number of research questions arise, primarily around the themes of the generation of knowledge in our typology, the management of consultancy firms and the actual work of management consultancies.

Footnote: An earlier version of this paper was published: Berry, A.J. and Oakley, K. (1993) "Management Consultancies: The Agents of Organisational Development", *Leadership and Organisational Development*, Vol.14.

ACKNOWLEDGEMENTS:

The authors are grateful for earlier discussion with Professor D. Littler (UMIST).

However, responsibility for errors and omissions rests with the authors.

INTRODUCTION

There has been a great deal of interest of late in the so-called "knowledge economy" Drucker, (1993) Badaracco (1991) Webber (1993) et al. As Badaracco puts it, "knowledge can take many forms; technology, innovation, science, know-how, creativity, information." Much of the literature on the knowledge economy focuses on one of these types, sometimes to the exclusion of the others. And almost all management literature currently preaches "effectiveness through working smarter". In this paper, we focus on an industry that typifies many of the characteristics that are coming to be associated with knowledge intensive industries. This industry is management consultancy and it is characteristic of what we call a "knowledge industry", and sometimes described as a Professional Service Firm.

A brief review of some of the approaches to Management Consulting firms is given in Section I, where these are compared to a simple knowledge typology. In Section II, the results of an initial survey of large consulting firms is presented. Discussion of these observations (Section III) is followed by conclusions, presented as a series of research questions.

I.   MANAGEMENT CONSULTING

There is a surprisingly sparse literature on management consulting, a fact that seems to be commented on by all those writing on the subject. Most of it seems to be about how to hire a consultant (Bennett 1990) or how to be one (eg. Kubr 1976, Blake and Mouton 1976, Bennis 1966). There is little consideration of consultancy as an industry, nor how it relates to other similar occupations, nor of its collaborative competitive dynamics.

Several reasons for the lack of research on consultancy have been advanced. In the first place most consultants stress client confidentiality as a major issue in their work - it is one of the core values of consulting that work for clients is not discussed in public. In addition, the partnership form of many consultancies means that they do not produce annual reports and are often coy even about their own structure and size. A further explanation of the secrecy is that it is difficult for the consultants themselves to distinguish between the impact of a consultancy and other factors on the success or otherwise of a client company.

Knowledge Firms

Winch & Schneider (1992) suggest that professional firms are basically selling one of three things, "creativity" (knowledge creation and praxis), "probity", or "technology" (knowledge application). They argue that management consultants distinctive competence is likely to be "creativity" in common with architects and advertising agencies.

Most knowledge industries have only their staff as assets with which to trade. In this they are distinct from other service industries which deploy assets such as fixed plant (eg. airlines), property (eg. hotels and retailing) or liquid capital (eg banks).(Winch & Schneider 1992). As distinct from the "facilitator" services such as estate agencies, which act as information brokers, knowledge industries add value in the sense of expertise or advice. (Maister and Lovelock 1982).

In addition, we can divide knowledge industries into those which transfer knowledge or expertise (eg. consultancy, training, education) and those which do not (eg. law, architecture). Further, business organisations in knowledge industries are heavy employers of graduate or post-graduate level employees who are "professionalised" but not necessarily professionals. For example, in the case of management consultants, the industry is not regulated in the same way as the traditional professions, but the model of the professional practice is often adopted as a useful organisational form.

In common with other service organisations, the knowledge firm does not sell a product. Some commentators argue that what it sells is a "capacity to produce" (Winch & Schneider 1992) ie. the knowledge, information or advice to allow others to produce further goods or services. The idea of adaptation to the client is important. Many knowledge industries provide services to corporate clients, which tend to be customised to these clients' needs. A further difference between a knowledge industry and other manufacturing or service industries is that in the latter, knowledge may one way to gain competitive advantage; in the former, it is the only way.

These criteria for recognition of a knowledge industry are typical of those in the literature and are not complete. However, we suggest a more abstract typology based upon three functions of a knowledge-based organisation; these are knowledge creation, praxis and knowledge application.

By *knowledge creation* we mean the development of theory in relation to the experienced world. This is the task of academic researchers, staff of research institutes and the research departments of professional service firms. We make no claims as to the stimulus for theory development, nor are we taking here a particular epistemological or methodological stance.

By *praxis* we mean the task of the fusion of theory and action in the continuing experience of working at serious problems which evade present classifications, current theory and simple pragmatism.

By *knowledge application* we mean the task of resolving and taking forward tractable problems with existing theory and models, usually contained in well-rehearsed problem solving routines in some well understood domains.

We note that each of these requires special expertise and insight and a recognition of the difficulties in doing any of them. We believe that the function of praxis - the fusion of knowledge and action is of special significance in management consulting, in that it acts as a bridge to knowledge creation and knowledge application.

Professional Service Firm

The category Professional Service Firms (PSFs) is somewhat more inclusive than knowledge industries as it includes "facilitator services" or information brokers (Maister, 1982). These include companies such as estate agents or travel agents, who Maister claims differ from what we would call knowledge industries in that the value added to the information is very low. The other professional service firms include consultancies, lawyers, advertising agencies and stockbrokers. To differentiate professional services from other services such as fast food or dry cleaning, he argues that the product is not standardised and that adaptation to client need is essential. Indeed he argues that the ability of a professional service firm to work with a client is more valuable than any specific expertise."Professionals are never hired because of their technical capabilities," he argues. Its less a case of can you do it than, do I want to work with you? Or more, succinctly, "In selecting a professional, I'm not just buying a service, I'm entering into a relationship." In this context we note that knowledge differs from other services in that it can be shared (both the provider and the client can have the same piece of knowledge simultaneously) and it is not consumed on use (though it can date or become irrelevant).

Maister's work suggests a typology of strategies that can be adopted by professional service firms. These are considered in terms of "distinctive competence" ie. the ability of a firm to do something better than its competitors (Fahey & Christensen 1984). The three types of strategies that firms can adopt are; "Brains", "Grey Hairs" and "Procedures" (Maister, 1982). He argues that clients seeking are the "3 E's" - expertise, experience and efficiency, though not necessarily in that order and probably not at the same time. Expertise is the skill least in demand, required only by clients in the minority of cases where the problems are truly complex, very ill-defined and probably being considered for the first time. These are the times when "Brains" strategies are required. Far more common is the need for "Grey Hairs", or experience. Clients recognise that their problem, although complex has probably been faced by other companies before and want an organisation that has past experience which it can bring to bear in solving these problems. The third and perhaps largest group of clients are seeking, "efficiency" or "procedure" firms. They have a well-defined and common problem which can probably be handled by a large number of firms so they will seek one that is low cost and can deliver what is required within the time constraints.

In Table 1 we suggest a correspondence between the suggested typology related to knowledge creation, praxis and application, and the more homely business function typology of Maister. Interestingly enough, Maister reflects something of the personalisation of consultants in his terms, Brains and Grey Hairs, perhaps implying a wise, experienced uncle, with a lesser credit to procedures, perhaps implying routine work for the juniors.

TABLE 1: Typologies Compared

Knowledge (this paper)	Maister	Greiner & Nees	Winch & Schneider	Hypothesised proposition of the business
Creators	"Brains"	Mental Adventures Strategic Navigators	Creativity	15-25%
Praxis	"Grey Hairs"	Friendly Co-Pilot		60-75%
Application	Procedures	System Architects Management Physicians	Technology	10-15%

These strategies, Maister would argue, can be adopted by different firms and by different parts of firms at different times. Other writers see these strategies as more characteristic of the firm itself and consider that the firm which seeks to articulate more than one strategy may end up weakening its marketing stance. Greiner & Nees (1984) argue that in the more competitive marketplace of the 1980s, firms were seeking to present themselves as competent in all areas, to play down differences and even specialities and in fact presenting a "look alike" front to the public. Behind this they argued was five distinctive types of firms which they called Mental Adventurers, Strategic Navigators, Management Physicians, System Architects and Friendly Co-Pilots, reflecting a perception on the organisational cultures of these companies and, of course, the personalising metaphors.

Greiner & Nees' first type of company is the Mental Adventurers (MAs) so-called think tank companies such as Arthur D Little or SRI (their examples) who they claim take a "scholarly" approach to the discipline of management and are "motivated more by intellectual challenge than by concern about either their clients or their own firms." Greiner and Nees suggest that they tend to tackle difficult issues, the ill-defined 5% or so of problems that are at the leading edge of the discipline and where they face little competition from less cerebral competitors.

Both MAs and SNs are concerned more with the environment that a company operates in rather than the internal workings of the company, according to Greiner and Nees, which differentiates them from the Management Physicians, who, as the name suggests, try to spot internal problems such as those within a companies' structure, culture or values. Research by these consultants tends to be clinical, rather than on computer and statistical models of the competitive environment. Management Physicians are deeply concerned with implementation and tend to work very closely with clients, which also means they tend to stress interpersonal skills as much as academic qualifications in their consultants. This of course is closer to Maister's idea of the professional service firm, who he suggests are generally hired for interpersonal skills rather than expertise. It is not surprising therefore that McKinsey is one of Maister's "one-firm firms" (Maister 1985).

System Architects (SAs) get involved in the design and implementation of specific systems with a company rather that look at its overall structure or strategy. The idea is to take on a narrowly defined project that requires a technical solution. These companies are clearly trading in experience, though Greiner and Nees argue that efficiency and delivery are also strong points of this type of consultancy work.

The fifth type is concerned with sole practitioners rather than firms, the so-called Friendly Co-Pilot who sells his or her experience and expertise on an individual level, usually to the Chief Executive. We locate these as working in praxis or knowledge application.

Greiner and Nees are insistent that it is the firms' style that dominates the professional values of the consultants it employs, a point taken up by Pennarola (1992), who stresses that firm culture, rather than professional culture, is the defining experience of management consultancy work. Indeed, Pennarola suggests that the degree of cohesiveness of consultants around core values, set at the firm level, is the only way to avoid the kind of interpersonal conflict that can lead to the breakup of these companies.

In contrast to the functional typologies of Greiner and Nees, Maister and the present author, Pennarola suggests a typology of genesis, in his suggestion of four roots. Taking Greiner and Nees as a starting point, Pennarola suggests that the background and experience of the founder(s) of a company heavily influence its organizational traits. The managerial root comes from the founder who had an important position in another industry before turning to consultancy. This type of company is characterised by the presence of a charismatic leader and the crisis, of course, comes when the leader's succession is in question. Firms can respond to this either by generating a looser, network-like organization, with different specialists or by splitting into different companies, possibly weakening themselves by loss of the "brand name". Important in most of Europe, and to less an extent in the UK, is what Pennarola calls the foreign root - the European subsidiary of a (generally) Anglo-American firm. They differ from one another in to what extent they exploit their international network or try to trade on their local expertise, however. What Pennarola calls professional root firms are often the spin-offs of interpersonal conflict in managerial root ones. The founders of the new firm are career consultants and methods and management systems will often be carried over from the previous firm. The new firm is likely to have a flatter management structure and avoid charismatic leadership if possible.

Pennarola's fourth type is the entrepreneurial root which, as the name suggests, is founded by young, inexperienced consultants often straight out of college. These firms attempt to emulate a knowledge creation strategy as they tend not to have the experience to deliver a praxis approach, though knowledge application is possible. The need to stay at the leading edge of management know-how however involves vast investment in training and a continual policy of hiring new graduates. If a firm can hire enough smart people to survive the first years it may succeed. If, as we and Maister suggest, clients only require this kind of leading edge expertise in a tiny minority of cases, it seems likely that these firms will quickly adopt other strategies if they wish to grow.

From a study of architectural practice, four generic strategies for better than average performance were proposed (Winch and Schneider, 1993). The first strategy is that of strong delivery, which corresponds to Maister's Procedures firm and emphasises routine designs, delivered at less than average cost with a stress on efficiency and heavy use of technology. Such firms maintain a relatively high level of profitability, despite not charging a great deal for their work, by employing a large ratio of technicians to architects and using standardised methods.

The second strategy is strong experience, where the clients' demands may be fairly exacting but where the firm is selling its experience rather than its expertise in bidding for the work: this process is reflected in the third strategy (strong ideas), which is articulated by those firms who can charge a premium because of their reputation for original and exciting ideas.

Winch & Schneider's final strategy is strong ambition, which corresponds to Pennarola's entrepreneurial root. They point out that such a strategy is not sustainable in the long term. Strong ambition firms, if they survive and win competitions become strong ideas firms. If they survive through specialisation they become strong experience firms and if they survive long enough they may develop a sustainable low-cost base and become strong delivery firms.

They argue further that most firms, earning average fees or slightly below, fail to articulate any of these strategies clearly and are "stuck in the middle". Whereas all architectural firms will claim that they provide a customised service and are able to handle any type of client, in reality being all things to all clients is rarely viable "and an almost certain recipe for ending up stuck in the middle."

Differences between architecture and management consultancy become apparent when considering strategies. Whereas architecture has an important and influential press, is very award-conscious at the top level and has a high profile in the public consciousness; none of this is true of consultancy. Although management consultants definitely do trade on reputation it is unclear how, in a profession which is traditionally publicity-shy and where the results have very little impact on the public consciousness, such a reputation is created and sustained.

Competitive Behaviour

While it is possible to note the convergence of the literature cited upon our typology of knowledge and its relation to organisation modes of functioning, we should note that environmental characteristics would affect organisations. Competition in those business services defined as "intermediate demand functions that serve as inputs into the production of goods or other services", eg. advertising, consultancy or market research was studied by O'Farrell, Hitchens & Moffat (1993), via a Porter approach. They concluded that while such an approach can be used, there are some shortcomings in a method which was basically designed for manufacturing industry. The major difference is that there are few if any, economies of scale in Professional Service Firms (PSFs), though they argue that economies of scope do exist, which could include: brand name awareness; shared external relationships; and shared learning processes.

Companies even take advantage of these economies of scope by cross-selling services eg. accountants selling consultancy services. These projects are not always successful though, eg. Saatchi & Saatchi's attempts to sell consultancy services on the strength of its "brand-name" in advertising. These authors suggest that a firm can use its reputation in one area to support other services, but a lapse in quality (reputation) in the new service could reflect poorly on the core business. In addition, the effects of such reputation may only be transferable between certain types of services eg. accounting and consultancy, but not say, advertising and consultancy.

O'Farrell, Hitchens and Moffat also stress that it is difficult for a firm which is seen as a low price/low quality supplier to move to a high price/high quality position, because of its reputation. This burden of reputation could create pricing problems for PSFs, with high quality firms unwilling to reduce prices in case they risk being seen as offering lower quality work. In their study of PSFs in Scotland and the South East of England however, these authors conclude that only a minority of PSF's are competing on price, most were attempting to differentiate their services or were stuck in the middle without a strategy.

A Further Typology - Task And Process
In addition to the issues of function, genesis and competition there is a further common typology of consultation,that of Task and Process, which suggests that some consultancies would focus mainly upon the work of their clients while other consultancies would focus upon processes within the client organisation. In simple terms the Task consultancies are concerned with the question of what to do, the process consultancies with improving the functioning and development of the client.

The primary tasks for a consultation have been described as a set of goals which justify the existence of the consultancy group, the reason that it was called together, its basic mission (Schein, 1986), and as that aspect of a situation presently causing the client's difficulty (Blake and Mouton,1976). Process in a consultation has been addressed in a variety of ways. The work involved in deciding what to do and then doing it involves processes. Similarly the work involved in developing a client's organisational processes also involves processes, both within the consultancy group and between the consultancy group and the client system. The foremost typology of process consultancy was that of Schein (1969) who in parallel with work at the Tavistock Institute developed understandings of the relationship of task and process, especially the notion that task is dominated by the richer and more complex issues of process. So to speak of process as the how of the task and the how of interpersonal,group, intergroup, institutional and inter-institutional relatedness, became common.

To illustrate this issue we point to four different ideas of process.

By Process O   we refer to the focal processes within the client system that in a more subtle reading is the task focus for a process consultation.

By Process I   we refer to the standard operating procedures adopted by a consultancy in doing its work, whether that work is with the what or the how e.g. planning, budgeting, control and reporting and so on.

By Process II   we refer to the configuration of roles and working patterns within the consultancy. This would include the manner in which consultancy teams are formed (inter alia Belbin, 1981) and the modes of intervention which are to be used,(Blake and Mouton 1976).

By Process III   we refer to the psychodynamic issues that arise within the consultancy and between the consultancy and the client organisation. This third notion of process is exemplified in the work of deVries and Miller (1984), Menzies Lyth (1988, 1989) and de Board (1978). We would include in this arena of process the work needed in order for members to overcome organisational defences (Argyris, 1990).

Hence the typology of consultancies into focus on Task or Process does not imply very much differentiation in their genesis, strategies, modes of organisation or competitive positioning. Nor does it imply any necessary difference in their position in our knowledge typology, creation, praxis or application. However it may imply differences in the way in which they choose to handle themselves in relation to the four types of process which we have identified. We would expect differences to be especially marked in the Process II and III, with Process oriented consultancy groups being more likely to use catalytic, and acceptant interventions styles and more likely to work with all of the issues of Process III than Task oriented firms.

The distinction between process and task (or what they call content) consulting is articulated by consultancy companies (Fullerton and West, 1992). They suggest that while consultants tend to view themselves as either task or process consultants, clients indicate that they prefer them to move freely between the two styles, and view neither "pure" style as effective, a point which supports our less rigid typology of task and processes. As might be expected, clients stress the practical side of the relationship, claiming to be more interested in whether consultants understand their business or not, avoid jargon and provide customised, rather than off-the-shelf solutions. Consultants are more interested in "relationship-building" and developing a rapport. Clients seem to feel this is less important than that there are clear aims and objectives, effective use of time and the consultant is viewed as giving value for money, that is, expecting effective Process I-II behaviour.

This brief review of management consultancy, the knowledge industries and the professional service firm has shown that the knowledge typology of knowledge creation, process and application does accommodate the functional approaches of Maister, Greiner and Nees, and Winch and Schneider, the common ideas of task and process, and does not conflict with the genesis model of Pennarola. While there has been no critical exploration of these classifications, they appear serviceable as a basis for examining some aspects of the practice of management consultancy.

II. THE SURVEY

In order to explore the larger part of the management consultancy market coopera-tion and data was sought from the companies which appeared in Management Consultancy magazine's survey of the market (1992), which contained some 40 companies. We also checked the figures supplied in the magazine survey, with all those firms who agreed to be interviewed and amended the survey figures, where necessary. We supplemented those firms with members of the Management Consultancies Association (MCA), the only trade body in the area specifically aimed at the company, rather than the individual consultant level. We sought cooperation from all members of the MCA regardless of whether they appeared in the Management Consultancy magazine survey or not. These firms were supple-mented by the Directory of British Consultants, and we contacted all the larger firms which appeared in that but in neither of the other two lists. The constraint was, as usual, in gaining co-operation from busy people in busy firms and of the companies approached, we were grateful that representatives from 26 agreed to be inter-viewed. This was done, on the telephone or in person, in the first part of 1993. The format chosen was a semi-structured questionnaire, supplemented with secondary material such as brochures, annual reports etcetera, provided by the companies.

We believe that these firms are adequately representative of the larger firms in the UK, though we accept that the top forty or so management consultancy firms may make up only 60% (or 40% depending on what figures are believed) of the UK market as there are an unknown number of very small firms and sole practitioners.

The findings from this survey are presented in the following sequence. Firstly, was the Knowledge typology useful in categorising the firms and were there any interesting differences between the firms so categorised? We examine this through consideration of our typology and how the firms describe themselves. Then we turn to an exploration the firms' sources of knowledge, knowledge networks, transfer of knowledge and/or expertise and consultant knowledge and skills.

The Typologies

In asking consultants to describe how their firm operates, we did not invite them to relate directly to our model of creation, praxis and application described earlier, but instead approached this through exploring with them what they regarded as the primary added value they provided to their clients. From their responses and with reference to our model, we present the typology as part of Table 2. From these data we have compiled Table 3. As can be seen companies which provide a mixture of praxis and application are the most common (50%), followed by companies which offer a mixture of all three i.e. a full range (32%), while a smaller number of companies,(12%) offer knowledge creation and praxis, with only one company being classified as only in application and one in praxis. Interestingly none of the companies in the survey could be classified as offering only knowledge creation and equally none were classified as offering knowledge creation and application. The first empty set was not surprising. However the second empty set, that of creation and application was interesting to us as this is the commonly perceived separation between academic research and commercial organisation, a separation which does not appear to exist in the world of management consultancy. In general the typology seems to capture the patterns of work of these respondents; however the breadth of the work in each category differed from firm to firm. For example a consultancy firm classified as offering a full range might have a different mix of that range than another firm so classified.

It appears that there are interesting differences in locus of work, domestic or international, total revenues and fee income per consultant in relation to our typology; see Table 4. Clearly the internationally oriented firms tend to offer the full range of our typology, be larger and have a higher fee income per consultant than the domestic firms. It is also clear that the fees payable for Praxis work are substantially higher than those payable for the more manageable work of Application. It would appear that full range consultancies earn more per consultant than the application workers.

In concert with Winch & Schneider's idea, the overwhelming majority of these respondents appeared to us to be selling "probity." The fact of being a disinterested outsider, "able to see the wood for the trees," was the primary added value most consultants thought that they were providing. This idea is, of course, applicable to each element of our typology.

In terms of markets served, 14 (50%) of the firms surveyed could be described as specialists, six of these describing themselves as specialists in "change management." The remainder, who would otherwise be called generalists, claimed to provide service in two or more specialist areas.

A difference between process and task consultants emerged. The process consultants describe their role in terms like "helping organisations learn," or "enabling them to do what we do when we leave." The task consultants tended to stress their role as providers of temporary skills, which where either not present in the organisations (hence they were selling expertise); or were present in the organisation, but were otherwise employed. They stressed sectoral knowledge and experience of having solved similar business problems before. In some ways this self description is somewhat misleading, especially when compared to the manner in which we addressed process in this article. We drew a distinction between task as the content of the work and three kinds of processes (operating procedures, the taking up of roles and the psychodynamics of a consultation). Our respondents seemed to have a typology of task and process more closely attuned to the distinction which Blake and Mouton (1976) drew between two modes or styles of intervention, that of Prescription and that of Theory/Principles; prescription is offering solutions to problems, both what to do and how to do it and Theory/ principles is about working with clients to jointly solve what to do and how to do it such that the client is enabled to learn how to do these things for themselves.

Most respondents regard general management knowledge, or knowledge of what they call process consulting skills, as their major body of expertise, rather than specific sectoral, or technical knowledge. Companies at the knowledge creation end of the scale however were more likely to mention knowledge of process consulting skills, or other specialities such as human resources and organisation design.

Sources of Knowledge

Respondents were asked to describe "where they got their knowledge". Their replies were categorised as follows:

Generated in-house
Derived from client practice
Derived from academic links/sources
Other

All but one of the respondents included the category "derived from client practice", and ten (40%) stated that, for them, this was the most important source. One respondent said that "95% of our knowledge comes from this", while another stated "people learn most or best from experience at clients". This knowledge is disseminated through the companies in a variety of ways; in larger consultancies and those with international offices, in-house databases of methods and practices were most popular. The majority of larger, full-service consultancies expressed a desire to give their consultants experience with more than one kind of client and with more than one sector. Smaller consultancies tend to share experiences in a more informal, face to face manner, though several respondents had formal training sessions in "best practice" given by members of the consultant staff. A similar story is told by Casey (1993). However it is not clear which methods were deemed the most effective for disseminating knowledge gained on clients sites. This type of in-house knowledge sharing, both of experiences and ideas, was cited as the second most important source of knowledge for consultancies, with links with academic institutions the third most important source.

Links with academic institutions in general were viewed as beneficial and, in a minority of our respondents (4, 20%), a major source of knowledge-asset building. Of those firms which specifically mentioned academic links, two were full range, one in praxis and one in knowledge creation and praxis. In addition, academic institutions or academics acting as consultants were viewed as competition in some 20% of cases. Aside from these links though, which tend to be informal, most consultancies still seem to prefer to operate as single entities. Only about 30% of respondents favoured links with other organisations - to provide expertise in areas where a firm is weak, for example. One respondent commented "there's only so much you can do yourself," but in many cases these links were informal, sometimes tied to specific pieces of work. If much knowledge sharing goes on in the consultancy market, it tends to be within companies. Outside of that, it would appear to be on the personal, networking level, rather than in formal alliances.

Apart from the firms which already were part of an international firm, only two of our respondents had deliberately created long term links with consultancies in Europe as a response to, or to take advantage of, the single market. This suggests that, to date, internationalism as an issue may be less important than many commentators suggest. Those consultancies which do have an international presence said that it was often a factor in their being hired, but for this initial survey we did not seek evidence for this.

In terms of economies of scope, few companies outside of the large, accountancy-based firms seem in a position to take advantage of them. The group of knowledge-based companies or organisations is a seductive idea, but we found little evidence of their existence.

Transfer of Expertise

We were concerned to explore the role of these consultancies in the transfer of expertise to clients, especially since many of the firms claimed to have that as a primary aspect of their work. Some 90% of respondents claim that they do transfer expertise to clients. About 70% say that is not only in specific, functional areas, but also in process skills. This evidence may appear to undermine our classification in respect of "task" and "process" but for some companies process is the task of consultancy. About 20% of respondents, see the transfer of expertise as the primary competency consultancies offer, with comments like,"If you don't do this, they (the client) won't follow through on plans." Or "It's very dissatisfying to a consultant if you think something will fall over as soon as you turn your back." The opposite viewpoint is much less often encountered, though one respondent commented, " as a client, you may not be interested in knowledge transfer, you may just want your problem solved." Again we could not observe a relationship of these attitudes with the type of firm in question, even those companies at the procedural end of the spectrum see knowledge transfer as a defining characteristic of their profession. It is evident from our survey that the primary method for transferring expertise seems to be by joint client/consultant teams working together over the course of a project.

Of less importance, mentioned by about 40% of respondents is transfer of expertise through specific training programmes, seminars, courses etc for client staff. This is favoured for task skills such as a new computer system, but not process skills. About 15% of respondents refer to "style" being transmitted to clients ie. clients learn a lot from watching the way consultants hold meetings/conduct reviews/devise business plans etc.

Only 20% of respondents in our survey mentioned training of staff as the way transfer of expertise is carried out. Most prefer the "team" approach, where client and consultant work in complementary teams until the project is complete. In one case (an IT Consultancy) "implementation" was taken to mean strictly systems implementation, but even in this case, it was carried out in conjunction with client staff.

Attitudes to "training" the client staff, as opposed to transferring expertise through collaborative teamwork, seem to vary between "process" and "task" consultants. Most of the "process" consultants say that they do some training. Others, notably the full-service, accountancy-based consultancies will generally offer training only as part of a consultancy assignment. This was partly because rates for management training were perceived to be much lower than for consultancy and there is a lot more non commercial eg. academic, competition. Not surprisingly, consultancies who do a lot of work in IT, are heavy providers of training, while others in areas such as strategy tended to the view that training was inappropriate.

Firms expressed concern for the effective implementation of this work, for it certainly seems to be the case that, as one respondent commented, "the days when you could just write a report and go," are over. All respondents said they do get involved in implementation - usually through joint client/consultant teams, in one case through management development programmes. All consultants are not involved in implementation in all cases though. One respondent said sometimes it is preferable to let the client be their own implementors and indeed it is possible that the ability of a client to implement the recommendation on their own would be a good indicator of how successfully clients had gained expertise. Implementation is not an inevitable event, for as one respondent commented, "sometimes the client doesn't want to implement our recommendations." In other cases, clients cannot afford to have consultants involved in the implementation process as well, though the respondents who cited cost as a factor, work for small and medium sized companies, rather than large organisations. This lends some weight to the belief that small and medium enterprises tend to purchase more standardised, off-the-shelf solutions, that are less complex to implement.

Consultant Skills

Maister's (1985) comment that, "unless their skills are truly unique, professionals are almost never hired for their technical capabilities," seems to be borne out by this research. Most (55%) of the consultancies in our survey place great stress on experience as a quality they look for in recruits, rather than specific technical expertise.

Those firms which did not mention business experience of some kind as a recruitment criteria tend to be the larger, full-service consultancies who recruit more junior staff and train them. Even in these cases, most mentioned two levels of entry to the organisation; at a junior level, with a first degree or MBA, or later on with several years of line management or other business experience.

Smaller consultancies prefer applicants to have experience of line management, or in several cases, experience of consultancy. This was seen as a positive thing as it accustomed people to the long hours, travelling and other pressures associated with this kind of work. In about a third of cases, specific sectoral experience was mentioned as a quality looked for in recruits.

There was a large degree of agreement as to what constituted the personal skills of successful consultants with 60% of respondents mentioning good social skills and ability to get on with people as a top priority. The ability to sell was mentioned by 25% of respondents, problem solving ability by 25% and business awareness or the ability to empathise with client problems, by 25%. A "good brain" was mentioned in 20% of cases and other skills such as, integrity, competitiveness and creativity merited one mention each. The picture that emerges here is of the need for applicants to possess a range of general as well as specific competencies.

The kind of knowledge required by successful consultants seems to be largely gained in practice. In this, the educational institutions are perhaps able to provide only a part of the required array of knowledge and skills. Specific educational qualification seem to be less in demand than experience or personal qualities.

Only one respondent said they <u>expected</u> staff to have a post-graduate degree. About 20% of companies said they liked staff to have a "professional" qualification eg. in accountancy and these were often gained as part of the in-company training. Most only expected a first degree or in about 20% of cases, had no educational requirements. Some 30% of companies did have staff with MBAs, though it was not a significant number in most cases and none had it as a mandatory entrance requirement.

There is little or no correlation, between the type of firm (ie. knowledge creator, praxis or applicator) and the educational requirements expected of recruits. MBAs in particular were viewed with suspicion in some firms, particulary in those cases were several years of line management experience was regarded as necessary at entry level. Several respondents commented that an MBA was more useful for dealing with large companies than with small or medium sized ones. As expected, therefore, those companies whose business is only with very large, blue-chip clients were keener than others to hire staff with MBAs. Other reasons for suspicion of the MBA seemed more at odds with one another though, with one respondent claiming that the knowledge gained in business school was at too low a level and too functional to be of any practical use, while another felt it was too high flown, "they're good at mergers and acquisitions, SWOT analysis etc, but this isn't the day to day work of most companies." Other post-graduate qualifications, including doctorates aroused less strong feelings, though one respondent commented that a PhD would be a "negative indicator" for them as it would suggest too narrow a specialisation.

A picture emerged of a requirement for applicants to be able to function with some knowledge and significant practical abilities. We were though, unable to distinguish between the capabilities required to undertake work in each of our typologies, though we would suggest that knowledge creation (whether academic or practical) and praxis would require some substantial educational attainment, for not to have such would clearly be disabling. For the more programmed work of knowledge application the lower qualifications sought were matched with lower fee earnings.

We compared the amount spent on research and training, by the various firms as an indication of how much they invest in their "knowledge assets". Such spending varied from 3% to 20% of annual fee income (or turnover), but there was no correlation of these figures with any other performance measure (eg. fee income per consultant, market share, or percentage of repeat business) or with the type of firm, according to our model. In addition, there is no correlation between the amount spent on research and training and the average size of client served.

Relationship to clients

All consultancies displayed a degree of adaptation to clients and over half, said their work was largely customised though even they often adopted a "toolkit" type approach ie. used standard tools/techniques in different combinations. 20% of respondents claim to use proprietary techniques and to market them as such. However this does not correlate with types of company and knowledge generators are no more likely to use proprietary techniques than knowledge application companies. Some 20% of the remaining respondents expressed the belief that clients are put off by anything which seems like a "packaged" solution. Several said that they referred internally to proprietary models, but did not market their skills in this way, preferring to be seen as presenting truly customised solutions, rather than standard procedures, even though these must exist and make cost estimation more reliable.

In the case of those consultants who do use proprietary techniques, assessments of their usefulness varied widely. Some saw them as the "crown jewels" of the organisation, while others believe they are only competitively useful for about 18 months at most. Only 15% of respondents have copyrighted their techniques and we need in future to find out why this is the case. It may be inherently difficult to codify this kind of knowledge in a form suitable for patenting, or it may be that the process of patenting is too difficult, too long and complicated.

It seems that transferring expertise does not prevent a company from getting repeat business. One respondent claimed that full-service consultancies are better placed in this regard, as "you can get repeat business even if you transfer skills, by offering them different services eg. training, market research, strategy etc." This seems sensible as the full range consultancies gain more repeat business than others (Table 4).

More than half the respondents get more than 50% repeat business per annum, though as one respondent warned," it's hard to quantify as although it may be the same organisation, it's often not the same person within the organisation that hires you." This would suggest that it is easier to get repeat business if your clients are large rather than small or medium sized companies and there does seem to be some evidence for this. In addition, consultancies with very high levels of repeat business (more than 70%), tend to have higher than average fee income per consultant and are international.

In terms of organisational forms, "the assets are the people" angle, has often been interpreted to mean that the partnership form is a vital component in the motivation and retention of consultancy staff. In recessionary times this may be less of an issue and the majority of respondents commented that staff turnover was currently lower than usual. Just over half of our sample were partnerships, but even those that are not claimed to be "run along partnership lines," by which they meant successful consultants could become principals or shareholders. For those respondents which are not partnerships and which do not have a partnership-like reward structure, intellectual challenge, variety and fun were among the methods of motivating staff. Money was mentioned in 50% of cases and many of the limited companies offer bonus payments etc. Some of the non-partnerships are less than ten years old and one director of a limited company commented that he thought partnership may be the eventual form as it was a more "effectively self-perpetuating motivational the eventual form as it was a more "effectively self-perpetuating motivational structure". Thus knowledge assets in the main are protected by a combination of salary and bonus, variety of tasks and sense of personal challenge and the opportunities to learn and build on one's own skills base. In addition, about half of the companies surveyed offer partnership as a reward for long service to the firm. The use of copyright of in-house knowledge is not widespread.

III. DISCUSSION

The survey results were limited by the sample of large firms which were kind enough to cooperate with us and of the limitations of the data that we were able to obtain. While the use of published data and interview data has limitations of thoroughness and scope we are content that the material does represent adequately the broad direction of the behaviour of consultancy firms.

Firstly, we can say that management consultancy firms display many of the characteristics of Knowledge Industries outlined. Their biggest single asset is the skill of their staff, which they build up from a mixture of recruitment, training and practical experience. This experience is transmuted through the organisation with the use of in-house databases of methodology, case studies, formal training sessions and informal "networking."

The "product" of the consultancy firm is certainly intangible and although many firms use standardised methodologies and models, they are rarely marketed as such and the idea of adaption to client needs remains strong.

Consultancy firms claim to add value to client organisations in the sense of expertise or advice, most importantly by bringing the experience of "having done something before" to the client in question. In addition, the consultants' position as outsider allows him or her the opportunity to provide a more dispassionate overview of the situation than those working closely with it (probity).

In the light of this, educational qualifications are part of some broader sense of capability in the profile of the consultant. Nonetheless, consultancies are largely staffed with graduate or above level personnel. These personnel have many of the characteristics of the other professionals, but their professional status remains ambiguous. There is little or no regulation or certification of the consultancy market and no agreed body of knowledge in which consultants must be versed.

Transfer of expertise is undoubtedly more important to consultancy firms' success than in other professional services eg. architecture, accountancy or medicine. There appears to be a division of opinion between suppliers; some regard it as a vital component of the service and others feel they are brought in to clients primarily to solve problems and any skills transfer that takes place is a by-product. This issue will need to be investigated further, particularly the degree to which end users require skills transfer and how successful they deem it to be.

In this initial survey therefore, in addition to our study of the usefulness of the typology of knowledge, we were concerned also to explore the common typology of "task" and "process" consultancy. Although the firms rarely used these terms to describe themselves, we have attributed them to two major groupings, largely in the sense of the distinction drawn by Blake and Mouton (1976) between interventions which are prescriptive and those which are based in theory/principles. In addition, there is a third grouping, which fits neither model exactly.

The relationship of the two typologies is rather rough and ready (see Table 5). However it does appear that the majority of the firms classified as primarily Task oriented are also classified as working with Praxis/Application modes, while those classified as Process oriented are more likely to be classified as working in Knowledge Creation/Praxis or full range. Note that the fee earnings per consultant are significantly higher for the firms classified as "Process" than those classified as "Task". Data is also given in Table 5 for those firms that we were unable to classify.

The first group of Task consultants are often accountancy-based (eg. Big Six) and generally organised as partnerships. They tend to recruit staff at two levels - either straight from University or Business School, or with about ten years' line management experience. They seem to be offering a mixture of task and process skills, though they emphasise their role as providers of temporary skills rather than management educators or developers. Fullerton & West (1993) however, suggest that clients want both and are happiest when consultants move between the two styles.

In the second group, the "Process" firms, we include the change management companies, the Human Resources and management development specialists and some of the IT-based companies which specialise in business process re-engineering. These companies are characterised by a specialist-orientation. They hire only experienced staff and are more impressed with personal skills than educational qualifications. In this group we would include many of those companies currently selling "business process re-engineering". The focus is on horizontal processes within organisations with a manner of consultation primarily based upon working with clients.

The "others" comprise a group of companies which we were unable to classify in either of the two categories. Some are smaller, accountancy-based companies, others are specialised in just one or two vertical markets. Most of them provide "task" or content, rather than "process" consulting.

Implications

We have attempted to support the validity of our knowledge-centred typology. In future, we would wish to focus more clearly on detailed questions concerning the type of knowledge used by consultants in their work. As Friedson (1970) points out, the practice or application of expertise is often analytically distinct from its knowledge base. If this is clear in a case such as medicine, with a well established and codified knowledge base, then it would be likely to be more pronounced in consultancy. The discourse knowledge that consultants draw on might be management science or one of the disciplines feeding into it e.g. mathematics, sociology, economics, psychology. In the case of some specialists the discourse might be from more applied areas such as human resources or information management.

These admittedly introductory speculations raise, with Friedson, the difficult issues of the distinction between the clearly highly valued practical knowledge used by consultants and the formal academic discourses. There is enough evidence from this survey to suggest that some, at least, of these firms are aware of the significance of knowledge creation, both academic and practical, and of networks to academic and research institutions. Hence there is an issue of how consultants relate discourse knowledge and practical knowledge. This is not a trivial matter for from ad hoc conversations with a small number of consultants it is clear that there is no simple way in which to apply either academic knowledge or practical knowledge to current work (which point suggests an opening in to understanding the work of praxis, which might be explored as working beyond the range of discourse and practical knowledge). Further we are aware that some scholars argue that the distinction that consultants make and that we use here are themselves products of a certain, perhaps simple, epistemological stance and from the view-point of, for example, Habermas (1984) would not be regarded as helpful or valid. This paper is not the place for an extended discussion of this important argument but it is a matter which scholars and consultants must attend.

We know from talking to consultancy firms that it is practical knowledge that they value most highly in recruits and which they regard themselves as "selling" to their clients? We also know that they think that work at client sites is where such knowledge is gained. However it was not clear what this process of the creation of practical knowledge might be, or whether there were consistent patterns in those processes. Although links with academic management science institutions were looked upon favourably,by some, as a source of new ideas and most consultants claimed to read at least some of both popular and academic work in the field, these experiences were rated a long way behind work at client sites in terms of building knowledge assets. This evidence lends weight to the earlier question as to what, in these consultancy practices, is the difference and relationship between practical knowledge and discourse knowledge? How do they and we recognise practical knowledge or discourse knowledge?

The "case" method is obviously used, both in academic training and within consultancies, several of whom claimed to document instances of "best practice" in certain cases and to disseminate these throughout the organisation. While lacking the standardised prescriptive remedies found in the health profession, consultancy does to some extent rely on symptomatic diagnosis. If is difficult to say however, to what extent organisations presenting the same symptom would be met with similar diagnoses from different firms, though one would guess that the solutions and pathways prescribed might differ more widely than in a well-established profession, though that could be a function of the particular type of work being undertaken

In addition to reassuring the public (and leaving aside the question of who constitutes the public in the case of consultancy), standards are used to pass on knowledge within a profession. Again, there is some evidence from our survey that this is how consultants learn from one another. Many spoke of both written and oral presentations of best practice and "war stories" from client sites, usually passed on informally and face to face. But, even if it were attempted the question arises, can such knowledge be usefully codified and if so how do consultancies develop a competitive advantage from it? As mentioned earlier, only a minority of the firms we spoke to had attempted to copyright their techniques and one respondent commented that the competitive advantage gained from such a move could only last about 18 months at most.

In addition, is it very difficult to discover criteria for the success or otherwise of such consultancy work. It seems that the studies and reviews which we know are undertaken by consultancies and by some clients are, understandably if regrettably, subjected to a data protection act all of their own. This is interesting when viewed in the light of the movement towards professionalism, which some consultancy firms and bodies such as the MCA and Institute of Management Consultants, support. The professionally ambiguous status of management consultants results partly from the fact that no agreed minimum body of knowledge or expertise exists, which the aspirant professional must possess in order to practice. Management consultancy has some way to go in what Larson (1977) calls the "dual project" of professionalism - to define a market for professional services and then to establish "monopolistic" control over it.

An interesting way of conceptualising expertise is to consider its relationship to four kinds of uncertainty commonly experienced (Baer, 1986). Firstly the collective uncertainty about what is known; this applies to both the public and to professionals. Second the "technical uncertainty" about cause-effect relationships. Coping with this technical uncertainty, he argued, is the basis for a profession, but the application of technical knowledge in context leads to the third kind of uncertainty - evaluative uncertainty. That is - how do I apply this knowledge in this instance? Finally there is "social" uncertainty which concerns the publics' attitude to the professions' expertise in general and practitioners' personal skills in particular.

Professionalization then is in part a process of uncertainty absorption or management by professionals on behalf of the public. Without wanting to dwell on the question of whether or not management consultants can call themselves professionals (the publics' attitude to their ability to deal with uncertainly is but one of a host of concerns standing between consultants and professional status) this discussion does focus an important and interesting question as to how consultants respond to these uncertainties and hence turn technical into practical knowledge.

Baer suggest that professionals answer the question by the use of "standards" based on the similarities of frequently encountered problems. As he puts it," why agonize de novo over the link between theory and action.....in each particular case if there is a standardised way of treating it?" He argues that occupations differ in the ways in which they formulate such standards - engineers and architects have tables of standards for commonly encountered structural problems, doctors have lists of symptoms and recommended prescriptions. Consultants however, from our research, seem both unwilling and unable to codify their knowledge to this extent.

Of course, professions establish rules and procedures for entry. While they express concerns at the standards of professional practice, they do not, on the whole, monitor professional behaviour. It is, at the least, possible that even in a well established profession (e.g. medicine) the development of professional competence through years of work might rest heavily upon notions of praxis as we have used them in this paper. Hence two notions of professional emerge, that of the approved new entrant and that of the maturer worker. In this second sense management consultants could readily claim professional standing. Further, the process of becoming the older, work-experienced, mature professional might involve similar processes in different professional occupations.

IV. CONCLUSIONS

Management Consultancy is a significant economic activity which is relatively ill-understood, both because of its work variety and confidentiality. From this initial survey, we observe that the proposed knowledge-based typology offered an illuminating way of classifying the limited data we were able to obtain. Further, the proposed typology complemented other approaches to professional service firms. However, the results and discussion raise a number of research questions.

1. Are consulting firms properly classifiable as a sub-set of professional service firms and knowledge industries?

2. While the knowledge typology that we used proved serviceable for this survey, would it be robust enough to aid a description and analysis of the internal world of consulting firms? Are the categories sufficiently independent?

3. What is the relationship of the elements of the typology of knowledge work and the organisational design and management of consulting firms?

4. What are the benefits to clients of consultancy work? How might these be assessed? Do these differ as between prescriptive and process consultancy work?

5. What do consultants actually do in the various stages of their work?

6. The typology of knowledge itself (e.g. discourse and practical) needs some critical exploration. Since formulating this project, we have noted the work of Blackler (1993) and the possibilities that are suggested for re-framing and analysis of consultancy as an activity system.

REFERENCES

Argyris, C. (1990) *Overcoming Organisational Defences*. Allyn and Bacon.

Badaracco, J. L. (1991) *The Knowledge Link*. Boston, Harvard Business School Press.

Belbin, M. (1981) *Management Teams: Why they Succeed or Fail*. Heinemann.
Barras, R. " New Technology and the New Services," *Futures*, 18, 6, pp 748-72.

Bennett, R. (1990) *Choosing and Using Management Consultants*. Kogan Page, London.

Bennis, Warren. G. (1966) *Changing Organizations*. McGraw Hill, New York.

Blackler, F. (1993) "Knowledge and the Theory of Organisations", *Journal of Management Studies*, 30, 6.

Blake, R. & Mouton, J. (1976) *Consultation*. Addison-Wesley.

De Board, R. (1978) *The Psychoanalysis of Organisations*. Tavistock Publications.

DeVries, K. and Miller, D. (1984) *The Neurotic Organisation*. Jossey Bass.

Drucker, P. (1989) *The New Realities*. Heinemann, London.

Enderwick, P. (1989) *Multinational Service Firms*. Routledge, London.

Fahey, L. & Christensen, H. (1984) "Building Distinctive Competences into Competitive Advantages", *Strategic Planning Management*, February.

Fullerton & West (1992) "Management Consultancy: Dimensions of Client/consultant relationships". Discussion paper No 99. Centre for Economic Performance, London School of Economics.

Greenwood, R. Hintings, & Brown, J. (1990) "'P2 -Form' Strategic Management: Corporate Practices in Professional Partnerships", *Academy of Management Journal*, 33/4 pp 725-755

Greiner, L. & Nees, R. (1984) "Seeing Behind the Look-Alike Management Consultants", *Organizational Dynamics*.

Handy, C. (1989) *The Age of Unreason*. London, Business Books.

Lovelock, C. (1988) *Managing Services*. Prentice Hall, New Jersey.
Machlup, F. (1962) *The Production and Distribution of Knowledge in the United States*. Princeton, Princeton University Press.

Machlup, F. (1982) *Volume 2 - The Branches of Learning*. Princeton: Princeton University Press).

Maister, D. (1982) "Balancing the Professional Service Firm", *Sloan Management Review*, Fall, pp 3 - 13.

Maister, D. (1985) *Professional Service Firm Management*, 5th edition. Maister Associates, Boston.

Marchand, D. & Horton, F. (1983) *Infotrends*. London, John Wiley.

Menzies Lyth, I. (1988) *Containing Anxiety in Institutions*. Free Association Books.

Menzies Lyth, I. (1989) *The Dynamics of the Social*. Free Association Books.

Masuda, Y. (1990) *Managing in the Information Society*. London, Blackwell.

Miles, I., etc (1990) "Mapping and Measuring the Information Economy" *Library and Information Research Report 77*, London.

O'Farrell, P N, Hitchens, D M & Moffat, L. (1993) "The Competitive Advantage of Business Service Firms," *Service Industries Journal*, Vol 13, No 1.

Payne, A. (1986) "New Trends in the Strategy Consulting Industry", *Journal of Business Strategy*, Vol 6, No 1 pp 43-55.

Pennarola, F. (1992) "Shared Professional Values and Organisational Forms in Management Consultancy Firms". Paper presented at the "Knowledge Workers in Contemporary Organisations Conference", Lancaster University, September.

Pettigrew, A. (1985) *The Awakening Giant, Continuity and Change at ICI*, Basil Blackwell, Oxford.

Porter, M. (1980) *Competitive Strategy* Free Press, New York.

Preston, P. (1989) "The Information Economy and the International Standard Industrial Classification (ISIC): Proposals for Updating the ISIC". *PICT Policy Research Paper No 6*, London, Economic and Social Research Council.

Rajan, A. (1990) *Capital People* The Industrial Society, London.

Rajan, A. with Fryatt, J. (1988) *Create or Abdicate*. Witherby and Co, London.
Raelin, Joseph A. (1985) *The Clash of Cultures, Managers and Professionals*. Boston, Harvard Business School Press.

Reich, R. (1991) *The Work of Nations: Preparing ourselves for 21st Century Capitalism*. London: Simon & Schuster.

Roach, Stephen. "The Information Economy Comes of Age", *Information Management Review*, Vol 1, Issue 1, 1986.

Rubin, M. and Sapp, M. (1981) "Selected Roles of Information Goods and services in the US National Economy", *Information Processing and Management*, Vol 17 pp 195-213.

Rubin, M. and Huber, M, Taylor (1987) *The Knowledge Industry in the United States, 1960 - 1980*. Princeton, Princeton University Press.

Schein, E. (1969) *Process Consultation*. Addison Wesley.

Schein,E.H. ( ) *Process Consultation: Lessons for Managers and Consultants*, Volume II. Addison Wesley.

Schon, D. (1983) *The Reflective Practitioner: How Professional Think in Action*. Basic Books, New York.

Sveiby, K. and Lloyd, T. (1987) *Managing Knowhow*. Bloomsbury, London.
        Webber A. M. (1993) "So what's so new about the new economy?" *Harvard Business Review*, January/February, pp 24-42.

Winch, G. & Schneider, E. (1993) "Managing the Knowledge-Based Organisation: The Case of Architectural practice". *Journal of Management Studies*, Vol.30, No.6

Zaltman, G. & Duncan, R. (1977) *Strategies for Planned Change*. New York, John Wiley and Sons.

Baer, W . (1986) Expertise and professional standards in Work and Occupations 13/4 pp 532-552

Bennett, R. (1990) Choosing and Using Management Consultants (Kogan Page, London)

Berry,A.J. and Oakley,K. (1993). Consultancies: Agents of Organisational Change. Leadership and Organisational Development Journal. Vol 14. No 5.

Casey,D. (1993). Managing Learning in Organisations. Open University Press.

Friedson, E (1970) Profession of Medicine: A Study of the Sociology of Applied Knowledge. (New York: Dodd, Mead)

Habermas, J. (1984) The Theory of Communicative Action. Beacon Press. (also 1991, Polity)

Raelin, Joseph A. (1985) - The Clash of Cultures, Managers and Professionals (Boston, Harvard Business School Press)

Table 2
Earnings per professional staff of firms interviewed (figures altered after consultation with firms)

Source: Management Consultancy Magazine and firms

Ranked in descending order of fee income per consultant, 1991.

	1991	Approx Fee Income (£m)	Typology	
1	£190,000	4.2	FR	Dom
2	£182,000	13.7	FR	Int
3	£144,000	3.6	FR	Int
4	£142,000	1.0	P	Int
5	£140,000	2.8	KCP	Int
6	£138,000	21.0	FR	Int
7	£133,000	2.2	KCP	Dom
8	£123,000	1.6	PA	Dom
9	£120,000	6.0	FR	Int
10	£110,000	160.0	PA	Int
11	£104,000	47.0	FR	Int
12	£103,000	172.1	FR	Int
13	£101,000	50.5	PA	Int
14	£100,000	12.0	PA	Int
15	£100,000	8.0	PA	Dom
16	£96,000	9.1	PA	Dom
17	£91,000	14.2	FR	Dom
18	£91,000	25.0	PA	Dom
19	£80,000	84.0	PA	Int
20	£62,000	0.5*	A	Dom
21	£56,000	70.0	PA	Int
22	£56,000	0.4*	PA	Dom
23	£51,000	1.8	KCP	Dom
24	£50,000	2.0	PA	Dom
25	na	na	PA	Int
26	na	na	PA	Int

Total   712.7

* 1992 fee income
Range (Source: Management Consultancy magazine and firms) £190,000 to £23,000.
Total no. of companies: 40.

  FR Full Range (all 3 types)
  KC Knowledge Creation
  P   Praxis
  A   Knowledge Application

Table 3
By Typology Total 26

	FR	KCP	P	PA	KC	A
Domestic	2	2		6	/	1
International	6	1	1	7	/	
TOTAL	8	3	1	13		1
	32%	12%	3%	50%		3%

Table 4
Fee Income Per Consultant (£)

	FR	KCP	P	PA	KC	A
Domestic	140,000	91,000	/	86,000	/	62,000
International	132,000	140,000	142,000	89,000	/	
Average for All	136,000	107,000	142,000	87,000	/	62,000

Table 5

	FR	KCP	P	PA	KC	A
Average Repeat Business	73%	33%	/	29%	/	50%

Table 6
"Task", "Process", Knowledge Typology and Earnings

	FR	KCP	P	PA	A
"TASK" £86,000	2 (103,000)	-	-	7 (86,000)	1 (62,000)
"PROCESS" £131,000	4 (158,000)	3 (107,000)	1 (142,000)	2 (106,000)	-
OTHERS £(95,000)	2 (118,000)	-	-	3 (72,000)	

MEETING THE CHALLENGE OF THE CASE

Philip Boxer and Barry Palmer, *Independent Consultants, London*

ABSTRACT

The paper explores the place or position taken up by anyone acting as a consultant. It is not primarily concerned with consultancy techniques, but with the ethical and epistemological assumptions which shape what the consultant does. The main work described is a series of workshops and its underlying assumptions about the nature of the consultant-client conversation. These assumptions underpin the design of the series, and two cases are used to show something of the process which resulted. In the authors' view, the challenge of the case is always also a challenge to the consultant's practice. They hope that they succeed in sharing something of this challenge with the reader.

INTRODUCTION

In early 1993 we ran a series of three workshops for practising and aspiring consultants. Our aim was to explore and generate understanding of the place or position taken up by anyone who undertakes to act as a consultant to any client system. We were not primarily concerned with consultancy techniques, but with the ethical and epistemological assumptions which shape what we do.

We ourselves are independent consultants, and so have had plenty of opportunities to think about this. Boxer works primarily as a strategy analyst with business organisations. He was at the London Business School, and is now an Associate of HKA Ltd and an Associate Member of the Centre for Freudian Analysis and Research. Palmer engages in organisation and management development, team-building and training, mainly in the public and voluntary sectors. He is an Associate of the Grubb Institute, OPUS Consultancy Services and Randolph Enterprise. In the course of this work we have found ourselves subject to, and responding to, a range of expectations: to come in as experts and fix something, to offer a diagnosis of an organisational dysfunction and propose some treatment, and (less frequently) to join our clients in their bewilderment and stuckness and work with them to find a way forward.

For us this poses epistemological and ethical problems. What is the status of the knowledge which we bring to, or generate during, this work. Or if, as we believe, we can have no certain knowledge or unquestionable theoretical framework, what is our justification for offering our services and accepting people's money? Worrying away at questions like this has led us to attempt to articulate the demands of consulting from what we have called the position of the 'fool'. This is the subject of this paper[1].

We have come to distinguish between three basic postures (cf Schein, Mintzberg)[2]:

- **bird**: the position of the consultant as expert, who supplies know-how which he or she is believed by the client to have, to solve a problem as identified by the client. (The term is mildly derogatory: the bird flies in and flies out again, leaving behind a solution to what is assumed by both consultant and client to be a known problem - a solution which, as long as the problem persists, may or may not prove to be welcome.)
- **guru**: the position of one who is asked by the client to use his or her insight and theory to define what the 'real' problem is behind the 'presenting problem' identified by the client, and to formulate what can be done about it. (Schein calls this the doctor-patient model, in which the process of diagnosis as well as the 'cure' are prescribed by the consultant.)
- **fool**: the position of the consultant who Schein called the process consultant. Here the client accepts the process of diagnosis of what the 'real' problem is as being problematic. In response to the 'identified problem' put forward by the client, the fool, like the client, accepts not knowing what the 'real' problem and its solution are, and is prepared to work with the client in a shared ignorance, learning with him or her the hard way how things can be different.[3]

These three position may be represented diagrammatically according to who is supposed to know what the problem is (rather than who knows how to solve a known problem):

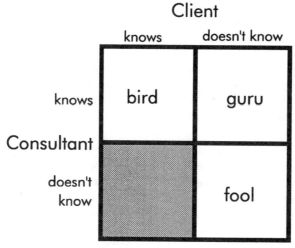

Although the blank position is one where someone can be providing a solution to a problem someone else has defined, it is not really a consultancy mode, though it is not unknown in practice: the consultancy firm sends along an **apprentice** consultant who knows how to apply a 'solution', but who has the opportunity to learn from the client what the problem is, at the client's expense!

Consultants may move between these positions during the course of a consultancy assignment. They form a repertoire of positions, in which we focus on the third mode not only because it is reached through the other two; but also because we believe it provides a stance from which to sort out the ambiguities into which consultants repeatedly wander, and which, in Winnicott's phrase, is a necessary condition for 'meeting the challenge of the case'[4]. Examining this stance leads us into intellectually and emotionally deep waters. It entails identifying the sources of our certainties and positioning ourselves outside them (although we know we never can); and hence steering into the unconscious anxieties from which we and our clients defend ourselves.

THE WORKSHOPS

We ran our series of workshops to explore this third position. The three workshops were run under the auspices of the Institute of Group Analysis, and constituted a single course. During the course participants were invited to present a current case, up to three times, and the rest of us acted as consultants to them. This is how we outlined the aims of the series:

"In this series of workshops we shall explore what it means to take up the place of a consultant in an organisation - whether as a manager or as an adviser. The aim is to give participants the opportunity to examine and develop their own practice.

In successive weekends we shall focus upon the activities of formulating, hypothesising, intervention and critical reflection through which we endeavour to 'meet the challenge of the case' and to face the questions which impale our practice. We shall be examining what is lacking in how participants seek to understand and work so as to open up new possibilities.

Participants will have the opportunity to examine this in small groups. This will involve adopting a 'Plus One' role from which to formulate questions for the group about what is ignored or 'bought into' without question in its deliberations. There will also be plenary sessions for theory and reflection."

The case material used in the paper is based on our notes from the workshops.

To give you an idea of the design of the workshops :

- participants moved between consultations in small groups, working on their cases, plenary sessions in which we endeavoured to look critically at these consultations, and spaces in which participants were invited to use a journal to record their reflections on their case;

- we provided theoretical notes for each weekend, which we introduced on the first evening. These covered speaking and listening (discussed here), power and knowledge[5], the theory of dilemmas[6], organisational viability and identity[7], and the impossibility of the 'Plus One' position (also discussed here).

- in every small group consultation one participant took what we called a 'Plus

One' role. The task of the Plus One was to listen critically to the client-consultant conversation, and to formulate questions about the account of 'reality' which was being constructed through this conversation. These questions were raised in the plenary sessions.

- the Plus One was a visitor from another group, except for the last weekend when the person presenting their case was the visitor. This meant in effect that every small group consultation was a new grouping of participants and consultants.

- we took part in the small groups in the same consultant role as other participants, but did not take the Plus One role. In this way we sought to avoid the Plus One role being identified with a guru position - not always successfully.

- in the periods between workshops participants continued to work on the projects they were presenting. We regarded these periods as an integral part of the workshops series.

THE THREE WEEKENDS

The three weekends, which were five to eight weeks apart, were designed to focus on successive stages in a consulting process:
1. In the first weekend, the presenter spoke about a case, and group members listened and offered readings of what was going on.

2. In the second weekend the presenter again described his or her case, but now presenter and group were invited to listen to this account, and to read it in terms of dilemmas in the client system - dilemmas which were manifesting themselves in the stuckness the presenter was being asked to address.

3. In the third weekend, the presenter again spoke about the case, but this time from the point of view of what they were learning about their own practice. This time presenter and group were invited to listen to the way the presenter was listening to her/his own account. In other words all of us moved towards a Plus One position.

In each weekend we suggested that those taking the Plus One role should focus upon a different question. In the first weekend the question was:

Are the presenter and consultants placing too much dependence upon one account of what is going on? (Are the consultants buying in to the presenter's story, as though he or she knew and could give a total description of the situation?)

In the second weekend we suggested they ask:

Are the presenter and consultants assuming that there is a right way to interpret the presented problem ? (eg is a psychoanalytic or group analytic or systems frame of reference being accorded unquestioned authority?)

In the third weekend, as we have said, everyone was in a Plus One role. Our questions was:

> **Where do the presenter and consultants 'draw the line' round the problem? Is the line being drawn in a way which includes or excludes themselves? (Who is part of whose problem in the problem-as- presented, and are the presenter and consultants able to formulate the problem in a way which includes themselves?)**

This third question pointed to what we regard as an essential aspect of the fool position which we pointed to in the pre-series flyer, quoting Robin Skynner:

> "The [consultant] automatically selects the ideal clientele in which to study himself or herself vicariously....., though the knowledge cannot benefit us.... until we acknowledge the fact that our work, however useful, has also been an evasion of the truth about ourselves."[8]

Since a consultancy project is an episode in the life of the consultant, as well as in the lives of others who make up the client system, becoming aware of the 'real problem' means becoming aware of a question about what we are up to, as well as what other people are up to - the question of our own desire in the matter. As we listen to our own interpretations, we become aware of how they are shaped by the desire of the one who formulates them, as well as by 'what is going on'. In Eliot's words:

> "....every moment is a new and shocking
> Valuation of all we have been.[9]

This is not to suggest that we should not make interpretations - only that in doing so we should act in the knowledge that we are doing so. It is in relation to this knowledge of our own participation that we find what is characteristic of consulting from the position of the fool.

THE CONSULTANT-CLIENT CONVERSATION

We explained the rationale of the design of the workshop process (and our view of the consulting process) in terms of the nature of the speaking and listening which takes place in a conversation. Everything said is said by some one to an other - thus even when you are speaking to yourself there is a listener. The presenter's account can therefore be understood as an endless chaining of speaking behaviour, so that any listening to this chaining involves selecting from the chain retrospectively - what we call 'punctuating' the chain. This punctuating can be thought of as a backward movement which makes sense out of the forward movement of speaking. Thus listening 'frames' the reality conjured up by the speaking through the way it punctuates the speaking chain:

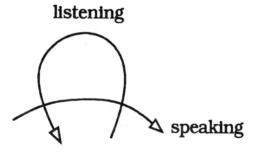

In the consultant-client conversation we can therefore distinguish between two positions:

- that of the manager or client who describes what is going on, and takes up the position of 'client system' for the consultant in their account;
- that of the consultant, who listens to the account coming from the client system, and forms a view, not only of what-is-going-on, but also of the client's view of the what-is-going-on. This view is expressed in an interpretation of the client's view:

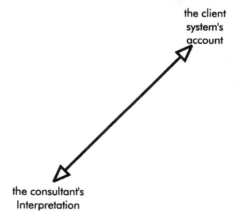

Such a conversation implies two other positions, from which it is impossible to speak, though sometimes we speak as if we could:

- That of 'what-is-going-on' - the organisation as it 'is'. The distinction between reality and fantasy implies the possibility of taking up this position; but in practice any account of this reality is always mediated by the speaker;
- that of a 'Plus One' process, which continues outside the consultant-client conversation, and seeks to articulate what is ignored or excluded by the terms in which the client's situation is described and

interpreted. Inevitably, the conversation constructs readings of the situation which highlight some aspects of the situation and how they are to be understood, and obscures others. It is like a torch shone into a room, which picks out what the beam strikes and leaves other things in darkness. The 'Plus One' position is an active refusal to forget this.

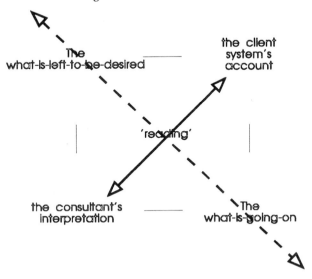

The three questions we have already discussed point towards this 'Plus One' position. The above diagram is adapted from Lacan[10]. In Lacan's terms, these questions are ways of probing what is wanting in the situation as described - in the colloquial phrase, what is left to be desired. The concept of desire is important in Lacan and in the scheme we are presenting. The client presents a problem. He (or she) cannot simply sit there and weep, so he formulates a problem and a request to the consultant in words. Of course the client may speak and weep (although it is unusual), or in some other way his desire may bend or trouble what he is saying. But even after everything has been said that can be said, still what is said in words can never express all that was in the weeping. That which remains left out, that which is left wanting, shows itself to us as what Lacan refers to as 'desire'. From the Plus One position we may note that something is not being said, and we may try to articulate what that is. But of course whatever we actually say is also inevitably lacking: it is uttered along the client-consultant axis, and is itself subject to the scrutiny of the other axis.

This second diagonal which we introduced into the diagram is an impossible axis. We suggest that the challenge of the case is only addressed insofar as the conversation is oriented in relation to this other axis: thereby becoming a continuously seeking after discovering 'what-is-left-to-be-desired' in relation to 'what-is-going-on', in the full knowledge that it can never be pinned down; and therefore a continuous asking of what the conversation as it is being conducted is causing to be ignored (forgotten: the word for truth in Greek is 'alhqeia' - 'unforgetting'.)[11]

This Plus One position must always elude us, because what ever we think and say is in language (or, in Maturana's terms, in 'languaging'[12]) and therefore embedded in its own assumptions. While we can do useful things from a bird or a guru position, our work is limited in its influence unless we are able to take up this fool position in which we know that we know nothing. The fool position is thus a sceptical position (not to be confused - as it often is - with the position of the cynic):

> "Scepticism does not mean the successive doubting, item by item, of all opinions or of all the pathways that accede to knowledge. It is holding the subjective position that one can know nothing.... Scepticism is something that we no longer know. Scepticism is an ethic. Scepticism is a mode of sustaining man in life, which implies a position so difficult...... that we no longer even imagine it...."[13]

We shall illustrate this progression of positions by describing (in a fictionalised form) how two cases unfolded through the three weekends. These accounts seek to communicate the _process_ of the two consultants' experience. The _content_ is an amalgam of several situations known to us - in other words, fiction.

JANET

I - Telling the problem

At the beginning of the course Janet introduced herself as a probation officer who had risen from the ranks to the position of Assistant Chief Probation Officer in the East Midlands service. She had become disaffected with the way probation was going, and had accepted an invitation to join a friend in the voluntary sector who was chief executive of a national organisation recruiting and deploying volunteers (the National Federation of Volunteer Centres). She was in her mid-fifties, and had joined the course because of concern about the management of expansion in the NFVC.

She began her session by launching into a description of what was happening in NFVC, without saying what she wanted from the group. There were about 250 volunteer centres within NFVC, throughout the UK, providing volunteers for local welfare and environmental projects. The NFVC supported these centres by providing information, advice and training, making recommendations about standards, and representing their interests at a national level. It was funded by the Home Office and a levy from local centres.

Janet had worked with the Director (Tom) for 12 years, and was now Assistant Director in charge of their five regional coordinators. Initially she and Tom had been the total HQ team; later they grew to a team of four.

Eighteen months ago, Tom had organised a merger with another agency. Janet had not been party to this decision and had felt alienated when she was told. Tom had agreed with the Director of the other agency, Charles, that he should become an Assistant Director and continue to coordinate, and be responsible for, his two coordinators, who serviced voluntary advisory agencies in the north and south of Britain. Janet had thought this was ridiculous: now they had two teams of

365

coordinators, sometimes servicing groups of volunteers in the same town or county. She had also felt that the ethos of the NFVC was under threat: their own volunteers were generally young and radical; the other agency comprised older, retired people from business who offered their advice as managers and accountants to charities.

Janet described ructions in the management team. They would shortly be moving into a new building in Birmingham, and would be together under one roof for the first time. She feared that if she could not contribute to the managing of all this, the organisation might disintegrate; but if she was successful, she feared that they might find they had one manager too many, and Charles would take over her job.

The responses from the others listening to her account were:

- One person said Janet had presented a no-win situation. She attracted a lot of sympathy from the group on the course. It was all the Director's fault.
- One saw a parallel with the centres they served, which were often run in amateurish ways: the Director had behaved unprofessionally too.
- One saw all this as a response to a world which was increasingly threatening to charities. Money was tighter, there was pressure for more accountability. Charities were being forced into trying to make economies which jeopardised their raison d'être.
- Some interpreted her story as though it was dream material, asking no questions which suggested that they wanted to know more about what was going on.

Janet appeared initially to have taken over the group, and the group in turn appeared to have swallowed her view of things whole. They were making no distinction between what-was-going-on (or what was going on in her inner world) and Janet's reading of all this. This created the illusion that they had direct access to the real problem, and could fix it (if only they knew how).

II - Hypotheses and dilemmas

At the beginning of the second weekend Janet said she had gone away feeling much greater clarity, and had used this clarity at various meetings. But she felt it has been 'too clear and too easy'. Had it been consultation or therapy?

This time she wanted to talk about the relationship between the HQ staff and organisers and the local volunteers and their committees. All were locally run and most were charities in the own right. They used the services of NFVC, but few of their members were interested in anything beyond their local scene. HQ were under pressure from the Home Office to demonstrate that their funding was well spent. They were also aware that the Charity Commission were tightening up on the management of charities. HQ had a policy of requiring local centres to introduce more quality control of volunteers, to tighten up their accounting systems, and to participate in nation-wide campaigns about things like the care of the elderly and environmental concerns.

But regional organisers (RO's) had a very variable impact upon individual centres. Some established effective relations and influence, others didn't. Local centres seemed to wait until the RO had gone away and then continue as they had before. To make matters worse, representatives on the central Council of NFVC were putting pressure on HQ to do more for them, and some were saying they might have to reduce their subscription.

Janet drew a diagram of the organisation to explain this, which represented the RO's as managers with the local centre committees under them. She talked about the professionalism she had learned in the probation service, and her frustration at the vagueness of her RO's and of local centres.

The group seemed to be having difficulty seeing the situation from any perspective other than that offered by Janet herself. She read the situation through her probation management spectacles, and could only see the volunteers as difficult staff who would not toe the line. One dilemma in the organisation seemed to be able to be expressed in terms of two imperatives:

- the organisation must be run according to professional standards;

versus

- the local centres must preserve their autonomy as local initiatives with a voluntary ethos.

So one reading of what was going on was that the more Janet and HQ sought to control the activities of local centres, the more local centres resisted and asserted their self-help values...

...and the more the local centres asserted their autonomy, the more HQ sought to get them to adopt national standards.

In this session the group were restricted by assuming that Janet's way of interpreting her own problem - as one of deviance from a normative hierarchical structure - <u>was</u> the right way (cf second critical question). The analysis of the situation as a dilemma offered a way out of this restricting perspective. At the third weekend it became apparent that the analysis had in fact been releasing for Janet.

III - What are you up to?

In the third weekend, we asked each presenter: what questions has this project raised for you about your own practice? Janet reviewed what had been happening to her during the course. Before the first weekend she had been off sick for eight weeks, and was ambivalent about going back - hence her anxiety about being squeezed out by Charles and the new organisation. She could now see how the group had 'bought' her version of the story, and not asked questions which would have brought to light how her own anxieties were shaping it.

She said that the second weekend had clarified a dilemma in the organisation, which she saw as top-down versus bottom-up. She had written a paper about this, to be presented to her colleagues shortly.

She had been thinking about Skynner's dictum (referred to earlier) that we choose organisations in which we can engage with our own conflicts, either to perpetuate them or to understand them and move on. Had she used her career to explore her own preoccupations with delinquency and control, and had she now got to change in some way? People responded to her professional persona, but she felt the course had touched something more personal.

She then talked about the situation in her own life, in which her husband had taken early retirement and was asking her to wind down and spend more time with him. She felt that her anxiety about this - about the possibility of being bored and losing all meaning in her life - had led her to cling to her job in the NFVC and to control the local centres, so that she had been unable to contemplate other options.

From these reflections, it appeared to us that Janet had moved closer to the challenge of her 'case', which was not just a cluster of management problems, but a problem in which the question of her own desire as a subject could no longer be ignored.

TRISTAN

I - Telling the problem

The Reverend Tristan had trained as a group analyst, and since he had given up his normal parish duties, had acted as a consultant to a number of different dioceses. The case he brought with him was a community in the north-east of England - a very depressed, dying new town which was in the process of reverting to its original boundaries.

Tristan had been asked by the Chairman of a group of 20 clergy to see whether he could do anything to help them stop the community breaking up, and had agreed to meet with them every other week at their weekly two hour meeting. His brief was to help the group cope with what was going on in the community, work together more as a team, and learn to complement each other.

The group of clerics were at each others' throats. They were a mixture of Anglicans, Methodists, Catholics, and Free Church with individual clergy in positions ranging from being legally responsible for the community to being private chaplains to those who paid the stipend. The clergy faced vandalism and murder in the community, and as a group were themselves split into two - the right wing high church clergy versus the low church and nonconformists.

Tristan worked with the group for a year, during which time his role became one of stopping them being horrid to each other. Tristan had been invited into the community because of his connections with the Bishop, and was even referred to at times by members of the group as "my lord bishop". Paid nine months in arrears from diocesan funds (the nonconformists paid nothing), he was wondering what he got out of it. Was it the pleasure of keeping a Christian community going?

Three months ago, the group had announced that "everything was under control". But the Chairman didn't want Tristan to leave, and at that point, Tristan's question had been: "What do I do? What should my role be now?" His answer had been to hold a two-day conference to find out. The conference was coming up in two weeks.

Tristan's own comments on the situation was that he felt very torn. The group was ready to explode when he left, the problems were going to go on for ever, and in effect all he had done was take on their dependency needs for a while, and then give them back to them. The question was what to do with the leadership. They needed an independent leader.

The rest of the group had a number of reactions:

- The clergy were collecting the violence and fragmentation of the community, and without a leader they lacked the commitment and structure to contain this.
- There was a tension between the group-analytic ideal that people should become independent, and the need to deal with the organisational lack in the community.
- Tristan's presence, supported by Anglican and Catholic churches who were paying, was concealing questions about the nature of the collaboration between the churches.

Tristan's comment at the end of the session was that he felt the listeners had theorised about the situation with very little information, that there had been no difference between the speaking and listening positions, and that both positions had appeared to know what the problem was - i.e. how to leave decently.

II - Hypotheses and dilemmas

Tristan had felt that the first weekend had been very powerful - it had taken him a week to recover, and he had felt reluctant to come back. This suggested that more was going on for him than his comment at the end of the first weekend had indicated. The two-day event had happened. It was the first time the clergy had got together with their respective heads for six years. Following the event, he had agreed to write a report on what had happened.

Only two people had turned up in clerical garb on the first day - Tristan and the Bishop. The senior clerics started out being very critical, and fed up with the Ecumenical project - there were too many clerics for the number of souls. The clergy had argued how good the process had been with Tristan, and by the beginning of the second day, the senior clerics' views had changed - they began to see the team as working in the Slough of Despond.

But as soon as the senior clerics left on the second day, the whole thing blew apart. Everyone went off on their own hobby horses. Tristan was identified as the hated bad guy, and there was no attempt made to plan for the future. In effect, the group had returned to where it had started, but worse, because now it had tried being supportive and it hadn't worked. Now, the only thing which united them was being against the seniors: they needed more money and more people, and the seniors had said no.

The hypotheses about Tristan's position were that he

- had got himself into a Messiah position and become too identified with their position,
- was trying to 'contain' them and be a kind of meta-cleric,
- was the little boy with the finger in the dike as far as the group's relations to the community were concerned.

These were seen as being responses to a number of dilemmas running through the situation:

- Ministry as being about rising above the particular situation to see the general good in it versus communion involving engaging with the particular nature of each others' concerns

- To intervene involving understanding the situation versus not to intervene meaning not wasting any more time and effort by getting further involved with the situation..
- If the group can sort itself out it can help the congregations versus if it helps the congregations it will come together
- The group's role is to hold together in order to be able to contain the community versus if the group lets go owning the community's problem and can carry its differences, then perhaps it can work something through for itself.
- Our vocation is to do good works. If we do, money will come versus Our duty is to help this community but we can only do this if we have the money to do it with.

These dilemmas added up to a questioning of who the client was, and what was the basis on which intervention was possible. By articulating the various positions possible in relation to those dilemmas, the group at the same time resisted identifying with any one of them, and thereby losing the Plus One perspective. But Tristan was certainly left at the end of the second weekend with a question about his approach to intervention.

III - What are you up to?
By the time of the third meeting, Tristan still had not written his final report, and was in a quandary over how it should be written. At the beginning of the workshop series, he would have written a pure 'guru' report. Now he was not so sure.

At the last session of the two-day event, the group had been very pleasant, but there had also been a lot of resentment that Tristan was not staying, couldn't cope and didn't have an answer. Tristan wondered what his role had been. He had been included, but had not been part of the system. Had he been unable to resolve their questions for them because he couldn't resolve them for himself? How helpful could it be to act out the needs of the people you were called in to help? Was it self-indulgent to try and solve your own problems through the client system? Where do you stop - where do you draw the line?

The problem with taking up the position of a priest was that he had been unable to be there for himself. In effect he had only existed for others, and insofar as he had been able to pursue his needs, it had only been possible via the needs of the others.

The invitation for Tristan to manage the meetings was a 'presenting problem', but doing that alone had not been adequate for addressing their stuckness. Had Tristan over-identified with his group analytic method and his priestly role? Had this rendered him unable to adopt a 'Plus One' perspective in relation to the form of his own engagement with them?

Tristan left the workshop series with some very different questions about his practice from those he started with.

CONCLUSION
Did we succeed in our aim to explore and generate understanding of the place or position taken up by the consultant? We think we did, although the participants

and ourselves were left with the question of "where do we go from here"? We saw that we had a lot of work to do to elaborate elements in the approach which we had so far only touched upon, including our way of understanding organisations. But we felt that we had shared something of the problematic nature of the practice of consulting, and a way of working with it.

NOTES

[1]   We are grateful to Lina Fajerman for her valuable comments on an earlier draft.

[2]   Schein, E.H. (1987), *Process Consultation* Vol II Reading Mass: Addison-Wesley pp22ff. Mintzberg coined the 'bird', 'guru' nomenclature at a seminar given at the London Business School.

[3]   It is a position in which the consultant (and the client) have to deal with their own anxiety around not knowing - not knowing what to 'do' about the presenting problem; and working with a faith in their own resourcefulness in being able to respond appropriately to the problem-as-presented. Hence "learning the hard way". This is the position which involves what Lacan refers to as 'paying with one's being' in *The Seminar of Jacques Lacan 1959-1960: The Ethics of Psychoanalysis. Book VII* Tavistock/Routledge 1992. It is further developed in Boxer's (unpublished) paper (1994) on the Ethics of Psychoanalysis.

[4]   D.W. Winnicott (1965) *Training for Child Psychiatry* in "The Maturational Processes and the Facilitating Environment". Hogarth Press

[5]   Developed out of Michel Foucault's work (1980) on *Power/Knowledge: Selected Interviews and Other Writings 1972-1977*. Harvester; and further elaborated by Boxer, P.J. (1994) in *The Future of Identity* in Richard Boot, Jean Lawrence and John Morris (eds) "Creating New Futures: A Manager's Guide to the Unknown. McGraw-Hill.

[6]   Cf Hampden-Turner, C (1990),*Charting the Corporate Mind*, Oxford: Blackwell

[7]   H.R. Maturana & F.J. Varela (1987) *The Tree of Knowledge: The Biological Roots of Human Understanding* Shambhala.

[8]   Skynner R (1991) *Institutions and How to Survive Them* London: Routledge.

[9]   Eliot, T.S. (1963), 'East Coker', *Collected Poems 1909-1962*. London Faber

[10]   See "Introduction of the big Other" in *The Seminar of Jacques Lacan 1954-1955: The Ego in Freud's Theory and in the Technique of Psychoanalysis*. Cambridge. 1988. pp243-247.

[11]   A way of formulating this is to say that the ethic of this direction is constituted in a passion for ignorance.

[12]   Boxer, P.J. and Kenny, J.V. (1992) *Lacan and Maturana: constructivist origins for a 30 Cybernetics*. Communication and Cognition Vol 25 No 1 pp73-100.

[13]   Lacan, J. (1977) *Ecrits: a selection*. Translated by Alan Sheridan. Tavistock. First published in French Editions du Seuil 1966. p223

TEAMBUILDING AT THE TOP

David Casey, *Independent Consultant, Shenfield Essex*

ABSTRACT

A short paper based on the empirical experiences of a practising consultant who works almost exclusively with top management teams. Starting from the academic framework which the author developed with Bill Critchley he warns against over-emphasis on working with feelings when helping top teams. Casey concludes that in the final analysis there is little difference between a fully functioning true team and a self-managed team.

INTRODUCTION

In this paper I intend to do three things: lay out a framework for thinking about top teambuilding; overlay it with challenging empirical ideas concerning processes; and argue that at the top of the organisation any genuine team must become self-managed.

The basic framework was developed ten years ago by Bill Critchley and me (1984) it has stood the test of time for me in a wide variety of organisation settings. The thoughts about processes and team leadership are derived from recent work at the top of a Public School, a very large international systems integration business, an electricity distribution company, a hospice, household name in the computer business, a London Borough and a County Council.

THE BASIC FRAMEWORK

Bill Critchley and I (1984) noticed a straightforward relationship between two variables: the need to be a team and the level of ambiguity in the work the group does. These two variables are directly proportional: highly ambivalent work demands teamwork, unambiguous work does not.

FIG I represents a most valuable insight and it is worth spending a moment on each axis. The vertical axis progresses through three convenient stages (FIG II) from no teamwork, through an intermediate level 'co-operating together', to full teamworking. Similarly the horizontal scale shows three levels of ambiguity in the work: simple puzzles, more complex puzzles and genuinely open-ended problems where the ambiguity is very high. An example of a genuine open-ended problem might be 'How does a hospice change from being a small hospital where people come to die, to become an educational influence in its local society to enable all families to come to terms with death?' Another might be 'Should a great boys boarding school stick to tradition or become a day school... and when do the girls arrive?'

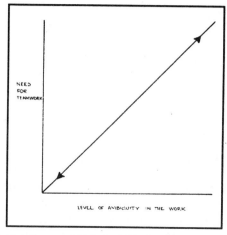

Fig I The Straightforward Relationship between Ambiguity
in the work and the need to be a Team

A glance at FIG II will make it clear just how important it is to **start** by asking of any group interested in teambuilding 'What work do you need to do as a group' The place to begin is with the work.

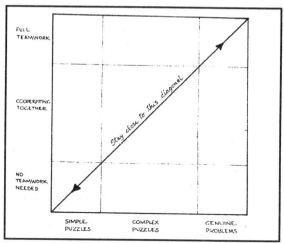

Fig II Genuine Problems Demand Full Teamwork.
Complex puzzles need no more than Cooperation

It is also becomes clear how important it is to stay close to the diagonal. Straying North of the diagonal is silly because it leads to painful and expensive efforts to build a team, when a real team is not needed. Straying East of the diagonal is futile, it is simply not possible to crack open-ended ambiguous problems in today's society, without teamwork.

The truth is that many top management groups shy away from daunting ambiguity and settle for handling complex puzzles; often they contrive to disguise their most fearsome challenges in more comforting simplified options: shall we do

373

A, or shall we do B? In practice their most common working mode is co-operating well together, rather than teamwork. And they are right: complex puzzles can be solved by cooperation.

This explains why the largest box in FIG II is in the middle of the diagram. Real teamwork (top North-east corner of FIG II) is rare indeed. The best teams can move adroitly up and down the diagonal of FIG II as they tackle different kinds of work from day to day.

THE PROCESS TRAP

Since most top teams spend most of their time in the middle box in co-operative mode, dealing with task puzzles using sophisticated task processes with great skill, it is natural that teambuilders come along advising them to move up the vertical axis of FIG II and bring more of their emotions into play.

The argument goes that emotions are always present and can be tapped into as a positive resource rather than ignored or denied, when they might well become a hindrance. This is correct in itself but leads in my into the trap of teambuilding becoming labelled as an excursion into feelings.

A polarisation takes place between two different kinds of work: proper work sessions when task is performed (using effective task processes) and teambuilding sessions off-site when emotions are released and effective emotion processes are invented for dealing with those released emotions. Because of this unfortunate separation people find it hard to pull together the four essential elements of teamworking:

(a) Task
(b) Task processes   (For more detail on processes see Casey 1993)
(c) Emotions
(d) Emotion processes

When badly handled, a dichotomy separates out in peoples minds and they come to the conclusion that (a) and (b) are legitimate and useful, whilst (b) and (c) are inessential luxuries.

I have come to believe that part of the problem lies in the propensity of teambuilders to concentrate on the vertical axis of FIG II, encouraging teams to reach up to open teamwork, sharing themselves fully. In the excitement this creates, it escapes everyone's notice that the team reaching up the vertical axis is not at the same time extending itself along the horizontal work axis. In these circumstances striving to uncover feelings and to find some ways to deal with those feelings is a dangerous waste of time and deserves to be labelled as inessential and self-indulgent, because the **only** work which justifies the pain and effort of emotional sharing is genuinely open-ended ambiguous problem solving.

Nowadays my own request to top teams is not 'Will you please extend yourselves up the teamwork axis and bring your feelings into the work'. Instead I find myself challenging them to move along the horizontal work axis and confront those frightening, hugh ill-defined monsters they have been avoiding for so long. I know that I am succeeding just as soon as someone blurts out. "I have no idea what to do!' And quite soon after that the heartrending cry 'I'm really scared!'

What this means is that emotions are coming out not because the teambuilder said it was a good idea but because the team is truly facing up to massive problems where the only honest statement is 'I haven't a clue and I'm frightened to death!' Once this stage is reached and emotions are present, the teambuilder becomes really helpful in suggesting ways these emotions might be handled by the group. Emotions are no longer an inessential luxury, they are at the centre of the team's legitimate concerns.

LEADERSHIP AND TEAMWORK

Not only do most top teams spend most of their time in the middle box of FIG II, cooperating well to solve task-centred puzzles, they also have a very clear concept of team leadership. Leadership in 1994 is still typically lodged in a clear leadership role, exercised by the Chief Executive, Head Teacher, Managing Director, Hospice Director. Yes, I agree with Charles Handy (1994) '...we shall increasingly run our organisations without hosts of people called managers' but the important word in that sentence is 'shall'.

What happens to leadership if a team makes genuine progress towards the North-east corner of FIG II? The journey towards this North-east corner must not deviate from the diagonal of FIG II, which is another way of saying that progress must be made at one and the same time along **both** the work axis and the teamwork axis, as I emphasised in the previous section.

In practice this faces the traditional leader with a whole range of new challenges and risks. Not only the exposed necessity to deal openly with those frightening strategic unknowns which are now forced on to the open agenda, but also to share with colleagues the risks involved. such a leader will share herself, her power, her grip on strategy - three of the things which tradition has ordained should not be shared. Historically many leaders have not shared much of themselves, have not shared much of their power and have not shared much of their strategic thinking. Say what you like about the comfort of sharing (a problem shared is a problem halved, and all that) it is my personal experience that to the person at the top this level of sharing feels like risk, risk and yet more risk!

Let's just take the sharing power - what does that mean? It does not mean empowering other people, which is no more than a paradoxical way of describing delegation. sharing power means letting go of power, walking away, without any clear idea what will happen to that power. Who will pick it up? The team? A dominant team member? A conspiracy? The hierarchy above you? Letting go of power is a gamble.

A leader working towards creating a genuine team is exposing himself, risking his power, letting go of strategy. so what is left? Not much... except the satisfaction that somehow the letting go has achieved everything - like the housemaster who sees his protégé become Prime Minster. Only the best can do it; it is a most generous way of working. Only the strongest can cope with being the leader of a genuine team. It means in a word encouraging the team to become self-managed.

I've done a lot of work with Digital (1993) helping them invent self-managed teams and I'll end with this quote from one of the best managers I've every worked with. This is how she experienced leading a genuine team:

'I had to invent a new way to add value to their contributions, being more visionary, looking father ahead, being a kind of catalyst to help them learn from their experiences, being the one who facilitates the explication of their feelings...'

CONCLUSION

Most top teams still work on task in a focussed way, by cooperating well together. This falls short of genuine teamwork. The challenge for teambuilders is to avoid the cul-de-sac of getting into feelings for their own sake and to encourage instead a broader view of task. The role of leader can no longer be pinned on one person and a corollary of this is that effective teams inevitably become self-managed, with threatening consequences for all but the very best team leaders.

REFERENCE

Critchley Bill and Casey David, 1984, Second Thoughts on Teambuilding. Management Education and Development Vol 15, Pt 2

Casey David, 1993, Managing Learning in Organisation, Open University Press

Handy Charles, 1994, Why we don't need mangers. The Times, 17th March 1994. Times Newspapers Ltd.

OFFERING A CONSULTANCY UMBRELLA

Maureen Scholefield, *Cullen Scholefield Associates, Haywards Heath*

INTRODUCTION
The paper explores the various forms of consultancy and establishes what is meant by an umbrella consultancy. The benefits of sheltering under such an umbrella are considered from a consultants perspective. The client's perspective is also looked at. The paper concludes with a look to the future and also reports on the group who attended this session.

1   FORMS OF CONSULTANCY
There has been considerable growth in the consultancy sector with many more consultants in the market place. How they present themselves to clients varies considerably but several forms are emerging.

1.1.   Employed consultants
These are consultants who are working for major and medium sized consultancies. They are likely to be paid a fixed salary with various incentives for attracting new business to the consultancy.

Many of the major consultancies have several young graduates working with senior consultants. This enables the senior consultant to secure the business and in many cases the younger and less experienced consultants carry out major parts of the project. Such consultancies are able to command a high daily rate and the client feels confident in the name and reputation of the consultancy.

Medium sized consultancies that is with ten plus consultants are less likely to use inexperienced consultants and more able to offer "wysiwyg" consultancy - what you see is what you get! Such consultancies are also in a particular niche, for example offering specialist consultancy to a specific sector.

1.2   One person bands
This type of consultancy is rapidly increasing. It is normally one individual with very specific skills for example marketing or financial skills. The consultant often starts as a result of employment no longer being an option. This could be as a result of retiring or redundancy. Some employers use the retainer principle to help a valued employee make the transition to consultant. In this way both sides win the employer does not lose the knowledge of the ex-member of staff and the new

consultant has the security of a regular client.

This form of consultancy is usually run from home and all the technological aids are employed to excellent effect. The downside of this is that the consultant can feel isolated and therefore needs to seek methods to remedy such feelings. If the consultant also needs to "bounce" ideas about there is no one to turn to.

1.3   Networks

This is why networks are growing in popularity. Consultants can belong to a number of such networks and this helps to give support and back up if a major project comes in. Most networks are small with two to five consultants linking together. They are unlikely to have a common brand name and will still trade under their own business names. Such networks form and break up with regularity. They have no formal structures.

Other forms of networks are those where consultant just meet. Membership of organisations such as AMED, local Chambers of Commerce and professional groups is invaluable.

1.4   The umbrella principle

This enables one person bands to shelter under a common brand. It enables a group of people to market collectively and to share the costs of administrative support and office space.

In some instances umbrella organisations will charge an entry fee which is normally between £2,000 to £5,000. This gives the lone consultant instant corporate identity. Such umbrella consultancies still expect the consultant to search for and grow their own client base.

1.5   The Cullen, Scholefield Associates umbrella

Cullen, Scholefield Associates currently has a core of three consultants who actively "grow" the business. These core consultants discuss and agree the direction taken by the consultancy, they are involved in marketing and financial decisions.

There are then six consultants who have worked with Cullen, Scholefield Associates for a number of years. In some cases the consultancy is the only or prime source of income. Each consultant brings particular skills and the consultancy quite often has "group thinks" to arrive at creative solutions or approaches to projects.

The outer ring comprises of ten consultants who work with Cullen, Scholefield Associates when their particular skills are in high demand - for example a major piece of research requiring field visits over a short period of time.

The consultancy started out by being London based and is now based in Haywards Heath, Sussex. It has a minimalist approach to office space and there is an office staff of three to support the activities of the business. Meetings with consultants take place at the most convenient location and all consultants are fully set up with their own offices at home.

2 THRIVING ON CHAOS

One of our consultants described us as being an anarchic organisation; whilst that may be true we have over the years needed to work to a set of principles. These are particularly relevant to Cullen, Scholefield Associates but they are relevant to anyone seeking to establish an umbrella consultancy.

2.1 Commitment to the consultancy

This is evidenced most by the core consultants who give time to develop the business. This can take the shape of attending meetings, marketing the consultancy and developing materials for the consultancy to use. Not all of these activities are rewarded financially.

2.2 Common values

All consultants need to share common values. Such values can be categorised into three headings:

 (a) personal values
 (b) professional approaches
 (c) business ethics.

Personal values

This is to do with openness, honesty, trust, empathy and a direct approach. Experience has shown that when any of the above items are doubted or not used the relationship is in danger.

Professional approaches

This is not about producing stereotyped solutions for projects. It is about respect for individuals professional competence and judgement. If the first strand of common values is in place - healthy and prolonged debate as to the best and most viable approach for a particular project occurs.

Business ethics

This is another area with the potential for misunderstandings to occur. It needs to be fully covered at the start of any business relationship. It can be raised by posing each other "what if" questions which explore situations that could occur. For example - "What if a client approaches you directly for repeat business, what would you do?"

During the life of Cullen, Scholefield Associates we have tried to formalise relationships with consultants by producing an agreement. When such agreements are put on to paper they inevitably shake the first strand of common values by questioning openness, trust and honesty. We have therefore abandoned paper bound agreements.

2.3 Quality approaches

This encompasses all aspects of how the consultancy deals with its clients. It falls into five categories:

(a)   formulating the brief with the client
(b)   approach to clients
(c)   value added versus dependency
(d)   presentation and house style
(e)   going the extra mile for the client

Formulating the brief with the client

All consultants subscribe to the view that solutions are not offered as a panacea to cure all ills. Time will always be spent ensuring that the brief finally agreed "fits" the client. On some occasions clients will pay to formulate the brief but most clients do not pay for such activities and the consultant will have to decide if "free" consultancy is being given.

Approach to clients

All consultants take the long term view with clients. Establishing the relationship often ensures that the client will return to the consultancy for a range of different projects. It is quite common for the client to use the consultancy again when they change organisations.

There is never a "heavy" sell. In some instances a relationship will be established before any business if ever done.

Value added versus dependency

This is about leaving skills in the organisation whenever it is feasible to do so. This is discussed when agreeing the brief. We do not wish to have clients dependant on our services as we feel that this is a negative result of consultancy. We would far rather the client return to us for innovative projects rather than to run a repeat of a training course for example.

Presentation and house style

This is where the image of the consultancy is projected by how clients are dealt with by support staff, how reports, letters and handouts are presented.

The office is the hub of the consultancy and it is essential to have an overview of consultant availability and an accurate and efficient message taking service. All support staff are encouraged to be more than message takers and if possible to progress the query.

Support staff have agreed a house style and whilst this is followed it is not set in tablets of stone and the style is constantly being improved and refined.

Going the extra mile for the client

This is normally making a mission impossible deadline! It is also about flexibility and responsiveness. All of which are not possible without a good team effort - consultants and support staff pulling together.

2.4   Project management processes

A project manager is appointed for major assignments. He or she has the responsibility of appointing consultants, liaising with the client, reporting on progress on a monthly basis and overseeing the budget to ensure that an overspend situation does not occur.

The project manager is normally drawn from the core consultants and may not be directly involved in the project.

3 BENEFITS OF CONSULTANCY UMBRELLAS TO CONSULTANTS

3.1 Marketing brand

An umbrella consultancy is able to offer the lone consultant a brand to work under. It is often difficult for a newly established consultant to talk about the range of projects that have been completed.

A lone consultant is also unlikely to be able to set up and maintain a database of existing and potential clients. They will be so concerned with the need to be out earning.

The expense of producing publicity materials is also likely to stop lone consultants producing newsletters or brochures.

3.1 Freedom and support

With an umbrella consultancy the consultant can have the best of both worlds. He or she can complete a pet project with a long established client not linked with the consultancy. Alternatively he or she can bring a project into the consultancy where it requires considerable administrative support or for any other reason. As long the common values are observed all benefit.

3.3 Power of "group thinks"

This should never be underestimated. Being part of an umbrella consultancy enables a consultant to put a particular project on the table as it were and seek the opinions and advice of others who he or she trusts and respects.

Working as a lone consultant can be lonely and worse still lack of exposure to other thoughts and approaches could have a negative effect on the advice given to a client.

3.4 Broad client range

Consultants bring with them contacts from a wide range of sectors and this in turn enables all to benefit by having access to a broad range of clients.

It also helps gain credibility with large organisations to be able demonstrate a broad range of clients.

3.5 Cost savings

A lone consultant cannot be all things to all people. Inevitably they will need some administrative support or access to desk top publishing or some other aid. The umbrella consultancy can also subscribe to a large number of professional magazines and certainly in Cullen, Scholefield Associates case a considerable resource library has been built up over the years.

4   BENEFITS TO CLIENTS

4.1   Wide range of expertise

Clients are able to have the benefit of a wide range of expertise. Cullen, Scholefield Associates have a team who are occupational psychologists, personnel specialists, management development specialists, generic trainers, developers of training materials and research specialists. When this expertise is coupled with industrial experience in a number of sectors the benefits to the client are doubled.

4.2   Long relationships with clients

As a result of our client approach, we gain in depth knowledge of the client and its organisational structure, products, culture and people. This proves to be useful for the client as they do not need to spend time briefing us on the organisation. If we introduce a new consultant and that consultant is approved by the client, the responsibility is ours.

4.3   Flexible and responsive

The nature of an umbrella consultancy is to be flexible. The consultancy whilst established is not likely to be complacent and it therefore will be responsive to the needs of the client.

4.4   Tried and tested source

The client will be buying from a known entity. The client will know about the reliability of the consultancy and their approach to projects. Trust will have been gained in the consultancy. The consultants they negotiated with will actually be involved in the project.

5   LOOKING TO THE FUTURE

There is an increased demand for consultancy support primarily as a result of organisations sub contracting services in an effort to make their organisation leaner and fitter during the recessionary years.

This trend can be expected to continue but there are some potential threats to the consultancy world. The main threat is that of inexperienced consultants who give the life to that old joke "if you can't do it - consult!"

There is a move to look at the competence of consultants and this trend will gain momentum. It is currently evidenced by Training and Enterprise Councils vetting consultants via a number of mechanisms. These include references from clients, financial viability, occupational competence and length of experience.

There is also potential for a less drastic exit for senior managers if organisations put valued managers on a retainer at a mutually agreed time. This would encourage those with an entrepreneurial spirit to use their considerable skills and enable the organisation to benefit from an expert outside.

6   REPORT ON THE SESSION

Eight consultants attended the session. Maureen Scholefield ran the session in the form of a discussion group. Some time was spent exchanging information about the varying nature of each consultant's specialist area.

The discussions were lively and the time allotted to the activity sped by. The group decided that they would stay in touch and Maureen volunteered to arrange a lunch time meeting. This was arranged after the conference and so another network begins!

7   SUMMARY

This paper has explored the nature of various forms of consultancy. It has also dwelt on the particular experiences of Maureen Scholefield, Senior Partner of Cullen Scholefield Associates by looking at how that consultancy has made the umbrella approach work for it.

The benefits of umbrella consultancies to consultants and clients were reviewed. Looking at the future umbrella consultancies could be one way to counter the threats posed to consultancy in general and provide a valid starting point for senior managers whose time in their organisation is coming to a close.

ORGANISATION HOLDING ENVIRONMENTS: THE KEY TO UNDERSTANDING AND MANAGING ORGANISATIONAL CULTURE

Lionel Frederick Stapley, *Independent Consultant, London*

ABSTRACT

This paper challenges the prevailing view that sees culture as something that an organisation *has*: something which can thus be managed and controlled. Working from the perspective that if you want to change something you need to know how it develops in the first place, a new theory of culture is presented. The view taken here is that culture is seen as something that the organisation *is* and that the process of culture develops out of the inter-relatedness of the members of an organisation and the organisation holding environment. This, in turn, provides us with the key to understanding culture and organisation change. While it is not possible to impact culture per se it is postulated that it can be managed and controlled, indirectly, by impacting the organisation holding environment.

INTRODUCTION

As an organisation consultant I have experienced many occasions when attempts to change the formal systems of goals, strategies and structures of an organisation have - to varying degrees - been unsuccessful because what was intended did not take place or that unintended consequences occurred. I came to believe that this had something to do with what is commonly called the 'culture' of the organisation, although why and how this should be so was not at all clear. I also discovered, when attempting to apply existing theory to practice, that while it may be a very attractive notion, the prevailing theory that culture is something that an organisation *has*, was just not borne out in my experience. There is a wide range of literature on both culture and change but it is my analysis that current theory does not provide a satisfactory explanation of this phenomenon.

Consequently, it was felt that there was a need to look at culture in a different light, to search for new ideas and that an original approach might prove more beneficial. I have sought to gain an understanding of the processes involved with the aim of putting forward what I believe to be an original conceptualisation of culture relevant to understanding organisational change. In doing so, I have particularly sought to provide an answer to a most basic and crucial question: that concerning how culture develops. The result is a theory that views culture as something that the organisation *is*: a process that develops out of the inter-relatedness of the members of the organisation with what I term the 'organisation holding environment'. From this position, I shall explain how it is possible to identify the key elements in the process of culture in order to gain a better understanding of organisational change.

1.   OTHER THEORIES

Several writers have taken the view that 'organisation culture' is a unifying force within the organisation that exists in a real and tangible sense and that management can identify and manage it as a controllable variable to enhance organisational effectiveness. For example, Peters and Waterman (1982) and Deal and Kennedy (1982) both talk of 'excellence' and 'winning' by having internalised uniform corporate values. Others have produced studies that on the face of it are more sophisticated. For example, the concept of 'organisational climate' as an individual's cognitive map, (Schneider, 1979); organisational learning (Argyris and Schon, 1978); the role of history and founders, (Pettigrew, 1985); and, basic assumptions, (Schein 1987). However, on closer examination all of these theorists promulgate the idea that culture is the collective consciousness of the organisation and that it is available to management to manipulate.

2.   TOWARDS A NEW THEORY

Viewed as above, culture can be seen as something the organisation *has* (Smircich, 1983). However, that is not my experience, or, for that matter, the experience of fellow consultants. If culture is something that an organisation *has*, I must confess that I have never been able to locate it. The view taken here is that culture is something that the organisation *is*. However, there is reason to suggest that culture and social structure can be distinguished. For example, the experience of attempting to change the formal systems of goals, strategies and structures, referred to in the introduction above, would suggest that the organisation's cultural system was not congruent with the sociostructural system - an experience that I feel sure is shared by many others working in organisations. In circumstances where attempts at change have resulted in industrial disputes the lack of congruence between the cultural system and the revised sociostructural system may be reasonably obvious. On other occasions the distinction may be far more subtle but nonetheless of considerable relevance.

I would therefore argue that in developing a theory of culture that helps us to understand organisational change there is a need to maintain a conceptual distinction between culture and social structure. In doing so, however, we need to bear in mind that culture and structure are both constructs, not tangible entities. As culture and social structure are not concrete entities but abstract concepts used by members of organisations and theorists to interpret behaviour we need to bear in mind the need of the researcher not only to study the culture or structure developed by the members of an organisation but more importantly, the behaviour of individual actors. An organisation, or part of an organisation, may be viewed as an association of individuals, and it is those individuals who develop the constructs that we categorise as structure and culture. Consequently, the behaviour of individual actors is considered to be a key concept in the study of culture.

3. HOW CULTURE DEVELOPS

3.1 INTRODUCTION

At the centre of the process are the individual members of an organisation and their mental processes. Culture being a construct, the source of that construct is the human mind. Consequently, in developing a theory and methodology we need to develop a means of interpreting the conscious and unconscious behaviour of the individual actors of various boundaried groups within organisations. Because of this, it was decided that the use of concepts from psycho-analysis were the most appropriate tools available to provide the sought after explanation of culture. The theory therefore builds on psycho-analytic theories about the development of the individual and in particular to a key concept of this paper, namely, the inter-relatedness of the individual with various 'holding environments' in the development of the personality.

3.2 PERSONALITY DEVELOPMENT

Starting from birth, the early relation is characterised by infantile dependence, that is, a dependence based on a primary identification with the object, and an inability to differentiate and adapt. The infant is part of a symbiotic relationship with his mother, that is, he is both 'held' by the mother and is part of the maternal holding environment. At this stage the holding environment is both 'psycho-' and 'socio-'. However, in spite of the closed nature of the holding environment between mother and infant, this is still an open system.

For the infant to develop there is a need for a 'basic trust' in the maternal holding environment and for what Winnicott (1971) has termed ' a good enough holding environment'. This 'basic trust' is developed as a result of the infant's perceived experience of his holding environment. From holding inside the mother's womb this extends to holding in the mother's arms. However, what we are referring to is much more than just physical holding. It is about the mother providing boundaries which help the infant to make sense of his world.

As the infant grows there then develops the use of a transitional object which leads to the recognition of external objects - of a 'me' and 'not me'. Gradually there develop several 'not me's' in the shape of father, siblings, playmates, and other relations. At this stage there also develops the use of true symbols and the use of language and words as symbols. Here the holding environment begins to split into an internalised psychological part and an external social and physical part. There also develops a succession of holding environments in the form of family, school, youth groups (eg, scouts and guides), university and work organisations.

To conclude this brief look at individual development, we can describe personality in the following way:

(a)	it is a psycho-social process
(b)	it is evidenced by sameness and continuity
(c)	it is influenced by conscious and unconscious processes
(d)	it is unique for each individual
(e)	it is a dynamic process
(f)	it is such that the individual will produce forms of behaviour which will be psychologically advantageous to him under the conditions imposed by the environment.

3.3   THE PROCESS OF CULTURE

The main thesis of this paper is that in the same way that personality develops out of the inter-relatedness of the individual with his holding environment(s) so the culture of an organisation develops out of the inter-relatedness of the members of an organisation with the organisation holding environment. The group (or members of the organisation) and holding environment are structured by and within each other but by virtue of treating 'the organisation' as if it were an individual the members interrelate with it 'as if' it were a holding environment.

In a manner similar to the relationship of the individual with his mother the organisation becomes a partly conscious and partly unconscious holding environment for its members. The conscious part of the holding environment may be termed the external holding environment. This is the sociostructural part which consists of the ruling coalition or leader, the formal goals, structures, strategies, policies and processes, roles of members, knowledge and skills, the shared private language, beliefs, values and attitudes. The unconscious part of the holding environment may be termed the internalised holding environment. This is the psychological part which consists of internal objects derived from phantasy activity about the holding environment, that is, by introjection of external objects.

Viewing organisations as open systems, the partly conscious and partly unconscious holding environment is influenced by activities in the external environment of the organisation. The inter-relatedness to symbolic objects may include those 'outside' the organisation. The degree of influence will depend on the degree of boundary control exercised on behalf of the members of the organisation. If there is a clarity of purpose external influences are unlikely to be great, whereas if the boundary is weak external influence may be considerable.

From the foregoing we may therefore describe culture in a similar manner to the description of personality:

(a)	it is a psycho-social process, which was explained by reference to the inter-relatedness of the members of the organisation with the organisational holding environment
(b)	it is evidenced by sameness and continuity to provide for the self-esteem of the members and their sense of reality with others
(c)	being a psychological as well as a social process it is influenced by conscious and unconscious processes

(d) both the uniqueness of the collective, perceived view of the members of the organisation and the organisational holding environment results in a unique culture in every organisation and part of an organisation

(e) because groups are ongoing structures as opposed to finished ones it is a dynamic and changing process

(f) the members of the organisation will produce forms of behaviour which will be psychologically advantageous to them under the conditions imposed by the environment.

Reliable holding is as important to the self-esteem of the members of an organisation as it is to the infant. If there is a basic trust in the holding environment there is likely to be a task supportive culture. That is, the culture is likely to be in synchronicity with the sociostructural system. However, if there is no basic trust and the holding environment is viewed as being either socially, physically and/or psychologically, 'not good enough' (to para-phrase Winnicott), there is likely to be an anti-task culture. In these circumstances there will be a lack of congruence between the cultural system and the sociostructural system. From the view of an outsider, the behaviour of members of an organisation may appear irrational. However, the behaviour needs to be viewed from the perspective of the members of the organisation. They produce forms of behaviour that are advantageous to them under what they consciously and unconsciously perceive are the conditions imposed by their holding environment. Thus, the rationality of organisational behaviour is one associated with the particular culture and not one associated with external criteria or societal values.

4. A METHODOLOGY FOR UNDERSTANDING CULTURE

4.1 INTRODUCTION

In order to make sense of the process of culture I have used categorisations that have previously been developed for the purposes of psycho-analysis. This provides not only a ready made structure for viewing this complex process but also a shared language that others may understand. However, in addition to developing a theory of how culture develops it is also necessary to develop a methodology that permits us to gain access to both the conscious and unconscious data involved in that process. The only place that the organisation and its holding environment exist is in the perceived reality of the members of the organisation. Consequently, in order to gain the sort of data required it is necessary to intervene directly into the lives of the subjects of the culture so that we and they may access the conscious and unconscious views of their organisation.

4.2 TRANSFERENCE

It is suggested that the way we gain this access to the conscious and unconscious views of the members of an organisation is to obtain an understanding of the transference in the situation. By deliberate intervention and the deciphering of the responses - that is, the way that the consultant is used and experienced and the feelings evoked in him - it is possible to develop hypotheses about the unconscious processes of the members of the organisation.

Thus a person (subject) exhibiting transference in a relationship experiences the other (object) in a way that does not correspond to the actual object and which cannot be accounted for on the basis of the current situation alone but is based on previous interpersonal experiences. Starting from this point and following Scheidlinger (1980), the consultant needs to ask, "What makes this client behave (speak or act) towards me in this particular way at this moment?" In other words, what role does he unconsciously try to push me into, what sort of relationship is he unconsciously trying to establish between us? In this way we arrive at a knowledge of the unconscious which, of course, is only as something conscious as we know it, after it has undergone transformation or translation into something conscious. A working hypothesis is that answers to these questions will enable the consultant to establish contact with the unconscious level of the organisation, which is essential if he is to understand culture.

5.   CASE STUDY

Working as a consultant in a large public sector organisation by deliberate intervention and deciphering the responses it was possible to gain an understanding of the culture of the organisation, including the unconscious relatedness of the members with their organisation holding environment. For example, through engaging with various groups it was possible to confirm, as others have previously stated, that groups of people within the same organisation may have different languages, beliefs and values. Sometimes this was a marked difference, at others a more subtle difference and at times there was little or no discernible difference. This supports the notion that parts of an organisation that are perceived by their members as boundaried groups enact - to varying degrees - sub-cultures of the main culture.

Perhaps more importantly, an analysis of the way the various groups involved in the interaction related to me, as consultant, provided data about how the members of the organisation related to their holding environment. At times this was expressed in the transference as helplessness and was accompanied by requests such as 'Tell us what to do and we will do it' or by calls for experts to assist them in their endeavours. They were in effect saying 'If we devise this new system we may get it wrong; therefore we will let someone else get it wrong or we will do as we are told; either way we cannot be wrong'.

At other times the feelings of the members of the groups were expressed in terms of questions such as, 'Have we got authority to do this?' There were also questions about the commitment of senior management and calls for firm and strong leadership. There was also avoidance of the current problem using proposed future structural change as an excuse to do so. This produced counter-transference feelings of a rejected father. There was also further examples of a lack of trust evidenced for example by questions such as, 'What are you really trying to do?' Here the feeling was of a father not trusted by his child. In all these circumstances the refusal to provide the sought after dependency or the challenging of the helplessness, denial and avoidance brought a transference reaction of anger, anxiety and hostility.

The anxiety that was being transferred onto the consultant was arising primarily at the unconscious level and was a representation of the internalised holding environment. An interpretation of this transference led me to believe that there was a lack of basic trust by the members of the groups in their holding environment. Furthermore, that this lack of trust had developed out of experience of the holding environment over a period of time. It was a representation of the psychological internalised part of the holding environment which - it will be recalled - consists of internal objects derived from phantasy activity about their holding environment. What was being introjected by the members here was not a comforting progressive experience but the sense of contentless anxiety referred to by Bion (1961).

What was not understood, at this time, was why there was no basic trust. To understand more fully what was happening it was necessary to go beyond the transference and try to interpret the counter-transference. That is, we need to be aware that what is repressed by the client may be expressed by the consultant and that this counter-transference can be used as a tool for understanding the transference. The overriding feeling in the counter-transference was one of guilt. Analysis led me to believe that the guilt that I was experiencing was that which was repressed by the members of the organisation and was the reason why the consultant was the object of such transference. Furthermore, it was the guilt experienced by the members which led to the anxiety and resistance to change.

The analysis led to the conclusion that the demands that produced a collective super-ego and subsequently guilt, had arisen over a period of years. Public calls for accountability coupled with the lack of an effective strategy, had resulted in a collective conscience which said, 'You must be right'. The effect was that the culture was one where being right was all-important and taking chances was far too risky to contemplate. This in turn imposed a sort of control on the organisation which was manifested in a demand for a static order and structure, the avoidance of change and the restriction to activities which the members felt they were good at. Thus, in this case, the everyday activities of the members were considerably affected by the inter-relatedness to symbolic objects in the 'outer' environment.

In effect, it is postulated that what had happened was that because of the combination of circumstances, for the members of the organisation, these exceptionally strong public demands had become an important integral part of the organisational holding environment. The culture was dominated by conscience and the forms of behaviour adopted by the members of the organisation that they felt would be advantageous to them under the conditions imposed by their environment were exercised to prevent the extreme anxiety arising from the feelings of guilt that the members experienced when they had doubts about the correctness of their actions. In turn, the inference is that the members had a serious lack of belief in themselves and a low self-esteem. The ambiguity presented by the holding environment prevented the necessary confirmation, consistence and continuity that was required by the members. In developing a culture they therefore reached a level that was least anxiety provoking for the members by adopting forms of behaviour that did not cause them anxiety and guilt.

6.   CONCLUSION

We need to bear in mind that all organisations are unique. Consequently, the question of what the organisation holding environment includes and what it does not include can only be organisation specific. The significance of various aspects of the organisation holding environment will also be organisation specific. We need to assess how open the organisation system is and what the significant aspects are. In the case reported the most significant aspect was the lack of an effective strategy and the influence of factors in the external environment. That will not always be the case. For example, looked at from this theoretical basis, a significant aspect of the holding environment for Kets De Vries and Miller (1987) in their 'neurotic organisations' was the leader. For Jaques (1955) and Menzies Lyth (1959) in their 'social systems as a defence against anxiety' the significant aspect was the inappropriateness of the formal structures and strategies.

In providing a means of interpreting the way that individual members of an organisation characterise their social reality this theory provides a richer explanation of organisational culture and it is, therefore, a more appropriate tool for understanding organisational change. If the consultant is to help his clients he needs to ensure that a state of mature dependence exists and to do this he must be aware why the members of an organisation adopt their particular forms of behaviour and the structures of meaning that they rely on.

In providing data about the way the actors interpret their holding environment the theoretical framework is helpful in diagnosing the cause of an organisational problem. Without such an understanding we would address the symptoms, by, for example in the case reported, responding to the lack of decision-making by providing more leadership training. In addition, the framework also provides data at a deeper level of understanding. Too much anxiety will prevent progression and mature dependence and may result in regression of the members of an organisation to paranoid-schizoid behaviour. A working hypothesis is that the consultant who is able to acquire such knowledge of the culture will be able to reduce the anxiety by providing the members of the organisation with a temporary holding environment while they adjust to new behaviour and a new meaning system.

The theory outlined above nullifies the notion that culture is something that the organisation *has*. Nevertheless, the explanation of the way that culture develops takes us some way down the road that such theories sought - namely, a means to manage and control organisation culture. The understanding that culture develops out of the inter-relatedness of the members of the organisation and the organisation holding environment provides us with the knowledge that if we want to change the culture of an organisation then we need to impact the key aspects of the organisation holding environment. Furthermore, that should we make changes to the organisation holding environment, particularly the key aspects, this will impact the organisation culture and will result in resistance.

7.   SUMMARY

The prevailing view, whereby, organisation culture is viewed as something that an organisation *has* which can be managed and controlled is challenged. On this view, culture is seen as something that the organisation *is*. However, there is reason to suggest that culture and social structure can be distinguished. At the centre of the process of culture are the individual members of an organisation. Culture being a construct, the source of that construct is the human mind. Personality theory shows how the individual first develops out of inter-relatedness with the maternal holding environment and then with a succession of holding environments.

The theory advanced here is that in a similar way to personality, culture develops out of the inter-relatedness of the individual members of an organisation with their organisation holding environment. The organisation holding environment may be seen to consist of a conscious part which may be termed the 'external holding environment' and an unconscious part which may be termed the 'internalised holding environment'. Reliable holding is as important to the members of an organisation as it is to the infant. The type of culture that develops will depend on the perception of the members of the organisation and the basic trust that they have in their holding environment.

It is suggested that we gain access to the conscious and unconscious views of the members of an organisation by deliberate intervention and deciphering the transference responses of the members. The case study provides an example of how the transference can be used to gain an understanding of the perceived views of the inter-relatedness of the members of an organisation with their organisation holding environment. In conclusion, the theory provides a means of establishing the key aspects of an organisation holding environment. Armed with this knowledge it should be possible to manage change more effectively. Thus, organisational holding environments are seen as the key to understanding and managing organisation culture.

REFERENCES

ARGYRIS C & SCHON D A (1978), Organisational Learning: A Theory of Action Perspective, Reading MA, Addison-Wesley.

BION W R (1961), Experiences in Groups and Other Papers, London, Tavistock.

DEAL T & KENNEDY A A (1982), Corporate Cultures: The Rights and Rituals of Corporate Life, Reading Mass., Addison-Wesley.

JAQUES E (1955), On the Dynamics of Social Structure, Human Relations 6: 3-24.

KETS DE VRIES M & MILLER D (1987), The Neurotic Organisation, London, Jossey-Bass.

MENZIES LYTH I (1959), The Functioning of Social Systems as a Defence Against Anxiety, in I Menzies Lyth (ed), Containing Anxiety in Institutions Volume 1, London, Free Association: 43-88.

PETERS T J & WATERMAN R H (1982), In Search of Excellence, London, Harper & Row.

PETTIGREW A M (1985), The Awakening Giant: Continuity and Change in ICI, Oxford, Blackwell.

SCHEIDLINGER P (1980), Psychoanalytic Group Dynamics, New York, International Universities Press.

SCHEIN E H (1987), Organisational Culture and Leadership, London, Jossey-Bass.

SCHNEIDER B (1979), Organisational Climates: An Essay, Personnel Psychology 28: 447-479.

SMIRCICH L (1983), Concepts of Culture and Organisational Analysis, Administrative Science Quarterly, 28: 339-358.

WINNICOTT D W (1971), Playing and Reality, Harmondsworth, Penguin.

CONSULTANCY AS 'WORKING WITH THE ENERGY' IN ORGANIZATIONS

A REPORT ON RESEARCH IN PROGRESS

Dr. Paul Tosey, *University of Surrey*

ABSTRACT

This paper describes research in progress into the notion of consultancy as 'working with the energy' of organizations and change, which has relevance to Organizational Transformation and Learning Organization approaches. The research is qualitative, broadly co-operative and grounded in style, exploring the phenomenology of energy as experienced by organizational change agents. Preliminary observations are that the concept of energy has meaning for participants and that it seems connected to a wide range of skills, beliefs and practices.

INTRODUCTION

This paper is very much a progress report. Since 1992 I have been exploring, through a variety of research processes, notions of energy and healing in relation to approaches to organizational change. This exploration has been linked to a developing conceptual perspective on organizations as flows of energy (Tosey 1994, forthcoming). In parallel, I have been inquiring with a number of organizational consultants what they mean when they refer to their practice as 'working with the energy' in organizations. This paper is a summary to date of the inquiry into these phenomenal worlds.

In the paper I describe the background to the research and outline some relevant sources which also develop the theme of energy. Attention is then given to the methodology and the research experience to date, followed by a section summarising observations and themes from the inquiry. Finally, there is brief commentary on emerging questions and next steps.

1. BACKGROUND

1.1 Aims and Focus

What is this research about? In a nutshell, it began as a process of being curious about the frequency with which change agents or consultants said, with reference to what they did, 'I work with the energy', or perhaps 'I think of myself as a healer'. The principal aim is to explore what, if anything, lies behind these types of expression. What specifically do these people do, and what specifically do they experience? How do they work, and do these represent ways that are different from what we find in texts on organizational change? If so, what beliefs, values, models, skills and so on are associated with this mode?

The purpose - the aim of this aim - is probably to encourage people who work in the consultancy field to explore their experience and consciousness. It is also, and not coincidentally, a project that is helping me to explore such areas for myself. The inquiry develops an hypothesis that people in general have available intuitive skills and awareness that may usefully be coded more specifically, and which are likely to be of practical use to consultants and managers alike. Such skills and awareness are connected to experiences that are probably common - for example, sensing that an atmosphere can be cut with a knife, or feeling a deep connection with another person.

The inquiry has therefore taken a phenomenological approach to people's experiences and meanings of energy. However, various approaches of direct relevance to organizations use this concept already. DeBoard (1978), for example, writes of a psychoanalytic approach to behaviour in organizations. He suggests that the notion of mental energy from Freud's theory of personality is also of great significance in understanding groups and organizations;

Mental energy powers the psychic apparatus...The psychic apparatus is the means by which mental energy, constantly generated through the instincts, is distributed and allocated throughout the total personality....The total amount of energy available at any one time is finite and therefore the investment of energy in one particular mental process means that less is available for any other. (DeBoard, R. 1978 pp130-132)

This approach is closely associated with the work of the Tavistock Institute. DeBoard describes energy as a relatively mechanistic 'force' which 'drives' the organization. Other, more recently emerging ideas about organizations parallel the 'new' physics rather than the 'old', exploring the fluidity and patterning underlying the material world. For example, Senge (1990) refers to 'the illusion that the world is created of separate, unrelated forces', and Morgan (1986) cites physicist David Bohm's notion of implicate order. Energy it is is relevant not only to the developing ideas and practices of the learning organization - Pedler et al (1991) describe their model of the learning company as essentially about energy flow - but also to the field of Organizational Transformation (see Adams 1984). Ackerman's flow state management (1984) is based on the idea that organizations can be seen as flows of energy;

Webster defines energy as "the capacity for action, or performing work."... The act of accomplishing, or performing work, is the very nature of energy - movement...The energy model we seek is contained in the verb, to organize, or, in the process of organizing. The movement is in the "act of," which is a constant phenomenon in life, as things are always changing. There is in fact perpetual motion in the organization. Managers are continually faced with new data and new challenges. Decisions always need to be made... Ideally, the core purpose of the organization is the one energy force that touches every person in common and ties them all together. (Ackerman. L. 1984 pp117-118)

Even this, though, continues to use mechanistic metaphors such as force, motion and critical mass, so that in the organizational field to date it seems these notions of energy may have predominated. Culturally, too, we may incline to this view. In a workshop I presented, participants commented that previously they had typically considered only the physical, motivational connotations of energy. Gregory Bateson frequently referred to the use of a physical science concept of energy as an *explanatory* principle in the world of human experience as an epistemological error (Bateson 1979). Bateson's work, and other non-organizational sources, suggest that there are other conceptions of energy too - for example, organic, emotional and spiritual. Energy figures prominently in many contemporary psychotherapeutic and developmental approaches (for example Lowen 1976), and in ancient wisdoms such as the chakra system (see for example Vaughan 1985). These emphasize more the qualitative aspects and significance of energy. Thus for Virginia Satir, energy 'is for support of the human soul as it moves towards its freedom' (1985).

It seems important to keep the focus broad if the intention of exploring the qualitative, human experience of energy is to be honoured. For illustration, here (figure 1) is a set of questions I gave to small groups of participants at the conference workshop to help define the scope of the theme and to prompt their own reflections.

What is the quality of your 'energy' here and now?
- what do you sense in/through/around your body? (e.g. where specifically are those sensations located? how would you describe their quality?)
- what do those sensations mean to you? (e.g. what do they remind you of? to what do you attribute them? what associations come to mind as you focus on the sensations?)
- can you change the quality of the sensations (e.g. intensify/ diminish)? what happens as you do this?

What does 'energy' mean to you?
- what do you understand by 'energy' in relation to organizations?
- can you give examples that illustrate your understanding and experiences of 'energy'?
- what do you think is the relevance of 'energy' to consultancy and organizational change, if any?

Figure 1: Questions offered in Consultancy Dynamics Conference Workshop

1.2 Origins and Influences

The research developed from a number of strands of interest, both substantive and more personal. First, I have a continuing curiosity about how change happens in organizations (Tosey 1993), and how consultants contribute to or enable change, as in the way McLean et al (1982) explored Organization Development practice through consultants' own accounts. I have been influenced by systemic thinking (Bateson and Bateson 1988, for example) and empathise with characterisations of consultancy such as that of engagement (Phillips and Shaw 1989). These sources lean towards treating the consultant's being and consciousness as their instrument, rather than seeing consultants as implementers of procedures and techniques.

Second, the notion of organizational paradigm shifts began to connect with themes of healing and spirituality, especially following the 'Joining Forces: Working with Spirituality in Organisations' conference at the University of Lancaster in 1989 (see MEAD special issue 1991). Then, in 1992, I was invited to a small conference into 'Energy and Organizations' initiated by Nic Turner, then of W.H. Smith. Nic noticed and catalysed various interests in energy and related topics that had been expressed at the first Learning Company conference (University of Warwick 1992). A member of this 'Energy' conference, Lynne Sedgmore, has been researching what lies behind the label Organizational Transformation both as a practitioner and as a researcher linked to my Department (Sedgmore 1992).

Third, the style of the research owes much to two sources in particular. As a research student at the University of Bath in the early 1980's I received much from the development of new paradigm research (Reason 1988), as noted in section 2 below. This included emphasis on research as a process of personal development (Marshall 1981), which in formulating this project has meant searching for a coincidence or alignment of inner curiosity and outer significance. Then, more recently, I experienced applying the potential of Neuro-Linguistic Programming to the exploration and coding of inner or subjective experience. The research approach is described in more detail below.

2. MODE OF INQUIRY

2.1 Methodology and Methods - a Summary

The various influences on and choices about the style of the research have resulted in the following approach (it is not the intention here to discuss methodological issues in detail).

First, I have aimed to work collaboratively with people who have chosen to participate because the inquiry process also meets their own purposes. The selection of participants - all of whom are consultants or change agents in a broad sense, including some managers - has been somewhat serendipitous, by following up expressions of interest from people I have met and talked with. My research process has encompassed several types of event, including conferences and personal development work, but the main format to date has been one-to-one interviews and working sessions set up explicitly as being for mutual benefit, with equal right to direct the encounter. Contracts have been for commitment to one initial session, any further involvement being the participant's and researcher's choice. I have undertaken to keep confidentiality and maintain anonymity for participants and their clients.

To date, ten people have participated in the individual work that has been the source of specific data and for which a definite research contract has been agreed. I have met with some of these people more than once, and six sessions have been recorded on audio tape. Many more people have had some involvement in the broad process, for example as workshop participants, and have therefore influenced the development of the project.

The approach was described by a peer in a review session as 'facilitating people in understanding the core processes they are using'. In some ways it addresses Rowan's (1981) concerns about alienation, and the ethics of co-operation and collaboration that developed in Human Inquiry (Reason 1988); in other ways, such as in my retention of the role of central contact to date, it does not. I own to a preference for working one-to-one in the first instance, and this has often seemed appropriately intimate given the vulnerability participants have felt in beginning to talk openly about some very private experiences. At this stage, too, I do not feel enthusiasm for trying to organize group events; at the same time I have evidently chosen to increase the sense of holding or taking responsibility for the process. I am offering to circulate to participants the names and addresses of those who wish to network.

Human Inquiry (Reason 1988) also recommends research cycling as a validity process, and I sense that the research needs to move soon into a further phase, facilitated by the sharing of findings to date. So far I have sent individual participants copies of their own tapes and/or transcripts and/or working notes. This paper is part of the processing of the inquiry so far and is intended to contribute to feedback of collective themes.

Generally I have used a method of relatively non-directive, qualitative interviewing, especially for tape-recorded sessions. Relatively non-directive refers to the fact that I have identified a number of themes (see figure 2) which it is my intention to explore. These represent a menu. Items on the menu are explored in varying depth, or not at all, according to what becomes figural during the session. This also means that present-time experience of the energy of sessions themselves has been not only relevant content but also an influence on the action, and so a way in which the research process mirrors the content.

What does 'energy' mean (to this person)?
- How do they describe their approach, and how have they come to work in this way?
- What beliefs and values are associated with this approach?
- How specifically do they experience energy?
- How specifically do they 'work with' energy (with examples)?
- What dilemmas and issues do they experience from working in this way in organizations?

Figure 2 Main themes for research interviews

People's verbal accounts of their experience therefore constitute a significant part of the data, with attendant issues of validity. There are, however, additional aspects. Neuro-Linguistic Programming (see for example Bandler and Grinder 1975) provides frameworks through which non-verbal and paralinguistic communication can be incorporated; it has been styled at times as 'the study of subjective experience'. This widens the focus to include aspects of the participant's account and experience such as related kinaesthetic sensations, (internal) visual and auditory imagery, metaphor and so on. Torbert (for example, 1991) similarly emphasizes attending to various domains of experience in inquiry, though from a different value stance.

NLP enables skills to be explored live through being demonstrated to, and modelled by, the researcher (ideally in the participant's working context). It becomes possible to inquire specifically and systematically into how participants experience energy, and how they work with it. Non-verbal data, witnessed and experienced directly by researcher and participant, can become sources of comparison with verbal data and so provide a form of triangulation. In principle, such coding also enables skills to be learnt easily by others, thus serving the practical aims of the research. The underlying values of NLP emphasize that it is at heart a methodology rather than a product; the potential of this for other forms of research seems great, and I hope to articulate the prospects and related issues in a later publication.

The lived experience of this research has had features and dilemmas that are probably familiar to qualitative researchers in general. My own energy fluctuates; sometimes I feel enthused and completely on track, at others it is hard even to articulate my purpose. Themes proliferate and diverge, requiring great tolerance of ambiguity and confusion, and then coalesce in an exciting way. Supervision has been drawn upon in several ways - for example, occasional peer supervision with a colleague, and a review session with a group of MSc students - but has been inconsistent, leaving me to weigh up the balance of self-direction and possible self-delusion. I have also oscillated between being certain that this research path is appropriate, and wondering how ready I am for the transpersonal areas it invites in. Casting the *I Ching* for guidance, I received the hexagram called 'The Shocking';

various experiences have reflected this, including extremes of approval and disapproval from people who have more training and experience than me in working with energies.

3. OBSERVATIONS AND THEMES

3.1 Notes on 'Working with Energy'

These notes reflect responses to the interview themes. I intend to communicate the flavours of 'working with the energy', but not to attempt a formal reporting of data. For the latter purpose, more grounded categories will need to emerge from the continuing analysis.

Participants have described themselves in different ways. For some, healing appears to be part of their identity (eg 'I see myself primarily as a healer') and related to their core purpose as a human being; others emphasize doing, so that 'working with energy' is a skill more than a matter of who they are. Some are comfortable and familiar with notions of spirituality and healing, while others either do not mention or specifically disassociate themselves from such areas. Nevertheless, it has been common for people to cite significant personal experiences as key influences on how they developed their interest in energy. For example, I have been told of formative experiences such as seeing auras, with the people concerned being afraid of what was happening or having their experience discounted; in such cases, 'working with energy' can represent a way of making sense of their worlds.

There is variation in what people have done to develop their practice. Some have had specific education and training in a spiritual discipline, or extensive experience of personal development; others have no such background. The views of what energy is thus range from the unitary notion mentioned earlier, which typically emphasizes physical activity and motivation, to more holistic, multi-faceted concepts, sometimes linked to particular spiritual frameworks. While these may still take the underlying view that everything is energy, it is seen as having many different qualities - physical, emotional, spiritual, archetypal and so on - and manifestations. Some distinguish between positive and negative energy, others see energy itself as neither good nor bad - it just is. In diagnosing organizational contexts, energy might be perceived by the practitioner as being, for example, out of balance or too low.

Potentially, some common metaphors (Lakoff and Johnson 1980) are emerging. These appear to include;

- Energy as a reservoir (it has a level which can be raised and lowered; if lowered completely it is drained; it has capacity and is finite in quantity; it can be tapped into)

- Energy as a fuel (it is generated and creates force; it drives and powers)

- Energy as a vibration (it exists as waves which emanate from people, buildings and so on; it can be sensed)

The beliefs, values and principles connected with 'working with energy' also differ. Characteristic of those who use the description of healing, for example, are a sense of valuing (eg 'a recognition of the real value and purpose of each individual... engaging with each individual on that level of heart'), and a notion that people are responsible for their own changes (eg 'I can only offer the healing, it is up to the individual to take it on if they so choose'). In particular connectedness is often emphasized - not only of consultant to client, but more widely. Consultants often perceive that work assignments have symbolic meaning and potential learning for themselves, a significance beyond the practical level.

Energy is sometimes perceived as being noticeable all the time, something obvious to our usual senses. Participants cite indications of energy such as people's posture and movement, or their tone of voice. The quality of what clients do, and of how they actually behave, is taken as more significant typically than their verbal, conceptual analyses of their situations. Some participants have described in detail how they will access an altered state of consciousness in order to sense or work with energy. There is variation in the extent to which such states can be accessed and left at will; indeed, on occasions it was a case of something happening to them that they feared they might not be able to return from.

Significantly, working with energy is not exclusive of or necessarily different from other forms that consultancy can take. Thus a training workshop led by someone who 'works with energy' may seem entirely familiar in its outward form. An awareness of energy is likely to inform and influence the trainer's actions and choices, so that they will respond to energies they sense in the place and the people; it is not a question of applying consciously particular frameworks or techniques and it is often the consultant's own energy - whether it is is clean or unblocked - that is cited as critical. Such awareness is likely to remain ground rather than figure, and energy will probably not become explicit content unless in its action-and-motivation sense, although it was mentioned that working in a healing mode can feel 'pretty normal' to most people.

The scope of application of such awareness appears to have few boundaries. Far from being confined to personal development workshops, participants have described using their sense of energy to work with business strategy and finance. While much emphasis is on a sense of energy as a background awareness as noted above, people have also described a wide range of specific skills, where they are conscious of how they use internal kinaesthetic and other signals. It seems characteristic that participants regard their own bodies as primary sensing mechanisms. Several, for example, have talked of referring to feelings in their heart area for one purpose or another, such as guiding them in selecting which pieces of work to accept, and which clients to work with. This relates again to the notion of connectedness.

A significant theme is of how explicit it is advisable or necessary to be in organizations about 'working with energy', particularly when it is associated with healing or spirituality. Several acknowledge, for example, that this is not the sort of thing one can currently go into organizations and sell. However, it is also recognised that some senses of energy can be very attractive to clients ('one of the things that organisations will buy into is the notion of energy efficiency').

Finally, what are perceived to be the outcomes of this way of working? Generally people have described 'working with the energy' as assisting them to be more effective in achieving the client's outcomes. It is recognised also that, as with personal development work in general, some people may begin to question their own and their organization's values. Thus people's approach is typically both practical and client-centred. Those with a more spiritual perspective also perceive themselves to be fulfilling their own purpose and contributing to global shifts in consciousness and paradigm. The latter types of shift, though, are seen as long-term and large-scale changes; nobody I have talked with has in any sense been a missionary with regard to their clients.

3.2 Emergent Themes and Reflections

What, therefore, is emerging from this research, and what briefly may be some implications for consultancy practice?

First, in the interviews and other events such as workshops people have related easily to the notion of energy; it has been meaningful to them in terms of their own experience. Of course, those who have attended and participated have chosen to do so in response to the theme being publicised.

I have also had fed back to me that recognition of the theme of energy, and that it seems to be connected to a range of subtle skills, has been affirming for many, particularly for those who feel they work in what may be characterised as an intuitive and female way. Thus one outcome may be to identify more clearly and value more highly what many people do already.

A curiosity is of how 'working with energy' and working intuitively may be related; this feels linked to the general theme of consultancy as doing and as being, and the notion of engagement with rather than simply intervention in the client system. Also there is a question of what aspects of 'working with energy' are peculiar to the field of organizational consultancy, and what may represent more general human abilities. Potentially, there is learning from this research about a variety of inner skills for consultants in general.

Beyond the skills level, I wonder too what the models and world views of these consultants may have to offer. What new insights, understandings and options for action might be provided by applying their beliefs, metaphors and concepts to organizations? What are the implications for practice and the potential benefits for clients?

Given the relative invisibility of much (certainly not all) of this work, there is a question of how to know how useful energies perspectives may be, and in what ways 'working with energy' is being effective. Many participants in the research experience this mode as being themselves; it is not a question of there being techniques that can be easily or formally assessed. I am aware that to date no clients have been included in the research, and I am certainly curious about how others experience the practitioners concerned.

However, right now I feel that the inquiry has reached a stage where in-depth processing of the data is needed, with detailed feedback to participants who can then choose whether and how to remain involved. Through this process I would hope the research questions and themes will be renewed.

4. SUMMARY

In Section One I outlined the background to the research, describing how I became interested in the theme of energy and noting relevant areas of knowledge and practice (Organizational Transformation; the learning organization; consultancy skills and dynamics; new paradigm thinking and research; and Neuro-Linguistic Programming). I summarised some existing usage of energy in literature relevant to organizational change, noting that I was interested in a wider view than the mechanistic and that the purpose of the research was to explore people's own meanings rather than to rely upon an authoritative definition. .

The following section summarised the methodology and practice of the research. This was qualitative in nature, and intended to be co-operative in the sense of participation being voluntary and mutually developmental. An innovation of the research has been to incorporate aspects of Neuro-Linguistic Programming for the exploration of personal experience.

Finally I described some of the flavour of and variation within people's accounts of 'working with energy'. Participants generally had coherent and detailed representations of their thinking and practice from this perspective, though had not necessarily articulated these representations prior to interview. The accounts included ways in which people understand and use energy, with reference to related beliefs, metaphors, skills and issues of practice. More detailed and specific description of these themes is expected from further analysis of the research data.

ACKNOWLEDGEMENTS

Thanks are due to all who have participated in various ways in the inquiry process, and who therefore have contributed to this paper.

REFERENCES

ACKERMAN. L. (1984) 'The Flow State: A New View of Organizations and Managing'. in ADAMS, J. (ed.) *Transforming Work* Miles River Press

ADAMS, J. (ed.) (1984) *Transforming Work* Miles River Press

BANDLER, R. and GRINDER, J. (1975) *The Structure of Magic; A Book About Language and Therapy* Science and Behaviour Books

BATESON, G. (1979) *Mind and Nature* Fontana/Collins

BATESON, G. and BATESON, M. C. (1988) *Angels Fear* Rider Books

BOHM, D. (1980) *Wholeness and the Implicate Order* Routledge and Kegan Paul

BOYDELL, T. (1990) *Modes of Being and Learning* Working Paper no.8, Transform,

Suite 55-56, 22 High Street, Sheffield S1 2GE

BRENNAN, B. (1988) *Hands of Light* Bantam Books

BURGOYNE, J. et al (eds) (1994) *Towards the Learning Company* McGraw-Hill (in preparation - reference details not confirmed)

DEBOARD, R. (1978) *The Psychoanalysis of Organizations* Tavistock Publications

DELOZIER, J. and GRINDER, J. (1987) *Turtles All The Way Down: Prerequisites to Personal Genius* Grinder, DeLozier and Associates

GENDLIN, E. (1981) *Focusing* Bantam Books

GERBER, R. (1988) *Vibrational Medicine* Bear and Co.

HARMAN, W. (1988) *Global Mind Change* Knowledge Systems Inc.

LAKOFF, G. and JOHNSON, M. (1980) *Metaphors We Live By* University of Chicago Press

LOWEN, A. (1976) *Bioenergetics* Penguin Books

MANAGEMENT EDUCATION AND DEVELOPMENT (1991) (Special Issue) *Joining Forces: Working with Spirituality in Organizations* vol 22 pt 3

MARSHALL, J. (1981) 'Making Sense as a Personal Process' in REASON, P. and ROWAN, J. (eds) *Human Inquiry*

McLEAN, A., SIMS, D., MANGHAM, I. and TUFFIELD, D. (1982) *Organization Development in Transition.* John Wiley and Sons

MORGAN, G. (1986) *Images of Organization* Sage

OWEN, H. (1987) *Spirit, Transformation and Development in Organizations* Abbott

OZANEIC, N. (1990) *The Elements of the Chakras* Element Books

PEDLER, M., BOYDELL, T. and BURGOYNE, J. (1991) *The Learning Company* McGraw-Hill

PHILLIPS, K. and SHAW, P. (1989) *A Consultancy Approach to Training* Gower

REASON, P. and ROWAN, J. (eds) (1981) *Human Inquiry* John Wiley and Sons

REASON, P. (ed.) (1988) *Human Inquiry In Action: Developments in New Paradigm Research* Sage

ROWAN, J. (1981) 'A Dialectical Paradigm for Research' in REASON, P. and ROWAN, J. (eds) *Human Inquiry*

SATIR, V. (1985) *Meditations and Inspirations* Celestial Arts

SEDGMORE, L. (1992) *Organizations as Mandala* Department of Educational Studies, University of Surrey (unpublished paper)

SENGE, P. (1990) *The Fifth Discipline* Century Business, Random Century

TORBERT, W. (1991) *The Power of Balance* Sage

TOSEY, P. (1993) 'Interfering with the Interference'. *Management Education and Development* vol. 24 pt 3 pp 187-204

TOSEY, P. (1994, forthcoming) 'Energies of Organization and Change' in BURGOYNE, J. et al (eds) *Towards the Learning Company* McGraw-Hill

VAUGHAN, F. (1985) *The Inward Arc: Healing and Wholeness in Psychotherapy and Spirituality* New Science Library, Shambhala

WHAT MAKES CONSULTANCY DIFFICULT?

ON INTERPRETING CONFUSION IN AN EAST-WEST CONSULTANCY

Adrian Ward, *University of Reading*

INTRODUCTION

The theme of this book is 'What makes consultancy work?', and my contribution reframes this question as 'what makes consultancy difficult?'. I shall be reporting on a difficult experience during a consultancy to a foreign government, and reflecting upon the nature of the difficulty and upon the ways in which we tried to tackle that difficulty, exploring connections between process and content in particular. My hypothesis is that because we were visiting a country in a state of complete upheaval at all levels, learning was difficult, confusion was inevitable and genuine exchange almost impossible, but my further hypothesis is that being ready to feel confused may be a necessary part of the process of consultancy.

1. THE CONSULTANCY

Background

The project described in this paper was part of a continuing exchange of ideas between our Department and the Russian Ministry for Education, the aim of which has been to help the Ministry in its plans to reform its system of residential care and education for troubled children. On this occasion a colleague and I had been invited to visit the Ministry in Moscow, and to visit St Petersburg University, with a view to helping them to pilot a national training programme for residential staff.

Task

There was some initial ambiguity in the invitation as to whether we were being asked to visit as trainers to the University staff, as consultants to the Ministry of Education, or as interested visitors to the Russian system; our working hypothesis was that we had been engaged as consultants to the Ministry. Equally our response to this invitation had been one of some ambivalence and uncertainty, for a variety of reasons. In particular we were reluctant to fall into a 'colonial' assumption that the British system was necessarily any better or more enlightened than the Russian system. At the same time, we felt that we did have something to offer, in that we had some experience as consultants, and had the recent experience of establishing an innovative training programme for senior staff in this field (Ward, 1993a), and we knew that they were interested in this course.

Process of work

Our time in Russia comprised roughly two full days' work at the State Pedagogical University in St Petersburg and two days in Moscow. At the University we had a range of meetings, including a 'round table seminar' comparing theoretical approaches to training, a public debate between senior Faculty members and Ministry officials, and a formal meeting with the Deputy Rector (Vice Chancellor). We also visited a special school for 'delinquents', and had a number of informal meetings and semi-formal meals in the University. We tried to utilise every opportunity both formal and informal for working towards the task of our consultancy, and mealtimes offered particular opportunities for informal reflections and clarification.

As the visit unfolded it appeared to us that we had been brought in by the Ministry as catalysts to a debate between Ministry and University which may have been simmering for a long time but which needed speeding up and resolving, although we could not be exactly sure what the process was that we were catalysing. Some of the meetings were harder to follow than others, partly because the standard of translation provided was variable, but partly because the arrangements and the order of events often bore no relation to the planned programme we had been given, and frequently changed with little notice or explanation. Even when we were presented with a revised plan during the day, the events themselves would often follow a different pattern again. We also began to gain the impression that, although we were being asked detailed questions by Faculty staff about our own training programmes and for comment upon their plans for similar programmes, they did not really need our advice, as they had well-advanced plans and were highly-experienced educationalists. At times we felt confused, frustrated and uncertain as to what was 'really' going on. Was this simple confusion, was there a plot to undermine our efforts, or was the original programme and its aim not so important after all?

On our third day we undertook the lengthy train journey to Moscow. It was on this journey that the two of us worked together on unravelling and interpreting our experience to date, and on deciding upon our proposed way forward. We also realised that we needed to take our confusion seriously and examine its sources and its meaning: the process by which we analysed this confusion is described in Section 2.

Outcome

The outcome of our reflection was that we agreed upon an Interim Report to the Ministry in the form a set of proposals and feedback, to include detailing the points upon which we were still confused, since we felt that, even though we had attempted several times to clarify some of these points without success, it was important not to give up. The feedback would also include recommendations to the effect that the Ministry and the University should simply proceed with the plans which they appeared to have in mind, to appoint a leader for the proposed training programme, and to set the machinery in motion for the national programme of training to be started. Although our trip as a whole was only half-way through at this stage, and many further negotiations took place in Moscow, we feel that we had already achieved our most significant learning as consultants by this stage, which is why this paper focuses primarily on this phase of our work.

2.   REFLECTING ON THE EXPERIENCE

Introduction
Our predominant experience during this consultancy was that of trying to unravel, interpret and find equivalents for the phenomena which we were encountering. We often felt confused, and sometimes hopeless, because frequently we could not understand what we were engaged in, what we were being asked to do, and where we or they were going. The elements in this confusion included the following:

Language and communication
The restricted resources of our hosts meant that professional interpretation was rarely available during our visit: therefore not only were we sometimes unsure as to the literal meaning of what was being said *to* us, but we were also not sure that our *own* meaning was being adequately conveyed.

Money and exchange
A second source of confusion arose from the dislocation between our nations in terms of currency. The process of financial exchange was unfamiliar in that we could not obtain roubles before entering the country, but had to bring in US dollars which could then be exchanged for roubles. The intermediary role of the dollar seemed to increase the distance between our systems, and to make the rouble seem even more unreal. Moreover, the move towards a free market and the consequent soaring inflation rate in Russia meant that the value of the rouble was almost impossible to estimate - if indeed it had value at all. We found it hard to grasp the meaning of the exchange rate, and formulated the issue to ourselves in terms of the question, both pragmatic and symbolic, 'How can there be exchange when there is no equivalence?'.

Cultural difference
Although we had been aware of the risks of appearing to adopt a superior attitude in our work, and we consistently stated that we saw our task as assisting our clients to produce Russian solutions to Russian problems, we had not fully appreciated the importance of the differences between our own culture and the Russian culture, and on the basis of such brief contact it would be difficult to specify these differences more precisely. We were also aware of a complex blend of feelings in our hosts about Western culture: in some respects Western values were idealized, while in other ways they were probably still regarded as shallow, untrustworthy, and perhaps unfathomable.

Change and uncertainty

Fourthly, some of our confusion arose from the frequent need to re-frame our assumptions because of changes of arrangement and sudden revision or mutation of what was being asked of us. Such changes, often requiring fundamental questioning of our assumptions and complete reframing of our thoughts and emotions, happened frequently. We decided eventually that what we were experiencing was probably in part an enactment of the much broader confusion and continual upheaval in which the Russian nation was living. Intentionally or - more likely - unintentionally, we were being made to experience what it feels like to be in a state of upheaval and unpredictable transition. It is well-established in the group-analytic literature (e.g. Foulkes, 1983; de Mare, 1989) that people's behaviour may unconsciously reflect not only their here-and-now preoccupations in relation to the group's task, but also their broader experience of 'macro-issues' in society. There is also recent evidence of the particular force with which such phenomena may arise where a society is in violent upheaval - see recent papers on Northern Ireland (Benson, 1992), on the former Yugoslavia (Trampuz, 1993) and on Russia itself (Semyonova, 1993), and the growing literature on 'The Psychodynamics of International Relationships' (Volkan et al, 1990 & 1991). The extent to which such upheaval permeates human interactions at every level was brought forcibly home to us, as was the degree of the upheaval in Russia at that time. (At this time the seizure and storming of the parliament building in Moscow were several months away and unguessed-at, but the dislocation in everyday society was already palpable.)

3. ON BEING CONSULTED: TRANSFERENCE AND COUNTERTRANSFERENCE.

Confusion and the interpretation of feelings

However, despite being able to identify the possible sources of our confusion, and thus to gain some rational perspective on our experience, we still remained confused! By the time we had completed our visit to St Petersburg, we could not understand what the problem was for our hosts. They appeared to know what they wanted to do, and we felt that all they needed to do was to appoint the staff for their new training course, design the curriculum and start the work, all of which was well within their capability. On the other hand, they appeared to be completely stuck: lacking a sense of direction, unable to identify suitable staff to lead and teach upon the course, and over-dependent on our advice. We tried to understand why they should need to feel stuck: it might perhaps be due to a lack of confidence following many years of state paralysis, or it might be due to unresolved conflict between the personalities whom we had met; but we were unsure, as we had been unable to 'read' the process by the normal methods.

In the absence of reliable observation of the other players in the process, we were thrown back onto our *ourselves*, and our own thoughts and feelings. We thought we were simply confused, but was this our confusion or theirs, and how can you decide where one stops and the other starts? On reflection, we realised that what we were calling confusion might in fact be a defence against other strong emotions. We could identify a number of conflicting and powerful emotions which had been evoked in us by our work and by the people with whom we had been trying to establish contact, emotions which we may have been attempting to disavow because they were especially painful or anxiety-producing. We found that our apparent confusion was at least in part the result of struggling to contain these powerful emotions rather than simply confusion over language or a complicated and conflictual task. We thus discovered that we *could* distinguish between actual confusion and absorbed or re-enacted confusion, if we paid as much attention to our own feelings as we paid to those of the others involved. Similarly, the paralysis which we felt, in not knowing how to respond to the 'stuck' situation which we felt we had encountered, was not 'simple' stuckness, but a paralysis which we had unconsciously absorbed through our intensive contact with people who them-selves felt stuck. We now knew that we did not have to feel paralysed: there was a choice. We realised, in other words, that in our consultancy we could trust our intuitive judgements, listen to our own experience of 'process', and learn from the countertransference.

Attending to the countertransference thus emerged as a central element in our work: indeed, it was only after we stopped regarding our confusion as a handicap and viewed it instead as a message that we were able to move forwards. Perhaps consultancy will always be likely to entail such experiences, because if the clients themselves did not feel seriously lost they would be unlikely to call in consultants (see Shapiro and Carr, 1991). In a sense, the consultants willingly place themselves into the line of fire, joining the system sufficiently to experience the powerful feelings inherent within it, but then stepping out enough to register what these are (see Ward, 1993b for further discussion).

4. CONCLUSION

I have described here a search for understanding amidst confusion, and reflected upon the interpretation of confusing and uncomfortable feelings during consul-tancy. Returning to my reframing of the conference title from 'What makes consultancy work?' to 'What makes consultancy difficult?', I would therefore propose that, once we really know what it is and confront it, it is sometimes what makes consultancy feel personally and professionally difficult that can eventually make it work.

REFERENCES

Benson, J. (1992)   The group turned inwards: a consideration of some group phenomena as reflective of the Northern Irish Situation. *Groupwork* 5 (3) 5-18

de Mare, P., Piper, R. & Thompson, S. (1990) *Koinonia: From hate through dialogue to culture in the larger group.* London, Karnac Books.

Foulkes, S.F. (1983) *Group-Analytic Psychotherapy.* London: Gordon & Breach. (Reprinted, London: Karnac Books, 1986)

Semyonova, N.D. (1993) Psychotherapy during social upheaval in the USSR. *Group Analysis* 26, 91-97

Shapiro, E.R. and Carr, A.W. (1991) *Lost in familiar places. Creating new connections between the individual and society.* New Haven & London, Yale University Press.

Trampuz, D. (1993) The 'Yugoslav Crisis' reflected in the large group in the Diploma Course in Zagreb. *Group Analysis* 26, 183-188

Volkan, V.D., Julius, D.A. & Montville, J.V. (eds) (1990) *The Psychodynamics of International Relationships. Volume 1: Concepts and Theories.* Lexington, Massachusetts, Lexington Books.

Ward, A. (1993a) The Large Group: the heart of the system in group care. *Groupwork.* 6. 1. 64 - 77.

Ward, A. (1993b) On Learning to Interpret Confusion in an East-West Consultancy. Unpublished paper delivered at *Making Links: Child Mental Health Services Abroad*, Workshop for the Association for Child Psychology and Psychiatry, October 1993, London.

DESIGNER CLOTHES & LABELS - OR THOSE THAT 'FIT'?: REFLECTIONS FROM CONSULTANCY EXPERIENCES

Michael John Walton, *Independent Consultant, Camberley, Surrey*

ABSTRACT

Drawing on three diverse case examples this paper considers insights from psycho-therapy can be used to complement conventional logical-rational approaches to reviewing behaviour in organisations. The literature on Organisational Behaviour (OB) and Organisation Development predominantly emphasise a focus on manifest structure and behaviour and relatively neglect the less tangible influences on individual and collective thinking and action in organisations. The most critical factors influencing the course of these cases however centred around the embedded organisational dynamics and the pre-occupations and concerns of the author.

The paper proposes more integration between the, somewhat normative, approaches of the conventional writings on OB with the insights and notions from psycho-therapy. It is not suggested that organisations can be psycho-analysed but that the psycho-dynamically aware organisational consultant may be equipped to more sensitively and productively intervene into the complex work-worlds of others.

1. INTRODUCTION

Much of the literature on Organisation Behaviour (OB) and Organisation Development (OD) is too neat and tidy. It presents carefully constructed ways of doing things which, if followed, are seemingly 'designed' to   productive, positive outcomes. It is 'as if ' by following the steps laid down in the books, lectures and videos the erstwhile consultant will - almost by default- be able to sort out the client's dilemmas and mend, remedy or guide the client to a better position. By donning on the 'designer clothes' of others - with little adjustments here and there - I expected to replicate the outcomes so clearly set out in the literature.

The rhetoric of organisational consultancy - and the whole business of trying to understand organisational life - seems to me too often presented as a rather straightforward activity. Effective interventions are usually reported as following a pre-determined sequence of:

    (i)   a careful diagnosis,

    (ii)   a rational analysis of the presented issues,

    (iii)   an exploration of the organisational structures and ways of working leading to

(iv)   shared clarity about what needs to change , and

(v)   following clearly defined sets of actions to achieve the desired results.

There seems to be an underlying unstated emphasis on addressing the tangible, and a preference for reporting on what 'should' happen from an almost idealised view of organisational life.

My experience over several years of organisational consulting is quite different. I have found that seeking to enter, engage with and influence the course of events in organisations is significantly more complicated, unpredictable, confusing and messy than much of the literature presents it to be. And there are 'things that go 'CRASH'in the night' that confuse, confound, upset and derail the best laid strategies and plans.

Three case examples of my work will be drawn upon on to (i) illustrate the added value of attending to the underlying messages and dynamics that are at play within organisational settings and (ii) the discrepancy I experienced between what 'should' have happened (the 'Designer clothes') and what actually occurred (the clothes that 'fitted' the situation).

2. THE WAY IT 'SHOULD' BE !

With a few notable exceptions (eg see Argyris 1990 et al), the OB/OD literature and 'conventional wisdoms' about what makes organisations 'tick' remain firmly wedded to logic and analysis and to tangible and manifest business activities. Yet much of what goes on in organisations appears from my experience to be far less rational than many writers on management would have us believe. For example there appear significant fault lines between how decision making is logically presented and what actually occurs; departments clash for seemingly ludicrous reasons; so called 'logical analysis' can fly out of the window in the face of emotional displays in meetings, and key decision makers will discard, deny or discount relevant information when it challenges the 'answer' they wanted all along!

My experience suggests that much of the taught theory of organisational behaviour is at best simplistic - and at worst illusionary - and that far from managers invariably seeking to objectively resolve problems they will tend to function with persistent and subjective self-interest to the fore. As Kets de Vries (1991) comments:'Whilst management science talks about rational choices, many observers and practitioners of organisational life have come to understand that the 'irrational' personality needs of the principle decision makers can seriously affect the management process. If these needs are not taken into consideration, it is only to be expected that many management models will fail to work.' (p. 2) and Schwarz (1990) comments how, 'Traditional organisational theory does not enable us to understand organisations that are fundamentally unhealthy. Our theories of organisation are basically functionalist theories, which assume that organisational processes make sense in terms of the overall purposes of the organisation. Within this paradigm, these overall purposes go unquestioned, and the validity of the fundamental organisational processes that carry them through is taken for granted.

Thus, within this paradigm, organisational disasters and the bad decisions that lead up to them must be seen as aberrations' (p73).

Over the years I have tried to match my experiences with the predominantly logical-rational explanations advanced by the 'leaned' writers on organisational behaviour. Often there was quite a difference between what I expected and what I encountered so, as I went about my consulting work I built up my own notions and models to help me to make my own sense of what I was experiencing and seeing in front of me (Walton, 1984,1989). Whilst valuing the 'designer labels' of the named leaders in OB I have found it necessary to create my own designs and styles that fit both me and my clients.

In spite of this something still seemed to be missing from my work, 'a lost dimension' almost, and I was left with a sense that much of what influences behaviour in organisations remained unaccounted through solely following a predominantly logical-analytical approach to business life. I looked towardspsychotherapy as a furtile area to explore further and this paper is about some of my tentative efforts at using insights from psycho-therapy in my consulting work.

3. SYNOPSIS OF THREE CASE EXAMPLES

Three case examples are outlined to provide material from which to consider how notions from psychotherapy can enhance the understanding of behaviour in organisations and offer insights to the management consultant that have generally been neglected.

In the first case I was a senior manager trying to review formal decision making procedures. Unexpectedly I got swept up in such intense emotional reactions to my work that I didn't know what hit me until I forced myself to look again at what might be going on, and what I might have blundered into. The second case concerns a successful consultancy that was so proud and pleased at itself that, seemingly, it was unable to handle internal challenges to its preferred view of itself. Unable to feel heard people who pushed for change left: the organisation remained successful. The third case notes how CEO behaviour patterns can become the sub-motif for the way the organisation does its business - even when such behaviour is seen as unhelpful others will perpetuate, and manipulate, such situations for their own advantage.

3.1 Case One : Southern Health District (SHD)

Southern Health District was a group of hospitals and health care services where I was the Personnel Manager and had taken on an action research project 'to review the adequacy of the committee structure and to make proposals for constructive change.' My findings indicated the current arrangements to be ineffective with very little productive work being accomplished during most of the formal committee meetings and general dissatisfaction with the current system.

These findings were not well received and I resisted increasing pressure to review, change and tone them down. I could not understand the intensely negative reactions I received from others and the unexpected personal distress I was feeling.

The intensity of these pressures led me to re-examine my material and to look again at the initial brief to see if I had misled others, misdirected my approach or simply had just not undertaken the work expected of me.

I inverted the original brief and looked at it with the possibility that my client did *not* want me to complete the review as stated but perhaps wanted me to confirm that the existing structure was OK as it stood with no need for change at all. It also seemed possible that the management team just did not expect there to be any need for change and so were shocked and confused when I suggested otherwise. This 'cynical hypothesis' however gave me a way of re-interpreting the reactions I had encountered and freed me to re-consider what may have generated their reactions.

Acknowledging the possibility of mutual shock and unease at my proposals (1) released me from feeling impelled to sort it all out and to defend myself against attack, (2) gave me a way of reflecting anew on the intense reactions my work had elicited, and (3) brought me to a closer appreciation of how my colleagues may be feeling about the findings I had reported. I became more able to work sensitively with my boss and the management team and I became more of an internal force for change rather than being perceived as an internally threatening object.

3.2 Case Two : Consultancy Services Limited (CSL)
This was a successful, well regarded and medium sized consultancy and concerns my attempts - as one of its senior consultants - to draw attention to inconsistencies in its internal ways of working, some of which contrasted sharply with its presented image, and to facilitate internal debate about the changing balance of work as the company expanded.

CSL promoted and fostered a culture of equality, personal assertiveness, mutual support & challenge, a belief in oneself and in the organisation. The organisation saw itself as unique; as an open, non-competitive, mutually developmental, privileged and exciting practice to be in - there was a lot of energy and a lot of positive spirit around the place. However the organisation was not wholly the idealistic entity it projected itself to be and there were internal tensions, internal competition and fears of falling out of favour with influential colleagues; in short there were differences between the espoused values and those practised. Yet life went on 'as if' all was ideal - the discrepancies were discussed with trusted colleagues but not fully explored openly.

The was an internal dynamic of self congratulation that was appealing and seductive to adhere to and helped generate an exceptionally strong desire for acceptance. I was cautious about the overly zealous way in which many of my colleagues mutually reinforced CSL as 'the greatest'. I believed we were a very effective force, had some outstanding performers and that we were productive and well regarded by our clients; but there were several ways in which the consultancy functioned that made me uneasy - we seemed too exclusive, too self-confirmatory and to have altogether too grandiose (narcissistic almost) a view of ourselves.

Through its strong presentation of itself to itself I believe it became increasingly difficult to acknowledge and address internal difficulties and growing pains. It seemed particularly difficult for CSL to work with colleagues who challenged the idealised view of the company and questioned the way CSL was developing.

3.3 Case Three : International Marketing Inc. (IMI)

This is an international commodity marketing organisation headquartered in the UK with a network of offices world-wide. Ineffective implementation of Board decisions - often primarily the wanted decisions of the strong MD - led this company to diagnose a need for change and as an external management consultant I was invited to begin working with the MD and the Board on internal communication matters.

My findings suggested a fragmented organisation divided against itself. There was a separation between the MD and his Regional Directors located in America, Asia and Europe and a separation between the Management Board and the rest of the staff - who rarely saw nor really understood what the MD and the Board did or wanted. There was a climate of hierarchical compliance, self-protection, of dependence, and an avoidance of contentious issues all of which contributed to 'organisational drift' whereby the company seemed unfocused and confused in what it wanted and how to attain its priority targets.

Whilst shocked by my analysis, which created an internal shockwave when shared with the top thirty-five directors and managers, the MD did not attempt to restrict my findings nor to ask me to lessen their impact even though they signalled aspects of his behaviour that were dysfunctional and affecting the organisation as a whole..

4. RE-VIEWING THE CASE MATERIAL

I identified several features that were common to each case and looked to see if there were any underlying themes which connected what was going on in these examples. The results (see Walton 1994) gave me some perspectives about *What* seemed to be most important, and *How* these showed themselves in practice.

What seemed most important were:

    (i)   concerns about internal power and political dynamics

    (ii)   the reinforcement of normative 'right' behaviours

    (iii)   the exercise of personal and collective influence as a means of maintaining organisation-centred behaviours.

Examples of *How* the above themes showed were through:

    (a)   *ego-centric decision making* : whereby 'I can't be wrong' and 'they must be at fault'

    (b)   strongly protected *boundaries*: 'in-and-out' groups, reinforcement of 'organisationally correct' ways to see, view and do things and through

    (c)   the *custody and ordering of others* : keeping people in their place, pressures to conform and follow the party line

These outcomes highlighted the importance of an organisation's *embedded culture* on the organisation yet - from my experience - this remains a relatively neglected area of attention for managers and organisational consultants. Business managers and leaders are not alerted about or trained to work with these dimensions in mind yet they appear to be factors of immense significance in the shaping of inter-personal, group and organisational relationships... and ... organisational performance.

If these case experiences are representative of what goes on in other organisations they may partly explain why so many 'conventionally' based attempts at improving organisational performance fail in that they concentrate on improving rational business procedures and give too little attention to the personal and organisational dynamics that emerged from these cases as being so influential. These reflections led me to look for perspectives on organisational behaviour that were complementary to, but different from, the logical-rational ones I usually followed. I looked to psycho-therapy.

5. PERSPECTIVES FROM PSYCHO-THERAPY

5.1 Introduction
Whilst, as Levinson (1984) points out, we do not psychoanalyse organisations the psycho-dynamically informed practitioner uses psycho-analytic theory and psychotherapeutic perspectives to plan, guide and interpret organisation interventions. Insights from psycho-therapy could have helped me to appreciate more fully some of the issues I encountered and experienced in these cases.

I now think that my work, through threatening to disturb the existing culture, also threatened to destabilise the internalised social defences and this resulted in some of the intense reactions I reported and four of the key areas I now see as important to consider from a psycho-dynamic perspective are briefly noted below:

5.2 An Organisation's Social Defence Systems
An organisations as a frameworks of social defences networks that fit with its history, its leaders and its business. Social defences as defences against anxiety protect the status quo and facilitate continued functioning especially when under experienced threat. The constructive outcome of these measures is the securing of the time needed to reassess the situation, consider what needs to be looked at and adapt; the dysfunctional outcome is a closing down of the organisation's external contacts and a disallowing of internal review processes (eg see Bion, 1961; Menzies-Lyth, 1959; Hirschhorn 1988).

5.3 The Organisation Ideal
The notion of the 'organisational ideal' underlies a good deal of normative organisation theory whereby, in one way or another, organisations portray a picture of themselves as they wish themselves to be seen. Attempt to maintain this ideal, even in the face of their failure to manifest it, can lead to the manipulation of business processes and information to sustain the desired myths and beliefs. The process of subordinating the perceptions of reality to the fantasy of the organisation ideal will lead to increasing organisational ineffectiveness whichSchwarz (1991)

refers to as 'organisational decay', noting that 'When the process of decay begins the organisation shifts its functioning from coping with reality to a preoccupation with maintaining an idealisation of itself ....' This can lead to a narcissistic organisation culture in which its members have become overawed by their own omnipotence, and begin to believe it undoubtingly.

5.4 Organisational Leaders: Heroes or Villains?

Leaders in organisations are subject to a heady blend of realistic, desired and idealised forces that are difficult for them to disentangle, contain and manage as organisations offer their lead managers a chance to realise a degree of immortality through reaching positions of power and authority. Kets de Vries (1991) notes that 'Clinical investigation shows that many organisational problems originate in the private, inner world of an organisation's senior executives in the way they act out their conflicts,desires, fantasies, and defensive structures' (p3); and Zaleznik (1970) has shown that patterns of unconscious anxiety affect the politics of organisational life, often preventing those in prominent leader roles from being open to and accepting genuine help and advice.

5.5 The dynamics of disruption: Management of Change

For some the organisation comes to represent their purpose in life whereas for others the organisation offers a means of defending themselves against life's uncertainties and traumas. Either way individuals' psychologically invest parts of themselves in organisations and in so doing they become stakeholders with a vested interest in any attempts to alter the(ir) status quo of the organisation in which they have invested. The result is that an organisation becomes a depository of highly charged personal - both individual and collective - interests, meanings and needs.

Far from being collectives of people brought together solely to accomplish formal tasks, organisations become intense socio-dynamic entities and attempts at change, are likely to be experienced as efforts which threaten to de-stabilise the existing psycho-dynamic equilibria. This will generate resistance and possibly the unleashing of dramatic emotional responses to even the most modest of attempts at change - leading to confusion and surprise in those initiating the change activities - and opposition and resentment in those seeking to maintain the status quo.

5.6 Summary

The following table briefly draws together some of my case findings and the principal reactions they elicited:

Summary of Case Findings & Reactions

Initial Focus	Findings	Internal Reactions	Impact on me	Organisational Defences
Case 1: Southern Health District				
Review of committees	ineffective meetings collusive practices covert systems at work prominent internal politics	denial, attack, shock, anxiety, rejection of my findings extreme unease	confusion, shock, felt attacked, fight back, felt persecuted, increasing anxiety	fight-flight covert coalition recourse to org rituals transference
Case 2: Consultancy Services Limited				
Address internal issues	gap between espoused values & those in force undercurrent of unease covert politics internal split emerging	denial, rejection of these observations, reinforcement of 'how good we are', covert attack, traitor?	began to feel dis-empowered, fight- then - flight, slowly distanced myself	narcissistic tendencies growth of 'org ideal' covert coalition 'deified' leaders seductive processes transference & counter - transference
Case 3: International Marketing Inc.				
Ineffective implementation of Board decisions Development of a management develop-ment strategy	organisation internally fragmented; 'distant' management; MD dominant; secretive, competative & compliant organisation too many priorities	shock by MD and senior management; preparedness however to work on issues; fragmented and uneven progress	initial anxiety then calm;	hierarcially dependent climate; org rituals important; projection prevalent; persecutory anxiety and fear organisational drift deified leader

6. SUMMARY - ENDPIECE

Superficially, the cases presented straightforward issues for attention yet in each cases additional less obvious, complex and dynamic issues emerged as factors ofconsiderable significance which affected the workings and performance of each organisation. In each case the inter-personal dynamics and the embedded culture of the organisation deeply influenced the work pre-occupations, the thinking and the enactments which took place. In each case the subjective 'truth' as seen by key players - including myself - exercised a critical colouring and shading of what was going on and of what needed to be attended to (or to be denied).

Organisations are generally construed as rationally ordered entities within which staff go about their prescribed tasks in a precise, effective and well ordered manner; resembling the myth of the business organisation as described by Galbraith (1977). This is a myth however and does not do justice to the complexity of their internal workings and the range of individual and collective dynamics and concerns that profoundly influence organisational behaviour.

One surprising outcome from these cases was the extent to which the formal structural aspects of the organisation emerged as less critical in shaping what goes on in an organisation than the literature and the rhetoric of management Gurus would have us believe. It was the psycho-dynamic relationships that exerted critical influences in determining organisational behaviour and this presents a very different picture to the more conventional pre-occupations about structure, role definitions and reward strategies that occupy much of the literature on organisational change.

This paper does not suggest psycho-therapy for organisations, nor that organisations can be psycho-analysed per se. It does though advocate a fuller utilisation of psycho-therapeutic insights, theories and philosophies - together with more conventional approaches to OB and OD to reach better understanding of behaviour in organisations.

REFERENCES:

Argyris, C (1990) *Overcoming Organizational Defences* Allyn and Bacon, Boston

Block, P (1981) *Flawless Consulting*   Learning Concepts, Austin Texas USA

Hirschhorn,L (1988) *The Workplace within* The MIT Press, Cambridge, Mass. USA

Kets de Vries, MFR (1991) *Organizations on the Couch*   Jossey-Bass, San Francisco

Kernberg, O (1980)*nternal World and External Reality: Object Relations Theory Applied* Jason Aronson New York

Levinson, H (1984) *Review of 'The Psychoanalysis of Organisations'*, Journal of the American Psychoanalytic Association 32, 784-6

Menzies, I (1959) *The functioning of social systems as a defence against anxiety*, Human Relations 13: 95-121 London

Miller, D (1990) *The Icarus Paradox* HarperCollins New York

Schwartz, H (1990) *Narcissistic Process and Corporate Decay* New York University Press, New York

Schwartz, H (1991) *Organizational Decay and Loss of Reality: Life at NASA* in Kets de Vries (1991) *Organizations the Couch*

Steele, F (1975) *Consulting for Organizational Change* University of Massachusetts Press, Amherst USA

Walton, MJ (1984) *Consulting Practice in the National Health Service : Some Empirical Studies* unpublished PhD Thesis, Birkbeck College, University of London

Walton, MJ (1989) *From Fragmentation towards Cohesion: a case example* Congress Paper - 4th West European Congress The Psychology of Work & Organisation, University of Cambridge, UK

Walton, MJ (1994) *Being in Organisations: reflections on some experiences* unpublished MA Dissertation, School of Psychotherapy and Counselling, Regent's College, London

ABSTRACTS

EMPOWERMENT: RELEVANT OR RHETORIC?

Brian Blundell, *South Bank Business School, London*

ABSTRACT

This paper has two parts. The first, which reviews the importance of empowerment espoused by some writers for organisations and the particular nature of 'empowerment' as a distinct concept, was prepared as the basis for a round-table discussion at the conference. The second, which considers the implications of empowerment on the dynamics and practice of consultancy was completed after the conference and was informed by discussion and other learning achieved during the proceedings.

This first part of the paper explores the extent to which empowerment, particularly in organisational contexts is based on relevant theory and practice or is just an expression of managerial rhetoric. The roots of the concept of empowerment are reviewed and both the promise and problems of the implementation of 'empowerment' in organisations is considered. The case for empowerment as a distinct concept which is worthy of further analysis and potentially important for consultancy is made.

Two examples drawn from current literature, one which seems to adopt the rhetoric of empowerment and the other which takes a more analytical stance, are reviewed.

As the basis of these analyses three discussion topics are offered: is 'empowerment' worth pursuing, or are there better models already in existence, is the concept of the 'empowering consultant' significantly different from current best practice, and how would one recognise an empowering organisation?

Some results from the necessarily short discussion session are offered, and although no firm conclusions were reached some interesting areas for further discussion and research were aired.

Full copies of the paper are available from:
Brian Blundell, South Bank Business School, 103 Borough Road, London SE1 0AA

BIBLIOGRAPHY

At the end of the conference session a number of delegates asked to be referred to books and other sources of information and debate around the topic of 'empowerment'. As well as the authors referred to in the paper anyone interested in pursuing the subject further may like to select from the following:

Belasco, J. A. (1990) Teaching the Elephant to Dance: Empowering Change in Your Organisation. London: Business Books.

Blyton, P., and Turnbull, P. (Eds) (1992) Reassessing Human Resource Management. London: Sage.

Byham, W., and Cox, J. (1991) Zapp! London; Business Books.

Froham, A. L., and Johnson, L. W. (1993) The Middle Management Challenge: Moving from crisis to Empowerment. New York: McGraw Hill.

Ketchum, L. D., and Trist, E. (1992) All Teams are not Created Equal: How Employee Empowerment Really Works. Newbury Park, CA.: Sage.

Marchington, M. (1992) Managing the Team: A Guide to Successful Employee Involvement. Oxford: Blackwells.

Myers, M. S., (1991) Every Employee a Manager. San Diego Calif.: Pfeiffer.

Oates, D. (1993) Leadership: The Art of Delegation. London: Century Business.

Plunkett, L. C., and Fournier, R. (1991) Participative Management: Implementing Empowerment. New York: John Wiley.

Scott, C. D., and Jaffe, D. T. (1991) Empowerment: Building a Committed Workforce. London: Kogan Page.

Suzaki, K. (1993) The New Shop Floor Management: Empowering People for Continuous Improvement. New York: Free Press.

Vogt, J. F., and Murrell, K. L. (1990) Empowerment in Organisations: How to Spark Exceptional Performance. San Diego, CA.: University Associates.

Wellins, R. S., Byham, W. C., and Wilson, J. M. (1991) Empowered Teams: Creating Self-directed Workgroups that Improve Quality, Productivity and Participation. San Francisco: Jossey Bass.

WAS NOAH'S ARK THE ORIGINAL TECHNOLOGICAL FIX?

Tony Emerson and Kamil Kellner,
South Bank Business School, London

SUMMARY

The argument for ecological sustainability is gaining a voice, it's effect can be seen in the rhetoric of politicians of developed countries and some action of governments and companies.

In this research project we are studying how a number of consultants - both internal and external - are intervening to bring about change in the environmental policies and practices of a variety of large organisations. Our aim is to explore the variety of types of green issues - the 'content' of change, in the language of Pettigrew - that might effect different firms, and the variety of external and internal 'contextual' factors may help or hinder the complex, green change process in organisations. In doing so, we identify some of the requirements for effective change agency in the transition to sustainability.

In this paper we report on our learning from this research.

We are finding a wide range of issues defined as 'environmental':
*   from issues involving the quality of peoples living environment * to fairly localised environmental health and safety issues
*   to issues relating to (global) sustainability; but also including such issues as cruelty to animals - and the 'greenness' of organisational culture or decision making style.

We explore the possibility of this ambiguity in definition leading to confusion, to the tackling of problems which may be of little or no ecological significance, even to collusion between change agents and clients on 'convenient' definitions of environment. For instance, one interviewee cited a large airline that focuses environmental discussion on noise (because it believes that problem can be solved) rather than on its contribution to global worming or upper atmosphere pollution. Particularly as many organisations are re-active rather than pro-active in facing environmental problems, and people find a great many pressures that keep environmental problems off the agenda.

Our interviewees discussed with us how to get sustainability, in particular, on the agenda, with the level and degree of change it implies. And what models might be applicable to this change process? From this discussion we suggest some components for a model for fundamental 'green change':

* the transition to sustainability is seen as part of a wider, more positive agenda, eg total quality management, long range strategic planning;
* the change agent as a variety of agencies playing a variety of roles, (rather than one person);
* the client system is seen as a complex web of groups, subgroups;
* in which specific behaviours may need to be changed (or substituted);
* but the underlying problems may be seen as an 'abuse', or 'painful condition', evolving, over time, in the context of a complex (internal and external) political system; with 'unspoken rules than cannot be challenged', in the words of Al Gore, which may need to be uncovered.

Gore is using the analogy of the family therapy process, which is based on systemic thinking. The management theories of Argyris, Senge and Stacey, derived from the same root, may be particularly helpful in emplaning organisational ecological abuse, and the difficulties of bringing about change.

We discuss the support, information access, specific training, and longer-term professional training, required by change agents involved in such a complex change process - and in the context of organisations whose cultures and climates are changing more rapidly, certainly more perceptibly, even than the climatic change which threatens life.

On the one hand, we suggest, change agents will require basic **informational clarity**: knowledge, or access to knowledge, in order to see the relevance and significance of a particular environmental issue, within a particular organisational context.

On the other hand, they need to be able to **live with total lack of clarity**: to be able to start where the client (and all its sub-systems) are, to appreciate the **breadth** of possible sustainability-related issues and the range of organisational contexts in which they might be raised - or not raised; and to appreciate **depth**: the complex historical organisational contexts in which environmental problems arise, the pressures that are likely to render problems 'undiscussable'.

So all the skills of management consultancy are required - particular those process consultancy skills required for intervention in the organisation facing very major change.

We discussed a range of options for pursuing the change process - all of which involve **collaborative teamwork**, over a **substantial period of time**, between people sharing responsibility for environmental action, whether primarily technical or 'people' specialists, whether within or without the organisation.

Full copies of the paper are available from:
Tony Emerson and Kamil Kellner,
South Bank University, London Road, London SE1 0AA

CO-DEPENDENCE IN CONSULTANCY: *FROM ENMESHMENT TO BOUNDARIES*

Hilary O'Donnell, *Cambio International, San Francisco, USA*

Whilst a significant body of writing and practice exists and continues to be developed on the subject of individual co-dependence, little exists on organisational co-dependence. This is an important workplace issue requiring further exploration, research and documentation because people living a co-dependent existence spend enormous energy dealing with the feelings which result from it. To exactly the extent they are so preoccupied, they lose mental, emotional and physical energy, with significant diminishment of the productive capacity that could be available to their employer. Co-dependence robs people, and the organisations they work in, of the best an employee has to offer. In addition, more needs to be discovered about the impact of co-dependence on the consulting relationship and the quality of consulting outcomes.

Co-dependence is a process addiction in which one person tries to control another (or him/herself) and to be responsible for the consequences of the behaviour of that other person. It results in enmeshment or overinvolvement of one person in the life of another where the former loses his/her own personality in the latter in some unhealthy manner. In the individual, it results when personal abuse, abandonment, neglect or enmeshment has been or is present.

In an organisation, the corollaries to the aforementioned personal causal conditions are depersonalisation, hierarchy, comparison and competition, poor communication patterns and lack of appreciation for whole life balance. Many, if not all, of these conditions are present in traditional, status, hierarchy and bureaucratic orientated and structured organisations. The feeling created by both sets of causal factors is shame. Thus, shame is the common denominator between personal and organisational co-dependence. Shame is defined as a feeling of constant, overwhelming inadequacy as a person. Shame, in turn causes people to feel violated, unworthy, unimportant. It is not difficult, therefore, to see the tremendous human potential lost when people are struggling with such powerful feelings on a regular and ongoing basis.

These feelings, in turn, drive behaviour which is characteristic in co-dependent organisations and can be observed in communication, interpersonal relations, management and decision-making style, organisation structure, customer relations and personnel processes and patterns. Since an organisation is a system, one would expect that every part of the system will show some symptoms of co-dependence if it is in operation anywhere in the system. One can observe in co-dependent organisations: control as the main mode of interpersonal relations, blaming, manipulation, competition, infighting amongst factions, power in the hands of a few (inner circle), lack of feedback, isolation from customers, crisis orientation, resistance to change, complex and paper-intensive procedures, focus on the logical and rational, indirect communication, gossip, secrets and confusion as a result of attempts at communication.

Examination of the causal factors for both personal and organisational co-dependence reveals that all are rooted in abuses of power which involve violation of boundaries. Thus the antidote to co-dependence is empowerment and creation of clear boundaries between the individual and the organisation. Although empowerment happens at the level of the individual, organisations can create dialogues, structures, and responses to facilitate and support individual empowerment. Organisational empowerment means moving decisions, authority, responsibility, skills and information to the lowest reasonable point in the organisation. Empowerment is a redistribution of power.

Consultants can assist organisational shifts to empowerment only to the degree that they are working on their own issues of co-dependence and empowerment. They also need to understand the nature and dynamics of process addictions and to understand and be able to work with systems change. Process addictions (co-dependence being one type thereof) are "burden shifting systems" in which the organisation opts for symptomatic solutions which gradually atrophy the ability to focus on the fundamental solution, over time weakening it, and increasing reliance on the symptomatic solution. This tends to produce periodic crises, followed by symptomatic solutions, then temporary relief accompanied by a weakening of the fundamental response. Over time, the basic ability to function is seriously impaired. If organisations continue to behave co-dependently, they can expect to bottom out just like any addict.

Leveraging effective change into these dynamics requires a combination of simultaneously strengthening the fundamental response and weakening the symptomatic response. Breaking this cycle requires long term orientation and a sense of vision as a starting point, backed by making decisions in the short term which are in concert with the support the long term. Simultaneously, one must resist the powerful pull to respond to the immediate situation or crisis as if it were an isolated instance and not a symptom of a larger pattern or system.

Unless consultants understand these dynamics and are working on the ways in which they personally "get hooked" into responding to and creating short term symptomatic "fixes", they will tend to respond to the presenting problem in a vacuum, thus compounding the addiction. Beyond that, one of the great tragedies of co-dependent organisations is that they make their members more and more debilitated over time. Thus, consultants who are working in these organisations will also become more and more debilitated.

The character of leaders, consultants and organisations is often revealed in their ability or inability to face into "shifting the burden" structures. As the expression goes, "It's difficult to remember to drain the swamp when you are up to your armpits in alligators". Refusing to respond to the immediate crisis and finding a way to "shift the burden" back to the fundamental response, which will have been weakened, is an act of courage and faith.

THE DYNAMICS OF LEARNING ABOUT MANAGEMENT:

THE IMPACT OF A PSYCHODYNAMIC APPROACH WITHIN A LOCAL GOVERNMENT MANAGEMENT DEVELOPMENT PROGRAMME.

RUSS VINCE
BRISTOL BUSINESS SCHOOL,BRISTOL.

ABSTRACT

This paper reflects on the experience of using a psychodynamic, group relations approach within the context of a Local Government Management Development Programme (MDP). The aim of the paper is to discuss how the approach makes it possible for managers to understand and work effectively with the management of change, both on a personal and an organisational level. The psychodynamic component of the course is a "large group" exercise which attempts to raise various key issues about management and organisational behaviour. The paper reflects on ten MDP courses over a period of five years, and discusses both the learning and the defenses to learning that have taken place. The paper considers the application of learning from the large group exercise into the organisation. It concludes that the large group work has succeeded in focusing the attention of managers on the processes that continually shape a changing organisation. This approach has had an impact on the culture of the authority, introducing managers to the processes that underlie their work; balancing the rationality and task obsessiveness of management; and stimulating engagement between individuals and groups. In this sense therefore it has promoted a potent understanding of what is involved in the management of change.

Full copies of the paper are available from:
Russ Vince, Bristol Business School,
Frenchay Campus, Coldharbour Lane, Bristol, BS16 1QY

A SMALL PARADIGM FOR CONSULTANCY PRACTICE

Bill Cooke, *Teeside Business School*

OVERVIEW

The basic theses of the paper are that

1) Much organisational consultancy, (organisation development, strategy implementation , TQM) carried out with large organisations, large in scale and ambitious in scope - "Big Consultancy" often fails to deliver practically.

2) The validity of such approaches is also called into question by the new perspectives on organisations, particularly those which, at the risk of oversimplifying question the unitarist (to use an industrial relations term) ideology implicit in much "Big" practice, and which try to set forth a more sophisticated understanding of the creation and sustaining of organisational realities.

3) Yet at the same time such perspectives are open to accusations of being at best voyeuristic - in that they are derived from observation and analysis, increasing our ability to understand but not to act - and at worst reactionary - in that they restrain and constrain our intervention in organisational realities, which however they are brought about are for their members nonetheless real.

4) An alternative, which may begin to acknowledge these practical and philosophical concerns is to adapt and develop a model of consultancy more typical of that carried out already by consultants working with small organisations - small businesses, voluntary organisations - "Small Consultancy". This might be applied in our work as consultants with large organisations in a literal sense - limiting the scale and scope of what we do - and in a metaphorical sense - for example, treating the consultancy that we do with large organisations as a series of small, discrete (a key word) projects.

5) The "Big" versus "Small" paradigm contrast (although it is more than a dichotomy) is important for the issues it seeks to address as well as the outcomes attributed to it. In other words even if it ultimately doesn't work, in reaching that conclusion we will have hopefullyarrived at a clearer understanding of what must inform our action as consultants.

BACKGROUND

The thesis has as its personal basis my own experience over the last five years - first as an internal Organisation Development Consultant with a well known large blue chip business, implementing TQM, Culture Change and Planning activities (or trying to), then as an external consultant to both small and large organisations, more recently combining that role with that of an academic in a Business School. That experience has been accompanied by a growing awareness of the issues and critiques derived from the perspectives alluded to above.

STRUCTURE

This outline structure represents the papaer as presented at the conference. In the light of that conference session, two subsequent papers are now being developed, both of which incorporate ideas from the original presentation. But the original was structured thus:

DEFINITIONS - The problems of defining "Big" and "Small" at a general level. At a consultancy level exploring definitions of Small that starts with organisation size in terms of people and develops to smallness being defined in terms of the closeness (organisationally) of the people with whom one is working to the person(s) with whom the original contract was made.

SMALL CONSULTANCY - Those distinctive elements of small organisation consultancy as it happens in this country which we can build into our model of more generic practice.

BIG CONSULTANCY - A contrasting model of archetypal big organisational consultancy.

THE PROBLEMS OF BIG CONSULTANCY - A presentation of the argument that there at least a prima facie case that Big consultancy is inherently problematic:

a)   in its own terms, whether it achieves what it sets out to do, if indeed that is ever clearly articulated

b)   in "objective" organisational terms whether the organisation benefits (eg whether it survives, in what state)

c)   from a philosophical perspective - in terms of consultancy as a would be constructor of organisational reality - where the question becomes, among other things "for whom is the consultancy working".

BIG IS SMALL (1) - THE SMALL ROOTS - The case that much which currently transpires as Big consultancy has in any case developed from archetypal Small approaches (in scope and or ambition - eg group interventions such as team development on a cross corporate scale) but which fails because it does not adopt the Small model of practice in its entirety.

BIG IS SMALL (2) - THE SMALL PRESENT - A presentation of a model of Small consultancy practice with large organisations

a)   anticipating the benefits of working in this way in practical, pragmatic terms.

b)   responding the need to examine the philosophical developments already mentioned.

SMALL PRACTICE - THE SMALL FUTURE- A concluding discussion of the benefits and drawbacks to consultants of trying to make a living as a "Small Consultant"

Full copies of the paper are available from:
Bill Cooke, Senior Lecturer, Teesside Business School, University of Teesside
Flatts Lane,Middlebrough, TS6 OQS

CLOSING SESSION
REVIEW

The closing session focussed on the dynamics and process of the conference as a temporary learning organisation. **Dr. Eric Miller** of the Tavistock Institute, who agreed to act as a participant-observer and a consultant to the conference, presented his observations of the event from his role.

OBSERVATIONS OF THE CONFERENCE

Dr Eric Miller, *The Tavistock Institute*

I had a curious feeling just as I came across to the podium: an image of a guillotine. I think this image of the guillotine may have to do with my awareness of things I have done wrong – my sins of omission and commission as a consultant over the years. I have been struck over the last two days by the amount of emphasis on how successful this or that was, and I was quite reassured this morning by Bill Critchley saying that actually it's possible to learn from experience and to change your mind. So what I was finding in myself just now was guilt about my failures to learn from experience, for which I evidently deserved punishment!

Let me give an example of this. A few months ago the Chief Executive of an organization came to see me and said what he wanted done was a brief organizational diagnosis. Now that sounded very attractive to me. Many years ago the head of a large research department in a major chemical company invited me to see him. He said they were doing extremely well, but they didn't know *why* they were doing so well: would I investigate and tell them? Now this was one of the most engaging assignments I had ever had. So when, a few months ago, this Chief Executive approached me, I was obviously attracted to the idea of spending a couple of days or so, during which I might initially sit in on the whole group and hear what they had to say, interviews and discussions with individuals and sub-groups, and then come up with some reflections and a diagnosis.

I made two mistakes. First of all, I said "Yes" far too quickly. I don't know if anyone else suffers from this problem. My analyst and I never quite worked it out, but I think it probably goes back to early infancy: if the breast is on offer, you take it, otherwise it may disappear forever! As a result of saying "yes" too quickly I made the second mistake: I assumed I knew roughly how big the organization was, and failed to check it out. The problem was that when I actually came along to sit in on the initial meeting of the whole group, I discovered that there were about four hundred people... So that is how I come to be here!

Of course, the role I chose to take means that I had no paper prepared in advance. On the one hand, that was quite a relief; but having to produce something with minimal time for preparation can generate quite a lot of anxiety.

So what do I bring to this role? I certainly bring my own values, which are part of my consultancy, that have to do with respect for the individual; encouraging, enabling people to exercise their own authority. This is a central theme of the Group Relations Programme which has been running for many years at The Tavistock Institute. Making proper use of 'human resources' is the term used nowadays; they were called 'people' when I was younger. I also bring a kind of conceptual baggage, carried in the back of my mind rather than in the forefront. A central concept is the primary task which enables one to compare the overt primary task which the organization is set up to perform with the tasks it is actually performing. That is set in the context of the organization as an open system, with inputs of raw materials and people, some kind of conversion process, and outputs. I also bring a psychodynamic perspective which means that when one thinks about such an organization one is thinking not only "How well does the organization carry out the task it's explicitly set up to perform?" but "What other latent tasks is it performing and how well is it performing those?" – the notion that organizations also serve as defences for those who work in them. Finally, I bring with me a socio-technical perspective. I believe it is extremely important to understand, or try to understand, the technology of an organization and the critical points at which that impacts on the human, social system.

A long time ago, one of my colleagues at The Tavistock Institute (who is here) was describing some work she was doing with a manufacturer of confectionery: sweets, toffees, and so on. In order to understand the technology she said to the manager she was interviewing, "Imagine I'm a grain of sugar, what would happen to me in this process?" Once one had got past the idea that she could look like a grain of sugar, in fact that was a very useful way of exploring technology: what happens to what goes through it in the conversion process. I was thinking that the process engaged in here was not unlike sugar refining. We had an initial situation of some four hundred granules of sugar, which were assembled in a warehouse. There they were packaged and labelled. (Some of them unfortunately were delivered to the wrong address.[1] They were then brought onto the factory floor in order to have hot air blown into them. (Some were processed in a separate annexe[2] – I'm not sure what the hot air felt like over there!) They were then separated into small clumps, and then other small clumps and ground up very finely, in an iterative process of blowing hot air and grinding, until ultimately every grain is separated, purified, polished, refined. I worked out – probably wrongly; my statistics are not very good – that the chances of any two grains surviving together throughout the process was about six thousand four hundred to one, against. But odd grains do tend to cling together I find! There has also, unfortunately, in this process, been a loss of some of these granules – I see some empty seats here in the auditorium and I don't know if there's anyone over there in the annexe or not at this stage!

We don't really know whether the purification process has been successful or not and may not know for a long time. I'll come back to that notion of purification. So the overt primary task of this enterprise is "to give participants" (if I'm quoting correctly) "opportunities to enhance their understanding and competence" in this field of consultancy.

So what is the input here? What are the raw materials? One question is why are there so many of us, and I'm sure it's not just through marketing (or Kamil Kellner's arm-twisting). What motivates people to be here? One thing is clear: there are more consultants around. It seems to be a very rapidly expanding occupation with many more ex-managers coming out of industry and commerce and becoming consultants. If one extrapolates the trend, soon consultants will be outnumbering managers: that should be quite an interesting stage. Also, of course, we have more solo consultants, with, I think, in many cases, attendant problems of isolation. Particularly if you are a solo consultant, there are the constant nagging questions: "Am I doing it right?", "Are others doing it differently, or better?", "Do they have tricks that I don't have?"

Two or three years ago, Tony Berry (Manchester Business School) and myself, with one or two others, organized a weekend conference for thirty or so people in the consultancy field. One of the things that struck me then was the question whether consultancy really is a craft, or is it a profession? It felt that for many of us, myself included, it was actually still largely a craft in the sense that we had been self-taught, or maybe apprenticed in the proper way in which craft people are developed, yet we were on the way to becoming a profession. (A small plug here: The Tavistock Institute runs the Advanced Organizational Consultation Programme, which is very much concerned with making a shift to greater professionalism of the consultant role.) So there is that uncertainty of being on the boundary of a craft and a profession.

Another thing that is happening is that our clients, generally, are getting a lot smarter, and as someone was saying to me this morning, "They are actually talking about the same issues as we are – the more sophisticated ones. They are maybe using slightly different languages but they are pre-occupied with the same issues". So the problem is also getting more complex and, as Ralph Stacey pointed out, the pace of change is becoming, in some areas, exponential with all the uncertainties and unpredictabilities which that brings. So that is attracting people here, and in particular, a search for a deeper understanding of change. We have heard that the learning organization is still important, but that, on the other hand, we may be moving on to the un-learning organization. So where do we go next?

The other attraction may lie within the title of this Conference: the word 'dynamics' may have been significant; it seems to be catching on. (Related to that, someone kindly suggested to me the hypothesis that really Eric Miller was the great attraction for the Conference; that's why people are here. However, given the number of people who are *not* here this afternoon, that hypothesis is falsified!)

One interesting motivation that has struck me, talking to people over the last two days, is (as one person put it) "I didn't want *not* to be here". I thought that was quite telling: not so much wanting to be here as not wanting not to be here, as though they were going to miss something. I had a notion of an underlying fantasy that there would be some revelation of the kind that our clients seem to be asking us for all the time. And that may link to the image of becoming refined and purified.

If that is the input of this Conference, what is the latent primary task? What can we understand about that? Certainly, it has something to do with opportunities for networking: this seems to have been very important. But beyond that, what this organization is called upon to do, is to meet some very varying individual needs and anxieties, and these have produced, and possibly still are producing, some quite complex dynamics. The big anxiety that I pick up, is the anxiety of discovering that I am less competent than I thought I was. What then is coming in with the input, the raw materials in this system? There is a wish to learn, undoubtedly, with the complication that that puts one in the student role, which implies dependency. I resist dependency; I don't want to be dependent; I resent it; it's a threat to my identity; I need to assert my competence... And so one gets challenge and fight. We share the role of participants, but at the same time we are competitors. Some of us are competing for the same clients in the same sectors. And so one has rivalry and a lot of envy. So these are the kind of dynamics that I see being brought in to this temporary organization.

The form of the organization for performance of the overt task has been quite neat. We have concepts and methods introduced by keynote speakers. There are parallel sessions with various choices in whatever we want to specialize in, with opportunities for both inputs and interaction. And there are the review groups for reflection and application. Intentionally or not of course, the organization is also designed to provide defences against anxieties relating to these complex dynamics, to provide psychological containment, and to meet basic dependency needs, including food. I seem unusual in having only one bodyguard here; most speakers have had two or three bodyguards, presumably to protect them against envious attack. So far the voice from the floor has been controlled out. Of course the review groups have provided much more room for individuality – indeed, for individualization, for people to become what they want to become. They have also served to contain any anger or competitiveness and prevent it from spilling over into the system as a whole.

So how has it actually worked? My own feelings are always important to me in undertaking a consultancy activity like this one. What I have felt is that I am supposed somehow to integrate the unintegratable, which is not an unfamiliar expectation placed on us as consultants. But alongside the experience of very high expectations I have also had a sense of being irrelevant. So it was a mixed transference to me. At the same time, I have also been sharing some of the membership experience: for example, very much valuing networking (and also becoming highly embarrassed at forgetting someone's name!). In the first twenty-four hours I also shared the experience of feeling lost, forgetting where I was just now, or where I was going: too many choices, all too much, wanting to withdraw and find a corner. Interestingly, when my wife and I went home and played a game of Scrabble on Friday night, we both found ourselves with all sorts of potential words that just wouldn't quite fit on the board. Except for the contradictory transference, which did confuse me a bit, this kind of experience is not unusual to me – or, I'm sure, to you – in engaging in a consultancy. I feel it is my task to absorb what is coming to me in terms both of hard data and of soft data like this, and to avoid premature generalization and crystallization. It is also very important to me to find space on my own to ruminate. (If anyone saw me coming from the pub over the road yesterday, what I had been doing was ruminating!) In that way we discover some of the complexity of conflicting dynamics that may have been engaging us.

By yesterday evening, through observations and discussions and from what I had picked up from meeting with the facilitators of the review groups, I had a sense of what I would call 'failed dependency', of people going to the wrong address.

Yesterday, they were complaining about lack of leadership, feeling crowded, part of a herd, and pushed around; being exploited; and a sense of a neglect of the individual. Then there was the tantalizing choice of workshops: how do I choose one out of fifteen? What have I missed? A lot of envy was also floating around. There was appreciation nevertheless of being able to opt in or out of the workshops but resentment at actually being assigned to review groups with "all sorts of incompatible people". Some of the review groups yesterday threw up a lot of ambivalences, with splitting: the theoretical versus the practical; process versus technical content; for or against the psychoanalytic approach. There was talk about "people in the other camp". I was interested in reactions to Ralph Stacey's contribution, for example: one set of people saying it was really stimulating and another saying they "didn't understand a bloody word". That is the kind of splitting that seems to be around.

Also in the review groups yesterday, and more generally, in the parallel sessions, I picked up a persistent competitiveness. There has been 'fight': facilitators in review groups have not been physically attacked, but put under very considerable critical scrutiny. I understand there was nearly an actual fight in one parallel session, but I was never able to discover which one it was. We also had 'flight' in that some people were skipping their review groups and others were fleeing away from the whole enterprise. There were other themes around in yesterday's review groups too: for example there was death – perhaps an anticipation of today's ending. The variety made me question Petrushka Clarkson's version of 'microcosm' – the notion of each part as a miniature representation of the whole: I got a sense amongst the review groups of a great many different parts of the whole being distributed and acted out in different locations. However, in last night's game of Scrabble we scored very well and we both got seven letter words: it was tremendous! Maybe integration was beginning to happen.

Moving onto this morning, I want to give you one quote that captured something for me: "It is scary to be with someone who has a different perspective that might have value." I personally found Bill Critchley's contribution enormously reassuring and I think others did too. He told us that it is OK to change your mind. You could have been into something five years ago and then realize that perhaps it was not now appropriate. Today, I am seeing an increasing emergence of splinter groups (or maybe "new creative configurations"!): a sense of people going off into small groups – and some of them in review group time – to make new relationships that may continue after the conference.

Overall, one thing that has bothered me, and I think others, is an assumption, that we are smarter than those managers out there; almost as though that is the basis of our identity as consultants. It may offer some reassurance, but I believe it is dangerous. Undoubtedly some managers are insensitive and obtuse, but we would be very unwise to underestimate the grasp and concern that many of them have for the kinds of issues that we are looking at here.

One other observation on the way we relate to clients, which I find reaffirming of my own picture of myself and my consultant role, is linked to what Jean Neumann was saying yesterday morning, about the possibility of the consultant/

client relationship becoming one of "mutual engagement". This connects with what I was saying about integration. We can't integrate the unintegratable, but I think it *is* possible for the individual consultant actually to have quite a repertoire of knowledge, concepts, skills and ways of operating which can be deployed in different ways, in different settings and at different stages in the consultant relationship. To use a word that has been around quite a lot, it means thinking about the consultant role as being "emergent". Millie Banerjie, on the first evening, talking about her experience as a client, made me think of about Winnicott describing how the baby teaches the mother how to become a mother. Similarly, we must allow our clients to teach us how to become consultants in relation to them.

I will simply conclude by saying that it has been a difficult two days for me. I have got quite a lot out of it; I hope you have. One thing that was reaffirmed for me, partly by what Larry Hirschhorn was saying yesterday, and also Bill Critchley today, that change is going to happen anyway and maybe the smart consultant is one who identifies the change that is ready to happen and takes the credit for it!

[1] A reference to confusion over the location of this conference: many participants initially went to the wrong address.

[2] Overflow lecture theatre with video.

CONCLUSIONS AND FUTURE DEVELOPMENTS

Kamil Kellner, *South Bank Business School, London*

The conference is now over and we have completed our primary task. As a temporary organisation we have reviewed our work, and are considering how we use our learnings from this experience.

As conference organisers, and it was our first conference, we have learnt a lot. (The feedback from both delegates and contributors has been very valuable, and it is summarised in Appendix 3.) We have also been delighted with the many offers of contribution to the development and implementation of another conference of this kind.

It seems that we have identified and (temporarily) met a need for a forum where practising consultants of different theoretical orientations to learn with and from each other. South Bank University will be considering the proposals listed below for meeting this need on a more permanent basis.

The Second International Consulting Conference

It has been heartening to have received so many offers of help with and contributions to the next conference, therefore there is a proposal for this to happen in Spring 1996. We would like the theme, focus and organisation of the conference to emerge from a planning conference in Autumn 1994, to which all those who wish to contribute will be invited. There will be many opportunities for being involved in various roles - planning, organising, marketing, sponsorship, facilitating, contributing, editing....

Centre for Organisational Consulting

The interest in the conference suggests that there is a need for a more permanent forum for learning, debate, research in the arena of organisational consulting. South Bank Business School will be conducting a feasibility study into developing a Centre for Organisational Consulting at the University.

Masters Programme in Organisational Consulting

Consultancy as a professional activity is growing and developing, yet there is at present no recognised professional qualification for organisational and management consultants. Currently Institute of Management Consultants is exploring a continuous development programme, National Vocational Qualification Council is considering a competence scheme for consultants, Tavistock Institute of Human

438

Relations has recently launched an Advanced Organisational Consulting Programme. South Bank Business School will be developing a new MSc. in Organisational Consulting to link with and build on the current initiatives in consultants' development.

We would welcome offers of collaboration on these proposals from both individuals and organisations.

THE LEARNING REVIEW GROUPS

Roger Casemore, *Kasmore Consulting*

The conference planning team decided at an early stage, that as part of the structure of the conference they would provide an opportunity for every participant to spend time in a facilitated Learning Review Group. This would provide participants with opportunities for self-reflection, integration of conference experiences application of the learning to the participants' own consulting practices. For my sins in pushing for this idea, I was asked to take on the task of designing and managing this part of the conference process. This chapter contains a description of the approach that was developed, an outline of the briefing that was given to Review Group Facilitators and some extracts from some of the reports that the facilitators produced after the conference.

The rationale behind the review groups was taken from my experience in the field of educating adults and my strong belief that it is important to pay as much attention to the process or dynamics of the learning situation as to the content of learning itself. In order to enable individual learners to focus on their own internal dynamics whilst they are in a learning experience, it is important to provide them with the right conditions in which this can occur. As this conference was intending to focus on the dynamics of consultancy, it seemed essential to give participants the opportunity to consider the dynamics of the conference and of their learning within it.

It was my view that as this was an adult learning experience, the Review Groups should be based on educational assumptions that might be different to those which are commonly used as the basis for learning. These assumptions were taken from studies of the work of Paulo Freire[1] and developed with a group of colleagues at Nottingham University[2]. I produced a briefing pack encapsulating my own approach to working with adult learning groups which would form the basis for working with the Learning review groups.

The Planning Group then set about recruiting the required number of facilitators who we thought would be able to work effectively in this way, or adapt it to fit their own style of working. Through using our own contacts on the Conference Planning Team we managed to identify some 28 individuals who agreed to work in this way and to attend a briefing/training session on the afternoon preceding the conference. Life being what it is on the last day we suddenly found ourselves having to recruit an extra four facilitators but somehow, we managed to do that in time for the start of the briefing session!

The briefing pack which is included at the end of this chapter, had been circulated to the possible facilitators to enable them to identify if they could work in this way. Recognising the level of work that I would now be carrying throughout the conference, Steve Moss another member of the Planning group offered to provide me with some support in working with the Facilitators. He and I then started the conference working by running a briefing session for the facilitators. In doing this I set out to model the way that I was suggesting they should work. We spent some two hours with the group of 30 facilitators, testing out the process and giving them permission to amend it to suit their own styles and skills. We agreed a contract with them about the way we wanted them to work and the support we would provide This included several support sessions for them as a group, at critical stages during the conference and a final debriefing session at then end after everyone else had left.

Some 21 brief reports were received from facilitators during the next few weeks which offered some fascinating insights into their experience and the dynamics of the conference. it was clear that for many of the participants the Learning Review Group process had added considerable value to the conference providing containment, the opportunity for reflection and growth and a means of heightening their learning. The following extracts are intended to portray some of that flavour.

Extracts from the reports of the Review Group Facilitators

Review Group 27 - Teresa Howard

In the first sessions we found ourselves lost on the limitless sea on the edge of chaos. any attempt to get people to reflect on this powerful image made them feel dropped into the abyss. Instead there was a desperate need to ward off anxiety either by competing or by withdrawing into angry silence. attempts by me to ground the group in the here and now of what people were feeling failed.

The theme of whether to deal with the process of the group or to discuss the content of the presentations continued through to the last session, when one member presented us with an ultimatum. "Either talk about this morning's presentation or I will leave". he left because the group did not respond to his proposal quickly enough. Others felt that we were spinning off into too much high level theory which had no applicability to the world that they were working in.

my experience tells me that when people need to polarise into irreconcilable opposites they are having to deal with intolerable anxiety which they are unable to contain. it is safer to stay with a perspective of the world that has always been held. the Review group it seems to me, brought us all up against our most powerful prejudices and for some this situation was intolerable. Given the provocative nature of some of the material presented by the key note speakers, it was imperative that safe places were provide to explore these unsafe issues. To be launched into the idea that the most creative place to be was on the edge of uncertainty on a limitless sea of chaos, at the beginning of the conference, without a safe boat, was almost beyond tolerance for most of us. In the last session several people talked about the will power they needed to stay with the group but felt that the effort had been rewarded. These people had earlier experiences that told them it was important to stick it out.

As a facilitator with a lot of experience, this was one of the most difficult groups I have encountered. mainly because the environment for our discussion had to be constantly prepared for both in the physical and the emotional sense.

Review Group 12 - Jean Woollard
The content of the group sessions was usually suggested by the member's most recent experience at the conference. People shared their thoughts and to a lesser degree their feelings about sessions that they had attended, relating these to their own experiences as consultants. There was some, but not much, attention paid to our own group process. as the trust between people grew within the group, members were able to disclose more personal information and to express their personal concerns as consultants.. Some of the issues we covered were:

- Chaos versus stability - It is OK to want some stability in our lives and work? Is it OK to aim for a balance?

- Our integrity as consultants - Doing what we believe is right despite the potential loss of income.

- What if any, are the boundaries between therapy and consulting? are there two distinct camps as represented at the conference?

- Destruction versus creation - is there a need for both? Can we acknowledge both impulses in ourselves and what does this mean for our work?

I can't say what other people learned but it did seem that learning was taking place. I know that I learned that it was important to strike a subtle balance between leading the group and participating within it as an equal member. I trusted my intuition and hope that what I chose to do and chose not to do worked!

Review Group 9 - Joe Walsh
The question of contracting into the group and establishing ground rules was raised and quickly decided against by the group.. However throughout the discussion the question of the contract - client/consultant, group member/group was continually referred to. The contract as an event was contrasted to the continuous activity of seeking clarification and feedback, of negotiating an appropriate relationship. In general the issue caused some irritation and undoubtedly was a vehicle for feelings of ambivalence and risk.

By the third day, discussion was animated and included a lot of personal sharing relating parallel session themes to work problems. Task and process issues were discussed with no reference to the original splitting and avoidance of that terminology on the first day. There were considerable personal contributions about personal feelings and dysfunctional, task avoidance, dynamics within the work setting.

A participant who had initially expressed anger at the process consultancy model, subsequently identified values in this approach which he had not previously seen. Another participant who had expressed great cynicism initially began to acknowledge that she had been avoiding difficult feelings and recognised that managing these was an aspect of the consultant's task which should be tackled rather than seen as a distraction to be avoided.

Review Group 19 - David Lawler
On the whole feedback from the group was positive. I felt that I was able to work with the experience that participants were having of the conference and this did further participants' ability to learn. There was a split between "psychodynamic" consultants and the "management " consultants which did not get worked through or understood fully, but this was due more to lack of time than willingness.

Review group 17 - Alan Turkie
I felt the review group concept to be a very good one. I experienced it for the majority of group members as a "holding" mechanism in the wider mêlée of the busy conference schedule. it provided an intimate setting and also offered continuity and a sense of "home team".

Review Group 20 - Colleen Homan
As the title of the conference concerned itself with understanding the dynamics of consultancy, I was surprised by some of the Review Group's members"surprise" that others wanted a space to explore dynamics within both the consulting relationship and the Review group itself.

The review group began with members splitting and refusing to work together in a large group. References to past experiences of "group therapy" were made which appeared to indicate the fears and fantasies of working in a large group. Working with these emergent issues created a new opportunity from which to learn. as this learning space was created the fight/flight dissipated and dependency emerged. Competition between the members was present and the role of the facilitator was constantly challenged. By Sunday the group felt safe enough for members to begin to challenge each other in a more constructive fashion.

Family life became a metaphor for process issues, with the emotion "love" within the consulting relationship being explored. This led to an exploration of the needs for individual support/ supervision in consultancy practice and issues of professionalism and accountability were salient. Feedback from the parallel papers and workshops was of limited value. However all the group agreed that the process involved in our working together had been a greater learning experience than the accounts of the academic content of different papers.

Review Group 5 - Lynn Macwhinnie
It may have been better if the Review Groups had followed the Keynote speakers which would have given an immediacy for questions and discussion as there was not the opportunity to do so directly with the speakers. None the less the group felt that the inclusion of the Review groups had provided an oasis in the proceedings, giving welcome time for integration, processing and networking. Comments included: integrity of consultant, professional rivalries, defences (microcosm and

macrocosm), fragmentation, values conflict, "fit"/harmonization, commitment, financial security, splitting of the task and process.

It was felt that any loss of diversity would be sad, although the emphasis on psychodynamics appeared to exclude pragmatic content. However there was an appreciation of the intellectual stimulus - " a smorgasbord of icons" was one comment.

The Review groups briefing pack was useful in creating a focus and the Facilitator Support Sessions were helpful in establishing the flexibility of the framework, thereby giving permission to interpret that according to the wishes of the Group and my own approach.

Review Group 23 - Bruce Lloyd

The first group meeting began with introductions from the seven participants and there appeared to be general mutual respect. Although there was little formal discussion of the ground rules, these seemed to be implicit and I was allowed to play a reasonably proactive role as facilitator, particularly over ensuring that everyone participated and on time keeping. Some of the content issues raised were:

- The need for more communication between psychodynamic professionals and others (ie practical/client driven consultants).

- There was some division between those who were primarily confected with changing the organisation, while others felt that it was more important to start (and end?) with changing individuals.

- It was valuable to exchange experiences on the client/consultant relationship.

In general it was felt that the content and process of the Conference, and the review Sessions were both enjoyable and useful.

Review Group 5 - Ron Metcalfe

The Group gelled and began to work together fairly quickly and easily. Disagreements and outbursts were dealt with in a matter of fact way and without the group becoming polarised. The group was able to act as a container for feelings and members were able to allow others their different points of view.

There were no deep or painful issues to work with, but this was not a "Group Relations" event looking at weighty unconscious processes. On the other hand, the group did begin to work together in a mature way and some intimacy had developed by Sunday.

I think it was important that I had not provided too strong or structured an initial lead. All members seemed to be experienced in groups and comfortable enough with my fairly non-directive role and occasional process commentary.

Review Group 9 - Jane Hicks

Instead of writing my version/opinion of what had happened during the Review group process, I took the opportunity of asking the members what they felt should go into a review of the proceedings. Their opinions were as follows:

There was agreement that the Review group had been a good place to hear about what had been going on over a range of parallel sessions during the conference. there was so much going on that people had felt worried about "missing" things. At least the Review groups gave them an opportunity to share different experiences.

In addition the review group became a "Home Group" - a more comfortable place to be in the midst of the conference hubbub (mayhem?). Somebody said "Even consultants are social animals" Expressing a view that the review group was a necessary place to reconnect with known faces.

The Review group was a place where people could start to think about, to digest, some of what they had heard. It "kept us here" (Grounded us) as someone stated.

There was agreement that the group should not be "led", that some chaos or uncertainty should be expected and endured.

finally someone said that the review group was an ideal way to hold the conference together - at which point someone else said "Ideal? For Whom?". Which in a nutshell says it all really!

Review Group 28 - Gail Dyos

The life of this review Group appears to have followed a not untypical early client and consultant relationship. initial attempts to connect focused on external pressures which were followed by obvious tensions created as client and consultant explored who they were, the best possible approach and the contract.

Interpersonal dynamics, recognised as potentially difficult were put aside later in favour of organisational problem solving. It was safer to use difficulties with the environment as an indirect scapegoat in favour of confronting each other. Finally in exploring global pressures and the preoccupation with resourcing, it seems that the client's underlying concern was to get on with the business of the consultancy task in hand, whilst the underlying anxiety for the consultant was to ensure prompt payment of fees in spite of the tensions between them

Review group 26 - Phil Mix

For me there are at least three lessons in all of this.

1   When using a review group mechanism with professional colleagues, keep the sessions predictably short. Forty five minutes was just right. expectations of intimacy are necessarily limited, yet important things can be said.

2   Once individuals decide that they may have the makings of a group (ie sufficient clarity about needs, context, possible tasks and time available) progress through the group formation cycle is inevitable. I suppose I've known this for years, but it was quite exciting to re-learn it!

3   The best way to facilitate a group of professional colleagues is by being clear and open in acknowledging that the facillitator's perceptions of the needs of the group are no more than projections of his/her own needs. This allows the facillitator to be experienced as professionally competent by the group.

Conclusion

For me these extracts reveal something of the richness of the learning experience for the participants and something of the struggle that they experienced. It reinforces my beleif in the importance of paying equal attention to both the process of learning and the content - and that is something that I believe more consultants should pay attention to.

REFERENCES

[1]   **Freire, Paulo** - Pedagogy of the Oppressed - New York: Herder and Herder 1970

[2]   **Nottingham Andragogy Group** - Towards a Developmental Theory of Andragogy - University of Nottingham , Department Of Adult Education - 1983

REVIEW GROUPS BRIEFING NOTE

The Review Groups have a number of purposes, within the overall purposes of the conference.The Review Groups are intended to provide a supportive small group environment which will offer participants an opportunity to:

1   Focus on their own internal dynamics as consultants.

2   Reflect on the inputs and workshop sessions and how those experiences have impacted on them.

3   Integrate the various experiences they are having at the conference.

4   Assess their learnings from the conference.

5   Consider how they might apply the learnings from the conference to their own consultancy practice.

6   Share their individual personal concerns about the stresses they experience in their work as consultants.

7   Use the dynamic process within the Review Group as further learning material.

It is important to remember that there is no "right" agenda for the review groups. Their purpose is to meet the needs of the participants in each small group. It is also essential to remember that the dynamic process in the Review Group (or what is happening in the group and the way that people in it treat each other and relate to each other) is of equal importance to the content of discussions. The role of the facilitator is to enable that process to happen.

RUMINATION: SOME POST-CONFERENCE REFLECTIONS FROM A DELEGATE

David Wasdell
Unit for Research into Changing Institutions (URCHIN), London

So what does make consultancy work? That all depends on what you mean by "Work". Desired outcome drives the evaluative framework within which the underlying dynamics can be understood and assessed. Where definitions of desired outcome are themselves in conflict, the same consultancy exercise may be subject to a wide variety of judgement ranging from "It worked brilliantly!" to "It was an unmitigated and destructive disaster!". A smoothly collaborative engagement between consultant and client may be seen from a different perspective as a dysfunctional exercise in collusion, reinforcing the defences of the management and encouraging the scapegoating of some of the most creative elements of the organisation.

A retrospective evaluation of the conference is subject to similar difficulty. The question "Did it work?" depends for answer on the intended outcome. The definition of outcome depends in turn on the perspective of the person or group concerned and in any case the outcome definition is likely to be complex and "fuzzy". The conference itself was an extremely complex and fuzzy event so any overall evaluation is likely to be to simplistic. The backgrounds, needs and current level of understanding and competence differed from each participant, as did the experience of the conference as a whole. The distillation of reflexive evaluation from this primeval soup of meaning is inevitably an exercise in subjective creativity. It offers an interplay between the reality of the conference and the autobiography, selectivity and projected fantasy of the author.

The conference can be described as a model organisation. It had an entrepreneurial founder who identified a market niche and brought together a management group. In order to realise its task it negotiated a relationship with a host institution which took the financial risk and profit and provided accommodation and support staff. The product was marketed and potential customers identified. A group of professionals was recruited to deliver the product within a pre-planned organisational framework. Management engaged a consultant to help them optimize performance.

The advertised product which attracted so many customers and for which they paid was a combination of information and insight: answers to the question "What makes consultancy work?" and deeper understanding of the dynamics in play. Product was delivered to the customers via the conduct of a two-day educational event involving plenary lectures, parallel-track workshops and small review groups. At another level the process of the conference as a whole provided opportunities for experiential learning about the dynamics of consultancy as each person took up a member role within a temporary organisation undergoing consultant input.

An examination of the processes, structures, boundaries, dynamics, implicit assumptions, emergent symbols and underlying paradigm of the conference provides a rich range of alternatives which could be woven in to the fabric of any future event of its kind. The cognitive framework, organisational design and operating procedures of any learning system provide both the facilitating environment and the boundary constraints of the learning possible within that system. At a deeper level the dominant anxiety defences and the collusionalmechanisms to which they give rise set the limits of tolerance beyond which the learning raises too much anxiety and is repressed, both individually and corporately.

The opening invitation was to explore and integrate the theory and practice of consultancy at a dynamic level in a process of double-loop learning, within the dynamics of the conference as a whole. One of the marks of effective learning systems is the high quality of community within which the learning takes place. The planning group gave some evidence of formation as a learning community over the nine months from conception to delivery of the conference but almost no attention was given to the task of community formation of the total conference membership. As a result learning was essentially individual. Except in the review groups (of which more anon), interaction between members was minimal. Even interaction between members and presenters was prohibited in the plenary sessions. Passive listening generates minimal learning. Increasing the quality of learning calls for frequent opportunities for interaction with peers, articulation, questioning, challenging, developing new ideas and testing out their relevance to practical working situations.

Then there is the issue of learning styles. Verbal learning is not the only model. Dominant learning mode is different for different people. It may also be visual, activity-based or emotive. Indeed current research into the most effective processes of communication indicates the necessity for integrating all four dimensions of words, images, actions and feelings. A few presenters did use the overhead projector, but only to display words (even though one presenter called them "pictures"!). The almost exclusive verbal dominance created an impoverished learning environment which could have been so much more effective. The ancient Chinese proverb: "I hear and I forget, I see and I remember, I do and I understand" can be enlarged to include "I feel and it becomes part of me".

The university setting within which the conference took place provided a powerful if largely unexamined framework for the learning experience, with its lectures, seminars and tutor-groups. One of the unexamined polarities was between teachers and students, knowers and learners. It offered a dependence culture which separated the ignorant from the wise. Paying customers were presumed to be the learners who needed to know what makes consultancy work and to understand its dynamics. Management and presenters were presumed to be the experts providing the answers for which the customers had paid. That may be a simplistic parody of what was going on but does raise questions about the existential integrity of the conference as a learning system. There was an immense reservoir of practical competence and theoretical understanding among the conference members which went almost untapped. Far from offering role-models of fast-track learning, learning rates appeared to drop off rapidly in proportion to the significance of position within the conference organisation.

Perhaps a future conference can seek to avoid the collusion with immature dependence needs and move towards a more mature adult inter-dependency. The resources of all participants need to be recognised and utilised to the full, while the conference culture as a whole would reflect the reality of a gathering of professionals working and learning together to expand the boundaries of understanding and to make more conscious those dynamic processes which remain unconscious even in the practice of the most competent.

The image of "knowers' Ark" emerged in one workshop as a refuge from drowning in the sea of uncertainty. Certainly there was a shift in the rescuer fantasy from consultancy as offering answers to the question "What shall we do?" to consultancy as providing meaning in the midst of chaos and unpredictability. The rescuer fantasy persists albeit in a different context. If the task of the consultant in conditions of turbulence and chaos is to enable managers "To know what to do when they do not know what to do", then presumably one task of the conference was to meet the same need in the gathered group of customers. Consultancy as revelation is still seduction into immature dependency in which Knower and his family provide a container for the anxieties of the population, reduced to animals in a pairing culture, to be carriedsecurely through the storms of chaos and landed safely on the South Bank when the threatening waters have begun to recede. Fascinatingly in the final plenary, the conference chairman introduced the conference consultant as having the task "To contain our experience".

As a temporary educational system, the primary task of the conference was the imparting of knowledge about the dynamics of consultancy from presenters to customers. Although learning was taking place as an implicit part of the task, that does not qualify the conference as itself a learning system. Single-loop learning would have required mechanisms for examining the way the task of the conference was being carried out together with effective feed-back loops which changed and enhanced the task performance as it was happening. No such mechanisms appeared to be in place. Indeed the procedures of the conference seemed to militate against any possibility of effective feed-back.

For the conference to operate as a double-loop learning system there would have had to be a second level of procedures which monitored and changed those mechanisms by which the task performance was itself being monitored and evolved. The anxieties of the planning group appeared to be so high that all such procedures were positively suppressed. One early presenter identified avoidance of double-loop learning as evidence of a collusional relationship between consultant and client, so it is likely that the anxiety defences of the customers were also too intense to tolerate participation in an effective double-loop learning system. Triple-loop learning could not even be conceptualised within the conference culture.

One structure did offer some potential as a learning system. All participants had the regular opportunity to work in a review group with eleven other customers and a facilitator. The twenty-seven facilitators also met as a group which was attended by the consultant to the planning group. One member of the planning group worked as a review-group facilitator. Presenters were not involved. When asked, the conference convenor described the function of this structure as one of "monitoring, since the structures and procedures of the conference were fixed in advance on reflection as a defence against input from the large number of 'aggressive' consultants". The conference consultant had no input to the conference as a whole until after all its formal proceedings had been completed. It is hardly surprising that his initial fantasies were of decapitation by guillotine or execution by firing squad. Sadly it would seem that the corporate paranoia of the planning group in collusion with presenters, facilitators, customers and consultant, aborted all possibility of running the conference as a model learning system.

In a negative kind of way the situation did offer an opportunity to explore the dynamics of consultancy since these powerful defences and intensely collusional processes are endemic in the consultant-client interaction. It was unfortunate that such learning had to take place in spite of the formal structures of the conference.

The analogy of the sugar refinery, introduced by the consultant in the final plenary, was a powerful symbol of conference process. Here customers were described as grains of sugar being polished in a giant machine. They were ground together in corridors and plenaries, separated into batches for further polishing, mixed together and separated by blasts of hot air followed by further batching, mixing and grinding until each grain was polished.

Several issues emerge. The image of a machine is used to describe the conference structure. Its production processes are pre-set and certainly not open for examination or modification by the grains of sugar! The power differential between machine and grain takes the infantilisation of the dependency culture a stage further as customers are reduced in size and treated as inanimate particles. The lapidiary action leads to surface polishing without internal change. Customers get their corners knocked off and emerge as somewhat smoother consultants through a learning process that is only skin deep. In response one person took the image further changing it to a toffee-factory. Here the experience is of melt-down and confusion as customers coalesce into an undifferentiated sticky mess with all individual boundaries dissolved.

Such symbols raise disturbing questions about the process of the conference. They may also reflect some of the depersonalising and disempowering dynamics of consultancy as experienced by the mass of employees subject to management implementation of a consultative report. Was the examination of the dynamics of consultancy from the perspective of the workforce really taboo?

Images of regression, infantilisation and oral dependency surfaced at various points, yet always with ambivalence. The conference consultant noted the dynamics of his appointment as oral seduction leading to a compulsive "lunge for the breast" offered by the client. In this symbol the client is the mother and the consultant presents infantile dependence needs for resources and care. A few minutes later he was using the image of a baby relating to its mother as a parallel to the relationship between client and consultant. Here the infantilisation was reversed. The co-dependency or crossed regression also emerged in the use of D.W. Winicott's concept of the "third space" between consultant and client. Just as a mother provides a safe enough holding environment within which her child can explore in creative play, so the consultant provides containment within which the client can explore creative new ways of being. At another point in the conference the client was described as providing the containment and security for the consultant to engage in creative activity. Ambivalence between container and contained was profound. Perhaps at the heart of the dynamics of consultancy is the mutual projection of unmet foetal and infantile needs and collusional carrying and caring in displacement.

Birth and death provided another polarity. For one member of the planning group the whole process of the conference from conception to delivery was like a pregnancy ending in birth. Ambivalence surfaced in the question as to whether the planning group had given birth to the conference or whether the group was itself the foetal content being forged together in the process into "a forceful tool for change involving both pain and pleasure". For the conference consultant the ending of the conference was coded with the symbols of death as anticipation of crossing the boundary of the event back into the working world. One of the most powerfully perseverant myths is the reversal of birth and death. We have no experience of death as the ground for such symbolism. What we do have is the experience of birth as a transition across a turbulent boundary from the safety of the known womb to the insecurity of the unknown world beyond. It is a transition accompanied by the fear of death, of annihilation, of discontinuity, which is itself projected to the end of life and fantasized as an image of dying. Symbols of death code, in displacement, the repressed impingement of birth, albeit without the hope of continuity associated with the symbol ground. This confusion is endemic in the Kleinian or object-relations paradigm of psychoanalysis which formed the interpretative framework of the conference.

For those least conscious of the role of the unconscious in human behaviour, the constant drawing on psychoanalytic insight was an unwelcome intrusion. For them the study of the dynamics of consultancy was restricted to the interactive force-fields of conscious activity. However, for those willing to look below the surface, psychoanalysis provided an essential tool for the exploration for the darker side of the corporate process. To be unconscious of the effects of projection and transference is to be caught up in collusional dynamics, whose dysfunctional and destructive potential can be catastrophic in the consultative engagement.

Here, however, we encountered a fundamental constraint on conference learning. During the last twenty-five years there have been major advances in psychoanalytic research with significant bearing on the dynamics of change in large systems. Breakthrough has come through recognition of the powerful part played by very early imprinting in forming the defences and dynamics of the common unconscious. In the USA, in Germany and here in the UK this paradigm shift in understanding is already opening new avenues of consultancyformation and intervention with the power not only to deepen understanding of the dynamics involved but to change them. Several conference participants expressed concerned that no account was taken of these developments. It was as if the psychoanalytic paradigm employed had become fixated in the 1950's and subsequently defended against all further insight. Are the British psychoanalytic institutions really that heavily defended? Although it takes time for new research to seep through to the field of practical application, in today's world that is no reason for depriving such an important conference of resources that could enrich the intellectual climate of British consultancy.

Perhaps the next step in understanding the dynamics of consultancy is to become conscious of how unconscious we are of the power of the human unconscious in shaping the dynamics of every aspect of human endeavour.

APPENDIX 3

CONFERENCE EVALUATION

It has been educative to analyze the feedback we had received (from about a third of the participants); both appreciative and critical comments have been extremely valuable. The main points which emerged are summarised below.

Why people attended
Participants attended for broadly three related purposes, congruent with the stated learning objectives of the conference:
*   networking, e.g.
        find new consultants for my organisation
        find potential associates/collaborators
        meeting peers
        seeing old and meeting new friends
*   benchmarking, e.g.
        comparing own work with others
        confirmation that what I do works, is good enough
        affirmation of own approaches <u>and</u> new ways of working
        to find out if consultancy is for me
*   professional development, e.g.
        establish and work on development needs
        get tools and ideas for own practice
        find out about "psychotherapeutic" models of consulting
        apply new models to own work
        see what is new in the field
        find out what works and why

To what extent were delegates' objectives met
Most of the people who provided feedback were satisfied with the way the event met their needs and objectives. There was not surprisingly a broad range of degree of satisfaction, from " a wasted weekend" to " an inspiring weekend", "great learning event that will live fondly in my memory", "the best conference I have been to". One delegate quoted T.S.Elliott:

> And what you thought you came for
> Is only a shell, a husk of meaning
> From which the purpose breaks through
> Only when it is fulfilled.
> If at all.....

If we can assume that the sample of respondents is representative, then the event provided a good enough experience for the participants.

* **What aspects of the conference were helpful/unhelpful:**
  The feedback on the different aspects of the event was varied, and often contradictory.
* **Overall structure**
  Some people found the shape of the event appropriately containing and helpful, others thought that it was too rigid, too much crowded into too little time, insufficient unstructured time for networking and personal reflection, too much or too little time allowed for the different components of the programme.
* **Plenary presentations**
  The plenary presentations were experienced as valuable and interesting by over 90% of participants. Many delegates would have liked more time in the plenaries and an opportunity to have entered into a dialogue with the presenters. Most people found role of the respondents irrelevant and unhelpful.
* **Parallel presentations**
  The parallel sessions offered an impressive range and variety of presenters; for some people this presented a difficult choice on the basis of the information provided, for others too many choices. The quality of the sessions was perceived as varied, some of them were also experienced as too didactic in style and not allowing for participation and experiential learning. For some participants the predominance of the psychodynamic perspective was limiting, even "incestuous", while others valued the opportunity for deepening their understanding of this approach and it's power in consulting.
* **Review groups**
  These were the most contentious aspect of the conference. The best and most vital for some; useful for many; the worst for others. Valuable space for reflection, debate, integration; a waste of time in listening to people with large egos; inappropriate attempt to run a therapy group. Suggestions included: special interest groups, groups meeting after the plenary, advance information about the groups. Overall they were perceived as very useful by 35%, useful by 30%, interesting by 25%, not useful by 10%.(The Learning Review Groups are commented on in Appendix 1.)
* **Organisation and domestic arrangements**
  While the size of the event was a source of the great richness for some, it was also unhelpful as some of the groups were too large to facilitate full participation, uncomfortable due to overcrowding, confusing when moving in between the many rooms of the building. The facilities were stretched to (or perhaps beyond) the limits and the lack of informal meeting places, unavailability of refreshments on demand, plenary sessions having to be televised, long queues for coffee, etc, suggest that the environment provided was not of sufficiently high standard for many of the participants.

INSTITUTE OF MANAGEMENT CONSULTANTS (IMC)

The Vision of the Institute is to be the Body that qualifies management consultants by establishing such professional standards that clients will want to use only members.

Founded in 1962, the IMC is the institute for professional qualified management consultants in the UK and Republic of Ireland. Members are admitted and certificated on the basis of an independent assessment of their competence and experience as management consultants.

Members, who include sole practitioners, partners, directors and employees of consulting firms, and internal consultants, affirm annually to abide by the Code of Professional Conduct and to commit to continuing professional development.

- The IMC promotes the profession, and the standards of performance and conduct of its members, through maintaining an active dialogue with government, clients, practices and the media.

- The IMC defines and publishes standards for training and professional development, and provides guidance on ISO9001 quality standards and ethical issues. It publishes guidelines, handbooks, the quarterly journal 'Consult' and the monthly members' newsletter 'Update'.

- The Client Support Service advises purchasers of management consultancy and provides clients with a shortlist of qualified consultants for specific projects.

- Through links with the International Council of Management Consulting Institutes (ICMCI) members are recognised and designated worldwide as CMC (certified management consultant) and enjoy reciprocal arrangements with institutes in many overseas countries.

The IMC has 3700 individual members and 300 Registered Practices of all sizes which support its aims and encourage membership.

Institute of Management Consultants
5th Floor, 32-33 Hatton Garden
London EC1N 8DL
Tel: 071 242 2140
Fax: 071 831 4597

SOUTH BANK BUSINESS SCHOOL

REALISE YOUR FULL MANAGERIAL POTENTIAL AND ENHANCE YOUR CAREER OPPORTUNITIES WITH THE SOUTH BANK BUSINESS SCHOOL

Central London location close to both the City and Westminster.

MBA PROGRAMME

Full or Part-Time. Evening or Day Release. Fully Unitised.

The MBA at South Bank Business School is the MBA for those with middle and senior management experience. The course is designed so that it builds on the diversity of experience amongst participants, giving a foundation in the theory of management as well as the skills to put that into practice.

The MBA currently has an intake of approximately 100 students per year, consisting of middle and senior managers drawn from a wide range of public sector, private sector and not-for-profit organisations.

Those on the full-time programme are normally experienced managers looking, as individuals, to equip themselves with the relevant knowledge and skills needed to broaden their prospects or change direction. Others are sponsored by their companies who wish to develop their managers through skills and knowledge development.

The part-time programme offers practising managers the opportunity to consolidate their experience, develop their skills, and acquire more versatility. The course thus enables managers to study and research, in depth, aspects of strategic management and change with particular reference to their employing organisations.

Units:
STAGE ONE
- **Managerial Context**
- **Managing Financial Information**
- **Marketing and Service Management**
- **Managing People and Organisations**

STAGE TWO
- **Strategic Management**
- **Organisational Management and Development**
- **Financial Management**
- **Options***

(* **Public Services Management, Small Business Enterprise, Project Management, International Finance, International Marketing, Arts Management**).

STAGE THREE
- **Research Methods/Dissertations (4 units)**

For further information contact the MBA Course Administrator, South Bank Business School, South Bank University, 103 Borough Road, London SE1 0AA. Tel: 071-815 8209. Fax: 071-815 8280.

The University of Choice

SOUTH BANK UNIVERSITY
•LONDON•

Programmes for the changing world of business and public service

These courses offer

- *Individuals* a wide range of courses enabling them to develop organisational effectiveness and the ability to manage change
- *Organisations* the opportunity to enter into collaborative postgraduate management development programmes

Diploma/MSc in Human Resource Management

Full and part-time routes are available, depending on prior qualifications and experience, for those wishing to develop their own careers in personnel management to a senior level.

MSc in Information Systems in Management

Full and part-time modes are available for those who want the key to better management of the increasing amount of business information available.

MSc Organisational Development

Can be completed in 12 months with attendance two days per week combined with self-managed learning. Particularly suitable for those wishing to work in an advisory/consultancy role, private, public or voluntary sectors.

MSc in Managing Change

The first Masters programme in managing change, provided by a partnership of Sheffield Business School and the Centre for the Study of Change, London. Designed for senior managers dealing with change issues.

Additionally Sheffield Business School offers a full range of other postgraduate programmes.

For further details please contact Programme Support Office
Sheffield Business School, Totley Campus, Totley Hall Lane
Sheffield S17 4AB. Telephone 0742 532820.

Sheffield
Business School